THE HASIDIC TALE

THE LITTMAN LIBRARY OF
JEWISH CIVILIZATION

Dedicated to the memory of
LOUIS THOMAS SIDNEY LITTMAN
who founded the Littman Library for the love of God
and as an act of charity in memory of his father
JOSEPH AARON LITTMAN
and to the memory of
ROBERT JOSEPH LITTMAN
who continued what his father Louis had begun
יהא זכרם ברוך

Get wisdom, get understanding:
Forsake her not and she shall preserve thee
PROV. 4: 5

The Littman Library of Jewish Civilization is a registered UK charity
Registered charity no. 1000784

THE HASIDIC TALE

◆

GEDALYAH NIGAL

Translated by
EDWARD LEVIN

London
The Littman Library of Jewish Civilization
in association with Liverpool University Press

The Littman Library of Jewish Civilization
Registered office: 4th floor, 7–10 Chandos Street, London W1G 9DQ

in association with Liverpool University Press
4 Cambridge Street, Liverpool L69 7ZU, UK
www.liverpooluniversitypress.co.uk/littman

Managing Editor: Connie Webber

Distributed in North America by
Oxford University Press Inc., 198 Madison Avenue,
New York, NY 10016, USA

First published in paperback 2012

Catalogue records for this book are available from the
British Library and the Library of Congress

ISBN 978–1–906764–41–8

Publishing co-ordinator: Janet Moth
Copy-editing: Gillian Somerscales and Lindsey Taylor-Guthartz
Proof-reading: Philippa Claiden
Index: Bonnie Blackburn
Designed by Pete Russell, Faringdon, Oxon.
Typeset by Hope Services (Abingdon) Ltd

Printed and bound in Great Britain by
CPI Group (UK) Ltd., Croydon, CR0 4YY

Contents

Note on Transliteration, Translation, and Names

THE transliteration of Hebrew in this book reflects consideration of the type of book it is, in terms of its content, purpose, and readership. The system adopted therefore reflects a broad approach to transcription, rather than the narrower approaches found in the *Encyclopaedia Judaica* or other systems developed for text-based or linguistic studies. The aim has been to reflect the pronunciation prescribed for modern Hebrew, rather than the spelling or Hebrew word structure, and to do so using conventions that are generally familiar to the English-speaking reader.

In accordance with this approach, no attempt is made to indicate the distinctions between *alef* and *ayin*, *tet* and *taf*, *kaf* and *kuf*, *sin* and *samekh*, since these are not relevant to pronunciation; likewise, the *dagesh* is not indicated except where it affects pronunciation. Following the principle of using conventions familiar to the majority of readers, however, transcriptions that are well established have been retained even when they are not fully consistent with the transliteration system adopted. On similar grounds, the *tsadi* is rendered by 'tz' in such familiar words as barmitzvah where they have entered the English language in that form. Likewise, the distinction between *ḥet* and *khaf* has been retained, using *ḥ* for the former and *kh* for the latter; the associated forms are generally familiar to readers, even if the distinction is not actually borne out in pronunciation, and for the same reason the final *heh* is indicated too. As in Hebrew, no capital letters are used, except that an initial capital has been retained in transliterating titles of published works.

Since no distinction is made between *alef* and *ayin*, they are indicated by an apostrophe only in intervocalic positions where a failure to do so could lead an English-speaking reader to pronounce the vowel-cluster as a diphthong—as, for example, in *ha'ir*—or otherwise mispronounce the word.

The *sheva na* is indicated by an *e*—*perikat ol*, *reshut*—except, again, when established convention dictates otherwise.

The *yod* is represented by *i* when it occurs as a vowel (*bereshit*), by *y* when it occurs as a consonant (*yesodot*), and by *yi* when it occurs as both (*yisra'el*).

Names of people have similarly been rendered in familiar form as far as possible. Where there is an accepted English form in common use for a personal name—Abraham, Moses—that has been used in preference to the Hebrew form of the name; where a name is not in common English use, the

Hebrew form has been used. Where rabbis are also known by an acronym formed from all their given names, both forms are used interchangeably. Where rabbis are commonly known by the titles of one of the books they wrote, the appropriate title is cited together with the rabbi's name the first time they are mentioned; thereafter both forms may be used interchangeably, and both forms are listed in the index.

The treatment of place names is more complicated. For example, many places acquired multiple names as borders changed: Grosswardein of the Austro-Hungarian Republic was known as Nagyvarad when it was part of Hungary and is today Oradea in Romania. Some places had Yiddish names that were rather different from those by which they were known in the local language: the Polish Nowy Sącz was known in Yiddish as 'Sanz', and the Polish Oświęcim (German 'Auschwitz') was known in Yiddish as 'Oshpetsin'. Just to make it more complicated, variant pronunciations of Yiddish have given rise to variations even in how the Yiddish name is rendered in English. There are also places that figure in these stories that have a well-established 'English' form in current use, either as a result of fashions in tourism—Krakow being the outstanding example (though some would say 'Cracow')—or through the scholarly literature on hasidism. In the light of these differences, and in an attempt to represent names in a familiar form, we have tried to use established English forms where they exist, and names that represent a Yiddish pronunciation in other cases. A gazetteer of all the central and east European place names mentioned, showing the country in which each place is currently located, together with its distance from a main town, is to be found at the back of the book. Thanks are due to Yehudit Malkiel for patiently compiling it from Gary Mokotoff and Sallyann Amdur Sack's *Where Once We Walked: A Guide to the Jewish Communities Destroyed in the Holocaust* (Teaneck, NJ, 1991), and to the publishers, Avotaynu Inc., for generously allowing us to use it. Following the editorial principles of this source, we do not use diacritical marks on place names.

In pursuit of the same ends of fluency and accessibility, we have avoided Hebrew terminology as far as possible, retaining only what is felt to be culturally vital because there is no other way to express the concept in question. Thus, for example, most *gigul*s are now reincarnations, but *agunah* has been retained throughout because there is no easy English equivalent.

A particular case in point is *parits*. The term does not really exist in modern Hebrew, in that it is defined in the Ben-Shoshan dictionary as a term 'that *used to be used* [emphasis added] by the Jews of the Diaspora to denote the Polish land-owning nobleman for whom the Jews used to collect taxes'. In fact, the term they would have used would have been not the Hebrew *parits* but the Yiddish *poritz*. Using a neutral English term such as 'Polish nobleman' or 'local Polish landowner' would remove the overtone of socio-cultural distance, perhaps even contempt, embedded in the Yiddish, and thus obscure a culturally significant connotation of the term; so in this instance we have retained *poritz*.

INTRODUCTION

No social or religious movement in the entire course of Jewish history has engaged so intensively in storytelling as hasidism; nor have stories occupied such a central and important place in any other intellectual movement within Judaism. New examples of the genre continue to be told and published to the present day. The central role afforded the tale in hasidism in general, and especially in certain strands within the movement, such as Bratslav hasidism, has been the subject of scholarly enquiry for some time,[1] but the underlying causes of the phenomenon have not been examined. This introduction begins by outlining the defining characteristics of the hasidic tale and explaining its importance, in particular to the early hasidic movement and its revered leaders.

THE CHARACTERISTICS OF THE HASIDIC TALE

The hasidic tale marked an innovation in Jewish literature because it was the first Jewish literary genre to focus on exemplary individuals and their followers. It may be defined as a story related by hasidim about their revered leaders, known as 'tsadikim' (or about pre-hasidic characters whom hasidim deemed to fit this category), or by the tsadikim themselves in order to communicate a religious message. A principal element is always the ability of the tsadik to channel the divine energy that emanates from God and to mediate heavenly decrees so as to help his followers, the simple folk who followed the path of hasidism.

An additional characteristic of the hasidic tale is its sanctified status: the esteem in which the tale was held by its teller and its audience alike. Both believed in the sanctity of the story, just as they believed in the sanctity of the tsadikim; they accepted the content of the story as true and understood the lesson it imparted. This explains why the genre has survived for so long—over two centuries, longer than any other Jewish literary genre—and why the changes it has undergone, both in content and in form, have been so minor.

[1] See Dan, *Hasidic Story* (Heb.); id., *Hasidic Novella* (Heb.); Piekarz, *Bratslav Hasidism* (Heb.).

The tales themselves have certain typical features:

1. The story generally revolves around a wondrous act by the tsadik.
2. The other hasidim in the story are usually secondary characters.
3. Many stories present an individual coming to the tsadik with a problem (usually in the realms of offspring, health, or livelihood), and the resolution of the problem, thanks to the tsadik.
4. Themes of landscape and nature are absent from the stories.
5. Both Jewish (hasidic and non-hasidic) and non-Jewish motifs are used.
6. There is a focus on the *tamim* (simple person), reflecting the hasidic belief that such individuals may be superior to scholars or persons of distinguished lineage in their spirituality, in accordance with the maxim 'God desires the heart'.
7. The same predilection for the virtuous but unrecognized individual lies behind the presence of the figure, unique to this genre, of the *lamed-vavnik*, the 'hidden tsadik'—one of the thirty-six (in Hebrew, *lamed-vav*) righteous individuals in whose merit the world continues to exist but whose identity as such is concealed.

Any social or literary formation owes its genesis to more than one factor, and the hasidic tale is no different in this regard. Scholars have already identified a number of factors contributing to the emergence of the hasidic tale and the status it enjoyed, in particular the following:

1. The emphasis that itinerant *mokhiḥim* (preachers) among the early hasidim placed on using parables and stories as a way of simplifying complicated ideas so that ordinary people could understand them.[2]
2. The significance ascribed to *siḥot ḥulin* (mundane talk) and apparently everyday matters in early hasidism,[3] which championed the principle 'In all your ways acknowledge him':[4] that is, the idea that God may be worshipped through any action, and even in *siḥah batelah* (idle talk).

[2] See Nigal, *Leader and Congregation* (Heb.), pt 2; id., 'On Proverbs and Aphorisms' (Heb.).

[3] See e.g. Jacob Joseph of Polonnoye, *Toledot ya'akov yosef*, 'Shemot', fo. 36*b*: 'And there are *yiḥudim* in all material speech and stories, and also, as I heard from my master [the Ba'al Shem Tov], he engaged in *yiḥudim* between himself and *aḥotah dematronita* [the Divine Presence] by means of material [or: mundane] stories, and he explained the reason . . .This rabbi also said that by speaking with the masses he draws himself closer to *aḥotah dematronita*, by means of material stories, and he explained the reason . . . This rabbi also said that by speaking with the masses he draws himself closer to them, and draw them closer to the Torah and the commandments.' And further: 'There are people who engage in prayer even when [seemingly] speaking of material matters with their fellows.'

[4] Prov. 3: 6. For the concept of *avodah begashmiyut* (literally, 'divine service in material matters': i.e. turning mundane affairs into part of the cosmological drama of elevating the sparks of holiness), see Jacob Joseph of Polonnoye, *Tsafenat pane'aḥ*, ed. Nigal, index.

3. The universal human desire to tell one's family and immediate circle about one's past, events in one's life, and one's views on various matters.
4. The tradition of recounting the wonders performed by the *ba'alei shem* (wonder-workers) throughout the generations, both orally and in writing.[5]
5. The direct and indirect influence of the narrative material present in Jewish literature throughout the ages, including elements derived from non-Jewish sources.[6]

However, in my opinion the most important factor underlying the centrality of the tale to hasidism is the imperative felt by generations of tsadikim—from the founder of the movement, the Ba'al Shem Tov, and the members of his circle through to the present-day *admorim* (hasidic grand rabbis)—and by the hasidim themselves to champion and promote the hasidic movement and defend it from every trace of criticism.

Hasidism was surrounded by opposition right from its inception in the first half of the eighteenth century. Criticism and derision were directed at the Ba'al Shem Tov and his followers both in the conversations of their contemporaries and in books and polemical literature.[7] Personal criticism of the Ba'al Shem Tov seems to have focused on his lack of rabbinic lineage and his lack of expertise in Torah and halakhah (Jewish law), the two realms that defined the status of every Jew in eastern Europe, and certainly of any public personage. As the new movement developed, the same criticisms were probably also directed at the tsadikim of all the different hasidic courts and dynasties. The opposition that the hasidim faced from the leaders of the traditional Jewish community, who came to be known simply as 'mitnagedim' (opponents), also influenced the content of the hasidic tales.

One of the prime responses to the attacks on hasidism was to engage in apologetics, using the hasidic tale as a way of countering criticism. The apologetics in which hasidic storytelling engaged was both direct and indirect. The direct form was most commonly aimed outwards, that is, towards the opponents of hasidism, whether Jews or non-Jews, but was also targeted inwards on occasion, i.e. towards the followers of hasidism. Conversely, the indirect apologetics, while occasionally targeted at non-Jews, was primarily aimed at the hasidim themselves. Since these criteria offer a useful way of classifying the stories, a few examples may be instructive here.

A prime example of stories that served as vehicles for outward-orientated direct apologetics are those describing confrontations between the Ba'al Shem Tov and doctors.[8] When the latter mockingly ask the Ba'al Shem Tov

[5] See Nigal, *Magic, Mysticism, and Hasidism*, ch. 1; id., 'New Light on the Hasidic Tale' (Heb.).
[6] e.g. narrative material from *Gesta Romanorum* that entered into the *Mayse bukh*.
[7] See Wilensky, *Hasidim and Mitnagedim* (Heb.).
[8] See Ch. 7 below.

where he studied medicine, and how he succeeds in effecting cures, he responds that he learned from on high; and that while doctors heal physical organs, he heals man's spiritual organs, in the course of which the physical organs are cured as well.

The stories in which tsadikim and/or hasidim vigorously counter the attacks of their accusers may be characterized as inward-aimed direct apologetics. In one such tale, the Ba'al Shem Tov is asked by the members of the rabbinical court what remedial action is required of a person who forgets to recite the *Ya'aleh veyavo* prayer on Rosh Hodesh (the day marking the appearance of a new moon). In an answer replete with derision and sarcasm, the Ba'al Shem Tov replies that this had never happened to him, and in any event his answer would be of no use to his questioners, since they would forget it by the next Rosh Hodesh.[9] Another example of such a counter-attack is the response by R. Elimelekh of Lizhensk to the challenge of a mitnagdic rabbi. This rabbi wrote in a letter: 'Since I have heard that his Torah eminence boasts that he experienced *gilui eliyahu* [seeing the prophet Elijah], let him please instruct me how I, too, may reach this level.' R. Elimelekh responded that he had never claimed to have experienced such a vision of Elijah, 'But now that his Torah eminence asks me, I say to him that even the most insignificant of my disciples has experienced *gilui eliyahu*; his esteemed excellency [= the mitnagdic rabbi], however, was not created for this, only for the revealed Torah. Let him follow this path in the future as well, and not occupy himself with concealed matters.'[10]

Most of the hasidic tales intended to aggrandize the hasidic tsadik fall into this category of indirect apologetics. In emphasizing the wonders performed by tsadikim, they repudiate any contention that the tsadik is merely an ordinary person who is not blessed with supernatural powers. The first hasidic storyteller was the Ba'al Shem Tov, and this tendency is apparent in two parables that he is said to have related about himself. In the first parable the Ba'al Shem Tov explains his modest circumstances,[11] and in the second he explains why his efforts to disseminate his teachings in a certain city were unsuccessful.[12]

The Ba'al Shem Tov unquestionably told his associates and disciples stories about himself. The veracity of the narrative material that was transmitted in later generations cannot be confirmed, but there is clear evidence that the

9 *Shivḥei habesht*, ed. Rubinstein, 280–1; Zevin, *Hasidic Tales: Festivals* (Heb.), 189; Sperling, *Reasons for the Customs* (Heb.), 46; and see Ch. 2 below.

10 Berger, *Eser tsaḥtsaḥot*, ch. 1, §22.

11 Jacob Joseph of Polonnoye, *Toledot ya'akov yosef*, 'Tsav', fo. 75*b*. Gershom Scholem writes, with regard to this parable, that 'the Ba'al Shem Tov regarded himself as destined to be a witness to all the suffering and distresses of the people whom he desired to save', and that it presents 'a touching and modest picture of himself' (Scholem, 'Historical Image' (Heb.)).

12 Jacob Joseph of Polonnoye, *Tsafenat pane'aḥ*, fo. 20*b*. Nigal, *Leader and Congregation* (Heb.), pt 2, 121, contains an erroneous reference to *Ketonet pasim*.

Ba'al Shem Tov related the story of his relationship with his mystical teacher, Ahijah the Shilonite,[13] to his disciple R. Jacob Joseph of Polonnoye, to his brother-in-law R. Gershon of Kutow, and to the other members of his circle. The message that the Ba'al Shem Tov sought to deliver through this story—both to his intimates and to anyone else who was interested—was that he was instructed by a heavenly guide, and that a teacher who is not of this world is certainly not inferior to a flesh-and-blood teacher. Furthermore, while an earthly instructor usually teaches only the revealed Torah, from Ahijah he learned the mystery of the esoteric Torah as well. For those who were attracted to hasidism, this conferred on the Ba'al Shem Tov legitimacy as a divinely inspired charismatic leader; for the mitnagedim, who opposed hasidism on the grounds that it was a perversion of Judaism, the claim was intended to show that the Ba'al Shem Tov was merely another link in the chain of the transmitters of the Oral Law throughout the generations.

A careful examination of the stories in the first major published collection of hasidic stories, *Shivḥei habesht*,[14] reveals apologetics at every turn.

The story about the Ba'al Shem Tov's parents,[15] in which his father is taken captive and subjected to tests of his faith in foreign lands, was meant to indicate the high moral and religious stature of the Ba'al Shem Tov's father. The message intended was clear: admittedly, the Ba'al Shem Tov did not possess the distinguished lineage usual for rabbis, and his father was neither a Torah scholar nor a *rosh yeshivah* (head of a yeshiva) nor a communal leader; but he possessed sterling qualities with which few are blessed, and character traits are of greater importance than lineage.

The Ba'al Shem Tov was well aware of the criticisms directed against him and his forebears. One tale relates that when he was staying in the mansion of two brothers, wealthy men of Slutsk, one sought to put the Ba'al Shem Tov to the test. As his wife was standing before the Ba'al Shem Tov's door, she heard him say: 'The fool wishes to test me!'[16] I have discussed at length elsewhere stories about attempts to cause the Ba'al Shem Tov and other tsadikim to engage in the sin of drinking non-kosher wine, a transgression that would presumably prove that they did not have supernatural powers to know things not immediately evident.[17]

As it developed, the hasidic tale exhibited an ambiguous attitude to the question of lineage. If elevated heritage made a person haughty it was frowned upon; on the other hand, the hasidic tale would always relate that a certain tsadik was among the descendants of a renowned individual. Naturally, the

13 See Nigal, 'Master and Teacher' (Heb.).

14 First edn Kapust, 1815; unless stated otherwise, all references from *Shivḥei habesht* are to the Horodetzky edn.

15 *Shivḥei habesht*, 36–9.

16 Ibid. 268. Cf. Margolioth, *Gedolim ma'asei tsadikim*, §12.

17 See Nigal, '*Sefer divrei no'am*', 136–9.

descendants of tsadikim are presented as being of distinguished lineage, and hardly any hasidic dynasty does not boast a founder who was among the disciples of one of the early hasidic leaders, or at the very least an attendant of one of these great figures.

Even the story of the Ba'al Shem Tov's marriage was formulated to demonstrate his stature as a Torah scholar.[18] R. Abraham, his future father-in-law, is engaged in litigation and hears from his co-respondent of a *melamed* (a teacher of young children) in their town who arbitrates between litigants, and whose decisions satisfy both sides. When R. Abraham comes to the Ba'al Shem Tov's house (for that was who the *melamed* was), he hears the latter engaging in a casuistic dispute regarding Maimonides. R. Abraham is so deeply impressed that he offers him his daughter in marriage, and suggests that the betrothal contract be written straight away.

Several of the stories in *Shivḥei habesht* contain a character who counsels against believing in the powers of the Ba'al Shem Tov;[19] as the story progresses, it usually becomes clear that this person is wrong. For example, physicians were prominent among the non-Jews who rejected the Ba'al Shem Tov's superiority,[20] and in all the stories in which there is a confrontation between the Ba'al Shem Tov and a physician, the former emerges victorious.

Many of the polemical writings of the mitnagedim argue that the Ba'al Shem Tov was not a scholar,[21] and accordingly many hasidic stories aim to demonstrate his erudition. Notable in this respect is the book *Sipurim nora'im* by R. Jacob Kaidaner,[22] which includes a number of stories about the Ba'al Shem Tov's erudition in Torah. Kaidaner relates that he heard from R. Simeon Rizes, a leading pupil of R. Shneur Zalman of Lyady, known as the Admor Hazaken ('Old Rebbe'), that someone had said of him: '*This* rabbi is a veritable *gaon* [genius], in both the revealed and the esoteric [Torah].' The person to whom he spoke responded that this was true, while the founder of hasidism 'was a *very simple* person, who was of no account as regards the revealed Torah' (emphasis added). R. Shneur Zalman heard this remark and reacted strongly. He told the doubters that he had heard his teacher, R. Dov Baer of Mezirech, attest that the Ba'al Shem Tov was superior to him in his knowledge of the revealed Torah, 'and that his sharpness and erudition were as one of the *tana'im* [rabbis of the mishnaic period]; he said that his method of studying the revealed Torah was actually as the *amora* Abbaye [one of the sages of the Talmud]'.[23]

Kaidaner's collection of stories also includes praises of the Ba'al Shem Tov by R. Meir Margoliouth, author of *Me'ir netivim*, who attested of the hasidic

[18] *Shivḥei habesht*, 46–51.
[19] See above, n. 16.
[20] See Ch. 7 below.
[21] See Scholem, 'Historical Image' (Heb.).
[22] See Kaidaner, *Sipurim nora'im*.
[23] Ibid. 32.

leader: 'He is as great for us as was R. Isaac Luria, of blessed memory.'[24] In another tale R. Nahman of Horodenka dreams of a disagreement in the heavenly academy between the Ba'al Shem Tov and R. Isaac Luria, the Holy Ari, regarding the mystical significance of the *mikveh* (ritual bath), which ended in Luria conceding victory to the Ba'al Shem Tov.[25] This deference is all the more striking because Luria was held in the highest esteem by hasidim. Menahem Mendel Bodek, author of *Seder hadorot heḥadash*,[26] indirectly attested to this in a comparison of the Ba'al Shem Tov with Luria:

> Our master the Ba'al Shem Tov, of blessed memory, followed R. Isaac Luria, of blessed memory, to reveal the Godhead in each and every item in this lowly and base world, for everything that R. Isaac Luria, of blessed memory, revealed in the heavens above, in the celestial spheres . . . the Ba'al Shem Tov revealed the Godhead here on earth.[27]

A study of each of the collections of hasidic tales reveals that the great majority of the accounts are intended to glorify one tsadik or another, and repudiate any alleged defect. This idealization was carried to such a degree that even if the tsadik's behaviour seemed improper, morally or otherwise, the story offers an explanation that justifies his conduct. For example, a life of luxury, which on the face of it does not redound to the tsadik's credit, is explained as being his way of serving the Lord; the tsadik's cursing of his servant is explained as being euphemistically a string of blessings; and so forth.[28]

THE HISTORY OF THE HASIDIC TALE

The Hasidic Tale in Early Hasidism

The hasidic storytelling genre was born in the unique encounter within the nascent hasidic movement between the extraordinary personality of the Ba'al Shem Tov and the phenomenon of *mokhiḥim*—the itinerant moralizing preachers who used parables, flowery language, and vivid images to illustrate their teachings. Add to this the natural appetite of ordinary people for stories that fire the imagination, and it is easy to understand why the hasidic tale, from its very inception, found an eager audience.

The first published instances of the hasidic tale appear in the earliest hasidic literature, namely in the writings of R. Jacob Joseph of Polonnoye

[24] Ibid. 34.

[25] Ibid. 37. See also Zeligman, *Beit tsadik*, §1.

[26] Bodek, *Seder hadorot heḥadash*, fo. 3*b*.

[27] The great esteem in which hasidim held the *kavanot* of R. Isaac Luria is apparent in the injunction by R. Uri of Strelisk that a hasid have a guest at his table at every meal, and 'then it would be considered as if he had engaged in all the *kavanot* of R. Isaac Luria, of blessed memory' (Uri of Strelisk, *Imrei kodesh*, 21, quoted in Donner, *Derekh ha'emunah uma'aseh rav*, 21).

[28] See Nigal, 'Nonuniform Moral Standards in Hasidism?' (Heb.).

(died *c.*1782). This indicates that hasidic storytelling emerged in the earliest stages of the hasidic movement; it was not a later phenomenon, as we might be tempted to think by the fact that the first major collection of such stories, *Shivḥei habesht*, was published only in 1815. Note that I am drawing a distinction here between the parable and the hasidic tale: while the parable centres on and is defined by its message, the hasidic tale has an existence independent of its message since the religious and ethical conclusions are not made explicit but rather left to the understanding of the individual listener.

Preachers have always used parables in their sermons, and the first hasidim were no exception. Given the difficulty in communicating abstract ideas—whether because of the preacher's inability to express himself or because of his audience's limited understanding—the first hasidim were only too happy to use parables to illustrate their message. Thus R. Jacob Joseph includes many parables in his writings, both those told by the Ba'al Shem Tov himself and those told by members of his intimate circle and his disciples. Furthermore, these preachers engaged primarily in delivering moral reproaches, and a fire-and-brimstone approach was considered liable to be counter-productive: the early hasidic preacher was warned 'not to open his mouth and loosen his tongue to speak of sin, the guilt of the people, [and] of each and every individual. Rather, let him choose a concealed reproof, speaking in allusions.'[29] He therefore needed a vehicle that would allow him to impart his teaching indirectly, while not differing essentially in function from the parable or novel interpretation of a religious text. As R. Jacob Joseph of Polonnoye explained,

> A healthy person drinks water to slake his thirst; that is not so for a sick person, who needs wine and milk. So, too, a person whose soul is healthy thirstily imbibes words of reproof and moral instruction; this is not the case for a person whose soul is sick and cannot taste the underlying sweetness of such a reproach, for whom it must be dressed in some parable and rhetorical language, so that it will taste sweet, so that [the listener] shall taste wine and milk, within which is the inner meaning of the moral.[30]

Moral instruction could be delivered to the wise in plain terms, without having to be made palatable by narrative and rhetoric; but for simple people, and certainly for the wicked, moral reproof had to be sugar-coated, presented in the guise of parables and stories.[31] This approach resulted in the construction of many parables, only a portion of which are preserved in R. Jacob Joseph's homilies.

It is possible that these preachers also related short stories, probably in the main personal ones. We possess a single example, the story of R. Judah Leib

[29] Jacob Joseph of Polonnoye, *Toledot ya'akov yosef*, 'Kedoshim', fo. 93*b*.
[30] Ibid., 'Re'eh', fo. 177*c*. [31] Ibid., 'Emor', fo. 104*c*.

Fistiner (called the Maharil). On one of his journeys he stayed in the house of the head of the community,

> and he considered whether he should study Torah before all [i.e. as an overriding priority]; he could not do so [i.e. at that moment] with the proper awe and respect, because this required bodily cleanliness, and there were also other inhibiting factors; or whether he should sit idle, when to do so would result in a great desecration of the name of God before those who would see that a great man was sitting without [engaging in the study of] Torah. In the meantime, slumber overcame him, and in a dream he was given the interpretation of the verse 'Let him sit alone and be patient, when He has laid it upon him' [Lam. 3: 28], [namely,] that it would be preferable for him to remain silent, if [Torah study under these conditions] would prove to be burdensome.[32]

This autobiographical story was told by the Maharil to his companions, and R. Jacob Joseph heard it, either directly from him or from someone in the Maharil's audience. This short anecdote includes several motifs typical of the hasidic stories in the later collections: the tsadik finding lodgings in a person's house, and what happens to him there; the tsadik's indecision as to how he is to conduct himself in a certain situation; and resolution of the problem following a dream (a low level of prophecy).

Thanks to R. Jacob Joseph we possess parables and short stories used by the Ba'al Shem Tov himself, both to explain his views and to illustrate the experiences and uncertainties in his own life. For example, one of the many parables that I have collected concerns a preacher who departed from the straight and narrow.[33] The Ba'al Shem Tov, though not a preacher himself, possessed very definite opinions on the subject of reproof and on desirable and undesirable ways of preaching. The following parable describes how a person with excellent intentions could forget his true objective and descend, in religious and moral terms, to the level of those sinners whom he sought to elevate:

> A parable: a certain hasid entered a city in which there were places of harlotry, and sought to determine the nature of the city's inhabitants. He said: I will go to the tavern, where there are many people, where [much] can be learned from what is related in stories and in speech, for the tongue is the quill of the heart. And so it was: one person told what he had done with a certain harlot, and similarly his fellow, and so on, until he was greatly grieved by this. When they realized that he was a renowned hasid, every one gave him a fine present, to propitiate him with presents. The following day he employed stratagems so that they would gather there, so that he would receive gifts from them, until, in the end, he did as they had.[34]

[32] Ibid., 'Ki tetse', fo. 191*d*.

[33] See Nigal, *Leader and Congregation* (Heb.), ii. 113–36.

[34] Jacob Joseph of Polonnoye, *Toledot ya'akov yosef*, fo. 201*b*.

The parables and stories that the Ba'al Shem Tov related about himself are of particular interest in this context. Two such parables attest to trenchant self-criticism. The first, the 'Parable of the Tall Man', describes in graphic fashion the Ba'al Shem Tov's failure to persuade the inhabitants of a large city to accept him as their leader and follow his ways:

A very tall man stood facing the rising sun, and the sun beat down fiercely. One wise man saw from afar how hot this tall man had become, for he could not find the remedy for himself, to cool his tired body with cold water. What did he do? He sat opposite him and took a vessel of water for himself, so that every time he drank, he [the tall man] would see what he was doing and would copy him. The one with the vessel of water, however, was short, while the other one was tall, and would have to bend his head and lower himself to take some water for his thirst. [The tall man], however, did not want to debase himself to take water from [the other], because of his coarse nature and his own tall stature, as if he needed the other person. The wise man understood this, but he could find no remedy so that the other would take some water from him. Finally, he was compelled to throw some water upwards, against the face of the [tall] man, so that perhaps he would take some water in his mouth for his thirst. He [the tall man] pursed his lips one against the other, so that no water would enter his mouth from the other, for this was not to his honour. The water fell back to the one who had cast it . . . until he [the tall man] died of thirst.[35]

In the second parable the Ba'al Shem Tov views himself as doomed to see the foolishness of people, unable to help them.

This is comparable to a king who appointed four ministers over the treasury, who took the treasury and fled. One came to his senses and returned of his own will; the second consulted with a wise man who persuaded him that he had been misguided, and he returned. The third came to a place where people are judged [for such crimes], and he returned out of fear. The fourth did not return. The king awarded greater standing to the one who returned of his own free will, since his mind had composed itself properly, to return. This was not so regarding the second, to whom he said, if he had not found a wise man to so counsel him, he would not have returned. As for the third, who returned because he saw that people were judged, the king appointed him to be the official there, to see this suffering. My master [the Ba'al Shem Tov] said this about himself; understand this.[36]

However, it cannot be said that humility is a prevalent feature of the Ba'al Shem Tov's autobiographical stories; indeed, there are a number in which the Ba'al Shem Tov portrays himself as a person well aware of his value and qualities. One, related by R. Jacob Joseph, makes the point that the uniqueness of the Ba'al Shem Tov was already evident while his soul was still in the upper realms, before its descent to earth:

[35] Jacob Joseph of Polonnoye, *Toledot ya'akov yosef*, fo. 201*b*, *Tsafenat pane'aḥ*, fo. 20*b*. See Scholem, 'Historical Image' (Heb.).

[36] Jacob Joseph of Polonnoye, *Toledot ya'akov yosef*, 'Tsav', fo. 75*b*.

For I heard from my master that he was shown that when he was brought under the Tree of Knowledge of good and evil, there were many people of Israel with him, but afterwards, when he was brought under the Tree of Life, they were few; and after this, when he was brought into the inner Garden of Eden, their number further diminished, until only a scant few remained.[37]

The main purpose of such stories, however, is not so much to extol the qualities of the Ba'al Shem Tov himself as to downplay the importance of elevated status. An additional (or perhaps parallel) version of this last tale is preserved in *Shivḥei habesht*, showing the continuity between the parables related by the Ba'al Shem Tov himself and his inner circle and the tales told later by the Ba'al Shem Tov's acquaintances and disciples. It reads as follows:

I heard several times from that rabbi [R. Jacob Joseph], may the memory of the righteous be for a blessing for the life of the world to come, that he told my father-in-law [R. Alexander] at the third sabbath meal, in the way of moral instruction, remember what the Ba'al Shem Tov told you: Once I went to the Garden of Eden, and many from Israel went there with me, but the closer I came to the Garden of Eden, the fewer the people, until by the time that I arrived at the Tree of Life, only a scant few remained with me; I saw you, too, Senderl [= Alexander], among them, and you remained *hinter shtelik* [behind].[38]

Early hasidic tales commonly describe the Ba'al Shem Tov's prophetic powers. He would be told things in a dream, after asking a 'dream question'; he also possessed the faculties of vision and hearing from afar.[39] His disciple R. Jacob Joseph writes that if it were not for the *kelipot* (referring to a kabbalistic concept: the 'shells' that were broken when the primeval light burst out of its enclosure) that fill our world, 'it would be possible to see from one end of the world to the other, to hear voices from the upper worlds, and to hear *keruzin* [heavenly pronouncements].' As proof of this claim, R. Jacob Joseph cited the example of the Ba'al Shem Tov, whose vision and hearing could not be limited by the forces of the Sitra Ahra (the 'Other Side' or forces of evil), writing: 'My master is a proof, for he saw from afar and heard *keruzin*, and this was actually so.'[40]

R. Jacob Joseph also cites narrative evidence to support the kabbalistic view that 'the names are the souls', writing that 'my master performed a wonder [illustrating] this, by calling by name a sleeping person, who was awakened by this'.[41] He further provides personal testimony about the Ba'al Shem Tov's knowledge of the future: 'And likewise, I heard from my master, may his memory be for the world to come, that when someone recited a certain *mishnah*, he would tell him what would be regarding material matters, as

[37] Id., *Ben porat yosef*, fo. 13*a*.
[38] *Shivḥei habesht*, 52.
[39] See Ch. 2 below.
[40] Jacob Joseph of Polonnoye, *Tsafenat pane'aḥ*, fo. 18*d*.
[41] Ibid., fo. 6*d*.

it once happened.'[42] The first printed testimony to the ascent of the Ba'al Shem Tov's soul to the upper spheres appears in R. Jacob Joseph's first book, as follows: 'For my master engaged in an ascent of his soul, and he saw how Michael, the great guardian of Israel, interceded on behalf of Israel, so that all their liability is [in fact] merit.'[43]

Of all the tales relating to the Ba'al Shem Tov's own life and experience, the one of most far-reaching significance is that of the Ba'al Shem Tov's otherworldly teacher. Fragments of this are scattered throughout R. Jacob Joseph's writings. In a few places he speaks of 'my teacher's teacher', but Ahijah the Shilonite is mentioned expressly in only a single disquisition.[44] Even the Ba'al Shem Tov's own detailed description of his meeting with his teacher, given in a letter to his brother-in-law R. Gershon of Kutow, does not mention Ahijah by name, probably on the assumption that R. Gershon would know who he was.

Two paragraphs (run together in the following extract) at the end of *Toledot ya'akov yosef* concisely summarize two stories (or possibly a single one) related by the Ba'al Shem Tov during his lifetime, in which Ahijah the Shilonite is revealed to him during a time of crisis and confusion, consoling and guiding his pupil:

> I heard in the name of my teacher that when he went on his well-known journey [i.e. the Ba'al Shem Tov's attempt to go to the Land of Israel], his teacher showed him that the journey that Israel took in the wilderness alludes to this place, on this journey, and the Torah alludes to all of a person's journeys. And likewise, when the ship was wrecked, and he greatly grieved, his teacher came and showed him which worlds he was in at the time. There were [divine] names, 'I will be', and combinations of 'I will be' . . . Then he became strengthened [i.e. returned to his high spiritual level] to effect a *tikun* [repair] [of the situation] at the [heavenly] root.[45]

The tales recorded by R. Jacob Joseph are important not only for their originality and immediacy but because they show that from the very beginning of the hasidic movement, tsadikim were already telling stories about themselves, and hasidim were telling stories about tsadikim. Although the hasidic concept of the tsadik does not appear in its classical formulation in R. Jacob Joseph's writings (being first set down in print in 1788 in *No'am elimelekh* by R. Elimelekh of Lizhensk), the key figures in the early stories share with the tsadik in the later hasidic tale a knowledge of the future and the ability to perform miracles. However, while storytellers of the first generation relate these wonders in a matter-of-fact manner and without elabor-

[42] Jacob Joseph of Polonnoye, *Ben porat yosef*, 'Derush leshabat shuvah, shenat 527' [Sermon for Shabat Shuvah, 1766], fo. 96*a*.

[43] Jacob Joseph of Polonnoye, *Toledot ya'akov yosef*, 'Omissions', fo. 202*b*.

[44] Ibid., 'Balak', fo. 156*a*. See Nigal, 'Master and Teacher' (Heb.).

[45] Jacob Joseph of Polonnye, *Toledot ya'akov yosef*, fo. 201*a*. For the Ba'al Shem Tov's attempt to go to the Land of Israel, see Ch. 17 below.

ation, versions told at a greater remove from the events related are much more ornate and intricate in their embellishment.

A small volume first published in 1794/5 under the title *Keter shem tov*, by R. Aaron of Apta, exemplifies the rapid development of the genre very well.[46] This book claims to be no more than collections of the words of the Ba'al Shem Tov from the writings of R. Jacob Joseph and the Maggid of Mezirech, but it is of great importance because its author also drew material from traditions that were not represented in the books of his two declared sources, as well as including some expositions of his own. The importance of the book for the current discussion lies in its inclusion of six hasidic stories that are scattered across the second part of the book, not presented as a single unit. These stories, which precede by twenty years the first printed collection of hasidic tales, *Shivḥei habesht*, may be divided into two categories: first, accounts whose central characters are anonymous hasidim; and second, those in which the Ba'al Shem Tov is the dominant figure (though those in the first group are also connected in some manner or other with the Ba'al Shem Tov).

The opening tale in the book, which falls into the first category, serves as an archetype in the hasidic tale of the motif 'God desires the heart': that is, the emphasis placed on intent. The story tells of 'a great hasid' who travelled to the Ba'al Shem Tov for Yom Kippur. Prevented by the difficulties of the journey from arriving on time, he was compelled to spend Yom Kippur in the fields. The hasid was greatly saddened by his failure to reach his destination and prayed from the depths of his heart. When he finally met the Ba'al Shem Tov, after the conclusion of the fast day, the latter received him very warmly, consoled him, and said that 'his prayer had been effective in raising up all the prayers of the people in the fields [i.e. the simple folk who lived in the villages]'.[47]

Another tale in this category makes a similar point about the benefits to the many deriving from the virtuous intent of a single individual. It tells of a righteous person who suffered greatly as a result of an illness. Every time the Ba'al Shem Tov passed through the forest, this ailing disciple would give the rabbi a *pidyon* (lit. 'redemption', i.e. a way of redeeming a wayward soul: a supplicatory donation), but to no avail. In response to the disciple's remonstrations, the Ba'al Shem Tov revealed to him that by his suffering he protected other Jews from murderers who lurked in the forest and sought to kill them. The Ba'al Shem Tov further disclosed that soldiers had already set out to seize the murderers, and that when these criminals were brought to the city as prisoners, the sick disciple would be cured of his ailments.[48]

[46] For the book, its author, and its date of publication, see Nigal, 'A Primary Source' (Heb.).

[47] Aaron of Apta, *Keter shem tov*, ii, fo. 5*b*.

[48] Ibid., fo. 21*b*. Another story tells of a proof-reader's wife in the city of Chmelnik whose

Two other stories from this group—that of the simple person whose prayer was accepted in heaven, and that of the wealthy leaseholder whose supplications were likewise acceptable to heaven—will be discussed at length in Chapter 13. Here it is sufficient to note the great esteem accorded by the hasidic story to the simple person who moves heaven and earth by his simplicity and humility and who brings succour to those in need, just as the tsadik effects such wonders by the nature of his being.

The second category of hasidic tales in *Keter shem tov* consists of two stories that are concerned with the early opposition to the Ba'al Shem Tov and the manner in which he attracted his followers. The author's emphasis on the credibility of these stories is noteworthy: he concludes the first tale in this group with the words 'I heard all this from truthful people'; the second begins with 'I heard from a certain hasid' and ends by asserting that '[the hasid] heard all this from the holy mouth of the rabbi, our master, Dov Baer, may his memory be for the world to come'.

The first story in this group teaches about the Ba'al Shem Tov's greatness in Torah. It introduces a Torah scholar who had vast knowledge of the Talmud and the *posekim* (the halakhists and their rulings) and who lived in the same city as the Ba'al Shem Tov, but resisted the latter's wish that he become one of his followers because he did not believe in 'his great [spiritual–supernatural] perception'. For weeks this learned Jew had difficulty in understanding a passage in the Tosafot (the standard medieval commentary on the Talmud), and was uneasy as a result. One night he dreamed that he entered the upper *heikhalot* (heavenly halls), where he saw the Ba'al Shem Tov studying at the head of a group of Torah scholars, to whom he presented a fine explanation of this passage. In the morning, when the scholar awoke and recalled the interpretation that he had dreamed, he examined this matter in the Talmud. Although he was inclined to accept this interpretation, he did not draw any conclusions from this episode; after all, he said, it was only a dream. None the less, on the sabbath he went to the Ba'al Shem Tov for the *se'udah shelishit*—the third of the three sabbath meals, eaten just before the end of the sabbath, and a time of heightened spirituality. When the Ba'al Shem Tov greeted him warmly and asked if he had already studied the Tosafot, in accordance with the explanation that he had given him, the scholar was completely astonished; at that moment he became a passionate follower of the Ba'al Shem Tov.[49]

The next tale in this group describes how R. Dov Baer, the future Maggid of Mezirech, became a disciple of the Ba'al Shem Tov. Here again we encounter a scholar who is 'sharp, great, and erudite in all the Talmud and all

husband asked the Ba'al Shem Tov to cure her; the latter refused, claiming that her righteousness and her weakness 'protected the city from the bandits in the forest'. See *Shivḥei habesht*, 131.

[49] Aaron of Apta, *Keter shem tov*, fos 21*b*–22*a*.

the *posekim*', but in addition is quite well versed in kabbalah. R. Dov Baer had heard that the Ba'al Shem Tov brought about 'great and awesome things' through prayer; doubting the reliability of this report, he resolved to travel to the Ba'al Shem Tov, 'to put him to the test'. On his arrival he was greatly disappointed, for the Ba'al Shem Tov merely told him trivial stories of what had happened to him on his travels. On the second day, too, R. Dov Baer heard more of these banal episodes, and decided to return home. Then, in the middle of the night, the Ba'al Shem Tov summoned him and asked him to explain a difficult paragraph in the kabbalistic book *Ets ḥayim* by R. Hayim Vital. R. Dov's explanation was not accepted by the Ba'al Shem Tov, who said that it lacked a 'soul'. When the Ba'al Shem Tov began to explain the passage himself, 'the entire house was filled with light, and the fire of the Lord blazed around him'. R. Dov Baer immediately resolved to remain with the Ba'al Shem Tov and learn Torah from him.[50]

The two tales in this group are complementary: in each we meet Torah scholars whom the Ba'al Shem Tov wishes to convert to hasidism. In each case he overcomes the scholar's opposition by demonstrating his superiority in the other's own field: to a master of the revealed Torah he demonstrates his superiority in understanding the plain meaning of a text; to one who is proficient in the esoteric Torah he demonstrates his knowledge in that realm. Supernatural elements are present in both tales: in the first, the Ba'al Shem Tov is present in the *heikhalot* of the upper realms; in the second, light and blazing fire envelop him. Inherent in these stories is the hasidic conception of the standing of such stories, since these reports regarding the Ba'al Shem Tov are simply an allegorical vehicle for conveying profound, concealed ideas.

It is noteworthy that two of the *Keter shem tov* tales appear, with minor variations, in *Shivḥei habesht*. These are the first story, about the 'great hasid' who travelled to the Ba'al Shem Tov for Yom Kippur, and that about the Torah scholar who was among the Ba'al Shem Tov's opponents.[51] Their appearance in the earlier book supports the argument that stories about the Ba'al Shem Tov were widespread in hasidic circles (orally, and apparently also in writing), considerably prior to their publication.[52]

[50] Ibid., fo. 30*a–b*. R. Hayim Vital also became a follower of R. Isaac Luria after hearing the latter's interpretations of the Zohar. See *Sefer hakavanot uma'asei nisim*, fo. 3*b*.

[51] *Shivḥei habesht*, ed. Rubinstein, 152, 97.

[52] Note should be taken here of the few stories within the homilies by R. Moses Hayim Ephraim of Sudilkov, the grandson of the Ba'al Shem Tov, in his book *Degel maḥaneh efrayim* (first published in 1810, five years before *Shivḥei habesht* appeared), 'Bereshit': 'as I actually saw with my own eyes several miracles that were performed for the father of my uncle, R. Gershon of Kutow, of blessed memory'. He later tells a story that also appears, with minor changes, in *Shivḥei habesht*, 67–8, concerning R. Gershon of Kutow, who went on the sabbath to a circumcision that was outside the halakhic bounds of the Land of Israel.

Shivḥei habesht and the Lemberg Period

The publication of *Shivḥei habesht* by R. Israel Jaffe in 1815 marked an important point in the annals of the hasidic tale. While the occasional hasidic tale was to be found in the writings of hasidic masters before this, now there was a collection of hundreds of stories about the Ba'al Shem Tov and his intimate circle. The collector of the tales, whose identity would become evident only in the second printing of *Shivḥei habesht* (published later that same year, in Berdichev),[53] was R. Dov Baer of Linitz, a son-in-law of the Ba'al Shem Tov's scribe, R. Alexander Shohat. Although R. Dov Baer was not personally acquainted with the Ba'al Shem Tov, he was close to people who were, and it was from them, among others, that he heard the stories that he recorded so diligently.

R. Dov Baer prefaced his collection with an 'Author's Introduction' in which he set out the factors that led him to commit the tales to writing—an essay that had a profound influence on those who followed him in publishing collections of hasidic stories.

First and foremost, R. Dov Baer wished to respond to those who dismissed the tales of wondrous events transmitted by word of mouth and mocked the plethora of versions in which they were told. R. Dov Baer defended the stories by claiming that 'everyone prophesies in a different manner', and that in his time, when miracles were on the wane, it was all the more necessary to record all the marvels of the Ba'al Shem Tov and his generation. In these days of the early nineteenth century, he wrote, 'belief has greatly declined, and several heresies [have come] into the world', leading him 'to write of the awesome things that I heard from men of truth'. The emphasis placed on the veracity of what was related would later become a characteristic feature of the introductions to the collections of tales. 'In every tale, I wrote from what I heard. God be praised, I enjoy God-given memory; I have neither added nor subtracted, everything is true and certain, and my mouth has changed nothing.' The author commits the stories to writing ostensibly 'as a remembrance for my children and my children's children', but there is no questioning his unspoken hope that the collection will reach a wider readership. R. Dov Baer explains to his readers that he wrote down the stories not 'in the manner of simple tales or history', but rather with a view to the moral lessons to be gained from a knowledge of the miracles they describe and to the 'belief in the sages'—that is, in the tsadikim and in their wondrous powers—that would consequently be strengthened.

The first publisher, R. Israel Jaffe, added his own introduction, from which we learn that he became a partner in the writing of the book, setting

[53] See Dubnow, *History of Hasidism* (Heb.), 411–16.

down the tales in the first part in the order in which he heard them from his rebbe, R. Shneur Zalman of Lyady.

The structure and subjects of *Shivḥei habesht*,[54] its many editions,[55] its translations into other languages, and its Yiddish versions,[56] have long been the subject of scholarly interest. The citations from the book given here follow the edition by S. A. Horodetzky (Tel Aviv, 1957), in which, unlike the first edition, the stories are grouped by subject.

The numerous editions of the book attest to its popularity and the affection in which it was held among hasidim. Notwithstanding this generally positive reception, some scattered reservations were expressed within the hasidic camp; it is not inconceivable that the detractors mentioned in the 'Author's Introduction' were not mitnagedim or maskilim, but critics from within the hasidic movement. Although printed expressions of such internal criticism are rare, it is clear that some individuals within the various hasidic circles were at best ambivalent towards this type of story; and such objections were inevitably directed at *Shivḥei habesht* as the first (and for a considerable time, the sole) representative of this literary genre. Even a tsadik such as R. Nahman of Bratslav, whose positive attitude towards the story in general cannot be questioned, maintained (according to the Bratslav tradition) that some of the stories in *Shivḥei habesht* 'were not well written'.[57] It is also clear from Jaffe's introduction that the publisher himself was not at ease with certain storytelling traditions, for he stated that he was printing the tales 'in the proper order', as he heard them 'from the mouth of the rebbe, may his soul rest in peace in Paradise', 'and in the name of the rebbe, the rabbi, may his soul rest in peace in Paradise'.[58] R. Shneur Zalman of Lyady, the founder of Habad hasidism, is not explicitly mentioned by name in the publisher's words, but reliable traditions maintain that Jaffe was a Habad hasid,[59] and there is evidence of the profound interest taken by R. Shneur Zalman (who died in 1803) in the tales of the Ba'al Shem Tov.[60] 'The rebbe' is mentioned

[54] See Dan, *Hasidic Story* (Heb.), 64–131.

[55] See Raphael, '*Shivḥei habesht*' (Heb.).

[56] See Ya'ari, 'Three Yiddish Translations' (Heb.); id., 'Two Basic Recensions' (Heb.); see also Shmeruk, *Yiddish Literature* (Heb.), 201 ff.

[57] Hazan, *Sipurim nifla'im*, 3.

[58] *Shivḥei habesht*, 39; ibid., printer's introd., 33; ibid. 39. Rodkinsohn, *Toledot ba'alei shem tov*, i. 13, notes that R. Israel Jaffe enclosed his additions within parentheses (see *Shivḥei habesht*, 41, 48, 77–8, 92, 124, 161–2). On the other hand, there are several comments within parentheses (e.g. pp. 124, 132, 133) that contradict Rodkinsohn's assertion.

[59] See Kaidaner, *Sipurim nora'im*, §20; see also A. Rubinstein, '*Hitgalut* Stories' (Heb.), 182: 'We have no basis [for concluding] that R. Israel Jaffe referred [with the term *admor*] to the founder of the Habad movement.'

[60] See the first tales in Kaidaner, *Sipurim nora'im*; cf. the view held by the maskil Pinhas Ruderman in *Hashaḥar*, 6 (Vienna, 1875), 92 n. 9: 'The book *Shivḥei habesht*, according to Habad hasidim, was fabricated by some mitnaged, or heretic, to defame the Ba'al Shem Tov with falsehoods and matters worthless in comparison with his holiness.' See a rejection of this view in Rodkinsohn, *Toledot ba'alei shem tov*, i. xii.

not only in the 'Publisher's Introduction' and at the beginning of the book, but also in two other places in *Shivḥei habesht*.[61]

Shivḥei habesht unquestionably contains historical facts and full or partial accounts of episodes that actually occurred, along with tales in which the imagined overshadows the real. The latter were influenced by many elements in addition to the creative ability of the storyteller and collector, including orally transmitted Jewish and Christian folk tales, and written sources from both these traditions.

Prominent among the Jewish influences are biblical narratives, rabbinic exegeses, and the kabbalistic *shevaḥim* (hagiographic) literature. The stories of R. Solomon (Shlomo Shlomel) of Dreznitz about R. Isaac Luria, which were written in 1607–9 and became known to Jews in eastern Europe through various works,[62] primarily *Shivḥei ha'ari*,[63] exemplify the penetration of motifs from this strand of literature into the hasidic storytelling genre, primarily into *Shivḥei habesht*.

Table 1, which sets out various motifs and stories that appear in both *Shivḥei ha'ari* and *Shivḥei habesht*, shows how material that originated in the kabbalistic *shevaḥim* literature reappeared in the hasidic tale.[64]

The appearance of *Shivḥei habesht* was followed by a fifty-year hiatus in the publication of collections of hasidic tales. Thereafter, several more volumes appeared, and the prominence in their genesis of the town of Lemberg, where several collectors, notably Rodkinsohn and Bodek, lived and published their books, has led to these later decades of the nineteenth century becoming known in this context as the 'Lemberg period'. The period comes to an end with the death of Aaron Walden in 1912.

R. Isaac Judah Yehiel Safrin of Komarno

The tsadik R. Isaac Judah Yehiel Safrin (commonly known as R. Isaac Eisik Safrin) of Komarno (1806–74) made a significant contribution to the hasidic storytelling genre by recording both his own intimate thoughts and the hasidic tales that he heard.

61 *Shivḥei habesht*, 41, 77. Rodkinsohn, in his discussion (see n. 60 above), states that R. Israel Jaffe enclosed 'exaggerated tales' in *Shivḥei habesht* 'within two half-moons . . . but we did not copy them, until their source was known; we also skipped and abridged some of his tales'.

62 e.g. Joseph ben Judah Yudel of Dubno, *Yesod yosef*, chs. 27, 33, 56, 61, 73, and the book by his disciple, Tsevi Hirsch of Koidanov, *Kav hayashar*, among others.

63 Three letters by Solomon of Dreznitz were published in 1629, entitled 'Writs of Praise and Esteem of the Greatness of R. Isaac Luria, of Blessed Memory'. These and other accounts (such as those published in *Sefer hakavanot uma'asei nisim*, fos 2a–13a, under the heading 'Shivḥei ha'ari') are similar to and exerted considerable influence on the tales in praise of the Ba'al Shem Tov.

64 Solomon of Dreznitz, *Shivḥei ha'ari* (Ostraha, 1794), pagination added; *Shivḥei habesht*.

Table 1. A thematic comparison of *Shivḥei ha'ari* and *Shivḥei habesht*

Shivḥei ha'ari		*Shivḥei habesht*	
folio[a]	**Motif/episode**	**page**	**Motif/episode**
1*b*	Elijah reveals himself to the father of R. Isaac Luria.	41	'And when he was on the way, Elijah, of blessed memory, was revealed to him [the father of the Ba'al Shem Tov], and he said to him: "By this merit, a son shall be born to you who shall illuminate the eyes of Israel."'
2*a*	At the time of the circumcision, Elijah told the father of R. Isaac Luria: 'Take the child and hold him, for a great light shall come forth from him to the world.'		
2*a*	The father of R. Isaac Luria dies after the circumcision.	41	The father of the Ba'al Shem Tov dies when the latter is a small child.
2*a*	Poverty compels R. Isaac Luria to go to Egypt.	41	The young Ba'al Shem Tov earns his livelihood as a teacher's assistant.
2*a*	R. Isaac Luria 'would go and speak with acuity, casuistry, and logic'.	45	The Ba'al Shem Tov 'was an extremely outstanding scholar, and was a great sage'; he spoke before his future father-in-law 'the simple meaning, with great acuity'.
2*a*	His uncle [consequently] gave him his daughter in marriage.	45	R. Abraham recognizes the Ba'al Shem Tov's scholarly prowess, offers him his daughter in marriage, and with him writes the betrothal document.
2*a*	Following the wedding, he secluded himself on the Nile river.	47	Following his wedding, 'he went into seclusion among great mountains'.
2*a*	'He returned home only on the sabbath.'	49	'And he came home on the eve of the sabbath, close to nightfall.'
2*a*	'And there [in seclusion] he received the spirit of divine inspiration. At times the prophet Elijah, of good remembrance, would reveal himself to him, and teach him the secrets of the Torah. Every night his soul ascended . . . to the academy in the heavens.'	45–6	The Ba'al Shem Tov experiences his first *gilui eliyahu*.

Table 1 (*cont.*)

Shivḥei ha'ari folio[a]	Motif/episode	*Shivḥei habesht* page	Motif/episode
		106–7	The 'ascent' of the soul of the Ba'al Shem Tov.
		161	The ascent of his soul to the heavenly chamber-palaces and study there.
2a	'And in those [heavenly] academies the secrets and hidden things of the Torah were given over to him.'	106	'And there he saw that there would be a great decree against Israel.'
		51	'And he spoke esoteric words of Torah that no ear had heard.'
3b	Elijah reveals himself to R. Isaac Luria when the latter is aged 36.	53	The Ba'al Shem Tov reveals himself at the age of 36.
4a	'He also possessed the spirit of divine inspiration, and revealed many future things.'	61, 92, 133	The Ba'al Shem Tov can read people's thoughts, and is capable of seeing and hearing from afar.
5a	'And he was cognizant also even of thoughts; he was cognizant of the wisdom of physiognomy, and he knew the souls of people, and transmigrations of the soul . . . from [their] commandments and transgressions . . . and he knew the chirping of birds.'	157	He would see the transgressions of people.
		86–7	The Ba'al Shem Tov knows 'the wisdom of the language of beasts and birds, and the language of trees'.
5b	'His conception and birth were in sanctity.'	41	'The Ba'al Shem Tov said that it was possible for his soul to continue only when the desire [of his father] had been annihilated.'
6b	R. Isaac Luria hears a heavenly proclamation.	62, 112–27	The Ba'al Shem Tov hears heavenly proclamations.

6a–7a	R. Isaac Luria has knowledge of a [divine] decree and cancels it.	140	The Ba'al Shem Tov has knowledge of a [divine] decree and cancels it.
16*b*	A fire blazes around the members of R. Isaac Luria's intimate circle.	98	The Divine Presence blazes around the disciples of the Ba'al Shem Tov.
18*a*	R. Isaac Luria sees a raven [in which the soul of a wicked person is reincarnated] who seeks its *tikun* from him.	48	The Ba'al Shem Tov encounters a frog [in which the soul of a sinner is reincarnated] who seeks its *tikun* from him.
19*b*	'Thousands and myriads of souls appear before him when he walks in the field.'	105	'And then the souls of the dead came by the thousands and myriads . . . and I [the Ba'al Shem Tov] effect a *tikun* for them, I pray for them and cause [their souls] to ascend.'
28*a*	'Before his death, he [R. Isaac Luria] said to his disciple that he would shortly return to this world.'	169	'If the righteous Redeemer shall not come within sixty years, I shall be compelled to come [back] to this world . . . He said that he would certainly be reincarnated in this world, but I will not be as I am now.'
3*a*	R. Isaac Luria said 'our teacher Hayim [Vital] is the soul of R. Akiva who is mentioned in the Talmud'.	158	'Once they heard the Ba'al Shem Tov say of the great rabbi, our master and teacher, R. Hayim Zanzer of Brod, that he is the spark of R. Yohanan ben Zakai.'

[a] Counted manually; original unpaginated.

The publication in full of *Megilat setarim*, his personal diary, offers the reader a glimpse into the soul of a hasidic tsadik with mystical and messianic leanings.[65] The second part of the work, 'Ma'aseh hashem' (The Acts [and Tales of the Acts] of the Lord), includes tales that Safrin heard from his uncle and teacher R. Tsevi of Zhidachov, his father-in-law and teacher R. Abraham Mordecai of Pintchov, and other 'truthful people'. Some of the tales have no parallel in earlier narrative sources, while others echo tales published prior to the composition of *Megilat setarim* (1845–58). The story of the Ba'al Shem Tov's going into seclusion in the mountains, his miraculous rescue on the point of falling into an abyss, the plot by robbers to kill him, and their

[65] Isaac Judah Yehiel Safrin, *Megilat setarim*.

recognition of him as a man of God is an example of the latter category. The brigands then offer to show him a shortcut to the Land of Israel; the Ba'al Shem Tov accepts the offer, but is prevented by the perils of the journey from achieving his goal.[66]

Important hasidic tales also appear in books by Safrin that were published during his lifetime, especially in 'Netiv mitsvoteikha' (the introduction to his *Otsar haḥayim*, Lemberg, 1858). Safrin's son, R. Eliezer Tsevi, notes in his introduction to *Zohar ḥai*, his father's commentary on the Zohar: 'he knew almost all the true tales that happened to the tsadikim of our generation . . . Also, I heard many stories from him; I heard a new story from him almost every day.'[67]

Michael Levi Rodkinsohn

Michael Levi Rodkinsohn, the most important collector of hasidic tales, was born in Dubrovno in 1845 into a distinguished hasidic family.[68] His father, R. Alexander Frumkin,[69] had married Rodke ('the redhead'), and Michael Levi's last name is a matronymic, 'Rodke's son'. Rodke was the daughter of R. Aaron of Staroselye, a faithful disciple of R. Shneur Zalman of Lyady, the founder of Habad hasidism; while still a youth Rodkinsohn heard hasidic stories in his parents' house, and his grandfather was apparently one of the major sources of them. Many years later, Rodkinsohn would attest that 'our father, may he live long, heard [stories] from his father-in-law, the holy rabbi, R. A[aron] Halevi of Staroselye, a pupil of the holy *gaon* of Lyady, who passed on to him what he had heard from his teacher, the great Maggid of Mezirech, of blessed memory'.[70] Rodkinsohn also stresses in his introduction to *Shivḥei harav* (In Praise of the Rabbi [R. Shneur Zalman]) that from his youth he had been in the company of hasidim who were close to the founder of Habad and his disciples. Every year on 19 Kislev (the anniversary of the liberation of the Old Rebbe, R. Shneur Zalman, from prison), when the hasidim would gather to celebrate, he would question the elderly among them about the founder of Habad. Even at this early age, he declares, he thirsted 'to inscribe these matters with an iron pen', to commit them to writing so that they would not be forgotten and so that they would serve as an educational model for future generations. Not surprisingly, in view of his background, Rodkinsohn's first book, *Shivḥei harav*, unfolds for the reader the entire episode of the Old Rebbe's arrest and subsequent release. In the

[66] Cf. Safrin, *Magilat setarim*, 34 and *Shivḥei habesht*, 47–8; and see Ch. 17 below.

[67] 'Introduction', in I. Safrin, *Zohar ḥai*. For R. Isaac Safrin, see also Yashar (Schlichter), *Beit komarno*, 31–81.

[68] See *Encyclopaedia Judaica*, xiv, col. 218 and bibliography; Dan, *Hasidic Story* (Heb.), name and subject indexes.

[69] R. Alexander died in Jerusalem on 22 June 1875, at the age of 78 (see Rodkinsohn, *Toledot ba'alei shem tov*, i, introd., p. xxxvi).

[70] Ibid., p. xii.

same year, 1864, Rodkinsohn published two more collections of hasidic stories: *Adat tsadikim* (The Congregation of Tsadikim) and *Sipurei tsadikim mehaḥut hameshulash* (Tales of Tsadikim from the Threefold Cord).[71]

Shivḥei harav. Many of the tales in this first of Rodkinsohn's books would later appear, with textual variations, in the book *Toledot amudei haḥabad* ('The History of the Pillars of Habad'; Königsberg, 1876). In his introduction the author explains that he was prompted to realize his wish to commit to writing the hasidic stories he had heard since his childhood by the appearance of a Yiddish booklet by Elazar Margaliot entitled *Ma'aseh r. zalmene*.[72] According to Rodkinsohn, this small book professed to relate the life of the Old Rebbe but in actuality was 'full of lies and foolishness', and its author, who came from Bukovina, was unfamiliar with the sources. Of his own work he wrote: 'I called the book *Shivḥei harav* because in all the lands of Poland and Volhynia . . . he [R. Shneur Zalman] is simply called *harav* [*the* rabbi].'

Adat tsadikim. This book was probably first published in the summer of 1864. A copy of this edition was bound together with the books *Sipurei tsadikim mehaḥut hameshulash* and *Ma'aseh tsadikim im divrei tsadikim* ('The Tale[s] of Tsadikim with Words of Tsadikim') and published in Lemberg in 1864 by the publisher and printer Y. M. Stand. The book, consisting of forty folio leaves (i.e. eighty pages), is partially numbered from fo. 9. Another edition was published by the Luria Press (Lemberg, 1868).

There are twenty-two tales in the book; most are about hasidim, the remainder concerning individuals who preceded this movement. One of the latter concerns an episode from the time of R. Samuel Edels (1555–1631, known as the Maharsha), and an additional three form a single unit, entitled 'Shivḥei harema' ('In Praise of the Rema [R. Moses Isserles, 1530–72])'. The tenth story (in my numbering) is a variant of a tale included in *Shivḥei habesht*.[73] The seventeenth story, describing how the Maggid of Mezirech became a follower of the Ba'al Shem Tov, is taken from the book *Keter shem tov* (discussed above), and that concerning the letter sent by the Ba'al Shem Tov to his brother-in-law R. Gershon of Kutow was taken from another secondary source.[74]

The 'Author's Introduction' is unsigned but an acrostic alludes to its author's identity. This introduction was apparently written under the

[71] For bibliographical details, see Bodek(?), 'A Chapter in the History of the Hasidic Tale' (Heb.), 103.

[72] The reference is to the *ma'aseh* (tale) written by Eleazar Margolies of Skalat. See Habermann, 'The Gates of Habad' (Heb.), 323–4.

[73] For the story of the large land-tenants in Lithuania, see *Shivḥei habesht*, 132–6.

[74] Rodkinsohn erroneously stated that the letter was published in Jacob Joseph of Polonnoye, *Toledot ya'akov yosef*; in fact it was printed at the end of his *Ben porat yosef*.

influence of the introduction to *Shivḥei habesht*. The author extols simple faith and its contribution to Israel's endurance among the nations of the world. He draws attention to the presence in every generation of righteous individuals who, capable of performing miracles and cancelling evil decrees against the Jewish people with their prayers, reinforce this belief. From the time of the Talmud on, he writes, the Jewish people had been blessed with sages and righteous ones; however, the passing away of the *gurei ha'ari* (Luria's disciples; literally, his 'cubs', a term deriving from the fact that the name by which he was known, 'Ha'ari', has the same Hebrew letters as the word *aryeh*, 'lion') had led to a spiritual nadir that ended only when the Ba'al Shem Tov revealed himself. Ever since that day, tsadikim have been present 'in every district and region', strengthening the people's spirit and *emunat ḥakhamim* (faith in the tsadikim). The author regards simple faith and *emunat ḥakhamim* to be synonymous.

Sipurei tsadikim mehaḥut hameshulash. This was the third of Rodkinsohn's books to be published in 1864; the copy in the Jewish National and University Library in Jerusalem is bound together with *Shivḥei harav*. Like the latter, this book was printed partly in Rashi script and partly in regular Hebrew letters. On the title page and in his introduction to the first edition the author states that the book contains material about R. Leib Sarahs, R. Israel Polotsker (= of Polotsk), and R. Azriel, 'who are three *metivei lekhet* ['those who carry themselves well': see Prov. 30: 29]'; hence the reference in the book's title to *haḥut hameshulash*, the 'threefold cord'. The book also includes tales of R. Leib, known as 'the Grandfather of Shpola', and later editions (printed in Lemberg, one later in 1864 and another in 1873) bore the title *Sipurei tsadikim me'arba'ah metivei lekhet* (Stories of Tsadikim: Of Four Who Carry Themselves Well). (The first of these included the name of R. Leib on the title page and in the introduction; the second also mentioned R. Leib on the title page, but did not contain an introduction.) At the end of the book Rodkinsohn appeals to readers to judge him favourably and not accuse him of making additions or omissions: 'I had', he notes, 'a great deal of work to select the fine flour from among the chaff of the tales'—certainly an admission that he had not transmitted the tales as he had heard them. Short introductions are attached to the stories, each of which concludes with a moral lesson.

*

In all these books, and especially in his introductions, Rodkinsohn emphasizes the veracity of the tales and the reliability of his sources, but he does not assume full responsibility for their truthfulness. He stresses the importance 'in our time' of strengthening *emunat ḥakhamim*, that is, the belief in the hasidic tsadikim and the wonders they perform, since 'by our many sins, there is an increase in the scurf from the maskilim of our people who have devoted themselves to the folly that they call Haskalah, to destroy every element of religion'.[75] He takes the view that the tales of the luminaries of hasidism may be able to counter the threat posed to the religion of Israel by the literature of the Haskalah (Jewish Enlightenment). Taking into account his audience, he wrote, he said, 'in very easy, low, and simple language', although he could have composed the tales in 'pure and fine flowery language'.

Rodkinsohn would eventually become a maskil himself, but he did not abandon his interest in hasidic topics. His ambitious plan to write a large four-volume work on the leaders of the hasidic movement, entitled *Toledot ba'alei shem tov* (A History of *Ba'alei shem tov*),[76] was not realized in full, but in 1876 two sections of it were published: the first section, *Or yisra'el* (The Light of Israel, a biography of the Ba'al Shem Tov), and the fourth, *Toledot amudei haḥabad* (The History of the Pillars of Habad). He strove for a scholarly, critical approach in these volumes, accompanying the text with useful footnotes; but despite this more academic approach, he still included some tales that he regarded as authentic.

After he became a maskil Rodkinsohn also wrote as a journalist, continuing to do so after his emigration to the United States in 1889. His mercurial personality was controversial even in his lifetime, and he did not lack enemies and detractors.[77] Nevertheless, his contribution to the genre is unquestionable and his tales found a ready audience; most found their way into Aaron Walden's book *Kahal ḥasidim*, and some even made their way into a story by the Nobel laureate S. Y. Agnon.[78] Rodkinsohn died in America in 1904.

Menahem Mendel Bodek

Menahem Mendel Bodek was very different from his contemporary Rodkinsohn in that he shrank from publicity and sought to remain anonymous. In his book *Einot mayim* (a commentary, unrelated to hasidism),[79] which

[75] Rodkinsohn, *Adat tsadikim*, introd.

[76] See Bodek(?), *Sipurei kedoshim*, 104–5.

[77] See Kohen-Tsedek, *Mikha'el hanehefakh lesama'el*; Deinard, *Mashgei ivrim*. Pesah Ruderman writes in Peretz Smolenskin's *Hashaḥar*, 6 (Vienna, 1875) that he heard from the maskil Aryeh Leib Schalit, a lumber merchant in Riga, 'that once when he travelled from Petersburg to Riga, he became friendly with quite a young man, who was dressed in European garb, and who also ate non-kosher food in the hotel. In the course of this conversation he admitted to Schalit that he was the author of *Sipurei hatsadikim*, stories the majority of which he had fabricated, and some of which he had heard from old women in Dubrovno, solely to fill his pocket after a great loss in commerce, in which he had lost almost all his money.' All the signs indicate that this was Michael Levi Rodkinsohn.

[78] Agnon, *Elu ve'elu*, 63–4 (the tale of the *ba'al habitaḥon*, the one with trust in God).

[79] Bodek, *Einot mayim*, printed at the press of David Hirsch Shrenzel. See Moriya, *Beit eked sefarim*, iii, letter *ayin*, §533.

was published in 1856, he affectionately mentions his wife, who 'labours with all her strength in commerce to give food and sustenance to his household', thus enabling him to engage in matters of the spirit. The rabbi of Lemberg and head of the city's rabbinical court, R. Joseph Saul Nathanson,[80] wrote an approbatory introduction to the work, noting that the author was a young man who managed to find time for Torah study despite his occupation with business affairs (supplementing his wife's labours).

Bodek's literary work falls into two categories. He wrote commentaries, including *Einot mayim* and a commentary on the mystical *Tikunei hazohar*; and he wrote hasidic literature, predominantly hasidic tales but also hasidic Torah teachings and thought. The latter category includes *Ma'aseh tsadikim*, *Pe'er mikedoshim*, *Kahal kedoshim*, and *Mifalot hatsadikim*. His *Seder hadorot mitalmidei habesht* (A Chronology of the Disciples of the Ba'al Shem Tov) purports to be historical but in fact belongs to the genre of hasidic tales. Several scholars have also attributed the book *Sipurei kedoshim* to Bodek but the attribution remains unproven.

Most of Bodek's collections of hasidic stories include introductions in which the author stresses the importance of tales relating to the tsadikim. He cites prominent tsadikim who advised their followers to recount their activities: the Maggid of Zlotchev, who commanded those in his intimate circle to recount the doings of tsadikim, 'for the letters of the story arouse the [heavenly] root of the miracles';[81] R. Shalom of Drohobitch, who ordered his coterie that whenever they gathered together they should speak of his practices, his prayers, 'and even of his horse and his carriage', for all were of the aspect of holy objects, like the mantle for a Torah scroll (as R. Abraham Joshua Heschel of Apta said when he came to R. Israel of Ruzhin); and R. Israel Dov of Vladnik, who said that not only are the miraculous tales to be recounted, but even the mundane conversations of tsadikim are to be accounted as the Holy of Holies.[82] According to Bodek, the importance of the stories consists of their intensifying the reader's *emunat ḥakhamim*: they would 'inflame his soul so that he would be filled with different emotions and great enthusiasm to fulfil all the words of the Torah that are established for us in the *Shulḥan arukh*'. The reader will be enthusiastic and fervent in his prayer and he will learn from the actions of the tsadikim; but, most importantly, he will believe that 'the tsadik has been given the power . . . to change Nature as he wishes, and the Lord is with him, for the halakhah is

[80] For R. Nathanson, see *Encyclopaedia Judaica*, xii, cols 866–8. See also the tale of a conversation between the rabbi and the tsadik R. Tsevi of Rymanow, in Moskowitz, *Otsar hasipurim*, iv. 14–15.

[81] Bodek, *Mifalot hatsadikim*, introd.; cf. id., *Kahal kedoshim*, introd.: 'They are a marvellous charm to arouse miracles, as I have written in my introduction to the first part of the book *Pe'er mikedoshim*.'

[82] Bodek, *Ma'aseh tsadikim*, introd.

with him, that is to say, his conduct in all the affairs of the world, both spiritual and material'.[83]

According to Bodek, the lessons of these stories will be absorbed more easily through reading them than from studying books of moral instruction.[84] The benefits afforded to the reader will include faith in the Lord and humility, as well as greater happiness; the stories will offer him 'solace in his distress, which will be transformed into rejoicing and salvation'; 'each person will meditate [on the tales] even when his heart sinks in the mire of concerns . . . and every person will find a remedy for his sadness, and all sadness and sighing shall flee, for he will be sated from the founts of deliverances'.[85]

Bodek, like Rodkinsohn, stressed the authenticity of his tales: 'I received them from one person [who received them] from another, from reliable people . . . and all are true stories, that I heard from the pious and men of good deeds.'[86] He declares that he has attempted to render the stories in fluent language, and that the stories are suitable for all, 'the young as the old, the wise as the foolish'.[87] Everyone can learn from them, each at his own level. However, since these tales are available to all, kabbalistic matters are not to be spoken of at length.[88] Even so, the reader senses Bodek's affinity with esoteric teachings and his inclination towards mystical beliefs: for example, the stories are replete with instances of transmigration of the soul.

One of the goals that Bodek set for himself in his writing was to silence the slanderers and disparagers of hasidism; he is blatantly sarcastic towards maskilim. His literary style was very different from that of most other hasidim, yet he showed a warm regard for the hasidic rabbis, their teachings, and the hasidic tale.

Bodek preferred not to reveal his identity; since the tales have intrinsic sanctity, he argued, the identity of the person who recorded them is of no consequence.[89] 'Let heaven be my witness that I have no intent of gaining a name for myself with this, such as the princes of Jeshurun, the holy people, to crown myself with a glorious diadem for my efforts';[90] 'I do not intend to aggrandize myself with such base labor.'[91]

Bodek died around the age of 40 (his exact date of birth is unknown) on 28 September 1864,[92] without completing his commentary on *Tikunei hazohar*. It was prepared for publication by his wife Reize and his son Shraga and published that same year in Lemberg, under the title *Zikhron menaḥem* (Memorial for Menahem).

[83] Ibid. [84] Ibid. [85] Bodek, *Kahal kedoshim*, introd.
[86] Id., *Ma'aseh tsadikim*, introd. [87] Ibid. [88] See Bodek, *Pe'er mikedoshim*, §16.
[89] Id., *Mifalot hatsadikim*, introd.; cf. id., *Pe'er mikedoshim*, introd.
[90] Id., *Mifalot hatsadikim*, introd. [91] Id., *Ma'aseh tsadikim*, introd.
[92] See id., *Zikhron menaḥem*, fo. 102*a*.

More than twenty of his tales were reproduced in the book *Kahal ḥasidim* (see below).

Ma'aseh tsadikim. The book *Ma'aseh tsadikim im divrei tsadikim* was published in Lemberg in 1864;[93] if the author's name had not been mentioned in one of Rodkinsohn's books,[94] his identity would have remained a mystery. As its title implies, the book is divided into two parts: tales about tsadikim (the Ba'al Shem Tov, R. Barukh of Medzibezh, R. Tsevi Hirsch of Zhidachov, R. Elimelekh and R. Zusya, R. Shmelke and his brother R. Pinhas, R. Hirsch Leib of Alik, the rabbi of Apta, R. Moses Leib of Sasov, R. Feibush of Bolshevetz, and R. Uri of Strelisk), and their ethical teachings and Torah insights.[95] This practice of setting tales about tsadikim alongside their explicit teachings was quite common in the later period of the hasidic story. The book contains a total of nineteen hasidic tales.

Pe'er mikedoshim. This book was first published in 1865.[96] The title page declares of the contents that 'they did not appear, neither in *Adat tsadikim*, nor in *Ma'aseh tsadikim*, nor are they known in *Sipurei tsadikim*', thus making it clear that all these books preceded it. Like *Ma'aseh tsadikim*, *Pe'er mikedoshim* was published anonymously. In the introduction to the first edition the author dismisses himself as 'the base and lowly writer'; in the introduction to the second edition he admonishes the reader: 'Do not seek to know who is the collector.'

The author frequently speaks directly to the reader. At the conclusion of the first tale, he explains why he positioned it at the beginning of the book: 'For it bears a moral lesson that pertains to all of humankind, including to beware of pride, haughtiness, jealousy, and enmity, and provides a rod for the back of the foolish, to cause them to submit before the holy Lord, and opens a gate for repentance, and a gate for introspection.'[97] The moral lesson in some cases precedes the tale, in other instances follows it; in yet other cases Bodek interrupts the narrative to alert the reader to the moral and religious values embodied in the story. In his commentary on the last story, Bodek reiterates and expands upon the importance of the tales. The book is divided into sections, each of which contains stories on a specific subject: some

[93] See Moriya, *Beit eked sefarim*, iii, letter *samekh*, §68.

[94] See Rodkinsohn, *Toledot ba'alei shem tov*, i. 46 n. 18, 102 n. 35.

[95] The ethical teachings and Torah insights appeared on pp. 48–63 in the (misdated) Lemberg edition that I used.

[96] The title page, erroneously, gives the date 1856. Cf. Dan, *Hasidic Novella* (Heb.), 183; id., *Hasidic Story* (Heb.), 212–13; Moriya, *Beit eked sefarim*, iii, letter *peh*, §18.

[97] Bodek, *Pe'er mikedoshim*, ii. 4. (This edition was printed in Lemberg at the press of A. Y. H. Drucker. For the various printings of *Pe'er mikedoshim* and of Bodek's other books, see Nigal, 'Chapter in the History' (Heb.)).

include non-hasidic tales. Bodek ends the book with a promise to present additional stories in a second collection entitled *Kahal kedoshim*.

Kahal kedoshim. This collection is the continuation of *Pe'er mikedoshim*, mentioned at the end of the latter (just as *Pe'er mikedoshim* was mentioned in the collection that preceded it), and, like *Pe'er mikedoshim*, was published in Lemberg in 1865.[98] The running head on fos 2–5 (my pagination) reads *Adat tsadikim*, and on the other pages, *Kahal kedoshim*. The structure and main features are typical of Bodek, who notes in his introduction that the tales are 'a solace for the soul when [a person's] soul is immersed in the mire of worries'. The first story emphasizes how a heavenly decree against a young man who was a follower of the Seer of Lublin was cancelled thanks to the intervention of his fellow hasidim (not that of the tsadik), and concludes with a moral of the importance of public prayer. The author links this tale with the one that follows: 'For we spoke of this [topic], how great is the participation of Israel in the suffering of their fellows. Accordingly, I shall now relate a story . . . of a tsadik among those who are hidden and concealed.' The third story is likewise linked to the second: 'And from my words concerning the hatred of the Ishmaelites, I shall relate another wondrous tale in which we shall see that Israel is delivered for ever by the salvation of the Lord.'

Like Bodek's other books, *Kahal kedoshim* also presents tales about individuals who were not hasidim, including Nahmanides (fos 7*a*–8*a*) and R. Mordecai Jaffe, author of the *Levushim* (fo. 11*a*–*b*). It also tells tales of distant lands ('And so it happened in the land of Spain . . . ': fo. 11*b*), and copies stories from other books ('I shall copy an awesome tale from a book that is entitled *Shem ya'akov*': fo. 13*a*).

The collector also emphasizes the reliability of his sources: 'I heard this tale from an aged hasid from the hasidim of Lublin, who was himself in Berdichev at the time of the episode' (fo. 30*a*). He also seeks to find rational explanations for the stories (fo. 9*a*).

Mifalot hatsadikim. The book *Mifalot hatsadikim im divrei meisharim* (The Deeds of the Tsadikim with Hasidic Commentaries [lit. 'upright speech']) was published anonymously in Lemberg, apparently in 1866, and was the last of Bodek's hasidic books. The title page states that the stories 'were not included in *Shivḥei habesht*, they do not appear in *Adat tsadikim* or *Ma'aseh tsadikim*, nor were they spoken of in *Pe'er mikedoshim*'. No mention is made of *Kahal kedoshim* here, probably because Bodek considered it to be the second part of *Pe'er mikedoshim*. The book consists of forty-nine passages: most of them are stories of wonders (*mifalot hatsadikim*) and the rest are hasidic commentaries (*divrei meisharim*).

[98] See ibid. 114–16.

Seder hadorot mitalmidei habesht ('The Generations of the Besht's Disciples'). This book was written after Bodek had begun writing his hasidic stories, and was published in Lemberg by Y. M. Stand. Its pages bear the running head 'Seder hadorot heḥadash' (The New *Seder hadorot*). It mentions *Shem hagedolim heḥadash* by Aaron Walden, published in Warsaw in 1864, and refers to a forthcoming work by R. Jacob Joseph of Polonnoye that was still in press and whose title the author did not know; this was *Ketonet pasim*, published in Lemberg in 1866. These indications point to a publication date in 1865.

In his introduction, Bodek indicates his great concern to intensify *emunat ḥakhamim*. He had, he said, collected the contents of the book 'from writers and books', and since he does not want to derive benefit from something that is not his, he does not put his name to the work. Not all of Bodek's sources have been definitively identified, but at least one was a written or printed source, namely, that of the tale that the collector found in 'a certain *kunetres* [booklet]'. The book has a historical orientation, but the author has none the less included numerous hasidic tales for the moral lessons they encapsulate, thus making the book quite different from *Shem hagedolim heḥadash* (see below): while the latter contains only a few stories, merely as adornment, stories form the core of Bodek's work. The first part of the book is divided into eleven chapters, as follows: ch. 1, 'On the Ba'al Shem Tov and his Disciples'; ch. 2, 'On the Maggid of Mezirech and his Disciples'; ch. 3, 'Tsadikim during the Time of the Maggid, Who Were not his Disciples'; ch. 4, 'R. Yehiel Mikhel of Zlotchev and his Disciples'; ch. 5, 'R. Elimelekh, his Disciples, and his Sons'; ch. 6, 'The Seer of Lublin and his Disciples'; ch. 7, 'R. Moses Leib of Sasov and his Disciples'; ch. 8, 'R. Solomon of Karlin and his Disciples'; ch. 9, 'R. Tsevi Hirsch of Zhidachov'; ch. 10, 'R. Shalom of Belz'; and ch. 11, 'R. Meir of Peremyshlyany.' The second part of the book, entitled 'Sifran shel tsadikim' ('Books of Tsadikim'), is a six-page list of some 140 hasidic works.[99]

Aaron Walden

Aaron ben Isaiah Nathan Walden (b. Warsaw 1835; d. 1912, probably in Warsaw) is most widely known as the author of *Shem hagedolim heḥadash*, published in Warsaw in 1864.[100] This work, which is a lexicon of the hasidic lead-

[99] A number of non-hasidic works found their way into the list, such as *Yosher levav* by Raphael Immanuel ben Abraham Hai Ricci and *Limudei ha'atsilut* by Hayim Vital (with an interesting comment by Bodek on this book). Rodkinsohn did not hold Bodek's *Seder hadorot heḥadash* in high regard. He writes in *Toledot ba'alei shem tov*, i. 102 n. 35: 'for the author of *Seder hadorot heḥadash* is that R. Mendel Bodek, and he is not superior to *Shem hagedolim heḥadash*'.

[100] The censor's approval for vol. i was given in May 1864, and for vol. ii in August of the same year. See Dubnow, *History of Hasidism* (Heb.), 383, §43. On Walden's dates, see Eisenstadt, *Dor rabanav vesoferav*, iii. 13–14; Y. Rubinstein, 'Notes on the Book *Shem hagedolim heḥadash*' (Heb.), 140 ff.

ers and their books, incidentally includes a number of tales within the entries on the various individuals. Walden's main contribution to the genre of the hasidic story, however, consists of his dissemination of tales in a book that does not bear his name (or the place and year of its publication): *Kahal ḥasidim*, which was published in a number of editions during Walden's lifetime, all anonymously, and apparently enjoyed very wide distribution at the time.

It seems that Walden did not set his name to the book because he was the author of only a very limited number of the hundreds of stories in the collection; the rest he copied from *Shivḥei habesht* and from the books by Rodkinsohn and Bodek. Bibliographers of the nineteenth century attributed *Kahal ḥasidim* to Walden,[101] but more recently Joseph Dan has suggested that the author of this work was none other than Michael Levi Rodkinsohn.[102] This question was discussed in detail at the end of my edition of *Sipurei kedoshim*.[103]

The Storytelling Genre from the Lemberg Period to the Holocaust: A Bibliographical Survey

Sheloshah edrei tson

The book *Sheloshah edrei tson* (Three Flocks of Sheep: see Gen. 29: 2) by Menahem Meneli Sofer was first published in Pshemishel in 1874, during the author's lifetime. Sofer came from Oshpetzin, but when the book was published he was living in the city of Mako. He was acquainted with many tsadikim, but did not become a follower of any hasidic dynasty.

The book was reprinted in 1930 in Piotrkow, and again after the Second World War by the author's grandson, R. Moshe Goldstein (Tel Aviv, 1948), with notes by Naftali Ben-Menahem. The work contains tales about R. Solomon, the head of the Kshanev rabbinical court and a disciple of R. Shmelke of Nikolsburg; of R. Dov Berisch, the head of the rabbinical court in Oshpetzin; and of R. Aryeh Leibush, the head of the Vishniets rabbinical court. Half the stories were later included by Isaac Singer in his *Seva ratson* (see below).

Sipurim nora'im

The book *Sipurim nora'im* by R. Jacob Kaidaner was published in Lemberg in 1875, at the press of R. Abraham Nissan Suess, who purchased the manuscript from Kaidaner's heirs. He printed it without pagination or division into chapters. The title page mentions that Kaidaner was from Vilkomir, and the author of *Matsref ha'avodah* (also known as *Vikuha Rabbah*).

[101] Lippe, *Bibliographisches Lexikon*, 516; Moriya, *Beit eked sefarim*, iii. 887, letter *kuf*, §164.

[102] Dan, *Hasidic Story* (Heb.), 189.

[103] Bodek(?), *Sipurei kedoshim*, 87–119. For an extensive treatment of the book and the manuscript, see Nigal, 'A Hasidic Manuscript' (Heb.).

The book contains sixty-two tales, some short, others lengthy and developed. The basic structure is chronological, with individual units for each tsadik included. There is also a preface that stresses the importance of the tales, and, especially, their authenticity.

A study of the tales reveals that the author had studied in the renowned Volozhin yeshiva under R. Hayim of Volozhin. He was very probably acquainted with the Old Rebbe of Habad, R. Shneur Zalman of Lyady, and his leading disciple, R. Aaron of Staroselye, but he actually became a follower of the hasidic movement only in the time of the 'Mitteler Rebbe', R. Dov Baer of Lubavitch.

In addition to the stories, the book also provides a considerable amount of historical information that sheds much light on individuals both within hasidism and outside the movement.

Mora'im gedolim

The book *Mora'im gedolim* (Great Awesome Things; the running head reads 'Inyanim nora'im', Awesome Matters), a 32-page booklet by N. Y. Reznik, was published in 1876 at the press of Hayim Aaron Zupnik in Pshemishel. The title page proclaims that it contains 'precious and authentic true stories, new ones that have not yet been printed, neither in *Kahal ḥasidim* nor in the other books that tell the praises of the tsadikim', a claim that seems to be accurate. Nine of the thirteen tales in the work focus on the dead, the transmigration of souls, the forces of impurity, the heavenly court, and repentant individuals. The reference on page 3 to the *Tanya* by R. Shneur Zalman of Lyady suggests that the collector might have been a hasid of Habad. Following the sixth story, the author interposes a direct explanation to 'my friend the reader'. One of the stories concerns a pupil of R. Isaac Luria, and the rest are about regular hasidim.

Ramatayim tsofim

The book *Ramatayim tsofim*, by R. Samuel of Shinova, which is a commentary on the midrashic work *Tana devei eliyahu*, was printed in two volumes in Warsaw in 1881. It begins with a list of the sixty-three tsadikim mentioned. At the end of his life R. Samuel was the head of the rabbinical court in Nashelsk, having previously served as rabbi in the cities of Wolodni, Shedlitz, and Lowicz. He was the disciple of R. Jacob Isaac (the Seer of Lublin), R. Jacob Isaac (the 'Holy Jew'), R. Simhah Bunem of Pshischa, R. Menahem Mendel of Kotsk, R. Solomon of Lentchna, R. Isaac Meir of Ger, and R. Isaac of Nezkizh. In his book he cites their teachings and stories that he heard from them, or in their name.

Many of the tales in the book would reappear much later in *Emunat tsadikim* (= *Kahal ḥasidim heḥadash*; see below).

Ma'asiyot peliyot nora'im venifla'im

The book *Ma'asiyot peliyot nora'im venifla'im*, printed first in Lemberg in 1883 and again in Lublin in 1904, consists of two works: *Ma'asiyot nora'im venifla'im* (Awesome and Wondrous Tales), and *Ma'asiyot peliyot* (Marvellous Tales); if the title page had not borne the combined title, we would assume that these two books had been bound together by chance. Each of the two books, which are of similar composition, contains many stories, only some of which are hasidic; each of the two ends with a standard Hebrew abbreviation meaning 'finished and completed, praise to God, the Creator of the Universe'. Many tales have initials at the end indicating the source, attesting to the intellectual honesty of the unnamed collector, who did not want to take credit for work not his own. Most of the hasidic tales in *Ma'asiyot nora'im venifla'im* were copied from *Netiv mitsvoteikha* by R. Isaac Eisik Safrin of Komarno (Lemberg, 1858). Some years later, R. Eliezer Shenkel copied the tales and published them in two separate books (see the section on Shenkel below).

Shivḥei tsadikim

The book *Shivḥei tsadikim* (Praises of the Tsadikim) was published in Warsaw in 1884. The collector and publisher, R. Mendel Tzitrin, states on the title page that the tales are 'new ones, never before published'. A statement on the second folio informs us that the stories are about the Thirty-Six Righteous (that is, the *lamed-vavnikim*, the 'hidden tsadikim' referred to earlier in this Introduction): their names are listed, and include pre-hasidic individuals, such as R. Isaac Luria, R. Naphtali Katz of Posen, R. Jonathan Eybeschuetz, and the Vilna Gaon, as well as hasidic tsadikim, beginning with the Maggid of Mezirech.

In his introduction, Tzitrin draws upon Maimonides' commentary on the tractate *Avot* to demonstrate 'that accordingly, this [telling tales of tsadikim] is not considered to be a waste of time, but [rather] the verse "genuinely truthful sayings" [Eccles. 12: 10] applies to all that has been remembered by the faithful'. The twenty-eight folio leaves of the book contain eighty-two different tales.

Temimei derekh

According to the title page of *Temimei derekh* (Those of Pure Way), which was first published in 1886, it was 'copied and published by Y.D. of Sudilkov'. In his introduction, the copyist relates that the tales were in a manuscript in the possession of a person from Sudilkov, and he purchased the manuscript and translated the stories into Hebrew, 'in pure and easy language'. The stories are preceded by a poem, signed by this Y.D., in 'eleven verses, of eleven syllables [each]', the acrostic thus formed spelling the name

'Jacob ben Samuel'. Two stories are about hasidim: R. Yehiel Mikhel of Zlotchev, and R. Mordecai, the brother of R. Leib Sarahs; the others are about non-hasidic individuals, including R. Samson of Coucy, R. Judah Hayat, and R. Naphtali of Posen.

Ma'aseh hakedoshim (Tale[s] of the Holy)

The book *Ma'aseh hakedoshim* was published anonymously in 1894 by the publishing house of R. Israel David (ben Abraham Nissan) Seuss in Lemberg. It contains stories of R. Meir Ba'al Haness and various *tana'im* and *amora'im*, passages copied from other books, and also a substantial number of tales of hasidim.

Among the first group of twenty stories, hasidic stories predominate. Story 20 (my numbering) is followed by the comment: 'Today, Thursday, the Torah portion of "Shemini", 13 Iyar 5693, Sniatin, March 30, 1893, by their reckoning [i.e. the Gregorian calendar; the actual Gregorian date should be 29 April 1893], Benjamin Dessler [should be: Ressler]'. It is unclear whether this was added by the collector of the stories, or by the censor. This note is followed by a number of passages giving accounts of non-hasidic personages: §21 is in the name of the worthy R. Michael Halberstadt of Berlin; §§22–3 are in the name of R. Jacob Tsevi Mecklenburg, a rabbi in Konigsberg; and §25 is in the name of R. David Luria. Most of this material was copied from *Sefer aliyot* by R. Joshua Heschel Levin (Vilna, 1855).

Years later, most of the hasidic stories would appear in the book *Ma'asiyot mehagedolim vehatsadikim* (Warsaw, 1909; see below), with the exception of two tales: that recounting how the Maggid of Mezirech brings a young man to repent (see Chapter 11 below, 'Apostasy and Apostates'), and a tale of R. Isaac Luria and the Devil.

Ma'asiyot vesihot tsadikim

The book *Ma'asiyot vesihot tsadikim* (Tales and Discourses of Tsadikim) was published in Lemberg in 1894 by the publishing house of R. Israel David Seuss. The running head reads 'Sihot tsadikim' (Discourses of Tsadikim), and, true to its name, the book contains many discourses and interpretations. The text was published again with a new title and different pagination by R. Feivel Munk (Warsaw, 1898). The title page of the Warsaw edition also appears at the beginning of the book *Ma'asiyot mehagedolim vehatsadikim* (Tales of the Great and the Tsadikim; Warsaw, 1909), despite the different content of the latter.

Kevutsat ya'akov

The book *Kevutsat ya'akov*, by R. Jacob Margolioth, was published in Pshemishel in 1896. The last part of the book contains a group of stories that would later be published separately (Jerusalem, 1946) under its original title, *Gedolim ma'asei tsadikim*; referring to this last part in his introduction, which he entitled 'Sheva einayim' ('Seven Eyes'), the collector writes:

I called this *Gedolim ma'asei tsadikim* [Great Are the Deeds of the Tsadikim], in which I wrote truthful and faithful things from the light of the world, the Ba'al Shem Tov, of blessed memory, mainly what my father, of blessed memory, related to me, that he had heard from his father, of blessed memory, the rabbi, the tsadik, our teacher and master, R. Samuel, the [hasidic] rabbi of Zolishtchik, what his eyes had seen and his ears had heard from the light of the world, the Ba'al Shem Tov, may his memory be for the life of the world to come, for he was on intimate terms with him, as will be explained in the text. And several additional tales of the holy ones who were after the generation of the light of the world, the Ba'al Shem Tov, of blessed memory.

The reader is told (see fo. 62*a*) that, many years prior to the book's composition, the author had been requested by the father-in-law of R. Menahem Nahum Duber, a son of the Mitteler Rebbe, to write down everything that he had heard from his father. When R. Menahem Nahum Duber learned of this, he, too, asked Margolioth to record the stories for him, and he gave the collection its name, *Kevutsat ya'akov*. The epilogue to the book, 'Amar hameḥaber' ('Author's Afterword'), was written in 1883.

All the tales of *Gedolim ma'asei tsadikim* in *Kevutsat ya'akov* were reproduced in the book *Emunat tsadikim* ('Faith in Tsadikim' [= *Kahal ḥasidim heḥadash*]; see below).

Notser te'enah

The book *Notser te'enah* was 'copied and published by S[imeon] R[abbi] of Tarnow' (Krakow, 1899). The work contains three tales: a story concerning the Tosafist R. Simeon of Coucy; an episode that occurred in Lemberg in 1679; and a tale 'that has not yet been published' concerning how R. Jacob Joseph of Polonnoye became a follower of the Ba'al Shem Tov.

Kahal ḥasidim heḥadash

The book *Kahal ḥasidim heḥadash* was first published in Warsaw in 1900, under the title *Emunat tsadikim*. The following declaration appears at the end of the work: 'This book was composed by an old man who acquired wisdom from the successors and worthies of the tsadikim, one of the many old hasidim who are God-fearing than most . . . and due to his great humility, he was not desirous of publicizing his name, but only in an allusion, in the abbreviation DBH.' The collector to whom this alludes is R. Isaac Dov Baer ben Tsevi Hirsch. Beginning with the second edition (Lemberg, 1902), the book was entitled *Kahal ḥasidim heḥadash*.

The title page of the new edition asserts that it contains more than two hundred stories that were related by the 'four who carry themselves well', namely, R. Isaac Eisik Safrin of Komarno, R. Isaac of Nezkizh, R. Meshullam Nathan Margolioth (whose stories were published by his son R. Jacob Margolioth in *Kevutsat ya'akov*), and R. Samuel of Shinova (in his book *Ramatayim tsofim*). An examination of the book confirms this, but the collector apparently drew upon other sources as well, including among others *Shivḥei habesht* (§28), *Shem hagedolim heḥadash* (§§103, 138), and *Sipurim nora'im*.

Derekh ha'emunah uma'aseh rav

The book *Derekh ha'emunah uma'aseh rav* was published in Warsaw in 1899. In his introduction the collector of the stories, R. Jacob Shalom Hakohen Duner, thanks his father, R. Nathan Neta, the head of the rabbinical court of Kolbiel, for his help in preparing the collection. The running head reads: 'Derekh emunah uma'aseh rav'. The book is organized as a kind of anthology, with the various hasidic teachings and stories grouped by subject. Page 7 contains a 'List of Abbreviations' intended to help the reader to find the sources used in compiling the book. The diligent collector made use of seventy-eight works, most of them standard hasidic works. Not surprisingly, the anthology was quite popular, and S. Y. Agnon probably drew upon it (without attribution) for his stories on the theme of hospitality (*Elu ve'elu*, 89–90).

Pe'ulat hatsadikim

The book *Pe'ulat hatsadikim* (The Activity of the Tsadikim) was published in Podgorze in 1900, and was prepared for publication by R. Isaac Singer of Rava Ruska, author of *Zoharei ḥamah* and *Zikhron tsadikim*. The book has a number of parts, each separately paginated. The content mostly derives from earlier works, such as *Mifalot hatsadikim* and *Kahal kedoshim* by Menahem Mendel Bodek, *Ramatayim tsofim* by R. Samuel of Shinova, and *Netiv mitsvoteikha* by R. Isaac Eisik Safrin of Komarno.

Seva ratson

The book *Seva ratson* (Satisfaction) was written by Isaac Singer and first published in Podgorze in 1900. It consists of two sections, the first relating the activities of R. Berish of Oshpetzin and the second those of R. Barukh of Medzibezh. Singer added to these the 1756 letter by R. Gershon of Kutow to his brother-in-law the Ba'al Shem Tov (these were taken from a manuscript and appeared here in print for the first time). The book contains no original material: the stories in the first section were copied from Menahem Meneli Sofer's *Sheloshah edrei tson* (Pshemishel, 1874), and those in the second section from Menahem Mendel Bodek's books *Ma'aseh tsadikim* and *Mifalot tsadikim*.

Hitgalut hatsadikim

The book *Hitgalut hatsadikim*, by R. Solomon Gabriel Rosenthal, the son of R. Mordecai Ze'ev (the head of the Kolbiel rabbinical court), was first published in Warsaw in 1901. In his introduction, Rosenthal speaks of the importance of the tales of tsadikim, drawing on statements by major hasidic rabbis; he thanks R. Simhah Gelernter, a rabbi in Klimentov, who agreed to pass on to him tales that he had heard from his grandfather, R. Meir Joshua, the head of the Klimentov rabbinical court. The two tales that begin the work (the first from *Ateret ya'akov* by Jacob Hager and Israel Berger; the second by the collector's uncle, R. Ephraim Fischel of Pilov) are followed by teachings from Rosenthal's father, R. Mordecai Ze'ev, on the weekly Torah portions and rabbinic dicta. These are followed by additional stories, some copied from other books (with attribution), and some contributed by various informants. The book concludes with further Torah teachings by the collector's father. At various places in the book Rosenthal adds explanations of the tales of a scholarly Torah nature, in the form of comments beginning with the words 'The collector said'.

The books of Isaiah Wolf Chikernik

Ma'asiyot uma'amarim yekarim (Precious Tales and Teachings) was published in Zhitomir in 1902. Its title page proclaims that it contains '[stories] that were never printed, of the Ba'al Shem Tov and his grandsons, the holy brothers, the holy rabbi, R. Moses Hayim Ephraim of Sudilkov, and his brother, the holy rabbi, R. Barukh of Medzibezh, may the memory of the righteous and the holy be for a blessing, may their merit protect us, Amen'. Many hasidic texts are mentioned in this work, including books by R. Jacob Joseph of Polonnoye and others such as *Avodat yisra'el* (R. Israel of Koznitz), *Peri ha'arets* (R. Menahem Mendel of Vitebsk), *Degel maḥaneh efrayim* (R. Ephraim of Sudilkov) *Tiferet shelomoh* (R. Solomon Rabinowich of Radomsk), *Be'er mosheh* (R. Moses Elyakym Beriah of Koznitz), *Shivḥei habesht*, *Raḥamei ha'av* (Jacob Kattina) *Notser ḥesed* (Isaac Eisik Safrin), *Butsina kadisha* (Nathan Neta Duner), *Siftei tsadikim* (Pinhas of Dinovitz), and Safrin's *Netiv mitsvoteikha*.

Sipurim neḥmadim (Pleasant Stories) was published in Zhitomir in 1903. The title page proclaims the origins of its contents: 'From the Ba'al Shem Tov and the holy rabbi, the Maharal of Prague [Judah Loew ben Bezalel], the holy rabbi, R. Issachar Baer of Zlotchev, the holy rabbi Azulai, the holy rabbi, R. Isaiah of Dinovitz, the rabbi, the *gaon* of Apta, and several additional tsadikim, may their merit protect us, Amen.' This book too mentions numerous hasidic works.

Sipurim uma'amarim yekarim (Precious Tales and Teachings) was published in Warsaw in 1903. The title page states that it contains tales 'of the four who carry themselves well: the . . . holy rabbi, David Leikes, the holy rabbi, R. Nahum of Chernobyl, and from his holy sons . . . the holy rabbi, R. Moses and his brother, the holy rabbi, R. Mottele of Chernobyl, may the memory of the righteous and the holy be for a blessing, and several additional tsadikim, may their merit protect us, Amen'.

Sipurim nifla'im uma'amarim kedoshim (Wondrous Tales and Holy Teachings) was published in Lemberg in 1908, bearing the running head 'Sipurim nifla'im'.

Eliezer Shenkel

Eliezer (Lazer) Shenkel of Tarnow published several collections of hasidic tales, a considerable number of which he took from earlier anthologies. His compilations also contain a significant amount of early narrative material from the rabbinic and medieval literatures. Shenkel copied a number of works in their entirety. Although his collections are not noted for their originality, they played a highly significant role in the dissemination of the tales among the different strata of Polish Jewry; his book *Yeshuot yisra'el* (see below) was of particular importance.

The following are the books by Shenkel that, in varying proportions, contain hasidic material.

Ma'asiyot nora'im venifla'im, published in Krakow in 1896, contains twelve tales, only some of which relate to hasidic personalities. Each story is followed by initials indicating the book from which it is taken. All of the material (with the addition of two new passages by Shenkel: pp. 38–9) was copied from the first section of *Ma'asiyot peliyot nora'im venifla'im* (Lemberg, 1883), also bearing the title *Ma'asiyot nora'im venifla'im*.

Ma'asiyot peliyot was also published in Krakow in 1896. The book contains twenty-four tales, again from both non-hasidic and hasidic sources, and here too the sources are indicated by initials. With the exception of the last three tales (paras 22–4), all the material was copied from the second section of the book *Ma'asiyot peliyot nora'im venifla'im*, also entitled *Ma'asiyot peliyot*.

Niflaot gedolim (Great Wonders) was published in Podgorze in 1900. The work contains five stories, two of which were copied from *Adat tsadikim* by Michael Levi Rodkinsohn (on R. Hayim, the brother of the Maharal, and on R. Moses Isserles).

Ma'asim tovim (Good Deeds) was also published in Podgorze in 1900. The work comprises twenty tales, only three of which are about hasidim.

Noraot anshei ma'aseh (The Awesome Acts of Men of Good Deeds), which also appeared in Podgorze in 1900, contains six stories, two of which are about hasidic personalities.

Ma'asiyot mitsadikim yesodei olam was published in Podgorze in 1903. One of its fourteen stories concerns hasidic individuals.

Sipurei anshei shem appeared in Podgorze in 1903. Of its twenty-three tales, eight are on hasidic subjects.

Yeshuot yisra'el was published in Podgorze in 1904. This work, which was printed in two volumes, is quite different from the other books published by Shenkel in being about a single individual. Its first volume portrays the hardships suffered by R. Israel of Ruzhin, and its second volume consists primarily of stories related by this tsadik. Each volume contains an introduction. In his introduction to the first volume, which implies that the author intended from the outset that his work should be published, Shenkel stresses his faithfulness to what is related. He has set down, he says, only what his eyes have seen, or what he has heard from the tsadik or from other reliable individuals; and he committed these records to writing during the tsadik's lifetime. In this same context, he quotes what the tsadik said about him: 'When I send Yosya to perform some mission, and he brings me an answer, I know clearly that he will neither add to nor subtract from the wording of this mission' (p. 4). This suggests that the author, who did all he could to conceal his identity, was in fact Yosya (a diminutive of Yosef) Rath (or Roth). Close reading of other passages of the work indicates that he lived in Kolomai (pp. 9, 12), and that he 'engaged in great commercial transactions' (p. 24). In 1839 or 1840 he was in Berdichev on business affairs (p. 5), subsequently emigrating to the Land of Israel (p. 23).

There is a certain affinity between the first volume of *Yeshuot yisra'el* and Rodkinsohn's *Shivḥei harav*, which also described the hardships, imprisonment, and release of one of the most prominent hasidic rabbis. However, while Rodkinsohn relied on oral accounts, and did not personally participate in the episodes he recounted, Yosya Rath was personally involved in the events that revolved around the tsadik of Ruzhin. The introduction to the first volume attests: 'This manuscript remained sixty-one years with his disciple, the concealed hasid', while the introduction to volume 2 states: 'This manuscript remained for sixty years [with his disciple].' This, then, indicates that the manuscript of volume 1 was written in 1843, and that of volume 2 in 1844; the main text, however, erroneously mentions the years 1847 and 1851 (p. 31) and, at the end of the first volume (p. 32), 1883. This discrepancy would appear to result from a simple typographical error: the number should have read כ"א (= 21) and not ס"א (= 61) years, with this error recurring in the second volume. The manuscript, which most probably was written in the Land of Israel (p. 23), therefore remained unpublished from 1883 until 1904.

The books of R. Dov Baer Ehrmann

Devarim arevim was printed in Munkacs in two volumes, in 1903 and 1905. The author, who says in his introduction 'I am a young man', asserts that he began writing the book in 1881 and completed it in 1903. He was apparently a Belzer hasid ('Stories of the Ba'al Shem Tov', §13). The composition is divided into sections containing, respectively, tales of the following individuals: the Ba'al Shem Tov; R. Elimelekh of Lizhensk and his brother R. Zusya; R. Levi Isaac of Berdichev; R. Israel, the Maggid of Koznitz; R. Moses Leib of Sasov; the Seer of Lublin; and R. Menahem Mendel of Rymanow.

Various dates are attached to events mentioned in the book (in contrast with other hasidic tales, most of which do not include dates)—1889 (fo. 2*b*), 1895 (fo. 36*b*), 1902 (fos 9*a*, 11*b*)—as are various hasidic and other books that can help date it: *Birkat avraham* ('Stories of the Ba'al Shem Tov', §21); *Tiferet shelomoh* (§30); *Sipurim nora'im* (§25); *Ma'or vashemesh* ('Introduction'); and *Kahal ḥasidim heḥadash* ('Corrigenda').

In 'Akdamot milin' (the Author's Introduction) Ehrmann writes at length of his sources and the subjects of the tales:

> I merely heard all these tales, and as they remained in my memory, thus I copied them and wrote them down to preserve them. Also, [the reader] will surely find some stories that I heard once or twice, once in a certain style and in the name of a certain holy one, and another time I heard it in a different style and in the name of another holy one. . . . The reason for this . . . [is that] because of the great amount of time and the multiplicity of tellers from one generation to the next, one matter may be exchanged by another. . . . There also are numerous stories that I heard from the same person, and afterwards he changed his manner, and the second time related it in a different fashion. . . . For this reason I have not cited in whose name each [tale] was told.

He adds, however, in the introduction, regarding the authenticity of the tales: 'And even if some fact is related in the name of a certain tsadik . . . and even if, in truth, this is a fabrication, and never had been, [the readers] will nevertheless know for a reliable certainty, that that tsadik was capable of exhibiting [i.e. of performing] this wondrous matter that is related in his name.'

The author begins his composition with the 'Corrigenda' list, which extends over several pages, evidence both of his desire to be precise and of the many errors that had entered the work.

Pe'er vekhavod was published in Munkacs in 1911, also in a number of sections, presenting tales of R. Moses Teitelbaum of Satmar, author of *Yismaḥ mosheh*; R. Jekuthiel Judah Teitelbaum, author of *Yeitev lev*; and the tsadikim R. Shalom and R. Joshua of Belz.

Zokhreinu leḥayim, Ehrmann's last book, was published in Munkacs in 1938. Ehrmann's descendants republished all his works in Israel in 1973, under the title *Devarim arevim hashalem*.

Divrei david

The book *Divrei david* by R. Israel Rapoport was published in Husyatin in 1904. The work is a collection of teachings and tales by the tsadik R. David Moses of Chortkov (one of the sons of R. Israel of Ruzhin), who died that same year. The collector was a relative and follower of R. David Moses. R. Israel, R. David Moses' only son and successor, conferred his approbation on the work; Rapoport states in his introduction that he had recorded what the tsadik had related after Kiddush and after Havdalah, and that R. Israel also had provided him with several teachings from his father.

Sipurei ya'akov

Sipurei ya'akov, an important collection of hasidic tales by R. Jacob Sofer of Dobromil, was printed in two parts, with a considerable interval between the two: the first volume (containing thirty-two tales: paras 1–32) was published in Husyatin in 1904, and the second (with thirty-three stories: paras 33–65) appeared in Lemberg in 1913. In the 'Introduction by the Author and Editor' Sofer emphasizes the authenticity of the tales, and asserts that he had been at the courts of sixty tsadikim and had heard stories that they related. Both this introduction and the index for the first volume are reprinted in the second.

The books of R. Abraham Hayim Simhah Bunem Michelsohn

R. Abraham Hayim Simhah Bunem Michelsohn, the son of R. Tsevi Ezekiel Michelsohn (head of the Plonsk rabbinical court), left a literary legacy of great scope and value. His œuvre is somewhat similar to that of his relative R. Israel Berger, who collected biographical material, teachings, and tales of forty hasidic tsadikim in his book *Zekhut yisra'el*.

Michelsohn's first book, *Shemen hatov* (The Good Oil), appeared in Piotrkow in 1905, in two volumes. The first volume includes teachings and commentary by R. Samuel Shmelke of Nikolsburg (from whom Michelsohn was descended), and the second contains stories culled from books and contributed by various informants. Michelsohn sent the work to his father, who added his comments and additions in a booklet entitled *Tsapaḥat hashemen* (The Jug of Oil).

Some five years later Michelsohn published several more books. *Dover shalom* (on the tsadik R. Shalom Roke'ah of Belz) and *Ohel yehoshua* ('The Tent of Joshua', on R. Joshua of Belz) appeared in Pshemishel in 1910, as did *Ohel elimelekh* ('The Tent of Elimelekh', on R. Elimelekh of Lizhensk). *Ateret menaḥem* ('The Crown of Menahem', on R. Menahem Mendel of Rymanow) was published in the same year in Bilgoray; *Ohel naftali* ('The Tent of Naphtali', on R. Naphtali Tsevi Horowitz of Ropshits) appeared in Lemberg in 1911, and the same year *Ohel avraham* ('The Tent of Abraham', on R. Abraham Abusch of Frankfurt) was published in Piotrkow.

R. Abraham Abusch was not a hasid, but the tales about him have much in common with the depictions of the hasidic tsadikim. *Mekor ḥayim* ('The Fountain of Life', on R. Hayim Halberstam of Sanz) was published in 1912 in Bilgoray.

The books of R. Israel Berger

The compendium *Zekhut yisra'el* by R. Israel Berger, the head of the Bucharest rabbinical court, consists of four books, each of which contains biographical material and discourses as well as the tales about specific hasidic tsadikim which make up the bulk of the contents.

Eser kedushot ('Ten Sanctities', Piotrkow, 1906) contains sections on the tsadikim R. Isaac Eisik Safrin, R. Tsevi Hirsch of Zhidachov, R. Moses of Sambor, R. Sender (Alexander) of Komarno, R. Judah Tsevi of Rozdol, R. Isaac Eisik of Zhidachov, R. Isaac Judah Yehiel of Komarno, and R. Judah Leibush of Rozdol.

Eser orot ('Ten Luminaries', Piotrkow, 1907) includes material on R. Duber (Dov Baer) of Mezirech, R. Pinhas of Korets, R. Levi Isaac of Berdichev, R. Isaac of Rozdol, R. Israel (the Maggid of Koznitz), R. Jacob Isaac of Lublin, R. Abraham Joshua Heschel of Apta, R. Israel of Ruzhin, R. Abraham Jacob of Sadigora, and R. David Moses of Chortkov.

Eser tsaḥtsaḥot ('Ten Brightnesses', Piotrkow, 1910) includes material on R. Elimelekh of Lizhensk, R. Moses Leib of Sasov, R. Menahem Mendel of Kosov, R. Isaac Eisik of Kalev, R. Uri of Strelisk, R. Naphtali Tsevi of Ropshits, R. Asher of Ropshits, R. Tsevi Elimelekh of Dynow, R. Hayim Halberstam of Sanz, and R. Abraham of Stretin.

Eser atarot ('Ten Crowns', Piotrkow, 1910) includes material on R. Moses of Drogichin, R. Abraham of Ulanov, R. Solomon Leib of Lentchna, R. Moses Tsevi of Savran, R. Meir of Premishlan, R. Abraham of Mikoliev, R. David of Zablutov, R. Shmelke of Sasov, R. Isaiah Shor, and R. Yehiel Mikhel.

Tiferet hatsadikim

Tiferet hatsadikim, compiled by R. Solomon Gabriel Rosenthal (author of *Hitgalut hatsadikim*), was published in Warsaw in 1908. Rosenthal's father was the author of *Kol haremez* (a play on words, meaning both 'The Voice of R. Mordecai Ze'ev' and 'The Allusion'), a commentary on *Midrash tanḥuma* and the Talmud, and Rosenthal added to *Tiferet hatsadikim* a collection of his father's writings, entitled *Hagahot veḥidushei haremez* (with reference to the title of his father's book). Rosenthal draws upon *Toledot aharon* by R. Aaron of Zhitomir (p. 10), and also includes stories from *Sefat emet* by R. Meshullam Feibush of Berzhan (pp. 47–9). Additional tales were related to the collector by his relatives: his uncle, R. Ephraim Fischel of Pilov (pp. 56–7); his father-in-law, R. Joseph Leib Schwotle of Kolbiel (pp. 64–5); another relative by marriage, R. Nathan Neta, the head of the Kolbiel rabbinical court (p. 61); and R. Jacob Koppel Silberberg of Warsaw (p. 62). Other stories appear with attribution to those from whom they were taken, and Rosenthal is careful neither to add to nor subtract from their words. So scrupulous about this is he that in one place he writes: 'because I did not remember it well, I did not wish to write it' (p. 63).

The books of Moses Hayim Kleinmann

Mazkeret shem gedolim (A Memorial for the Name of the Great Ones), published in Piotrkow in 1908, is divided into eighteen sections, each dealing with a different tsadik. Most of the book's content is copied from other books, as noted at the end of the tales or homilies. Kleinmann writes in his introduction that if no source is given, he heard it from 'truthful tellers'.

The full title of *Zikhron larishonim*, which appeared in Piotrkow in 1912, is *Zikhron larishonim arba'ah metivei lekhet* (A Memorial for the Early Ones, Four Who Carry Themselves Well). As this title implies, the book offers teachings and tales of four tsadikim: R. Isaac of Drohobitch, R. Aaron of Karlin, R. Yehiel Mikhel of Zlotchev, and R. Levi Isaac of Berdichev.

Or yesharim arba'ah metivei lekhet (The Light of the Upright, Four Who Carry Themselves Well), printed in Warsaw in 1924, contains teachings and stories of R. Mordecai of Lachowicze, R. Noah of Lachowicze, R. Moses of Kobrin, and R. Abraham of Slonim.

Layesharim tehilah (Praise to the Upright) was published in Piotrkow in 1910. The 'four who carry themselves well' of this book are R. Jacob Joseph of Polonnoye, R. Elimelekh of Lizhensk, R. Hayim Haike, and R. Mordecai of Nezkizh.

Ma'asiyot mehagedolim vehatsadikim

The book *Ma'asiyot mehagedolim vehatsadikim* (Tales of the Great Ones and the Tsadikim) was published in Warsaw in 1909 by the Lewin-Epstein brothers. The title page does not correspond to the content of the book, and is actually the title page of *Ma'asiyot vesiḥot tsadikim* (Tales and Discourses of Tsadikim; Warsaw, 1898). The book also contains 'Indexes' (a listing of the individuals and tsadikim around whom the tales revolve).

Close examination of the book reveals that the tales were copied from *Ma'aseh hakedoshim* (Lemberg, 1894), and that this is, indeed, the same work, but with a different title.

Sipurei tsadikim heḥadash

The book *Sipurei tsadikim heḥadash* (New Stories of Tsadikim), with the running head 'Sipurei tsadikim', was compiled by R. Abraham Isaac Sobelman (the head of the Zinkowitz rabbinical court) and published in Piotrkow in 1909/10. A considerable number of tales were passed on to the author by various individuals, including his father, R. Asher Enzil, who had also served as head of the rabbinical court in Zinkowitz and was intimately acquainted with R. Israel of Ruzhin. Although *Sipurei tsadikim heḥadash* was not itself reprinted many times, the stories it contained (in Yiddish) were printed in different combinations and under different names and were quite widely distributed. Sobelman also left manuscripts that include hasidic tales (some of which were not printed in his book) and hasidic teachings that he had heard from the hasidic rabbis of Chortkov.

Niflaot hatsadikim

The book *Niflaot hatsadikim* (The Wonders of the Tsadikim) was published anonymously in Piotrkow in 1911, at the press of Abraham Joseph Kleinmann of Warsaw. The unnamed collector states in the introduction that he has appended to the beginning of the book a special booklet on love of one's fellow Jews, entitled 'Roots and Branches in the Character Trait of Love of One's Fellow Creatures'. At the end of this booklet he notes that he saw fit to include in his collection tales that he had heard from reliable individuals, and especially (in the first seventeen pages) stories that he had heard from his relative R. Jacob Aryeh of Turbin, whose wife was the granddaughter of the tsadik of Belz. The anonymous collector also stresses that his tales are 'new tales that have not been printed'.

The 'Author and Collector's Introduction' to *Magdil yeshuot malko* (Jerusalem, 1955; see below) indicates that the collector of the tales in *Niflaot hatsadikim* was Yekutiel Zalman Lemberger, who lived for thirty years in Ostrovy in the Lublin district and then emigrated to the Land of Israel.

The 1939 Warsaw edition of *Niflaot hatsadikim* contains two stories that do not appear in the first edition.

Me'orot hagedolim

The book *Me'orot hagedolim* by R. Aaron Zeilingold, published in Bilgoray in 1911, contains fifty-five tales, along with hasidic Torah teachings. The ten tsadikim mentioned on the title page are R. Israel Ba'al Shem Tov, R. Dov Baer of Mezirech, R. Solomon of Karlin, R. Ze'ev of Zhitomir, R. Barukh of Medzibezh, R. Levi Isaac of Berdichev, R. Abraham Joshua Heschel of Apta, R. Asher of Stolin, R. Israel of Ruzhin, and R. Aaron of Karlin. Much of the subject-matter relates to relations between rich and poor, and problems related to matchmaking and marriage.

R. Judah Yudel Rosenberg and his books

R. Judah Yudel Rosenberg was born into a family of rabbis in Skarishov in 1860. Rosenberg, who was a hasid, studied in the Lublin yeshiva before taking up a rabbinic post in Warsaw; from there he moved to Lodz, before migrating to Toronto in 1913. In 1919 he was offered a rabbinic post in Montreal, where he died in 1936.

Rosenberg edited a monthly journal entitled *Kol torah* (The Voice of Torah) as well as books on halakhic and homiletical subjects. He also published a translation of the Zohar into Hebrew (*Zohar torah*), with a concise commentary entitled *Ziv hazohar* (The Brilliance of the Zohar). In addition, he exhibited a propensity for aggadic literature and tales. His popular works include: *Niflaot hamaharal* ('The Wonders of the Maharal' [= R. Judah Bezalel Loew of Prague], Piotrkow, 1909), containing sayings of the Maharal and stories about the golem he created; *Eliyahu hanavi* ('The Prophet Elijah', Piotrkow and Podgorze, 1911), containing tales and legends of Elijah; *Rafa'el hamalakh* ('The Angel Raphael', Piotrkow, 1911), on remedies and charms for various maladies; and *Divrei hayamim* ('Chronicles', Piotrkow, 1914), containing tales and legends of King Solomon.

His only hasidic work is *Tiferet maharal*, which was first printed in Lodz in 1912. The book contains many tales about R. Aryeh Leib, the 'Grandfather of Shpola', some of which are extremely long and complex. Rosenberg writes about the contents of the book in his introduction: 'And I collected from books, from writers and Torah scholars, and especially from the writings [i.e. manuscripts] that I obtained from the grandsons of R. Eisik Skverer, of blessed memory, . . . who was one of the first hasidim, and who attended the holy Grandfather almost his entire life.' Rosenberg claimed that he had obtained the worn manuscripts from two of R. Eisik Skverer's descendants ('R. Eisikel Urschotow and R. Hatzkile Kalmanovitch'), corrected them, and 'ordered them correctly'. In *Niflaot hamaharal*, however, Rosenberg had claimed that a relative of his had copied for him a manuscript in a library in Metz that was written by the son-in-law of the Maharal of Prague. This is without doubt a new literary work, and the only questions are who exactly the author is—the relative, or Rosenberg himself—and which early legends and tales he used. In *Tiferet maharal* Rosenberg admits at the outset that he has introduced changes into the works he has collected and set them in a new order. The mention of the descendants from whom he obtained the manuscripts, and references (at the end of the book) to the sources from which he copied the tales, along with the publication of letters by various people from whom he requested details on the life of R. Aryeh Leib, seem to indicate that Rosenberg took pains to transmit accurately what had come to him, and that his statement about the work is to be taken at face value. Nevertheless, it seems to me that *Tiferet maharal* is an original work by Rosenberg himself, albeit based on tales that he absorbed from his surroundings.

Rosenberg's references to the tales that he copied are as follows: chs 13, 31: from *Siftei kedoshim* (Lemberg, 1876 [= *Sipurei tsadikim* by Rodkinsohn]); ch. 32: from *Seder hadorot heḥadash*; ch. 35: from *Zikhron tov*; ch. 39: from *Mifalot hatsadikim*. He corresponded with R. Aaron Mordecai Kramer, the head of the Shpola rabbinical court; R. Tsevi Ezekiel Michelsohn, the head of the Plonsk rabbinical court; and R. Abraham Segal Ettinga of Dukla.

Sifran shel tsadikim

The book *Sifran shel tsadikim*, by R. Eliezer Dov Gemen, was published in Warsaw in 1914. The collector, a grandson of the Maggid of Riki, was born in Koznitz and at the time of the book's publication was living in Miechov. The collector heard many of the tales from the tsadik R. Yerahmiel Moses of Koznitz. The book comprises forty-nine chapters, each devoted to a hasidic master, and each divided into a number of sections containing tales, a guide to proper conduct, and discourses; the tsadik's death date (usually commemorated as a religious event, *yom hilula*); is given at the end of each chapter.

Darkhei ḥayim

The book *Darkhei ḥayim*, published in Krakow in 1923, sets down the religious customs observed by R. Hayim Halberstam, the tsadik who founded the hasidic dynasty of Sanz, along with some tales of his wondrous deeds. These were committed to writing by the tsadik's attendant, R. Raphael Halevi Segel Zimetbaum, who mentions in his introduction how he became a follower of R. Hayim: his mother, who was the granddaughter of the wife of R. Asher of Ropshits, was raised and educated in the home of the tsadik, who also arranged her marriage. Zimetbaum himself was raised in the home of the tsadik of Sanz, and when the latter required a physically 'strong person' to serve as his attendant, he turned to Zimetbaum, who was 'awake with him several nights'. A few years before R. Hayim passed away, Zimetbaum was asked to be his permanent attendant, a task that he faithfully fulfilled, without pay, until the tsadik's death. A letter of thanks and recommendation that the tsadik gave Zimetbaum on the eve of the sabbath of the Torah portion of 'Vayera' in 1866 is printed in his introduction.

The first part of the book, entitled 'Practices of Our Holy Master of Sanz, May his Merit Protect Us', includes 129 subsections. The second part, containing 69 subsections, consists of stories, each with an appropriate title. The third part, which runs to only two pages, records novel insights into the Torah that Zimetbaum heard from R. Hayim.

Ma'aseh hagedolim heḥadash

Ma'aseh hagedolim heḥadash, by Matityahu Tsevi Slodovnik, was published in Piotrkow in 1925. At the age of 65 Slodovnik, a scribe by occupation, decided to collect and publish hasidic tales. An entire section of the book is devoted to tales of hospitality, a subject that was close to Slodovnik's heart because of his many wanderings during the course of his lifetime. Tales and Torah teachings that he heard appear in the first fourteen pages of the book, and he apparently copied the fifty-seven tales on pp. 15–88 from earlier books.

Besorot tovot

The book *Besorot tovot*, by D. Meller, was published in Bilgoray in 1927. The book consists of three parts: I, Discourses and Tales; II, Letters; and III, Good Practices. Meller writes in his introduction that he heard these things at *melaveh malkah* gatherings (quasi-ceremonial occasions intended to prolong some of the atmosphere of the sabbath) and at *hilula* celebrations (banquets held to mark days of festivity, e.g. anniversaries of the death of famous rabbis), 'and every time I recorded what I heard'. Initially he had not intended to publish his collection, but when he saw how the generation was declining, so that 'there was hardly any house in which there are no newspapers' (taken as a sign of cultural assimilation and degradation) and 'heretical books were widespread', he resolved to take action to halt this degeneration by making his compilation more widely available. He cites in his introduction statements by the Ba'al Shem Tov, R. Nahman of Bratslav, R. Israel of Ruzhin, R. Shalom of Belz, the Seer of Lublin, and others, of the importance they ascribed to tales of tsadikim. He found it surprising, he said, that the leading Torah scholars of the generation attacked licentious behaviour with casuistry, instead of arousing people's minds and hearts with stories of tsadikim, and thereby overcoming heresy and irreverence.

Migdal david

The book *Migdal david*, by R. Mordecai Brukman, was published in Piotrkow in 1930. Most of the material in this volume, which consists of tales about R. David of Lelov, a well-known tsadik and a disciple of R. Elimelekh of Lizhensk, was taken from other books, but it also contains more traditional tales that Brukman had heard from various hasidim. The collector initially intended also to include teachings by R. David, but the high cost of printing forced him to limit himself to the stories. Thus, although the title page states: '*Migdal david.* Volume One', a second volume was never published.

Ḥutim hameshulashim

The book *Ḥutim hameshulashim* by R. Abraham Stern (Montreal, 1953) is divided into three sections. The first, entitled (in Yiddish) '*Hasidische maaises*' (Hasidic Tales), includes several dozen stories. In his general introduction to the book Stern writes (in Hebrew) that he committed the tales to writing 'to strengthen the faith of the holy ones of Israel in the good Lord . . . who performs wonders by his holy servants, the true tsadikim'. In his 'Introduction to the Hasidic Tales', which is written in Yiddish, he notes that the stories were transmitted to him from reliable sources, one person to another, and that they had never been published. Although many of the tales in the book represent oral traditions, the book also contains tales that, in one version or another, had already appeared in print. A striking example of this is the account of the Ba'al Shem Tov's attempted emigration to the Land of Israel, and his prevention of a planned persecution of the Jews in Constantinople. Stern himself writes (p. 36, in Yiddish): 'What happened to the Ba'al Shem Tov during his journey is well known and [i.e., already] described.' Mention is also made in the book of *Keter shem tov* by R. Aaron of Apta.

The tales were transmitted by various individuals from the author's town (Tishvitz), including the town's rabbi. Tale 11 is related in the name of Stern's father, the ritual slaughterer R. Issachar, and Tale 13 in the name of his father-in-law, R. Israel Dov Shuv of Shevershin. Of particular interest is a tale that the author claims to have seen in print (in Yiddish) as a child; for fear that the book had been lost during the Second World War, he committed it to writing. What is noteworthy is the chain of transmission of the tale, as described by Stern: the first teller of the story was R. Hayim Ibn Atar (1696–1743, the hero of the story), who related it to the Hida (R. Hayim Joseph David Azulai, 1724–1806); an old man who heard it from Azulai retold it (at the age of 90) to R. Tsadok Hakohen of Lublin; R. Tsadok Hakohen transmitted it to R. Simhah Goldberg, the head of the Shevershin rabbinical court; and Stern heard it from Goldberg.

Magdil yeshuot malko

The book *Magdil yeshuot malko* (He Accords Great Victories to his King), published in Jerusalem in 1955, consists of tales and teachings that R. Yekutiel Zalman Lemberger heard from the rabbi of Barniv, R. Abraham Simhah Horowitz. Horowitz (b. 1848; emigrated to Jerusalem; d. 1916) was the great-grandson of R. Naphtali Tsevi of Ropshits and served as attendant to many hasidic tsadikim, including R. Hayim of Sanz, R. Joshua of Belz, and R. Meir of Zhidachov. He related to his hasidim the stories that he had heard from his teachers.

In the 'Introduction by the Author and Collector', Lemberger describes how his ties with the rabbi of Barniv were forged after the author emigrated to the Land of Israel, and how he wrote down the tales. Once in Jerusalem, Lemberger also heard tales from R. Leib Shov that he wanted to include in a second section of his book; and he planned a third section that was to contain tales 'from faithful people, and from the kabbalists of Jerusalem'. These sections, however, which were meant to make up the second half of the work, are absent from the printed version. Although most of the material was related by the rabbi of Barniv, Lemberger defined himself as the 'author–collector'. Lemberger undoubtedly stylized the material and made some additions; the book's editor, R. Isaiah Margolies, also added glosses on various passages. Lemberger's introduction speaks of 'my books', in a reference to *Magdil yeshuot malko* and *Niflaot hatsadikim*, published in Piotrkow in 1911 by Abraham Joseph Kleinmann of Warsaw (see above); if it had not been for this reference, we would not know the identity of the unnamed collector of the latter work. The editor of *Magdil yeshuot malko*, R. Isaiah Asher Zelig Margolies (another follower of the rabbi of Barniv, stories about whom also appear in *Otsar hasipurim*), relates that the manuscript of this work remained unpublished for some forty years: Lemberger had actually written the introduction and the stories between 1911 and 1915. This explains why, when the book finally went to press, the blessing for life addressed to the rabbi of Barniv was placed in parentheses, and a blessing relating to the memory of the dead was added.

Lemberger died in Jerusalem on 21 June 1928.

ONE

THE HASIDIC TALE AS PERCEIVED BY HASIDIM

THE HASIDIC TALE has been an integral part of the hasidic movement from its very beginnings, through every stage of the development and formulation of hasidism, generation after generation.[1] The stories themselves may have appeared in published form only at a relatively late stage; but, irrespective of the differences between one storyteller and another, and among the various collectors of the tales, this literary phenomenon has been inseparable from the history of hasidism from the time of its founder, the Ba'al Shem Tov.

The extensive use of this literary genre expressed a profound psychological need on the part of the early hasidim, who afforded it a prominent place in their thought. Its popularity and longevity are also attributable to the inclination of tsadikim in later generations to sing the praises of their teacher–predecessors,[2] and the desire of the simple hasidim to relate to their children and acquaintances all that their eyes had seen and their ears had heard.

The tale would generally be considered to belong to the halakhic category of *devarim betelim* (idle matters), or at best that of *siḥot ḥulin* (mundane talk); but in the teachings of the Ba'al Shem Tov the telling of stories was sanctified, on the assumption that through this genre it would be possible to elevate the 'holy sparks' dispersed in the world; in this way, the tale could be a way of serving God, just like Torah study, prayer, and the observance of the commandments. This belief intensified in the generations following the Ba'al Shem Tov. The sanctification of the story that is characteristic of hasidic thought has already been the subject of scholarly research,[3] and the discussion in this chapter seeks merely to expand this examination. I will

[1] See Dan, *Hasidic Story* (Heb.), 35; see also Nigal, *Collectors of the Hasidic Story* (Heb.).

[2] e.g. when R. Menahem Nahum of Chernobyl learned of the death of the tsadik R. Abraham Hamalakh (the Angel), he began 'to tell his praises' (see *Shivḥei habesht*, ed. Rubinstein, 140).

[3] Dan, *Hasidic Story* (Heb.), 40–52; Piekarz, *Bratslav Hasidism* (Heb.), 85–101; Shmeruk, *Yiddish Literature* (Heb.), 198–260.

explore the virtues and roles that hasidism assigns to the story, the reasons it offers to justify its intense preoccupation with tales, and the attitude of the tsadikim themselves to the stories that were told about them.

THE POWER OF THE TALE

One of the important attributes that hasidism ascribes to the story is its ability to carry hidden meanings: it was commonly held that with simple words and tales the tsadik could work great wonders. R. Kalman Kalonymus Epstein of Krakow (d. 1823), author of *Ma'or vashamesh*, spoke of the ability of tsadikim to elevate sparks 'even in simple things, such as the words of one person to his fellow'.[4] Although the words and stories of the tsadik seem straightforward to the simple person, because 'they enwrap their aim in garments whose inner thought cannot be comprehended by the listener',[5] the full meaning is nevertheless different from what the common folk perceive. R. Shimon of Dobromil stresses that several tsadikim 'attire their words in simple matters from the way of the world, while their true meaning concerns profound matters and hidden principles', so that the simple folk will not fully understand their thought.[6]

An intellectual basis for the story and its spiritual and mystical influence appears in the writings of R. Israel of Ruzhin, the great-grandson of the Maggid of Mezirech and one of the major hasidic storytellers (see below). He maintained that the tsadikim of the first generations after the Ba'al Shem Tov were on a higher level of *gadlut* (literally, greatness), meaning a higher mystical–religious level, than his own generation and could act on behalf of the public and congregation by merit of their Torah learning and their prayer; 'but now, when the world is of the aspect of *katnut* [smallness], therefore, when the tsadik must act on behalf of the world, he does so only by means of tales and simple matters'.[7]

The sanctity of the tale and its lofty status were accepted not only within hasidic circles, but also by those who collected and circulated such stories. R. Israel Rapoport writes in the introduction to *Divrei david*, 'An everyday conversation by sages is comparable to the entire Torah' (see *Yalkut mishlei* on the verse 'the words of the wise and their riddles', Prov. 1: 6). He adds

4 Epstein, *Ma'or vashamesh*, 'Toledot', fo. 24*b*, s.v. *ve'od*.

5 Ibid., 'Vayigash', fos 27*b*–28*a*. In contrast, Ze'ev Wolf of Zhitomir, *Or hame'ir*, Ecclesiastes, 255*d*, writes that even simple people know 'that even the most earthly stories contain a kernel of wisdom'.

6 Shimon of Dobromil, *Naḥalat shimon*, 'Devarim', fo. 21*a*.

7 Israel of Ruzhin, *Irin kadishin*, 'Likutim', fo. 55*b*; H. A. Rabinowitz, *Shemuot tovot razin de'oraita*, fo. 19*b*; also cited in Alexander, *Niflaot hasaba kadisha*, introd.; Piekarz, *Bratslav Hasidism* (Heb.), 102.

that he heard from R. David Moses of Chortkov that R. Levi Isaac of Berdichev 'possessed a notebook [in which] was written every jot and tittle of mundane conversation that he had heard from his teacher, the great Maggid of Mezirech, may his memory be for a blessing for the life of the world to come, may his merit protect us, and he would always endeavour to understand the profound intent of each and every utterance.' The natural conclusion to be drawn from this is that there is no difference between sacred and mundane talk, since the 'commonplace' talk of the tsadik is such only for those who have not grasped its full profundity. The same approach is attributed to R. Samuel Shmelke of Nikolsburg, who interpreted the statement in the Talmud (BT *Sukah* 28*a*), 'I never in my life engaged in mundane talk', as meaning: 'even when he spoke idle, material matters, as it seemed to the multitude and was so understood by them, in truth, even these did not constitute mundane talk, rather, he performed great *yiḥudim* [mystical unifications] with them. . . . Likewise, R. Levi Isaac could be on an elevated spiritual plane the entire day and be occupied with things that seemed to be mundane talk and idle matters, while [in actuality] he performed awesome *yiḥudim* with them, as [one on] the level of Rav, the great *tana* [teacher of the mishnaic period].'[8]

R. Isaac Eisik Safrin writes in the same vein:

> I saw that my holy masters took exceeding care in guarding their mouth and tongue, so that all their speaking would relate to *yiḥudim*, [holy] names, ethical teachings, and the ways of the unity [of God], even though they might be relating tales and matters concerning bodily needs, and the like. . . . I saw that when my holy master, my uncle [R. Tsevi Hirsch of Zhidachov], related some matter pertaining to the affairs of this world, or when he spoke with people who had certain needs connected with the affairs of this world, he would [in reality] speak wondrous and spiritual things, sublime and lofty esoteric matters.[9]

In his collection *Beit tsadik*, Eliezer Zeligman discusses at length the telling of stories by tsadikim and states his view that there is 'undoubtedly enwrapped in these words, in concealment . . . a profound idea, one that our knowledge and mind are too limited to comprehend'; this leads him to conclude that

[8] Rapoport, *Divrei david*, introd.; Berger, *Eser orot*, 'Levi Isaac', §21; Bodek, *Mifalot hatsadikim*, §14, fos 13*b*–14*a*; Zevin, *Hasidic Tales: On the Torah* (Heb.), 422. Cf. *Shivḥei habesht*, ed. Rubinstein, 152: in a mundane conversation with the brothers R. Pinhas and R. Shmelke, the Maggid of Mezirech concealed his response to a question that he had been asked concerning a teaching in the Zohar.

[9] I. Safrin, *Zohar ḥai*, cited in Teomim, *Ateret tiferet*, 'His Holiness, the Holy Rabbi, R. Tsevi Hirsch of Zhidachov', §24. See also I. Safrin, *Zohar ḥai*, 'Bereshit', pt 2, 395: R. Abraham Joshua Heschel told stories 'with profound wisdom'. R. Tsevi Hirsch of Zhidachov could not sleep on a sabbath eve after he heard a story from R. Abraham Joshua, 'and he said that the tale that he had heard from the rabbi did not let him sleep, because of the deep wisdoms and secrets that it contained'.

'mundane talk and tales by and about tsadikim are as one with their Torah teachings [i.e. those that are defined as such], for all are directed to the will of the Lord, may he be blessed, and are intended to please him'.[10] Just as the Zohar explains the narratives in the Bible as profound esoteric matters, so the tales by the tsadikim also contain 'exalted profundity, hidden and concealed secrets'. Zeligman argues that belief is reinforced by stories, and that 'these matters are not [to be understood] as their simple meaning; rather, concealed within them are the mysteries of wisdom and discernment'.[11]

A similar approach is adopted by Michael Levi Rodkinsohn, who took the view that 'every utterance [by tsadikim], even [the telling] of tales, is Torah'. Moreover, even the mundane speech of common folk, when they speak of tsadikim, constitutes Torah: 'even if they have no knowledge of the inner dimension of the Torah scholar, and their talking consists solely of chatter concerning the external nature and behaviour of the sage, this, too, is good'.[12]

On one occasion R. Naphtali of Ropshits, the great Ropshitser rebbe, was a guest of R. Menahem Mendel of Rymanow, and the two men were conversing privately. R. Menahem Mendel's son, who was at the time a small child, hid in the room in order to listen to the conversation of the tsadikim, and he heard them talking about the number of types of dog there are in the world. When the tsadikim left the room, the child also left his hiding-place. When he encountered the Ropshitser, he asked the visitor about the conversation he had overheard, to which the tsadik replied: 'You should know, that not even man's seventy years suffice to disclose the secrets that are concealed in this matter!'[13]

R. Meir Shalom, the head of the Parczew rabbinical court, would frequently speak on matters that seemed of no consequence, and would do so even when sitting at table on the sabbath and festive days; at times he would even joke with children. The rabbi told the compiler of the collection *Derekh tsadikim*: 'Do not think, heaven forbid, that the things he [i.e. R. Meir Shalom] said were [to be understood] as their simple meaning', explaining that through such speech he was performing 'sublime divine service'.[14]

This way of thinking is also evident in the tendency on the part of the collectors of tales sometimes to provide, along with the stories themselves, an intellectual basis for their content, usually in their introductions to the volumes of tales. The various writers cite narrative passages containing

[10] Zeligman, *Beit tsadik*, 4; cf. Goldberger, *Darkhei hatov vehayashar*, fo. 11*a*: R. Meir of Premishlan would tell stories, 'and all the world would say that they were the secrets of the Torah'. Cf. also A. M. Rabinowitz, *Keter hayehudi*, introd., 7: R. Solomon of Radomsk said 'that a story from the deeds of the tsadikim is Torah'.

[11] Zeligman, *Beit tsadik*, 5.

[12] Rodkinsohn, *Shivḥei harav*, introd.; cf. Bodek, *Mifalot hatsadikim*, introd.: R. Israel Dov of Vladnik said that Torah is to be sought in the mundane words of tsadikim.

[13] Kamelhar, *Em labinah*, 'Beit menaḥem', §7, p. 40.

[14] Yellin, *Derekh tsadikim*, 16.

hasidic thought from the expositions of the hasidic teachers as well as oral traditions that do not appear in the hasidic homiletical literature.

In his introduction to *Shivḥei habesht*, R. Israel Jaffe, its first publisher, refers the reader to the Ba'al Shem Tov's statement that 'whoever relates the praises of tsadikim is regarded as if he engages in *ma'aseh merkavah* [lit. 'the work of the chariot': i.e. mystical contemplation of the divine]'.[15] This was a common adage among the hasidim, and is cited many times in the introductions by the compilers of the story collections.[16] An extreme formulation of it is attributed to R. Menahem Mendel of Rymanow: 'Tales from tsadikim are the *ma'aseh merkavah*, for the tsadikim are the Merkavah [God's chariot-throne].'[17] A scriptural interpretation based on wordplay and ascribed to R. Jacob Joseph of Ostrog (also known as R. Yeivi) likewise accords a high spiritual value to the words of the tsadik: '"I will lay sapphires [*sapirim*] as your building stones" [Isa. 54: 11]—this refers to the stories [*sipurim*] of the tsadikim.'[18]

In addition to this hidden, esoteric significance, the hasidic tale also has a revealed, literal meaning and aim: under the influence of the story, the average person is likely to recall his sins and repent.[19] R. Kalman Kalonymus Epstein, author of *Ma'or vashamesh*, notes this effect of the hasidic tale: '[The tsadik] would relate a story, that would seem to be actual idle speech, and everyone took for himself from this story a great moral. Even if a hundred people or more were listening, each one thought that the tsadik was relating these matters [especially] for him.'[20] The originator of the didactic narrative method was R. Elimelekh of Lizhensk, Epstein's teacher; R. Elimelekh 'would stand before his house, and people encircled him. He

[15] *Shivḥei habesht*, 149. Gershom Scholem is of the opinion that this teaching has its origins in Shabatean literature. See Scholem, 'Neutralisation of the Messianic Element', 51.

[16] See e.g. Joseph ben R. A., *Mifalot tsadikim heḥadash*, introd.; Slodovnik, *Ma'aseh hagedolim heḥadash*, introd.; *Ma'asiyot noraot*, title page; Meller, *Besorot tovot*, introd. In the introduction to his book *Sha'ar ha'emunah*, Nathan Nata Donner cites this dictum, and adds: 'Our masters understood this, on condition that the heroes of the tales be true tsadikim, and that the story be true.' He wrote in a similar vein in his introduction to *Butsina kadisha*.

[17] Gemen, *Sifran shel tsadikim*, introd. Cf. Alexander, *Niflaot hasaba kadisha*, introd.: 'For anyone who tells the praises of the tsadikim is regarded as if he engages in *ma'aseh merkavah*, for tsadikim are the chariot of the Omniscient.' R. Solomon Gabriel Rosenthal writes in his introduction to *Tiferet hatsadikim* (Piotrkow, 1912), in the name of R. Tsadok of Lublin (in the latter's book *Tsidkat hatsadik*) regarding the tsadikim: 'they are the chariot in which the Lord, may he be blessed, rides'. Cf. N. N. Donner, *Butsina kadisha*, introd. For the source of all this, see *Genesis Rabbah* 47: 8, and elsewhere: 'The Patriarchs, they are the divine chariot.'

[18] Gemen, *Sifran shel tsadikim*, ch. 16, §7; ibid., introd.; Slodovnik, *Ma'aseh hagedolim heḥadash*, introd.; Brukman, *Migdal david*, introd., 11.

[19] See Epstein, *Ma'or vashamesh*, 'Devarim', fos 193*a*–*b*; cf. Abraham of Slonim, *Beit avraham*, 163: tales of tsadikim, especially on the sabbath, curb desires and refine the soul.

[20] Epstein, *Ma'or vashamesh*, 'Devarim', fo. 193*b*.

would stand in the centre and relate to them a story on some subject, and each one of them thought that he was relating this tale for him, alluding to his adverse deeds.'[21]

The third goal of the hasidic story was to rouse its hearers into action for the service of God. Several compilers of hasidic stories quoted the dictum by R. Elimelekh that 'it is an auspicious sign for a person if, when he hears what is related regarding the virtues of the tsadikim and their faithful holy service of the Lord, may he be blessed, his heart beats at that time with desire and very great fervour that he also merit faithfully to serve the Lord, may he be blessed; this is a good sign that the Lord is with him'.[22] The compilers of the hasidic story found an additional theoretical basis for their work in the teachings of R. Nahman of Bratslav, whose views on the hasidic story have been the subject of extensive scholarly examination.[23]

The very power of the hasidic tale wins adherents to hasidism. Many people, among them some outstanding individuals, have been drawn to hasidism by its stories. R. Menahem Mendel of Kotsk, one of the leading hasidic tsadikim, said of himself that 'he was made a hasid by an old man who told stories about the holy tsadikim'.[24] The Ba'al Shem Tov excelled in his

[21] Ibid. fos 194*a*–*b*.

[22] Elimelekh of Lizhensk, *No'am elimelekh*, 'Shemot', fos 32*c*–*d*. See Donner, *Derekh ha'emunah uma'aseh rav*, introd.; Hazan, *Sipurim nifla'im*, introd.; Slodovnik, *Ma'aseh hagedolim heḥadash*, introd.; Alexander, *Niflaot hasaba kadisha*, introd. to vol. ii. Shmeruk, *Yiddish Literature* (Heb.), 204, views Elimelekh's statement about the importance of the stories as evidence of their currency at the time (before 1787). He concludes (pp. 206–7) that R. Elimelekh (*No'am elimelekh*, 'Kedoshim', fo. 62*c*) 'manifestly denigrates' the hagiographic *shevaḥim* stories that were directed to 'those weak in study and in observance'. R. Elimelekh stresses that the tsadik should not engage in self-aggrandizement ('do not detail your fine attributes and deeds'). The praises of the tsadik are to be left for those who are close to him, that is, the hasidim, 'who will tell of your good deeds' (ibid.). This approach is quite consistent with his fierce opposition to any form of pride and self-aggrandizement by the tsadik; he also demands that those who tell stories about tsadikim not exaggerate (see *No'am elimelekh*, 'Bo', fo. 36*d*).

[23] See Piekarz, *Bratsav Hasidism* (Heb.), 83–131. The introductions of the following books draw upon R. Nahman of Bratslav for support: Rakats, *Tiferet hayehudi*; *Ma'asiyot vesiḥot tsadikim*; Alexander, *Niflaot hasaba kadisha*; Rosenthal, *Hitgalut hatsadikim*; A. M. Rabinowitz, *Keter hayehudi*; Brukman, *Migdal david*; [Lemberger], *Magdil yeshuot malko*. Echoing the view held by R. Nahman (Nathan of Nemirov, *Shivḥei haran*, §52) that 'the glory of the Lord is proclaimed by everything, for "his glory fills all the earth" [Isa. 6: 3], and the glory of the Lord, may he be blessed, is proclaimed even from the stories of non-Jews, as well', R. Isaac Safrin writes, in *Notser ḥesed*, fo. 18*c*: 'One can also learn from a non-Jew in the marketplace when he tells him some story. . . . He will understand that he does not hear this without a reason; rather, he should learn from this some good mode of behaviour, or a good way.'

[24] Rakats, *Siaḥ sarfei kodesh*, vol. i, §365; Arten, *Emet ve'emunah*, §791, p. 120. Cf. Brukman, *Migdal david*, introd., 11: 'And several great and tremendously awesome tsadikim related that their awakening to the Lord, may he be blessed, was primarily by means of tales of the tsadikim.'

ability to attract new followers by this means. A classic example of this is the narrative of the conversion to hasidism of R. Dov Baer of Mezirech, who became the Ba'al Shem Tov's outstanding disciple and went on to assume the mantle of leadership of the hasidic movement as 'the Maggid' after the death of his teacher:

And behold, afterwards, when he [the Maggid] came to the Ba'al Shem Tov, may his memory be for the life of the world to come, he thought that he had heard Torah from him. The Ba'al Shem Tov had [in fact] related a story to him, how he had travelled for several days, and had no more bread to give to the Gentile [servant] of the wagon owner . . . more stories such as this. Afterwards, on the second day, [the Maggid] came again to the Ba'al Shem Tov, and [the Ba'al Shem Tov] told him how on this journey there was no more fodder to feed the horses. . . . All the stories that the Ba'al Shem Tov told contained wonderful and copious wisdom for the one capable of comprehending.[25]

At the time, however, R. Dov Baer did not understand this, and after two days of apparently trivial talk had already resolved to return home. Had it not been for a midnight conversation between the two men, in which the Ba'al Shem Tov asked the future Maggid the meaning of a difficult passage in the book *Ets haḥayim* by R. Hayim Vital, from which he realized the greatness of the questioner, he would have left the following day. The Maggid himself would later talk of horses and carriages at a sabbath meal; but his audience then was composed of hasidim, who sensed that this related to matters abounding in the mysterious.[26]

Similar elements are to be found in the narrative of the adoption of hasidism by a second leading pupil of the Ba'al Shem Tov, R. Jacob Joseph of Polonnoye. R. Jacob Israel of Cherkassy begins his account thus:

Once the Ba'al Shem Tov came to the city of Sharigrad . . . early in the morning on a summer day, when they were leading the cattle to graze, and he stood with his wagon in the city street. He called to one person, who was leading animals to pasture, and he told him some tale. And when someone else passed by the same way, he bent his ear to hear what he was saying, and the story appealed to him. Afterwards, yet another person came to him, and similarly several additional people, until the Ba'al Shem Tov attracted with his stories all the people of the city,

[25] Aaron of Apta, *Keter shem tov*, fo. 30*a*–*b*; Donner and Wodnik, *Sefer ba'al shem tov*, introd. ('Kuntres me'irat einayim'), §8. Cf. the Yiddish edition of *Shivḥei habesht*, ch. 23. See Nigal, 'A Primary Source' (Heb.), 138.

[26] See Zeilingold, *Me'orot hagedolim*, 'His Holiness, the Holy Rabbi, R. Dov Baer of Mezirech', §7, pp. 32–5. See Gemen, *Sifran shel tsadikim*, ch. 40, §14: R. Jerahmiel Moses of Koznitz would tell stories during the third sabbath meal, in order to prolong the sanctity of the sabbath.

who all came, and stood there to hear tales from him. The beadle from the synagogue also stood among them.[27]

R. Jacob Joseph, who was a young rabbi at the time, noticed to his displeasure that the gates of the synagogue had not been opened as they should have been, and remonstrated with the beadle for neglecting his duties. When he asked why this had happened and was told about the storyteller who had distracted the beadle, he sent for this disruptive individual. The Ba'al Shem Tov presented himself to the furious rabbi and said: 'Do not be angry; I will tell you a story!' The rabbi was profoundly moved by the tale that he heard, and his anger turned to admiration. The Ba'al Shem Tov went on to tell R. Jacob Joseph two more stories, and by the end of the third there stood before him a passionate hasid who would eventually become his faithful disciple.

A fourth characteristic of the hasidic story is its intrinsic ability to perform miracles and wonders. The Ba'al Shem Tov was asked by R. David Forkes how one could pray for a sick person by means of mere stories,[28] and indeed, tsadikim succeeded in healing the ill in this manner: R. Berisch of Oshpetzin healed a sick woman through stories,[29] and a young man who suffered from melancholy was cured in the same way.[30] Problems of many other kinds, too, were solved by the power of the tsadik's storytelling. R. Israel of Ruzhin told the following anecdote:

Once a tenant came to my lord, my father, may the memory of the righteous be for a blessing for the life of the world to come, and he told him that his master wanted to cancel his lease before Passover. My father, of blessed memory, was sitting and telling stories the entire time that [the tenant] was speaking. Before he left, the [tenant] said to him: 'My master, what is his [= your] response to this?' He [the tsadik] replied: 'I have already acted on your benefit. Go in peace!'[31]

[27] Chikernik, *Ma'asiyot vesipurim yekarim*. According to another version (Sobelman, *Sipurei tsadikim heḥadash*, §11), R. Jacob Joseph travelled to see the Ba'al Shem for himself, but returned home after two or three weeks, 'and he did not yet desire to be one of the followers of the Ba'al Shem Tov, for he did not approve of the latter's way, which was almost alien to him. He did not understand his way in holiness, for the tales that he heard and the inner meaning they contained were the most secret [esoteric knowledge].' For an additional version, see S[imeon] R[abbi], *Notser te'enah*, 14: R. Jacob Joseph heard the Ba'al Shem Tov tell stories during a wedding banquet, and when he saw that these related to incidents from his life, he became a hasid. Cf. A. Stern, *Ḥutim hameshulashim*, 28–30.

[28] *Shivḥei habesht*, ed. Horodezky, 167, ed. Rubinstein, 182–3; see A. M. Rabinowitz, *Keter hayehudi*, introd., 8.

[29] Singer, *Seva ratson*, fo. 4*b*.

[30] Sobelman, *Sipurei tsadikim heḥadash*, §45.

[31] Shenkel, *Yeshuot yisra'el*, introd. to vol. ii, p. 3; also cited in the introd. to Rosenthal, *Hitgalut hatsadikim*. Gemen relates in *Sifran shel tsadikim*, ch. 40, §14, that the story he was told by R. Jerahmiel Moses of Koznitz facilitated his wife's recovery: 'Thus was his way, that the relating of the story was greatly beneficial to one who was in need of a remedy.'

Prominent among those who benefited from the stories of the tsadikim were women experiencing difficulties in childbirth. Once some people came to R. Nahum of Chernobyl with a request to pray for a woman who was having difficulties in labour. The tsadik sent them to his son-in-law, R. Shalom Shakhna (the father of the Ruzhiner), who exclaimed when they came: 'I have nothing to do with what is concealed, nor do I know anything [about that]!' The delegation returned to R. Nahum, who sent them back to R. Shalom Shakhna with an order to aid the woman. R. Shalom Shakhna related an 'awesome story' about a Jewish woman who succeeded in escaping from an Ishmaelite who wanted to rape her. The woman's husband was convinced that she had not been defiled, since—by an astounding coincidence—he was told this by the Ishmaelite himself, who was unaware that the man to whom he was talking was the woman's husband. The tsadik emphasized that the couple rejoiced greatly at this outcome, and added: 'Go home, and you, too, will have a *mazal tov* ['congratulations': i.e. a cause for rejoicing], for the infant is born now.' After the group had left, R. Shalom Shakhna said that this story was a wondrous charm to be related to anyone suffering from a difficult birth.[32]

Once R. Mordecai ('Mottele') of Chernobyl and R. Israel of Ruzhin met, and they received a request to help a woman who was having a difficult birth. The Ruzhiner started telling a story,[33] and when he had finished, he called out 'Mazal tov!' He then turned to the woman's husband and said to him: 'Go home, for your wife has given birth to a son.' To the tsadik from Chernobyl this was a miracle, and the Ruzhiner explained that he had learned to provide help by means of a story about the servant of Abraham. When the servant saw that *dinim* (evil decrees or punishing powers) were present in the food that was placed before him, he said: 'I will not eat until I have told my tale' (Gen. 24: 33), and by his speaking he transformed the evil into good. The rabbis referred to this when they said (*Genesis Rabbah* 60: 11, *inter alia*): 'The conversation of the servants of the Patriarchs is better than the Torah of the sons.' The tsadik added: 'And also by this story, even if it is told by a simple person, help will be effected!'[34]

[32] Rakats, *Siaḥ sarfei kodesh*, ii, §476. See Ehrmann, *Devarim arevim*, 'Stories of the Holy Brothers R. Elimelekh and R. Zusya', §6: the brothers ordered the telling of what had happened to them with a woman who experienced difficulty in childbirth 'every *Wachtnacht*' (see Ch. 4 below), 'and this was considered to be a charm'. See also Moses Hayim Ephraim of Sudilkov, *Degel maḥaneh efrayim*, 'Vayeshev': 'I heard and saw my master, my grandfather, may his light shine [= the Ba'al Shem Tov], relate stories and external matters, and thereby serve the Lord with his unblemished and pure wisdom.' See also A. Stern, *Ḥutim hameshulashim*, 31.

[33] A Christian tale concerning a female pope that was transformed into a hasidic story. See Gans, *Tsemaḥ david*, 284.

[34] Slodovnik, *Ma'aseh hagedolim heḥadash*, §37. See the discussion below of the stories of R. Israel of Ruzhin.

The beadle of the tsadik of Kaminka told a tale from the time of the Ba'al Shem Tov about a treasure. According to him, the tsadik said that the story 'acts as a charm for livelihood, and it is good to tell it at the *melaveh malkah* meal'.[35] R. Shalom Roke'ah of Belz asserted that it was commonly said, in the name of tsadikim, that retelling one of the stories of the Ba'al Shem Tov after the end of the sabbath is a charm for livelihood. The tsadik added that stories bring about benefits not only in matters of livelihood, but in every area, and not only after the end of the sabbath, but at any time; also, not only stories from the Ba'al Shem Tov, but also stories from other tsadikim are highly effective.[36]

Hasidic thought subscribes to the belief that the recounting of a miracle is likely to bring another one in its wake. R. Solomon of Lutsk, a pupil of the Maggid of Mezirech, wrote: 'Similarly, when by speech and recollection the miracle is related, the aspect of that miracle is also aroused and is drawn down; consequently, it is a commandment to retell of the Exodus from Egypt.'[37] A similar idea surfaced in a later generation, in the writings of R. Tsevi Elimelekh of Dynow, based on the thought of his predecessors:

Our holy masters, the tsadikim of our generations, receiving from those blessed with divine inspiration, wrote: When a person needs some succour, such as for healing and success, or to pass through the depths of the sea without hindrance, then he is to mention with his own mouth the miracles that were performed in like circumstances for the tsadikim of the generations. . . . For by the accounts of miracles in similar straits, they shall be delivered in view of all.[38]

Despite the commonly accepted assumption regarding the decline of spiritual power over the generations, even the tsadikim who doubted their own ability to perform wonders firmly believed that the telling of a miraculous

[35] Ehrmann, *Devarim arevim*, 'Stories of the Ba'al Shem Tov', §2.

[36] See Ehrmann, *Pe'er vekhavod*, 26. The tsadik added, 'Even stories about us': Meller, *Besorot tovot*, introd. See also the title page of *Ma'asiyot noraot*: 'and acting as a charm for livelihood, and success in spiritual and material pursuits'; Rakats, *Tiferet hayehudi*, introd.: R. Isaac Meir of Ger said that when people speak of the Holy Jew (R. Jacob Isaac of Pshischa), this is a charm for piety; Rosenstein, *Pe'er layesharim*, fo. 20*b*: 'And the world [i.e. everyone] says that one must speak of the Ba'al Shem Tov, of blessed memory, upon the departure of the holy sabbath [i.e. Saturday night].'

[37] Solomon of Lutsk, *Dibrat shelomoh*, on the book of Esther, cited in Donner, *Rishpei esh hashalem*, 'Introduction by the Son-in-Law of the Rabbi, the Publisher'; id., *Derekh ha'emunah uma'aseh rav*, introd.; Hazan, *Sipurim nifla'im*, introd. Cf. the statement by R. Yehiel Mikhel of Zlotchev: 'The letters of the story arouse the [heavenly–spiritual] root of all miracles': Jacob Isaac (the Seer of Lublin), *Divrei emet*, 'Beshalaḥ'; *Mifalot hatsadikim*, introd.; Donner, *Derekh ha'emunah uma'aseh rav*, introd.; Slodovnik, *Ma'aseh hagedolim heḥadash*, introd.; Hazan, *Sipurim nifla'im*, introd.

[38] Tsevi Elimelekh of Dynow, *Igra dekalah*, 'Ekev', s.v. *ki tomar bilevavekha*, fo. 93*a*; Donner, *Rishpei esh hashalem*, 'Introduction by the Son-in-Law of the Rabbi, the Publisher'; Hazan, *Sipurim nifla'im*, introd.

story was likely to bring about a new miracle. R. Shneur Zalman of Lyady was asked to take action to prevent the impending apostasy of a young man. He responded that it was not within his powers to bring the young man back to his faith, but that he could relate a story concerning the return to Judaism of a candidate for conversion that had taken place during the time of his teacher, the Maggid of Mezirech; and true enough, after he told this story the young man who was about to embrace Christianity returned to his family and his original faith.[39]

Another story shows the decline of the generations: what the tsadikim of former times could do in contrast to the limited capabilities of those born later.

> Our holy teacher [R. Israel of Ruzhin] told a story of the Ba'al Shem Tov, of blessed memory. One time there was a great matter of life and death involving an only, and very good, son. . . . He [the Ba'al Shem Tov] ordered that a waxen candle be made. He went to the forest, affixed the candle to a tree, [performed] other actions, engaged in *yiḥudim* and the like, and with the help of the Lord, may he be blessed, effected great deliverance. Afterwards, a similar occurrence happened to our grandfather, the holy Maggid [R. Dov Baer of Mezirech], who also did the same. He said: I do not know the *kavanot* [mystical intents] and *yiḥudim* in which the Ba'al Shem Tov engaged, but I will act on the basis of the intent employed by the Ba'al Shem Tov, and [his action] was accepted, as well. Afterwards, a similar occurrence happened to the holy tsadik, R. Moses Leib of Sasov, of blessed memory, who said: We, we do not have the power to do thus; rather, I will relate and the Lord, may he be blessed, will help! And so it was, with the help of the Lord, may he be blessed.[40]

R. Jacob Kaidaner heard from R. Pinhas Reises of Shklov that

> once he was on the way with the holy *rebbe* [R. Shneur Zalman of Lyady], when the skies suddenly grew dark and a pouring rain began to fall. His honoured holiness said that once the Ba'al Shem Tov had been travelling, and a pouring rain began, and he recited a single verse and the rain stopped. He told us the verse that he [the Ba'al Shem Tov] had recited, and he also expounded for us the mystical intent of the verse. And before he finished the exposition, we saw a true wonder, namely, a torrent on both sides of the wagon, while the wagon itself was completely dry, indescribably so, not a single drop . . . and when we came to the inn and his holiness took his feet out of the wagon, it immediately was filled from the rain.[41]

[39] See Ch. 11 below.

[40] Zak, *Keneset yisra'el*, 23. Cf. Scholem, *Major Trends*, 349–50; Agnon, *Sefer sofer vesipur*, 439; Piekarz, *Bratslav Hasidism* (Heb.), 102–3.

[41] Kaidaner, *Sipurim nora'im*, §49, p. 121: 'The Ba'al Shem Tov further decreed that the rain [that fell by his decree] would continue to fall, but that no rain should fall in the middle of the road, where the wagon was going, and so it was.' Mondshein, *Migdal oz*, 'Sha'ar hama'aseh', 152.

Elsewhere it is related that R. Ezekiel of Shinova wanted to light his pipe, but the wind extinguished the match, and this happened a number of times. The tsadik related an incident that had happened to R. Menahem Mendel of Rymanow. The wind had extinguished the sabbath candles in his house, and R. Menahem Mendel had exclaimed: 'Master of the universe, I require the lights of the holy sabbath!' After this the candles no longer went out. When the tsadik of Shinova finished his story, he asked that a match be lit for him, and this time it was not extinguished by the wind. The tsadik admonished: 'Do not say that this is a wonder! Rather, if people want to perform a miracle, they can do so by telling of something that happened to some tsadik, because the stories that are related concerning tsadikim have great power to effect deliverances.'[42]

R. Benjamin Munk, a bookseller in Lemberg, came to R. Joshua of Belz to seek his help because his newborn infant was losing blood. The tsadik told Munk how the Ba'al Shem Tov advised stopping such bleeding by using the ashes of a frog, and then added: 'And now it is the autumn, and it is impossible to obtain a frog. Accordingly, let this story be a remedy, as if the action had been performed, and may the child be healed and regain his strength.' And when the anxious father returned home, he found that the words of the tsadik had been fulfilled.[43]

THE STIMULUS FOR DISSEMINATING HASIDIC STORIES

The stimulus for disseminating hasidic stories was not only their mystical power to change the world but also the desire to increase popular faith in the tsadikim and their power to perform miracles, and to refute the claims of those who doubted them.

The need to strengthen faith was regarded as of pressing urgency against a background of constantly waning belief. This sense of decline from one generation to the next, and the conviction that it could be halted through the telling of stories about tsadikim, was shared by several collectors of hasidic stories.[44]

In his introduction to *Shivḥei habesht*, R. Dov Baer of Linitz asserts that even in his time 'faith has declined greatly, and several heresies [have] appeared in the world'. Wishing to ensure that each reader would learn a moral lesson from every story, he had initially intended to write such a moral

[42] Hazan, *Sipurim nifla'im*, §13; Moskowitz, *Otsar hasipurim*, i. 3; Agnon, *Sefer sofer vesipur*, 440.

[43] A. Michelsohn, *Ohel yehoshua*, §6.

[44] See e.g. Zeligman, *Beit tsadik*, 6: 'To strengthen belief, that has been somewhat weakened in our time'; Meller, *Besorot tovot*, introd.

explicitly at the end of each tale, but decided against this for fear of having to be too concise when a lengthy exposition was required.[45] Most of the collectors therefore sought to extol the deeds of the tsadikim, so that the reader could learn from them 'some manner of conduct and good character trait for the service of the Lord, may he be blessed'.[46]

R. Reuben Hayim Aleksander notes in his introduction to *Niflaot hasaba kadisha* (The Wonders of the Holy Grandfather) that the tales of the tsadikim had a greater influence on him in his youth than books of *musar* (ethical teachings): 'For while I still was a child and I looked in the books of the righteous and holy that were printed every day, my heart within me was aroused to the service of the Lord, may he be blessed, even more than when I studied *musar* books.' The primary, shared goal of the collectors was to ensure that these deeds were not forgotten;[47] but they also had their own additional, individual aims, for example that the stories would constitute 'a remedy for the melancholy' of the collector,[48] or even serve as a memorial for him.[49]

Stories were told by many tsadikim,[50] the most outstanding of whom (with the exception of R. Nahman of Bratslav, whose stories deserve a separate study) was R. Israel of Ruzhin. As mentioned above, the Ruzhiner maintained that in a deficient generation, one characterized by *katnut*, the tsadik is capable of influencing his followers only 'by stories and simple matters'.[51]

45 *Shivḥei habesht*, author's introd., 36. See Rodkinsohn, *Shivḥei harav*, introd. Later collectors did, in fact, adopt this methodology: e.g. Rosenthal, *Hitgalut hatsadikim*.

46 Joseph ben R. A., *Mifalot tsadikim heḥadash*, introd. Nathan of Nemirov, *Siḥot haran*, §138, contains testimony by R. Nahman of Bratslav, attesting of himself that 'his awakening to the service of the Lord was, in truth, due mainly to the stories of the tsadikim'.

47 Rodkinsohn, *Shivḥei harav*, introd. Cf. Rakats, *Tiferet hayehudi*, introd.: 'And the stories that were known among the hasidim were forgotten due to the many worries of the time.'

48 Bodek, *Kahal kedoshim*, introd.

49 Slodovnik, *Ma'aseh hagedolim heḥadash*, introd. The collector, Matityahu Tsevi Slodovnik, was apparently childless.

50 The Seer of Lublin 'told stories about the tsadikim' ([Lemberger], *Magdil yeshuot malko*, 26); see e.g. the story in Gemen, *Sifran shel tsadikim*, ch. 9, §3. When the Maggid of Koznitz came to pray, 'he would wrap himself in his *talit* and hand *tefilin* on his holy hand, and before binding [the *tefilin*] he would speak of new things in the world, that seemed to be worthless things, heaven forbid' (Rosenthal, *Tiferet hatsadikim*, 143). See I. Safrin, *Zohar ḥai*, ii, fo. 395, for his custom of relating stories. R. Abraham Joshua Heschel of Apta was also very fond of storytelling: see, among others, Rodkinsohn, *Adat tsadikim*, §2; Reznik, *Mora'im gedolim*, §26, p. 55. R. Naphtali of Ropshits would tell stories to his wife, but the listener (R. Isaac Safrin, as recorded in his *Zohar ḥai*, 'Vayeḥi'; A. Michelsohn, *Ohel naftali*, §37) knew that these were parables about washing the hands and the ritual bath.

51 Israel of Ruzhin, *Irin kadishin*, 'Likutim', fo. 53*b*; Shenkel, *Yeshuot yisra'el*, introd. to vol. ii; Alexander, *Niflaot hasaba kadisha*, introd.; Piekarz, *Bratslav Hasidism* (Heb.), 102–3. Stories are scattered among the expositions in *Irin kadishin*, e.g.: 'Miketz' (on Habad hasidim in Jassy who mocked the sermon by the rabbi of Apta); 'For Purim' (about R. Menahem Mendel of Vitebsk); 'Vayikra' (on the rabbi of Apta and R. Elimelekh); 'For Shabat Hazon [the sabbath

An example of this is his story of how his father had acted on behalf of a tenant who was about to be evicted.[52] R. Israel of Ruzhin also said that his great-grandfather, the Maggid of Mezirech, was a storyteller: 'When my [great-]grandfather R. Dov Baer would tell a simple story, the bed would be agitated. What does "agitated" mean? It would rise up and descend.'[53]

R. Israel of Ruzhin never tired of stressing the difference between the early days of hasidism and his own time. It was related in his name that the innovation of the Ba'al Shem Tov consisted of his performing *yiḥudim* 'so that there would no longer be any way in the world for Samael [an ancient Jewish name for Satan] to gain the ear of people; this, therefore, [is the true meaning of] speaking what seem to the eye and ear of people to be idle matters, and to thereby truly perform holy and wondrous *yiḥudim* to the Lord, may he be blessed'.[54] The tsadik of Ruzhin told R. Hirsch Gershon that faith would wane greatly prior to the advent of the messiah, and that the remedy for this was to tell stories.[55] On one evening a group of hasidim were sitting in the study hall of R. Hayim of Kosov and telling stories about tsadikim, including the Ba'al Shem Tov. Their storytelling went on late, until close to midnight, when someone, finishing a story about the Ba'al Shem Tov, he sighed and asked: 'Where do we find a *ba'al shem* like that today?' At that moment they heard the footsteps of R. Hayim, coming down from his apartment to the study hall. Entering the hall, he told them: 'In every generation there is a *ba'al shem tov*, but then he was revealed, while now he is concealed.'[56]

before the Ninth of Av]' (on the rabbi of Apta); 'Collections' (about R. Zusya); s.v. *yesh tsinorot hashefa* (on R. Hirsch Leib). Cf. J. Sofer, *Sipurei ya'akov*, ii, §53: R. Israel of Ruzhin proposes that his in-law, R. Hayim of Kosov, should influence sinners with words of Torah or with stories. When the latter claimed that he could not do so, R. Israel proclaimed: 'I will tell!' and he related a story. See also Breitstein, *Siḥot ḥayim*, 24 (a parable about himself); ibid. 36 (a story for a rich man in whose house he stayed). See also Goldberg, 'Hasidic Story' (Heb.).

52 See H. Rabinowitz, *Shemuot tovot razin de'oraita*, fo. 19*b*.

53 Shenkel, *Yeshuot yisra'el*, introd. to vol. ii, p. 3; Gemen, *Sifran shel tsadikim*, ch. 4, §1; A. M. Rabinowitz, *Keter hayehudi*, introd., 9; also, in Heb. (trans. from Yiddish) in Agnon, *Sefer sofer vesipur*, 438.

54 Rosenthal, *Tiferet hatsadikim*, 143. R. Israel acted in similar fashion. He was heard in conversation with R. Judah Tsevi of Stretin, apparently discussing the price of grain, while in fact they were speaking of wondrous affairs (ibid.).

55 Sobelman, *Sipurei tsadikim heḥadash*, preface, p. 6. See Slodovnik, *Ma'aseh hagedolim heḥadash*, introd., comment on Mal. 3: 16: ' "Then they that feared the Lord spoke [*nidberu*]": it does not say *dibru* [the simple 'spoke'], but *nidberu* [the *nifal* form, meaning 'spoke together'], meaning that they spoke of they that feared the Lord; then "the Lord hearkened and heard", meaning that before the advent of the messiah, all of [man's] vitality [comes from] the telling of stories of the God-fearing.' Cf. also Goldberger, *Darkhei hatov vehayashar*, 16*b*; Meller, *Besorot tovot*, introd. For R. Israel of Ruzhin telling stories before praying, and thus once missing the time for prayer, see A. M. Rabinowitz, *Keter hayehudi*, introd., 7.

56 H. Kahana, *Even shetiyah*, 53.

Although the mitnagedim from within the traditional Jewish community were deemed to have played their part in the general spiritual decline, its primary cause was identified as the Haskalah, the Jewish Enlightenment. The danger that the average reader would not distinguish between the stories of tsadikim and those of the Haskalah literature intensified as more of the latter were published, and the fear grew that these would come into the hands of hasidim. R. Dov Baer of Linitz took pains to emphasize 'that I did not write this in the manner of mere tales and history';[57] and in a later generation R. Jacob Sofer would write: 'Do not imagine that these stories are like the simple tales that are sold by the booksellers.'[58] At times, however, the hasidic author–collectors did point out to their readers that 'you will be able to enjoy them [the stories] as you please', in order to avoid putting off readers who might otherwise turn to 'tales, novels, and the like, worthless stories'.[59] The collectors of the hasidic story were well aware of the criticism levelled at this genre by mitnagedim and maskilim, and explicitly confronted it in their introductions. While the detractors attacked by the author of *Shivḥei habesht* are not specified, in the introductions by Rodkinsohn and Walden the identity of those who deride the hasidic story is made quite clear.[60] These authors excoriate the Haskalah as *sapaḥat* [a skin disease]: an affliction that, if unchecked, risks destroying everything worthwhile in the Jewish nation. It may be assumed that neither author would have directed such fierce criticism against the maskilim if he had not been familiar with their attitude to the hasidic story.

Echoing these authors' perception of the hasidic story as a sort of barrier preventing the Jewish community from being inundated by the literature of the Haskalah, another story collector advocated the fostering of this type of literature 'especially in our times, in which secular knowledge abounds, faith is absent, and falsehood is increasing in the world'.[61] In a later generation, too, the collectors viewed the hasidic tale as a shield against the spread of the Haskalah and assimilation: 'our time, when people have lost belief, and heresy and irreverence intensify daily . . . is the most fitting time for the

57 *Shivḥei habesht*, ed. Rubinstein, author's introd., p. 32.

58 J. Sofer, *Sipurei ya'akov*, i, author's introd.

59 See *Mifalot hatsadikim*, introd. The tsadik of Gostynin once heard that youths, and even householders, were reading 'useless novels on the sabbath'. He reproached his audience in the synagogue for this practice (Rakats, *Siaḥ sarfei kodesh*, i, §188). Cf. the title page of *Ma'asiyot noraot*: 'And today, due to our numerous sins, nonsense, worthless things, [and] love stories, are printed, and all our teachings should not be like their worthless speech.' Abraham Isaac Sobelman notes in the preface to *Sipurei tsadikim heḥadash* (p. 7) that during the week people are occupied with problems of livelihood, 'but when the holy sabbath day arrives, on which all rest, they will sit and derive enjoyment from reading such stories [about tsadikim]'.

60 See the introductions to Rodkinsohn, *Sipurei tsadikim*, and to A. Walden, *Kahal ḥasidim*.

61 M. M. Sofer, *Sheloshah edrei tson*, introd.

propagation of these stories, to increase in the hearts of the Israelites belief in the Lord, may he be blessed, and in his servants, the tsadikim'.[62]

Most hasidim were only entrenched in their belief in the tsadikim's stories by the criticism of the maskilim and the mitnagedim.[63] However, the collectors of these stories did also have to reckon with internal criticism, which was raised on various grounds. The most important charge levelled at them was that these stories were 'worthless things' that distracted men's minds from study; that 'it is better to study some pages of Talmud than to gaze at such tales'.[64] In this case the author counters that those who raise such claims against him are hypocritical, since they themselves engage in activities considerably inferior to reading stories of tsadikim. In his opinion, it is better to read hasidic stories than to engage in 'the reading of newspapers, or to speak slanderously of some tsadik'.[65]

A second strand of criticism from within hasidism disputed the stories' contemporary relevance. The same collector apparently heard, from within the hasidic camp itself, questions such as: '"What is this service to you?" [Exod. 12: 26]. Who needs such stories in our period? Who will buy this, and who will pay attention to them?'[66] In his response, he unleashed a scathing attack against the 'contemporary [i.e. modern] people' who 'when they gather with hasidim who may truly be called by the name of "hasidim", asked in their confusion: Is this conceivable, things that exceeds the bounds of Nature? How is it possible to change Nature?' His answer to such scepticism is that miracles have occurred in all the generations, and they occur in our time as well; whoever desires to see them need only open his eyes.[67] He also takes issue with those hasidim 'who believe only in their own rabbis', regarding the wonders that are related of other tsadikim as mere invention.[68]

62 Alexander, *Niflaot hasaba kadisha*, introd.

63 See e.g. the introd. to Hazan, *Sipurim nifla'im*: 'And the sanctimonious among them say that the stories are lies and fictitious.'

64 Alexander, *Niflaot hasaba kadisha*, introd.

65 Ibid. The author lists 'political affairs' among their other occupations.

66 Ibid.

67 Ibid., introd. Questions were asked primarily about dybbuks and the exorcism of evil spirits. Cf. also Kamelhar, *Em labinah*, 15, who cites Ephrati, *Toledot anshei shem*, 17: 'A *gaon* and tsadik said, in his fine language, that "his signs, his wonders [occur only in] the land of Ham" [Ps. 105: 27].' 'It is related of the Mitteler Rebbe [R. Menahem Mendel Schneersohn, the 'Middle Rabbi' of Lubavich] that he did not desire to debase himself to attain the level of wonders, that belong to the level of the forty-eight lesser combinations of the name of God, as in the phrase "his signs, his wonders, against the land of Ham" [i.e. corresponding to the numerical value (48) of the letters composing the Hebrew word *ḥam*]' (Mondshein, *Migdal oz*, 193). For an additional hasidic response to this derisive exposition by the opponents of wonder-working, see Alexander, *Niflaot hasaba kadisha*, introd. See also Zevin, *Hasidic Tales: Festivals* (Heb.), introd.

68 Alexander, *Niflaot hasaba kadisha*, ii, introd. See also Kattina, *Raḥamei ha'av*, §25, 'Hasidism'. Cf. another version (using 'Torah' instead of 'wonders') in Chikernik, *Sipurim neḥmadim*, 6: 'It is written in the introduction to the book *Toledot yitsḥak* by the holy rabbi, R. Isaac of Nezkizh, may the memory of the righteous and the holy be for a blessing, that after

Much of the internal hasidic criticism coalesced around opposition to the accentuation of wondrous acts,[69] an aversion that several stories trace to the Ba'al Shem Tov himself. For example, R. Menahem Mendel of Rymanow said, upon returning from a visit to the tomb of the Ba'al Shem Tov, that '[the Ba'al Shem Tov's] anger was aroused against the people who tell of the wonders and signs that he performed, but do not speak of his fear of the Lord'.[70] The following stories have a similar theme:

One time the holy circle of the Ba'al Shem Tov, may his merit protect us, were sitting together after his departure from this world, and were telling stories about him. In the meantime, the son of the Ba'al Shem Tov, Rabbi Tsevi, of blessed memory, fell asleep, and he saw his holy father. He [the Ba'al Shem Tov] asked: 'Why are they relating stories about me? Of what benefit is this to them? Instead of this, they should speak of my service in this world of the Lord, may He be blessed, and this will be beneficial both for them and for me!'[71]

One time the pupils of the Ba'al Shem Tov were sitting after his departure from the world and were telling of the wonders that the Ba'al Shem Tov had performed. One of them was seized by slumber, and he saw the Ba'al Shem Tov. He [the Ba'al Shem Tov] said to him: 'What favour are you doing for me, and what benefit do you have, from this? It would be better if you were to tell of my piety; this would be beneficial for both you and me.'[72]

The book *Shivḥei habesht* was the subject of controversy on this point. When the son-in-law of the Mitteler Rebbe (R. Menahem Mendel) saw the book in his father-in-law's home, he said that it was not acceptable to him.[73]

the death of the Ba'al Shem Tov, may the memory of the righteous and the holy be for a blessing, the circle of his holiness's pupils gathered, concerning Torah teachings that they had heard from his holy mouth, each according to his comprehension. And the Ba'al Shem Tov appeared to them in a dream, and reproached them: Why are you setting your minds to the words of my teachings, and are not setting your minds to the fear of heaven that I possessed?' This is also cited in Donner and Wodnik, *Sefer ba'al shem tov*, 'Ekev', fo. 193, n. 21 (quoting Isaac Landau, *Zikhron tov*, fo. 22c).

69 Shmeruk, *Yiddish Literature* (Heb.), 203, notes the reservations expressed by hasidim who regarded the storytelling literature as inferior to the exegetical literature, and is inclined to attribute to them the late appearance of the hasidic *shevaḥim* literature, and even the temporary lull in the printing of such books that followed the publication of *Shivḥei habesht*.

70 Bromberg, *Toledot haniflaot*, 44.

71 Abraham of Slonim, *Beit avraham*, on Shavuot, 161. Cf. ibid. 12; Agnon, *Sefer sofer vesipur*, 441. Cf. also Brandwein, *Degel maḥaneh yehudah*, §23: when the book *Shivḥei habesht* was published, R. Judah Tsevi of Stretin observed: 'Is this *Hashivḥei habesht* [i.e. the praises of the Ba'al Shem Tov]? We, too, can perform all these signs and wonders, but the fear [of God] and love of the Ba'al Shem Tov, this is the praise of the Ba'al Shem Tov!' Cf. Agnon, *Sefer sofer vesipur*, 409.

72 Moses Modner, *Kitvei kodesh r. m[osheh] m[e'odner]*, 6.

73 Cf. what is cited in the name of R. Nahman of Bratslav in Hazan, *Sipurim nifla'im*, 3 n. 3. This tradition confirms the reliability of the stories in *Shivḥei habesht*, 'except for a very few of them that [R. Nahman] said were not written well'.

The tsadik replied: 'All that is written in *Shivḥei habesht* is as nothing compared to the greatness of the Ba'al Shem Tov.' He further related: 'I heard from my grandfather [R. Shneur Zalman of Lyady], may the memory of the righteous and the holy be for a blessing, that he heard from his teacher, the great Maggid of Mezirech, may the memory of the righteous and the holy be for a blessing, that he said that the Ba'al Shem Tov had physical sight capable of seeing four hundred parasangs [= 1,600 miles] by four hundred parasangs.'[74]

At times the debate centred on the reliability of a certain tale. It was reported that R. Isaac of Nezkizh was asked about a story concerning R. Barukh of Medzibezh that was printed in the book *Kahal ḥasidim*, 'and he stated that it was not true, but that they [nevertheless] hitched their wagon [attributed the story] to a great tsadik'.[75]

From its inception the narrative hasidic literature stressed its credibility, with the collectors of these stories making copious use of official endorsements and claiming links with the leading hasidic masters. R. Aaron of Apta concludes one of the stories in his book *Keter shem tov* with the comment: 'All this I heard from men of truth.'[76] In the story of how the Maggid of Mezirech became a follower of the Ba'al Shem Tov, R. Aaron emphasizes that he heard this report from a hasid who had heard the episode from the Maggid himself.[77] R. Dov Baer of Linitz, whose 'Author's Introduction' to *Shivḥei habesht* may be regarded as a classic example of the genre, was extremely sensitive to the issue of credibility and well aware of the derision that was already directed at the tales, including the charge that 'everyone prophesies in a different style'. R. Dov Baer stresses in his introduction to *Shivḥei habesht* that he wrote only 'the wonders that I heard from men of truth, and I wrote each story from the one from whom I heard [it]. Thanks to the Lord for having blessed me with memory, and I neither added nor subtracted; everything is true and certain, and things did not change in my mouth.'[78] The collector of *Shivḥei habesht* took care to record from whom he had heard almost every story—a practice that was followed by many

[74] Chikernik, *Ma'asiyot uma'amarim yekarim*, 6. Cf. Rodkinsohn, *Toledot ba'alei shem tov*, i: *Or yisra'el*, introd. See the discussion of *Shivḥei habesht* above. Rodkinsohn relates in this book (pp. 15–16) that R. Menahem Mendel of Lubavitch rebuked the family members treating a sick person who engaged in idle conversations. He told them: 'The book *Shivḥei habesht* lies before you, why do you not relate tales from it, for they are not worthless things, heaven forbid!'

[75] Isaac Landau, *Zikhron tov*, 'Inyanei tefilah', §6. Cf. Shenkel, *Yeshuot yisra'el*, introd.: R. Barukh of Medzibezh 'at times would tell some story with different letters and words'.

[76] Aaron of Apta, *Keter shem tov*, fo. 22*a*.

[77] Ibid., fo. 30*b*. See Nigal, 'A Primary Source' (Heb.), 138.

[78] *Shivḥei habesht*, 36. Cf. Donner, *Derekh ha'emunah uma'aseh rav*, introd.: 'And nothing that did not come to pass in the world appears in all our words.'

subsequent story collectors. On rare occasions a literary source is cited instead.[79]

The veracity of the stories is a prominent theme in most of the introductions to the various collections. Eliezer Shenkel, the compiler of *Yeshuot yisra'el*, writes:

Before I begin to speak and relate to the latest generation all the deliverances and wonders that [the Lord] performed for his holy one, the holy one of Israel, [Israel's] diadem and glory [i.e. R. Israel of Ruzhin], I hereby request of my brethren, the honoured readers, not to be so bold as to imagine in their mind and spirit that I invented these words from my mind, heaven forbid, or that I allowed myself to include here some story without first being sure that the person who related it to me is reliable, that he would neither lie nor be false to me. [By] my witnesses on high and those testifying in heaven, all the stories that are included here, from the beginning to the end, either I was an eyewitness to them, or I heard with my ears these stories, coming from his holy and pure mouth in holiness and purity, with the holy spirit speaking from his throat, or I heard them from the speakers of truth who would not talk falsely for any sum, and whose utterances originate from the source of truth.[80]

He then goes on to explain that the tsadik of Ruzhin told a single story in several different ways according to the appropriate 'level' for each particular time and place of its telling. This explanation for discrepancies is also given by R. David Moses of Chortkov (see below).

However, the ways in which these authors determined the veracity of the stories were relative and subjective. Some collectors, like Rodkinsohn, who testifies that he heard the stories from the elders of the Habad hasidim,[81] state that they were raised among hasidim; others state that they heard their stories directly from the tsadikim. R. Jacob Sofer writes: 'I merited to be with sixty tsadikim, the pillars and holy ones of the generation . . . and I heard from them these stories and tales.'[82] Similarly, R. Israel David Weiss writes: 'From my childhood, I grew up among those who fear and serve the Lord, and I loved to hear them telling of the tsadikim who lived among them.'[83] Some storytellers regarded the very dissemination of the story as a mark of its reliability. Thus we find emphasis placed on the fact that, for example, a particular story was known and famous throughout Volhynia.[84]

[79] It is stated in Bodek(?), *Sipurei kedoshim*, §5, that the life story of R. Solomon Ephraim of Luntshits was copied 'from the communal register of the holy community of Prague' (in other versions of the story: from the register of the Altneuschul). *Continued in Appendix.*

[80] Shenkel, *Yeshuot yisra'el*, 3. Cf. M. M. Sofer, *Sheloshah edrei tson*, introd.: 'All that I wrote, I actually saw with my own eyes.'

[81] Rodkinsohn, *Shivhei harav*, introd.

[82] J. Sofer, *Sipurei ya'akov*, i, author's introd.

[83] *Ma'asiyot vesiḥot tsadikim*, introd.

[84] [Isaac Dov Baer ben Tsevi Hirsch], *Kahal ḥasidim heḥadash*, §202. Cf. ibid., §203: 'This story is well known throughout all the districts of Podolia.'

Not everyone was convinced by these claims to authenticity. Particular criticism was levelled by R. Abraham Hazan, a Bratslav author, at the tales written in books published recently. These, according to Hazan, in comparison with the stories by R. Nahman and his disciples, were as darkness to light. He lists *Adat tsadikim*, *Kahal ḥasidim*, *Pe'er mikedoshim*, and *Shivḥei tsadikim* among the books that were published within this relatively short period, and alleges that they are of questionable reliability because 'most of the stories [were told] while drinking wine, with the teller standing between the third and fourth cup, and the listener sitting and snoozing, to the extent that more than nine parts [out of ten] of them are false, and the little truth is grafted, altered, exchanged, and mixed'.[85]

One of the charges against which the collectors of hasidic stories frequently had to defend themselves related to variants of the stories. The existence of different versions of the stories was known both to the tsadikim and to the various collectors, and the latter found it necessary to provide a plausible explanation for this phenomenon. R. Israel Jaffe noted in his introduction to *Shivḥei habesht* that he had recorded the events related in accordance with the version of the Old Rebbe, and in the portion that he edited we find two parallel versions, his own added to that of the Old Rebbe.[86] The collector R. Dov Baer of Linitz also mentions the existence of different versions of the same story.[87] The tsadik R. David Moses of Chortkov heard that R. Israel of Ruzhin told the same story, once in a certain manner, and another time differently, to which he commented: 'The stories that the tsadikim relate are in accordance with what is required at that time.'[88] The recorder of this statement, R. Israel Rapaport, adds: 'I, too, heard a tale, with some changes, from *maran* [our master], *admor*, the righteous [who] is an everlasting foundation, may his merit protect us.'[89]

The collectors frequently feared that readers might regard the many different versions as their handiwork, and thus charge them with prevarication or distortion. Not all variations were justified or accepted. Rodkinsohn writes:

You perhaps will find in the book something that you know with a slight change, or find that I have subtracted from, or added to, what you heard. Do not let your

85 See Hazan, *Sipurim nifla'im*, 3 n. 3; id., *Kokhvei or*, 'Anshei moharan', 35–6; cf. Yellin, *Derekh tsadikim*, 23: 'The story that is cited in *Kahal ḥasidim* in the name of the Ba'al Shem Tov, regarding the book *Ḥemdat hayamim*, is something that never happened in the world.'

86 See e.g. *Shivḥei habesht*, 48 ('Some say').

87 'There are several versions of how the Maggid [of Mezirech] came to the Ba'al Shem Tov' (*Shivḥei habesht*, ed. Rubinstein, 126); 'and I heard several versions of this story' (ibid. 86); 'another version' (ibid. 146).

88 Rapoport, *Divrei david*, fo. 30*a*; cf. Shenkel, *Yeshuot yisra'el*, 3.

89 Rapoport, *Divrei david*, fo. 30*a*.

spirit be vexed, to judge me to be a liar, heaven forbid, [rather] know that I sifted all the stories in a sieve and strainer, and I presented to you the purest and the choicest that I selected from them, according to my understanding; they are accepted by hasidim, tsadikim, and the wise.[90]

Many assumed that corruptions had entered the stories over the course of time, and had to be corrected. R. Jacob Kaidaner, author of *Sipurim nora'im*, went so far as to write: 'The corruptions of stories have increased. . . . Most of them are totally false, and what is heard from a private person also must be examined. We must also investigate whether the story has been passed from mouth to mouth, from many mouths; the matter could possibly have been totally changed.'[91] Another hasidic collector writes: 'I know that just as it is not possible to have wheat without chaff, so is it impossible to have stories and traditions without different versions. None the less, if the story contains even a grain of truth, my labour and toil are worthwhile.'[92]

The struggle with variant versions continued in the twentieth century. One of the compilers writes that he sometimes hears the same story told about different tsadikim, and even a story that is attributed to a single teller is liable to exist in different versions. This collector resolved the problem by taking an original view: even if these things did not actually happen, they were worthy of happening, by merit of the tsadik! As he put it: 'if some fact is told regarding some tsadik . . . and even if, in truth, this is a fabricated matter, and never happened, nonetheless, know, faithfully and for a certainty, that this was within the power of that person, the tsadik, to perform this wondrous happening that people relate in his name'.[93]

[90] Rodkinsohn, *Shivḥei harav*, introd. Cf. Rodkinsohn's introductory remarks to *Sipurei tsadikim*: 'The stories have been greatly distorted by the masses: each person, as he hears it, adds or detracts.' *Continued in Appendix.*

[91] Kaidaner, *Sipurim nora'im*, §35, p. 100.

[92] A. Michelsohn, *Ohel avraham*. Alexander's introduction to *Niflaot hasaba kadisha* proclaims: 'Unlike the stories of our time, many of which are fictitious or strange exaggerations, I am not so, rather, the majority is what I heard and received from reliable sources. There are some things that were reproduced a number of times, that I heard in a number of ways. Because this is so dear [to me], I also presented the second version—choose whichever you please.' A statement in a similar spirit appears in the introduction to Gemen, *Sifran shel tsadikim*: 'And I also beg the reader, if he shall find in my collection some words of Torah, or a story in the name of some tsadik, that the reader heard in the name of another tsadik, or in a different version, do not assign guilt to me, for as I heard, I wrote.'

[93] Ehrmann, *Devarim arevim*, introd. Cf. Moses of Kobrin, *Amarot tehorot*, 34: 'We are required to believe all the stories, signs, and wonders that are related of the Ba'al Shem Tov, may his memory be for the life of the World to Come. We must also believe even if they did not actually happen, because they were so potentially.' Cf. I. Landau, *Zikhron tov*, 'The Deeds of the Tsadikim', §26 (in the name of R. Mordecai of Nezkizh): 'He takes no notice of stories that tell anecdotes concerning tsadikim, for many of the anecdotes are fabrications and include mistakes, except for the stories that are told of the Ba'al Shem Tov, may his memory be for the life of the World to Come; for even if the incident did not happen in actuality, the Ba'al Shem Tov had the potential to effect everything.'

The various collectors reached different conclusions as to how this issue was best dealt with. Rodkinsohn sifted what he had heard; the father of Jacob Margolioth, author of *Kevutsat ya'akov*, stressed that he related only what he heard from his own father, saw with his own eyes, or heard with his own ears, 'because confusion has occurred in the stories of the *olam* [literally, 'world'; here meaning the hasidic world, and specifically the simple people, rather than the tsadikim]'.[94] The ambivalent attitude to miraculous stories within certain hasidic circles is expressed most strongly in Agnon's quotation of Professor Zvi Meir Rabinowitz, in the name of his grandfather, the tsadik R. Solomon Rabinowich of Radomsk: 'Whoever believes the stories in *Shivḥei habesht* is a fool, whoever denies the stories in *Shivḥei habesht* is a heretic.'[95]

Behind all these considerations of veracity and reliability lay the primary obligation to tell stories of the tsadikim, a duty imposed by the tsadikim themselves in mandates to their disciples that are cited by the compilers. The origin and nature of this obligation are spelt out in the well-known story of R. Jacob, an attendant of the Ba'al Shem Tov who became a renowned teller of stories. The motivation combines three elements: the practical advantage likely to derive to the storyteller; the sign from heaven to the listener; and the natural desire of the tsadik that he and his actions not be forgotten after his passing. Before the Ba'al Shem Tov died, he revealed to his servant that the latter would gain his livelihood from stories. This prophecy was realized some years later, when R. Jacob happened to be in the home of a wealthy Jew in Italy. He told his host a story from which the latter learned that he had been forgiven for a sin that he had committed in the past, as the Ba'al Shem Tov had told him he would many years earlier. In return, this person heaped great riches upon R. Jacob.[96]

This is not the place to mention all of the stories attributed to the Ba'al Shem Tov, as found in *Shivḥei habesht* and in later collections of hasidic tales,[97] but one in particular is worth mentioning as evidence of the importance attached to their dissemination. The Ba'al Shem Tov saved the flock of

[94] Margolioth, *Kevutsat ya'akov*, fo. 53*a*. Cf. Rabinovitz, *Ma'aseh neḥemiyah*, 5, 8.

[95] Agnon, *Sefer sofer vesipur*, 410; I heard this also from Professor Zvi Meir Rabinowitz.

[96] Rodkinsohn, *Adat tsadikim*, §8; see Ch. 11 below. For R. Jacob, the Ba'al Shem Tov's servant, see also *Shivḥei habesht*, 144, a story that he told to R. Gedaliah of Linits. Cf. also Gemen, *Sifran shel tsadikim*, ch. 1, §5: the Ba'al Shem Tov told a hasid who had come down in the world that the latter would regain his wealth if he would set forth as the Ba'al Shem Tov's agent 'to a place where no one has heard of the Ba'al Shem Tov, nor of the city of Medzibezh'. Once there, far away, this man told 'several stories' of the Ba'al Shem Tov, resulting in these people coming to the Ba'al Shem Tov and having their requests fulfilled by him. In the Yiddish edition of *Shivḥei habesht*, R. Jacob is mentioned as preparing medicines for the Ba'al Shem Tov.

[97] See e.g. *Shivḥei habesht*, 145: the Ba'al Shem Tov told rural Jews who happened to be in Nemirov a story whose moral was not to have a non-Jewish servant engage in work on the sabbath.

a non-Jewish shepherd from wolves, blessed him with longevity, and informed him that a Jew named Israel would come to him, and that he must tell this Jew the story of his rescue. And, indeed, many years later the tsadik R. Israel of Ruzhin came to the shepherd, who told him what had happened and then immediately dropped dead.[98] This teaches that the Ba'al Shem Tov, who saw far into the future, knew that the Ruzhiner would be greatly interested in hasidic tales. The introduction by R. Israel Jaffe to *Shivḥei habesht* also reflects the importance attributed by the early hasidic masters to their disciples continuing to tell stories about them. Here he writes that, after his immigration to the Land of Israel, R. Menahem Mendel of Vitebsk was once sitting at the third sabbath meal, 'and with him was an old man, one of the disciples of the Ba'al Shem Tov, and he was telling the praises of the Ba'al Shem Tov. Once the rabbi, the Maggid [of Mezirech], came to this rabbi in a dream and told him: "You [Menahem Mendel] are my disciple, why do you, too, not relate my praises?"' R. Menahem Mendel accepted the remonstrations of his teacher the Maggid and intended to tell about him during the third sabbath meal. At that time, however, the old man once again began to tell of the Ba'al Shem Tov, and prevented R. Menahem Mendel from telling his stories. The old man was consequently punished, and died soon afterwards.[99]

The printer of *Shivḥei habesht* regarded this story about the Maggid's insistence that his followers tell stories about him as sufficient reason to engage in the publication of hasidic stories; and later compilers took a similar stand. In his introduction to *Mifalot hatsadikim*, R. Menahem Mendel Bodek mentions the desire of tsadikim that stories be told about them. According to Bodek, R. Yehiel Mikhel of Zlotchev ordered his followers to 'tell one another the deeds of the tsadikim, continually'.[100] R. Shalom of Drohobitch commanded 'his people who were close to him, that whenever they sat in a single party, or together in one company, they should speak of his practices, and even of his horses and wagon, his prayers, and the like'.[101] Rodkinsohn writes in one of his introductions: 'And, similarly, I heard in the name of the holy rabbi, R. Shalom the son of the Malakh [the 'Angel': R. Abraham of Mezirech], that he told his followers: When you are together,

[98] See Joseph ben R.A., *Mifalot tsadikim heḥadash*, 31.

[99] *Shivḥei habesht*, ed. Rubinstein, printer's introd., 24. See Margolioth, *Kevutsat ya'akov*, fo. 56*a*: R. Yehiel Mikhel of Zlotchev would not recite grace after meals in the third sabbath meal (thus concluding the meal) until he had related something about the Ba'al Shem Tov.

[100] Bodek, *Mifalot hatsadikim*, introd.; Donner, *Derekh ha'emunah uma'aseh rav*, introd.; Slodovnik, *Ma'aseh hagedolim heḥadash*, introd.; Hazan, *Sipurim nifla'im*, introd.; Alexander, *Niflaot hasaba kadisha*, introd. to vol. ii. R. Yehiel Mikhel was himself an outstanding storyteller. R. Isaac Safrin (*Megilat setarim*, 40) writes that his teacher and father-in-law, R. Abraham Mordecai Pinchev, passed on to him many stories that he had heard from his teacher, R. Yehiel Mikhel.

[101] Bodek, *Mifalot hatsadikim*, introd.

speak about me, and if you are finished with sayings of mine—speak about my chairs and my benches.'[102] An examination of this literature leaves no doubt that the tsadikim and hasidim amply fulfilled these commands.

It would be a grave error to posit any fundamental distinction between the type of stories related by tsadikim about themselves or other tsadikim and the type of stories told by the hasidism about the tsadikim. Right from the time of the Ba'al Shem Tov there were stories that the tsadik told about himself, and stories that his disciples told about him. This duality would continue. An examination of the names of those relating the stories, from *Shivḥei habesht* to the last collections (with the exception of the stories of R. Nahman of Bratslav, which have a singular character of their own within the genre) demonstrates that such a distinction is groundless.

A complete list of all the storytelling tsadikim would exceed the limits of the current discussion; nevertheless, it is worth mentioning a number of individuals, including some of the leading hasidic rabbis, who excelled in relating hasidic tales. Judging by the extant tales, one of the early hasidic leaders who was renowned for his inclination to tell stories was R. Shneur Zalman of Lyady, the Old Rebbe and founder of the Habad movement, who apparently bestowed this ability on later Lubavitcher *rebbe*s. R. Israel Jaffe, the first publisher of *Shivḥei habesht*, also performed a kind of editorial role, ordering the tales in the first part of the book in accordance with what he had heard from R. Shneur Zalman.[103] It is perhaps not coincidental that some other collectors of hasidic stories, such as Michael Levi Rodkinsohn and Jacob Kaidaner, were of Habad origin or were themselves Habad hasidim, and had heard the stories from a reliable source (or had even been present at the actual events described).[104]

'Some deeds of the tsadikim' were related in the synagogue of R. Menahem Mendel of Lubavitch, after the day's studies were concluded.[105] Once R. Shimon Manasseh of Hebron came to the third Lubavitcher Rebbe, the Tsemah Tsedek (1789–1866), and sat among the hasidim as they were telling of the tsadikim. The Tsemah Tzedek entered and asked: '"Of whom are you telling now?" They answered, "Of R. Mendele of Rymanow." He responded: "Many candles must be lit!" The Tsemah Tsedek himself

[102] Rodkinsohn, *Shivḥei harav*, introd.

[103] According to a quite plausible Habad tradition, R. Israel Jaffe was a follower of the 'Old Rebbe' (R. Shneur Zalman of Lyady). The *admor* (*rebbe*) mentioned in the printer's introduction to *Shivḥei habesht* (and also in the body of the work) is R. Shneur Zalman of Lyady. For confirmation of this identification, see Kaidaner, *Sipurim nora'im*, §20: 'Once the hasid R. Israel Jaffe, the printer of the holy community of Kapust, came and [R. Hayim of Volozhin] delayed him [Jaffe] until the sabbath. . . . During the meal he implored him to tell him of those same sublime things that he had heard from his holy master from Lyady.'

[104] For these two authors, see above, pp. 53, 64, 68, 69–70, 71.

[105] Sobelman, *Sipurei tsadikim heḥadash*, §32.

began to speak, and said: "I will tell you who was the rabbi, R. Mendele of Rymanow"'—that is, a great tsadik.[106]

R. Israel of Ruzhin, one of the greatest tellers of the hasidic tale, told stories of the Ba'al Shem Tov,[107] of R. Pinhas of Korets,[108] of the Maggid of Mezirech,[109] and of many other great hasidim and tsadikim.[110] R. Israel also used stories/parables to explain his views to his followers.[111] Although most of his stories are scattered among various hasidic books, some are concentrated in the second half of the book *Yeshuot yisra'el*, which was written by his devoted disciple Eliezer Shenkel.[112]

Some tsadikim, such as R. Isaac of Nezkizh, would recount their stories at the sabbath meal;[113] others would do so on special occasions, such as memorial days,[114] or on festivals and other holy days.[115] R. David Biderman of Jerusalem would always pray in the Ohel Mosheh synagogue in the Old City of Jerusalem. After the morning prayer, he would remove his *tefilin* and tell of the early tsadikim.[116]

The continuing practice of publishing collections of hasidic stories, including some that have not previously appeared in print,[117] clearly attests to the vitality of these stories, which have retained their force for over two centuries.

[106] Moskowitz, *Otsar hasipurim*, iv. 7.

[107] See e.g. Kaidaner, *Sipurim nora'im*, §4, p. 45; *Ma'asiyot vesiḥot tsadikim*, 20.

[108] See Bodek, *Ma'aseh tsadikim*, §14, pp. 30–3.

[109] See Zeilingold, *Me'orot hagedolim*, §9, p. 20; Sobelman, *Sipurei tsadikim heḥadash*, §71.

[110] e.g. a story concerning the Baḥ (R. Joel Sirkes): J. Sofer, *Sipurei ya'akov*, ii, §40.

[111] See e.g. Rosenthal, *Hitgalut hatsadikim*, 133; Berger, *Eser orot*, 'R. Israel of Ruzhin', §10; Gemen, *Sifran shel tsadikim*, ch. 5, §4.

[112] The second section of the book contains twenty-five stories.

[113] See Zeligman, *Beit tsadik*, introd., 4; also the stories recorded by R. Isaac Landau in *Zikhron tov*.

[114] R. Shalom of Kaminka would tell stories on the anniversary of the death (of R. Naphtali?) in Ropshits. See Bodek, *Pe'er mikedoshim*, §1.

[115] R. Eliezer of Azipolia would relate a certain story 'every Sukkot' (Brandwein, *Degel maḥaneh yehudah*, §115); R. Pinhas of Korets did so every Purim (Milik, *Sipurim nifla'im*, §4); on Passover R. Isaac Meir of Ger (the author of *Ḥidushei harim*) would tell a special story to those close to him (T. E. Michelson, *Toledot ya'akov*, 16); on the seventh day of every Passover, R. Israel of Vladnik would tell of the Ba'al Shem Tov's journey to Istanbul (Rodkinsohn, *Adat tsadikim*, §3); cf. Shalom of Koidanov, *Divrei shalom*, 'For the Seventh Day of Passover', fo. 46*c*, for the Ba'al Shem Tov's crossing of the Dneiper River. R. Meir of Premishlan would tell of R. Samson Weiner every Shavuot (J. Sofer, *Sipurei ya'akov*, i, §28, p. 90); R. Mordecai of Husyatin was accustomed to tell his stories on the third and seventh nights of Hanukah (Zak, *Beit yisra'el*, 160); for the reading of stories about tsadikim by R. Hertzke of Ratzferd, see Miller, *Beit mordekhai*, i, introd., 7.

[116] Moskowitz, *Otsar hasipurim*, xv. 7.

[117] See e.g. R. N. Kohen, *Shemuot vesipurim*.

THE ESSENCE OF THE HASIDIC STORY[118]

Although the attitude of the hasidim to the hasidic story, as outlined in this chapter, was a novel and distinct one, it is difficult to identify innovations in form or content in the stories themselves. In great measure, the hasidic story is a continuation of the hagiographic *shevaḥim* literary genre, exemplified in works such as *Shivḥei ha'ari*, in praise of R. Isaac Luria (the Ari), or *Shivḥei r. ḥayim vital*. Although this genre has parallels in the non-Jewish world, especially in the Christian cultural sphere, with numerous obvious parallel motifs, an examination of its authentic Jewish elements is of importance to our discussion. The latter originate in the internal Jewish narrative tradition as it developed from the biblical and midrashic narratives to the hagiographic literature of the Safed community in the sixteenth century.

Formal structures were at best secondary in the view of the hasidic storyteller, who emphasized the primarily didactic content. The majority of the tales focus upon an exemplary individual, who might be a revealed or a hidden tsadik, some other hasidic leader, or a pre-hasidic figure; or might be a simple person who possesses mannerisms and traits worthy of emulation, such as an unlettered shepherd or even an ignorant youth. The hasidic storytelling genre does not present its hearers and readers with an orderly hasidic teaching, such as those set out in the theoretical and exegetical hasidic literature; rather, it teaches hasidic ethical values by presenting exemplary behaviour. While the theoretical exegetical literature was intended for the educated and therefore a relatively small circle of readers, the hasidic storytelling genre translated the practical portion of hasidic teachings into the language of the simple folk, women, and children. There was, it seems, no propagandistic literature that spoke to the hearts of the Jewish masses in the villages and towns as forcefully as the storytelling genre, which had its origins in the oral tradition. The story enables the materially poor, whose lives were replete with trials and tribulations, to find balm for their personal suffering in the miraculous acts that were performed for the wretched and the oppressed, to identify with them, and even to hope that their own problems would be solved by the merit of the exemplary individuals of their own generation.

Consequently, the hasidic story is, on the whole, optimistic. It is conscious of misfortunes and suffering, but generally describes problems solved and remedies found for the ills of the body and the soul. The few stories that do not depict the total victory of good over evil also teach the hearers or readers how to protect themselves, and how to see the positive nucleus in life's realities. Admittedly, tales of the innocent and simple abound, but since these

[118] See Nigal, *The Hasidic Book and the Jewish Holidays* (Heb.).

were role models with which the masses could identify it made it easier to remember the plots when telling the stories to their children and grandchildren.

The hasidic story is composed of a series of events, not a single episode. Some stories relate the annals and deeds of an exemplary individual, but even in these apparently historical accounts the simple hasid can find a moral. Another type portrays the miracles wrought by the tsadik, in which those asking his help find solutions for problems relating to health, livelihood, and other areas of their life. The audience therefore achieved profound identification with the story on two levels: first, with the unfortunate who was saved; and second, with the wonder-worker who had saved him.

Depictions of landscapes and the natural environment are totally absent from the hasidic tale, and even man's immediate surroundings and their non-human inhabitants—dogs and cats, domesticated beasts and horses, fields and forests—receive only incidental mention. Two factors explain this. First, the vegetable and animal worlds did not much interest the simple Jew who was engaged in earning a livelihood and troubled by personal problems. Second, the time-honoured tradition was that while the spiritual was held in primary regard, material matters were given attention only to the extent that they were necessary for an orderly life. Those suffering the travails of the Exile had no leisure to gaze at the beauty of the sunrise or the sunset, or to contemplate the splendour of flower and tree. On the contrary: under the influence of kabbalistic literature and the kabbalistic *shevaḥim* literature, cats, dogs, pigs, and other 'beasts of prey' represented in great measure the evil forces of the Sitra Ahra in their war with the Creator and those who follow in his path. It is not incidental that a priest–sorcerer will probably appear to the hasid in the form of a rat or devouring beast, just as the forest is a place of demons, robbers, and murderers.

The language of the stories is often confused. All of them were first told in Yiddish, being translated into Hebrew only when committed to writing, and much of their lack of clarity is attributable to the process of translation. The original Yiddish versions did not make copious use of metaphors or wordplay: the purpose of the story lay in its content, not in the aesthetic pleasure associated with its form—a pleasure, indeed, to which most of the listeners were not attuned. More precisely, the aesthetic criteria of the audiences of the hasidic story were different from those of contemporary readers of stories, and the pleasure gained by the very hearing of the plot should not be disparaged. The unique artistic means employed by this genre still await scholarly linguistic enquiry.

TWO

THE TSADIK, HIS FOLLOWERS, AND HIS OPPONENTS

IN THE HASIDIC STORY, the tsadik is gifted with superhuman qualities that raise him to the level of prophet. The tsadik's abilities to hear from great distances,[1] to see from afar, and to know the future all ensue from divine inspiration. The tellers of the hasidic story assert confidently that 'tsadikim see with divine inspiration',[2] or, in the well-known formulation of the Ba'al Shem Tov, 'everything is with divine inspiration'.[3] The Ba'al Shem Tov once said, 'When I go to the ritual bath, I close my eyes once, and I see all the worlds';[4] and on another occasion, having prophesied to a certain individual what would happen to him when he got home, he asked that person to send a messenger back to tell him what had taken place, adding, 'even though, praise be to God, I have eyes to see from afar'.[5]

THE TSADIK AND HIS SPECIAL POWERS

The superhuman vision of the Ba'al Shem Tov is graphically illustrated in many stories. He saw a Jew who was forced to spend the sabbath in a field,

[1] *Shivḥei habesht*, 123: 'He tilted his ear as if to hear, said that they were speaking in the court of a [blood] libel, and declared that there was nothing of which to be afraid.' Cf. p. 268: 'And the Ba'al Shem Tov heard in the inn something that he was speaking to her in bed.' See also Jacob Joseph of Polonnoye, *Tsafenat pane'aḥ*, fo. 18*d*. For the concepts of tsadik and hasid in Jewish thought and kabbalah, see Tishby, *Wisdom of the Zohar*, ii. 1407 ff.

[2] J. Sofer, *Sipurei ya'akov*, ii, §58, p. 178; cf. §35, the statement by R. Hirsch of Chortkov to the Ba'al Shem Tov: 'For you see with the spirit of divine inspiration.' *Continued in Appendix.*

[3] Sobelman, *Sipurei tsadikim heḥadash*, §4. See *Shivḥei habesht*, 45 (ed. Horodezky), 49 (ed. Rubinstein). *Continued in Appendix.*

[4] *Shivḥei habesht*, 65; and emphasizing that the *mezuzah* in the rabbi's house was unfit (pp. 49–50). Cf. the same occurrence in the house of R. Jacob Joshua Falk, the author of *Penei yehoshua* (A. Stern, *Ḥutim hameshulashim*, 33).

[5] *Shivḥei habesht*, 110; ibid. 51: the Ba'al Shem Tov 'saw in advance' that 'the leading hasidim' and the rabbi went forth to accept him formally as their spiritual leader.

and a thief who had been exiled and who was about to murder him, and took action to rescue the Jew.[6] He saw from afar someone who was suffering;[7] he witnessed a transgression committed by his brother-in-law, R. Gershon;[8] he knew about the death of R. Eliezer of Amsterdam;[9] and he gazed all the way to Koznitz, to the home of the elderly bookbinder R. Shabetai.[10] The Ba'al Shem Tov saw and understood the thoughts of R. Nahman of Kosov;[11] he knew where Torah scholars erred in their prayers,[12] and where mitnagedim were not praying in the proper spirit.[13] His vision extended beyond the borders of his country: on one occasion, during the sabbath eve prayers, he sought R. Gershon and 'did not find him in the Land of Israel'.[14] He was even capable of seeing the future. Using this ability, he could write a letter to the leaders of the Brod community—who would be elected twenty years later! Obviously, he also knew that the letter, which he gave to an ill-fated Jew, would be forgotten, found twenty years later, and given to the communal leaders on the day that a son would be born to the wife of one official, and a daughter to the wife of another.[15] His knowledge, indeed, was so wondrous, that he said of himself: 'I know all!'[16]

At times the Ba'al Shem Tov's vision was aided by means such as gazing in a copy of the Zohar. It was related in the name of the Ba'al Shem Tov that 'upon opening the book, the tsadik could effect all his wishes, and engage in

[6] *Shivḥei habesht*, 129; see also ibid. 148 (a similar rescue effected from afar).

[7] Ibid. 61–2. Elsewhere (ibid. 152) the Ba'al Shem Tov sees from afar a person in danger of drowning, and advises him how to rescue himself.

[8] Ibid. 65–6.

[9] Ibid. 124.

[10] See Rodkinsohn, *Adat tsadikim*, §1. Cf. Bodek, *Pe'er mikedoshim*, end of §6. On the other hand, 'when he [the Ba'al Shem Tov] so desires, he cannot be seen' (*Shivḥei habesht*, 148).

[11] *Shivḥei habesht*, 92.

[12] For R. Abraham Abba, see *Shivḥei habesht*, 152–3; for R. Abba, the head of the Krivitch rabbinical court, see ibid. 108. See also Chikernik, *Ma'asiyot uma'amarim yekarim*, 15; Hazan, *Sipurim nifla'im*, §14, p. 29.

[13] *Shivḥei habesht*, 159: the Ba'al Shem Tov informs a householder who did not hold him in high regard that whenever he sought to have the proper intent during the recitation of *Shema yisra'el*, Jesus stood before him.

[14] Ibid. 67. At that time, R. Gershon was at a place that is not halakhically regarded as within the boundaries of the Land of Israel. See also the stories in Donner and Wodnik, *Sefer ba'al shem tov*, i, 'Me'irat einayim', 18.

[15] See Rodkinsohn, *Adat tsadikim*, §2. Cf. A. H. Michelson, *Ohel naftali*, §82: 'It was the way [of R. Naphtali of Ropshits] to tell the future, for the generations following him . . . and not a speck of his holy words was left unfulfilled.' Cf. also Brawer, *Pe'er yitsḥak*, §5: 'Many times our master [R. Isaac Eisik of Zhidachov] beheld with his spirit of divine inspiration and told things that were fulfilled twenty or thirty years afterwards, after our master was already in the world of truth.' See also Samuel of Shinova, *Ramatayim tsofim*, fo. 26*a*, regarding the rabbi of Pshischa, 'who said that he knows what everyone had done from the day of his birth . . . [saying,] for I am a man of signs and I possess the spirit of divine inspiration'.

[16] See J. Sofer, *Sipurei ya'akov*, i, §1, p. 18.

a sort of prophecy'.[17] Once, as he was looking into the Zohar, he even saw oxen that had been stolen from their owner.

R. Joseph asked the Ba'al Shem Tov: 'Is this written in the Zohar?' He replied: 'This is what the sages said on the verse [Gen. 1: 4] "God saw that the light was good," and they said that it was good that it be concealed. For by the light of the six days of Creation, people could see from one end of the earth to the other. And where did the Holy One, blessed be he, conceal it? He concealed it in the Torah. And what he said regarding the righteous [see BT *Ḥagigah* 12*a*, regarding his reserving the light of Creation for the righteous in the time to come] means: for the tsadikim who will appear in the world, and whoever merits to find the concealed light in the Torah gazes by means of it from one end of the world to the other. And do you think that it was only the oxen that I saw? In that same look I saw an occurrence in the holy community of Amsterdam.' And he related to him the event.[18]

Hearing the holy text could be as efficacious as reading it: 'when [the Ba'al Shem Tov] heard a person learning, he would know what would happen at the end of the year'.[19]

The Ba'al Shem Tov also had *aliyot neshamah* (out-of-body experiences of the soul leaving the body at night and ascending to the upper spheres),[20] in the course of which he revoked decrees against the people of Israel: for example, during such an experience while sleeping in Istanbul he negated an evil decree that hung over the Jews of the city;[21] and in another instance of impending calamity he was able to annul the evil, thanks to his knowledge of what had been decreed in the heavenly court.[22] The hasidic story also

[17] Pinhas of Dinovitz, *Siftei tsadikim*, 5 (my pagination), and further (ibid.), quoting the Maggid of Koznitz: 'And now, in the bitter Exile, the tsadik is capable of seeing everything that is written in the book, and this is the meaning of: "all your deeds are written in a book" [Mishnah *Avot* 2: 1].' See also Mondshein, *Likutei reshimot vema'asiyot*, §7, pp. 2–3: the Maggid of Mezirech looked in the Zohar, and saw a distant conflagration.

[18] *Shivḥei habesht*, 126; cf. 121: the Ba'al Shem Tov addresses a merchant who initially did not believe in him, but later recanted his doubt: 'You are a fool! For the light that the Holy One, blessed be He, created during the six days of Creation . . . where did He conceal it? In the Torah. Accordingly, when I open the book of the Zohar, I see the entire world, and I do not err in what I see with the help of God, may He be blessed.' Cf. Moses Hayim Ephraim of Sudilkov, *Degel maḥaneh efrayim*, 'Bo': every day the book of the Zohar has a new interpretation. See also *Shivḥei habesht*, 123: 'R. Tsevi Sofer recites from the Zohar before him, and the Ba'al Shem Tov responds after him, and he becomes greatly excited, and his face is inflamed.'

[19] *Shivḥei habesht*, 142–3. Cf. Jacob Joseph of Polonnoye, *Ben porat yosef*, fo. 96*a*.

[20] See *Shivḥei habesht*, 106–7. Cf. the description of the ascent of the soul in a letter by the Ba'al Shem Tov to his brother-in-law R. Gershon of Kutow, printed at the end of Jacob Joseph of Polonnoye, *Ben porat yosef*. Cf. also Kaidaner, *Sipurim nora'im*, §3; §11: the ascent of the souls of R. Pinhas of Korets and of R. Isaiah of Dinovitz at the same time; §52: the protruding eyes of the 'Old Rebbe' during the nightly ascent of his soul. See Nigal, *The Hasidic Book and the Jewish Holidays* (Heb.), 21–8.

[21] See Bodek, *Ma'aseh tsadikim*, §5, p. 10.

[22] See *Shivḥei habesht*, 68–9; cf. ibid. 65–6; J. Sofer, *Sipurei ya'akov*, ii, §34.

ascribes to him the hearing of heavenly voices. On one occasion he heard from such a voice that he was to depose the ritual slaughterer of the community of Kaminka;[23] on another occasion, that he should make haste to save R. Jacob Joseph, who was about to die as a result of his many fasts;[24] and on yet another that R. Joseph, a teacher from Chmelnik, was near death, prompting the Ba'al Shem Tov to stop what he was doing and effect a remedy for the ailing man.[25] Sometimes the voices spoke to the Ba'al Shem Tov of his own condition: one such voice forced him to choose between two punishments,[26] and another informed him that he had lost his portion in the world to come; some time later, however, he heard another heavenly voice announcing the restoration of his portion in the hereafter.[27] These heavenly voices are introduced with standard forms of words, namely: 'And I heard in the heavens',[28] and 'It was revealed to him from heaven.'[29]

Lower degrees of prophecy are manifested in questions asked in dreams,[30] or the ability of the Ba'al Shem Tov to understand 'how the birds speak, and how the beasts and animals speak',[31] both of which afford him knowledge that is withheld from ordinary people. Thus the Ba'al Shem Tov could reproach his servant R. Jacob for the theft of some gaiters, saying: 'The dog calls you a thief—and you deny it?'[32]

[23] See *Shivḥei habesht*, 127. Here the Ba'al Shem Tov follows in the footsteps of R. Isaac Luria, who 'would hear a heavenly voice announcing every thing' (*Sefer hakavanot uma'asei nisim*, fo. 2*b*). [24] See *Shivḥei habesht*, 62. [25] See ibid. 112.

[26] See ibid. 129; ibid. 114: the Ba'al Shem Tov heard a heavenly voice telling him where to lodge; ibid. 61: when R. Aryeh Leib Geliner, the *mokhiaḥ* of Polonnoye, heard a heavenly voice (saying that the enemy of R. Jacob Joseph would die, and that the city of Sharigrad would burn down), the Ba'al Shem Tov became enraged, and shouted at him: 'Fool, do you, too, hear heavenly voices?' [27] See Rodkinsohn, *Adat tsadikim*, §3.

[28] *Shivḥei habesht*, 67 (he heard Maimonides deliver a ruling).

[29] Ibid. 120; cf. Jacob Joseph of Polonnoye, *Toledot ya'akov yosef*, 'Vayera', fo. 38*d*: 'he was told from heaven [the reason for the tarrying of the messiah]'.

[30] A question asked in a dream is mentioned in the writings of R. Jacob Joseph of Polonnoye. Cf. *Shivḥei habesht*, 39: R. Eliezer, the Ba'al Shem Tov's father, asks a question in a dream concerning the proper conduct of the war; ibid. 43: R. Adam Ba'al Shem Tov asks in a dream to whom the writings are to be given.

[31] See *Shivḥei habesht*, 86–7: R. Aryeh Leib, the *mokhiaḥ*, desired to learn 'the language of animals and birds, and the language of trees'; the Ba'al Shem Tov taught him, and then withdrew the ability. Also cited in Zevin, *Hasidic Tales* (Heb.), 482–3; and see Nigal, 'On R. Aaron Samuel Hakohen' (Heb.), 257 n. 27; A. Michelsohn, *Dover shalom*, §342n.; Kamelhaar, *Mevaser tov*, 'Pinḥas', 37–8. *Dover shalom* continues by relating that, on the wedding day of a young couple, the Ba'al Shem Tov heard a bird say: 'Among these is the land to be apportioned' (Num. 26: 53), from which he understood that they were destined to divorce, because of the husband's desire to go to the Land of Israel. *Continued in Appendix.*

[32] *Shivḥei habesht*, 144. For R. Elimelekh's knowledge of the language of dogs, see I. Safrin, 'Netiv mitsvoteikha', 'Shevil emunah', 5. Cf. the following story: 'It happened that a certain non-Jew was sitting with Rabbi Judah Hehasid, and a sheep came from the river and bleated. The non-Jew said to R. Judah: "Since you know secret things and the future, tell me what the

These abilities attributed to the Ba'al Shem Tov were also ascribed to other tsadikim in later generations, albeit to a lesser degree. It was generally assumed in hasidic thought and in the hasidic story that the statement in the Talmud (*Ḥagigah* 12*a*), 'A person could see by the light that the Holy One, blessed be he, created on the first day from one end of the world to the other. . . . he arose and concealed it. . . . And for whom did he conceal it? For the righteous [tsadikim] in the future time', refers exclusively to the hasidic tsadikim.[33] As noted above, the ability to see afar was attributed to the Ba'al Shem Tov even by his own generation, and it is not surprising that all the tellers of the hasidic story, from *Shivḥei habesht* on, accepted this view. Supernatural vision was ascribed to many tsadikim, but the most outstanding possessor of this trait was R. Jacob Isaac, known in recognition of this gift as the Seer of Lublin. Once, when he was asked about a married woman who was meeting in private with a man (contrary to Jewish law), he replied: 'I can see by means of my divine inspiration that she did not defile herself.'[34] He also said that he could see 400 parasangs (1,600 miles), and that when he was born, he saw from one end of the world to the other.[35] The Maggid of Koznitz attested of the Seer that his vision was as powerful as the priestly oracle, the Urim and Thummim.[36] On one occasion the Seer saw that severe judgments had been issued against a certain hasid, and later saw how they had been ameliorated by drinking a *leḥayim*, a toast to life.[37] While at a third sabbath meal he once saw a relative of his, a wine merchant, in danger in another place and saved him.[38]

R. Israel Abraham of Cherny Ostrov said, 'I can see 15 parasangs [60 miles] around Ticheniz.'[39] R. Mordish of Prinsk once asked the tsadik R. Mordecai of Nezkizh:

sheep is bleating." R. Judah answered: "The sheep is bleating and telling you that your wife is being unfaithful with a certain non-Jew now." The non-Jew went to his house, and he found it was as R. Judah said' (see *Mayse bukh*, fos 42, 48*a*).

[33] R. Menahem Mendel of Lubavitch related that the 'Old Rebbe' heard from the Maggid of Mezirech that the Ba'al Shem Tov 'possessed the material sight to see four hundred parasangs by four hundred parasangs' (Chikernik, *Ma'asiyot uma'amarim yekarim*, 6). Cf. Brandwein, *Degel maḥaneh yehudah*, 'Introduction by the Author's Nephew'.

[34] [Isaac Dov Baer ben Tsevi Hirsch], *Kahal ḥasidim heḥadash*, §126. See also Bodek, *Kahal kedoshim*, §11, fo. 2*b*.

[35] Samuel of Shinova, *Ramatayim tsofim*, fo. 55*b* (p. 110), §23. Cf. Sobelman, *Sipurei tsadikim heḥadash*, §28.

[36] *Niflaot anshei ma'aseh*, §11; Berger, *Eser orot*, 'R. Jacob Isaac', §1. Cf. Sobelman, *Sipurei tsadikim heḥadash*, §56: the rabbi of Apta claimed that asking his advice was like consulting the Urim and Thummim. Cf. Breitstein, *Siḥot ḥayim*, 45–6: during the wedding of a disciple of R. Moses Eliakum Briah of Koznitz, mitnagedim sought to embarrass him by posing halakhic questions. Another disciple, R. Isaac Meir of Ger, answered in the groom's stead and saved him from humiliation. Cf. ibid. 56.

[37] See Sobelman, *Sipurei tsadikim heḥadash*, §31.

[38] [Isaac Dov Baer ben Tsevi Hirsch], *Kahal ḥasidim heḥadash*, §§123, 199.

[39] Sobelman, *Sipurei tsadikim heḥadash*, §26.

'Is it true what the world says about my master, that he hears and sees everything?' He answered him: 'And what is new in this? For the rabbis, of blessed memory, said: "A seeing eye and a hearing ear" [Mishnah *Avot* 2: 1]. This means: that man was created to see and to hear all that he desires, but on condition that "all your deeds be in a book" [ibid.], [the word *sefer* (book)] meaning brilliance and clarity. And whoever does not spoil his eyes and his ears by his actions is undoubtedly able to see and hear in this manner.'[40]

Those who contend that this is an extravagant claim, or that this ability was attributed to the tsadik only in later generations, must confront the statement by R. Isaac Eisik Safrin in his personal diary, where he wrote: 'From the day that I was two years old, until I was fifty years old, I attained wondrous sights and I spoke prophecies "like an oracle sought from God" [2 Sam. 16: 23], and I gazed actually from one end of the world to the other.'[41]

Kefitsat haderekh (also *kefitsat ha'arets*),[42] a miraculous shortening of the way, is among the miracles mentioned as early as the rabbinic period and in the post-talmudic literature.[43] Not surprisingly, the hasidic story attributes *kefitsat haderekh* to some of the tsadikim, as well as to individuals who preceded hasidism.[44] For example, it is related that R. Abraham Abusch of Frankfurt asked R. Zalman of Posen, the rabbi of the nearby Friedberg community, to accompany him on his journey to a circumcision. The ceremony was to take place in a remote village, a trip of about four or five hours. Since it was a Friday, R. Zalman declined, maintaining that he had to be in his

[40] I. Landau, *Zikhron tov*, §25, p. 27. Cf. Jacob Joseph of Polonnoye, *Ben porat yosef*, 'Derush leshabat shuvah, shenat 526', fo. 96*a*.

[41] I. Safrin, *Megilat setarim*, 9. Cf. id., *Heikhal haberakhah*, 'Ve'etḥanan': 'In the generations preceding ours, the heads of the generation would see from one end of the world to the other, and would speak with the spirit of divine inspiration.' Cf. also Rabinovitz, *Ma'aseh neḥemiyah*, 8, regarding R. Nehemiah Yehiel, the son of Jacob Isaac of Pshischa ('the Holy Jew'), who related: 'When I was 9 years old, when I saw a person and I looked in his face, I comprehended all that he had done from the day of his birth until then . . . and I prayed to the Lord, may he be blessed, to take this from me, but my prayer was to no avail.'

[42] See Rashi on Gen. 28: 17; see Nigal, *Magic, Mysticism, and Hasidism*, ch. 2 ('*Kefitzat haderekh*: The Shortening of the Way').

[43] *Kefitsat haderekh* occurred for three individuals: Eliezer, the servant of Abraham; Jacob; and Abishai son of Zeruiah (see BT *San.* 95*a*; *Ḥul.* 91*b*). It is related of the father of Samuel that 'he came by means of a [divine] name' (BT *Kid.* 73*a*, Tosafot, s.v. *mai ika miut arusot*; Kayara, *Halakhot gedolot*, 337–8: 'He came by means of a [divine] name . . . and he returned by means of a name to his house'); see also B. M. Lewin, *Otsar hagaonim*, 'Ḥagigah', 16: 'The master, Rav Natronai Gaon, may the memory of the righteous be for a blessing, came to them from Babylonia by means of *kefitsat haderekh*.' For the *kefitsat haderekh* of R. Isaac Luria, see *Sefer hakavanot uma'asei nisim*, fo. 10*b*.

[44] See J. Sofer, *Sipurei ya'akov*, i, §2, p. 9. The miracle happened for R. Recanati by means of 'a name of *kefitsat haderekh*'. See Shenkel, *Ma'asim tovim*, §14: Nahmanides, too, used the special name to bring about *kefitsat haderekh* when he escaped from Barcelona in a boat.

home for the sabbath. R. Abraham, however, assured him that he would indeed spend the sabbath in his home; and, by means of *kefitsat haderekh*, he brought the other rabbi back to his city before the beginning of the sabbath.[45]

In a similar story, it is related that the Ba'al Shem Tov once brought a wealthy man from the city of Lyubar back to his house on the eve of the sabbath. This man had participated in the circumcision of the son of a friend of his in Ostropol. His friend had promised him that the circumcision would be held early in the day, but the Ba'al Shem Tov was late and the ceremony was delayed, leading the rich man to doubt whether he would be able to get back home in time for the sabbath. The Ba'al Shem Tov felt obliged to respond to the other's anxiety: *kefitsat haderekh* occurred, and the Ba'al Shem Tov spent the sabbath as a guest in the wealthy man's house.[46]

The many hasidic stories relating to the *kefitsat haderekh* of the Ba'al Shem Tov make it possible to arrive at an archetype of this miraculous ability. *Kefitsat haderekh* usually occurs either before the sabbath, when the goal is to reach a particular destination (or to return home) before the advent of the sabbath, or on Saturday night, after the end of the sabbath, when, according to these accounts, the Ba'al Shem Tov would usually set out on special journeys. The tsadik and those accompanying him—perhaps his disciples, or one or more guests—take their places in a wagon, the non-Jewish wagon driver takes the reins, and the horses begin to trot. Some time later, after they have left the city from which they set out, the driver falls asleep, or turns his back to the horses, and the miracle begins. The horses, left to themselves, gallop at a tremendous pace, and it seems to the passengers in the wagon that they are soaring through the air as they begin to see fields, towns, and villages pass by at dizzying speed. The wagon once again takes its normal place on the ground only when they are nearing their destination, and the horses canter along until they stop before a certain house—to discover that their journey, which would normally have taken several days to complete, has been shortened to a number of hours, or to a single day.

In *Shivḥei habesht*, *kefitsat haderekh* saves the Ba'al Shem Tov from the anticipated anger of the wealthy leaseholders in Slutsk: 'And he travelled from there in the middle of the night by *kefitsat ha'arets*, some fifteen parasangs [60 miles], until he had left their territory for another land.'[47] The same miraculous ability saved the Ba'al Shem Tov in another instance, when he had fallen into the hands of murderers, who sought to intoxicate the tsadik so that they could kill him.[48] According to another tale, the Ba'al

[45] See A. Michelson, *Ohel avraham*, §17.

[46] See Chikernik, *Sipurim neḥmadim*, 12.

[47] *Shivḥei habesht*, 133. Cf. ibid. 134: 'I heard from other people that he came to his house in three days, by means of *kefitsat haderekh*, despite the heavy rains.'

[48] See I. Safrin, 'Netiv mitsvoteikha', 'Shevil hayiḥud', 4, fo. 21*b*.

Shem Tov once left his home on a Wednesday night 'and travelled a great distance on that day, as he is known to all to do when travelling'. When the Jewish tax-collector with whom he was staying asked where he was headed, he said that he was going to participate in a wedding that was to be held in Berlin on Friday. The tax-collector was amazed by this answer, for Berlin was a long way away; he asked the Ba'al Shem Tov if he might accompany the tsadik on his journey. The next day, to the surprise of his host, the Ba'al Shem Tov was in no hurry to set out, and only towards evening did he order that the horses be harnessed. They travelled the entire night—and in the morning they entered Berlin. As it transpired, the purpose of the Ba'al Shem Tov's trip was to save a bride from death.[49]

Another lengthy journey undertaken by the Ba'al Shem Tov with miraculous speed, also in the company of a stranger, was from Brod to the city of Posen. A wealthy man's son-in-law, a native of Posen, who had not seen his parents for three years, asked the Ba'al Shem Tov to take him with him. They set out on Thursday, and the son-in-law did not believe that they would arrive in Posen in time before the sabbath; but they did, and they also returned on Saturday night, again by means of *kefitsat haderekh*. There was a threefold purpose to the Ba'al Shem Tov's trip: on the way, to effect a *tikun* for the souls of two Jews who had been murdered and were buried along the route; to meet with a hidden tsadik who was fit to be the messiah, if his generation was worthy; and in Posen itself, to elevate the soul of a professor who would subsequently convert to Judaism.[50]

Once the Ba'al Shem Tov came to Brod by *kefitsat haderekh* in order to cancel a ban that had been proclaimed against him;[51] and on another occasion, when R. Abba of Drohobitch asked him to come immediately and heal his wife, who had gone mad, the Ba'al Shem Tov recited the afternoon prayers in Podhaitza and the evening prayers in Drohobitch![52] There are many more examples of the Ba'al Shem Tov's use of *kefitsat haderekh*. One Saturday-night journey achieved 'by the [divine] name [written on parchment; i.e. a charm] that effected *kefitsat haderekh*' brought succour to the Ba'al Shem Tov himself, through atoning by means of his suffering for a sin he had committed against an orphan girl who had been raised in his house.[53] There was also an instance in which an emissary of the Ba'al Shem Tov experienced *kefitsat haderekh*,[54] while on another occasion the Ba'al Shem Tov employed *kefitsat haderekh* to

[49] See Rodkinsohn, *Adat tsadikim*, §4.

[50] See Kaidaner, *Sipurim nora'im*, §4, pp. 38–45: a story that was told by R. Israel of Ruzhin. See A. Stern, *Ḥutim hameshulashim*, 18–19.

[51] See Moskowitz, *Otsar hasipurim*, viii, §1.

[52] Shenkel, *Ma'asiyot nora'im venifla'im*, §18.

[53] See Bodek, *Mifalot hatsadikim*, §36, fo. 19*b*; also ch. 8 below.

[54] See Sobelman, *Sipurei tsadikim heḥadash*, §10.

go to the city of Radom, where a certain Jew denied God, because his brothers became rabbis;[55] and on yet another occasion, he saved a woman from apostasy by the same means.[56]

Not many other tsadikim were said to have experienced *kefitsat haderekh*. With the Ba'al Shem Tov's help, R. Yehiel Mikhel of Zlotchev succeeded in returning home by this means to his wife, who was experiencing a difficult childbirth;[57] R. Leib Sarahs experienced *kefitsat haderekh* on his journey to Vilna to cancel an antisemitic decree,[58] and R. Meir of Premishlan was granted the same miracle as he hurried to rescue a child from drowning.[59]

THE TSADIK'S FOLLOWERS AND SUPPLICANTS

Believing all these things of the tsadik—that he is blessed with divine inspiration, sees and hears in supernatural fashion, and is capable of annulling decrees [from heaven]—and that his blessing is given heavenly sanction, hasidim travelled to him to submit their petitions.

Several different stories describe the journey to the tsadik, but the actual stay in the court of the tsadik is given a broader description. Key features are the presentation of the *kvitl* (a written account of one's problems and requests) and the *pidyon* (or *pidyon nefesh*: accompanying monetary contributions); the blessing by the tsadik; and taking one's leave of the tsadik.

The stories of those who became adherents of hasidism—both simple people and those who eventually became leading disciples of tsadikim—occupy a prominent place in the hasidic storytelling genre. Especially instructive are the stories depicting how the disciples of the Ba'al Shem Tov, such as R. Dov Baer of Mezirech and R. Jacob Joseph of Polonnoye, were first attracted to their teacher and master.[60]

[55] See I. Safrin, *Notser ḥesed*, fo. 29*a*. [56] See *Shivḥei habesht*, 163. [57] See ibid. 91.

[58] See Rodkinsohn, *Sipurei tsadikim*, §1, p. 5. See also A. Stern, *Ḥutim hameshulashim*, 60.

[59] Berger, *Eser atarot*, 'R. Meir of Premishlan', §2. See Drickerman, *Temimei derekh*, fo. 25*b*: a concealed tsadik travelled to R. Elimelekh of Lizhensk with *kefitsat haderekh*.

[60] For the future Maggid becoming a follower of the Ba'al Shem Tov, see *Shivḥei habesht*, 70–1: 'and there are several versions of how the Maggid came to the Ba'al Shem Tov'. Cf. Aaron of Apta, *Keter shem tov*, fo. 30*a*–*b*; the Yiddish edition of *Shivḥei habesht*, ch. 23 (a version close to that in *Keter shem tov*). See also A. Stern, *Ḥutim hameshulashim*, 31 (two versions). On R. Jacob Joseph's becoming a hasid, see *Shivḥei habesht*, 61. Shimon Rabbi, under the name of 'S. R. of Tarnow', printed three stories in his book *Notser te'enah*; on the title page he says that the third of these, which tells of R. Jacob Joseph becoming a follower of the Ba'al Shem Tov, 'has not yet been published'. A. Stern, *Ḥutim hameshulashim*, contains two versions of how R. Jacob Joseph became a follower of the Ba'al Shem Tov: ibid. 27–8, an unknown version; ibid. 28–30, R. Jacob Joseph hears the Ba'al Shem Tov telling stories in Sharigrad. See Ch. 1 above. Cf. the tale of R. Hayim Vital becoming a pupil of R. Isaac Luria by virtue of the latter's interpretations of difficult passages in the Zohar (*Sefer hakavanot uma'asei nisim*, fo. 3*b*).

Most individuals who became attached to a tsadik did so after hearing of his spiritual status and ability to work wonders, but some declared their loyalty as the result of an order from heaven. Thus, R. Yehiel Mikhel of Zlotchev related 'that he was commanded by heaven to accept the Ba'al Shem Tov as his master . . . and when the Ba'al Shem Tov died, he was commanded to accept the great Maggid, R. Dov, as his master'.[61]

A hasid entering the presence of the tsadik would usually give the latter a *kvitl* or *tsetl* (note) on which was written his name, his mother's name, and a short account of his request.[62] The tsadik would bless the applicant with the formula 'May the Lord, may he be blessed, help you';[63] some tsadikim placed their hand on the head of the person who submitted the request.[64] Many stories mention the *kvitl* and the *pidyon*, since these were an integral part of the audience with the tsadik. The request could relate to any sphere of life, most concerning one of the areas defined by hasidism as *benei ḥai umezonai* (offspring, health, and livelihood), but *pidyonot* were also given on behalf of the dead.[65] The *kvitl* was usually presented by the applicant himself, but if he was prevented from doing so (for example, by ill-health), he would send it and the *pidyon* with a relative or friend. Often a single emissary would bring several *kvitlakh*, writing the names on a single piece of paper and representing all those who had sent him. Should a tsadik find himself in distress, he would himself send a *tsetl* to one of his fellow hasidic masters to request assistance.[66]

Although the great majority of tsadikim accepted *kvitlakh* and *pidyonot*,[67] not all did so without reservation. The tsadik R. Judah Tsevi of Rozdol once said, with subtle humour, to a person who gave him a *kvitl*: 'Now you give me a request with a *pidyon nefesh*, thinking that I am a *guter yid* [literally, 'good Jew': i.e. a tsadik]. What shall I do in the world to come, when you

61 *Shivḥei habesht*, 72.

62 In *kvitlakh* submitted to the tsadik of Komarno on marital matters, it was customary to write the names of the groom, the bride, and their parents. See Ehrmann, *Devarim arevim*, 'Stories of the Holy Rabbi, of R. Z[evi] H[irsch] of Zhidachov', §2.

63 See Teomim, *Ateret tiferet*, 'His Holiness, the Holy Rabbi, R. Tsevi Yude of Razla', §27.

64 See e.g. *Shivḥei habesht*, 72: 'The Ba'al Shem Tov took his hand and placed it on the head [of the Maggid of Mezirech] and blessed him.' *Continued in Appendix.*

65 See e.g. Brandwein, *Degel maḥaneh yehudah*, §87.

66 See e.g. ibid., §22: for years, every Rosh Hodesh Elul, R. Mordecai (Mottele) of Chernobyl would send a *kvitl* to R. Tsevi Judah of Stretin, while the latter would send a *kvitl* and *pidyon nefesh* to the Seer of Lublin (Brandwein, *Degel maḥaneh yehudah*, §29). See also Breitstein, *Siḥot ḥayim*, 24: before travelling to Ruzhin, the tsadik of Mogielnica would collect *kvitlakh* and *pidyonot* from those close to him and bring them to Ruzhin. See Yashar, *Beit komarno*, 60 n. 72: a laundry ticket was mistakenly sent to the tsadik of Komarno, but the tsadik 'read' all the requests of the applicant, and gave answers to those that were written on the original *kvitl*.

67 It was surprising if a hasid came to the court of the tsadik but did not submit a *kvitl*. See Sobelman, *Sipurei tsadikim heḥadash*, §38. For the *pidyon nefesh*, see also J. Y. Rosenberg, *Rafa'el hamalakh*, 75–97; see also Wertheim, *Law and Custom in Hasidism* (Heb.), 161–4.

realize that, in truth, I am not a *guter yid*, and you will demand that I return the *pidyon nefesh*? From where will I take it to return it to you?'[68]

A Jewish leaseholder once promised to give the Ba'al Shem Tov half of his possessions if his sick son were to recover. The Ba'al Shem Tov replied: 'I do not desire possessions; instead, give such and such [a person] a *pidyon nefesh*, immediately.'[69] In a story in which he points out that the founder of hasidism was not initially held in the high regard he later enjoyed, R. Israel of Ruzhin cites a case in which the Ba'al Shem Tov received only 10 zloty for reviving the son of a wealthy man, while he himself, he said, 'even for a smaller wonder than this, would not want to proceed for less than 300 zloty!'[70]

Some tsadikim were satisfied with a small *pidyon*,[71] while others demanded large sums of money. Once a person came to R. Abraham of Trisk and asked him to pray for his son, who was ill. R. Abraham asked for 18 roubles as the *pidyon*. When the supplicant said that he did not have this sum, the tsadik ordered that the horses be whipped up and he continued on his way. When the same person came to R. Mordecai Joseph of Izbica, he was asked to give the tsadik only 18 *gedolim* (literally, 'big ones'), meaning high-value coins, but of lesser worth than roubles. The tsadik explained: 'Some tsadikim have a profound mystical intent in the taking of much money from people who seek benefit from them; but under extenuating circumstances, when the distressed person does not have [such large sums], the tsadik also is obliged to participate in their suffering and be satisfied with the means of the supplicant.'[72] There is quite a detailed portrayal of the practice of R. Isaac of Nezkizh in this regard:

Regarding *pidyonot*: besides his having a *pidyon* of the number 18, and the number 160, he also had a *pidyon* of the number 24. And in former years he was accustomed not to order that he be given money; when people would ask him how much to give as the *pidyon* for that request, he would say: 'It is not my way, heaven forbid, to

[68] Teomim, *Ateret tiferet*, 'His Holiness, the Holy Rabbi, R. Tsevi Yude of Razla', §17; Zevin, *Hasidic Tales* (Heb.), 235.

[69] Rodkinsohn, *Adat tsadikim*, §4. Cf. J. Sofer, *Sipurei ya'akov*, i, §23, p. 74: the Ba'al Shem Tov asks a land-tenant if he has 'several *perutot* [small coins] for *pidyon*'.

[70] *Ma'asiyot vesiḥot tsadikim*, 20. Cf. Zimetbaum, *Darkhei ḥayim*, §51, p. 74: a village Jew, who had been saved from attempted murder, went in to R. Hayim of Sanz, and gave him a *kvitl* and ten roubles as a *pidyon nefesh*. The tsadik said to him: 'For something like this you give a *pidyon nefesh* of ten silver rubles? You should give one hundred silver rubles!'

[71] See Ehrmann, *Devarim arevim*, 'Stories of the Holy Rabbi, Our Master, R. Meir of Premishlan', §14: R. Meir of Premishlan did not want large sums of money and returned a large *pidyon* to the person who sent it; ibid., 'Luaḥ hatikun' (Corrigenda): R. Aaron Mashiah refused to accept more than what he had requested from the husband of a sick woman. It is recorded in Ze'ev Wolf of Zhitomir, *Or hame'ir*, 38–9, that R. Meir of Premishlan ordered his son R. Abraham to copy every *kvitl* into a ledger, and to place the ledger in his grave upon his death, so that he would be able to intercede for all those whose requests had not been granted.

[72] [Lemberger], *Niflaot hatsadikim*, 32. Cf. Ch. 4 below.

command that I be given money, rather, however much a person has to give me, so does the Holy One, blessed be He, send to the mind of the one giving.' And it seems that many times he would not look at all at how much they would leave for him as a *pidyon*.[73]

When R. Isaac was still a young man, a person decided to test him by giving him a blank *kvitl*. To the 'supplicant's' surprise, the tsadik appeared to read the note in the same manner as he usually read these petitions, 'and granted his request'.[74]

Once, while a disciple of R. David Moses of Chortkov, R. Tsevi Judah complained to his master about the great numbers of *kvitlakh*, and said that he would need a great deal of time to read them all to the tsadik. R. David Moses replied that they should do just as R. Abraham Joshua Heschel of Apta had done on a similar occasion, when

> there were many *kvitlakh* before him on Rosh Hashanah and on Yom Kippur, and he did not have sufficient time to read them all. The tsadik of Apta, may his merit protect us, had many pockets in his garments. He took the *kvitlakh* and placed them in his pockets. He put his hands over the pockets, and said in his holy words: 'I bless all the people of the *kvitlakh* that are here in my pockets with offspring, long life, satisfactory livelihood, and a good year.'[75]

So the tsadik of Chortkov collected all the notes in his handkerchief, and blessed them.

When R. Elimelekh of Lizhensk secluded himself during the month of Elul, he would receive *kvitlakh* only on matters of life and death, and only 'extremely brief' ones.[76] R. Elimelekh, moreover, would not receive a note from anyone who was not sincere—in contrast with his mentor, the Seer of Lublin, who would accept requests even from the wicked, in order to draw them closer.[77]

[73] I. Landau, *Zikhron tov*, §29. For the 160 coins, see also J. Y. Rosenberg, *Rafa'el hamalakh*, 77.

[74] I. Landau, *Zikhron tov*, §40. Cf. Brawer, *Pe'er yitsḥak*, ch. 12, §4: a young man mistakenly gave a blank note to R. Isaac Eisik of Zhidachov, and learned of his error only after leaving the tsadik. The latter, by means of an agent, informed him that even from the blank paper he read all the young man's requests, 'and he also will be blessed'. In another instance, the tsadik knew the request of a rabbi who had had a dream, even before the *kvitl* had been presented to him (ibid., ch. 14, §8); similarly, a *kvitl* that was given to him by a woman had already been 'read' by his son (§5).

[75] Rapoport, *Divrei david*, fos 21*b*–22*a*.

[76] See Sobelman, *Sipurei tsadikim heḥadash*, §35; Ehrmann, *Devarim arevim*, 'Stories of the Holy Rabbi, R. Israel of Ruzhin', §2: the tsadik immediately discarded a *tsetl* that was presented to him by an informer, without reading it. Cf. also Brawer, *Pe'er yitsḥak*, ch. 14, §1: a rich woman from Moldova came to the tsadik R. Isaac Eisik of Zhidachov and gave him a *kvitl* accompanied by a *pidyon*. When the tsadik looked at the note, he threw the money to the ground, and shouted at her to leave immediately, for he had seen her many sins.

[77] See M. M. Sofer, *Sheloshah edrei tson*, 48. See also Singer, *Seva ratson*, fo. 5*a*: the Seer draws transgressors closer.

Hasidim who sent *kvitlakh* and *pidyonot* with the same request to two tsadikim feared their anger over such an affront to their honour.[78]

The *pidyonot* comprised the chief source of income for the tsadikim, who used most of these funds to maintain their courts and to make charitable donations; R. Tsevi Hirsch of Lesko, for example, would distribute the *pidyonot* money to the indigent, many of whom received a fixed sum from him every week. He also sent money to distant locations to help poor people, especially to the Land of Israel.[79] Some hasidim would place the *pidyon* money on the graves of tsadikim, such as the young man who deposited two *pidyonot* on the grave of R. Dov Baer of Lubavitch.[80] Some of this money would be distributed for charity; some of it was used to purchase oil to illuminate the grave of the tsadik.[81]

THE TSADIK'S CRITICS AND OPPONENTS

Opposition to hasidism took various forms, from derision to actual physical blows, persecution, and informing on hasidim to the authorities. It was therefore only to be expected that the hasidic tale should give a prominent place to accounts of the behaviour of those opposed to hasidism. Hasidic readers no doubt derived much pleasure from stories in which the tsadik emerged victorious and the mitnagedim were defeated, admitted the superiority of the tsadik, and sometimes even repented and became loyal hasidim.

One of the later collections contains a dramatic tale about the persecutions suffered by the Ba'al Shem Tov at the hands of the mitnagedim. His adversaries attempted to intoxicate him, with the intention of killing him while he was inebriated. The Ba'al Shem Tov knew of their evil design and ate apples so that the strong drink had no effect on him. His enemies had closed the gates of the fortress, so that he could not escape; but upon his command they opened, and the Ba'al Shem Tov fled, employing *kefitsat haderekh*. The punishment of these opponents took the form of a fire and a plague that erupted among them, their descent into poverty, and the birth of deformed children. The wives of the wicked pleaded with the Ba'al Shem Tov, begging him to cancel the punishment, but he agreed only to postpone it for twenty years.[82]

[78] See e.g. Brandwein, *Degel maḥaneh yehudah*, §85.

[79] See Goldberger, *Darkhei hatov vehayashar*, fo. 11*b*. Cf. what is related in Ehrmann, *Devarim arevim*, 'Stories of the Holy Rabbi, R. Israel of Ruzhin', §2: that he had three collection boxes for *pidyonot*—one for religious needs, a second for the needs of his household, and a third for the purchase and upkeep of horses.

[80] See Kaidaner, *Sipurim nora'im*, §36.

[81] Ibid., §37.

[82] See I. Safrin, 'Netiv mitsvoteikha', 'Shevil hayiḥud', fo. 21*b*; Zeilingold, *Me'orot hagedolim*, 13. R. Abraham of Butchatch, in contrast, decided not to place a ban on a mitnaged who locked

Two leading early mitnagedim in particular loom large in the hasidic stories of opposition to the new movement: R. Hayim Sanzer and R. Moses Ostrer, two of the heads of the *kloyz* (synagogue/study hall) in Brod.[83] It is related that they plotted to proclaim a ban against the Ba'al Shem Tov, but he frustrated their evil design. In the end they were reconciled with the Ba'al Shem Tov, and R. Moses Ostrer even presented him with a copy of his book *Arugat habosem* (printed in his lifetime in Zlotchev).[84]

The hasidic stories list among the opponents of the Ba'al Shem Tov a number of people who would eventually become his friends and disciples, after acknowledging that they had misjudged him. These include the pietists R. Ze'ev (Wolf) Kiytses and R. David Forkes, who according to *Shivḥei habesht* initially considered the Ba'al Shem Tov to be 'of no import', because 'the name given him, of Ba'al Shem Tov [*ba'al shem* = wonder-worker], was not fitting' for someone who claimed such elevated status.[85] R. Nahman of Kosov, a contemporary of the Ba'al Shem Tov, had originally been among those opposing the Ba'al Shem Tov, himself defining the enmity between them as 'an ancient argument, that had existed between Saul and David, may he rest in peace, and afterwards between Hillel and Shammai'.[86]

The hasidic tale itself admitted that the early opposition to the nascent movement concerned matters of ritual and practice. Changes instituted by the hasidim in the prayers used in the synagogue and their insistence upon '[totally] smooth knives [for ritual slaughtering]' aroused the ire of their opponents.[87] R. Nahman of Kosov enraged the worshippers in the synagogue not only by leading the prayers without having received permission, but also by daring to follow *nusaḥ sefarad*: a Sephardi version of the prayers, much beloved by mystics but not accepted in the traditional Ashkenazi community. When some of them came to him after the prayer service and

him in a toilet, for fear that his intent might not be for the sake of heaven, and that personal considerations and defence of his own honour might have been involved in the issuing of such a ban (Ehrmann, *Pe'er vekhavod*, fo. 30*a*, cited in Agnon, *Hakhnasat kalah*.

[83] A. Stern, *Ḥutim hameshulashim*, 26: the second tsadik (R. Jacob) of Husyatin (d. in Tel Aviv), gave an account of the Ba'al Shem Tov in Brod, and of how R. Hayim of Sanz became his follower.

[84] See Moskowitz, *Otsar hasipurim*, viii, §1.

[85] *Shivḥei habesht*, 56. Cf. Chikernik, *Ma'asiyot uma'amarim yekarim*, fo. 6*b* (cited in Donner and Wodnik, *Sefer ba'al shem tov*, i. 13): R. Israel Harif of Satanov said to the Ba'al Shem Tov: 'And for this [knowledge of the correct simple meaning of texts], I would love you, if only you would not be a *ba'al shem*.' *Continued in Appendix.*

[86] *Shivḥei habesht*, 93.

[87] On the changes introduced in prayers, see Wertheim, *Law and Custom in Hasidism* (Heb.), chs. 3 and 4 (pp. 83–143). There was also internal hasidic criticism of various matters relating to prayer (bodily movements during prayer and praying after the halakhically prescribed times, among others). See e.g. Elimelekh of Lizhensk, *No'am elimelekh*, 'Mikets', fo. 23*a*; ibid., 'Ki tisa', fo. 52*c*; Kattaina, *Raḥamei ha'av*, §25. On ritual slaughter, see Shmeruk, 'Social Significance of Hasidic *Sheḥitah*' (Heb.).

challenged him—'How did he dare to stand before the Ark [i.e. lead the prayers] without permission, and to change the version [of the prayers], [to one that] our fathers and our fathers' fathers did not recite?'—he responded with a question of his own—'And who says that they [their forefathers] are in Paradise [i.e. were right]?'—that not only failed to mollify those questioning him but inflamed them further.[88] A similar incident occurs in the story of the Ba'al Shem Tov's visit to Slutsk on the invitation of the wife of one of the leading leaseholders in the city. During the afternoon prayers the congregants heard that the Ba'al Shem Tov was praying in *nusaḥ sefarad*, which greatly vexed them. Even before this, when they wished to invite him to a meal, he had demanded first to see the slaughterer's knife; on both counts the members of the community wondered how he dared to act thus in such a large city and such respected company.[89]

The first mitnagedim accused the early hasidim of being illiterates and ignoramuses, deriding the unlettered hasid or tsadik, as in the following story about the Ba'al Shem Tov.

One time, during an assembly of the [Council of the] Four Lands, the first communal leader was the rabbi and *nagid* [communal leader] R. Abraham Abba [of Lublin]. He proposed that, according to what they had heard about the Ba'al Shem Tov, he was an ignoramus; how then could he be blessed with divine inspiration? For 'the unlearned cannot be pious [*ḥasid*]' [Mishnah *Avot* 2: 5]. They sent him from the assembly to the Ba'al Shem Tov, to summon him before them immediately. And so he did. When he [the Ba'al Shem Tov] appeared before them, this rabbi was the main speaker. He said to the Ba'al Shem Tov: 'According to your behaviour, it seems that divine inspiration rests upon you. But some say that your honour is an ignoramus. Accordingly, let us hear from you if your honour knows some law.' This took place on Rosh Hodesh [the New Moon]. He [R. Abraham] asked him [the Ba'al Shem Tov]: 'A person forgot [to add in the Amidah for Rosh Hodesh] *Ya'aleh veyavo* ['Our God and the God of our fathers, let there rise . . .']; what is the law?' The Ba'al Shem Tov answered: 'This law is not needed, neither by his honour nor by me, for even if his honour were to repeat [the Amidah, as would be required if this passage were omitted], he would forget a second time (that actually was the case, that he forgot to recite *Ya'aleh veyavo* a second time as well), but as for myself—I certainly would not forget.'[90]

[88] See *Shivḥei habesht*, 95.

[89] Ibid. 133.

[90] Ibid. 152–3; Zevin, *Hasidic Tales: Festivals* (Heb.), 189. Sperling, *Reasons for the Customs* (Heb.), 46, writes that he saw this tale, but does not recall where. Cf. Israel (the Maggid of Slutsk), *Sefer havikuaḥ*, fo. 9*b*; and what is related about R. Meir Margoliouth in Chikernik, *Ma'asiyot uma'amarim yekarim*, 15. For the claims of the mitnagedim that the Ba'al Shem Tov was not learned, see Margolioth, *Kevutsat ya'akov*, fo. 54*b*, for a story of a test to which the Ba'al Shem Tov was subjected, in which the teller indirectly admits that the Ba'al Shem Tov did not exhibit expertise in Jewish law. Cf. the opposition of two Torah scholars to R. Isaac Luria and the test to which they subjected him: *Sefer hakavanot uma'asei nisim*, fo. 3*a*.

The gibe directed against the learned mitnaged was clear: even if he knew the law, it would be of no avail; the Ba'al Shem Tov's knowledge of hidden things, in contrast, revealed that he was blessed with divine inspiration. A similar charge was raised against R. Elimelekh of Lizhensk (see Chapter 16), and his response was similarly caustic.

Shivḥei habesht tells of a learned schoolteacher and contemporary of the Ba'al Shem Tov called R. Moses Kades, who dismissed the Ba'al Shem Tov as of 'no importance'. On one occasion R. Moses struggled for two weeks with a comment in Tosafot, but could not find an acceptable interpretation. Then one night he dreamed that the Ba'al Shem Tov told him the correct interpretation. The teacher did not attach any great significance to the dream, but when the Ba'al Shem Tov invited him to the third sabbath meal and repeated his interpretation of the comment, R. Moses acknowledged his greatness, 'became a follower of his, and became a great tsadik'.[91]

As another story would have it, the Ba'al Shem Tov even punished an arrogant scholar by stripping him of all his learning, so that from that time on he understood nothing whenever he opened a book. The former scholar came to the Ba'al Shem Tov and asked that his erudition be restored to him, upon which the Ba'al Shem Tov reproached him: 'And is it for contention and vexation that one engages in Torah study?'[92] Here again, as is common in stories of this type, the scholar went on to become a fervent hasid.

The tales report many derisive gibes uttered by the mitnagedim concerning the ignorance of hasidim and their deficiency in Torah study, often prompted by a seemingly simple person being accepted as a hasidic rabbi. A teacher in Lvov complained to R. Mordecai Ze'ev about R. Moses of Pshevorsk, saying: 'Here is a Jew wearing an outer garment [of a type worn by distinguished individuals]. See the honour afforded him by the hasidim, and he is an ignoramus!'[93] After the death of his rabbi, R. Moses of Kobrin, R. Abraham of Slonim was asked to serve as rabbi and leader of his hasidim, even though he had formerly been a mere schoolteacher. This aroused the ire of the head of the city's rabbinical court, who was a scholar and an outspoken mitnaged:

He summoned R. Abraham to him, and when the latter came, he greeted him with a sullen face, and said to him: 'What is this with you? Is Abraham also among the

[91] *Shivḥei habesht*, 97. Cf. Aaron of Apta, *Keter shem tov*, fos 21*a*–22*a* (about an unknown Torah scholar). See also Chikernik, *Ma'asiyot uma'amarim yekarim*, fo. 6*b*: R. Israel Harif of Satanov became a follower of the Ba'al Shem Tov following the latter's resolving a difficult passage in Tosafot. Cf. *Arba'ah arazim*, 103–4: the prophet Elijah revealed the resolution of a passage in Tosafot to R. Zusya, to which the scholars raised the objection: 'It is said that you [hasidim] do not know how to learn; how is it, then, that you offered such a fine and acceptable answer?' [92] *Shivḥei habesht*, 116. [93] *Ma'asiyot vesiḥot tsadikim*, 30–1.

prophets? Why, yesterday I knew you as one of the masses, and now you have been enthroned over your congregation of fools. You seclude yourself, and you shall be called a holy man. And from where did you take for yourself the title of holy?'[94]

The tales make it clear that the hasidim were quick to respond to such attacks. One describes a meeting between the 'Holy Jew', R. Jacob Isaac of Pshischa, and the sworn opponent of hasidism R. Azriel Horowitz of Lublin at a circumcision. R. Azriel asked:

Why is it that when you hasidim meet one another and want to act in an amiable manner, you imbibe strong drink together, and by this you seek to become friendly and act affectionately to one another? We mitnagedim do not [act] thus; rather, when we meet each other we become friendly with words of Torah, by striving together in new Torah interpretations, and in this manner we attain affection and amity. It therefore would be better if you, too, could become friendly to one another by the might of Torah study, and not by the drinking of wine.

According to the continuation of the account, the 'Holy Jew' admonished the mitnaged: 'Drinking is more effective to draw people closer to one another than are words of Torah.'[95]

The great numbers of hasidic tsadikim were another target for derision by mitnagedim, who regarded the wish to lead a congregation in the hasidic way as a sinful craving. The Torah scholar R. Anzil of Stry said to the tsadik of Rozdol: 'It seems to me that [the wish to attain] the institution of *rebishkeit* [the state of being a hasidic rabbi], to be a *guter yid* [i.e. a tsadik] is a desire like any other!' The tsadik responded to this charge: 'This is true, but this desire cannot be merited until all the desires are first broken!'[96]

R. Isaac Eisik Safrin tells of a similar incident that ended with the conversion of the mitnaged:

Once our divine master [= the Ba'al Shem Tov] travelled from Brod, and the rabbi, the *gaon* [genius], our master and teacher, R. Hayim Cohen, [was going] from Lvov to the holy community of Brod, and they met one another. The scholarly rabbi asked, in a joking manner: 'Israel, they say that you are gifted with divine inspiration?' Our master replied: 'Why is my master laughing? For it is taught in books[97] that one who recites "You endow [man with knowledge: part of the weekday Amidah prayers]" on the sabbath will worry the entire week; then why is my

[94] Lemberger, *Niflaot hatsadikim*, 27.

[95] *Shivḥei habesht*, 33.

[96] Teomim, *Ateret tiferet*, 'His Holiness, the Holy Rabbi, R. Tsevi Yude of Razla', §10; Zevin, *Hasidic Tales: On the Torah* (Heb.), 338–9. For the view held by the Ba'al Shem Tov that the proliferation of tsadikim delays the messianic redemption, see *Ateret tiferet*, 'His Holiness, Our Master and Teacher, R. Isaac Eisik of Komarno', §69, quoting I. Safrin, *Otsar haḥayim*, 'Ki tetse'.

[97] Judah Ashkenazi, *Be'er hetev* on *Shulḥan arukh*, 'Oraḥ ḥayim', 'Hilkhot shabat', 365 (in the name of R. Isaiah ben Abraham Halevi Horowitz (?1565–1630), author of *Shenei luḥot haberit*).

master laughing?' And no one in the world knew that this had happened to the rabbi that sabbath. He stood and kissed him on his head.[98]

Scepticism about the Ba'al Shem Tov's superhuman abilities, especially his capacity to see from afar, also appears—and is confounded—in the story of the merchant's son whose parents became worried when he was late in returning from Breslau. His mother, who believed in the Ba'al Shem Tov, urged her husband to turn to the tsadik to find out what had befallen their son. The merchant agreed, but reluctantly, addressing the Ba'al Shem Tov scornfully: 'My wife says that you know some things. Accordingly, I have come so that you can tell me, where is my son?' The Ba'al Shem Tov, responding in kind to the caustic tone of the mitnaged, replied: 'Things like this I look for while I am in the toilet [*beit hakise*]', and then informed him that his son was still in Breslau.[99]

One story counters the scorn levelled at the tsadikim with reference to heavenly disapproval of it. R. Isaac of Drohobitch senses that he has descended from his customary spiritual level; he understands that he has sinned, and that the heavenly court will restore him to his former level only when he has repented. When he examines his deeds, he recalls that he was present when people were making fun of the Ba'al Shem Tov, and did not protest. R. Isaac therefore journeys to Medzibezh and asks the Ba'al Shem Tov's forgiveness.[100]

In some stories the opponents of the tsadik set out to test his power or his prophetic ability, with the intention of proving that he is nothing out of the ordinary. An important leaseholder in Slutsk tells his wife that he wishes to test the Ba'al Shem Tov in this way. Later, when the woman is standing at the entrance of the inn where the Ba'al Shem Tov is staying, she hears him

[98] I. Safrin, *Megilat setarim*, 33. Cf. *Shivḥei habesht*, 159. The Ba'al Shem Tov discerned that, whenever a certain leading rabbi sought to have the proper intent during the reading of the Shema, Jesus stood before him. According to the Ba'al Shem Tov, 'his remedy is not to think of the great tsadikim'. Bodek, *Ma'aseh tsadikim*, 46, tells of a learned mitnaged who came to the Maggid of Mezirech, and believed that the Maggid undoubtedly knew that he was a Torah scholar and would therefore extend a cordial greeting to him. When the Maggid did not do so, the mitnaged thought to himself: 'The hasidim who say that he is wrapped in the spirit of divine inspiration, and that he is cognizant of a person's whole desire from his face, are lying.' See Zevin, *Hasidic Tales: Festivals* (Heb.), 23.

[99] *Shivḥei habesht*, 140. Horodezky mistakenly reads the Hebrew abbreviation *beit-heh-kaf* as *beit hakeneset* (synagogue) instead of *beit hakise* (toilet). A similar story appears in [Lemberger], *Magdil yeshuot malko*, 42–3: a mitnaged came to the Seer of Lublin to ask him about his missing son. Upon the Seer's return from the toilet, even before he washed his hands, he said: 'Your son is in such-and-such a place.' The mitnaged asked, derisively: 'Does the rabbi possess the spirit of divine inspiration in the toilet, as well?', to which the tsadik responded: 'And where shall I recall you [i.e. the mitnagedim], if not in the toilet?'

[100] [Isaac Dov Baer ben Tsevi Hirsch], *Kahal ḥasidim heḥadash*, §51.

saying, 'The fool wants to test me', thereby demonstrating his ability to hear from afar.[101] The Ba'al Shem Tov is put to the test in the two following stories as well—and of course, in both he bests his opponents.

Once the Ba'al Shem Tov came to Brod for the sabbath, and one worthy individual decided to try the powers of the tsadik. On this man's porch was a special corner where he kept non-kosher wine for non-Jews. He told his servant to fetch wine specifically from this corner for the Ba'al Shem Tov. The servant was ordered to give the bottle to the tsadik as a present, and to see whether he would drink from it or not. The Ba'al Shem Tov opened the bottle, gazed at it a number of times, and then drank. After the servant reported to his master that he himself had seen the Ba'al Shem Tov drink the wine, the latter told everyone that the Ba'al Shem Tov had drunk the wine prepared by non-Jews. When the Ba'al Shem Tov heard this slander, he summoned the worthy and his servant: it transpired that the servant had not taken the bottle from the corner for non-kosher wine, as he had been ordered, and the bottle that he had brought to the Ba'al Shem Tov had contained kosher wine.[102]

The second tale takes place in Tarnopol, whose residents, according to the account, were sworn opponents of the Ba'al Shem Tov. The latter examined the lung of a sheep that had been slaughtered, and determined that the animal was kosher. The slaughterer later found a perforation in the lung, but the Ba'al Shem Tov replied that the animal was kosher, and that he would eat from its meat on the sabbath. When the rabbi of Tarnopol and those opposed to the Ba'al Shem Tov heard of this, they decided to embarrass the hasidic leader by telling everyone that the tsadik had passed unfit meat as kosher. Their plot came to nothing, however, because a mad youth, whose malady the Ba'al Shem Tov was treating, mentioned that he had punctured the lung—after the animal had been slaughtered, when such a defect no longer affected its *kashrut*.[103]

Some people would come to a tsadik in order to get the measure of him. A scholar came to the Maggid of Mezirech in order to assess his worth in this way. The Maggid did not give him a warm welcome, but when the scholar

[101] *Shivḥei habesht*, 268. In Slutsk 'they suspected [the Ba'al Shem Tov] of falsehood', that is, they thought that he merely pretended to possess the ability to exorcise demons and the like. Generations later, R. Israel of Ruzhin related how the Ba'al Shem Tov had not been held in high regard in his time, and how he was considered to be a *kuntsen-makher* (trickster) (*Ma'asiyot vesiḥot tsadikim*, 20).

[102] [Isaac Dov Baer ben Tsevi Hirsch], *Kahal ḥasidim heḥadash*, §12. Brandwein, *Degel maḥaneh yehudah*, §114, tells of a similar matter. Someone wanted to test the tsadik R. Eliezer of Azipolia, and set before him non-kosher wine for kiddush. When the tsadik gazed at the wine, the flask shattered and the wine spilled out. The would-be challenger then recognized the holiness of the tsadik, and became his follower. See Nigal, *West and East Studies* (Heb.), 171–4.

[103] [Isaac Dov Baer ben Tsevi Hirsch], *Kahal ḥasidim heḥadash*, §12. For the opposition to the Ba'al Shem Tov by the people of Tarnopol, see Margolioth, *Kevutsat ya'akov*, fo. 53*a–b*.

came to take his leave, the Maggid, seeing into his thoughts, explained to him the various special abilities of the individual tsadikim.[104] Another story describes a prank dreamed up by one mitnaged, who presented himself before R. Hirsch of Rymanow dressed in woman's clothing and asked to be blessed with children. The 'woman' complained to the tsadik of her bitter fate: she had not borne any children to her husband, and now he wanted to divorce her. The tsadik, well aware of the deception, blessed the 'woman' and told her that she would speedily conceive—and for the next nine months the prankster suffered from stomach aches.[105]

Opposition to the tsadikim and criticism of them were voiced by common people as well as by the educated mitnagedim. A villager who sold milk and butter in Belz would say to the servant of the tsadik, 'Your master has much money that he amassed easily, without any labour.' This villager would sell his wares to the tsadik at exorbitant prices, more than he asked from other people, and one time even refused to let the servant leave his premises until he had purchased something.[106] The Ba'al Shem Tov's claiming of supernatural powers, such as seeing from afar, was sometimes challenged by the simple folk. A thief who was discovered by the Ba'al Shem Tov asked, 'Since his exalted excellency knows and sees how thieves steal, as well as their place and their sleeping, you obviously can also see better things. Why should you peer upon base matters? It is better to gaze upon good things!'[107] On another occasion, when the Ba'al Shem Tov was asked to intervene on behalf of a woman who suffered from bleeding during pregnancy, the tsadik was asked why he did not know that fact, when he knew from afar other details about this woman (such as her having been given an additional name during her illness).[108]

Other detractors focused on the habits of various tsadikim. It was the practice of R. Israel of Ruzhin, for example, to hum *bim-bam* while walking about in his study hall. A mitnaged who mocked the tsadik was asked why he laughed, and told the truth. The tsadik said to him: 'But it is written in the Torah [Deut. 6: 7]: "Recite them [*bam*]."' Some time later, this mitnaged also began to hum '*bim bam*'. When the tsadik of Ruzhin asked him why he did so, he replied: 'Why, the rabbi also says [i.e. hums] this, for it is written in the Torah!' The tsadik replied: 'But it is also written [Hos. 14: 10]: "The righteous [tsadikim] walk in them [*bam*], while sinners stumble on them [*bam*], for

[104] Bodek, *Ma'aseh tsadikim*, §33, pp. 46–7. The story does not relate whether or not the scholar accepted the tsadik's explanation. In other instances, hasidim decide to assess a certain tsadik, and discover that he knew their thoughts. See e.g. Brawer, *Pe'er yitshak*, ch. 14, §19.

[105] Moskowitz, *Otsar hasipurim*, xv. 11–12. For R. Israel Lebel and his admission of how he attempted to put tsadikim to the test, see A. Rubinstein, 'Possible New Fragment' (Heb.), 181 n. 29.

[106] See [Lemberger], *Niflaot hatsadikim*, 33.

[107] *Shivhei habesht*, 138. The Ba'al Shem Tov later delivered a discourse on this 'question'.

[108] See ibid. 123 for the question and the response by the Ba'al Shem Tov.

everything follows the intent, and from now on, whoever wishes to speak [= hum] may do so!'[109]

The hasidic storytelling genre is replete with accounts both of individuals who believed in the tsadikim and who were aided by them, and, on the other hand, of people whose opposition to and hatred of the tsadikim led them to shun them and deny their power to save them. *Shivḥei habesht* contains stories in which one spouse believed in the Ba'al Shem Tov while the other adamantly refused under any circumstances to turn to the tsadik for help.[110] The boundary between the two was not, however, absolute. Given the numbers of people in their communities who regarded the tsadikim with derision, many of those who did believe in their powers were apprehensive about travelling to seek assistance from the *rebbe*;[111] on the other hand, there were mitnagedim who in time of distress did not hesitate to turn to the tsadik and accept his help.

Among those opposed to the tsadikim were obviously the maskilim, the enlightened adherents of the Haskalah. In contrast with the numerous stories concerning mitnagedim, there are only a few involving maskilim, and they appear in a relatively late period. Fierce attacks on the Haskalah and maskilim, however, appear in the introductions to collections of hasidic tales by Rodkinsohn and Walden, who call the Haskalah 'a skin disease' (see Chapter 1 above).

Among all the collections of hasidic stories, Aaron Zeilingold's *Me'orot hagedolim* is especially noteworthy for its stories relating to maskilim. We hear, for example, of a young man from Polonnoye who studied in Volozhin, was attracted by the Haskalah, and went to Vienna to study medicine, his studies being financed by his father-in-law. He returned to Polonnoye as a poor physician. However, as a result of a journey to R. Levi Isaac of Berdichev, he repented (the story assumes that most physicians made light of the observance of Jewish law) and even became wealthy.[112] In another story we learn how yeshiva students were ensnared by the Haskalah. One young man was incited to read Haskalah books by a friend. The widow with whom the young man boarded wanted him to marry her daughter, but when he refused, she informed the *mashgiaḥ* (the yeshiva's spiritual supervisor) of his reading habits, leading to his expulsion from the yeshiva. There is a story of one of two sons-in-law of a wealthy hasid of Ruzhin joining the maskilim, who are portrayed in *Me'orot hagedolim* as 'void of all Torah and wisdom . . . [men] who wantonly rush to everything that is despicable'. Upon returning

109 Ehrmann, *Devarim arevim*, introd.
110 See e.g., among other examples, *Shivḥei habesht*, 111–12, 114, 121.
111 See e.g. Singer, *Seva ratson*, fo. 2*b*.
112 Zeilingold, *Me'orot hagedolim*, §19, pp. 72–7.

from a trip, the father-in-law, upon the advice of the tsadik, brings gifts for his two sons-in-law: for the scholar he brings a set of the Talmud, the *Mishneh torah* of Maimonides, and other such tomes, while the maskil son-in-law receives a deck of playing cards. When the latter expresses his anger at the cheap present, his father-in-law responds derisively, 'You wore your *talit* [prayer shawl] only once, and you will not wear it again!'[113] Yet another yeshiva student, the son-in-law of a rich man, became a maskil, started to associate with ill-behaved youths, went to theatres, and began to complain of shortcomings in his wife.[114]

R. Simhah Bunem of Warka advised against precision in the public reading of the Torah, in opposition to the explicit halakhah, 'because they [the maskilim] hold on to it [precision in reading] for dear life'.[115] The *Biur* commentary on the Torah, whose writing was inspired by Moses Mendelssohn, came to symbolize the maskilic books that were not to be opened on any account. It was decreed in heaven that R. Levi Isaac's prayers would not be accepted for thirty days because he had once read the *Biur*.[116] Another tsadik was not capable of praying properly during a visit to Hungary; when a copy of the *Biur* was discovered in his house, the reason for this inability was easily understood.[117]

113 Zeilingold, *Me'orot hagedolim*, §38, pp. 130–1.

114 Ibid., §35, p. 119. In contrast, see ibid., §50, p. 156, for a maskil whose intercession with Tsar Alexander II led to the release of prominent members of the community, during the time of R. Aaron of Karlin.

115 Rakats, *Siaḥ sarfei kodesh*, v. 105. Cf. Tsevi Elimelekh of Dynow, *Ma'ayan ganim*, ch. 14, §6, quoting R. Moses Sofer of Pshevorsk.

116 Moskowitz, *Otsar hasipurim*, viii, §18.

117 Ibid., §19.

THREE

MATCHMAKING AND MARRIAGES

THROUGHOUT THE AGES Jews have used the services of matchmakers; indeed, only rarely were marriages arranged without them.[1] The finding of a suitable spouse for a son or daughter was a difficult matter, and not only because of the great expense entailed in conducting the wedding ceremony and providing the dowry. Parents made high demands in respect of any prospective spouse for their offspring. Lineage was important, and after the writing of the marriage terms the two sides would sit and tell of their respective illustrious ancestries.[2] The character and personal attributes of the bride and groom were also scrutinized most carefully: in most cases the family of the groom sought a God-fearing bride and a proper dowry, and the family of the bride a Torah scholar. The payment of the dowry imposed a heavy financial burden on the family of the bride, and the prospect of a daughter's remaining a spinster for lack of an adequate marriage portion forced many fathers to take up the wanderer's staff in order to collect charity. Providing a dowry (known as *hakhnasat kalah*) was considered a religious obligation of the first order, to which even the miserly were willing to contribute, and over which many good souls expended much time and energy. Fulfilling the obligation to marry off orphans was considered especially virtuous, and thought to be efficacious in warding off plagues.[3]

Under such conditions the institution of matchmaking flourished. To prosperous families the matchmaker would offer 'princes, of magnificent

[1] For example, when two business partners arranged a match for their respective children.

[2] See e.g. Kamelhar, *Mevaser tov*, 24; Shenkel, *Yeshuot yisra'el*, i, §9; R. Margaliot, *Tiferet adam*, fo. 5*a*. Cf. Zeilingold, *Me'orot hagedolim*, 'His Holiness, the Holy Rabbi, R. Dov Baer of Medzibezh', 28.

[3] See A. Michelsohn, *Ohel elimelekh*, §153. Cf. Teomim, *Ateret tiferet*, 'His Holiness, the Holy Rabbi, R. Tsevi Hirsch of Zhidachov', §35; cf. also Gemen, *Sifran shel tsadikim*, ch. 3, §2: R. Mordecai of Nezkizh joined in marriage a pair of orphans that he had raised in his house. R. Nehemiah Yehiel, the son of Jacob Isaac of Pshischa ('the Holy Jew'), engaged in the same meritorious deed: see Rabinovitz, *Ma'aseh neḥemiyah*, 42–3, 70.

Torah scholarship, and of fine lineage',[4] 'lords, rabbis, princes', and 'renowned scholars', and received a hefty fee for each acceptable match actually concluded.[5] The heads of yeshivas also played their part in matchmaking, since the wealthy would look for scholarly sons-in-law who would be a credit to the family; sometimes they offered their help out of piety and goodwill alone, at other times in return for payment. But in many cases, and especially for the simple folk, it was the tsadik who acted as matchmaker, troubling himself on their behalf without expecting anything in return.

Some tsadikim even engaged in the labour of collecting money for the bridal fund. Thus it is related that R. Duber (Dov Baer) of Radoshitz once rejected the request of a poor man who had come to ask him to help collect money to pay for his daughter's wedding, on the grounds that he had already made such collections too many times. When, however, he heard from this poor person that the Seer of Lublin advised him to do so, he relented and collected the necessary sum.[6] R. Pinhas of Korets acted in similar fashion according to a story cited later in this chapter. Another tale describes how a villager came to R. Elimelekh of Lizhensk and told him that he had a 36-year-old daughter and no money to marry her off. With the consent of the father (the mother was no longer alive), the tsadik introduced the woman to a baker six years her junior, and the nuptial contract was drawn up. R. Elimelekh summoned two tailors to sew the wedding garments for the bride and the groom, and he and the members of his household prepared everything else needed for the wedding, which was held with great rejoicing among the large congregation who had gathered to celebrate it.[7] R. Joseph Saul Nathanson, the head of the Lvov rabbinical court, collected money for the wedding of an old friend of his who had been reduced to poverty. Together with the *parnas* (synagogue warden) the rabbi drew up a list of the wealthy, worked out how much was needed, and set about collecting the money.[8] Some tsadikim even waived the dowry altogether, and set the wedding date without it.[9]

At times the efforts made by tsadikim towards *hakhnasat kalah* included miraculous acts. Every Passover eve R. Abraham Joshua Heschel of Apta would tell the story of the miracle that had occurred to enable R. Isaiah

[4] See Sobelman, *Sipurei tsadikim heḥadash*, §9. [5] Bodek(?), *Sipurei kedoshim*, §13.

[6] See Slodovnik, *Ma'aseh hagedolim heḥadash*, §5. H. Kahana, *Even shetiyah*, fo. 34*b*, relates that R. Menahem Mendel of Kosov appeared in a dream (after his death) to one of his wealthy hasidim, and asked him to contribute to the bridal fund of a poor scholar's daughter.

[7] See A. Michelson, *Ohel elimelekh*, §127; and, for a slightly different version, ibid., §153. See also Breitstein, *Siḥot ḥayim*, 43: R. Meir of Premishlan advised a rabbi from Ostila how to obtain 300 roubles for his daughter's wedding expenses. R. Meir himself demanded a similar sum from a woman who regretting having engaged in sewing on the sabbath for her remedy, and then gave this money to a poor tailor for the wedding of his daughter. See Moskowitz, *Otsar hasipurim*, xv, §13.

[8] See *Sipurim ḥadashim ve'amitiyim*, §21. [9] See Ehrmann, *Pe'er vekhavod*, fo. 5*a*.

Slutsker to arrange a marriage for his daughter, despite his extreme poverty. R. Isaiah was a righteous person and a poor man, with three adult daughters living at home. Having no other choice, he began to collect alms for *hakhnasat kalah*. People in his immediate surroundings gave generously, since they knew him and his sterling character. When, however, he travelled further afield and came to a large city, his hopes were dashed, for no one here would give him anything. A matchmaker came to him, and when the latter heard the rabbi's name, he mistook it for that of his uncle, who was a well-known man of wealth and standing. The matchmaker proposed marrying his eldest daughter with the son of a *nouveau riche*, who had not inherited money from his father, but who had become wealthy by his own efforts. The poor rabbi agreed, and the rich man was glad to hear that 'the renowned worthy' R. Isaiah Slutsker had consented to the marriage of his daughter with his son. The father gave the matchmaker his fee, purchased a present for the groom as was the custom, and returned home without a penny in his pocket. There he resumed his studies and tried not to think of the dowry, to the tune of 2,000 zloty, that he had undertaken to pay. When the time of the wedding drew near, and the wealthy father of the groom had already arrived in the town, a miracle occurred that saved the marriage: the bride, who had been sent to the butcher's to slaughter a chicken, found a gold treasure. Now R. Isaiah could pay the dowry, and the wedding was conducted.[10]

Once the Ba'al Shem Tov ordered that a wedding ceremony be conducted for two servants who had joined forces to redeem a Jewish leaseholder and his family who faced death as a result of becoming mired in debt. The seven *ushpizin* (literally, 'guests': the seven biblical figures traditionally invited to enter the sukkah) came to the wedding, and each announced the gift that he was granting the couple, including a stable full of cattle and an inn. The gifts that were promised did indeed miraculously come into the hands of the newlyweds.[11] According to another (apparently earlier) version, the Ba'al Shem Tov told his followers to prepare everything necessary for a wedding, because they would be setting out to attend such a ceremony. When they came to a forest they encountered a Jewish servant and maidservant, who had been wandering in the forest for twelve months, but had still retained their virginity. The pupils of the Ba'al Shem Tov taught the groom the laws of marriage and wrote the *ketubah* (wedding contract), and the Ba'al Shem Tov himself conducted the ceremony. The couple were given gifts by the *ushpizin*, and the Ba'al Shem Tov assured them a village and fields, a promise that was speedily fulfilled.[12]

[10] See Bodek, *Pe'er mikedoshim*, §15; cf. Kaidaner, *Sipurim nora'im*, 27–9; Sadan, *Hebrew Literature* (Heb.), 109. Cf. Nigal, *S. Y. Agnon and his Hasidic Sources* (Heb.); Holtz, *The Tale of Reb Yudel Hasid* (Heb.).

[11] Sobelman, *Sipurei tsadikim heḥadash*, §30; cf. A. Michelsohn, *Mekor ḥayim*, §182; Zimetbaum, *Darkhei ḥayim*, 28–9.

[12] See A. Walden, *Kahal ḥasidim*, fo. 20*c–d*; Kohen, *Shemuot vesipurim*, 2–3.

A formerly wealthy person who had come down in the world came to Lemberg to collect money for his daughter's bridal fund. After dark, he met a man who went with him to a certain factory, where the accountant opened the cashbox and gave him a great deal of money; when the man was about to thank his benefactor, the latter vanished, and the factory along with him.[13]

A young man complained to the Maggid of Mezirech that no one considered taking him as a bridegroom because he was so poor. The tsadik advised him to consent to the first match that was proposed to him. The young man came to a certain inn, where a group of layabouts were drinking heavily. They asked him where he was from and where he was headed, and in his innocence the young man told them what the Maggid had counselled him about finding himself a bride. One of the revellers offered him his divorced sister, and the young man agreed. When his friends saw how innocent the young man was to consent to such a 'match', they took advantage of the innkeeper's absence to suggest that the young man in fact marry the innkeeper's daughter, who had stayed in the inn. The young man took up their proposal in all seriousness. He himself wrote the *ketubah*, and conducted the wedding as was proper. The next day, when the innkeeper returned to his inn, the young man greeted him with '*Shalom aleikhem* [peace be upon you], father-in-law!' The innkeeper was enraged, and beat the young man. When he heard, however, that his new son-in-law had acted in accordance with the advice of the Maggid of Mezirech, he agreed to travel with him to the tsadik, of whom he would demand a writ of divorce. However, when they stood before the Maggid, the tsadik instead commanded the innkeeper to give a thousand roubles to his son-in-law, adding: 'This young man is from a fine family, and he is perfect in all respects, except that he has no money. Now he has one thousand roubles, and it is my opinion that you will not find a better groom than him with such a sum. I tell the two of you that he is her match; therefore, go back home in joy.'[14] And so they did.

In another instance it was innocence rather than poverty that prevented a young man from marrying. R. Hirsch of Rymanow, the attendant of the tsadik R. Menahem Mendel of Rymanow, was an outstanding individual, but considered so naïve that no one wanted to make a match with him. Once the tsadik sent him away, and in doing so helped him find a wife. The attendant came to an inn where he fell in with what seemed to be some jaded Jewish merchants, who in reality were divine angels. The innkeeper was away, and in his absence the merchants asked his wife and her daughter to alleviate

[13] Ehrmann, *Pe'er vekhavod*, fos 22*b*–23*a*.

[14] *Ma'asiyot vesiḥot tsadikim*, 28–9; Zevin, *Hasidic Tales: On the Torah* (Heb.), 57–9. In E. Z. Stern, *Siḥot yekarim*, the Maggid of Mezirech advises a woman who has let her youth pass while waiting to find a Torah scholar as a husband to marry the first person who is offered to her. A poor tailor is matched with her, and their son is R. Uri of Strelisk.

their boredom with a 'play', choosing the presentation of a wedding ceremony for their entertainment. The two women readily agreed to participate in the 'fiction'. One of the merchants filled the role of the scribe who wrote the *ketubah*, another was the rabbi who conducted the ceremony in accordance with all the requirements of Jewish law, and the tsadik's servant took the part of the groom. When the innkeeper returned the following day and saw the remains of the festive wedding banquet he was extremely angry; but the marriage was valid, and the clock could not be turned back.[15]

A version of this story that appears in an earlier source has a slightly different ending. Here too, when the innkeeper returned home and heard of the marriage of his daughter to the poor youth he became enraged. He demanded that his new son-in-law tell him his life history, and when he learned that he was under the tutelage of the tsadik from Rymanow he travelled to R. Menahem Mendel with the young man. As he entered the house of the tsadik, the latter greeted him with his congratulations, and went on, 'I saw that your daughter was the match for this young man, and I did not know how this would turn out, because you are a wealthy man, and you would not straight away desire such a poor one as this; so I sent him away. And now the matter has been resolved in the best possible manner, and your daughter has a husband.'[16]

Another story tells that R. Leib Sarahs looked after one of those close to him, a wealthy merchant who had become a widower, and who had also lost all his property, in a most original manner. When he was asked to heal a young and affluent widow, he made his assistance conditional upon the young woman's marrying whomever he might stipulate, 'even if poor or lame, and even if he were to suffer from boils'.[17] At the appropriate time, the tsadik sent the merchant, in rags, to the woman's residence in Moscow. However, when the woman's uncle and other associates of the family heard that he wished to marry the rich widow, his request was met with general derision. No one could imagine that this wealthy woman, who had rejected some excellent matches, would be willing to give her hand to this pauper. But her uncle, who was angry at his young niece for having turned down previous offers of marriage, welcomed the chance, as he saw it, to humiliate her, and so agreed to set the man's proposal before her. The wealthy woman looked in her mirror, and when the countenance of R. Leib Sarahs appeared before her she knew that this match came from him; and so she married the suitor.[18]

[15] See Moskowitz, *Otsar hasipurim*, iv, §1.

[16] Shenkel, *Sipurei anshei shem*, §16, pp. 22–3. An identical story is related about a learned orphan boy who was expelled from the yeshiva by the tsadik R. Abraham of Stretin (Brandwein, *Degel maḥaneh yehudah*, §87).

[17] Bodek(?), *Sipurei kedoshim*, §13. For the story in Yiddish, see *Ma'aseh nora*, 3–13.

[18] Bodek(?), *Sipurei kedoshim*, §13.

In another version, R. Leib Sarahs rebuffed a certain young man in the city of Lutsk who wished to become one of his followers, saying that he would permit him to become one of his hasidim only if he were to lend him a large sum of money for a year. The young man was forced to sell all his wares cheaply in order to obtain the necessary amount, and having given the loan to the tsadik was left penniless; then, as if this were not enough, his wife died during the year that followed. At the end of the year R. Leib returned half of the sum to the young man and ordered him to use it to purchase fine clothing, and then to go to the city of Vilkovisk, where he was to contact the matchmaker R. David, who would match him with the daughter of a well-known and highly respected local figure. When he applied to the matchmaker, R. David laughed and replied, 'Are you making fun of me, or do I lack madmen, that you have come to make me a laughing-stock?' The matchmaker told him of the lineage and great wealth of the girl he mentioned, and offered instead to search for a woman on his own level. However, the sum of money that the young man gave him persuaded him to propose the match despite all his reservations. To R. David's surprise, the rich young woman agreed to marry this suitor, albeit first taking care to see that he had the appearance, at least, of a prosperous businessman. Only two years later, when R. Leib Sarahs came to their home (to repay the remainder of the loan), did the wife reveal to her husband that she knew the tsadik. She reproached her husband:

'Fool, did you think that when you sent the matchmaker to me I was insane and heeded him? I will tell you how it was: that old man would come to me evening and morning and say to me: "If a person from Lutsk, named so-and-so, were to come, become his wife." But I did not heed him. Then, my father and my mother came to me in a dream, and told me, "This old man is a great tsadik, and he knows that this is your true match." Nor did I pay attention to this, until I fell deathly ill, when the old man came and told me: "Choose one or the other—either you shall die from this illness in the flower of your youth, or you shall marry the man of whom I speak to you," and then I was forced, against my will, to consent to what he demanded. I promised him that when you would come here, I would marry you.'[19]

R. Meir of Premishlan saw with his supernatural faculties that a Jew from the Land of Israel had arrived in his city, after the latter's wife had compelled him to go abroad and collect funds so that they could find matches for their three daughters. The tsadik gave him a box full of money, for he had been commanded by heaven, from the time of the girls' birth, to save one coin

[19] Sobelman, *Sipurei tsadikim heḥadash*, §9, pp. 13–15. For instructions in a dream (variously from a deceased father and an anonymous instructor), see also Bodek(?), *Sipurei kedoshim*, §1; Shenkel, *Yeshuot yisra'el*, ii, §18.

after another for their weddings. When the money was counted, the box was found to contain 300 gold zloty.[20]

Sometimes miracles were performed for a third person, in return for which he would act charitably towards a needy person who had turned to the tsadik for assistance, either by giving money or by performing a certain task. R. Joshua, the tsadik from Belz, told the following story:

The Ba'al Shem Tov had a disciple who was a very exalted, righteous, and pious person. This man had two daughters who were of marriageable age, but he was destitute, and had no money for dowries and wedding costs. His wife advised him: 'You are always travelling to the Ba'al Shem Tov, why don't you tell him something about our daughters?' He promised her that he would do so, but when he got there, he could not muster the courage to speak of his problem to the tsadik. After a while, when his wife had heard nothing from her husband, she went to join him. When this hasid saw that his wife was there, he was forced to go in to the Ba'al Shem Tov and tell him all that was on his heart.

The Ba'al Shem Tov responded that the hasid had not acted wisely by concealing his sorry plight from him; he instructed him how to stop the bleeding of a newly circumcised infant, and sent him on his way. Shortly thereafter, while travelling, this hasid stayed with a rich Jew, five of whose sons had died as a result of bleeding following circumcision. Here he could put to use the advice he had been given by the Ba'al Shem Tov: he circumcised the man's remaining sons, and the happy father gave him the dowry for his daughters, and sufficient money to defray the expense of their weddings.[21]

Once a distant woman relative came to the Maggid of Koznitz and asked for his assistance in marrying off her daughter.

He said to her: 'What do you want from me? I give you an ague!' The woman left his room, disappointed, because she had confidently expected him to give her all that she needed, since the tsadik was known to be very generous even to those distant from [unrelated to] him, and certainly to relatives. The holy rabbi then told his wife: 'You should know that this woman is my relative; therefore, draw her closer in all manner of ways.' She did as he requested, and made a banquet, as for important people, with this woman sitting within, with an angry expression on her face. After the banquet, the holy rabbi summoned her to his room and commanded her: 'Think of your daughter's needs!' She thought of the dowry and the wardrobe, and all the other items she needed, which would cost 50 zloty in all. He then said to her: 'Very well, very well, tomorrow I will give you a fever!' The woman went out, disappointed, for the second time.

It was [this tsadik's] way also to perform miracles for non-Jews. The next morning a rich non-Jewish woman came to the holy man from far away. She had been

[20] Sobelman, *Sipurei tsadikim heḥadash*, §90.

[21] See A. Michelson, *Ohel yehoshua*, §6. For the wife's role in persuading her husband to travel to the tsadik, see Slodovnik, *Ma'aseh hagedolim heḥadash*, §5.

suffering from ague for an entire year, and even the great physicians had all failed to heal her. She said to him, 'Our holy master, I heard of your good reputation, that you also perform kindnesses for non-Jews. I therefore request of your honoured holiness that you cure me of my bitter illness, and whatever you decree, I will give.' He replied to her: 'The illness of fever, for such a long time, is worth fifty zloty to cure.' She wasted no time, counted out for him 50 zloty, and left him—completely healthy. Afterwards, he summoned his relative and gave her the 50 zloty, telling her: 'Here you have an ague: go and organize your daughter's wedding, may it be with good luck.' He gave her money for travelling expenses and a blessing, and she gladly went on her way.[22]

In another instance R. Eisik, the son of R. Uri of Strelisk, came to R. Shalom of Belz to ask for the money he needed to arrange his daughter's wedding. The tsadik sent him to a rich man in Berdichev whose daughter suffered from mental illness, assuring this man that his daughter would recover if he gave the hasid sufficient money to cover all his expenses; the wealthy man did so, and his daughter was duly cured of her affliction.[23] Similarly, R. Mikhel of Jassy was healed of an illness for having given money to pay for all the expenses of the wedding of R. Uri's granddaughter.[24]

R. Yerahmiel Israel of Aleksandrow had among his followers a wealthy man, a miser who in his entire life had never given any money to charity. He lived in a small town near Aleksandrow—as did a poor schoolteacher who could not afford to arrange marriages for his four daughters. These two hasidim happened to meet, and the schoolteacher found the courage to ask the rich man for a loan of 100 roubles to enable him to make a match for at least one of his daughters. The miser, outraged at the poor man's insolence, ignored his request. The schoolteacher saw no other way out of his difficulties than to turn to the tsadik and tell him of his troubles. R. Yerahmiel Israel heard his tale of woe and sighed deeply. Suddenly the rich miser came into the tsadik's court with a note in his hand and an accompanying monetary donation. The tsadik asked, 'What happened to bring you to me today?' The

[22] Kaidaner, *Sipurim nora'im*, §20, pp. 77–9. Cf. Shenkel, *Yeshuot yisra'el*, ii, §22; Kleinmann, *Mazkeret shem gedolim*, 120; and (a somewhat different version) Yehiel Moses of Yadimov, *Likutim ḥadashim*, fo. 52*a*. In E. M. Stern, *Siḥot yekarim*, §18, pp. 12–13, the Maggid of Koznitz gives a poor father a letter to a wealthy man, in which he asks the latter to give the bearer of the letter 300 roubles for the wedding of the poor man's daughter. The rich man refuses, and comes down in the world as punishment. The request of the tsadik to another recipient is honoured, and the charitable person is rewarded with great riches. For a corresponding story concerning R. Dov Baer, the Maggid of Mezirech, see Gemen, *Sifran shel tsadikim*, ch. 4, §4. See also the letter of recommendation given by R. Elimelekh of Lizhensk to his relative, R. Tsevi Hirsch Bachrach of Tiktin, printed at the end of *Ma'amar kedishin*; also appearing in Berger, *Eser tsaḥtsaḥot*, end of the section on R. Elimelekh; A. Michelson, *Ohel elimelekh*, §353.

[23] See [Lemberger], *Niflaot hatsadikim*, 13; Ehrmann, *Pe'er vekhavod*, fo. 23*a–b*. Cf. Teomim, *Ateret tiferet*, 'His Holiness, the Holy Rabbi, R. Hayim Halberstam of Sanz', §34.

[24] See Moskowitz, *Otsar hasipurim*, ix, §1.

wealthy man explained that his wife had fallen ill and all the physicians despaired of curing her, and he asked the tsadik to pray on her behalf. The tsadik said:

'You undoubtedly prayed today, and paid attention to the words of the Talmud [BT *Shabat* 127*a*, repeated in the morning prayers]: "These are the observances whose fruits a person enjoys in this world, while the principal remains for him in the world to come," and what is stated there: "Visiting the sick, providing for a bride, and accompanying the dead." This poses a difficulty: why did the *tana* [mishnaic sage] insert "providing for a bride" between "visiting the sick" and "accompanying the dead"? To tell you that if, heaven forbid, there is a sick person in your house, and you wish to be saved from accompanying the dead—fulfil the commandment of providing for a bride. If you want your wife to recover, give the schoolteacher from your city four hundred roubles in order that he can get his daughters married.'

The tsadik told his attendant to summon the teacher, and the wealthy man gave him the sum he needed to arrange his daughters' weddings.[25]

The Ba'al Shem Tov had promised R. David Forkes 800 zloty for his daughter's wedding, but as the time for the wedding approached he had not yet received any of the money. Setting out to see the tsadik, R. David met a worthy who was on his way to the same destination. The Ba'al Shem Tov received both men very cordially and told them the following story. A rich merchant was on his way back from the Leipzig fair when his servants, who had gone with him, rose up against him, intending to murder him. The merchant vowed then that if the Lord would save him from his assailants he would give half of his money to charity. He asked his servants to permit him to recite the *vidui* (confession recited before death) and they moved away from him, so that they would not be moved to mercy by his prayers. A *poritz* who was passing by in his carriage heard the sound of the merchant's weeping, stopped, and rescued him; the servants fled. Then, however, the merchant thought that it would suffice to give only one-quarter of his property to the poor; so he did not fulfil his vow in its entirety. And then his wife fell sick, and the physicians could do nothing for her . . .

Upon completing his story, the Ba'al Shem Tov turned to the wealthy man and asked: 'Did I speak truly?' The man—who was none other than the rich merchant in the Ba'al Shem Tov's story—fell to the ground in shame; then he made his calculations and gave the Ba'al Shem Tov 800 zloty, which the Ba'al Shem Tov gave to R. David for the wedding of his daughter.[26]

An almost identical story is related of R. Ze'ev (Wolf) Kiytses, whose daughter had been of marriageable age for some time, but who did not have

[25] Slodovnik, *Ma'aseh hagedolim heḥadash*, §3.
[26] See Ehrmann, *Devarim arevim*, 'Stories of the Ba'al Shem Tov', §8.

the money he needed for her wedding and dowry. The Ba'al Shem Tov told him to lose no time in arranging a match for his daughter, and R. Wolf accordingly sent a special emissary to the city of Jassy to write the *tena'im* (marriage conditions). When the time of the wedding drew near, and with it the time for paying the dowry, R. Wolf became anxious, but the Ba'al Shem Tov encouraged him and told him that everything would be resolved in the best possible manner. When a letter came from the bride's future father-in-law, announcing that he and his son the groom were about to arrive, R. Wolf set off, sad-faced, to show the note to the Ba'al Shem Tov. On the way he met another person who was also going to see the tsadik. When they arrived, the tsadik greeted the guest and began to tell a story. A wealthy Jewish merchant had been transporting lumber on a raft to Prussia. His enterprise had been profitable, and he was returning home in a magnificent carriage, bringing all his money with him. The non-Jewish carriage driver fell upon the merchant and demanded his money, and also planned to kill him, lest the robbery become known. The merchant asked permission to recite the *vidui* before his death; the driver agreed to allow this, but only after he had chained the merchant to a tree. The Jew pleaded with his maker, and vowed to give a tithe of his wealth to charity if he were saved. The forest watchman heard his cries, freed him from his bonds, and handed over the driver to the police. The rich man forgot to fulfil his vow, and his only son contracted a severe illness that looked like being fatal. All the physicians despaired of healing him. The merchant heard that the Ba'al Shem Tov lived in Medzibezh and went to him to beg that his son's life be spared . . .

When the guest who accompanied R. Wolf heard the words of the Ba'al Shem Tov, he recalled everything that had befallen him (for he was the merchant in the Ba'al Shem Tov's story), and immediately gave 4,000 zloty to R. Wolf, with which he paid for his daughter's marriage.[27]

There are echoes of this motif—provision for a poor family's bridal fund being made through another person's atonement for a former shortcoming—in other stories: for example, that in which R. Meir of Premishlan told a woman who had contracted leprosy for having violated the sabbath that if she gave 300 silver coins to a tailor who needed to marry off his daughter, she would be cured of her disease.[28]

Sometimes the focus is not on atonement for past misdeeds but on future reward for present generosity. In another story, a merchant saw a weeping woman in the marketplace; when he asked her why she was in such distress, she said that if she did not pay 400 silver coins before her daughter's wedding, the girl's fiancé was likely to leave her. The merchant gave her all his

[27] See Zeilingold, *Me'orot hagedolim*, §10, pp. 22–3.
[28] Cf. Kaidaner, *Sipurim nora'im*, §20, pp. 77–9.

money so that she could make the payment—and in reward for this good deed he later became extremely wealthy.[29]

In some cases the reward that a person receives for having acted charitably towards a needy bride is given him in the world to come. Thus it is related that a certain wicked rich man, who gave a pauper the money needed for his daughter's wedding, was later defended by this poor person before the heavenly tribunal.[30] A similar story was told about a man who had been blessed with three daughters who were now of marriageable age, but had no money with which to provide for their marriages. The anxious father consulted R. Menahem Mendel of Rymanow, who advised him to make a match for the eldest daughter and promise a dowry. He did so, but when the time came to pay the sum was unable to fulfil his obligation, and the marriage was cancelled. The tsadik counselled the same course of action with the second daughter; and the same thing happened. When R. Menahem Mendel advised him to act in the same manner with the third daughter as well, the poor man's wife became so incensed that he left his home and was afraid to return. As he stood in desperate distress on the road, he met a follower of the tsadik of Rymanow, a sinful person. The latter asked why this unfortunate man was weeping so bitterly; having heard the entire story (which he later confirmed when he arrived at R. Menahem Mendel's court), he pulled out of his pocket the money needed to get all three girls married. Shortly after this both the pauper and his benefactor died. The tsadik of Rymanow interceded on behalf of his sinful follower before the heavenly court; and, by virtue of having fulfilled the obligation of *hakhnasat kalah* (as well as having continued to support the tsadik financially), he was permitted to enter paradise.[31]

R. Pinhas of Korets once undertook the obligation of *hakhnasat kalah* while serving as head of the Ostrog rabbinical court. He had completed all the preparations for a wedding and was about to conduct the ceremony when the groom got up and declared that he would not stand under the wedding canopy until he had received the *talit* he had been promised by his future in-laws. It was late in the evening, but R. Pinhas set out to obtain the money needed to buy it. He found a tailor (whose depravity was common knowledge) who agreed to underwrite the purchase on condition that the tsadik R. Pinhas assured him that he had a portion in the world to come. The tsadik attended the tailor's funeral, and ensured that, by virtue of this good deed, he was saved from the heavenly accusers and granted eternal life in the

29 See Ehrmann, *Pe'er vekhavod*, fo. 20*b*.

30 Reznik, *Mora'im gedolim*, §10, pp. 20–3. For a non-Jew from the city of Pilov who gave a Jew 100 zloty for the expenses entailed in marrying off his daughters, see Rosenthal, *Hitgalut hatsadikim*, 9.

31 See Ehrmann, *Devarim arevim*, 'Stories of the Holy Rabbi of Rymanow', §3.

world to come.[32] A similar story was related about R. Hayim of Sanz, who went with his friend R. Moses Rapoport to collect money for *hakhnasat kalah*. A wealthy man, who was not particular in his observance of the commandments, gave them the sum they lacked for the purchase of the customary *talit* and *shtreimel* for the bridegroom. After the death of their benefactor, R. Hayim followed his bier, in order to drive away *malakhei haḥabalah*, the destructive angels who seek to kidnap a dead person.[33]

All these stories demonstrate the degree of importance that was attached to the religious obligation of *hakhnasat kalah*. The dowry was perceived as an important element of any match, and from it developed the practice of the bride's father granting a specified value or term of *mezonot* (living expenses) to his son-in-law as part of the marriage agreement. Usually, a number of years was stipulated for which the groom, with his new family, would dine at his father-in-law's table (*kest*: literally, 'board'). R. Solomon of Kishinev, for example, stated that he had been promised two years of *mezonot* after his wedding.[34] Men of standing were especially willing to support young Torah scholars in this way, in order to persuade them to marry their daughters. One story describes how a well-to-do man asked the principal of the yeshiva to propose a groom for his daughter, offering in addition 'a proper present [for] the yeshiva head'.[35] It was common for a man in this position to take his intended son-in-law under his wing, with the blessing of the head of the yeshiva. Such was the experience of the young Solomon Ephraim of Luntshits when he was in Pressburg: a prominent local man who 'wished to take him as a husband for his daughter' took him into his house and supplied his every want.[36]

According to one hasidic tale, R. Hayim the son of R. Bezalel, the brother of the Maharal of Prague (R. Judah Loew ben Bezalel, *c.*1525–1609), requested that a matchmaker find him a match that would enable him to dwell in his father-in-law's house and devote himself totally to Torah study. This, he said, was his top priority; he did not mind if the family was 'not a family of upper [standing]'; that is, he was prepared to marry into the lower classes if the family was otherwise suitable.[37] Another tale describes how the nephew of R. Isaac Luria lived outwardly as a simple mill-worker, despite his great knowledge of both the revealed and the esoteric Torah. This pretence greatly distressed the bride and her parents, and their joy knew no bounds

[32] See Lieberson, *Tseror haḥayim*, §19, pp. 11–12; Slodovnik, *Ma'aseh hagedolim heḥadash*, §4. A wagon driver purchased a *talit* for the groom, so that the latter would not tear up the *tena'im* and cancel the wedding. The Seer of Lublin wrote on the note: 'May this person's name shine exceedingly brightly' (Bodek, *Seder hadorot heḥadash*, fo. 29*b*).

[33] See [Lemberger], *Niflaot hatsadikim*, 26–7.

[34] See Singer, *Seva ratson*, fo. 3*a*.

[35] See Sobelman, *Sipurei tsadikim heḥadash*, §28.

[36] Ibid., §5.

[37] See Rodkinsohn, *Adat tsadikim*, §22; Shenkel, *Niflaot gedolim*, §2.

when it eventually became widely known that the groom was both a scholar and of distinguished lineage.[38] Tsadikim, for their part, made special efforts on behalf of indigent yeshiva students: R. Israel of Ruzhin once told the parents of a marriageable girl to match her only with a scholar, even if he was poor.[39] In another instance he advised an only son, who was hunchbacked and gaunt, and who had difficulty in finding a match, to marry an orphan girl.[40]

Sometimes it is the mother, not the father, who turns to the yeshiva head in the search for a husband for a daughter;[41] and in some cases, where a second marriage was at issue, the prospective bride herself took the initiative. For example, a rich widow heard of a worthy young man in Krakow, a Torah scholar, who had become a widower. She summoned the matchmaker and gave him 100 roubles to present her to this newly eligible man, asking that he be informed that she possessed enormous riches and was an honourable and modest woman. The matchmaker greeted her request with derision, but nevertheless went to the widower as instructed, since he did not want to forgo the fee that the woman had offered. The widower was favourably impressed by the woman and married her in a proper Jewish wedding.[42]

Notwithstanding the salience of this theme, hasidic stories also voice criticism of the excessive selectiveness of families in choosing a bridegroom, not only in respect of money or lineage, but also regarding scholarly achievements. This critical note is latent in the story of the nephew of R. Isaac Luria mentioned above, and appears more prominently in the following story. The son of a shoemaker worked as a servant in an inn, where he met a maid, whom he married. They became wealthy and purchased a small inn of their own; but when their daughter reached marriageable age, they had difficulty in finding a husband for her. The mother rejected all the offers by the matchmakers, seeking a truly outstanding scholar for her daughter; but the best scholars were not interested in the girl, because of her mother's low standing. The tsadik of Ruzhin, who happened to be in Berdichev (where the parents lived), suggested to the father a match with a simple craftsman. The wife strenuously opposed such a match, and eventually married her daughter to a poor scholar. Before long, this scholar began to find fault with his wife, and in the end he stole her jewellery and fled, leaving her an *agunah*. When

38 See Bodek(?), *Sipurei kedoshim*, §1. Cf. Breitstein, *Siḥot ḥayim*, 28: R. Israel of Ruzhin spoke of the groom's lineage before the wedding ceremony. See also Zevin, *Hasidic Tales: Festivals* (Heb.), 141.

39 See Zeilingold, *Me'orot hagedolim*, §38, p. 128.

40 Ibid., §41, p. 137: this match did not result in a marriage.

41 Sobelman, *Sipurei tsadikim heḥadash*, §9.

42 See Slodovnik, *Ma'aseh hagedolim heḥadash*, §8.

R. Israel of Ruzhin came to Berdichev a second time, and the father lamented their fate to him, the tsadik replied, 'You should have heeded my advice! Now go to Odessa, where you will find her husband; he will give your daughter a bill of divorce.' After being freed from her first marriage, the divorcee married a widowed shoemaker, the father of adult children, and bore him further offspring.[43]

Another story concerning R. Israel of Ruzhin echoes that recounted above in which a wedding is cancelled when the bridegroom declares himself unwilling to proceed simply because the promised *talit* has not been provided, showing himself in a poor light and forcing R. Pinhas of Korets to seek money urgently to purchase it. A match was arranged between the children of R. Israel and R. Tsevi Hirsch of Rymanow. R. Israel told R. Tsevi Hirsch that he would not permit the writing of the marriage terms before the latter had paid half the dowry, namely 600 gold zloty. The groom died a few weeks later, and new marriage terms were written between the bride and the dead groom's brother.[44]

The cancellation of a match was considered to be a drastic step, especially if it was taken by the groom, since it brought great humiliation for the bride. In the hasidic story such an action would result in grave consequences for the groom, and the tsadik would accordingly seek to avoid its happening. In one instance, the family of the groom sought to cancel the marriage terms when they learned that the bride was ugly. R. Levi Isaac of Berdichev intervened and persuaded them to avoid withdrawing from the match.[45]

In another case the bride died after a match was cancelled: the groom married another woman, but as punishment did not have any children. Only after appeasing his first bride (who appeared for this purpose in her former earthly guise) was he pardoned.[46]

[43] See Zeilingold, *Me'orot hagedolim*, §36, pp. 121–4.

[44] See Kamelhar, *Mevaser tov*, 23–4; Shenkel, *Yeshuot yisra'el*, i, §9. Cf. Rodkinsohn, *Adat tsadikim*, §15: 'If I do not pay the dowry to him [the father of the groom] within three days, he will sever the bonds of the match, and make another one.' Chikernik, *Ma'asiyot uma'amarim yekarim*, 28–30, relates that R. Solomon of Karlin married his son to the daughter of R. Barukh of Medzibezh. When he did not send the promised dowry, R. Barukh wanted to cancel the *tena'im*. R. Solomon sent people to collect money for the dowry, but three times he gave to charity the amount that had been gathered. In the end, R. Barukh decided to forgo the dowry, and the wedding was conducted without this sum of money.

[45] See Zeilingold, *Me'orot hagedolim*, §14, pp. 56–8.

[46] See Rodkinsohn, *Adat tsadikim*, §15. Cf. ibid., §4: an agreement sealed with a handshake that was broken, and that almost resulted in the death of the bride. In Zeilingold, *Me'orot hagedolim*, §17, p. 38, a sum of money is given to a young man to appease him for *tena'im* that were broken; see also §42, p. 84: a rich person who broke his promise to marry his son to his friend's daughter became impoverished and also almost drowned. He regretted his actions and vowed to keep his promise, but broke it a second time; in the end, his store burned down and he was left penniless.

In the following story, on the other hand, the cancellation of a marriage both entailed a miracle and brought happiness. A child who had been lost to his parents during their escape from imprisonment was given a parchment by a rabbi, who ordered him to open the scroll and read it only on the eve of his wedding. When the young man unrolled the parchment, he saw the sentence: 'How can a brother marry his sister?' The young man began to investigate the origins of the bride's family, and he discovered that his father-in-law was in actuality his biological father, and his bride was his sister. The cancellation of this match did not cause any unhappiness: on the contrary, the joy of all the family members at their reunion knew no bounds.[47]

[47] See Kaidaner, *Sipurim nora'im*, §10. Cf. Teomim, *Ateret tiferet*, 'His Holiness, the Holy Rabbi, R. Hayim Halberstam of Sanz', §33; Kleinmann, *Zikhron larishonim*, 81 n. 56; Kohen, *Shemuot vesipurim*, 212–14. Cf. also J. Y. Rosenberg, *Tiferet maharal*, §16, pp. 21–4. For the cancellation of a match because of a despicable act committed by the mother of the bride, see Brandwein, *Degel maḥaneh yehudah*, §88; Slodovnik, *Ma'aseh hagedolim heḥadash*, §45.

FOUR

THE BLESSING OF CHILDREN: BIRTH AND OFFSPRING

THE HOPE OF HAVING children was one of the most common reasons why people came to the court of the tsadik. The childless would ask the tsadik for his blessing; once given, according to the hasidic story, this generally resulted in the birth of a son.

The Ba'al Shem Tov blessed childless couples in order that they might have issue, and, according to the testimony of the stories, his blessings were effective.[1] Some of these couples brought great tsadikim into the world, at times even in their old age: indeed, the most prominent example in the hasidic tale of the birth of a great spiritual leader to an elderly couple is that of the Ba'al Shem Tov himself, which in turn is reminiscent of the births of Isaac and Jacob.[2] R. Israel ben Shabetai, the Maggid of Koznitz, was born to his aged parents upon the blessing of the Ba'al Shem Tov, because his mother preferred a male child to material wealth.[3] The tsadik issuing the blessing often also chose the name of the baby that would be born,[4] quite frequently on the request of the supplicant hasidim themselves.[5]

[1] Sobelman, *Sipurei tsadikim heḥadash*, §12. Cf. *Shivḥei habesht*, 115, 135; Gemen, *Sifran shel tsadikim*, ch. 1, §7. *Continued in Appendix.*

[2] *Shivḥei habesht*, 41. For the births of Isaac and Jacob, see Gen. 21 and 25: 19–24.

[3] Rodkinsohn, *Adat tsadikim*, §1. Cf. Moskowitz, *Otsar hasipurim*, vi, §5. Gemen, *Sifran shel tsadikim*, ch. 39, §1, states that R. Yehiel Jacob of Koznitz once saw a childless elderly couple who were cleaning beans. The tsadik asked them: 'Perhaps there will be a *shalom zakhar* [celebrating the first sabbath of a baby boy's life]?' As the tsadik spoke, so it was, and a son was born to the elderly couple.

[4] The Ba'al Shem Tov said: 'And name him Israel, like my name' (Rodkinsohn, *Adat tsadikim*, §1). R. Nahman of Bratslav selected the name (Nahman) for a child that would be born (Hazan, *Sipurim nifla'im*, 13). Cf. Vital, *Sefer haḥezyonot*, fo. 2*a*: R. Hayim Ashkenazi blessed Vital's father, saying, 'And there [in the Land of Israel] a son shall be born to you, and you shall name him Hayim, like my name.'

[5] 'Behold, there is a well-known custom among those who believe in the tsadikim, that when a person's wife is pregnant, he enquires of his rabbi what name to give the child that his wife shall bear' (Chikernik, *Sipurim nifla'im uma'amarim kedoshim*, fo. 12*b*). R. Isaac Meir of Ger picked the name for a girl who was about to be born (Yellin, *Derekh tsadikim*, 'Kunteres divrei harim', 61).

In some instances tsadikim promised a son to their hosts, as an expression of gratitude for the hospitality that was extended to them.[6] Thus, for example, it is related that when the Ba'al Shem Tov was on his way to the Land of Israel, he stayed with a rich man in Constantinople who had no children. After their return from the synagogue on the sabbath eve, when the Ba'al Shem Tov had recited the kiddush over wine, he said, 'Now, I know your desire, for you are childless. Accordingly, for your having sustained me, I swear to you that this your wife [pointing to her with his finger] shall give birth to a son.'[7] The continuation of the story is most enlightening: the Ba'al Shem Tov heard a herald proclaim that he, the Ba'al Shem Tov, had lost his portion in the world to come, because he had troubled the Holy One, blessed be he, to change the order of nature, since this man and his wife were both naturally infertile. The Ba'al Shem Tov was not saddened by this; on the contrary, he rejoiced that from then on he would be able to serve the Lord with no thought of personal gain. For this selfless reaction, his portion in the world to come was returned to him.

Sometimes conditions were attached to the tsadik's blessing, which would take effect only when the husband and wife met these stipulations. A wealthy old man had contributed a large sum of money towards the construction of a synagogue in Ostrog, and in return was to lay the cornerstone for the edifice. He gave this honour instead to the Maharsha (R. Samuel Eliezer ben Judah Halevi Edels).

Then the rabbi stood up and asked the old man, 'What is your wish, and what is your request? It shall be fulfilled.' The old man replied, 'Behold, I have grown old, and I have no sons, this is what I request of the rabbi: a promise of a male child.' The rabbi responded, 'Yes, I decree that this time next year you shall be granted a male child', to which the old man responded, 'It is my wish that he be as great a sage as you!' The rabbi answered, 'You have asked a difficult thing, you have asked a great thing. Only if you accept all that I tell you will you be able to receive that which you have requested.' The old man responded, 'I accept everything!' In response the rabbi declared, 'At first you shall lose all your possessions, and you shall be a poor man who goes begging from door to door. You and your wife shall be ceaseless wanderers and shall live lives of travail. And when your wife shall be with child—you shall die, and when she gives birth to the son—she, too, shall die after the circumcision.'[8]

[6] See J. Sofer, *Sipurei ya'akov*, ii, §45, p. 143. One of the Ba'al Shem Tov's disciples promised a son to Odel, the Ba'al Shem Tov's daughter, in exchange for shoes: *Shivḥei habesht*, 99; Zevin, *Hasidic Tales: Festivals* (Heb.), 174. Cf. Bodek(?), *Sipurei kedoshim*, 41.

[7] Rodkinsohn, *Adat tsadikim*, §3; I. Safrin, *Notser ḥesed*, ch. 4, §22. *Continued in Appendix.*

[8] J. Sofer, *Sipurei ya'akov*, i, §8; [Lemberger], *Niflaot hatsadikim*, §21, pp. 24–5; cf. Hazan, *Sipurim nifla'im*, 67. See A. Michelson, *Ohel elimelekh*, §255, for a condition that the new mother would die in childbirth, and her son would die at the age of 13. In *Shivḥei habesht*, 116, the Ba'al Shem Tov promises offspring, but the children will have a physical defect (a humpback).

In this case, both the husband and the wife so greatly desired male offspring, to continue the chain of the generations, that they agreed to the harsh conditions set by the Maharsha.

A man who asked the Ba'al Shem Tov's blessing received the reply: 'You have asked a difficult thing, for I see that if you give birth to a son, he will be a thief . . ., and [in order for this to happen] you will immediately be compelled to be a downtrodden pauper, and, additionally, you shall die and depart from the world, even before the birth of the son; the widow and her son, too, will suffer great want in their livelihood.'[9] The man asked the Ba'al Shem Tov whether the son would subsequently repent; and when the tsadik replied in the affirmative, he and his wife accepted the conditions.

In a similar spirit, the Maggid of Koznitz told a person who had entreated him for the blessing of a son, 'If you are eager to lose all your money—you shall have sons!' The man and his wife both agreed to this condition, and were sent by the Maggid to the Seer of Lublin. The Seer revealed to them the reason why they had hitherto had no children: in his youth, the husband had cancelled a match. If, however, he were to go and placate the bride, a child would be born to them.[10]

R. Meir of Premishlan promised a barren women that she would conceive and give birth if she purchased a horse and wagon for an elderly porter; the woman fulfilled the tsadik's condition, and was blessed with a son.[11]

At times the tsadik demanded a stiff financial price for his blessing. R. Hirsch of Rymanow was passing through a certain village when a childless Jew, about 50 years of age, approached him and gave him a *kvitl* and a large *pidyon*. The tsadik promised him a son, on condition that the supplicant give him 72 silver coins; he agreed to accept a down payment of only 10 coins, with the rest to be delivered after the birth, at the time of the *pidyon haben*

Cf. Yellin, *Derekh tsadikim*, 'Kunteres menaḥem tsiyon', 44: The parents of R. Menahem Mendel of Rymanow were given their son, provided that they consented to the conditions, first, that they would become wanderers, and second, that when the wife conceived the husband would die, as would the mother when the child reached the age of two years.

[9] J. Sofer, *Sipurei ya'akov*, ii, §38, p. 116. Cf. Hazan, *Sipurim nifla'im*, 12. *Continued in Appendix.*

[10] Rodkinsohn, *Adat tsadikim*, §12. In another incident, the Maggid of Koznitz sent a childless person to receive the blessing of a hidden tsadik, who was a cattle herder (Ehrmann, *Devarim arevim*, 'Stories of the Holy Rabbi, the Maggid of Koznitz', §1). A. M. Rabinowitz, *Keter hayehudi*, 46–7, relates that the 'Holy Jew' promised a son to the wife of the Seer of Lublin, on condition that she would cease to slander him. After her son was born, she once again maligned the tsadik, and the son fell ill, but the tsadik forgave her. She later sinned against him yet again, and the son died.

[11] Berger, *Eser atarot*, 'R. Meir of Premishlan', §22. For another story on this subject that is connected to R. Meir, see T. H. Rosenberg, *Raza de'uvda*, 'Sha'ar ha'otiyot', 104–5. Brawer, *Pe'er yitsḥak*, ch. 26, §6, relates that R. Isaac Eisik of Zhidachov requested fifty-two silver coins (corresponding to the numerical value of the word *ben*—son). The promised son was born seventeen years after the death of the tsadik.

(a ceremony following the birth of a firstborn male child).[12] Another incident involving this tsadik is related by R. Margoliot, in the name of his teacher, the rabbi of Barniv. When the tsadik came to a city, he proclaimed that 'he had some male children, and he desired to sell them for large sums'. One woman (who would later be the mother of the rabbi of Barniv) requested his blessing, for which he demanded the sum of 150 Reinish. The woman consulted with her husband and her father-in-law, and the latter advised her to give a *shterntikhel* (ornate sabbath head-covering). The tsadik accepted the head-covering, and the woman bent her head to receive the tsadik's priestly blessing, as was the custom. This time, however, he remained silent, and then said: 'You are already pregnant, with a male child!'[13] R. Tsevi Hirsch of Zhidachov offered to bless the (childless) daughter of his master, R. Naphtali of Ropshits, with a son, in exchange for her *shterntikhel*. Time passed because of her reluctance to make the gift, and she did not have a son her entire life.[14]

An exceptional case is depicted in the following story. A couple from a village came to the Maggid of Mezirech, asking to be blessed with children. After the Maggid demanded of them ten gold zloty, the man said to his wife: 'If the Maggid agrees to bless us with a male child only in exchange for ten gold zloty, then the Lord will help us without him, as well.' The Maggid proclaimed: 'The words of the villager were heard in heaven, and you shall have a male child!'[15]

[12] J. Sofer, *Sipurei ya'akov*, ii, §48, p. 151. Cf. the testimony by Dr Rubin concerning his barren aunt (Horodezky, *Hasidism and Hasidim* (Heb.), iv. 112). See Kamelhar, *Mevaser tov*, 20–1: R. Tsevi Hirsch of Rymanow gave a blessing in return for eighty gold coins. R. Tsevi Hirsch would at times give his blessing on condition that he was invited to perform the *pidyon haben* ceremony (Moskowitz, *Otsar hasipurim*, ix, §1). R. Nehemiah Yehiel received 400 gold coins from the 'Holy Jew' for a blessing for offspring (Rabinovitz, *Ma'aseh neḥemiyah*, 42–3).

[13] Moskowitz, *Otsar hasipurim*, ix, §2. Cf. Mondshein, *Likutei reshimot uma'asiyot*, §16, p. 4: R. Solomon of Karlin gave a person a blessing for a son, on condition that this person would give him a certain sum of money upon his wife's giving birth; when he came home, the man learned that his wife was already pregnant. In [Lemberger], *Magdil yeshuot malko*, 12, it is told that R. Elimelekh of Rudnik would travel to Hungary, and 'before his journey from his home, he would count the number of children that he took with him in his sack to distribute to barren women, so many males and so many females'. According to Rakats, *Siaḥ sarfei kodesh*, i. 295, the rabbi of Kotsk told R. Hirsch of Tomashov, who did not have the money to meet his travelling expenses, 'I give you two sons for barren women. Whoever gives you much money—give to him!' The Mitteler Rebbe told a woman who requested sons: 'I had another few sons in my pocket, they are yours' (Mondshein, *Migdal oz*, 192).

[14] Ehrmann, *Devarim arevim*, 'Stories of the Holy Rabbi of Rymanow', §20. For the sale, after much soul-searching, of a head-covering with inlaid pearls (*shterntikhel*), see Goldberger, *Darkhei hatov vehayashar*, fo. 13*b*.

[15] Shenkel, *Yeshuot yisra'el*, ii, §24; Gemen, *Sifran shel tsadikim*, ch. 4, §6, 'New Collections', fo. 52*a*. Cf. Kleinmann, *Mazkeret shem gedolim*, 132: once the Maggid of Koznitz was told of a childless couple, about 50 years old, who had been blessed with a son. The Maggid remarked: 'The Lord, may he be blessed, acted very well, for the entire world forgets the Lord, may he be blessed, since anyone who desires sons, or other things, would run, either to me or to the rabbi of Lublin, and now the Lord, may he be blessed, has shown that he, too, is capable of giving a son!' (cited in *Sifran shel tsadikim*, ch. 4, §6, 'New Collections', fo. 52*a*).

The hasidic story is also concerned with the main events connected with the conception and birth of a child as a result of the tsadik's blessing, namely immersion in the ritual bath, birth, and circumcision, with all the difficulties and dangers that they entailed, and the aid provided by the tsadik in overcoming these problems.

Several stories portray the various circumstances that could put obstacles in the way of a Jewish woman's immersion in the ritual bath at the end of her menstrual period, by which she becomes ritually clean and permitted to have sexual relations with her husband.

The future mother of the Maggid of Mezirech had not been to immerse herself at the appropriate time because her husband was away from home and she thought that he would not return that day. In fact, her husband came back late that night; and so she went to awaken the bath attendant. When he refused to open the bath, because of the late hour, she went and awakened the rabbi. As a result of her stubbornness and forcefulness the ritual bath was opened for her, and by virtue of fulfilling the commandment she conceived the Maggid that very night.[16] In another case the bath attendant refused to permit a woman to enter the bath on the night of the Fast of Esther because she could not pay, and turned the embarrassed woman away. An elderly couple—in fact, the biblical Abraham and Sarah—came to her aid, and through their intercession she was enabled to fulfil the commandment of immersion.[17]

The future mother of the Grandfather of Shpola (Aryeh Leib of Shpola) exhibited unswerving dedication of purpose in repeating her immersion three times, each time having become impure by contact with animals that were in fact agents of the Sitra Ahra.[18] The Devil sought to prevent the woman's purification both because impurity is his realm and out of a desire to cause the woman and her husband to engage in prohibited relations. In a similar fashion, Satan is described as coming in the guise of a good customer to the store owned by the mother of R. Menahem Mendel of Vitebsk when she was about to go and immerse, and trying to delay her. The woman, however, passed the test: overcoming the monetary temptation, she went to immerse, rebuffing her 'customer'.[19]

16 Sobelman, *Sipurei tsadikim hehadash*, §17.

17 *Ma'aseh hakedoshim*, §17. Cf. *Ma'asiyot mehagedolim vehatsadikim*, 31–2.

18 J. Y. Rosenberg, *Tiferet maharal*, 8: a black cat jumped on her, a black dog barked, and a pig alarmed her. See Eleazar ben Judah of Worms, *Sefer haroke'aḥ*, 202; *Shulḥan arukh*, 'Yoreh de'ah', 'Hilkhot nidah', 198: 48 (gloss): 'Women are to take care when they go forth from their immersion [in the ritual bath] . . . not to first encounter any impure thing.' See Shabetai ben Meir Hakohen, *Siftei kohanim*, ad loc., and the commentary of the Vilna Gaon. Judah Yehiel of Rozdol, *Lev same'aḥ haḥadash*, 108: a woman who returned from immersion entered a ruin so that men would not see her. In the ruin she saw an evil spirit in the form of a soldier with a large dog. She fled from the ruin, and in the night the destructive agent came and sought to rape her.

19 See Sobelman, *Sipurei tsadikim heḥadash*, §13.

The rabbi of Vishniets gave a certain herb to the husband of a chronically ill woman who had not had a child, and ordered the husband and wife to drink water containing the herb on the night of the woman's immersion. The sick woman recovered, conceived, and gave birth.[20] The grandmother of R. Ezekiel Schraga Halberstam saw in a dream a long-dead woman being led to immersion. In response to the old woman's question, the dead woman replied that she was now required to immerse herself for every immersion that had not been conducted at its proper time.[21]

Especially difficult was the plight of women who did not have a ritual bath where they lived, and who were forced to immerse in rivers or lakes, even in the harsh north European winter. Once a woman went with her husband to a river on the night of immersion, and left her clothes on the wagon while she went to immerse herself. Suddenly, the horse bolted with the wagon and her clothes (and the husband). An informer who found the naked woman clothed her and brought her home. Prompted by the bad reputation of this informer, the husband asked his rabbi a formal halakhic question: 'Is my wife to be believed in her claim that she was not raped by this informer?'[22]

In some instances tsadikim appear to their followers in dreams to prevent them from engaging in prohibited sexual relations.[23] In other cases the same effect is achieved by biological manifestations that prevent the purification of the woman as required by Jewish law. Thus the mother of a *mamzer* (child of a forbidden union), who had unwittingly married her own child, saw an issue of menstrual blood every time she went to immerse and therefore remained in a state of uncleanness. Since sexual relations are forbidden under such circumstances, she was kept from engaging in incest.[24]

The following two stories also tell of women who could not easily undergo purification.

[20] Singer, *Seva ratson*, fo. 6*b*.

[21] See Moskowitz, *Otsar hasipurim*, ii, §6.

[22] Rodkinsohn, *Adat tsadikim*, §15. Cf. Rakats, *Siaḥ sarfei kodesh*, ii, §476: a Jewish woman in Istanbul was kidnapped by an Ishmaelite on her way to the ritual bath, but she succeeded in escaping, and she was not defiled by him. Breitstein, *Siḥot ḥayim*, §10, p. 9, tells of an army officer in Tomashov who oppressed the Jews and bathed in the ritual bath, thereby preventing women from immersing themselves. See also Goldberger, *Darkhei hatov vehayashar*, fo. 3*a*: a miracle was performed for the mother of a (future) tsadik when, on the night of her immersion, a small pool expanded to become a proper ritual bath. For more regarding immersion in a river, see Moskowitz, *Otsar hasipurim*, xv, §13.

[23] The Maggid of Koznitz appeared in a dream to a hasid on the night of his wife's immersion, and warned him not to engage in sexual relations; lo and behold, his wife had a menstrual flow (Bromberg, *Toledot hanifiaot*, 37). R. Elimelekh of Rudnik saw his rabbi, the tsadik of Ropshits, in a nocturnal vision; in this instance too the tsadik's warning proved to be true (A. Michelson, *Ohel naftali*, §30). See [Isaac Dov Baer ben Tsevi Hirsch], *Kahal ḥasidim heḥadash*, §58, concerning the rabbi of Pshemishel's wife, who 'was wicked and despised immersion [in fulfilment of] the commandment, and only the maidservant knew of this'.

[24] Sobelman, *Sipurei tsadikim heḥadash*, §9. For the Christian source of the story, see Nigal, 'A Hasidic Manuscript' (Heb.), 840–2.

One woman could not become pure for her husband [because constant menstruation prevented her immersion], and she engaged in all the remedies, but they were to no avail. She travelled to the rabbi of Lublin, may his merit protect us, and he instructed her to go to Koznitz, to the *saba kadisha* [Holy Grandfather], where she would find relief. When returning from Koznitz, she should travel via Lublin, to tell him [the Grandfather's] answer, and so she did. She returned via Lublin, and related to him that the Grandfather of Koznitz had given her an amulet in his handwriting. The rabbi of Lublin opened the amulet, and found written there: 'He shall then be clean from the flow of [*mimekor*] her blood' [Lev. 12: 7], but with the first letter ***mem*** of the word ***mimekor*** effaced. The rabbi of Lublin commented: 'How wondrously did he act by expunging the first *mem*, for if he had not done so, not a drop of blood would have been left from her flow. Consequently, he erased the ***mem***, so that there would be a flow, or rather, that it would become clean.'[25]

The second story runs as follows:

A woman who could not become pure to her husband came to the rabbi and tsadik R. Aaron of Tetiyev, the son of the holy R. Tsevi, the son of our master the Ba'al Shem Tov, may his merit protect us, and asked him for a relief and remedy for this. He told her that she should give him a promissory note for 50 silver roubles, and she would speedily be cured. She gave him this note, signed by her husband, and was immediately cured. She remained [capable of being] in her clean state, as is the normal way of women, for a long time, until the death of this tsadik R. Aaron. He left a son, the tsadik R. Tsevi Hirsch of Skvira, who searched his father's estate and found the promissory note from the woman's husband. He knew this woman well, and he sent to her asking that she pay him the money that was due his father, of blessed memory, in accordance with the promissory note. The husband immediately sent him the full amount. As soon as the holy rabbi R. Tsevi received the money, the woman became weakened and began to suffer once again from the same condition, and she could not become pure to her husband. Several times she travelled with her husband to the holy rabbi R. Samuel of Kaminka, who gave them several amulets, but they were not effective. After this, it happened that this holy rabbi R. Samuel chanced to be in company with the holy rabbi R. Tsevi Hirsch of Chudnov, of blessed memory, who also was a grandson of the Ba'al Shem Tov, of blessed memory, and he told him about this woman: that when she owed the debt, everything was well, but that after the debt was paid she fell ill again, and several great tsadikim had been unable to help her. The holy rabbi R. Tsevi explained to him: 'There is nothing strange in the tsadikim's inability to do anything after the debt was paid. This holy rabbi R. Aaron, of blessed memory, had initially acted with profound wisdom in taking from them a bill of indebtedness, for the tsadik is from the *sitra dekedusha* [the side of holiness], and menstruation is from the *sitra aḥra*. So, when the tsadik took a bill of indebtedness from the woman, because 'the borrower is a slave to the lender' [Prov. 22: 7], the kingdom of holiness would reign over the *kelipah* [here, the 'evil' represented by menstruation]. After the money was repaid, the kingdom of holiness left the *kelipah*, and

[25] [Isaac Dov Baer ben Tsevi Hirsch], *Kahal ḥasidim heḥadash*, §157.

therefore the great tsadikim could be of no avail afterwards.' The holy rabbi R. Samuel of Kaminka wondered greatly at this, and said that this must certainly be the truth, and that such a holy idea could be uttered only by someone who was of the stock of the holy Ba'al Shem Tov, may his merit protect us.[26]

In all these instances the tsadik helped the woman to perform the immersion, and that was followed by the long-awaited pregnancy.

Hasidic stories do not depict problems encountered during pregnancy, but they devote a lot of attention to the difficulties of giving birth. The woman who has difficulty in delivering her child is as frequent a supplicant for the blessing of the tsadik as the barren woman, and tsadikim regarded the alleviation of birth pains by means of their blessing as one of their responsibilities. R. Isaac of Nezkizh related in the name of his father, R. Mordecai, that 'Anyone who is within fifty miles of the mother giving birth, who does not feel the actual birth pangs just as she does, in order to pray for her, so that it will be well for her—how can he be called by the name of "tsadik"?'[27]

Once the Ba'al Shem Tov laughed loudly. When he was asked why, he explained that a woman 'was having great difficulty in her childbirth, and the Devil desired to endanger both the woman and the infant, almost causing their death. I acted with this prayer of mine so that the foetus would emerge safely from his mother's womb.' The child that was born to this woman was to become R. Menahem Mendel of Vitebsk.[28]

[26] Ibid., §178. See also Gemen, *Sifran shel tsadikim*, ch. 1, §5: the Ba'al Shem Tov expelled *ḥitsonim* (see Ch. 10 below) from the ritual bath, thus enabling a woman who experienced a menstrual flow each immersion night to immerse herself and thereafter be able to sleep with her husband. See Ze'ev Wolf of Zhitomir, *Or hame'ir*, 9: R. Elimelekh cured the wife of R. Aaron Leib ben Meir the Great, who could not immerse herself. Cf. Kamelhar, *Mevaser tov*, 26; see also A. Stern, *Ḥutim hameshulashim*, 17–20: the Ba'al Shem Tov expelled demons from a ritual bath on behalf of a woman who could not become ritually clean for her husband. G. Levi, 'Teshuvat hamishkal', 64, tells that the Maggid of Chernobyl expelled demons from the ritual bath and sent them to the wilderness. See Tzitrin, *Shivḥei tsadikim*, §29, p. 63: R. Zelig of Sherensk blessed a young man, telling him that his wife, who was a leper and could not ritually cleanse herself, should go to the river and immerse herself, and she would emerge clean: she was indeed cured.

[27] I. Landau, *Zikhron tov*, 'About the Days of His Youth', §2. For stories that served as a charm for a woman experiencing a difficult childbirth, see Slodovnik, *Ma'aseh hagedolim heḥadash*, §37; Rakats, *Siaḥ sarfei kodesh*, ii, §476. For charms and amulets for such women, see J. Y. Rosenberg, *Rafa'el hamalakh*, introd. and pp. 62–5. See also Ch. 9 n. 18 below. For a kabbalistic story of the successful birth of twins by a woman who was experiencing a difficult childbirth, by placing the sign of the circumcision of R. Moses Galante ('who never in his life had a nocturnal emission') in the woman's mouth, see Benayahu, *Sefer toledot ha'ari*, 224–5.

[28] Sobelman, *Sipurei tsadikim heḥadash*, §13. On a Friday the Ba'al Shem Tov commanded R. Yehiel Mikhel of Zlotchev to return home, and revealed to him that his wife was undergoing a difficult childbirth. If R. Yehiel Mikhel whispered in her ear an incantation that he was taught by the Ba'al Shem Tov, she would give birth to a son (*Shivḥei habesht*, 91). Cf. A. Stern, *Ḥutim hameshulashim*, 25. The long-dead mother of R. Tsevi of Lesko appeared in a dream to the mother of a woman having difficulty in giving birth. She commanded the latter mother to go

R. Isaac Eisik Safrin told a story that combined knowledge of the language of the animals with the motif of the woman experiencing difficulty in childbirth:

Once our master Elimelekh was sitting with the renowned tsadik R. Moses, who asked him, 'Do you understand what this dog speaks?' He replied that he was saying that he is bearing a letter to our master. He further asked, 'And more than this, our master does not hear?' To which he responded, 'He is saying everything that is written in the letter, that there is a woman who is having a difficult childbirth, and who needs [divine] mercy.' As they were speaking, the wagon driver struck the dog. Our master took offence and asked, 'Why did you beat it, causing it to become confused, for it told me the name of the woman, and when you beat it it became confused, and I do not know if [her name] is Sashi or Rashi!' Shortly afterwards, the emissary came with the letter, and all the details were confirmed.[29]

Once Aryeh Leibush Harif, a rabbi in Plotsk, was asked in the middle of the night to act on behalf of a woman experiencing a difficult childbirth. The rabbi ritually washed his hands, opened a volume of the Talmud, and began to study. He then prayed as follows: 'Master of the Universe, by merit of my just having resolved a difficulty in the Talmud raised by Tosafot, thus release the woman so-and-so the daughter of her mother so-and-so from her difficulties in giving birth',[30] and the woman's travail came to an end.

In another case a man went to the tsadik of Sasov to ask for his intercession on behalf of a woman from his village who was undergoing a troublesome labour. The emissary arrived late at night and came to the house of the tsadik by chance; he was invited to spend the night, still without knowing who lived there. In the morning, the tsadik informed him that the woman had already given birth to a boy.[31] A messenger from another village was sent on the same errand to R. Tsevi Hirsch of Zhidachov. Night came, and he knocked on the door of R. Tsevi Hirsch's house. Although the attendant did not want to disturb the sleeping tsadik, the latter none the less awoke and went to immerse himself in the icy winter river. The tsadik almost drowned; by virtue of his readiness to sacrifice himself on behalf of 'two souls from Israel', the woman succeeded in giving birth. When he returned home, he told the emissary: '*Mazal tov*, the woman has already given birth to a son.'[32] Another such emissary, a wealthy individual, came to the rabbi of Lizhensk

to her own son, R. Tsevi, and to give him a coin so that the woman would be saved (Breitstein, *Siḥot ḥayim*, §62, pp. 50–1).

[29] I. Safrin, 'Netiv mitsvoteikha', 'Shevil emunah', 5; M. Berger, *Divrei elimelekh*, §7.

[30] Tzitrin, *Shivḥei tsadikim*, §18, pp. 42–3; Rabinovitz, *Ma'aseh neḥemiyah*, 69. The tsadik R. Nehemiah Yehiel berated and humiliated one of his hasidim; the humiliation suffered by the husband because of R. Nehemiah's words served to counter the harsh divine decree that at that moment, unknown to him, was causing his wife to have difficulties in labour.

[31] Bodek, *Ma'aseh tsadikim*, §23, pp. 38–9; Zevin, *Hasidic Tales* (Heb.), 40–1.

[32] Bodek, *Seder hadorot heḥadash*, fos 34*b*–35*a*.

early one Sunday morning, while it was still dark, to request his help in a similar case. The rabbi went to immerse himself in the icy water before praying. On his way he passed by the house of R. Eliezer Lippa, a descendant of R. Elimelekh, and heard the singing and dancing of the *melaveh malkah*, the festive Saturday night meal. When R. Eliezer Lippa learned why the rabbi was walking past, he said: 'Let the distinguished gentleman give us two measures of honey-water, and the woman will directly give birth.' And so it was.[33]

While R. Eliezer, the son of R. Elimelekh of Lizhensk, was staying in the house of the Maggid of Koznitz, some people came on behalf of a woman experiencing a difficult birth, 'and the Maggid ordered that the ritual bath be heated for him. The rabbi, R. Eliezer said: "Donate the wine for the *melaveh malkah* banquet, and she will find succour."' They did as instructed, and were immediately informed that the child was born, and all was well.[34]

The wife of R. Tsevi of Kaminka was a righteous woman, and as soon as she stepped over the threshold of any woman suffering in labour, the woman would give birth with ease. As it was outside the Land of Israel, so it was within it: once the daughter of an important non-Jew in the Land of Israel requested her help, in return for which the righteous woman requested permission from the authorities to go down to the Cave of Makhpelah (where the matriarch Sarah is buried).[35]

Concern for the woman in labour, rooted in powerful love for one's fellow Jews, is depicted in the following story.

The holy rabbi, the divine kabbalist, our master and teacher, the rabbi R. Tsevi of Zhidachov, of blessed memory, was going to [the rabbi of] Sasov, to 'shelter under his shadow' and learn Torah from him. Once the holy rabbi, our master R. Tsevi, said: 'I shall take care to watch the conduct [of R. Moses Leib of Sasov] regarding *tikun ḥatsot*' [the prayer recited in the middle of the night for the destroyed Temple]. The greatness of the latter's interest in *tikun ḥatsot* was so well known that it was said of him that 'my beloved knocks' [S. of S. 5: 2] for him precisely at midnight. . . . The holy rabbi, our master R. Tsevi, therefore concealed himself to

33 Ehrmann, *Devarim arevim*, 'Stories of the Holy Rabbi, R. Elimelekh', §12.

34 Gemen, *Sifran shel tsadikim*, ch. 9, §6; ibid., ch. 40, §15: when R. Eliezer of Pokshivnitza, the grandson of the Maggid of Koznitz, heard of a woman who was having difficulty in delivering, he ordered: 'Pour a drink, because she has undoubtedly already found relief!' He looked at his watch, and said, 'Not yet!' He looked again, and said: 'A son!' A telegram arrived shortly afterwards, with the news of the birth of a son. See also Zimetbaum, *Darkhei ḥayim*, 36: the tsadik's handkerchief, which he placed on the woman giving birth, was a charm for a swift and easy birth. And see Judah Yehiel of Rozdol, *Lev same'aḥ heḥadash*, 68 n. 3: 'And so there was no woman in his city who experienced difficulty in childbirth, for he ordered that his charm be placed on the woman's stomach, and she would deliver' (see also introd. to Gottlieb, *Ḥidushei maharaf*; R. Pesah Gottlieb was head of the Nemirov rabbinical court).

35 Pinhas of Korets, *Beit pinḥas*. Cf. Breitstein, *Siḥot ḥayim*, 43: the rabbi of Ostila prayed for a non-Jewish woman having a difficult childbirth, and she delivered successfully.

see how he [R. Moses Leib] conducted himself. Once at midnight our holy master R. Moses Leib, of blessed memory, took the clothing of non-Jews and wore it; he also took a large piece of wood with a lamp and went outside. The holy rabbi, our master R. Tsevi, followed so that he could understand fully what was happening. He went to a certain place, where a Jewish woman had given birth to a son. She was extremely poor, and her house was very cold, because this was during the nights of winter, that were extremely cold. This woman's very bones were quaking from the cold and frost. The holy rabbi went there and spoke in the language of the non-Jews: 'I have logs to sell, please buy, I am selling them cheaply now!' The woman argued, 'But I do not have a single coin', to which he responded, 'I will take the money from you tomorrow, please, take the wood.' She then said: 'Of what use is this thick log to me? I will have to split it into small pieces to heat the oven, and there is no axe here.' To this he replied, 'I have everything with me, and I will do everything for you!' The holy rabbi took the axe and split the log into chips. Having split the log, the holy rabbi recited *Tikun le'ah*. After this, he fired the oven, and recited *Tikun raḥel*. He then hurried to his home and changed his garb. When the holy rabbi of Zhidachov saw this, it was as a wonder in his eyes, and he recited the scriptural passage [Ps. 77: 20]: 'Your path was through the mighty waters, your tracks could not be seen.'[36]

The tsadik's blessing was not, however, the only remedy sought to alleviate the travail of giving birth, and some women even had to resort to charms by non-Jews. The daughter-in-law of R. Moses, the rabbi of Kutow, experienced difficulty in childbirth and turned for help to non-Jewish sorcerers, who placed a castrated rooster under the threshold of her house.[37] R. Israel of Ruzhin would tell the well-known story of the woman who became pope as a charm for women suffering in labour.[38]

A miraculous account of what looked like being a premature birth, with the contractions brought to a halt so that the birth could take place at its proper time, was given by the tsadik R. Judah Tsevi of Rozdol. His father, R. Moses of Sambor, married his mother, and, behold, after six or seven months

he [the foetus; i.e. the storyteller] was tired of doing nothing in his mother's womb, and the birth pangs began. R. Moses of Sambor, who had gone to the study hall to pray for the mother's health, saw how the young men were laughing and whisper-

[36] Bodek, *Ma'aseh tsadikim*, §25, pp. 40–1. Cf. the story by Peretz, 'Perhaps Even Higher'; for the sending of money by the Ba'al Shem Tov to a new mother, see *Shivḥei habesht*, 157. Cf. Ze'ev Wolf of Zhitomir, *Or hame'ir*, 42–3: R. Meir of Premishlan brought to a new mother the meat for the Passover Seder meal (which his wife had obtained with great effort).

[37] *Shivḥei habesht*, 84.

[38] Slodovnik, *Ma'aseh hagedolim heḥadash*, §37, pp. 38–9. In a well-known Christian story from the Middle Ages, a girl who wanted to be a priest dressed and acted like a boy, studied in a seminary, became a priest and eventually became pope. One day, in the middle of a sermon, she gave birth . . . From then on, it is said, as part of the process of electing a new pope, the candidate is seated on a chair and a young novice priest checks his genitalia.

ing that the woman had become pregnant wantonly. When the father returned home, his wife joyously told him that the birth had already begun. R. Moses sighed deeply. The wife understood the meaning of this, placed her hands on her stomach, and declared: 'My child, know the truth, that you are the son of your father the tsadik. Heed my voice, and wait another two months, to be saved from the shame of people's slander!'

The rabbi of Rozdol concluded: 'I immediately retracted my head, and I tarried there two more months, since I was no longer doing nothing, for I was fulfilling the commandment of honouring my mother!'[39]

It was believed that a great future lay ahead of a baby born surrounded by a halo.[40] On the other hand, danger awaited such an infant at the time of the circumcision, and in the days preceding the ceremony. Especially perilous was the night before the circumcision, the *wachtnacht* (the night of watching), during which the newborn had to be closely guarded. It was only natural that as long as the baby had not been circumcised and thereby become a Jew, the forces of the Sitra Ahra wanted to keep him within their dominion. Once the Ba'al Shem Tov came to the house of a Jewish leaseholder who had lost four sons in infancy, in each case on the *wachtnacht*. The Ba'al Shem Tov succeeded in overcoming the priest–sorcerer who had been responsible for the deaths of the infants, and saved the newborn.[41]

The tsadik delivering the blessing for offspring often requested of the father-to-be that he be given the honour of being the *sandak* at the infant's

[39] Berger, *Eser kedushot*, 'R. Judah Tsevi of Rozdol', §4; Teomim, *Ateret tiferet*, 'His Holiness, the Holy Rabbi, R. Judah Tsevi of Rozdol', §4; Zevin, *Hasidic Tales: On the Torah* (Heb.), 184–5. Another story, in which the tsadik refused to hasten the birth of a child with his prayers, involved the Hatam Sofer (R. Moses Sofer) and his wife. Although the latter was having a difficult childbirth, the husband did not pray on her behalf, 'for I do not wish to shorten the life of another tsadik' (Yellin, *Derekh tsadikim*, 10). For R. Solomon of Karlin's reluctance to pray for a woman experiencing difficulties in childbirth (because a mortally ill worthy would die at the time of the birth), see Gemen, *Sifran shel tsadikim*, ch. 12, §14; and see Ch. 9 n. 18 below.

[40] See e.g. Rakats, *Siaḥ sarfei kodesh*, v. 101: when R. Abraham Bornstein of Sochatchev (the author of *Avnei nezer*) was born, 'the entire house was filled with light, as [at the birth of] Moses'. For the light that was seen upon the birth of R. Menahem Mendel of Kosov, see H. Kahana, *Even shetiyah*, 'Shivḥei ḥakhamim', ch. 1; see also Bodek(?), *Sipurei kedoshim*, §5. For an extensive discussion of the subject, see Ch. 16 n. 4 below.

[41] Rodkinsohn, *Adat tsadikim*, §1. See also Dan, 'History of the Hebrew *Akdamot* Story' (Heb.), 197 ff. Cf. Brandwein, *Degel maḥaneh yehudah*, §2: on *wachtnacht* priest–sorcerers, who had seen a 'great light' in the house of the new mother, came and wanted to harm the infant. However, by virtue of the hospitality that the woman had extended to guests, their evil designs were thwarted. For a circumcision performed in a prison, see Kaidaner, *Sipurim nora'im*, §10; see also A. Stern, *Ḥutim hameshulashim*, 18. For the nine children of a Jew, each of whom was 'kidnapped on the night of watching', while the tenth was saved by the Ba'al Shem Tov, see Gemen, *Sifran shel tsadikim*, ch. 39, §3. For R. Elimelekh and R. Zusya ordering that their experiences as accoucheurs, a circumcisor, and a *sandak* should be related as a charm on *wachtnacht*, see Ehrmann, *Devarim arevim*, 'Stories of the Holy Brothers R. Elimelekh and R. Zusya', §6.

circumcision, as the Ba'al Shem Tov did of the parents of R. Israel of Koznitz.[42] R. Berish of Oshpetzin promised a son to a man who had hitherto sired only girls, on condition that he be honoured by being the *sandak*.[43] In many other cases the same suggestion was made by the parents, who regarded it as a great honour to have the tsadik fill this role at their son's circumcision.[44] Sometimes the honour of serving as *sandak* would be granted to a person who assisted at the circumcision, such as the cobbler in the story cited below about R. Gedaliah, who was none other than the patriarch Abraham.

It often happened that the father of the newborn son got himself into difficulty by promising this honour to two people, as in the following story.

The tsadik of Lublin, may his memory be for the life of the world to come, went to visit the rabbi, the tsadik R. Barukh of Medzibezh, may his memory be for the life of the world to come. There was a woman there who had difficulty giving birth, and her husband came to the Lubliner—for it is the way of the world, that when a tsadik comes from another city, his renown is magnified—and the Lubliner asked him, 'Will you honour me with the role of *sandak* if there is a son?' The father replied, 'Yes!' In the meantime, this supplicant also came before the Medzibezher, who also asked him: 'Will you honour me with the role of *sandak*?' And he responded, 'Yes!' The woman gave birth to a son, and the father hid on the day of the circumcision, because he did not know how to take counsel and decide to whom to give the role of *sandak*. Eventually he calmed himself and went to the Medzibezher, told him the entire course of events, and asked what he should do. The Medzibezher took the role of *sandak* for himself, and said: 'The Lubliner will probably remain for another sabbath [= another week], and everything will come out right.' . . . And this was so: there was another circumcision there, and the Medzibezher gave the Lubliner the honour of being *sandak*.[45]

One of the problems faced by the parents of a newborn son was obtaining the services of a *mohel* to circumcise the child. This could be almost impossible for parents who lived in a remote village, especially in times of emergency. Parents in such circumstances were saved by those *mohalim* whose dedication and self-sacrifice knew no bounds, and who were willing to risk their very lives to perform this commandment.

[42] Rodkinsohn, *Adat tsadikim*, §1.

[43] M. M. Sofer, *Sheloshah edrei tson*, 34; Singer, *Seva ratson*, fo. 3*b*. Cf. the promise made by R. Tsevi Hirsch of Zhidachov (Teomim, *Ateret tiferet*, 'His Holiness, the Holy Rabbi, R. Tsevi Hirsch of Zhidachov', §23).

[44] Sobelman, *Sipurei tsadikim heḥadash*, §12.

[45] I. Landau, *Zikhron tov*, 'The Deeds of the Tsadikim', §10; [Isaac Dov Baer ben Tsevi Hirsch], *Kahal ḥasidim heḥadash*, §86; it is related in Rosenthal, *Hitgalut hatsadikim*, 29, that on one occasion the honour of officiating as *sandak* was promised to the Seer of Lublin, but he was late for the circumcision (and missed receiving the honour). He was joyful during the banquet, and not angry at all. When he was asked about his good mood, he replied that, although the deed of being a *sandak* is great, it cannot be free of foreign thoughts and interests, and he was therefore happy not to have been given the task. See also Rakats, *Siaḥ sarfei kodesh*, iii. 243.

Once an emissary came to R. Gedaliah from the village next to Zelechow, asking him to go there to circumcise a baby and enter him into the covenant of our father Abraham. R. Gedaliah was a *mohel*, but this was during wartime, and everyone feared for his life, if he were to set out from the bounds of the city, for killing was rife and the villages lived in terror. This R. Gedaliah said: 'No matter what!' and travelled to the village. When he came to the house of the new mother, he saw her crying for her husband, who had gone away; out of his fear that a robber would come, he had fled into hiding. This made the rabbi anxious, for he could not be both *sandak* and *mohel*, and there was no [other] Jewish man in the village. He went outside to the road; perhaps the Lord would provide for him. From a distance, R. Gedaliah saw a man with a shoemaker's bench on his shoulder. He asked him to come and assist with the circumcision of the infant. This person served as the *sandak*, and R. Gedaliah circumcised the baby boy. The stranger also produced from his bag a bottle of wine, so that they could recite the blessing 'who sanctified the produce of the womb'. Then, all of the sudden, the guest-*sandak* vanished, as if he had never been there. When R. Gedaliah next met his master, the Maggid of Mezirech, the latter asked him: 'Did you think perhaps that the guest was the prophet Elijah? You should know that this person, without whom there could not have been a circumcision, was our father Abraham himself.'[46]

At times the *mohel* was also a ritual slaughterer, as is evident from the following story. Two sons of a certain man had died during their circumcision, and now a third son was born to him. He asked R. Menahem Mendel of Vitebsk to come to the circumcision, saying that the virtue attached to his presence would prevent any harm coming to the infant. Since the circumcision was on the sabbath the tsadik could not attend it in person; but he promised to send his ritual slaughterer, who also was a *mohel*, saying that this would be accounted as if he himself were present at the ceremony.[47]

One of the hasidim of R. Levi Isaac of Berdichev was a cattle dealer. At one time stock prices dropped so steeply that he was afraid he would suffer heavy losses, and he went to the tsadik to ask his advice. R. Levi Isaac asked

[46] Walden, *Shem hagedolim heḥadash*, ch. 3, §9 ('I heard from an outstanding rabbi, the great one of his generation'); [Isaac Dov Baer ben Tsevi Hirsch], *Kahal ḥasidim heḥadash*, §138; Kleinmann, *Or yesharim*, 22–3; Moskowitz, *Otsar hasipurim*, i. 5–6. S. Y. Agnon used this tale in his story 'Belevav yamim' (*Elu ve'elu*, 523). In Breitstein, *Siḥot ḥayim*, §59, p. 47, the *sandak* was indeed Elijah. Cf. Brukman, *Migdal david*, 26. For a *mohel* who was asked to circumcise a child on the eve of Yom Kippur, and the difficulty of finding a *sandak*, see Breitstein, *Siḥot ḥayim*, 58–9. For the patriarch Abraham in the home of R. Kalman Kalonymus Epstein (author of *Ma'or vashemesh*), see A. Michelson, *Ohel elimelekh*, §245. For people who refused to serve as *sandak*, see Ch. 16 below.

[47] Sobelman, *Sipurei tsadikim heḥadash*, secs 32, 28. On the ritual slaughterer, see also Ch. 12 below. Some tsadikim acted as *mohalim*, including among others the Ba'al Shem Tov (*Shivḥei habesht*, 141), R. Levi Isaac of Berdichev (Ehrmann, *Devarim arevim*, 'Stories of the Holy Rabbi of Berdichev', §5), and R. Aaron of Karlin (Zeilingold, *Me'orot hagedolim*, §51, p. 158). R. Samson Weiner was once saved by the merit of being a *mohel* (J. Sofer, *Sipurei ya'akov*, ii, §32).

him: 'Do you sometimes engage in [the performance of special] commandments?' The cattle dealer replied that he was a *mohel*. The tsadik continued to question him: 'And what do you do when the infant bleeds excessively?', to which he replied that he did such and such. The tsadik then told him, 'I will give you a herb; if there is bleeding, put the herb on the place of the circumcision.' The hasid asked: 'And what about the oxen?' The tsadik responded: 'But I told you, if the infant bleeds excessively, apply the herb, and, with God's help, he will be immediately be cured.'

The cattle dealer set off to return home. On the way he stayed in a Jewish inn, where he happened to learn that the innkeeper's son had not been circumcised. When he asked the innkeeper why this was so, the latter replied that the child's brothers had died as a result of their circumcision. The dealer asked him: 'If a remedy could be found that would enable the circumcision of your son [to be performed] with no fear for his life—how much would you agree to pay the *mohel*?' The innkeeper responded: 'Four hundred silver roubles.' The dealer declared: 'I am willing to circumcise him, and if, heaven forbid, anything were to happen, [an additional] four hundred rubles—my pledge—shall be yours!' They agreed that the dealer–*mohel* would remain at the inn for four weeks following the circumcision. When the infant began to bleed profusely after the circumcision, the merchant applied the herb, and the son was cured. At just that time the price of oxen rose, and the dealer wanted to get back home and sell his cattle; but, insisting on the fulfilment of the agreement they had made, the innkeeper refused to let him go. Finally, at the end of the agreement, the dealer set out—with a total of 800 roubles in his pocket, and with the price of cattle reaching new heights.[48]

Another story concerning the stopping of bleeding was told by the father of the circumcised infant himself. This was R. Nahman Munk of Lvov, who asked the tsadik R. Joshua of Belz, who had been the *sandak* at the circumcision, to pray for the child's health. The tsadik opened his mouth and began to tell a story. Once a person came to the Ba'al Shem Tov and asked his advice on obtaining the money he needed for the dowries and wedding expenses of his daughters, who were of marriageable age. The Ba'al Shem Tov told him: 'You did not act wisely by concealing your bitter fate from me until now. And

[48] Rakats, *Siaḥ sarfei kodesh*, v, §16, pp. 20–1; Zevin, *Hasidic Tales: On the Torah* (Heb.), 277–9. R. Aaron Moses, a disciple of the Seer of Lublin, did not want to give a blessing to a boy of about 12 years old, since he sensed that he was uncircumcised. This boy had not undergone the ceremony at the proper time because his brothers had died as a result of circumcision (Bodek, *Mifalot hatsadikim*, §23, fo. 17*b*). See also Zevin, *Hasidic Tales: On the Torah* (Heb.), 209: R. Zusya suggested holding a *se'udat mitsvah* in order to stop the bleeding of the newly circumcised infant, and the haemorrhaging did, in fact, cease. The story originally appeared in M. Berger, *Divrei elimelekh*, 'Interpretations on *isru ḥag* [the day following a festival]' (cited in Donner, *Menorat zahav*, 62), where it is related that R. Pinhas of Korets 'circumcised an infant, and could not stop the bleeding', and then R. Zusya appeared.

now I will tell you of a proven remedy for a child that bleeds as a result of circumcision, namely: take a frog . . . and burn it entirely, apply the ashes to the place of the circumcision, and the bleeding will immediately cease. And now, go on your way, and may the Lord cause you to prosper.' On his way home, the hasid passed through a village where he stayed in the house of a wealthy Jew. To his surprise, the hasid learned that the man's son was not circumcised. He declined the villager's invitation to dine with him, asserting that he was not willing to taste anything in a house that did not observe the commandment of circumcision. The householder began weeping, and told the hasid that his first five children had died following circumcision, and the rabbi had ordered him not to circumcise any more of his children. And, in fact, in addition to the child that the hasid had seen, he had two other sons who also were uncircumcised. The hasid recalled the words of the Ba'al Shem Tov and circumcised the child, using the remedy against bleeding—and the child quickly healed. He similarly circumcised the other sons of the villager, who gave him a sum of money sufficient to cover the wedding expenses of his daughters, as a token of his gratitude. R. Joshua of Belz said: 'It is autumn now, and no frog can be obtained. Let the story be as if the action was done, and the child be healed.' The infant quickly recovered.[49]

Relatives and friends would be invited to the circumcision banquet, with poor wayfarers being seated at a separate table.[50] The Grandfather of Shpola, R. Mordecai of Nezkizh, and the *shaliaḥ tsibur* (lay prayer-leader) of Zaslov met on such an occasion.[51] R. Barukh of Medzibezh would come to circumcisions in weekday clothes, while the Seer of Lublin would wear his sabbath finery.[52] At such a *se'udat mitsvah*, when relatives and in-laws would gather, they would deliver Torah discourses and tell of their illustrious forebears;[53] and they would also tell stories. R. Isaac Meir of Ger (author of *Ḥidushei harim*) once commanded that a story be told during a circumcision, and one of the hasidim present told the story of the cattle dealer reproduced above.

[49] A. Michelson, *Ohel yehoshua*, §6. In a similar story it is R. Israel of Ruzhin who gives the advice. See Ehrmann, *Devarim arevim*, 'Stories of the Holy Rabbi, R. I[srael] of Ruzhin', §23. For charms to stop bleeding after circumcision, see J. Y. Rosenberg, *Rafa'el hamalakh*, 24; see also Lewinski, 'Water instead of Blood' (Heb.), 68–70; id., 'Precious Stones' (Heb.), 93–101.

[50] A story of a man who was believed to be dead and, his wife having remarried, returned home on the day of the circumcision of his wife's son, contains a description of the circumcision festive meal: 'The new mother gave sweets and dishes with her own hand to every guest' (A. Michelsohn, *Shemen hatov*, §51). 'And this man [the husband] also came among the poor people and sat among them at the table, and food was set before them' (*Ma'aseh hakedoshim*, §12).

[51] See Rodkinsohn, *Sipurei tsadikim*, §14, p. 30.

[52] Bodek, *Ma'aseh tsadikim*, 16; Singer, *Seva ratson*, fo. 12*a*.

[53] At a circumcision banquet, R. Aaron of Karlin said to the child's other grandfather, R. Elimelekh of Grodzisk: 'We are accustomed, at religious celebrations, to tell of our lineage' (Kleinmann, *Zikhron larishonim*, 28).

FIVE

AGUNOT

AN *agunah* is a married woman whose husband has disappeared. According to Jewish law, such a woman may not remarry until her husband is found and gives her a writ of divorce, or until testimony is received of his death.[1] The phenomenon of *agunot* is an ancient one and has many causes; however, during the period of the Diaspora it was increasingly prevalent, becoming an integral part of the reality of Jewish life.[2] Many factors contributed to this development: the systematic assaults against Jews in recent centuries; the wanderings of Jewish communities throughout the Diaspora, exacerbated by anti-Jewish persecutions and wars; the fact that Jewish blood was free for the taking, so that any Jew who travelled was at constant risk of attack; the occupation of many Jews in peddling and in trade, which forced them, notwithstanding this ever-present danger, regularly to set out on long journeys. All this led to an increase in the number of *agunot* and provided fertile ground for the growth of a ramified halakhic literature on the subject, as well as a storytelling genre that reflected the situation in its own way.

In every generation *agunot* appealed to the leading halakhic authorities in their attempt—at times in desperation—to be released from this state of bondage. It was therefore only natural that upon the rise of hasidism many women, from both hasidic and non-hasidic families, would turn to the tsadikim for aid. The belief in the ability of the tsadik to see afar and to know concealed things gave the *agunah* hope that he could help her to find her lost husband, and either bring him home or obtain the necessary writ of divorce from him. In the hasidic stories on this subject the leading roles are played

[1] For the halakhah regarding *agunot* and their release, see Y. Z. Kahana, *Sefer ha'agunot*, 7.

[2] e.g. the *Ḥavatselet* newspaper, nos 37–42 (Jerusalem, 1893) contained the following announcement: 'The request of a deserted wife: about five years ago my husband abandoned me and went to America. When he came to the city of Hamburg he sent me two letters, and since then all trace of him has been lost and he did not send me any more letters. I and my son have been left with no staff of bread. I therefore request of my brethren, the Children of Israel, that anyone who knows of him, or who saw him, to inform me. These are his distinguishing marks: a young man, about 28 years of age, a short person, black beard, named Avraham Zelig Glick, from the city of Leisuva, Kovno district. The petitioner, Feige Glick.' *Continued in Appendix.*

by the wife, the tsadik, and the husband, with secondary parts occasionally given to additional figures such as a relative, or friends of the husband. Most of the stories begin with a description of the situation and the sorry state of the *agunah*, and end with the resolution of the situation by the tsadik. His counsel encourages the wife and helps to locate the husband; in most instances his blessing is effective in bringing the husband home, or in obtaining a writ of divorce from him. Thus a majority of these stories do, indeed, have a 'happy ending'.

The hasidic tale is distinguished from all other kinds of story concerning the freeing of *agunot* by the central place accorded to the supernatural capacities of the tsadik. He can see from afar and perform miraculous acts; he can harness the forces of nature, such as the wind; he employs supernatural powers that bring spirits into the world; he can even revive the dead for short periods of time. Even so, the hasidic stories, like other tales on this theme, are also full of ordinary human efforts and actions, including the imposition of pressure on, and even threats against, husbands who are in hiding. Nor are the circumstances that result in women becoming *agunot* in the hasidic story fundamentally different from those in regular stories. Sometimes the husband leaves the marital home because of poor relations between the couple, thereby solving his own problem in a highly selfish manner and at the cost of creating a much more serious religious, moral, and human problem. In other instances the conflict is not—or not only—directly between husband and wife, but between husband and father-in-law. For example, a young man vehemently hated his wife, but out of fear of his violent father-in-law did not demand that they divorce: instead, he fled to the yeshiva of R. Jonathan in Prague, where he presented himself as a bachelor.[3] Another young husband who was 'detested . . . by his wife' also ran away, and became a schoolteacher.[4] A third fled due to quarrels in his house,[5] while yet another bolted out of his anger at his father-in-law, who did not agree with the path of study that he had chosen.[6] In a few cases the husband apparently has no option but to flee, as in the case of the *mamzer* Torah scholar who had unwittingly married his mother; when he learned the truth, he fled, leaving her an *agunah*.[7]

The husband may have disappeared after setting out on an apparently normal journey to trade or seek work, with his wife's consent. He may have planned in advance not to return home, or be prevented from doing so by events that occur during the course of his trip. It may be that some calamity

[3] Bodek, *Mifalot hatsadikim*, §24, fo. 18*a–b*.

[4] See J. Sofer, *Sipurei ya'akov*, ii, §55.

[5] Bodek, *Pe'er mikedoshim*, §9.

[6] Zeilingold, *Me'orot hagedolim*, §38, p. 131.

[7] Sobelman, *Sipurei tsadikim heḥadash*, §9, from the original version in *Gesta Romanorum* (in German trans.: Leipzig, 1905, 67–86). See the extensive discussion in Nigal, 'A Hasidic Manuscript' (Heb.).

befalls him along the way; or it may happen that he opts for a new life, succeeds in business, even establishes a new family. He may adopt non-Jewish ways or descend to the world of crime. In extreme cases he converts to another religion, either willingly or under duress, thus creating an additional obstacle to freeing his deserted wife.

In many instances, however, the husband has died during his journey, but no witnesses can be found to attest to this. In such cases, the tsadik's ability to see from afar is not sufficient to free her, since the halakhah forbids releasing an *agunah* without human witness. These circumstances therefore called for exceptional actions, such as the locating of hidden witnesses and even the performance of miracles.

In every instance, the freeing of an *agunah* was taken very seriously, because of the possible complications that could arise, especially if the woman remarried. If it became evident that a husband who had been presumed dead was still alive, or that the writ of divorce that had been delivered to the wife was invalid or forged, the woman and her children from her second husband were placed in an intolerable situation. Sometimes a tragic mistake was made; in other cases individuals engaged in malicious deception for monetary gain, forging writs of divorce or giving false testimony to a supposed death. The tsadik's supernatural vision, even though it could not of itself free an *agunah*, sometimes enabled him to prevent such additional tragedies.

In many cases the husband had left his home for economic reasons: typically, because he could not earn a living there, and so set out to seek better fortune elsewhere. It may reasonably be assumed that in most such instances the husband left with the full knowledge and consent of his wife. Obviously, she did not imagine that her husband would not return, and that she would be fated to become a 'widow of the living'. Such a situation is exemplified in the story of how the Grandfather of Shpola succeeded, by means of threats, in forcing a deserting husband to return home. The story emphasizes that the husband's extended absence in distant regions, without communicating with his home, was not the result of any evil intent, but rather of his engagement in business affairs. The beginning of the tale is illuminating, 'Now, in one city among the towns around Shpola there was an *agunah* who had been deserted by the husband of her youth, and for fifteen years she had heard nothing from him. He had gone to trade in Danzig, and he did not part from her unamiably, nor did he send her any report. The wife despaired of him and lived as a widow of the living, for she thought it was impossible for her husband, who loved her and she loved him, to be alive and not send her any tidings.'[8]

[8] Rodkinsohn, *Sipurei tsadikim mehaḥut hameshulash*, §10, 33–6. See Ben-Yehezkel, *Sefer hama'asiyot*, v. 214–18, who notes that he copied the story from the book *Siftei kedoshim*, which is identical to *Sipurei hatsadikim mehaḥut hameshulash*. Cf. also J. Y. Rosenberg, *Tiferet maharal*, 71–2.

In contrast with most of the *agunot* in the hasidic stories, there was one wealthy *agunah* who managed her business affairs unaided by her husband, and who even travelled to tsadikim to seek their help. When her maid, who came from Shpola, attempted to persuade her to travel to the Grandfather in the hope of learning whether her husband was alive or dead, the *agunah* replied, 'Of what use will it be to me if he were to tell me that he is dead, since for such a report I would not be permitted to [re]marry, if there are no witnesses.' The maid, however, gave her mistress no respite, and advised her that if her husband were dead, the tsadik would tell her where she could find him, or find witnesses who could attest to his demise. The *agunah* was finally convinced and went to the tsadik, who assured her that her husband would shortly return and even set the precise date for his arrival. Everything happened just as the tsadik had predicted, and as a result of his vigorous efforts: for when the tsadik learned that the husband was a merchant in Danzig, he demanded, under threat of death, that the husband wind up his business affairs there and return home.

Many of the same elements also appear in the story which begins, 'A certain woman, the daughter of a worthy, had been an *agunah* for . . . about fourteen years. She lived in her father['s home], and her father established a business for her. She had become permanently embittered.' Here, too, the *agunah* is jolted into action by a maid, who had previously served in the home of R. Elimelekh. This maid spoke of the wonders and miracles she had seen the tsadik perform, and advised the *agunah* to go to see him: just as he had helped many other *agunot*, so too he could certainly assist her in finding her lost husband. The deserted wife travelled to R. Elimelekh, and he informed her that her husband was alive, in such-and-such a city, and that he would return home in two months' time. He asked that she conduct a banquet that evening and prepare herself for her husband's return. Upon his arrival, the husband said that he had forgotten that he had a wife, but an old man had appeared to him and urged him to return to his wife, threatening him with death if he were not to do so.[9]

A story founded on a similar set of circumstances was told by R. Isaac of Nezkizh about his revered father R. Mordecai:

Now, I am not as amazed about all the awesome and wondrous acts performed by Father, may his memory be for the life of the world to come, the signs and wonders [that he performed], and his reviving the dead, as I am about the following occurrence. A certain *agunah* begged Father to free her from that condition, and came before him many times. On one occasion he could not bear her suffering, and he asked her, 'What shall I do for you?' She replied, 'Is it too wondrous for our

[9] *Ma'asiyot vesiḥot tsadikim*, 36; M. Berger, *Divrei elimelekh*, §15; Berger, *Eser tsaḥtsaḥot*, 27–8; and, in a slightly different version, Ehrmann, *Devarim arevim*, 'Stories of the Holy Brothers R. Elimelekh and R. Zusya', §26 (the story is also printed in *Niflaot hamagid*, 21).

master and teacher to bring him back to me?' He, of blessed memory, answered, 'And is he here, that I can offer you relief? Here is a cup of water, perhaps he is there?' In her pure faith, she believed that no vain talk would issue forth from his holy mouth. She gazed into the cup that stood there, and shouted, 'Here, I see him, sitting in the cup!' He asked her, 'How is he sitting?' And she replied, 'With a *yarmulke* [skullcap] on his head, without a hat.' He ordered her, 'Show me the *yarmulke*.' The woman put her hand into the cup, and took out the *yarmulke*. What happened was that her husband was a tailor, and he was sewing in a courtyard far away. He was sitting before an open window, with his *yarmulke* on his head, and all of a sudden the wind snatched the *yarmulke* off his head and bore it away; then he realized that this had not happened by chance, and he resolved to return home. His wife showed him the *yarmulke*, which he recognized [as his], and she was freed from being an *agunah*.[10]

In this case the husband's long absence from home, without contacting his wife, was a result of carelessness and laziness, but without malice; and he had not totally forgotten his spouse, as was proved by the fact that when something extraordinary happened to him, he regarded this as a sign from heaven to return to his deserted wife.[11]

In a more complex tale that nevertheless includes similar elements, the deserting husband took a second wife in his new place of residence, and even had children by her, but eventually granted a writ of divorce to his first wife. In this story, the deserted wife found her husband through the good offices of R. Israel ben Shabetai, the Maggid of Koznitz. The *agunah* herself, her brother, and other people who witnessed these events related the story to one of the reliable sources used by Kaidaner, author of *Sipurim nora'im*: R. David, a disciple of R. Asher of Stolin.

One time an *agunah*, whose husband had abandoned her several years [previously], came with her brother to his honoured holiness [the Maggid of Koznitz]. They asked his honour whether, with his divinely inspired spirit, he could find the place where he [the husband] is residing, to obtain a writ of divorce from him. He told

[10] I. Landau, *Zikhron tov*, 'Me'avdut hatsadikim', §27; Donner, *Rishpei esh hashalem*, 'Kunteres shivḥei moharam', §28; Kleinmann, *Mazkeret shem gedolim*, 'Ezrat yisra'el', 122–3; Ben-Yehezkel, *Sefer hama'asiyot*, v. 228–32. See also Sadan, 'The Tailor and his Skullcap' (Yiddish). For an *agunah* whose husband was imprisoned by the authorities, and who obtained a writ of divorce by the efforts of R. Mordecai of Nezkizh, see I. Landau, *Zikhron tov*, 'Ma'amar siyum batov', §6; Kleinmann, *Mazkeret shem gedolim*, fo. 47*a*; Donner, *Rishpei esh hashalem*, 'Kunteres shivḥei moharam', §23. Cf. Mondshein, *Likutei reshimot uma'asiyot*, §49, p. 10: by following the counsel of the Tsemah Tsedek (R. Menahem Mendel Schneersohn, the third Lubavitcher Rebbe), an *agunah* found her husband, who had been imprisoned by the police because he did not possess a passport. Cf. Zevin, *Hasidic Tales: On the Torah* (Heb.), 141. For mendicant deserting husbands, see Mondshein, *Likutei reshimot uma'asiyot*, §44, pp. 8–9; §53, p. 10.

[11] Cf. the story in which a tsadik advised an *agunah* to blow on burning embers, and to pray that the same wind would inflame longing to return home in her husband's heart, as indeed happened (A. Michelson, *Shemen hatov*, 'Stories', §135).

his servant to bring a vessel full of water, which he did. The holy rabbi said to the woman, 'If you will, look in the water', and the woman did so. Then he said to the woman, 'What do you see in the water?' and she replied, 'I see a large city and many houses.' He told her, 'Look at the street where the marketplace is.' She did so, and she said, 'I see the marketplace.' Then he instructed her, once again, 'Look in the windows of the houses.' She did so, and she looked into the windows. All of a sudden, she cried out loud, 'Look, here is my husband in one of the houses! He is a tailor, and he is sitting with many workers and is sewing clothes, with a sleeve in one hand.' He ordered her, 'Grab the sleeve from his hand!' She extended her hand into the vessel with water, and plucked out the sleeve, which was still warm from the hot iron. The rabbi urged the woman to keep the sleeve, and all actually saw the miraculous wonder.

After this, the holy rabbi said to the woman and her brother, 'Now go in peace, and you will quickly obtain the writ of divorce from your husband.' She asked him, 'Our holy master, reveal to us in which direction we should make our way.' He answered, 'In whichever direction you please.' They asked, 'How will we be able to obtain a carriage, for the carriage-driver will ask in which direction we are travelling, and we will not know what to tell him?' He reassured them, 'Go, go in peace, and the beneficent and merciful Lord will prepare for you what you need. With the Lord's help, everything will be ready.'

They went from his honoured holiness along the city street to obtain a carriage, and they saw a non-Jew riding in a carriage hitched to two horses. They asked the non-Jew, 'Do you wish to take us?' He replied, 'Sit in the carriage.' He neither asked them which way he should go, nor mentioned what payment he would ask. They rode for about half an hour until they came to a city. They did not know where they were going; they simply rode along, believing in the tsadik. Suddenly they were overcome by slumber. The non-Jew overturned the carriage and they fell to the ground; awaking from their sleep, they found themselves lying on the ground in a forest. They could find neither the non-Jew nor the carriage, and they were greatly distressed, for they seemed to be as if shipwrecked at sea, since they did not know where the road led, nor which city they needed to get to. At a loss, they walked for nearly half an hour, until they reached the edge of the forest, from where they saw a large city nearby.

When the woman saw this, she rejoiced greatly, and said to her brother, 'Blessed be the Lord, the words of the holy tsadik are honest and true. Here, this is the city that I saw in the water.' When they came to the city, the woman said, 'Let us walk through the streets of the city; perhaps the Lord will provide for us the marketplace that I saw in the water.' They walked for a while in the streets of the city, and presently the marketplace became visible to the woman, who exclaimed to her brother, 'Blessed be the Lord, this is the marketplace that I saw!' She entered the marketplace, and looked through the windows until the Lord provided for her the house where her husband was. When she saw her husband through the window, her brother said to her, 'Let us go to the [local] rabbi and take counsel on the matter; perhaps he will deny that he is your husband.' So they went to the rabbi, who asked them, 'Where are you from?' They told him, 'From Koznitz.' The rabbi commented, 'That is a long way, about eighty parasangs [approximately 320 miles].' They told him, 'We came from Koznitz today.' The rabbi marvelled very greatly at this wondrous story, and said, 'Blessed be the Lord, who has not withheld his kindness from his people Israel, that the tsadikim of our time are blessed with the spirit of divine inspiration.' The woman gave the rabbi a description of the appearance of the house and of her husband's countenance. The rabbi responded, 'I know him very well, he has been residing in this city for several years, and he has a wife and children here. But do not be concerned, if the Lord wills it, everything will turn out for the best, only guard the sleeve.' The rabbi shut the woman and her brother in the room, and sent for the tailor. The tailor immediately came to the house of the rabbi, who asked him, 'Do you have a wife?' The tailor responded, 'My master, does his excellency not know that I have a wife and children?' The rabbi said to him, 'I know that, but I ask you if you have another wife, from before your marriage to this wife?' The tailor denied this, saying, 'I never had another wife, for before my marriage to this woman, I was a bachelor at the time of my arrival here.' The rabbi questioned him, 'What garment did you sew today?' The tailor responded, 'My master the rabbi, I will relate to his excellency a wondrous story of what happened to me today. I was sitting at my table, and my workers also were sitting at the table. We were sewing garments, and I had in my hand one sleeve for the garment of a certain minister, to press it with my hot iron. And now, I am holding the sleeve in my hand, and here, we all see how the sleeve runs from my hand like a flying bird and disappears from us. We searched throughout the entire house, but we could not find it at all. And this was a great wonder to us.'

The rabbi asked him, 'What will you give me if I give you the sleeve?' The tailor responded, 'That is impossible!' The rabbi declared, 'It is indeed possible!' He went and opened the door, and said to the woman, 'Come here and bring your husband his sleeve!' The woman entered and placed the sleeve on the table. When the tailor saw the sleeve, he was greatly agitated, and exclaimed, 'My master the rabbi, that is my sleeve!' In his excitement, he still did not see the woman's face. The rabbi told him, 'In truth, this is your sleeve, but it seems to me that this woman is your first wife!'

When the tailor looked at the face of the woman, he recognized her and fainted. When he regained consciousness, the rabbi told him the entire story. The tailor confessed, and gave her a writ of divorce.[12]

In the following story we meet another deserting husband with no conscience: this time he was discovered by means of his distinctive characteristics. The *agunah* was fortunate in that the husband was found only a few days before he was about to emigrate to America.

A shoemaker and his wife lived in the city of Sanz. Suddenly he left his home, and his wife did not know where he had gone. The woman went to the tsadik of Sanz to

12 Kaidaner, *Sipurim nora'im*, §21, pp. 79–81. The story also appears, with some changes, in Ehrmann, *Devarim arevim*, 'Stories of the Holy Rabbi, the Maggid of Koznitz', §10, a version that was copied in Berger, *Eser orot*, 'R. Israel, the Maggid of Koznitz', §51. The version in *Devarim arevim* also appears in the Yiddish *Niflaot hamagid*, 21–2.

ask his advice. She told him that her husband had a wife prior to her in Kolomai, and also in Stanislav and in Tarnopol, and that she was his fourth. He husband had distinctive features: when he spoke, he talked quickly and his eyes darted from side to side; he had a long neck, and one leg had been amputated. In reply, the tsadik told her to travel to a large city, and there she would find him. The woman asked, 'To which city? To Stanislav? Or to Kolomai? Or to Tarnopol?' The tsadik answered, 'No!' She asked him, 'Perhaps to Lvov?', and he replied, 'Yes!' The woman asked the tsadik to give her money for travelling expenses, because she was a poor woman. The tsadik did not give her anything, advising her instead to go first to Tarnow and ask people there: she should tell them why she was having to make the trip, and they would have mercy on her and give her [money] for the expenses of the journey.

She did this, and went to Tarnow. There, at the railway station, she met an innkeeper from Lvov named R. Moses. He took pity on her, and another person who was there also took pity on her, and they gave her travelling expenses to Lvov. R. Moses went with her, and in Lvov she stayed in his inn. R. Moses sent one of his servants to search among all the shoemakers in Lvov for a person who possessed the features described by the wife. Finally he found him, and told him to repair his shoe. As he was engaged in the repair, the servant thanked the man thus: 'My compliments to you for having repaired the shoe well and properly. And now, I can offer you a fine match here.' The shoemaker answered that he had already been in contact with a certain person from a village near Lvov, and was to be married the following day; and after the wedding he was going to sail to America. R. Moses [already] knew, from the shoemaker's wife, that every time that he took a new wife his father would send him 25 roubles from Russia; so, when the servant told him about his meeting with the shoemaker, R. Moses sent his servant to him a second time, with instructions to tell him to come to R. Moses, the owner of the inn, because 25 roubles had been received for him from Russia, from his father, who did not know his address. The shoemaker believed this and came straight away to the house of R. Moses. As soon as he got there, R. Moses sent for the police to come and force him to give a writ of divorce to his wife; and he asked the shoemaker about the wives that he had. He admitted that he had a wife in Kolomai, and also in Stanislav and in Tarnopol, and said that he had divorced them; and that in Sanz he had had a wife, who died.

When this wife, who was in an inner room in the house of R. Moses, heard this, she straight away came into the room where her husband the shoemaker was, and slapped him on the face: 'You spoke truthfully that I am dead, and yet alive! And now, if you give me a writ of divorce immediately and return to me three hundred silver [roubles], it will be well, but if you will not give me the money—you will be bound in iron fetters!' When he heard this, he gave her the money, and immediately gave her a writ of divorce as well. When she returned home and related these events to the tsadik, he said to her, 'You have seen that I acted well with you, by not giving you expenses for the journey. The affair thereby became known, and you could ask that person to help you.'[13]

[13] J. Sofer, *Sipurei ya'akov*, ii, §62, p. 185. For the source of the story, see A. Michelson, *Mekor ḥayim*, §§101, 316. See also Ben-Yehezkel, *Sefer hama'asiyot*, v. 245–50.

A woman could also become an *agunah* as a result of a natural disaster. For example, a fire broke out on the wedding night of R. Samson Weiner, and many people died. The bride and groom were among those who fled for their lives, each thinking that the other had been burned to death. The bride was an *agunah* until the groom succeeded in finding her before he married another woman.[14] In another instance, a fisherman was swept away by a storm to a distant place, where he was taken captive and enslaved by peasants. His *agunah* appealed for help from R. Levi Isaac of Berdichev, who advised her to enquire after her husband in the Caucasus region. The woman's intensive searches bore fruit, and she succeeded in discovering where he was held captive and extricating him.[15]

In contrast with the exhaustive searches conducted by this *agunah*, another deserted wife was lucky, and did not need to trouble herself at all. Her case was brought before R. Leib Beile of Dunaberg, who asked the opinion of R. Menahem Mendel of Lubavitch. No reply was received from the tsadik, and in the meantime a major conflagration erupted in the city. To her total amazement, the *agunah* identified her husband among the spectators. The husband was brought before the rabbi and agreed to give his wife a writ of divorce.[16]

A story of the tsadik from Nezkizh concerns a deserting husband who adopted non-Jewish practices. The tsadik blessed an *agunah*, praying that the Lord would send her his aid and that she would speedily find her husband.

And she went to the village of Zafridiye . . . and she sat to rest in the tavern. A soldier in the Polish army, who was mounted on a horse, also rode up to the tavern and drank whisky. He went to sit next to the *agunah*, but she kept away from him, as is the custom of Jewish women. The soldier mocked her, saying, 'But we are

[14] See Bodek, *Pe'er mikedoshim*, §10, pp. 21–2. The Yiddish version of the story appears in *Sipurei niflaot mehagaon hatsadik hashelaḥ hakadosh*, 16–23. A slightly different version of the story, related by R. Samson Weiner (= R. Samson Wertheimer), the author of *Tosafot ḥadashim*, appears in Heilperin, *Menaḥem meshiv nefesh*, §9, fo. 6*a*, as a story that he heard in his family. The book is also cited by A. M. Habermann in his glosses on Halperin, *Yefeh anaf*, 25. For more stories about R. Samson Weiner, see Bodek, *Pe'er mikedoshim*, §9, pp. 17–21.

[15] Zeilingold, *Me'orot hagedolim*, §22, p. 47; Ben-Yehezkel, *Sefer hama'asiyot*, v. 219–27.

[16] Kaidaner, *Sipurim nora'im*, §58. It is related in Kohen, *Shemuot vesipurim* (p. 54), that R. Menahem Mendel Schneersohn, the Tsemah Tsedek, did not initially grant private audiences to *agunot*, but began to do so in response to his wife's entreaties following her illness. This tsadik revealed to ten *agunot* the whereabouts of their husbands (Mondshein, *Migdal oz*, 208); ibid. 207: 'For it is found in books that gazing upon the countenance of the tsadik is a wonderful charm for *agunot*.' Cf. ibid. 142–3: the counsel of the fifth Lubavitcher Rebbe, R. Shalom Duber, that resulted in an *agunah* finding her husband. See also Z. Horowitz, *Horowitz Family* (Heb.), 78: the Seer of Lublin sent an *agunah* to Vienna. As she walked about in the streets of the city, she was pushed by a couple; when she looked at the husband, she recognized her husband who had abandoned her, and who was now willing to give her a writ of divorce.

related, so why should you move away?' He told many stories, and she recognized him, exclaiming, 'Here is my husband!' He admitted to knowing all the signs [that she gave]: the names of their parents, signs from their intimate life, and distinguishing marks on her [body]. Some other people were present and heard this, and they bore witness to it. Suddenly, another soldier like the first came riding up, and he also entered the tavern. In the meantime, the horses became entangled one with the other and fought [in Aramaic in the original—taken from the *piyut* (liturgical poem) *Akdamut milin*]; then the two soldiers came to blows, and the second one arose and killed the first . . . and [the woman] was therefore permitted to the world [i.e. she was no longer married].[17]

This man had become a soldier after he left his home; other deserting husbands degenerated and became robbers, even murderers. A husband fled from his wife in the city of Pruzhany, and eight years of searching for him yielded no results. When the *agunah* came before the tsadik R. Asher of Stolin, he told her to search for him in the forest, where she would find him. This advice was greeted by derision by the mitnagedim in the city, but the woman, who believed in the tsadik, hired a carriage and drove to the forest. On the way, the carriage-driver attempted to rape her, and she fled from him into the depths of the forest, where she managed to elude him. Then she came to a lonely house, where, to her misfortune, she was seized by robbers who were also cannibals; then it became clear to her, beyond any doubt, that the chieftain of the robbers was her husband. The woman used various stratagems to pass information to the police about her situation and where she was being held. Her husband the robber was captured by the police and executed. Before his death he admitted, in the presence of Jewish witnesses, that he was the husband of the *agunah*.[18]

Getting an apostate husband to supply a writ of divorce could be extremely difficult, since the apostate's hatred for Judaism frequently hardened his heart towards his wife the *agunah*. Not all apostates refused to divorce their deserted wives, however, as is apparent from the following stories.

An *agunah* and her brother came before R. Menahem Mendel of Lubavitch and asked him to use his spirit of divine inspiration to reveal to them where her

[17] I. Landau, *Zikhron tov*, 'Ma'amar siyum batov', §5; Donner, *Rishpei esh hashalem*, 'Kunteres shivḥei moharam', §22; [Isaac Dov Baer ben Tsevi Hirsch], *Kahal ḥasidim heḥadash*, §92; Kleinmann, *Mazkeret shem gedolim*, 'Parashat mordekhai', 92–3; Zevin, *Hasidic Tales: On the Torah* (Heb.), 204. For another deserting husband-soldier, see Mondshein, *Likutei reshimot uma'asiyot*, §72, p. 14. Cf. A. Michelson, *Shemen hatov*, 'Stories', §4, p. 20, for the story of R. Isaac Meir of Ger, 'that once an *agunah* came to the rabbi [the author of] *Or haḥayim*, and it appeared to him that she was permitted [to remarry]. He found it difficult, however, to unhesitatingly state that she was permitted, and eventually, the [presumably] dead [husband] came on his own two feet.'

[18] Zeilingold, *Me'orot hagedolim*, §30, pp. 102–6. See Ben-Yehezkel, *Sefer hama'asiyot*, v. 254–62.

deserting husband was. The tsadik replied to them, 'I am neither a prophet nor the son of a prophet!' The brother of the *agunah* said that he too sought the blessing of the tsadik, for he intended to emigrate to the Land of Israel. The tsadik advised the *agunah* to accompany her brother, suggesting that perhaps they would find her husband during their travels. Wherever they went, they questioned the local Jews about the woman's husband, but to no avail. Then, when they were travelling at night in the vicinity of the city of Jassy, they took a ride on a mail-wagon in the dark. The wagon-driver shouted and cursed in Russian, and the woman recognized her husband's voice. When the wagon arrived at the inn where the brother and sister were staying, they asked the Jewish inn-keeper about the driver, and were told that he was an apostate Jew. They also learned that getting the writ of divorce would be very difficult, because he was a very wicked person. Some time later the apostate entered the room, and lost no time in roundly cursing whoever had dared to enter his wagon at night. As he was doing so, his eyes fell on his wife: he recognized her, did not deny the facts of her claim, and gave her the writ of divorce, without even asking for any money in return. All those present were greatly surprised by his ready compliance with the woman's request; then the apostate explained. On his journeys he had to pass by a ruin that was inhabited by demons, and whenever he approached the place he was seized by deadly fear of the fiends; it was this fear that caused him to give a writ of divorce to his wife, on the assumption that the merit of this act would protect him from harm.[19]

The *agunah* therefore obtained her writ of divorce by following the counsel of the tsadik, as did the woman in the next story.

Once a woman who had been an *agunah* for several years came to his honoured holiness. He told her: 'Travel via Polotsk, and when you are thirsty on this road, do not drink water, but only alcoholic drink.' The woman was travelling near Polotsk and she became extremely thirsty. She could not obtain any liquor in the inn, but she did not want to drink water and act counter to the command of his honoured holiness. She was informed that there was a courtyard, at a distance of a parasang from the inn, where she could obtain strong drink. Driven by her extreme thirstiness, she went to this courtyard and obtained her drink there—where she also found her husband, who had been an apostate for several years, and in Polotsk he gave her a writ of divorce.[20]

[19] Kaidaner, *Sipurim nora'im*, §59, pp. 139–40. Ben-Yehezkel, *Sefer hama'asiyot*, v. 238–44, provides a version 'as it was related [*mipi hashemua*]'. In contrast with this story, the granting of a writ of divorce was often conditional upon the payment of a considerable sum of money to the deserting husband. The 'Old Rebbe' also aided *agunot*: once he instructed an *agunah* to travel to Vilna, where she would find her husband. With the help of R. Meir Raphaels, who found the name of the deserting husband in a list of prisoners, the husband was located, and he gave the woman a writ of divorce (Kohen, *Shemuot vesipurim*, §49).

[20] Kaidaner, *Sipurim nora'im*, §63, p. 145; [Isaac Dov Baer ben Tsevi Hirsch], *Kahal ḥasidim heḥadash*, §204. For a deserting husband who became an apostate, see also Rakats, *Siaḥ sarfei*

The same pattern occurs in another story.

I heard . . . that a certain *agunah* from our country [Romania] travelled to my great uncle, our master and teacher, author of *Tsemaḥ tsedek* [of Lubavitch], may he rest in peace. He ordered her to return to her country, and that she should travel from place to place in it in search of [her husband]. However, when she came to any place, for her first [meal] she should not eat bread without honey. Once, when she came to a certain place, the innkeeper could not provide her with honey, but told her that in a nearby place, outside the city, lived a certain man who sold honey. She went there to buy from him, and she recognized him: he was her husband.[21]

Sometimes apostasy was the result of being taken captive. The young husband of a woman was taken captive during the war between the Russians and the Turks. After engaging in fruitless searches (during the course of which her parents had died), the *agunah* resolved to leave her home and go far away to stay with her rich uncle who lived in Constantinople. There one day she heard the sounds of music from a religious procession—and was astonished to see that the regal figure who was marching at the head of the procession was none other than her lost husband. When she told all this to her uncle, he thought that the woman's troubles had driven her insane. Fortunately for her, the tsadik R. Jacob Samson of Shepetovka happened to be in Constantinople at the time, and he advised her how to obtain a writ of divorce from her husband. The woman did indeed receive her writ of divorce, and in the end the lost husband also returned to the Jewish faith.[22]

The book *Shivḥei habesht* contains only one *agunah* story,[23] but according to the later hasidic collections the Ba'al Shem Tov was very active in this field. The common theme in all the following stories is that the Ba'al Shem Tov reveals the deserting husbands by means of his capacity to see distant things. However, since all these sinning individuals have been defiled, he requires an unclean environment in order to discover them.

R. Jacob Sofer (author of *Sipurei ya'akov*) relates how R. Hirsch Sofer, head of the Chortkov rabbinical court, travelled to see the Ba'al Shem Tov in order to form an opinion of him, as told to him by R. Hirsch himself.

And when he came there, he saw many women in his house who were *agunot*, and he [the Ba'al Shem Tov] told them where their husbands were. Two women, whom he had not yet told [about their husbands], remained. He went to the toilet, and

kodesh, iii, §373. See MS JNUL 6289, fos *6b–7a*, for an apostate deserting husband in Zlotchev during the time of R. Meir of Premishlan: the *agunah* was instructed to take the twentieth carriage that came along and travel with its occupant to Premishlan. On their arrival, the tsadik called him 'Moshe [Moses]'; the husband realized that he had been found out, and gave the woman a writ of divorce.

21 Mondshein, *Migdal oz*, §33, p. 259.

22 *Mifalot tsadikim*, §1. See Ben-Yehezkel, *Sefer hama'asiyot*, v. 219–27.

23 *Shivḥei habesht*, 140; this *agunah* was a leaseholder.

upon his return from the toilet he informed them that their husbands had already died. R. Hirsch asked him, 'You see with the spirit of divine inspiration that rests upon you, why did you not tell them until after you returned from the toilet?' He replied, 'Their souls are in an unclean place, and therefore I had to search for them in polluted places.'[24]

R. Hirsch later became a teacher in the Ba'al Shem Tov's home. Another version of this story is presented by Abraham Hayim Michelson, author of *Shemen hatov*, in the name of the tsadik R. Israel of Chortkov, who told it during the third sabbath meal. According to this version, R. Hirsch went from Chortkov to the Ba'al Shem Tov,

and when he came to his house, he found there two women, *agunot*, who were standing there in the house. The Ba'al Shem Tov was not in the house then, for he had gone out to the toilet. Our grandfather [R. Hirsch] waited until the Ba'al Shem Tov came and washed his hands. He explained to the two women that one's husband was in such-and-such a city, and the husband of the other was in such-and-such a city. Afterwards he greeted our holy grandfather, and said to him, 'Welcome, the rabbi of Chortkov.' . . . He [R. Hirsch] asked him, 'Why did you enter the toilet before you gave an answer to the wives, as to where their husbands are?' The Ba'al Shem Tov answered that when he is in a clean and pure place, his eyes see in the upper spheres and in the high places, but when he must look with his eyes in base places and the lower worlds, in order to seek some person in the latter, then he must enter the toilet, where he cannot gaze into the upper realms. Then he sees from one end of the lower world to the other end, and in this manner he found the husbands of those women.[25]

In other stories similar to the first version, the Ba'al Shem Tov rescues *agunot* whose husbands have become apostates. In one such tale it is related that when R. Jacob Joseph of Polonnoye became a follower of the Ba'al Shem Tov, an *agunah* came before the latter, seeking his help in locating her husband. The Ba'al Shem Tov went to the toilet, and upon his return told her that her husband had become an apostate. He advised her to travel to a certain place, where she would find her husband, and that he would be willing to give her a writ of divorce. When R. Jacob Joseph wondered why

[24] J. Sofer, *Sipurei ya'akov*, ii, §35, p. 111. In Mondshein, *Likutei reshimot uma'asiyot*, §4, p. 2, the Ba'al Shem Tov informs an *agunah* that he is unable to assist her, 'for your husband had died, without witnesses'. Cf. the report delivered by R. Barukh of Medzibezh to the tsadik of Shepetovka: 'I searched for your husband everywhere, from one end [of the world] to the other, even in perdition [i.e. Gehinnom], but I did not find him' (Lieberson, *Tseror haḥayim*, §49). For the toilet as a place of demons, see Tsevi Hirsch of Koidanov, *Kav hayashar*, §69. For the requirement that the tsadik think on other than holy matters while relieving himself, see Kohen, *Shemuot vesipurim*, §16: the Maggid of Mezirech revealed the identity of the thief to a person whose property had been stolen. The thief admitted: 'In truth, the rabbi saw what I stole, but cannot the rabbi see better acts than this?' The Maggid replied: 'I saw this while sitting in the toilet!'

[25] A. Michelson, *Shemen hatov*, 'Stories', §99; cf. the variant in §109; cf. also A. Stern, *Ḥutim hameshulashim*, 15.

he had answered the woman only after returning from the toilet, and why he did not wash his hands before speaking, the Ba'al Shem Tov replied,

Now, I searched for her husband in the *sitra dekedushah*, and I did not find him; I understood that he is in the *sitra detumah* [respectively, the side (or sphere) of holiness, and the side (sphere) of impurity]. Accordingly, I went to the toilet and I searched for him in the *sitra aḥra*, and I found him there, where he had become a heretic [i.e. converted to Christianity] . . . and I did not desire to speak of him after washing my hands.[26]

An additional story that mentions activity by the Ba'al Shem Tov on behalf of *agunot* uses the motif of handwashing to a different end. In this tale, not washing the hands is considered to be a flaw in the behaviour of the Ba'al Shem Tov, who needs to have resort to prophecy (which requires cleanness) in order to locate the deserting husbands. The reason given by the Ba'al Shem Tov for his conduct is that in such matters no time is to be wasted, not even for washing one's hands. (It is noteworthy that all these stories involve people who initially doubted the Ba'al Shem Tov, but who became his followers as a result of what they witnessed with their own eyes.)

Once the Ba'al Shem Tov was in a certain city, and the rabbi of the place was a great man, who did not believe in the Ba'al Shem Tov. When he heard the great things and wonders that were related of the Ba'al Shem Tov, he greatly desired to see him and speak with him, but he did not wish to detract from his honour by going to the Ba'al Shem Tov. He said that as he was the *mara de'atra* [rabbi of the city], it would be more fitting for the Ba'al Shem Tov to come to him, to his house. When this was reported to the Ba'al Shem Tov, he said, 'It is not enough that he does not come to me, to greet me, but he even wants me to go to him!' In the end, this rabbi went to the Ba'al Shem Tov. When he came to his room, the Ba'al Shem Tov was not there, having gone outside; and a certain woman, an *agunah*, was standing there waiting for him. When the Ba'al Shem Tov returned to his room, and took a vessel with water to wash his hands, this woman cried and importuned him urgently to give her an answer regarding her husband, not giving him time to wash his hands. The Ba'al Shem Tov informed her that her husband was at present in such-and-such a city, and that she should go there, where she would find him. The rabbi said to the Ba'al Shem Tov, 'If the words you speak are words of prophecy, should you not have first washed your hands, and afterwards spoken the words of prophecy to her?' The Ba'al Shem Tov replied, 'Now, when you see in your house that precious glass vessels are standing on the table, and roosters are jumping on the table and want to break the vessels, will you wait until you have washed your hands, and in the meantime let the vessels be broken? I see, may the Lord be blessed, that her husband is walking about in a certain city, and he is before my very eyes, just as the vessels and the roosters stand on the table, with you standing and seeing them. This woman is standing, bitter-hearted, and is screaming before me—can I wait until I have

26 Sobelman, *Sipurei tsadikim heḥadash*, §7. *Continued in Appendix.*

washed my hands? In the meantime, until I answer her, her heart is bitter and she suffers agonies, and by my telling her where her husband is, I have revived her soul!'[27]

The fundamental, troubling question in the life of the *agunah*, whose husband has vanished, was always: Is he still alive? If so, then she is still bound to him; whereas if he is dead, then she is a widow, and free to remarry. The following stories concern *agunot* who were released on the strength of direct or indirect testimony to the death of their husbands, including such testimony obtained by miraculous acts.

R. Moses Isserles, the famous Rema, freed an *agunah* whose husband had left six months earlier, because he himself had turned the husband into 'a pile of bones' (i.e. killed him), when he caught him engaging in adultery.[28] A similar story is told of R. Meir of Tiktin. In his time, a Jewish merchant and a Jewish woman pedlar used to go about together through the villages. When they vanished without trace one day, R. Meir freed the wife of the merchant and the husband of the pedlar from their marital bonds. The public did not understand why he had done this, but no one dared to ask their revered rabbi. Before his death R. Meir said that at the time it had been revealed to him by heaven that the cholera that was rampant in the city at the time had come as punishment for the sin of the merchant and the pedlar. The rabbi had taken the ritual slaughterer with him and together the two men had killed the couple when they were engaging in adultery in an abandoned ruin. The disease was curbed, but the rabbi feared that if he told what he had done someone would inform on him to the city governor, and he so waited to make this sensational revelation to his congregation until the day he died.[29]

An *agunah* came before R. Abraham Tartakower of Polotsk to be released as a result of the death of her husband. The rabbi wanted to free her, but was reluctant to rely on a single opinion, and so he sent a query to the leader of the Habad hasidic movement, R. Shneur Zalman of Lyady. The tsadik added at the end of his response the verse (Ps. 27: 5), 'He will hide me in his pavilion on an evil day, conceal me under the cover of his tent, raise me high upon a rock.' R. Abraham concluded from the letter that the tsadik did not agree with him that the *agunah* should be freed, but could not find any connection between this verse and the woman's case; nor could the scholars with whom he consulted offer any plausible answer. After some time, it occurred to him that the tsadik might have been suggesting that they search for the deserting husband in hiding places. Then it was recalled that the husband of the *agunah* had not left his place of residence, as so many other deserting husbands did,

[27] Chikernik, *Sipurim nehmadim*, 5–6.
[28] Rodkinsohn, *Adat tsadikim*, §23.
[29] See A. Michelson, *Shemen hatov*, 'Stories', §129. For a plague that afflicted children as punishment for adultery, see Kohen, *Shemuot vesipurim*, 230–1.

but had disappeared suddenly. It was also recalled that the courtyard of the *agunah*'s house contained an old ruin with a cellar that no one had entered for many years. In the ensuing search by candlelight, they discovered the body of the husband, his head crushed by a large rock. Now everyone understood the reason why the tsadik had appended the verse: there was no need to free the woman on the basis of a halakhic consideration. The man was indeed to be found in a hiding place—to which he had gone on 'an evil day', that is, when he had done some evil deed—with a rock on his head.[30]

This motif of scriptural inspiration for the resolution of the *agunah*'s situation appears also in the following story.

My father, of blessed memory, heard in Lubavitch of an instance in which an *agunah* came before my great uncle, the Tsemah Tsedek, and complained about her bitter fate. Her husband had vanished several years previously, leaving her no word. The rabbi, may his merit protect us, asked her whether at that time there was some hut built in their courtyard, to which she replied in the affirmative: there was an old booth there that had collapsed, and the bricks and wood remained, to the present, where they had fallen. He ordered her to go home and search under that pile of ruins, and so it was that his body was found under the ruins, where he had died, may the Merciful One save us. When the rabbi, may he rest in peace, heard his followers speaking about the 'miracle', he said that there was nothing miraculous here; rather, when the woman stood before him, he was studying the verse, 'He will hide me in his pavilion . . .', and he applied this verse to her situation.[31]

Again, when the Tsemah Tsedek was asked about a man and a woman who had vanished from a wedding celebration, he wrote in answer as follows: 'and an ox or an ass falls into it [i.e. a pit]' [Exod. 21: 33]. The hasid who brought the issue before the rebbe decided to search in the wedding hall where they had disappeared, and he found a wall that had fallen on these sinners (the man and woman were married, but not to each other).[32]

In the next story the deserting husband had died some time previously, but because this had not happened in the absence of witnesses his wife became an *agunah* and could not be released. During the time of R. Naphtali Katz, the rabbi of Posen, a deserting husband joined a band of thieves and murderers, initially under duress though he then stayed with them of his own free will. This husband was eventually killed by his fellows during a quarrel, but as there were no witnesses to the event his wife knew nothing of this. The *agunah* and her father repeatedly entreated R. Naphtali for his assistance. Finally the rabbi's compassion was aroused, and by means of his supernatural powers he succeeded in raising the dead husband from

[30] See Kaidaner, *Sipurim nora'im*, §63, pp. 145–6. For a letter that was delayed in transit, with the husband returning in the meantime, see Ehrmann, *Devarim arevim*, 'Stories of the Holy Rabbi, the Maggid of Koznitz', §3.

[31] A similar story is printed in Mondshein, *Migdal oz*, 258.

[32] Ibid. 202–3.

Gehinnom and bringing him back to life, so that he would be killed a second time, in the presence of the wife and Jewish witnesses, thereby enabling the release of the *agunah*.[33]

Family tragedies resulted from erroneous reports of a husband's death. Hasidic stories relate how the supernatural powers of the tsadik prevented such calamities.

A tsadik who sought to free an *agunah* from the city of Kalyus found that when he took a book in his hand to study, it fell to the ground. The tsadik pitied the woman and wanted to write the document releasing her, but 'the quill fell from his hand, and the ink spilled on the paper', from which he understood that her husband was still alive. Some time later she went to the marketplace in Jassy, where she encountered a man who called her by name. This person was none other than her husband, who gave her a writ of divorce.[34]

A similar version of the story is told about an *agunah* from Kalisz who came before R. Joseph Landau, a rabbi in Jassy, to request her release, but was turned away. The tsadik of Ruzhin gave her a letter of recommendation to R. Landau, who was his pupil, but he rejected her appeal this time, as well, explaining to the rabbi of Ruzhin that every time that he wanted to study a book it fell from his hand, and when he took up a pen to write, it too would fall from his hand. It later happened that the *agunah* found her husband in the marketplace in Jassy.[35] R. Joseph Landau, a great scholar, was the great-grandson of R. Menahem Mendel of Ber, and knew R. Levi Isaac of Berdichev and the rabbi of Apta.[36]

A similar 'warning' occurred when R. Meir Margoliouth of Ostrog, author of *Me'ir netivim*, decided to free an *agunah*. Because of the tremendous responsibility that such a decision entailed and the extreme gravity of the matter, he fasted before affixing his signature to the release. As he was about to sign the document, his hand shook, and the quill that he held between his fingers fell to the floor. He therefore refused to endorse the release, and fasted again; when he came to sign this second time, his hand began to shake again; and the same thing happened the third time, upon which the rabbi said to the woman, 'Your husband is alive!' She went out into the streets of the city, where she did indeed find her spouse.[37]

[33] J. Sofer, *Sipurei ya'akov*, i. 34–6. *Continued in Appendix.*

[34] M. Landau, *Toledot yosef*, 17–18.

[35] *Writings of the Early Hasidim* (Heb.), 36–7.

[36] At the age of 22 R. Joseph Landau served as rabbi of Litin and in Kamenets-Podolski, and afterwards, from 1834 to 1853, in Jassy, upon the recommendation of R. Israel of Ruzhin. See D. Assaf, *The Regal Way*, 146.

[37] Margolioth, *Kevutsat ya'akov*, fo. 60*a*; [Isaac Dov Baer ben Tsevi Hirsch], *Kahal ḥasidim heḥadash*, §55. Cf. Ben-Yehezkel, *Sefer hama'asiyot*, v. 177–8. Mondshein, *Likutei reshimot uma'asiyot*, §72, p. 14, depicts an instance in which R. Ezekiel Landau (the author of *Noda biyehudah*) released an *agunah*, while R. Shmelke of Nikolsburg ruled that she was still a married woman and also helped her to find her husband.

Another tsadik was prevented by different physical obstacles from erroneously giving an *agunah* her release before he discovered that the husband was still alive.

A query concerning an *agunah* was sent from Vilna to the holy *gaon*, the rabbi R. Heschel of Krakow, of blessed memory [the teacher of R. Shabetai ben Meir Hakohen (author of *Siftei kohen*, known as the Shakh), and of R. David ben Samuel Halevi (author of *Turei zahav*, known as the Taz)]. He was inclined to free her. This was in the year 1648, which was a time of crisis, in the period of Chmielnicki, may his name be blotted out. The emissary who was sent with the release returned; he could not enter Vilna because of the disorder caused by the troops. This happened several times, and each time the emissary brought the release back to R. Heschel, who could not fathom the meaning of this wonder. He travelled a little way outside the city of Krakow to compose himself and to examine the matter once again, and a certain young man came and stopped him, saying, 'How can the rabbi travel with *kila'im* [mixed species of plants, which may not be planted together]? For a dog is tied underneath the carriage [see *Shulḥan arukh*, 'Yoreh de'ah' 297: 15].' When the rabbi saw that the young man was learned, he set out before him the case of the woman's release. The young man disputed his opinion, arguing that the woman should not be freed. After a lengthy casuistical discussion, the young man said, 'How can the *agunah* be released if her husband is alive and well, and stands and argues with the rabbi?' R. Heschel understood that the Lord, may he be blessed, had saved him from committing a halakhic error, may his Maker be praised.[38]

The opposite also happened when a case concerning an *agunah* came before R. Ezekiel ben Judah Landau, author of *Noda biyehudah*, who ruled against releasing her. The rabbi of Shepetovka told him to free the woman. R. Ezekiel asked him, 'Who are you?' to which the rabbi replied, 'I am the most insignificant of the pupils of R. Jacob Joseph, author of *Toledot* [*ya'akov yosef*]!' Afterwards, R. Zusya came to the court of R. Landau when the *agunah* requested permission to remarry. R. Landau said, 'I cannot release you, perhaps the poor one [R. Zusya] can help you.' R. Zusya examined the case and freed her, while the following day R. Landau also studied the case. They went to the river, where they saw the woman's (dead) husband among the passengers on the boats there. The husband told the rabbinical court that R. Zusya had come to him in a dream and demanded that he tell the court that he had abandoned his wife. What had happened was this: the husband had gone to a faraway land, where he had fallen ill, and had a will drawn up before he died. The local rabbi forgot to send the will back to his wife, and all trace of the dead husband was lost. The details of the case were examined and found to be true, and the woman was released.[39]

38 Moskowitz, *Otsar hasipurim*, xx, §19.

39 Ehrmann, *Devarim arevim*, 'Stories of the Holy Brothers R. Elimelekh and R. Zusya', §9.

Another tale about a husband who was in fact still alive is told about R. Jacob Lorbeerbaum, the *gaon* of Lissa. The rabbi wrote a responsum freeing an *agunah*, but when he was about to sign the document the inkwell fell over on it, and the rabbi set his ruling aside. A few days later the 'dead' man appeared in the city.[40] Again, a woman from the Maramaros district came before R. Eliezer Ze'ev of Kshanev to receive his blessing. She had been an *agunah* for eighteen years, and after much effort and exertion had obtained permission to remarry. When the tsadik heard her request, he disclosed to her that her husband was alive, that a letter would arrive from him shortly, and that after that he would himself return; and all this happened as he had predicted.[41]

Once an *agunah* went to R. Meir of Tiktin and, in a state of extreme agitation, asked him to release her. R. Meir replied that the rabbi of the city from which she came was responsible for her release, while the latter said that R. Meir should begin the deliberations. R. Meir argued that he was not inclined to free the *agunah*, since it was revealed to him from heaven that her husband was still alive. He was forced, however, to assure her that if her husband did not return within three months he would issue her the release. The husband did indeed return, and thus the problem was resolved.[42]

A different case involved R. Shmelke of Tarnow (the grandfather of R. Samuel Shmelke of Nikolsburg), who freed an *agunah* and only afterwards was informed from heaven that her husband was still alive. He demanded that the woman not remarry, despite his ruling, but this aroused the ire of the community worthies, who argued that once he had released the woman he could not countermand his decision. R. Shmelke died of his distress over this incident, and from the next world he demanded, on pain of death, that the husband immediately return to his home. His return, unfortunately, did not solve the problem, for in the meantime the woman had borne a son to her new husband.[43]

In another story that begins with similar circumstances but ends differently the leading Torah scholar of the time releases an *agunah*, only for her deserting husband to appear on the day of her remarriage. This causes a great commotion, but the rabbi asserts, 'The Torah is not in heaven [i.e. though the Torah is of heavenly origin, it was given to human beings to

[40] T. E. Michelson, *Toledot ya'akov*, §48, pp. 13–14.

[41] T. H. Rosenberg, *Raza de'uvda*, 'Sha'ar ha'otiyot', 113–14.

[42] See A. Michelson, *Shemen hatov*, 'Stories', §123. Cf. Mondshein, *Likutei reshimot uma'asiyot*, §13, pp. 3–4: an *agunah* came before R. Meir Hafets with testimony taken by *dayanim*, and asked him to release her. The rabbi was inclined to grant her request, but he sent a messenger to the 'Old Rebbe' to ask his opinion. The tsadik rejected the grant of permission to remarry and advised waiting for two weeks—and within this period, the husband returned.

[43] Samuel of Shinova, *Ramatayim tsofim*, §117, p. 16; [Isaac Dov Baer ben Tsevi Hirsch], *Kahal ḥasidim heḥadash*, §76; A. Michelson, *Shemen hatov*, 'Stories', §159; id., *Ohel naftali*, §92. See also Z. Horowitz, *Horowitz Family* (Heb.), 61–2.

interpret and apply]. I released the woman by Torah law, and if her husband came after the release, as he came—so shall he go!' and the deserting husband immediately died.[44]

When the tsadik R. Feivel was appointed rabbi and head of the rabbinical court in Gritza, a long-standing *agunah* and a single witness who attested to her husband's death came before him. After investigating the matter the tsadik was willing to free her, but he nevertheless sent a letter to his teacher, R. Jacob of Lissa, asking his opinion. His teacher's reply was that under no circumstances was the woman to be released, lest the law be perverted. R. Feivel summoned the *agunah* and informed her that he could not free her, advising her to await her husband's return. Instead of doing so, the woman went instead to another city, where the local rabbi permitted her to remarry. After she had borne sons and daughters to her new husband, the first husband returned. The rabbi ruled that 'she must be divorced from each [husband], and her children from the second [husband] are *mamzerim*', thus revealing to all that the rabbi of Lissa possessed the spirit of divine inspiration.[45]

In another case R. Jacob Samson of Shepetovka refused to release an *agunah*, arguing that the testimony to her husband's presumed death was faulty. The husband eventually returned, and the rabbi's wisdom was commonly acknowledged.[46] The following story depicts a similar chain of events.

A certain merchant from Hamburg sailed on a ship, accompanied by his friend. They were seized by pirates from the land of Algeria and put up for sale in the slave market. The master who purchased them gave each a plot of land to harrow and plant. He allotted a certain amount of time for them to complete their labours, telling them that if they did not finish in time they would be put to death. The merchant, who was pampered and soft, could not perform his work, to which he was unaccustomed. His master took him to be executed, but forgot his knife, and therefore tied him to a tree while he returned home and fetched it. In the meantime the merchant's friend came to talk with him before he died. The merchant asked him to attend to his burial, which he promised to do, and the friends took tearful leave of one another.

In the meantime, another master passed by with a negro slave whom he had bought in the slave market. He asked the merchant who had tied him to the tree, and the latter replied that he was condemned for failing to complete his work, having been unable to do so because as an important merchant he was used to soft

[44] Ehrmann, *Devarim arevim*, 'Stories of the Holy Rabbi, the Maggid of Koznitz', §3.

[45] See Frankel and Frankel, *Ḥen tov zevaḥ tov*, 'Kunteres aḥaron', fo. 149*c*, for a non-hasidic response to the activity by tsadikim relating to *agunot*.

[46] Sobelman, *Sipurei tsadikim heḥadash*, §27. Cf. Emden, *Megilat sefer*, 6–7, who relates that reliable witnesses testified that an old man had been killed, and a great rabbi released the wife. Some time later, it was learned that the witnesses had erred; but, fortunately for the elderly couple, the husband returned home before his wife remarried.

living. The master took a liking to him and released him from his bonds, tying up his negro slave instead. He took the merchant with him and went on his way.

Then the first master came back, with his knife in his hand, and straight away cruelly attacked and killed the person tied to the tree, without looking to see if this was indeed his slave. The merchant's friend kept his promise and buried the dead man, without knowing his identity.

Some time later, the merchant's friend escaped from slavery and returned to Hamburg. He recounted what had happened to the *gaon* R. . . . Horowitz, who permitted the merchant's wife to remarry, after engaging in halakhic discussions with the great Torah scholars of the land. A match was arranged for the woman with one of the prominent men of the city, for she was extremely wealthy. The couple wrote an announcement in the journals to proclaim their marriage, as was the practice of the monied classes. The merchant [assumed to be dead] was in America at the time, and he too had become very wealthy. When he saw in the journals that his wife had been permitted to remarry he was very grieved. He left behind all his wealth and travelled to Hamburg, where he arrived on his wife's wedding night. He came to the *gaon* R. [Horowitz], wept bitterly, and told him all that he had undergone. When he [the rabbi] heard this, he threw himself to the ground and tore at his hair, for he thought that a prohibited act for which he was responsible had certainly already been committed, and he lay on the floor in a swoon for half the night. After that, he arose and said that he had been informed from heaven that no prohibition, heaven forbid, had yet been committed [i.e. the newly married couple had not yet engaged in sexual relations]. This was so, and the next day he [the merchant] returned to his home, that is, his wife, hale and hearty.[47]

The difficulties entailed in finding a missing husband and obtaining a writ of divorce from him created many opportunities for swindlers. A wealthy man's daughter from the vicinity of Vienna married a young Torah scholar, the son of poor parents. Before long their home was the scene of many quarrels. The women neighbours egged the wife on against her husband, and she began to hate him. Eventually the young man fled his wife's persecution, leaving her an *agunah*. In the end the woman regretted her actions and went to her father, blaming him for everything. A young man in the city, who desired the beautiful *agunah*, offered the father his services in finding the deserting husband or, alternatively, in obtaining from him a writ of divorce. To be on the safe side, the father of the *agunah* sent another person with this young man, and promised generous compensation to them if they were successful, either in finding the deserting husband or in obtaining a writ of divorce from him. In a distant city the two emissaries found an accomplice, who agreed to pretend that he was the deserting husband. He was brought before a rabbinical court in that city and, after initially feigning stubborn

[47] A. Michelson, *Shemen hatov*, §168, quoted from *Matamei yitshak*; also cited in id., *Ohel naftali*, §225; see also §246.

opposition, finally consented to grant a writ of divorce to 'his *agunah*'. The agents immediately returned, quite happily, to their city, bringing the long-awaited writ of divorce to the father of the *agunah*. Now the young man intended to marry the woman himself, and her father went to R. Samson Weiner to inform him of this. The tsadik, however, sensed that something was not right with the writ of divorce and delayed the wedding. In the meantime, the deserting husband decided to return home, so that, thanks to R. Samson, it was proven to all that the writ of divorce was false.[48]

Another version of the story was told by R. Shalom of Belz, and was communicated to the author of *Sipurei ya'akov* by one of his sources. A single passage from the story will suffice for present purposes.

> The young man Israel became the son-in-law of this rich man. After some years R. Israel was despised by his wife, and thought to himself: 'Why should I be here? My wife, my father-in-law, and my mother-in-law look at me as if I were a thorn in their sides. It would be better for me to go away and be a teacher, and live a life of tranquillity.' And, having resolved to take this action, he did so. He moved several parasangs away and was accepted as a tutor in the house of a rich man, who was a follower of the Ba'al Shem Tov, where he taught for some years. R. Israel's wife regretted what she had done to her husband: she was sorry for having caused him to flee from her, leaving her an *agunah*.
>
> Then a fiendishly wicked preacher came from the land of Lithuania, and learned that the rich man's daughter had become an *agunah* and was bereft. He therefore went to the rich man and said, 'I know where he is, in which city he teaches, and if you wish, I will bring a writ of divorce from him for your daughter.' The rich man responded, 'If you will succeed in bringing a writ of divorce for my daughter, I will pay you generously for your trouble.'

In the continuation of the tale, the preacher (who wants his son to marry the rich man's daughter) finds another scoundrel who agrees to pretend that he is R. Israel, the deserting husband. He also finds two false witnesses who testify that this impostor is the deserting husband, and thereby obtains a writ of divorce from the rabbinical court. Meanwhile the deserting husband, R. Israel, travels with his employer to the Ba'al Shem Tov, who reveals to him that he has been informed from heaven that his *agunah* is about to marry another man. The Ba'al Shem Tov advises R. Israel to turn to the non-Jewish court and tell them everything that has happened, and to give the court

[48] Bodek, *Pe'er mikedoshim*, §9, pp. 17–21. A falsification of another sort was committed when, after an *agunah* had been permitted to remarry, the enemies of her second husband forged a letter that, so it was claimed, had been written by the first husband. However, the rabbi who had released the *agunah* revealed the forgery. He related: 'Before I released the *agunah*, I examined the matter thoroughly, and I was certain that there would be no adverse consequences. . . . Moreover, even if her first husband were still alive, he would have passed away when I released her' (Donner, *Sha'ar ha'emunah*, introd., quoting from the end of *Meshivat nefesh*).

official two ducats. This he does: the official then comes to the wedding ceremony, slaps the preacher and his son on the face, and arrests both of them. He then presents R. Israel to the guests, and they all bear witness that he is the *agunah*'s husband. When the official realizes that the preacher had falsified the writ of divorce, he orders that he and his son be whipped. R. Israel returns in peace to the city of Reisha.[49]

Of especial importance is the hasidic story on which S. Y. Agnon based his well-known story 'Vehayah he'akov lemishor' [And the Crooked Shall Be Made Straight].[50] The plot concerns an *agunah* whose husband has travelled far away, taking a letter of recommendation in order to collect charity and raise the money necessary to restore his family's finances. His wife has heard nothing from him in his absence. After the letter of recommendation is sold (or, in another version, stolen) and the purchaser (or thief) has died, the deserting husband is assumed dead; his wife is released from her status as an *agunah* and remarries.

There are three extant versions of this story, one in Yiddish and two in Hebrew. The first, entitled 'Der yored' (The One Who Came Down in the World), was written by M. Dyk (version A).[51] The second version (B) is reproduced here in its entirety;[52] the third version (C), which differs from the first two, was first printed in the anonymous book *Ma'aseh hakedoshim*.[53]

The following is the text of version B.

In the city of Nikolsburg, in the time of R. Shmelke, lived a rich man named Israel Abraham Pokanti, who was generous and gave money to the poor. As time passed, he lost all his property and became penniless. He resolved to travel to other cities far away to restore his livelihood, by collecting charity from generous Israelites.

Knowing that the name of the rabbi R. Shmelke was widely known, and that upon hearing his name all desired [to give a proper donation], he presented himself and requested a letter of recommendation openly attesting to his honesty and

[49] J. Sofer, *Sipurei ya'akov*, ii, §55, pp. 171–2; for an additional writ of divorce of which a rabbi disapproves, see M. M. Walden, *Ohel yitsḥak*, 86. See Ben-Yehezkel, *Sefer hama'asiyot*, v. 179–87.

[50] Agnon, *Elu ve'elu*, 61–127. Agnon wrote the story in four days, at the age of 24, and it was first published in instalments in the bi-weekly/weekly periodical *Hapo'el hatsa'ir* in 1912. (Agnon writes of an *agunah* who went to the second R. Meir of Premishlan in his story 'Bilevav yamim': *Elu ve'elu*, 504–5.)

[51] Published in 1855 in Warsaw. The possible connection between this story and Agnon's literary product was first identified by Ya'ari, 'Miscellaneous Bibliographical Notes' (Heb.), 502. In his article 'From Popular Story to Literary Story' (Heb.), Ya'ari writes: 'Unquestionably, Agnon did not see Dyk's notebook, but they both drew upon a single source.' See also Nigal, 'Hasidic Elements in a Work by Agnon' (Heb.).

[52] A. Michelson, *Shemen hatov*, 'Stories', §51.

[53] *Ma'aseh hakedoshim*, §12; repr. in *Ma'asiyot mehagedolim vehatsadikim*, 24–6; also appears in Slodovnik, *Ma'aseh hagedolim heḥadash*, §29, p. 55. See Ben-Yehezkel, *Sefer hama'asiyot*, v. 188–93, 194–8, for both versions (with minor stylistic changes).

virtue, saying that when he was wealthy he had given from his money to the destitute and beseeching the benevolent to repay him in kind, so that everywhere he went money would be collected for him, and people would look kindly upon him at every opportunity.

R. Shmelke replied that he was not accustomed to write letters of recommendation for anyone. [Reb Israel Abraham] was not satisfied with this, and argued that an exception should be made in his case on the basis of fairness: the rabbi R. Shmelke, he said, knew very well his former condition, and that when he was a wealthy man he gave abundant charity to whomsoever requested it; so how could he not now have compassion on him in his distress, seeing him suffering from want and hunger?

Faced with so earnest an entreaty, R. Shmelke was compelled to tell Israel Abraham openly that he had to turn him down, for he saw that such a letter would be of no use to the petitioner, and could even be to his disadvantage. When he saw that all his words were to no avail, Israel Abraham tried a different approach. He went to his old friend the head of the city [*prezident*],[54] and pleaded with him to act on his behalf, to go to the rabbi and forcefully demand that he fulfil his request. The official consented, and went to the rabbi and demanded of him why he did not take pity on this poor unfortunate, who could be saved by a few lines from him. The rabbi immediately responded that he could not agree to Pokanti's request, because misfortune would come to him as a result. The head of the city was not satisfied, and was emphatic in his demand that the rabbi, R. Shmelke, nevertheless do as Pokanti wished, threatening that if he did not do so he [the official] would have his revenge. Without saying another word, R. Shmelke immediately wrote a letter of recommendation for Israel Abraham Pokanti and put it in his hand, stipulating that immediately upon his return home he [Pokanti] would return the letter to him. Reb Israel Abraham Pokanti put the letter of recommendation in his pocket, and travelled to places where he was not known. Thanks to the letter of recommendation by R. Shmelke he collected substantial sums of money, for the rabbi had many admirers and followers, and when they saw that he supported Pokanti's case people were willing to aid the traveller wherever he went.

After Reb Israel Abraham Pokanti had collected a considerable sum of money, he decided to return home and pick up his former business activities. When he was on the way, he heard from an innkeeper that the rabbi R. Shmelke had passed away, and his voice had been stilled for ever. He believed the report and thought to himself, 'Now I have been freed from the promise that I made to the rabbi R. Shmelke to return his letter to him', and before he reached the city of Nikolsburg he sold the letter of recommendation to a passer-by. The person who bought the letter began to rove through the countryside under the name of Israel Abraham Pokanti, and he too collected a great deal of money, before he died in a certain city. After his death the people of that city searched through his clothes and found money, other possessions, and also the letter from R. Shmelke, all of which they sent to Nikolsburg, to the address of Israel Abraham Pokanti. When the latter's wife received the money and possessions, and also the letter from the rabbi

[54] Parentheses in the original.

R. Shmelke, together with a letter informing her that Israel Abraham Pokanti had died in that far-off city, she thought that her husband was certainly dead, and she married another man from a different city.

As for Israel Abraham Pokanti himself, while he was still in that village not very far from the city of Nikolsburg robbers came and took from him all the money that he had with him, and he was left naked and penniless. Thus he was forced to go about in the world a second time and collect charity, for his shame prevented him from returning home empty-handed. But he could not do this in an honourable manner as he had before, when he had possessed the recommendation by the rabbi R. Shmelke; this time he was just another common beggar. Eventually, on his way home, he happened to come to a city that was close to Nikolsburg, and heard that there was a circumcision banquet there. Together with the other visitors in the city he went to the banquet, where the new mother herself handed out sweets and dishes to every guest. When it was the turn of Israel Abraham Pokanti, her real husband, she recognized him, and swooned out of grief and suffering; only after great efforts were made to revive her did she regain consciousness. None of those present knew what this was all about, and only later did it become common knowledge. 'Now I admit', Israel Abraham Pokanti declared, 'that the rabbi R. Shmelke spoke truthfully, that his letter of recommendation would be to my disadvantage.' The *prezident* who had dared to threaten the rabbi R. Shmelke was struck with paralysis until his dying day. And this was for a wonder.

Versions A and B are very similar, and both differ in many details from version C. In the first two versions the plot begins in Nikolsburg, in the time of R. Samuel Shmelke, the city rabbi, while version C occurs in Prague, during the time of R. Ezekiel Landau. The name of the newly impoverished merchant is almost identical in versions A and B: in the Yiddish version, Tsadok ben Abraham Pokanti; in version B, Israel Abraham Pokanti. Version C, in contrast, provides only a first name (Solomon), with no mention of a last name. The rabbi's attitude towards the writing of a letter of recommendation is definitely negative in the two similar versions, for the same reason (the letter will have adverse consequences for its bearer); in version C the rabbi writes it willingly and without hesitation. In versions A and B the letter is sold by its subject (according to A, to a preacher, and according to B, to a passer-by), while in version C the letter is stolen by a cunning preacher of Russian origin, who even desecrates the sabbath in order to make a fast getaway with his booty. In all three versions the new possessor of the letter dies some time later and the letter is discovered among his possessions; the Jewish community learns of his (erroneous) identity from the letter of recommendation, and informs the city rabbi (the composer of the letter) and the family of his death. Version A has the preacher dying in Nemours, France, with the *agunah* arriving with her only son, who is 16 years old, to receive his money and possessions. According to this version, therefore, the couple were not childless; indeed, it begins with them pleading with the rabbi to take pity on them and on their child (in the Yiddish: *und oif zeire kleine kinder*). The couple also have children in version C, since after the death of the possessor of the letter, the rabbi gives the remaining money to the wife 'so that it shall be for her and for the fruit of her loins, for their livelihood'. Version B, on the other hand, makes no mention of any offspring. According to versions A and B Pokanti is robbed after the sale of the letter and is forced to continue collecting alms; otherwise, he would have directly returned home, and the tragic ending would have been avoided. Version A is the most detailed regarding his second period of wandering, undoubtedly because the geographical details were important to its author, M. Dyk. This version relates that Pokanti went to Vilna, where he met someone from his city who persuaded him to return home, and even gave him money to this end.

In each version the hero returns to his city without being recognized, either because he arrives in the dark (version A), or because his appearance has changed as a result of the hardships he has undergone. In all the versions he arrives on the day of the circumcision of his wife's son. According to version C, the woman (who was then aged 55) vowed at the time of her second marriage that if, at her advanced age, she were to give birth to a son, she would host a banquet for the poor. The meeting of the deserting husband and his wife occurs while the new mother is distributing money (version A) or sweets and food (version B) to the poor. According to version A, the man sought to flee, but was restrained by those present. Version B has him asking to see the face of the new mother, a request that is approved by the rabbi. In each version the wife recognizes her husband and faints. In version C she faints and dies, but the rabbi prays and she comes back to life. At the end of Version A of the story Pokanti is driven out of the city; the rabbi punishes those who compelled him to sign the letter of recommendation and orders that the episode be recorded for posterity in the city register. According to version B, Pokanti admits that the rabbi was right, for the letter was indeed detrimental for him, and the *prezident* who forced the rabbi to sign is paralysed for the rest of his life. In version C the wife is divorced by both husbands.

It is quite possible that Dyk made use of a written source, which means there must have been an earlier version that no longer exists. If there was no such written (or printed) source, it may be assumed that Dyk heard the story and committed it to writing, as did the authors of *Shemen hatov* and *Ma'aseh hakedoshim*. The absence from the story of clearly hasidic motifs enabled the hasidic collector to attribute it to R. Ezekiel Landau, who was known for his opposition to hasidism, while a maskil author could ascribe it to a rabbi belonging to the hasidic camp (albeit not one with a typical hasidic 'court'). Agnon, too, in 'Vehayah he'akov lemishor', portrays the rabbi in the story not as a hasidic tsadik, but as the rabbi of the city; indeed, the question of *agunot* was a general Jewish concern, not one specific to hasidim.

It would seem that we now possess the first version of the story, which Dyk (and possibly Agnon too) might have heard. At the end of this version, which was first printed fairly recently, is a record of the transmission of the story from one generation to another. This record reads as follows:

This was told by R. Dubrovsky, of blessed memory, in the name of our teacher and master, R. David Tsevi Hen, may the memory of the righteous be for a blessing, who heard it from his father, our teacher and master, R. Peretz, may the memory of the righteous be for a blessing, in the name of the holy rabbi R. Hayim Abraham, may the memory of the righteous be for a blessing, who heard it from his father, who is our great master, the Old Rebbe [R. Shneur Zalman of Lyady].[55]

Such a precise list of transmitters has the ring of authenticity, an impression strengthened by the fact that the Old Rebbe, who is not known as one of the transmitters of the hasidic story, is the first in the chain of transmission, and by the circumstances in which the story was related, which deserve to be quoted here in full.

When the Old Rebbe was ill, heaven save us, he was required to take baths. When he was sitting in the bath, his holy sons would sit with him and talk with him about tsadikim (apparently so that he would not think of words of Torah [which is forbidden under such circumstances]). On one such occasion they mentioned the holy *gaon*, R. Shmelke of Nikolsburg. Our holy master immediately told them, 'Shh! Shh! Do not speak of him.' When he left the bath, he told them why he had stopped them and would not allow them to speak of him: because he did not wish to speak in the bath of a man of God who actually revived the dead. He then told them the following story.

When R. Shmelke was in Nikolsburg, there was a certain worthy man there whose fortunes had been reversed and had come down in the world, so much so that he did not even have the wherewithal for a loaf of bread. He requested of the holy *gaon* R. Shmelke that he give him a letter in which he would write so that people should aid him wherever he came and give him generous donations, so that he would not be forced to go from house to house. The holy rabbi consented to his request, and gave him such a letter. His letter naturally was very effective, and wherever he went he was not forced to go from door to door, and he was given substantial contributions. After he had collected a satisfactory amount, he was about to return to his city when he met in the hotel a poor man who had set out to collect charity for his sustenance and the sustenance of the members of his family. When this man learned that the other person had a letter from the holy rabbi R. Shmelke, he proposed, 'Here, you are going home, and you have no further need of the letter, sell it to me for whatever price you please. Benefit will come from this for both of us: I will not be forced to go begging from door to door, and you will gain a sum of money.' The first man agreed, and sold him R. Shmelke's letter for a satisfactory price.

[55] Kohen, *Shemuot vesipurim*, 210.

The pauper who purchased the letter died a few days later, and when the burial society found in his pocket the letter by R. Shmelke, they thought that he was the first poor man. They sent to his house a message that he had died; the wife thought that her husband had passed away, the rabbinical court permitted her to remarry, and she married a wealthy man. All of the money of her first husband, who was about to return to his home, was stolen from him, nor did he have the letter any longer. And so he was left without anything, and he was forced to go begging from door to door for pennies. Once again he went around the towns as before, but without the letter he received only paltry sums. As soon as he had collected a small amount of money he decided to go home, and when he arrived in his city, he heard of all that had transpired in his house. He was told that his wife had remarried, a son had been born to her, and the day of the circumcision had arrived.

He, too, went to the circumcision and sat among the paupers. People did not recognize him because his countenance had changed, and also because of the rags in which he was dressed, which altered his appearance. And now, as he was sitting at the table, among the other poor people, he began to cry, and ate nothing. The new father asked him, 'Why are you weeping?' He replied, 'I wish to see the new mother, I cannot eat until I see her.' The father, out of the goodness of his heart, and also so as not to impair his joy and that of the relatives, led the pauper to the new mother, and left him at the entrance to her room. When the new mother saw her former husband, her soul left her and she died, heaven forbid.

There was great turmoil, until this became known to the holy *gaon*, R. Shmelke, who became extremely agitated and said with great force, 'The woman is in no way guilty, she married with full permission, and this disgrace that has come about is solely the fault of the man, who sold the letter. I therefore decree the opposite: that the man shall die, and she shall live!'

'And so it was', the Old Rebbe finished his tale, 'that when I was in the bath I did not wish to speak of such a man, who actually revived the dead.'[56]

Notwithstanding the gravity of the matter and the danger of family tragedy resulting from the release of *agunot*, Torah scholars and tsadikim did everything in their power to free such women from their unfortunate lot. In one case the rabbi of Kovla and others were unsuccessful in finding a release on halakhic grounds for an *agunah*. When his *meḥutan* R. Abraham of Trisk came to him, he studied various halakhic works and marked a certain page in one of the books. When the *agunah* came before him, in tears, he asked the rabbi of Kovla, 'Why do you not take pity on a daughter of Israel and free her from being an *agunah*?' The latter apologetically explained that he had searched many times for grounds for release, but had not found any. R. Abraham told him to study the book whose page he had marked, where he did indeed find halakhic support for releasing the *agunah*.[57]

[56] Ibid. 209–10: R. Shmelke of Nikolsburg revives the dead. See Nigal, 'Hasidic Elements in a Work by Agnon' (Heb.).

[57] Chikernik, *Sipurim uma'amarim yekarim*, 27–8. Cf. ibid. 28–9, for a similar episode that occurred in Zhitomir.

APPENDIX

The phenomenon of *agunot* in more recent times is attested in the following passage, which appeared in *Maḥazikei hadat* (the weekly paper of the Belz hasidim), Lvov, on 4 October 1907.

'*Takanat* [an announcement of an] *agunah*'

A certain person from here, Falk (Philip) Mayerson, left six months ago to travel to Galicia, to earn from his profession of playing the harmonica instrument, and left his wife and their two daughters without prop and stay. We were explicitly informed that he played in Lvov with some singers or musicians, and then journeyed on from there. Accordingly, she bitterly cries to the readers of *Maḥazikei hadat* in Lvov and in Galicia, that anyone who knows him should delay him in any way possible and to send information here, to the address below, and this will be regarded as a great and magnificent mitzvah.

His distinguishing marks are: his age, twenty-eight years—of average height, with yellow [blond] hair, cleanshaven—thin in appearance—shortsighted in one of his eyes, with a conspicuous scar from an operation in his youth.

Bert Drimer, Rabiner Dorohoi (Romaenien)

SIX

A LIFE OF SIN

ADULTERY is viewed in the hasidic story as a grave sin that brings down harsh punishment on the community at large. An act of adultery was considered to be the cause of the plague that raged in Krakow during the time of R. Moses Isserles, when 'one of the wealthy men of the city [was] engaging in licentious behaviour with two women, each of whom was married to someone in the city';[1] in another instance an epidemic broke out because of a man who was having a sexual relationship with a married woman.[2] The hasidic tsadik appears in these tales as the voice of moral authority, calling those who have gone astray back to the straight and narrow;[3] among the manifestations of his greatness is his ability to reveal adulterers.

In some stories of adultery and other sexual misconduct the woman is portrayed as being the sinner; in others, the blame falls on the man. Many include the motifs of seduction, on the one hand, and of withstanding temptation, on the other. There is a predominant tendency, however, to paint the woman in a negative light. The few stories telling of women who withstood temptation are greatly outnumbered by the accounts of those who could not resist, or even initiated the seduction.[4] The latter include women who came to despise their married life and deserted their husbands.[5] In such instances the tsadik helps the betrayed husbands, just as he comes to the assistance of *agunot*.[6]

Once a certain man, whose wife had deserted him several years previously, came to his honoured holiness [R. Menahem Mendel of Lubavitch] and desired to receive

1 Rodkinsohn, *Adat tsadikim*, §23. Cf. *Ma'asiyot mehagedolim vehatsadikim*, 63.

2 *Ma'aseh hakedoshim*, §9.

3 See e.g. the admonishment by R. Zusya of Hanipoli in Bodek(?), *Sipurei kedoshim*, §4; the reproof by R. Elimelekh in Rosenthal, *Hitgalut hatsadikim*, 79; and a story that caused an adulterer to repent: Brandwein, *Degel mahaneh yehudah*, §55.

4 See Jacob Joseph of Polonnoye, *Toledot ya'akov yosef*, fo. 200*b*; I. Safrin, 'Netiv mitsvoteikha', 'Shevil emunah', §§1–2; Shenkel, *Ma'asiyot nora'im venifla'im*, §8; Ben-Yehezkel, *Sefer hama'asiyot*, iii. 310–19, 434; Piekarz, *Bratslav Hasidism* (Heb.), 104–5; Nigal, 'A Hasidic Manuscript' (Heb.), 840 n. 46. For a God-fearing woman who was not tempted by a sorcerer see Shenkel, *Ma'asiyot nora'im venifla'im*, §2 (see Ch. 10 n. 45 below).

5 Bodek[?], *Sipurei kedoshim*, §12, relates a story of adultery that originated in *Gesta Romanorum*.

6 See also Ch. 5 above.

from his honoured holiness permission to take another wife. His honoured holiness told him: 'We shall examine this matter. Perhaps you will not need this permission. For, in truth, it is not common that a wife deserts her husband. If so, then she undoubtedly was wanton and belongs in a house of prostitution; perhaps you will find her there!' The man asked him [sceptically]: 'Shall I search all the houses of prostitution in the land?' He replied: 'None the less, check once. Now, the large city of Vitebsk is close by, perhaps you shall find her there?' The man did so: he went to houses of prostitution, where they have taverns. He asked for whisky and fish, which he received. Afterwards, he paid with a silver rouble for what he had eaten, and he was given small coins in change. The owner said: 'Rebeka, give the man change from the silver rouble!'—this was his wife. When she saw him and recognized him, she straight away fainted and fell to the floor. The man immediately went outside and gathered some people, so that she could not flee. Afterwards, she confessed and took a writ of divorce from him.[7]

In another case a husband whose wife had deserted him came before R. Menahem Mendel, who sent him to search for her in distant regions. In the course of his travels he happened to come to the house of the local rabbi in a certain town as the same time as a woman who had come to ask the rabbi to conduct her wedding ceremony. The woman claimed that she was divorced, but had lost the writ annulling her marriage. The husband recognized his wife, and gave her the writ of divorce that she wanted.[8]

Another story concerns the wife of a tailor from the city of Pest who 'left him abandoned' (*me'ugan*, literally 'anchored': the term is usually applied to women in such a plight). In this instance, too, the husband wished to give his wife a writ of divorce, but did not know where she was. When he came to the tsadik of Sanz he was the subject of general derision, but the tsadik instructed him to travel to R. Abraham Isaac, the head of the Kleinwardein rabbinical court, where he would obtain the writ. But when he arrived in Kleinwardein, everyone who heard his story merely laughed at him, and he went home, empty-handed. A few days later, however, the deserting wife came to the rabbis, apologized for her actions, and agreed to be divorced. The rabbi wrote to Pest, the tailor came back to Kleinwardein, and the writ of divorce was duly issued.[9]

These stories do not give the reasons for the wife's flight from her home, but others contain various allusions to the reasons leading up to her adultery. One woman was seduced by a member of a band of travelling actors and went away with him, leaving her husband in the lurch.[10] Other women

[7] Kaidaner, *Sipurim nora'im*, §60, p. 141.

[8] Mondshein, *Likutei reshimot uma'asiyot*, §47, p. 9.

[9] See Teomim, *Ateret tiferet*, 'His Holiness, the Holy Rabbi, R. Hayim Halberstam of Sanz', §44.

[10] J. Sofer, *Sipurei ya'akov*, ii, §61, p. 183. Thanks to the efforts of the tsadik of Sanz, the husband found his wife and gave her a writ of divorce.

engaged in sexual liaisons while still living at home; some of them seduced men, or sought to do so.

In some instances these acts of infidelity were committed with non-Jews;[11] it may be assumed, for example, that the itinerant actor mentioned above was not Jewish. A story of the adultery of a married woman with a priest, which originated in a medieval Christian collection, made its way into a hasidic collection, with the woman now a Jew.[12] Another tale depicts a Jewish woman who bore a son to a non-Jew and killed the child.[13] Once R. Solomon of Karlin was asked by a villager to officiate as *sandak* and circumciser for his son. When the tsadik asked the villager what name he wished to give the child, he answered: 'Ivan Ivanovich [i.e. Ivan the son of Ivan].' When the new mother heard what her husband said, she confessed that she had engaged in relations with a non-Jew, and that the child was not her husband's.[14]

These stories depict the infidelity of married women. Others give accounts of unmarried woman who acted immodestly. A young woman claiming to be a virgin who had been possessed by a dybbuk was sent by R. Levi Isaac of Berdichev to Chernobyl by boat. On the way, she was seen 'sporting with gentiles . . . as was her wont, engaging in illicit sexual conduct, and making love to many non-Jews'.[15] Most stories on this subject, however, tell of women who engage in illicit sexual relations with Jews.

A complex story, in which the tsadik R. Abraham Joshua Heschel of Apta was personally involved, begins in the fish market in Jassy, during a severe shortage of fish. The wife of the tsadik, wanting to buy some fish for the sabbath, asked two fishermen to catch some for her. As she was about to receive their catch, the wife of a local worthy, who was also having trouble finding any fish, came and grabbed it from the hands of the fishermen; cursing the tsadik's wife and casting aspersions on her honour, she threw the payment at the fishermen and hurried away in her carriage. The wife of the tsadik returned home in tears and told her husband what had happened to her. The tsadik sent the local beadle to this worthy, to bring the fish back, and ordered him that, if he would not agree to return the fish, the beadle should

[11] See e.g. *Shivḥei habesht*, 140, 163; see also Nigal, 'Women in the Book *Shivḥei habesht*' (Heb.), 139.

[12] Bodek(?), *Sipurei kedoshim*, §12, pp. 47–51.

[13] Zeilingold, *Me'orot hagedolim*, 'His Holiness, the Holy Rabbi of Apta', §26, pp. 95–7. Cf. A. Michelson, *Ohel avraham*, §21: the wife of a worthy in Frankfurt bore a son to an army officer, and R. Abraham Abusch refused to serve as *sandak*.

[14] Zeilingold, *Me'orot hagedolim*, 'His Holiness, Our Master and Rabbi, A[aron] of Karlin', §50, pp. 157–9.

[15] Ibid., 'His Holiness, the Holy Rabbi, R. Levi Isaac', §18, pp. 39–40. See ibid., §17, pp. 38–9, for a rich widower who married his niece. The latter engaged in adultery with the family physician, whom she married after her divorce from her uncle. After she contracted leprosy, the physician fled abroad, was accused of espionage, and died in prison.

tell the worthy's wife that she was an adulteress.' The emissary, who was well aware of the power possessed by this worthy, at first refused to perform this mission, and the tsadik was forced to threaten him with a ban of exclusion from communal life. When the woman refused to return the fish, the beadle told her what he had been commanded to say, and then fled for his life. The worthy incited the townsfolk to banish the tsadik. When they demanded that he prove his accusations, the tsadik summoned the entire community to the assembly hall, where he raised the soul of a dead person.

He said: 'You are so-and-so the son of so-and-so, please tell the entire congregation how an act of adultery came to be committed between you and this harlot.' And then a voice emerged from behind the curtain: 'Hear me, my brethren and my people! I was ensnared by this harlot, for I was the secretary and writer of accounts for this worthy. It happened once that the worthy travelled to Bucharest, and I was in his house, examining his accounts. The worthy's wife commanded me to come and spend the night there, for she was afraid to remain alone in the house. She was lying in the bedroom, far from the accounts room, where the money was. No sinful thoughts arose in my mind, and it seemed to me that in truth she feared to remain alone in the house, with her husband not home; I came to spend the night, and did so in the accounts room. But in the middle of the night she came to me, passing through four rooms, when I was sleeping, and she lay with me. When I awoke I greatly feared, and I asked: 'Who are you?' And she said, 'I am the worthy's wife, I have come to you for you to satisfy my lust, and I will give you great riches. But if you will not listen to me, you will come to a bitter end, for I will accuse you of stealing all my husband's money, and I will place you under arrest.' She embraced and kissed me, and promised me all manner of good things, and I was like an antelope caught in her net. And now, woe to me, for there is no remedy for this in the world of truth.'

In the end the worthy's wife admitted her guilt; her husband gave her a writ of divorce, and the tsadik prescribed her a *tikun* for her repentance. The dead person also was given a *tikun* to effect repentance by the tsadik, who left Jassy some time later to assume the position of rabbi in Apta.[16]

In another tale in a hasidic collection, a scholar's wife in her early fifties was unfaithful to her husband with a watchmaker, the father of four children. When they were persecuted by the community, the man and woman converted to Christianity.[17]

Journeys provided convenient opportunities for acts of adultery. The God-fearing man who withstands enticement by the innkeeper's wife is a common theme. The young R. Jacob Isaac (the future Seer of Lublin) was staying in an inn while on his way to Lizhensk. The wife of the innkeeper

[16] Rodkinsohn, *Adat tsadikim*, §13. Cf. Breitstein, *Siḥot ḥayim*, §20, p. 15.

[17] Zeilingold, *Me'orot hagedolim*, 'His Holiness, Our Master and Rabbi, A[aron] of Karlin', 15.

desired him, and demanded that he engage in sexual relations with her. When he withstood temptation and ran for his life, the angry woman accused him of trying to rape her, saying that when she had screamed, he had fled.[18] Another version of the story reads:

And as he was going into the village towards evening, he could go no further, because the sun had gone down, and he was not dressed well. He therefore entered the tavern, where a Jew lived, to spend the night. The innkeeper was not there, because he had travelled to the city with his wife for some matter of importance to them, and only the publican's daughter was there. When the Lubliner entered, she saw his beauty, and desired him. . . . She lit for him the winter oven, so he could warm himself, and also gave him food to eat, for he was hungry, to revive his soul. He thought to himself that she was a proper and hospitable woman. After he finished eating . . . she came to him and demanded that he do her bidding. . . . And also, that this be immediate, and if not—she would force him to do so, since she knew of her own strength and daring.

In this instance, too, R. Jacob found some excuse and fled.[19]

R. Menahem Mendel of Rymanow found himself in a similar situation when he was on his way to R. Elimelekh of Lizhensk:

And when he was in an inn close to the city of Lizhensk, he could go no further, because night had spread its wings over the entire world, and he was on a road that was unfamiliar to him. He asked the woman innkeeper to let him spend the night there, among the other guests who had found accommodation in the inn. When she saw the splendour of his countenance and his very fine appearance, she greeted him very hospitably, and, with great honour, gave him a fine spot in a special room. He did not know that something baneful had taken root in her. He lay down to rest, to revive himself somewhat from the strains of the journey. When slumber fell upon everyone, and all were lying about, drowsing in their sleep, the innkeeper arose from her room, came stealthily into his chamber, and stripped him of his clothes. The man was greatly afraid, and he left all that he possessed with her and fled outside, naked and barefoot, on the road that goes to Lizhensk.[20]

While the heroes of those stories are tsadikim who were travelling to R. Elimelekh, another story depicts R. Elimelekh himself as the one who withstood the test. He was on his way to his master, R. Dov Baer of Mezirech, and arrived at his lodgings tired and hungry. The woman innkeeper gave him supper and tried to seduce him, telling him: 'I am unmarried and

[18] J. Sofer, *Sipurei ya'akov*, i, §31, p. 98. Cf. Ehrmann, *Devarim arevim*, 'Stories from the Holy Rabbi of Lublin', §12; A. Michelson, *Ohel elimelekh*, §122; see also Z. Horowitz, *Horowitz Family* (Heb.), 172–3.

[19] Sobelman, *Sipurei tsadikim heḥadash*, §28. *Continued in Appendix.*

[20] Kamelhar, *Em labinah*, 12; A. Michelson, *Ohel elimelekh*, §182: in a house at the end of the city, people took pity on him and clothed him, and R. Elimelekh greeted him with the words: 'Welcome, Joseph the righteous!'

[menstrually] clean.' R. Elimelekh jumped out of the window and fell on the road. He was picked up by a carriage full of hasidim, but they set upon him and beat him: for they had just come from the inn, where the woman had told them that a hasid like them had attempted to seduce her and had then fled, 'leaving his possessions with me'. However, when they arrived in Mezirech, the Maggid come forth to greet R. Elimelekh and treated him with honour, at which point the hasidim realized that they had acted wrongly towards him.[21]

Some stories do not name the man, simply stressing the wantonness of the woman. In the city of Brod, people accused the district rabbi's wife of loose morals, and when this charge was investigated by the rabbis of the local study hall, the accusations were found to be true. The government-appointed district rabbi forbade the scholars of the study hall to punish his wife; furthermore, he declared that anyone who spoke against her would be flogged, or fined one hundred gold coins. Three of the scholars sanctified the name of God by defying the rabbi (despite the danger this entailed) and, standing before the entire public, declared three times that his wife was licentious and was therefore forbidden to her husband.[22]

Some of these seductresses were non-Jewish women. A wealthy countess fell in love with a Jew who came to trade with her. His knowledge of Polish facilitated their business dealings, after which the duchess attempted to seduce him, offering to forgo the payment due her for the merchandise that he had purchased. 'Then this man's urge increased, and the desire for money joined together with his physical cravings. He could not overcome his desire, and he did for the duchess all that she wished.'[23]

The righteous man who withstands temptation is a frequent theme in these accounts. The rabbi's wife Zissel told a story about her first husband, Reb Mordecai, a handsome merchant and a simple but God-fearing person. Once he travelled to the market in Debrecen, and a wealthy noblewoman who saw him through the window and was struck by his good looks summoned him to do business with her. He came in; she locked him in the room, and at gunpoint demanded that he engage in sexual relations with her. Thanks to his knowledge of Hungarian and his quick thinking, while pretending to be amenable to her wishes he succeeded in escaping through the toilet.[24]

[21] See Breitstein, *Siḥot ḥayim*, §61, pp. 49–50. Cf. the story concerning R. Elimelekh and R. Zusya: J. Y. Rosenberg, *Tiferet maharal*, §14; the story contains three attempts at adultery and the withstanding of temptation in each.

[22] [Isaac Dov Baer ben Tsevi Hirsch], *Kahal ḥasidim heḥadash*, §33.

[23] Rodkinsohn, *Adat tsadikim*, §14. See also *Pinkas ostraha*, 61–6, containing the story by Yosef Finkelstein, 'A Trial with a Dead Person', that was presumably copied from 'memoirs from the Ostrog communal register', but is none other than the story summarized here.

[24] See Ehrmann, *Devarim arevim*, 'Corrigenda'.

R. Hirsch Leib of Alik similarly managed to overcome his sexual desire in an encounter with a non-Jewish woman.

This rabbi made a long and tiring journey to his *rebbe*. When he was on his way, he encountered a matron of unparalleled beauty who was riding in a magnificent carriage. When she saw this awesome and handsome rabbi, she lusted after his beauty, and she commanded her servants who accompanied her to seize him. She held him tightly, sat him with her in her carriage, and began to seduce him. This rabbi said to her: 'I have no potency', but she did not believe him, and she attempted to arouse him for several hours. This righteous rabbi shed all his material being . . . and became as an actual dead person, thereby causing her to believe him. In her great anger she cast him from her carriage, and he went on his way.[25]

It is related that the Grandfather of Shpola withstood a non-Jewish woman who came to tempt him to transgress.[26] Another Jew who had similarly sanctified the name of God was placed next to R. Mordecai of Chernobyl in the world to come. In this world, the young man had been a handsome tailor, unparalleled in his beauty. Once, when he was working in the home of a *poritz*, the *poritz*'s daughter hungered after his comeliness, and fell ill when he did not requite her love. After she revealed her love to her father, he locked the tailor in a room with his naked daughter, thinking that the Jew would not be able to withstand his physical urges. The young man, however, was not enticed, the daughter died of grief, and the *poritz*, in his rage, murdered the young Jew.[27]

The discovery of a Jewish woman's infidelity to her husband usually resulted in divorce, but in some instances the supernatural powers of the tsadik inflicted a more severe punishment on the adulteress. An example of this is the action taken by the Hida (R. Hayim Joseph David Azulai) in the city of Leghorn in the rabbi's old age:

A very important person, who was a *kohen*, came to him . . . with a complaint against his wife, that she had been secluded with another man. The *gaon* was sitting there together with the leading rabbinical judges of the city, and he told the man that, as the Torah commands, he must divorce his wife. The judges could not restrain themselves, especially since they were related to this woman, and they wanted to defend her. They said to him: 'Let our master teach us, whence he has the source of this law, to deliver judgment without witnesses; this is plainly prophecy, and it [the law] is not in heaven! If the law and judgment were delivered by the spirit of divine inspiration, the result, heaven forbid, would be a perversion of judgment, for at the present time, due to our many sins, we have neither priest

[25] Bodek, *Mifalot hatsadikim*, §27, fo. 21*a*. Cf. Abraham of Slonim, *Beit avraham*, 22, which tells of R. Naphtali the Great, who was desired by a princess. He persuaded her, however, 'that he was incapable of this, and had no connection to such matters'. Cf. also Ze'ev Wolf of Zhitomir, *Or hame'ir*, 'Ḥayei sarah', fo. 14*b*.

[26] J. Y. Rosenberg, *Tiferet maharal*, 79–82.

[27] Kleinmann, *Mazkeret shem gedolim*, 160.

nor prophet, but only the teachings of the rabbis, in accordance with the words of our holy Torah.' The *gaon* did not reply to them, but said a second time to the man, the woman's husband: 'Heed my voice and divorce this woman.' When they [the judges] saw that he did not answer them, they went to the woman's relatives, who were the dignitaries of this city; they told them everything, and the entire congregation protested against him. When the *gaon* heard these contentious words, and the spirit of divine inspiration rested upon him, he summoned the woman. She came to him, to the upper storey, where he had his room for study and his prayer room. When he saw her he arose from his chair and he went to the closet where the Torah scrolls were placed. He took a Torah scroll and read in her ears the portion of the *sotah* [the ritual prescribed for a woman suspected of adultery], with its proper intonations and notes. And when she turned around to leave, the *gaon* Azulai read over her out loud: 'If you have not gone astray' and 'But if you have gone astray' [Num. 5: 19, 20, from the portion of the *sotah*]. And when she placed her foot on the first step . . . her face became jaundiced and her eyes protruded, and at the sound of her screams, the judges and many of the townsfolk came, to see this horrific sight, and they were greatly alarmed. They proclaimed: 'Bring forth this accursed woman and cast her down, so that she shall not defile the house of our master.'[28]

The *sotah* also features in another story told of R. Hirsch Leib of Alik, this time concerning his temptation by a Jewish woman:

Once this rabbi and tsadik was on the way when the sun suddenly set, and he was forced to spend the night in an inn on the main road, against his will. During the night, after he had eaten, while the candle was still burning, the woman innkeeper came to him, adorned and naked, and demanded, with all manner of enticements and soothing words, that he be with her, to lie with her. He was dismayed, and, behold, there was a *ḥumash* [Pentateuch] on the table. The rabbi opened it, and it opened to the portion of the *sotah*. The rabbi began to read the portion of the *sotah*, and as he read there, so it was fulfilled in that woman.[29]

Hasidic stories also depict men as the initiators of acts of sexual wantonness, including instances of rape, in which the woman is afraid to reveal the assault.

In some of these the sinning man is a non-Jew. An attempted rape occurred in the time of R. Asher of Stolin, when a non-Jewish carriage-driver took a Jewish *agunah* in search of her deserting husband through a forest. The woman resisted his assault, cursed the man, and succeeded in escaping.[30] In

[28] Y. Rubinstein, 'Notes on the Book *Shem hagedolim heḥadash*', ch. 8, §29; A. Walden, *Kahal ḥasidim*, fo. 57*b*; [Isaac Dov Baer ben Tsevi Hirsch], *Kahal ḥasidim heḥadash*, §103; Chikernik, *Sipurim neḥmadim*, 17–18; Shenkel, *Ma'asiyot peliyot*, §4; Moskowitz, *Otsar hasipurim*, ix, §4. The story appears in Yiddish in Shenkel, *Sipurei anshei shem*, 32–3. See also Nigal, 'A Chapter in the History of the Hasidic Tale' (Heb.), 119 n. 86.

[29] Bodek, *Mifalot hatsadikim*, §28, fo. 21*b*; cf. the story told about the Hida above and in n. 28.

[30] Zeilingold, *Me'orot hagedolim*, 'His Holiness, the Holy Rabbi, R. Asher of Stolin', §30, p. 103.

another story, a new mother admits that she had been raped by a non-Jew when she went down to the cellar to fetch a bottle of wine;[31] another new mother confessed 'that she had been violated by a non-Jewish official'.[32]

Most of the stories, however, present the male transgressor as a Jew, whose actions can be discovered by the tsadik employing his special powers. R. Uri of Strelisk gazed at the face of a worthy and discerned the signs of adultery, saying, 'he has recently committed [this transgression with] a married woman'.[33] Once R. Aaron of Karlin went to purchase *tefilin*. As the scribe handed the new *tefilin* to R. Aaron, the tsadik shouted: 'Yesterday you had relations with a married woman—and today you sell *tefilin*? Wicked one, make a confession!' And the man admitted his sin.[34] There is also a story about a *shaliaḥ tsibur* (a lay prayer-leader) who 'transgressed with two betrothed maidens for a long time'.[35] A woman who had fled from her home, because she had been married to a hunchback, hired herself out as a servant in the home of a wealthy man. She was soon compelled to leave this house too, because the wealthy man's son attempted to violate her. She continued to be dogged by misfortune: when she was a servant in yet another house, she learned that the affluent master of the house was none other than a habitual adulterer.[36]

Stories abound concerning Jewish men engaging in extra-marital affairs with non-Jewish women. This frequently resulted from contact in business affairs and other worldly matters. Dr Gordon, the personal physician of the Prussian king, had been a known adulterer before he became a hasid and a follower of the Maggid of Mezirech. In his sinful life he had taken 'lovers, harlots, women' with him on his travels.[37] It was also said of a tailor from Lemberg, who would sew garments in the homes of non-Jewish ministers and dignitaries, 'that he was suspected of engaging in licentious behaviour, heaven forbid'.[38] Jews in rural areas also came into contact with non-Jewish women: one story tells of a Jewish villager who transgressed with such a woman, who was a water-carrier and lighter of ovens.[39] A young man who had fled from his wife and went to study in a yeshiva passed himself off as

[31] See *Shivḥei habesht*, 181.

[32] A. Michelson, *Ohel avraham*, §42. *Continued in Appendix.*

[33] Bodek, *Ma'aseh tsadikim*, §28, pp. 42–3. Cf. also Brandwein, *Degel maḥaneh yehudah*, §46: R. Judah Tsevi of Stretin 'saw the signs of adultery' on the foreheads of two merchants.

[34] *Shivḥei habesht*, 72; Kleinmann, *Zikhron larishonim*, 29.

[35] Kaidaner, *Sipurim nora'im*, §15, pp. 71–2. Cf. Kleinmann, *Mazkeret shem gedolim*, 64–5: R. Zusya charged a *shaliaḥ tsibur* who had mocked him with adultery.

[36] Zeilingold, *Me'orot hagedolim*, §41, pp. 137–40.

[37] Rodkinsohn, *Adat tsadikim*, §17: when he approached Mezirech, he sent them all away, each in turn. For Dr Gordon and the Maggid of Mezirech, see also Abraham of Slonim, *Beit avraham*, 203.

[38] Chikernik, *Sipurim neḥmadim*, 15.

[39] Kaidaner, *Sipurim nora'im*, §14, p. 71. Cf. Kleinmann, *Mazkeret shem gedolim*, 64.

unmarried. Before the High Holy Days he was sent out of the yeshiva to seek a wife, as was the practice for bachelors at that time. In his wanderings the young husband came to a village; he remained there until the end of the holidays, and while there he engaged in sexual relations with a non-Jewish woman.[40] There were also men who kept mistresses in their homes; such was the rich man who came down in the world, and became an alcoholic and 'a well-known reprobate'.[41] An extra-marital relationship with a non-Jewish woman often ended with the Jewish adulterer converting to Christianity.[42]

Some people were deterred at the last moment from committing the sin of adultery. Once the Devil tempted a certain hasid, after showering great riches on him, to travel to a fair, where 'there is a harlot . . . who takes much money as her wages'. As the hasid was strolling with the prostitute 'among the fine trees in her garden', he felt remorse and refrained from transgressing with her.[43]

The Ba'al Shem Tov's brother-in-law, R. Gershon, was harassed by a certain God-fearing and brilliant Torah scholar and complained to the Ba'al Shem Tov about him. When the Ba'al Shem Tov asked the scholar why this was so, the latter answered that he saw many flaws in R. Gershon. The Ba'al Shem Tov responded: 'Nor are you free of sins!' When the scholar denied this and claimed that he had never transgressed, the Ba'al Shem Tov set before him a non-Jewish woman (who had already died) with whom he had sinned in the past. The Torah scholar begged the Ba'al Shem Tov for a *tikun*, and the Ba'al Shem Tov agreed.[44] In another instance, the Ba'al Shem Tov refused to sleep in a certain bed because he sensed that someone had engaged in sexual relations with a non-Jewish woman on it. The householder admitted that it was in fact his son-in-law who had committed such an act.[45]

Incest features in several stories. A ritual slaughterer was accustomed to sleep with his daughter-in-law, until this shameful act became generally known;[46] in another story, a grandfather engaged in intimate relations with his daughter-in-law.[47]

[40] [Isaac Dov Baer ben Tsevi Hirsch], *Kahal ḥasidim heḥadash*, §157. Cf. Shenkel, *Ma'asiyot mitsadikim yesodei olam*, §8.

[41] Kleinmann, *Or yesharim*, 26. The man repented as a result of the efforts by the emissary of R. Mordecai of Lachowicze.

[42] See Ch. 11 below.

[43] See Reznik, *Mora'im gedolim*, §5, pp. 11–12. Cf. the attempt by the devil to entice the ritual slaughterer of R. Menahem Mendel of Vitebsk (Sobelman, *Sipurei tsadikim heḥadash*, §32).

[44] See Ehrmann, *Devarim arevim*, 'Stories from the Ba'al Shem Tov', §23.

[45] See *Shivḥei habesht*, 153.

[46] See Bodek(?), *Sipurei kedoshim*, §6. For a slightly different version, see A. Walden, *Kahal ḥasidim*, fos 25*c*–26*a*.

[47] See J. Sofer, *Sipurei ya'akov*, ii, §47. Cf. Kohen, *Shemuot vesipurim*, 13.

Some stories depict virtuous Jewish women who withstand temptation. An unsuccessful attempt to seduce a married woman—a sort of reverse 'wife of Potiphar' narrative (see Gen. 39)—occurred in the time of R. David of Mikoliev. While travelling, the tsadik once stayed at the house of the head of the community, where a travelling preacher was also enjoying hospitality.

And when everyone was asleep, sleep escaped the preacher, and he lusted, heaven forbid. He thought that the head of the community was asleep, and his wife would not recognize him. His evil inclination tempted him—he succumbed, and he went to her. The merit of the Torah, however, restrained him, for when he approached her, the wife awoke, and she cried out: 'Who are you? Come, tell me!', for she knew that her husband was asleep. And she was struck dumb like a silent dove [see Ps. 56: 1]. When she could no longer hold him, she seized his robe to detain him until the people of the household awoke.[48]

Another story tells of a preacher who sought to seduce a woman innkeeper; she refused, arguing that such an act was a sin. The preacher responded that to atone for the sin he would study a chapter of Mishnah. The tsadik R. Menahem Nahum of Chernobyl, who was spending the night in the inn and who understood what was happening, dispersed the darkness by lighting a candle, thereby confounding the criminal importuning of the preacher.[49]

Sexual relations that ran counter to the halakhah at times resulted in the birth of offspring called *mamzerim*, an appellation given to them in the stories even when they were not so defined by the halakhah. Thus, a young man 'adhered to non-Jewish women and begat *mamzerim*'.[50] If the sinner repented, the problem of a *mamzer* offspring was 'solved' by the infant's dying of natural causes. An old woman came to the tsadik R. Aaron of Karlin to complain that her only son had left the straight and narrow path and 'adhered to non-Jewish women and begat *mamzerim*'.[51] This young man was summoned to the tsadik, but refused to present himself. Only after he was put in chains and his head was shaved did the man regret his actions and request a *tikun* for repentance from the tsadik. His request was granted by the tsadik, and the *mamzerim* died.[52]

A related story tells of a householder who had fathered two *mamzerim*. Hearing his children's teacher reading with them from the book *Reshit ḥokhmah* by R. Elijah de Vidas on the subject of repentance, this man repented of his own misdeeds and travelled to R. Shneur Zalman of Lyady,

[48] Rodkinsohn, *Adat tsadikim*, §9.

[49] Bodek, *Mifalot hatsadikim*, §53, fo. 26*b*; Yehiel Moses of Yadimov, *Likutim ḥadashim*, fo. 54*b*.

[50] Zeilingold, *Me'orot hagedolim*, 'His Holiness, Our Master, Rabbi A[aron] of Karlin', §51, p. 159.

[51] Ibid. 158.

[52] Ibid. 159.

from whom he requested a *tikun* for repentance. The two children died, and the man became a virtuous individual.[53] In yet another story, both the children and the men who fathered them died.[54] Sometimes the birth of a *mamzer* would result in a lawsuit: the ritual slaughterer of the Chotch community was sued by the non-Jewish court for failure to support financially a child that a non-Jewish woman claimed was his son.[55]

R. Samuel Shmelke of Nikolsburg once spent the night in an inn. The (Jewish) innkeeper sent a non-Jewish woman to him, but the tsadik paid no attention to her. It later transpired that the innkeeper, who had had a child with this non-Jewess, incited the woman to send blackmail letters to the tsadik, demanding that he provide for the child's upkeep, which R. Samuel Shmelke did until the child died. The innkeeper eventually admitted that the child was his. When the tsadik was asked why he had remained silent all those years, he replied that he did not want to cause the desecration of the name of God and bring great disgrace on Israel.[56]

Innocent people were often the victims of slanderous accusations, and the term 'harlot' was often used against women who had done nothing worse than arouse someone's anger. One woman was provoked by the Karlin hasidim who would not let her sleep at a Simhat Beit Hasho'evah celebration (held during the Sukkot festival, recalling the 'water libation' performed in the ancient Temple). She cursed and reviled the tsadik, and one of the hasidim insulted her in return, calling her a 'harlot'.[57] Another woman bribed people to testify falsely that the wife of her husband's business partner was an adulteress.[58] Even Havaleh, a granddaughter of R. Nahum of Chernobyl, was the victim of slander.[59] Evil tongues claimed that the wife of R. Moses of Sambor, who had married when she was 'a virgin of advanced years', had given birth to a child conceived out of wedlock when her labour pains began in the seventh month of her pregnancy.[60]

Nor were men immune from such false charges. It was said of the brother of the Maharal (R. Judah Loew ben Bezalel) of Prague that he had sinned

53 See Bodek, *Ma'aseh tsadikim*, §13, pp. 28–9.

54 Cf. Bodek(?), *Sipurei kedoshim*, §4.

55 See A. Michelson, *Ohel elimelekh*, §169; Berger, *Eser tsaḥtsaḥot*, 'R. Tsevi Elimelekh', §4. Cf. J. Sofer, *Sipurei ya'akov*, ii, §47; cf. also Zeilingold, *Me'orot hagedolim*, 'His Holiness, Our Master, Rabbi A[aron] of Karlin', §51, p. 94; Ze'ev Wolf of Zhitomir, *Or hame'ir*, 22: the ritual slaughterer has two children with a non-Jewish woman; he initially supports his misbegotten offspring, but later abandons them. His shame at the truth's coming to light leads him to drown himself.

56 See A. Michelson, *Shemen hatov*, 'Stories', §47.

57 *Ma'asiyot vesiḥot tsadikim*, 34.

58 Rodkinsohn, *Adat tsadikim*, §22; Rakats, *Siaḥ sarfei kodesh*, ii, §473; Zevin, *Hasidic Tales: Festivals* (Heb.), 331–2.

59 Sobelman, *Sipurei tsadikim heḥadash*, §51.

60 Berger, *Eser kedushot*, 'R. Judah Tsevi of Rozdol', §4; Teomim, *Ateret tiferet*, 'His Holiness, the Holy Rabbi, R. Judah Tsevi of Rozdol'. See also Ch. 4 above.

'with a certain woman';[61] and in the continuation of the story referred to above, an adulterous preacher accused R. David of Mikoliev of having slept with the wife of a fellow Jew. In most of these instances, the truth came to light.[62]

[61] See Rodkinsohn, *Adat tsadikim*, §22.

[62] See ibid., §9; see also [Lemberger], *Magdil yeshuot malko*, 9: a Jew is falsely accused of adultery with a non-Jewish woman.

SEVEN

ILLNESS AND PHYSICIANS

AMONG THE ABILITIES with which the hasidic story credits the tsadik is the power to heal the sick, and to restore to life people presumed to be dead. The enmity between professional non-Jewish physicians and the tsadikim, whom they regarded as no better than witch doctors, is evidenced in many hasidic stories; in the competition between the two, the tsadik is naturally victorious. The attitude to Jewish doctors is more varied: those who have abandoned the Torah way of life are treated with contempt, but those who have found their way back to Torah observance are accorded respect, and particularly if they become adherents of hasidism.

Stories of the healing of both Jews and non-Jews by tsadikim are so numerous that to list them all would require a separate volume. Inherent in each is the belief that the tsadik possesses supernatural power, and that he succeeds where the accredited physicians fail. *Ba'alei shem* had traditionally dispensed remedies, as did the Ba'al Shem Tov, for whom this was a source of livelihood. *Shivḥei habesht* relates that in the city of Radvil 'people began coming to him to seek cures, and so everywhere, until he brought livelihood for his home'.[1]

According to one of these accounts, a person who had lain in sick in his bed for ten years, paralysed and mute, 'without hands or feet, and without sleep', was summoned by the Ba'al Shem Tov to complete a *minyan*. The Ba'al Shem Tov first sent emissaries and gave them his walking stick, but the man did not move, let alone rise from his bed, and they returned with their mission unfulfilled. The Ba'al Shem Tov dispatched them a second time, this time giving them his hat, with orders to place it on the sick man's head and to put his walking stick in his hand. According to the story, the man came to the prayer service, and thereafter lived hale and hearty for a further ten years.[2]

Another story relates that the Ba'al Shem Tov came to a city where two brothers, who were followers of his, lived, and heard that their brother was dying. This brother was a mitnaged, and would not hear of receiving a blessing from the Ba'al Shem Tov. The Ba'al Shem Tov nevertheless went to him, and said,

[1] *Shivḥei habesht*, 147. [2] Ibid. 134–5.

'Give me your hand!' He gave him his hand, and he [the Ba'al Shem Tov] raised him up. The rabbi then ordered him to lower his legs from the bed, which he did. The rabbi then ordered him to put on some clothes and wash his hands, and he did everything as he was commanded. After this, he went with him to the synagogue, recited the Musaf prayer with everyone, and he recovered, with the help of the Lord, may he be blessed.[3]

The Ba'al Shem Tov demonstrated to those who doubted his powers that he was capable not only of healing them, but also of causing the illness to return. Thus he restored the sight of a blind child from Istanbul for a period of time, but then, in order to punish his impudent mother, restored the child's blindness.[4] Some individuals whom the Ba'al Shem Tov cured became his followers and disciples as a result: a classical example is R. Dov Baer of Mezirech, who first visited the Ba'al Shem Tov—according to one of the accounts of his becoming a hasid—to ask for the tsadik's help in obtaining a remedy.[5]

Other tsadikim, too, were blessed with such healing powers. In the city of Jaslo, a young woman fell into a deep sleep, and the physicians could not rouse her. When her relatives brought the girl to the tsadik (R. Hayim Halberstam of Sanz), the latter blessed her. When the party left the city, they saw that the sick girl had opened her eyes.[6] Worried parents came with their ailing son to this same tsadik, and his blessing restored their son to health.[7]

One person suffered from a swollen gland in his throat, and the physicians could not cure him. He could not swallow anything, and his condition rapidly deteriorated. The tsadik R. Mordecai of Nezkizh ordered him to drink a little liquid from the *shirayim* (food left over from the rebbe's table), and he was healed.[8]

A similar incident involved a non-Jew whose throat had been damaged. The physicians were afraid to operate on him, and warned him against drinking any liquids, saying this would be harmful to him. R. Yehiel Meir, the tsadik of Gostynin, sent a bottle of wine to the man, who believed in the tsadik; he drank the wine and was cured.[9]

The Ba'al Shem Tov, as noted above, would receive payment for curing the sick, and most other tsadikim did likewise. Some refused to accept

[3] Ibid. 157.

[4] Ibid. 111–12. Cf. Bodek, *Mifalot hatsadikim*, §7, fo. 11*b*: the wife of a sick man refuses to give a *pidyon nefesh* for her husband, claiming that the tsadik cannot help him.

[5] See *Shivḥei habesht*, 72.

[6] See Teomim, *Ateret tiferet*, 'His Holiness, the Holy Rabbi, R. Hayim Halberstam of Sanz', §35.

[7] Ibid., §34.

[8] I. Landau, *Zikhron tov*, 'Matters Concerning Eating and Sleeping', §8.

[9] See Rakats, *Siaḥ sarfei kodesh*, iii, §40. Sobelman, *Sipurei tsadikim heḥadash*, §64, relates that the tsadik of Koznitz healed the mute daughter of a non-Jew. Bodek, *Ma'aseh tsadikim*, §3, p. 7, depicts how a tsadik cured the daughter of the governor of Pistin.

remuneration; by contrast, others on occasion demanded to be paid for their remedies. This money, like that accompanying other requests to the tsadik, was known as a *pidyon* or *pidyon nefesh* (literally, 'redemption of the soul'). In one instance, a father who sought relief for his sick daughter after the physicians had despaired of curing her asked the tsadik how much money he had to send, and the latter set the sum of 500 roubles.[10] In another story a hasid describes his son's illness and the action taken by the tsadik:

As regards my very self, my son Joseph [was sick] with *sharlikh* [scarlet fever], heaven forfend, and I mentioned him every time before our master. The child, however, became so weak that the sound of his breathing could no longer be heard. I held a consultation with the physicians, and they drove me to despair. Once again I went to our master and mentioned him. This was on the sabbath night, and we set a guard over the child. Upon the departure of the sabbath [i.e. Saturday night], our master told me that he desired to perform a *pidyon nefesh*. I brought him 160 *keserlikh* [silver coins], and he performed the *pidyon*.[11]

The relations between tsadikim and physicians, and their mutual distrust and lack of respect, occupy a prominent place in the hasidic stories telling of the healing of the sick. The tension that existed between the Ba'al Shem Tov and physicians is illustrated by the story concerning the illness of R. Abraham Podlisker, one of the Ba'al Shem Tov's disciples:

[This rabbi] sent for the Ba'al Shem Tov, because he was gravely ill. The Ba'al Shem Tov spent much time with him, and was engaged in his remedy. When the rabbi's sons saw that this was having no effect, they sent for a doctor from the holy community of Ostrog, but he had gone to Sedeh Lavan (Belaya Tserkov). The Ba'al Shem Tov saw that the doctor had left, and he said to the rabbi: 'I am leaving here, because the doctor of the holy community of Ostrog is coming here.' The rabbi knew nothing of this, and he greatly implored him not to depart, and he [the Ba'al Shem Tov] remained for the night because of [the rabbi's] entreaties. He said that the doctor was spending the night two parasangs from the city. This doctor had raised his hand against the Ba'al Shem Tov for some time, and he said: 'When I see the Ba'al Shem Tov, I will kill him with my fire-stick [i.e. rifle].' In the morning the Ba'al Shem Tov made haste to depart, but the sick rabbi detained him until the doctor's arrival in the city. The Ba'al Shem Tov declared, 'Here, the doctor is arriving in the city.' He took his leave of the rabbi, got into the carriage, and departed. When he was opposite the inn of the doctor, he descended from the carriage, entered the building, and greeted the doctor. [The doctor] asked him: 'From where do you know doctoring?' to which [the Ba'al Shem Tov] replied: 'The Lord, may he be blessed, taught me!' and he went to his home. The sick rabbi's sons

[10] Teomim, *Ateret tiferet*, 'His Holiness, the Holy Rabbi, R. Hayim Halberstam of Sanz', §36.

[11] Ibid., §37. For additional instances in which tsadikim were successful when physicians had despaired of curing their patients, see Kaidaner, *Sipurim nora'im*, §55, p. 131; Bodek, *Ma'aseh tsadikim*, §3, p. 7; Tzitrin, *Shivḥei tsadikim*, fo. 14*b*; Sobelman, *Sipurei tsadikim heḥadash*, §28.

brought [the doctor] to their father, and for everything that the doctor told them to do, they responded: 'The Ba'al Shem Tov has already done this!' and the doctor left, disappointed. Then the sick rabbi complained to his sons: 'What have you done? Even though I did not have a remedy from the Ba'al Shem Tov, at least when he came in to me, I knew that the Divine Presence accompanied him, but when the doctor came in to me, it seemed that a *galaḥ* [literally, 'shaved one': a contemptuous term for a Christian priest] entered.'[12]

In conversations with physicians, the Ba'al Shem Tov was frequently asked about the source of his medical knowledge, as in the following instance:

It once happened that a sick individual, whom an important Jewish doctor had despaired [of curing], was no longer capable of talking. The Ba'al Shem Tov came to that place, and he summoned this sick person. He ordered that a meat soup be cooked for him, and he would immediately begin to speak. He was given soup to eat, and he treated him until he recovered. The doctor asked him [the Ba'al Shem Tov]: 'How did you cure him? I knew that the [vocal] cords had been spoiled, and there is no cure for those cords!' The Ba'al Shem Tov replied: 'You treated the patient in material fashion, while I treated him in a spiritual manner. For the human [body] contains 248 members and 365 tendons, corresponding to the 248 positive commandments and the 365 prohibitions. When, heaven forbid, a person spoils [with his actions, i.e. sins], the corresponding member or tendon is spoiled. If a person transgresses many prohibitions, many tendons are spoiled, the blood does not issue forth from them, and the person is in danger. I spoke with his soul, that it accept upon itself to repent, and it did so, thereby repairing all the members and tendons, and I was able to heal him.'[13]

At times a tsadik initiates a conversation on the difference between the power of the tsadik and that of the physician, in order to sanctify the name of heaven. The Jewish physician (and, obviously, his non-Jewish counterpart) was generally considered to be a heretic, and the tsadik's triumph over him was considered to be a sanctification of the divine name.[14]

A butcher was seriously injured, and the physician declared that his arm would have to be amputated. R. Berish of Oshpetzin cured the man, and asked him to go to the physician and show him his (now healthy) limb. He also told him: 'He will undoubtedly ask you, "Who cured you?", and you will tell him: "The rabbi of Oshpetzin cured me!" And if he asks you: "Where did he learn the knowledge of medicine?", you will tell him: "He never studied! The Lord, may he be blessed, teaches him all these things when they are required!"'[15]

There was an incident in which a physician sent a written indictment to the academy in Vilna, charging the tsadik R. Mordecai of Nezkizh of

[12] *Shivḥei habesht*, 109. [13] Ibid. 113; Zevin, *Hasidic Tales: On the Torah* (Heb.), 199.
[14] See Singer, *Seva ratson*, fo. 1*a*.
[15] M. M. Sofer, *Shelosh edrei tson*, 40–1; cf. Singer, *Seva ratson*, fo. 1*a*.

sorcery.[16] This was a grave allegation, and so, to impart a seemingly physical aspect to his cures, the tsadik would give medicines to the sick who came to him, although in actuality he healed them by his prayer.

R. Menahem Mendel of Lubavitch similarly took care 'that his sense that is "above nature" was not seen; rather, he would clothe all his marvellous and awesome wonders in completely natural garb'. Once a man came to him with his son, who had not acted normally for years, and who had not responded to any of his efforts to cure him by means of 'those using [divine] names and sorcerers'. The tsadik prescribed a medication and advised the youth's father to ask the sick boy to prepare a certain amount of the drug. The physician ridiculed this medicine, claiming that, according to medical science, this elixir was not only useless but could even be harmful. And, indeed, there was no change for the better in the youth's condition. The tsadik observed that the physician had undoubtedly not prepared the exact weight he had requested. The youth's father asked the physician, who admitted that he had not weighed the medicine at all, since as far as he was concerned, the preparation was total nonsense. When he re-weighed it according to the tsadik's orders, the youth's health was restored.[17]

In another story the Ba'al Shem Tov avoids treating a sick person and the physician's therapeutic efforts subsequently fail.

Once, as the Ba'al Shem Tov was on his way to Chmelnik, he heard a divine voice proclaiming that R. Joseph, a schoolteacher from the community, would die. When he came to the city, the townspeople came to pay him to heal [R. Joseph], but he declined to cure him, without revealing the reason. After the Ba'al Shem Tov left, a certain doctor came and treated him, and he recovered. The doctor was still there when the Ba'al Shem Tov returned to that city, and was informed that this R. Joseph had been cured by the medicine of the doctor who treated him. As the Ba'al Shem Tov was standing there, this R. Joseph asked the doctor to prepare a dressing to remove the lice from his head, which had greatly multiplied as a result of his illness. The doctor gave him a certain salve to apply to his head, he applied this ointment to his head—and he died. Then the Ba'al Shem Tov revealed the reason why he did not want to treat him, because of the heavenly voice that he had heard.[18]

Yet another story makes the point that the Ba'al Shem Tov diagnoses both the physical and the spiritual or moral defects of the person before him, while the physician is concerned solely with the physiological aspect of his patients, and lacks the ability to enter the spiritual realm.

Once a great and famous doctor came to the countess in the city, and the countess waxed eloquent in praise of the Ba'al Shem Tov, that he was a great person as well

[16] [Lemberger], *Niflaot hatsadikim*, 15–16.
[17] Kaidaner, *Sipurim nora'im*, §55, p. 131.
[18] *Shivḥei habesht*, 112.

as being knowledgeable in medicine. The doctor said: 'Summon him to come here.' She replied, 'This is below his dignity; rather, a magnificent carriage should be sent, as is done for high officials, for he is a great personage.' He was sent for, and he came before them. The doctor asked the rabbi if it were true that he was knowledgeable in medicine. He replied: 'It is true.' He [the doctor] asked: 'From what place, from which expert did he learn?' He [the Ba'al Shem Tov] answered: 'The Lord, may he be blessed, taught me!' The doctor found this laughable, and he further asked him if he understood the pulse. The rabbi said, 'Here, I have some defect [i.e. malady]; test my pulse, and I will test your pulse.' The doctor took the rabbi's pulse, and he understood that there was some defect, but he did not know what it was. For, in truth, he was lovesick for the Lord, may he be blessed, and that was beyond his [the doctor's] comprehension.

The Ba'al Shem Tov, on the other hand, learned from the physician's pulse that he had stolen precious articles from the house of the countess.[19]

The physician, then, is not a positive character, being capable even of stealing from people who have sought his help. That story concerns a non-Jewish physician, but at times Jewish physicians too appear in a negative light. They are not careful in their observance of *mitsvot*, and sometimes even commit serious transgressions such as adultery. One physician was caught in the act of adultery with the young wife of a wealthy old man.[20] Even Dr Gordon, the court physician of the king of Prussia, who would later become a disciple of the Maggid of Mezirech, is depicted—as noted in Chapter 6—as lustful, as well as someone 'who did not observe the Jewish religion'.[21]

Tsadikim did not all hold the same attitude to physicians; the attitudes expressed in the stories range from total repudiation to outright admiration. R. Aaron of Chernobyl declared: 'I fear the wicked physician!'[22] R. Simhah Bunem of Pshischa was of the opinion that physicians know nothing.[23] R. Aaron of Karlin told one of his followers not to pay attention to physicians, but afterwards asked, 'Why did he not heed the physicians?' and forgot what he had previously said.[24] R. Nahman of Bratslav expressed extremely negative opinions of physicians, but he, too, needed their help.[25] R. Barukh of Medzibezh, by contrast, had a good opinion of physicians.[26] R. Dov Baer, the Maggid of Mezirech, told one sick person that

it is not the medicine that the doctors prescribe that heals the patient, rather, the doctors themselves cure, for each doctor has a different *mazal* [literally, 'luck',

19 Ibid. 113.
20 See Zeilingold, *Me'orot hagedolim*, §17, pp. 69–70.
21 Rodkinsohn, *Adat tsadikim*, §17.
22 Zeilingold, *Me'orot hagedolim*, 89.
23 [Isaac Dov Baer ben Tsevi Hirsch], *Kahal ḥasidim heḥadash*, §162.
24 Zeilingold, *Me'orot hagedolim*, 151.
25 Nathan of Nemirov, *Siḥot haran*, §3 ('Concerning Doctors and Cures'); id., *Ḥayei moharan*, §16, and *passim*.
26 Rodkinsohn, *Adat tsadikim*, §17.

'fortune'], who are the angels responsible for medicine. An angel accompanies each doctor, and it is they who heal a person. Medicines are only for appearance's sake. The angel Raphael himself accompanies the greatest of the doctors, to heal the sick.[27]

The continuation of the story relates that the aforementioned Dr Gordon heals this person, without medicines. In the wake of his conversations with the Maggid of Mezirech, the physician draws closer to the tsadik, and eventually becomes his disciple.

The rise in the number of Jewish physicians in eastern Europe in the nineteenth century is described by a story that is connected with R. Levi Isaac of Berdichev. Under the influence of a friend, an outstanding student who studied in the Volozhin yeshiva began to read 'books in non-Jewish languages' and scientific tracts, until he was expelled from the yeshiva. He moved to Vilna, where he completed his studies in the grammar school. A rich man wanted to take him as his son-in-law. They agreed that the wealthy man would finance his medical studies at the university in Vienna, following which the young man would marry his daughter. The rich man kept his end of the bargain and supported the young man until he received his degree. Suddenly, his patron came down in the world and died, and the young man excused himself from honouring their agreement. Luck did not shine upon him: after returning to his city, he was the target of general derision ('the son of the *melamed* [schoolteacher] has become a physician'). He went with his father to the tsadik R. Levi Isaac, who instructed him to marry his intended bride from Vilna.[28]

Other physicians followed the path of Dr Gordon and returned to Judaism, repenting and abandoning their secular ways. A physician who was an unbeliever, and who was not successful in healing himself, was cured thanks to the efforts of R. Berish of Oshpetzin. The physician became observant, ordered his wife to maintain the Jewish laws concerning menstrual purity, and broke all the dishes that had become non-kosher.[29] The aptly named R. Hayim Doktor of Piotrkow, a well-known physician at the time, used to belittle the injunctions of the Jewish religion, as many Jewish physicians of the period were wont to do. Once, while on his way to treat a patient, he passed through the city of Lemberg, where he entered the house of the tsadik R. David. The tsadik advised him to promise much money (to charity) in a time of danger. On continuing his journey, the physician did indeed find himself in great peril; he followed the advice of the tsadik, and was saved. He subsequently became observant and began to travel to the

[27] Ibid. See Rechtman, *Jewish Ethnography and Folklore* (Yiddish), 152–7, who includes the story and provides details concerning the life of R. Aaron ben Samuel Gorda (Gordon) and his grave. [28] Zeilingold, *Me'orot hagedolim*, §19. [29] Singer, *Seva ratson*, fo. 9*a*.

tsadik, 'until it was said of him that he was on a high [spiritual] level, and that the spirit of divine inspiration rested on him. Towards the end of his life he accepted *kvitlakh*', that is to say, became a tsadik himself.[30]

On the other hand, there were physicians (and healers) who were not alienated from the Jewish way of life and who observed all the *mitsvot*. One such was Reb Yudel, who apparently had never studied in a school of medicine, but nevertheless possessed professional knowledge in this field. He was 'pious and God-fearing, expert and knowledgeable in the medicines of physicians, and in his city he was given the title of physician'. A relation by marriage of R. Yudel was apprehensive because of the rabbinic adage (BT *Kidushin* 82a), 'The best of physicians are destined for Gehennom [hell]', but R. Mordecai of Chernobyl explained to him that there are two types of physicians: one, who thinks that healing is dependent upon the Lord; and the other, who thinks that he himself heals. R. Yudel, said the tsadik, belonged to the first type.[31]

[30] Samlung, *Eser zekhuyot*, 'From Our Master of Warka', §36; Rakats, *Siaḥ sarfei kodesh*, i, §161. Bromberg, *Toledot haniflaot*, 43, relates that he was standing by the sickbed of R. Hayim Meir of Mogielnica when the latter expired.

[31] Bodek, *Mifalot hatsadikim*, 57.

EIGHT

THE DEAD, BURIAL, AND THE WORLD TO COME

THE BENEFIT to be derived from the powers of the tsadik is not limited to this world, since the tsadik has influence upon the heavenly court as well. Thus, for example, it is related that R. David of Lvov told the heavenly court how to conduct itself.[1] The rabbi of Apta told a dead person who appeared to him in the middle of the third sabbath meal not to worry or fear, since his [the tsadik's] opinion was decisive in the 'Chamber of Merit' (the venue of the heavenly court): as he ruled, so it would be.[2] On the other hand, it was said of the Ba'al Shem Tov that an attempt by him to intervene in the heavenly proceedings almost cost him his own place in the world to come. Once he decreed that a childless couple would be blessed with offspring. A heavenly voice proclaimed that he had lost his portion in the hereafter. The Ba'al Shem Tov accepted his fate with love, and a heavenly voice was heard a second time, declaring that, in reward for his acceptance of the divine verdict, his place in the world to come had been restored.[3]

It was within the tsadik's power to promise an individual a place in the world to come, and he was also entitled to impose conditions. On one occasion the Seer of Lublin urgently required a large sum of money. A rich villager was willing to give him this amount, on condition that he be assured of a place in the world to come, one that was close to the tsadik. Some time later, the Seer had second thoughts about their agreement, but the villager was unwilling to forgo his warranted reward. The Seer told him: 'That which I promised you was on condition that you would be with me every Rosh Hashanah.' Some time later, the villager became impoverished and was forced to wander far and wide, but he made sure to spend every Rosh Hashanah at the Seer's court. One year, as Rosh Hashanah approached, he was still far from Lublin. When he saw the carriage of R. Shalom of Belz, who was on his way to Lublin, he asked the tsadik to take him with him, and in return, he promised him his place in the world to come. After the High

1 See e.g. Tzitrin, *Shivḥei tsadikim*, §3, p. 17.
2 See Sobelman, *Sipurei tsadikim heḥadash*, §52.
3 Rodkinsohn, *Adat tsadikim*, §3. Cf. p. 115 above.

Holidays the tsadik of Belz studied with the villager until the latter reached the spiritual level that, as the tsadik stated, assured him of his portion in the world to come.[4]

R. Menahem Nahum of Chernobyl promised a place in the hereafter to a wealthy man who donated 300 roubles for the construction of a ritual bath.[5] R. Pinhas of Kolomai made a similar promise to a woman apostate, on condition that she recited the Shema every day, at the time of the morning and evening prayers.[6]

The tsadik acted as an advocate for the deceased, at times ascending to the upper spheres to plead their cases. In a story about the children of R. Yehiel Mikhel of Zlotchev recounted later in this chapter, the Ba'al Shem Tov is portrayed as someone who is at home in the *alma dekeshut* (the 'world of truth', i.e. the world to come) and whose words are not to be disregarded; and, indeed, in this case his request is immediately accepted by the heavenly court. A similar motif appears in a story (also described below) in which R. Mordecai of Chernobyl acts as advocate for a dead man. In some instances, the tsadik causes a person to suffer while still in this world, so that he will not lose his place in the world to come. A village innkeeper, who was a concealed tsadik (see Chapter 14), cursed the Ba'al Shem Tov and his disciples. This malediction was meant to punish the Ba'al Shem Tov, and thereby restore the latter's portion in the hereafter.[7] According to another story, the Ba'al Shem Tov lost his place in the world to come because of his cruelty to an orphan girl whom he raised in his home. She later married a concealed tsadik, and when the Ba'al Shem Tov stayed as a guest in her home she punished him with a sabbath of suffering in order to restore his portion in the hereafter.[8]

In other stories, the tsadik defends the deceased both from demons and from the prosecutors accusing him in the heavenly court. A wealthy man who 'made light of the customs and laws of Israel' fulfilled the obligation of *hakhnasat kalah* by giving R. Hayim of Sanz and R. Moses Rapoport the money needed to purchase a *talit* and fur *shtreimel* for a bridegroom.

And it came to pass than when the wealthy man's time came, and he was about to die, R. Hayim learned of this, and he ordered his attendant to inform him when he [the wealthy man] was brought to the cemetery. The attendant did so, and R. Hayim walked after the bier. On the way, R. Hayim ordered that they stop with the bier, which he approached, extended his hand to and fro, and then did so a second time. When [the funeral entourage] came to the courtyard of the cemetery, he drew near to the bier, waved his hands, and turned them upward and to the four directions. After this, he returned home. All the people saw, and marvelled. They

[4] Ehrmann, *Pe'er vekhavod*, fo. 74*a*–*b*.
[5] Bodek, *Mifalot hatsadikim*, §19, fo. 15*b*.
[6] Resnik, *Mora'im gedolim*, §12, pp. 25–7.
[7] Bodek, *Mifalot hatsadikim*, §26, fo. 20*a*.
[8] Ibid., fo. 21*a*–*b*.

could not understand this, because R. Hayim was not accustomed to interrupt his studies and attend the funeral of someone who was not renowned . . . One person gathered [his courage] and asked the rabbi: 'Why did you see fit to perform all the things that you did concerning the funeral?' R. Hayim told him what the rich man had done, concerning the giving [of money] for the *talit* and *shtreimel* to enable the wedding to proceed; for this reason, he was grateful to the man and followed the bier. When, however, he had walked for some distance after the bier, he saw a camp of demons all around, who encircled the bier and sought to seize the deceased. He therefore extended his hands here and there to drive them away from the corpse.[9]

R. Abraham of Stretin received a *pidyon* to act on behalf of a certain dead person, and asked to be informed when the funeral procession passed by his house. He joined the procession, and from time to time would ask the pall-bearers to stop; when they did so, 'every time he raised the staff in his hand, and he did so several times'. The tsadik undoubtedly succeeded in banishing the fiends who wanted to snatch away the deceased.[10] R. Solomon of Karlin inserted 'a small piece of a wooden staff' in the grave of a sinner who had supported the tsadik's household, thus preventing the angel Dumah (i.e. the Angel of Death) from touching this man in the grave.[11]

Not only was the tsadik capable of seeing the demons who surrounded the dead person, but on occasion he could even see the Angel of Death himself. The Ba'al Shem Tov saw the Angel of Death, who was invisible to others, dancing after a certain tax-collector.[12] He also saw the Angel of Death close to his own demise, and spoke with him, saying, 'I concede two hours to you, do not torture me!' He told his attendant, who could not see the Angel of Death, that the latter had always fled from him, but 'now that he has been given dominion over me, he has become all-powerful, and he exhibits great joy'.[13]

A person who is about to die assumes missions to be performed in the next world. It is related that R. David of Talnoye gave a dying yeshiva student a *kvitl* to deliver to his father, R. Mordecai ben Nahum of Chernobyl, in the 'world of truth'. Two years later, the deceased appeared to R. David and told him that at first he had not been permitted to approach the dead tsadik; only when all those who had given charity were summoned to greet a very charitable individual who had passed away was he able to deliver the note.[14]

In many stories a person makes a commitment, marked by a handshake or in some other manner, to return to this world after his death and deliver information to his relatives and friends concerning the world to come and

9 [Lemberger], *Niflaot hatsadikim*, 27.

10 Brandwein, *Degel mahaneh yehudah*, §86. Cf. A. M. Rabinowitz, *Keter hayehudi*, 36: the daughter of the 'Holy Jew' requested that the bed that she had received from her father be placed in her grave, for the tsadik had said that it would always protect her.

11 See Zeilingold, *Me'orot hagedolim*, §10, pp. 42–3.

12 See *Shivhei habesht*, 119.

13 Ibid. 168.

14 Libersohn, *Erets hahayim*, §159, p. 51.

what happened to him after he passed away. This theme is older than the genre, having appeared earlier in medieval works on ethical behaviour,[15] and also in the halakhic literature.[16] A mortally ill patient promised his friend that he would come to him in a dream after his death and tell him all that had happened to him, and in particular whether R. Mordecai of Chernobyl had kept his promise to act on his behalf before the heavenly court. The agreement was sealed with a handshake and the man died. On Friday night, as the rabbi led the sabbath prayers in the synagogue, everyone present saw him motioning to summon an unseen person, causing great wonder. That night the deceased appeared to his friend in a dream, in fulfilment of his promise. This is what he told him:

Immediately after my death, I was given over to the demons, and they acted with me as is written in the books, omitting no [torture]. It was a time of trouble for me, and the details of what I underwent need not be told. In my great misery and distress, I lay in the ground, and did not think to ask for succour from the holy rabbi, for I had completely forgotten his help. Only afterwards, during Kabalat Shabat [the introductory Friday night prayers], when the heavenly voice went forth and proclaimed: 'Let us go forth to greet the sabbath queen', I was immediately abandoned by the fiends. They fled and I saw them no more, but I did not know where to turn. Then I saw, behold, the oppressed souls running very quickly, and I, too, ran after them. Then I heard a voice proclaim in heaven: 'Go and hear how the rabbi, the tsadik, our master and rabbi, Mordecai of Chernobyl, receives the sabbath, with song and praises.' Then I instantly awakened, as a person awakens from his sleep, and I remembered that that rabbi was my rebbe when I was still alive, and I began to run extremely swiftly. When I came to a certain study hall, that was replete with windows, that were filled with brilliant splendour, like the sun at noon, I wanted to enter the study hall, but I couldn't find the door. I also saw other souls entering, but I was tired from looking for the entrance. I begged them to show me some way by which I could enter, but 'there was no sound, and none who responded' [1 Kgs 18: 26]. I went to the west side, because I knew that the entrance to a study hall should be in the west. I stood there for some time and wanted to go in, but I could not find the entrance. I looked through the window, and I saw—behold, the rabbi, the *admor*, standing before the reader's lectern [i.e. leading the prayers], enwrapped in his *talit*, as was his custom, and praying. My sorrow was redoubled, for my not being able to appear before him. Only, with the help of the master of all, afterwards, when he recited 'Enter in peace' [from the *Lekha dodi* hymn of the Kabalat Shabat service], he turned to the west. When he saw me

[15] Samuel Hehasid et al., *Sefer ḥasidim*, §324, p. 102, asserts: 'If two good people during their lifetime took an oath or put their trust in one another, if one were to die, he would inform his fellow, in a dream, how it is in that world.'

[16] See *Shulḥan arukh*, 'Yoreh de'ah', §179: 'It is permitted to adjure the sick person to return to him after death, that he tell what he will have been asked.' See the opinion of Rema ad loc., who permits the adjuration of a dead person, provided that the oath is administered to the soul, and not to the body. See also Potchowsky, *Gan hadasim*, ch. 6.

standing there, and another one with me, he beckoned with his finger, that we come in to him. The entrance was instantly opened for me, and I entered. I am still there [in the study hall], and they could not drive me out of there, but I cannot ascend to a higher level.'[17]

The rabbi of Sanz related that a sick disciple of the Ba'al Shem Tov agreed with a friend, sealing the pact with a handshake, that he would return to him after his death and tell of the heavenly world. And, indeed, he appeared on the third day after his demise and related that at the time of his death it seemed to him that he was falling, 'until he came to a broad plain' (the rabbi of Sanz explained that this was the lower level of Paradise), where he walked about. The deceased then spoke about Torah study in those worlds. 'I saw the holy Ba'al Shem Tov with the holy Ari, of blessed memory, studying a passage from the Zohar, and they disagreed . . . They concluded that they would ask R. Shimon ben Yohai [to whom authorship of the Zohar is traditionally ascribed], of blessed memory, himself.'[18] The continuation of the story indicates that this passage does not refer to the Ba'al Shem Tov after he passed away, but rather to the time when he was still alive and active among his disciples, while at the same time studying in the 'heavenly academy'. When the Ba'al Shem Tov taught this passage in the Zohar to his disciples, and asked them what they thought to be its simple meaning, the disciple replied that his dead friend had told him about the disagreement [in heaven] between the Ba'al Shem Tov and the Ari. The Ba'al Shem Tov said: 'I saw him there, walking about.'[19]

In *Shivḥei habesht* we encounter the Ba'al Shem Tov as the teacher of Torah in the upper worlds. The Ba'al Shem Tov assured a sick disciple of R. Ze'ev Kiytses and R. David Forkes that although he had not carried out the prescribed remedial activity for a certain sin, he would nevertheless enter paradise. His friends asked him to pledge that he would return after his passing and tell 'how he had been treated after his death', again sealing the promise with a handshake. Later the dead disciple appeared and related that he had been granted entry to paradise but that, because of the crowding there, he was being pushed from one place to another; he was still wandering, and he did not know his place. At one point he saw that everyone was going to a certain *heikhal* [heavenly hall]; he went with them, and he saw the Ba'al Shem Tov sitting 'and speaking words of Torah'. He (the Ba'al Shem Tov) posed questions to the members of the academy (of this *heikhal*), before resolving the questions himself. The dead person asked the Ba'al Shem Tov why he (the disciple) had no place in paradise. The Ba'al Shem Tov

[17] Bodek, *Mifalot hatsadikim*, §7, fos 11*b*–12*a*.

[18] Zimetbaum, *Darkhei ḥayim*, §43, p. 70. Cf. Bodek, *Mifalot hatsadikim*, §7, fo. 11*b*: a sick person agreed with his fellow, with a handshake, to inform the latter what became of him.

[19] Zimetbaum, *Darkhei ḥayim*, §43, p. 70.

responded that he had given his hand in pledge, but had not kept his promise (to tell his friend what happened to him).[20]

As a result of a similar agreement between two friends (once again sealed with a handshake), we learn of how a hasid was treated by the heavenly court after his death. Two friends, one a mitnaged and the other a hasid, agreed that the one who died first would appear to the other in a dream and tell him of his experiences in the upper worlds. The hasid was the first to pass away, and, by means of a charm that he had been given by the Ba'al Shem Tov, he ascended from one heavenly gate to another. All of a sudden, he came to a halt, and the charm no longer worked. An old man asked him why he was standing still and then told him: 'This is not good, for if you stay here without continually moving upwards, then, heaven forfend, you are liable to lose your spiritual vitality.' The old man also related that he had heard in this *heikhal* that the reason why the deceased was kept in this place was that he had given his hand to his friend but had not kept his promise. The deceased then went and told his friend all that had happened to him. He also related that every sabbath afternoon the Ba'al Shem Tov expounded in the 'heavenly academy'.[21] In another tale a dead person came to R. Judah of Graydung to tell the rabbi what had happened to him, as R. Judah had requested before the other's death.[22]

The usual pattern in these stories is that the one who has made the promise to reappear after death usually does not so do immediately, resulting in complaints by the living person against the deceased. The dead person eventually appears in a dream, when it is learned that the delay in delivering his report from the afterlife was caused by factors beyond his control. A man in Ruzhin related that he and his brother had pledged to one another that the first to die would give a report to his surviving brother of all that he had undergone. Twenty years, however, had passed since his brother had died, and he had not kept his word. When his brother finally appeared to him in a dream, he explained that it was only then that he had been given permission to appear. He stated that R. Shalom of Probisht had died on the same day as he had, and a heavenly voice had pronounced that all the tsadikim were to go forth to greet R. Shalom. Other heavenly voices were heard, too, announcing that anyone who died on that day would be exempt from the punishment received in the grave (by the denizens of the afterlife who torture the

20 See *Shivḥei habesht*, 56–7. For Torah study in the 'heavenly academy', see also J. Sofer, *Sipurei ya'akov*, i, §5. See Brandwein, *Degel maḥaneh yehudah*, §30: R. Uri of Strelisk observed that it was not surprising that his disciple R. Judah Tsevi of Stretin offered new insights into the Torah, 'for at the time that I received this teaching in the heavenly academy, in the most high Garden of Eden, he, too, was standing there and listening'.

21 Ehrmann, *Devarim arevim*, 'Stories from the Ba'al Shem Tov', §28: the dead person asked the living one to absolve him, from then on, from fulfilling his promise.

22 Sobelman, *Sipurei tsadikim heḥadash*, §21.

wicked in Gehinnom), all who had seen R. Shalom in this world would escape the abyss, and anyone who had given money to the tsadik would be exempt from all harsh judgments.[23]

A person who was about to die promised R. Elimelekh of Lizhensk, with a handshake, that he would appear before him and tell what befell him, in exchange for a pledge by the tsadik to care for the deceased's son and raise him. The dead man did not keep his word until the son's wedding day. Shortly before the ceremony, however, the dead man appeared, and said that at the time of the third sabbath meal in the upper spheres, he had heard R. Elimelekh speaking words of Torah.[24]

In all the cases mentioned so far, the connection between the living and the dead was initiated by the deceased; in other cases, however, it was made by the living. The overwhelming majority of such appearances occurred in dreams, but a seemingly corporeal manifestation was also possible. It is attested in *Shivḥei habesht* that one Saturday night a person who had already passed away entered the Ba'al Shem Tov's home, in his sabbath finery and wearing a hat. As he entered, he loudly wished the Ba'al Shem Tov a good week. R. Joseph Ashkenazi, the Ba'al Shem Tov's stepfather, fainted upon seeing the apparition, and the Ba'al Shem Tov passed his hand over his face, 'and he saw him no more'. Then the Ba'al Shem Tov said to his stepfather: 'If your spiritual aspect were stronger, you would have heard what he said to me; you, too, would have asked him whatever your heart desired, and he would have answered you. And not only that, you would have become actual acquaintances, and you would have seen him constantly!' The Ba'al Shem Tov then stressed, referring to the book *Sha'arei kedushah* by R. Hayim Vital, that seeing the soul of a righteous one is a level of prophecy.[25]

R. Baer of Oshpetzin saw his rabbi 'standing on his grave in a white garment, with a *shtreimel*, as well', and his body was a sort of spiritual essence (*ḥaluka derabanan*: the spiritual 'cloak' that a person weaves for himself with his good deeds).[26] It was told of R. Menahem Mendel of Rymanow that every year he would see his father's countenance on the anniversary of the latter's death (*yahrzeit*).[27]

Information concerning the afterlife is also delivered by sick people who lost consciousness and were considered dead but came back to life. The son of R. Yehiel Mikhel of Zlotchev was gravely ill. Since the tsadik had to travel

[23] Libersohn, *Erets haḥayim*, §261, p. 81; see ibid., §159, p. 51: it was declared in heaven that all those who had given charity would come to greet R. Joshua Eleazar of Berdichev, who was well known for his philanthropy.

[24] Moskowitz, *Otsar hasipurim*, xiii, §1.

[25] See *Shivḥei habesht*, 129–30.

[26] M. M. Sofer, *Sheloshah edrei tson*, 33; Singer, *Seva ratson*, 4. Cf. Sobelman, *Sipurei tsadikim heḥadash*, §3, regarding a corpse whose body did not decompose and who arose from his grave to bless the Ba'al Shem Tov.

[27] Reznik, *Mora'im gedolim*, §6, p. 14.

on urgent business, he requested that if, heaven forbid, his son were to die, his funeral be delayed until his return. After his departure, the son lost consciousness ('called in German *hinerflet*'),[28] and it was thought that he had died. When he awakened from this state of unconsciousness, three days later, he related:

As soon as his soul went forth, a certain angel took it and brought it to a certain *heikhal*; the angel was not permitted to venture into this *heikhal*, and only he entered, by himself. He stood by the entrance, witnessing the [heavenly] Great Court in session, and he immediately saw agents [of the court] bearing a book in which all sins were recorded, which was a heavy burden for them. A certain angel then came with the book of merits. They were not equal to the others, until a third book was brought, that of the suffering that he had endured, in accordance with the teaching of the rabbis [BT *Arakhin* 16*b*]: 'How far shall tribulations be administered?', and many of his sins were expunged. They none the less wished to sentence him to death, because of [the transgressions] that remained, and write his sentence. His father, the rabbi, our master and teacher, this R. Michael, immediately came, with much clamour and a great outcry, for their desiring to burn these books [by R. Jacob Joseph; see immediately below] . . . When he saw his son standing at the entrance, he asked him: 'My son, what are you doing here?' And he replied: 'I have been standing here for some time, but I do not know why or for what; I ask that you intercede on my behalf.' The father promised his son that he would do so, provided he [the father] did not forget the request, for [he was occupied with] his cries before the heavenly court concerning the danger that the books of R. Jacob Joseph would be burned. He promised to ask for divine mercy for the youth, if he did not forget, but he did not remember. And a great noise was immediately heard, for all the worlds trembled and proclaimed: 'Clear the way, for the Ba'al Shem Tov himself is coming to the *heikhal*!' The youth also asked the Ba'al Shem Tov to act on his behalf. He did so, and the youth was sent home, although he wished to remain a bit longer, to see what the Ba'al Shem Tov was doing there, but he was not allowed to do so.[29]

In some instances the souls of the dead come to the tsadik to receive a *tikun*. It is related that R. Isaac Luria sent one of his disciples to Babylonia, to effect a *tikun* for the souls of those who had been murdered while travelling.[30] Other stories state that the souls of some tsadikim, such as that of R. Leib Sarahs, descended to this world in order to effect *tikunim*.[31]

[28] For *hiner-bet* (or *hinerflet*), i.e. brain death, see Guedemann, *Hatorah vehaḥayim*, 174 n. 5. For the reports by the ill and those in a faint regarding the world to come, see Ben-Yehezkel, *Sefer hama'asiyot*, v. 438–9.

[29] *Shivḥei habesht*, 66.

[30] See Farhi, *Mora'im hagedolim*, §3, pp. 7–8.

[31] See Bodek, *Seder hadorot heḥadash*, fo. 20*b*. For a *tikun* that he effected, see Rodkinsohn, *Sipurei tsadikim*, §2, p. 7. 'A *tikun* for a *yahrzeit*: one time the tsadik R. Tsevi of Zhidachov forgot the anniversary of his mother's death. She came to him in a dream and said: "For your not reciting Kaddish, I forgive you; for your not studying *mishnayot*, I forgive you; but I cannot forgive your not having given a *tikun* [refreshments served in the synagogue on a *yahrzeit*, for the

Once R. Levi Isaac of Berdichev was on a journey, and his horses stopped and refused to budge. Those accompanying the tsadik heard him say: 'Wait for us in such-and-such a village!', and then the horses continued on their way. In the continuation of the story, we learn that the horses stopped on account of the spirit of someone who had died hundreds of years previously, but who, because of his numerous sins, had not been found worthy even to enter Gehinnom. This spirit requested, and received, a *tikun* from R. Levi Isaac.[32]

The nature of this measure taken to rescue the soul, and the manner in which the latter is 'elevated', are usually not described; reading between the lines, however, we learn that it consists of advocacy before the heavenly court by the tsadik on behalf of the deceased. At times the activity by the tsadik for the dead soul is called *asiyat tovah* (literally, 'performing a boon'). An example of such an act of benevolence performed for a non-Jewish servant and his Jewish master was related by the Ba'al Shem Tov to villagers who were staying in the city of Nemirov. 'Once I saw in a dream that I was walking in a field, and in the dream, I saw some kind of fog, from a distance . . . I had had a non-Jewish servant for several years, until he left me. I saw him walking with a very heavy load of wood on his shoulders, but when he saw me, he cast off the wood and threw himself at my feet.' The servant said that he had observed the sabbath as long as he had been in the service of the Ba'al Shem Tov, but afterwards, when he was in the employ of a Jewish tax-collector, he was forced to work on the holy day, and bring lumber from the forest to the village. 'And now both of us are dead, and I must bring logs on the sabbath to Gehinnom, until the tax-collector has enough for the entire week.' The dead man also told the Ba'al Shem Tov of the great esteem in which the latter was held in the world of truth, and requested that he act on his behalf. The Ba'al Shem Tov asked to be shown the servant's place in the afterlife. 'He accompanied me, and he showed me a *heikhal*, which I entered. I spoke on his behalf, and the decree against him was revoked. When I spoke in favour of the non-Jew, I also acted as advocate for the Jew, and he, too, was released from the heavenly decree.'[33]

R. Hayim of Kosov effected a *tikun* for the soul of a person who had been punished by the avenging angels for having drunken non-kosher wine.[34]

tikun of the dead person's soul] to restore the soul of one of Israel [that is, to abate the hunger of one of the congregants, who would have partaken of these refreshments]." Alarmed, [the tsadik] called his followers and studied *mishnayot*; while he did not recite Kaddish, he did give a *tikun* [refreshments]' (Moskowitz, *Otsar hasipurim*, xx, §17). For the lighting of candles on the *yahrzeit*, see J. H. Schwartz, *Mo'ed lekhol hai*, ch. 3, 'The Eternal Life', §12; Sperling, *Reasons for the Customs* (Heb.), 482.

32 See Rodkinsohn, *Adat tsadikim*, §9; see also Brandwein, *Degel mahaneh yehudah*, §11.

33 See [Lemberger], *Niflaot hatsadikim*, 10.

34 Kahana, *Even shetiyah*, 54.

R. Israel of Ruzhin related that the *ḥazan* (cantor) of Zaslov had acted in the upper worlds on behalf of a certain soul.[35] A dead person appeared before R. Isaac of Drohobitch to request a *tikun*.[36] R. Aryeh Judah Leib Geliner, the *mokhiaḥ* (preacher) of Polonnoye, effected a *tikun* for the soul of a dead person even before the grave had been closed.[37] Conversely, an old man had been granted the right to enter paradise, but then the Heavenly Adversary argued that one sabbath eve he had not worn clean undergarments; the heavenly court then ruled that he was forbidden to hear the Friday evening Kabalat Shabat prayer in heaven.[38]

In some instances the dead person sends an emissary to request that the tsadik act on his behalf. Thus, a young man's dead mother appeared to him in a dream and asked him to travel to Chortkov and entreat the tsadik to perform a *tikun* for her soul.[39] A dead person who had been doomed to Gehinnom was saved from this fate by the merit of R. Menahem Mendel of Rymanow, who had asked this person to tell him what became of him.[40]

Some tsadikim refused to act on behalf of the dead. On the day that the Ba'al Shem Tov died, a soul came to him and requested a *tikun*. The Ba'al Shem Tov reproached him, saying: 'For eighty years you have been wandering about, and you did not hear until today that I exist in the world? Depart, wicked one!'[41] The tsadik of Husyatin initially rejected the plea of a dead petitioner, since the latter had spoken ill of the tsadik's granddaughter. In the end, however, he was persuaded by R. Barukh of Medzibezh to forgive the deceased and to effect a *tikun* for him.[42]

Other dead souls appear to the living to demand satisfaction for affronts, to demonstrate that they had been wronged, to reveal hidden matters, to give testimony, or to complain about various injustices. Others still are brought to 'trial' before the tsadik. In such cases the deceased generally appears before the tsadik in order to fulfil some 'necessity of his [the deceased]'.[43]

In the following tale, the deceased brings a living person to justice. During the time of R. Israel ben Shabetai, a butcher named Eisik, who was the victim of malicious gossip, lived in Koznitz. After his death he came in a dream to the ritual slaughterer and demanded that he submit himself to judgment. After this dream had recurred three times, the slaughterer went to R. Israel, the Maggid, and a date was set for a trial by Torah law. An attendant was sent to the cemetery to summon the dead butcher, and a special

35 Reznik, *Mora'im gedolim*, §7, pp. 15–17. Cf. *Ma'asiyot vesiḥot tsadikim*, §45, p. 39: the tsadik, upon his death, raised up with him (to heaven) a soul that had been in limbo for 400 years.

36 See [Isaac Dov Baer ben Tsevi Hirsch], *Kahal ḥasidim heḥadash*, §52.

37 See ibid., §59.

38 *Ma'asiyot vesiḥot tsadikim*, §45, p. 39.

39 See Sobelman, *Sipurei tsadikim heḥadash*, §40.

40 See Reznik, *Mora'im gedolim*, §1, pp. 3–4.

41 *Shivḥei habesht*, 168.

42 See Sobelman, *Sipurei tsadikim heḥadash*, §51.

43 See *Shivḥei habesht*, 129–30.

place was allotted for him to stand. When the departed appeared, he claimed that the slaughterer did his work improperly and had rendered the animals he had sold him non-kosher, thus causing the butcher to sink into debt, and now he had no rest in the afterlife. The slaughterer could not deny these accusations, and a ruling was issued in favour of the dead butcher. The Maggid asked the dead person: 'In your lifetime you were the object of slander, but now you say that you have been forgiven everything, except for your debts? How did this happen?' The butcher replied that he had saved righteous people who had been seized by murderers, and he had been granted entry to paradise for this meritorious deed.[44]

In another tale, one merchant stole a sum of money from another, indirectly leading to the premature death of the victim, whose wife and children were left with no means of sustenance. The deceased appeared in a dream to the thief, and summoned him for judgment before the heavenly court. The merchant ignored the dream, but when it had come to him three more times, he resolved to travel to R. Aaron of Karlin and ask the tsadik's counsel. R. Aaron advised him to refuse to appear before the heavenly tribunal, but to agree to be judged before the tsadik. The deceased gave his consent to this, and a date was set for the trial. The tsadik stood by the window, looking out, apparently to hear the claims and arguments raised by the dead merchant. The latter demanded that the death sentence be imposed, but the tsadik ruled instead that the thief assess the value of his own property and give half of this sum to the widow and orphans.[45] In another instance, a person who did not honour his promise of marriage was required to reconcile himself with his betrothed after her death. To this end, she was temporarily brought back to life, and she appeared before him in the flesh.[46]

In another instance, the tsadik's attendant was sent to the cemetery to summon a dead person to testify as to where a sum of money was hidden. The deceased came and revealed the hiding place, but the petitioner did not see him.[47] The rabbi of Apta likewise sent his attendant to the cemetery to summon a dead person, in this case to give testimony regarding an adulteress.[48] The dead Maggid R. Joseph of Medzibezh appeared to the Ba'al Shem Tov and asked him why no one was visiting a sick youth who had attended to

[44] Gemen, *Sifran shel tsadikim*, ch. 36, §12.

[45] See Sobelman, *Sipurei tsadikim heḥadash*, §43.

[46] See Rodkinsohn, *Adat tsadikim*, §15. The Seer of Lublin stipulated reconciliation with the (dead) bride as a condition for the promise-breaker's having offspring.

[47] A. Michelson, *Ohel naftali*, §216. I. Landau, *Zikhron tov*, 30, relates that R. Leib Sarahs once ordered a person to lend him a sum of money, giving the lender in return a promissory note. In the meantime the tsadik died, and the lender wept bitterly over his grave. A hand emerged from the grave and paid him the amount he was owed.

[48] See Rodkinsohn, *Adat tsadikim*, §13.

the Maggid before the latter's death. When this youth himself passed away, the Ba'al Shem Tov saw R. Joseph walking before the bier.[49]

On occasion the dead complain about where they have been buried, or the condition of their grave. A dead person appeared before R. Mordecai of Chernobyl and related that he had been buried in the same grave as a woman, and requested that this sorry situation be corrected. The tsadik reproached the burial society, and the two corpses were separated.[50] A young man who had died appeared to the beadle and claimed that he had been buried in a plot other than the one he had purchased in his lifetime. The rabbi ruled that the dead person was to move to his own plot, and some time later the corpse was found in the plot that he had claimed was his.[51] One time R. Zusya went with a dead person to show him his grave (which was in dispute), while the beadle was afraid to accompany him.[52]

As several of the stories already mentioned in this chapter show, the afterlife is depicted as a place of Torah study. This is illustrated by, for example, the story of R. Elimelekh of Lizhensk, and a number of descriptions of the Ba'al Shem Tov studying in the 'heavenly academy', including those of his disagreement with R. Isaac Luria and his addressing R. Shimon bar Yohai to resolve a difference of opinion, among others. It is related of the Ba'al Shem Tov that 'on Friday, during the Minhah prayer, which is the time of the ascent by the soul to the highest spheres . . . he ascended to the *heikhal* of the Tosafists . . . to the *heikhal* of Maimonides'.[53] R. Tsevi Hirsch of Krostchov appeared posthumously to his father-in-law and revealed to him that the way of the Ba'al Shem Tov was beloved in the world of truth.[54]

At times the dead come to study with the living. After his death, R. Elimelekh engaged in the study of his book *No'am elimelekh* with the tsadik of Ropshits;[55] the Ba'al Shem Tov taught his son R. Tsevi Hirsch a certain divine name and promised him that if he were to meditate upon this name after his (the Ba'al Shem Tov's) death, he would come and study with him.[56]

The righteous, whose place is in paradise, take pity on the souls fated for Gehinnom, and seek to intercede on their behalf before the heavenly court. R. Israel of Ruzhin related that R. Joel Sirkes (known as the Bah, after his book *Bayit ḥadash*) was righteous in all his being. Once he coughed in the street, and this act indirectly caused a sin to be committed. Consequently, the heavenly court decreed that he pass through Gehinnom on his way to paradise. Thirty days before his entrance to Gehinnom, it was cooled down,

[49] See *Shivḥei habesht*, 150.
[50] See Chikernik, *Sipurim uma'amarim yekarim*, 24–5.
[51] See Hazan, *Sipurim nifla'im*, §32, p. 50.
[52] See Reznik, *Mora'im gedolim*, §4, pp. 9–10.
[53] *Shivḥei habesht*, 161.
[54] [Isaac Dov Baer ben Tsevi Hirsch], *Kahal ḥasidim heḥadash*, §102.
[55] See A. Michelson, *Ohel naftali*, §278.
[56] See *Shivḥei habesht*, 169.

so as not to harm this righteous soul. When he entered, 'he stood there and did not want to move . . . until all those in Gehinnom were granted permission to depart from there, and if they were not, he, too, would [remain] with them'. His wish was granted, and Gehinnom was completely emptied that day.[57] R. Abraham Hayim, author of *Oraḥ leḥayim*, once saw in a dream the dead R. Yehiel Mikhel of Zlotchev standing outside paradise. R. Abraham Hayim fasted a number of times, until R. Yehiel Mikhel appeared to him in a dream and told him to cease these futile mortifications. He went on to say:

Immediately [following my death], they wanted to bring me to paradise, while I said that I desired to take with me some souls from Gehinnom, and elevate them together with me to paradise. I was told in reply that, according to the letter of the law, they could not yet be exempted from Gehinnom, to which I responded: As long as those souls are not given to me—I shall not enter paradise![58]

When R. Moses Leib of Sasov came to the upper spheres, he immediately ran to Gehinnom, and did not want to enter paradise. He argued that having spent his entire life redeeming captives, he could not now dwell in paradise while Jews were still inhabiting Gehinnom. A ruling was therefore issued to calculate the number of (earthly) captives (including those yet to be born), and a total of 60,000 was reached. R. Moses Leib was accordingly granted permission to remove the corresponding number of souls from Gehinnom—but he also 'stole' several hundred additional sufferers, plucking them from the netherworld.[59]

Following *bedikat ḥamets* (the search for leaven just before Passover Eve), R. David Moses of Chortkov related that after R. Moses Leib of Sasov died,

when he came to the upper spheres and was brought to paradise, he stood and wept, and did not want to enter paradise. When he was asked why he was crying, he replied that he desired one of the following: either to be admitted to Gehinnom, where he would be with the people who had given him money in this world, or that those people be taken with him to paradise.

The ruling was that he would go to Gehinnom for a single hour. The *admor* concluded his story: 'When he departed from Gehinnom, he drew along with him all the ones who were deficient [i.e. sinners].'[60]

A common theme in the hasidic story is the revelation in which the tsadik

[57] See J. Sofer, *Sipurei ya'akov*, ii, §40, p. 124. The story also appears, with slight changes, in Luria, *Likutim yekarim*, 'and this was the cause of the proliferation of dybbuks in this world'. R. Joel Sirkes's soul transmigrated into his grandson, R. Joel Ba'al Shem, 'who was a renowned tsadik, who engaged in the *tikun* of souls and dybbuks, may God save us'.

[58] Margolioth, *Kevutsat ya'akov*, fo. 59*b*; [Isaac Dov Baer ben Tsevi Hirsch], *Kahal ḥasidim heḥadash*, §49.

[59] See Libersohn, *Erets haḥayim*, §321, p. 95.

[60] R. Margaliot, *Tiferet adam*, 14.

is told who will be next to him in paradise. When the tsadik travels to this person's place of residence, to examine him and find out why he merits this honour, he usually sees nothing out of the ordinary regarding this individual and his conduct. More exacting examination in most cases reveals that this person has performed an outstanding act of self-sacrifice at some time in his life, or even that the tsadik's heavenly 'neighbour' is a concealed tsadik whose great spirituality and righteous deeds are hidden from those around him.

R. Israel of Ruzhin related that R. Joel Sirkes asked in a dream who would be next to him in paradise. When he examined the individual whose name he had been given, he saw only a simple person, apparently in no way out of the ordinary. However, when he persisted in his enquiries, the man stated that on the day of his daughter's wedding to the son of a worthy, he heard one of the guests weeping. He learned that the child of this man had been engaged to be married, but the match had been cancelled when he had come down in the world and could not afford to pay the dowry. R. Sirkes's 'neighbour' in paradise persuaded the father of his prospective son-in-law to give his son in marriage to the first bride (the poor man's daughter), while he himself paid the sum of the dowry. This marvellous act sufficed to afford him the privilege of being next to R. Sirkes in the world to come.[61]

The burial of the dead has always been regarded in Judaism as an important religious obligation, and individuals who were not necessarily personally observant commonly made financial contributions so that funerals could be conducted properly. Once a poor tailor died, and his family could not afford the expenses of the burial. The money was contributed by a follower of R. Menahem Mendel of Rymanow who, although he believed in the tsadikim, was a *ba'al ta'avah*, that is, someone who sinned because he could not control his passions.[62]

Jews made great efforts to ensure that they themselves would receive a Jewish burial, and to inter their dead in a Jewish cemetery.[63] The graves of tsadikim were considered worthy places for prayer, and hasidim would travel long distances to pray at the *tsiyun* (tomb);[64] some would leave a *kvitl* there.[65] As several Habad tales attest, prayer at the tombs of the *rebbe*s of

[61] See J. Sofer, *Sipurei ya'akov*, ii, §40, pp. 123–6; cf. *Midrash tanḥuma*, ed. Buber, introd., 135–6; and the sources cited in Heller, ' "Gott Wunscht das Herz" ', 384–6.

[62] Reznik, *Mora'im gedolim*, §1.

[63] Thus even the decapitated head of an *ilui* who had met his end in a torture chamber requested that it receive a Jewish burial (Bodek, *Pe'er mikedoshim*, 5). Jewish merchants provided a Jewish burial for a woman apostate who returned to Judaism (see Ch. 11 below), and even for an apostate who repented on Yom Kippur (Reznik, *Mora'im gedolim*, §11).

[64] See e.g. [Isaac Dov Baer ben Tsevi Hirsch], *Kahal ḥasidim heḥadash*, §72. R. Elimelekh of Lizhensk appeared in a dream to his disciple R. Kalman Kalonymus Epstein (the author of *Ma'or vashemesh*), and reproached him for telling a woman not to travel to his tomb, where she wished to pray (Bromberg, *Toledot hanifiaot*, 5).

[65] See e.g. M. M. Sofer, *Sheloshah edrei tson*, 33; Singer, *Seva ratson*, fo. 2*b*.

Habad was effective. A beggar whose money was lost found it after praying at the grave.[66] Miracles occurred in the vicinity of the tomb: a *pidyon* that was placed by a woman who wrote the *kvitl* when she was impure was flung away from the tomb;[67] and a plaque that fell was reaffixed 'by itself'.[68] Even the sick were healed by means of earth from a grave.[69]

Hasidim took especial pains to commemorate the *yahrzeit* of the tsadik; a hasid who studied Mishnah on this day would be allowed to see his dead mother and grandmother.[70]

A person who was about to die could be certain that his offspring would dutifully recite the Kaddish prayer praising God on the deceased's behalf; for those who had no children, the duty was more problematic. The severed head of a murdered Jew asked an *ilui* (talmudic prodigy) to recite Kaddish in his memory;[71] the rabbi of Apta promised a guest who had died in his house during Sukkot that he and his offspring after him would recite Kaddish in his memory on every *yahrzeit*.[72]

The daughter of Odel (the daughter of the Ba'al Shem Tov) initially had no sons, and the Ba'al Shem Tov promised her male offspring. A son was born and named Israel, after the Ba'al Shem Tov, but at the age of two he fell ill and died. His mother placed the dead child on the tomb of the Ba'al Shem Tov and declared: 'Here, this is the son that you promised me,' and left. People found a live child sitting on the tomb, and brought him back to his grandmother (i.e. Odel). The Ba'al Shem Tov appeared in a dream to his granddaughter, and said to her: 'If you had come to pray at the tomb [when the child was ill], you would have been saved [i.e. the child would not have died]. But [after the child had died], you caused me great trouble, once the soul of the child had already come among the myriads of souls, and I had to labour greatly to find him.'[73]

[66] Kaidaner, *Sipurim nora'im*, §39, p. 106; see ibid., §37.
[67] Ibid., §42.
[68] Ibid., §41.
[69] Ibid., §40.
[70] Ibid., §30.
[71] See Bodek, *Pe'er mikedoshim*, §5.
[72] See Sobelman, *Sipurei tsadikim hehadash*, §54.
[73] Moskowitz, *Otsar hasipurim*, xx. 11–12.

NINE

TRANSMIGRATION OF THE SOUL AND DYBBUKS

THE HASIDIC BELIEF in *gilgul neshamot* (transmigration of souls) had its origins in kabbalah.[1] According to this notion a person's soul could return to the earthly world once or a number of times, manifesting itself not only in human but also in animal, vegetable, or even inanimate forms.

Shortly before he died, the Ba'al Shem Tov prophesied that he would return to this world within sixty years if the messiah had not come in the meantime.[2] R. Israel of Ruzhin sat at the third sabbath meal and told of several tsadikim of his generation who were the reincarnations of souls from times past; he attested that he himself was the reincarnation of King Solomon.[3] It was reported that the Ba'al Shem Tov was the reincarnation of R. Sa'adiah Gaon,[4] or of Enoch,[5] while Mordecai Banet was said to have 'received a note from heaven' informing him that he was the reincarnation of the biblical Mordecai, and that he must convene one hundred rabbis to do battle with heretics.[6] The

[1] See Vital, *Sha'ar hagilgulim*; id., *Sefer hagilgulim*; *Ḥemdat hayamim*, iv, ch. 4; Azikri, *Sefer ḥaredim*, fos 41*a*–42*a*; Scholem, *Elements of the Kabbalah* (Heb.), ch. 9, 'Transmigration', pp. 308–57; Benayahu, *Sefer toledot ha'ari*, index, s.v. *gilgul*; Scholem, s.v. *gilgul-neshamah* (metempsychosis), *Ha'entsiklopediyah ha'ivrit*, x, cols 753–7; see also the book by the kabbalist Judah Moses Jeshua Ftayya, *Ruḥot mesaperot*. Kalman Kalonymus Epstein (*Ma'or vashemesh* on Ruth, fo. 151*d*) credits the Ba'al Shem Tov and R. Elimelekh of Lizhensk with being the originators of the emphasis placed on repentance: 'It is desirable for a person to repent . . . during his youth, for a person must remedy what was blemished in the [previous] *gilgul*.'

[2] *Shivḥei habesht*, 169. Cf. the statement by R. Tsevi of Zhidachov (quoted in I. Safrin, *Megilat setarim*, 15) that 'our master the Ba'al Shem Tov is in this world a second time, and is greater in his ability to perform *yiḥudim* by several degrees than what he was, but I [R. Tsevi] do not know where he is'. Cf. also Solomon of Dreznitz, *Shivḥei ha'ari*, fo. 25*a* (pagination added): 'Before his [Luria's] death, he said that he would shortly return to this world.'

[3] Shenkel, *Yeshuot yisra'el*, ii, §13. Cf. Rapoport, *Divrei david*, fo. 29*b*. Zak, *Keneset yisra'el*, 39: 'The rabbi, the tsadik, R. Shalom, the firstborn son of our master of Ruzhin, said as follows: My father is in this world the third time, but in none of them was he in such a state of perfection as now.'

[4] *Shivḥei habesht*, 108. For the Ba'al Shem Tov being 'from the soul of King David, may he rest in peace', see ibid. 92; Abraham of Slonim, *Beit avraham*, 161.

[5] Ehrmann, *Devarim arevim*, 'Stories of the Ba'al Shem Tov', §11.

[6] Shenkel, *Ma'asiyot mitsadikim yesodei olam*, §7. The source is Banet, *She'elot uteshuvot parashat mordekhai*, §134a. For the transmigration of the soul of Queen Esther, see Weberman, *Ma'aseh nisim*, 62.

Maharal of Prague was said to have transmigrated into his grandson, the Grandfather of Shpola,[7] and R. Yudel, a close follower of R. Nahman of Kosov, was supposed to be the reincarnation of the prophet Samuel.[8] R. Tsevi of Zhidachov told his brother, R. Moses of Sambor, that in one of his transmigrations he had been the High Priest Ishmael ben Elisha.[9] R. Shalom of Belz knew who his son had been in former lives.[10] In his old age R. Naphtali Katz, the head of the rabbinical courts in Ostrog, Posen, and Frankfurt, arrived in Constantinople on his way to the Land of Israel. There, on his deathbed, he revealed to every individual present 'from what *gilgul neshamah* he had come'. Of himself he attested that he was the reincarnation of King Hezekiah of Judah, and requested to be buried next to the monarch in Hebron.[11]

According to the hasidic tale, then, the tsadik—like R. Isaac Luria, the father of kabbalism—knows the history of every individual's reincarnations. The Ba'al Shem Tov would reveal this knowledge to people if the information helped him explain their situation to them. For example, it is related that a Torah scholar in Medzibezh lacked the money needed to arrange marriages for his sons and daughters.[12] His wife persuaded him to tell his troubles to the Ba'al Shem Tov, who sent the man to the distant city of Kazmir, where he was to make thorough enquiries about a certain craftsman; he would then find respite from his troubles. The poor man travelled to this remote city, where he learned that the craftsman in question had been an exceedingly wicked man and had died sixty years ago. Disappointed, he returned to the Ba'al Shem Tov and told him all that he had found out. The latter explained to him:

You are learned in the Torah, and you undoubtedly believe with perfect faith in *gilgulim*, as the Ari taught. Know for a certainty that you are that person, the soul

[7] J. Y. Rosenberg, *Tiferet maharal*, 7. See ibid. 60–1: the Grandfather of Shpola showed Graf (Count) Potocki the previous incarnations of Meir Pinsker and R. Baer Halavan; ibid. 92: the Grandfather of Shpola said that his name had been Leib in all of his *gilgulim*. Before his last incarnation, he had been wandering through the heavenly realm for three generations, and had not wanted to descend to the material world until the Ba'al Shem Tov came and forced him to do so.

[8] *Shivḥei habesht*, ed. Rubinstein, 177; this is omitted in the Yiddish edition. *Continued in Appendix.*

[9] Berger, *Eser kedushot*, 'Our Master and Teacher, the Rabbi and Tsadik of Zhidachov', 39.

[10] J. Sofer, *Sipurei ya'akov*, ii, §55. R. Shalom of Belz himself was a spiritual descendant of Cain: see Bodek, *Seder hadorot heḥadash*, fo. 35*b*; Ehrmann, *Pe'er vekhavod*, fo. 18*b*. Bromberg, *Toledot haniflaot*, 39, tells that the grandson of R. Hayim Meir Yehiel of Mogielnica (who died at the age of 4) possessed the soul of R. Dov Baer, the Maggid of Mezirech. A. Michelson, *Ohel elimelekh*, §141, cites the statement by the Seer of Lublin to R. Zelke of Grodzisk that their love for one another ensued from the fact that in their first incarnation they had been father and son.

[11] *Ma'asiyot peliyot nora'im venifla'im*, §2, p. 34. See Nigal, *West and East Studies* (Heb.), 93–7. *Continued in Appendix.*

[12] Bodek, *Ma'aseh tsadikim*, §1, pp. 4–5.

of this wicked individual, who did not leave untouched a single sin in the world, that has been in transmigration for some sixty years. And now you have come, in this reincarnation, to correct what you damaged in the world these sixty years. And now, you still desire human delights and pleasures?

The collector of this story, R. Menahem Mendel Bodek, adds his own conclusion that a person should never complain of his misfortune[13]—a theme that recurs in the stories cited in this chapter.

The tsadik is often asked to find a remedy for the wandering soul; we know that such petitions were addressed to R. Isaac Luria and to the Ba'al Shem Tov.[14] In instances where the soul reappears as a dybbuk (entering the body of a living person, who already possesses a soul of his or her own), the tsadik is asked to free the body of the invasive spirit.

There are two main causes of transmigration: the soul returns either to fulfil some task, or to complete a *mitsvah*, that the deceased had begun in his lifetime; or to atone for a sin committed while the person was alive.

In the first category we have a case of an infant who died at the age of two, whose mother was informed by the Ba'al Shem Tov that in a previous life her son had been a king who had converted to Judaism; he was required to come into the world a second time, in order to live his first years as a Jew.[15] In another instance the Ba'al Shem Tov asked a poor travelling woman to give him her son to raise, for which he would pay her handsomely. The boy grew up to become a prodigious Talmud scholar; many matches were offered him, but the Ba'al Shem Tov rejected them all. He sent his attendant to ask an onion-seller in a distant city for his daughter's hand in marriage for the young scholar. The emissary even promised that the Ba'al Shem Tov would pay the wedding expenses and provide everything that this poor man lacked. When asked why he had turned down good matches for his protégé and instead sought out a poor man's daughter for him, the Ba'al Shem Tov explained that these young people had been married to each other in a previous life. The young man, in an even earlier reincarnation, had been a young prince who had converted, and had to be reincarnated in order to live his first years as a

13 Ibid. 5.

14 'Thousands and myriads of souls' came to the Ba'al Shem Tov when he was at prayer and asked that he effect a *tikun* for them and elevate them (see *Shivḥei habesht*, 104–5). According to *Sefer hakavanot uma'asei nisim*, fo. 2*a*, Elijah revealed, among other things, to the father of R. Isaac Luria that by means of his son who would be born 'several souls who are in *gilgul* will find [their] *tikun*'; cf. fo. 2*b*: 'He would know from a person's countenance what soul he contained, even if it he had been reincarnated for many years, how many times it had been reincarnated, and what was to be remedied by its coming.' In Solomon of Dreznitz, *Shivḥei ha'ari*, fo. 19*b*, R. Isaac Luria tells his disciple that souls come to him by the thousands and myriads: 'When he walks in a field he sees all the trees filled with them, and also in the river: countless [souls] pour out into the pools of water.'

15 *Ma'asiyot vesiḥot tsadikim*, 21–2; Zevin, *Hasidic Tales: On the Torah* (Heb.), 138–40.

Jew. His wife consented to his death, on condition that he promised her that in his second transmigration he would once again marry her. All the Ba'al Shem Tov's efforts were to facilitate the fulfilment of this pledge.[16]

During the time of R. Isaac Luria, a Torah scholar choked to death during his wedding banquet. Luria, who was present at this incident, did not grieve over the death, but said that the act of choking had remedied a deficiency in the soul of the young man and thereby completed its role in this world.[17]

There is a fascinating story by a tsadik regarding his own transmigration. R. Isaac Eisik Safrin tells the following tale in his *Megilat setarim*: 'I was my father's firstborn, and the machinations [of Satan] . . . were responsible for my misplaced transmigrations [i.e. in the wrong bodies], for if he [the father] had effected *tikunim* for my soul, I would not have been required to come to this world . . . I was not in this world more than a year.' When his soul came into the world a second time in his (R. Isaac Eisik's) body, 'I immediately came to my mother from the upper spheres and told her: Mother, they restored me to you, for so it was decreed.'[18]

The truly righteous, then, are reincarnated only to fulfil some mission. For the most part, however, they refrain from returning to the world, even in pursuit of some sublime goal, lest their deeds in their transmigrations be improper. The Ba'al Shem Tov saw R. Akiva and all the other holy martyrs who were killed in a pogrom in Pavoloch, and he asked them to take revenge upon the foes of the Jews. R. Akiva and his fellow martyrs told him that when they had entered paradise they had made such a request, but they were told, 'You must accept upon yourselves reincarnation.' These righteous ones feared lest they irremediably decline in their next life, and so they chose not to exact vengeance.[19]

16 Ehrmann, *Devarim arevim*, 'Stories of the Ba'al Shem Tov', §7. In Moskowitz, *Otsar hasipurim*, xx. 2, the Ba'al Shem Tov reveals that in a previous life the groom (whom the Ba'al Shem Tov had raised in his home) had been a prince who had converted to Judaism, and that the bride (the daughter of an impoverished scribe) had, in a previous *gilgul*, been a princess who had married that prince, and they had to come into the world a second time and be born as Jews. The bride and groom bore the symbolic names Elimelekh (God is my king) and Malkah (queen). Cf. *Midrash vayosha*, cited in J. Y. Rosenberg, *Eliyahu hanavi*, 43–4. See Vital, *Sha'ar hagilgulim*, introd. 20, concerning someone who had sinned and was required to transmigrate, that 'his spouse also transmigrates, so that she is reincarnated with him, for his benefit'.

17 Bodek, *Ma'aseh tsadikim*, §2, p. 6.

18 I. Safrin, *Megilat setarim*, 7–8. *Continued in Appendix.*

19 See *Shivḥei habesht*, 139; cf. above, n. 14, and Benayahu, *Sefer toledot ha'ari*, 250 n. 1: 'He possessed the hidden knowledge of *gilgulim*, both new and old.' For details concerning R. Akiva, the rabbi of Pavoloch, his martyrdom and that of his fellow Jews, and the memorial stone erected in their memory, see Rechtman, *Jewish Ethnography and Folklore* (Yiddish), 133–5; S. An-Ski, *Collected Writings*, xv. 146–7. See also Jacob Joseph of Polonnoye, *Toledot ya'akov yosef*, 'Tsav', fo. 77*d*: 'By our many sins, several martyrs were killed in this year, 1753, in the land of the Ukraine.'

Many stories belong to the second category of transmigration, in which a single soul can be reincarnated a number of times: two, three,[20] ten,[21] fifteen,[22] and even one hundred times![23]

One hasid had to undergo reincarnation because he had pronounced the words of the prayers improperly;[24] another, for having prayed until *Hodu* ('Give thanks . . .': a passage from 1 Chron. 16: 8–36 that begins the introductory Pesukei Dezimrah section of the morning prayer service) without *talit* or *tefilin*;[25] and yet another for making light of his obligation to conduct the *melaveh malkah* meal.[26] Some individuals were required to return because they had studied Torah not for its own sake, but only for self-aggrandizement.[27] One person was subjected to reincarnation because he had mocked the hasidim in his city,[28] while another was so punished for having mercilessly persecuted the daughter of a tsadik.[29] This heavenly decree was also imposed on someone who had vexed the tsadik himself and slandered his daughter.[30]

R. Shalom of Belz described how one young man had been the subject of deliberations in the heavenly court. One judge supported his acquittal, on the grounds that his wicked wife had pestered him and provoked him into bad habits. Another judge did not share this favourable opinion, and asked the rhetorical question: 'When the words of the master and the words of the pupil [are in conflict], whose are heeded?' (BT *Kidushin* 42*b*). This judge, who wanted the young man to be found culpable, aroused the ire of heaven, and it was decreed that the judge was to return to this world and marry a wicked woman so that he would be forced to withstand such a trial himself. The tsadik ended his story by stating: 'You should know that this judge was one of the greatest ones of his generation and a leading hasid, and he always comes to me.'[31]

20 Vital, *Sefer haḥezyonot*, fo. 5*a*: 'And if one of these shall not be wholly perfect, he must die, and afterwards return in a transmigration, until his *tikun* is completed.' Cf. Tsevi Hirsch of Koidanov, *Kav hayashar*, chs. 19, 40; Moskowitz, *Otsar hasipurim*, i, §18; Ehrmann, *Pe'er vekhavod*, fo. 1*b*.

21 See I. Landau, *Zikhron tov*, 'Me'avdut hatsadikim', §6.

22 See Bodek, *Pe'er mikedoshim*, §2.

23 See Shenkel, *Ma'asiyot peliyot*, §24.

24 Bodek, *Kahal kedoshim*, §11. For additional reasons for the transmigration of souls, see the following stories in this chapter. For a person whose soul wandered because of a sin that he did not commit, see [Lemberger], *Magdil yeshuot malko*, 7–8.

25 Ehrmann, *Devarim arevim*, 'Stories of the Ba'al Shem Tov', §30.

26 Lieberson, *Tseror haḥayim*, ch. 1, §§14, 70; Libersohn, *Erets haḥayim*, §45, p. 27. *Continued in Appendix.*

27 See Shenkel, *Ma'asiyot peliyot*, §24.

28 See *Shivḥei habesht*, 53.

29 [Lemberger], *Niflaot hatsadikim*, 21–2.

30 [Isaac Dov Baer ben Tsevi Hirsch], *Kahal ḥasidim heḥadash*, §100. This story resembles in large part the preceding story: in each case someone persecutes the daughter of the tsadik. *Continued in Appendix.*

31 Ehrmann, *Pe'er vekhavod*, fo. 22*b*.

A halakhic authority was sentenced to reincarnation because he ruled that a kosher chicken was not kosher.[32] In another instance, a rabbinic judge could have permitted the consumption of a goose, on the basis of halakhic considerations of 'considerable loss' and the honour of the sabbath (when this dish was to be served), but he chose to be strict, and ruled it non-kosher. When the judge died, the goose came before the heavenly court and claimed that it contained a reincarnated soul; by declaring it unfit, the judge had prevented its release. The heavenly court punished the judge with reincarnation; eventually, the Ba'al Shem Tov effected a *tikun* for this soul.[33]

The soul of one person was compelled to undergo transmigration twice, because he had denied the basic precepts of Judaism. By merit of the Ba'al Shem Tov, however, he died repentant and was not required to undergo a third reincarnation. The tale unfolds as follows: R. David Leikes and R. David of Mikoliev were miraculously sent by the Ba'al Shem Tov, by means of *kefitsat haderekh*, to bring to him the rabbi of a distant city on a Saturday night, after the conclusion of the sabbath. Upon their return, the Ba'al Shem Tov told the rabbi: 'Go home, for you will die this very night!' During the rabbi's funeral, the Ba'al Shem Tov declared:

Hear my words, old man. Know that you have lived in this world three times. The first time, you lived eighty years, and all that time you studied and prayed in a proper manner, and you engaged in good deeds. But before your death you denied the God of Israel, and a ruling was issued by the heavenly court that you must be reincarnated. This second time was precisely as the first, and a decree went forth that your soul would return yet a third time. This third time, as well, you studied Torah and performed meritorious deeds, and I know your Torah and your divine worship . . . I took pity on your soul, for if you were to behave a third time, heaven forbid, as you did the first two times, then, heaven forbid, you would be lost. I therefore sent a young man to bring you here, so that you would die repentant.[34]

Once R. Isaac Eisik Safrin told, in the name of the Ba'al Shem Tov, of the transmigration of the soul of the first person to strike the prophet Zechariah:

[32] I. Safrin, *Megilat setarim*, 39.

[33] Ibid.

[34] Chikernik, *Sipurim neḥmadim*, 7–10, based on Zohar, *Tikunei zohar*, 'Tikun' 32 (fo. 76*b*): 'It is said of sinners who do not repent during three *gilgulim*: "I will cause that person [literally, soul] to perish" [Lev. 23: 30], and he descends to Gehinnom, where he is forgotten for ever and ever.' See also Zohar, *Tikunei zohar*, 'Tikun' 70 (fo. 138*a*); 'Tikun' 32 (fo. 76*b*): 'All the souls that were reincarnated three times but did not receive their *tikun* are called the sinners of Israel, "a mixed multitude" [Exod. 12: 38].' See also Zohar, iii, fo. 216*a*: 'The wicked do not transmigrate more than three times.' Cf. Gelernter, *Revid hazahav*, fo. 14*a*: 'Into an animal, or into other things, one can transmigrate even several times, but within a human being one cannot transmigrate more than three times.' See also *Ḥemdat hayamim*, iv, ch. 4, fo. 55*d*; Azikri, *Sefer ḥaredim* (1897 edn), 58. For a woman whose soul transmigrated because she did not believe in the exodus from Egypt, see *Sefer hakavanot uma'asei nisim*, fo. 10*a*.

In the cities of Ashkenaz there was a righteous man who said, before his death, that he would come to an unnatural demise at the hands of murderers, and that he had already been in this world one hundred times, and each time he had been killed. During the time of the Temple he had been the head of the Sanhedrin, of fierce intellect, wise, and learned in the deadly poison of the Torah [i.e. his learning was wrongly applied]. He was the first to strike the cheek and face of the prophet Zechariah[, saying]: 'You commoner, how do you engage in prophecy?' He was responsible for the completely wicked masses falling upon [Zechariah] and killing him. He ordered that the following be inscribed on his tombstone: 'Here lies the one who killed the prophet Zechariah.' And he said that he had already received his *tikun*.

The tsadik of Komarno then added: 'Our master [the Ba'al Shem Tov] would relate this, as a moral lesson, showing that a person should take care not to study Torah not for its own sake, [for that would then be] a deadly poison and the bitter waters [i.e. that are given to a wife suspected on infidelity]', citing as examples those 'scholars' engaged in *Wissenschaft des Judentums* in Berlin, Breslau, Prague, and Hamburg, where little remained of traditional Judaism.[35] If the Ba'al Shem Tov did indeed tell this story, he would have been alluding to the flawed Torah study of the 'scholars', that is, the early mitnagedim. And in fact, Torah scholars feature prominently in many hasidic tales in which transmigration occurs to correct some blemish in the soul.

Another tale also concerns the person who was the first to cast a stone at the prophet Zechariah. The Maggid of Koznitz healed someone whose body had been entered by a dybbuk. The reincarnated soul related that it had been the first to throw a stone at Zechariah in the Temple, and promised to depart from the young man's body, leaving him unscathed, in exchange for a pledge by the Maggid to study *mishnayot* every day on his behalf, and a similar pledge by the young man to recite Kaddish.[36] The first person to harm the prophet Jeremiah was also required to undergo reincarnation.[37] The souls of the notoriously wicked must transmigrate in order to amend their iniquities: the soul of Jeroboam returned in the body of R. Josiah Pinto,[38] who effected

[35] I. Safrin, *Notser ḥesed*, fo. 21*b*; also included in Sperling, *Reasons for the Customs* (Heb.), 530; Chikernik, *Ma'asiyot uma'amarim yekarim*, 23. In Breitstein, *Siḥot ḥayim*, 17–18, the rabbi of Mogielnica related that a dybbuk that was brought before the Maggid of Koznitz (and afterwards before the Seer of Lublin) revealed: 'I was chief of the thousand, I lived during the time of the First Temple, and I delivered a blow to the prophet Zechariah in the Temple.' Cf. Goldstein, *Masaot yerushalayim*, fo. 25*a*; Jacob ben Ezekiel Halevi of Zlotowa, *Shem ya'akov*, fo. 17*a*: 'A certain spirit said that it had thrown the first stone at the prophet Zechariah, may he rest in peace.'

[36] Kaidaner, *Sipurim nora'im*, §22; also cited in Roth, *Shomer emunim*, fos 316*b*–317*a*, in 'Additions and Clarifications' added by Roth's son-in-law, R. Abraham Isaac Kahan; also in Ben-Yehezkel, *Sefer hama'asiyot*, vi. 297–9. For dybbuks, see Nigal, 'The Dybbuk in Jewish Mysticism' (Heb.).

[37] Bodek, *Pe'er mikedoshim*, §2.

[38] Ibid., §3.

a *tikun* when he destroyed an object used for idolatrous purposes. The soul of King Manasseh of Judah, who placed a statue in the Temple, returned in the body of a tax-collector who uprooted idolatrous statues placed at crossroads;[39] the soul of Ishmael son of Nethaniah, the would-be assassin of Gedaliah, suffered a similar fate.[40]

Once the Ba'al Shem Tov told of a rabbinical judge, a man with a reincarnated soul, who vexed the city rabbi. The Ba'al Shem Tov sought to effect a *tikun* for the judge, but without success, since 'the wicked remain wicked'.[41]

R. Ze'ev Wolf of Zbarazh, the son of R. Yehiel Mikhel of Zlotchev, passed through Lemberg, where a wealthy man was among those who received him. The rabbi told the following story. There were two brothers, one rich and the other poor. The wealthy brother loaned the impoverished one 1,000 roubles as capital to trade with, on the understanding that he would return the capital when he himself became a man of means. As time passed, the wealthy brother came down in the world, but the previously indigent brother, who in the meantime had become wealthy, refused to repay his loan, leaving his needy brother to die penniless. Some time later, the newly rich brother also passed away. The heavenly court decreed that the souls of both would return, the wicked brother as a rich person, and the righteous one as a poor man; the latter would collect charity throughout his life from the rich man, until he had obtained the sum of 1,000 roubles. When, in this second reincarnation, the pauper came to the rich man (his wicked brother) and begged for a single coin, the wealthy man sent him away empty-handed, at which point the poor man collapsed and died. R. Ze'ev Wolf told the wealthy man, who was among those receiving him: 'You are this wicked one! Yesterday you did such-and-such to the poor man who was your brother, who had loaned you one thousand roubles in an earlier incarnation!'[42]

A comparable story, this time about friends rather than brothers, was told by R. Shalom of Kaminka, in the name of the Ba'al Shem Tov, when the leading tsadikim gathered in Ropshits for the *yahrzeit* of R. Naphtali of

[39] Bodek, *Pe'er mikedoshim*, §4. Cf. Tzitrin, *Shivḥei tsadikim*, 50; Chervinski, *Teshuot ḥen*, i. 33–4; cited in Ben-Yehezkel, *Sefer hama'asiyot*, vi. 447. Ahab, king of Israel, was said to be reincarnated in a wealthy person who lived during the time of R. Isaac Luria (*Sefer hakavanot uma'asei nisim*, fo. 6*a*); and in a young man who was killed during the time of the Maharsha (R. Samuel Eliezer ben Edels) (Hazan, *Sipurim nifla'im*, 64–6).

[40] Rodkinsohn, *Sipurei tsadikim*, §22, pp. 40–2.

[41] Ehrmann, *Devarim arevim*, 'Stories of the Ba'al Shem Tov', §4. For the punishment of a rabbinical judge who did not judge properly and was compelled to come into the world a second time, see Shenkel, *Ma'asiyot mitsadikim yesodei olam*, §5.

[42] [Isaac Dov Baer ben Tsevi Hirsch], *Kahal ḥasidim heḥadash*, §83. Cf. Walden, *Shem hagedolim heḥadash*, s.v. Wolf of Zbarazh. See also J. Sofer, *Sipurei ya'akov*, ii, §60: the Maggid of Mezirech explains 'injustice in judgment' in relation to a monetary debt incurred in a previous life. For more on a reincarnated soul who returns money to its owner, see al-Hakam, *Nifla'im ma'asekha*, §40, p. 30; §103, pp. 94–6. See Nigal, *West and East Studies* (Heb.), 133–44.

Ropshits. A woman cried out to the tsadikim that she had lent 1,000 roubles to her partner, who had then disappeared without trace. The assembled tsadikim made various promises to her, but R. Shalom declared that all these assurances were worthless, and that there was no hope for this woman, 'for who knows what *gilgul* [reincarnated soul] proposed to this man to take the money, that the woman had given him to repay her debt [i.e. as a former *gilgul* of hers to a former *gilgul* of the partner]?'[43]

The Ba'al Shem Tov taught the Maggid of Mezirech the secret of the transmigration of souls through the case of a horseman who had lost his purse. This money was then found by a person who in a former life had wrongly paid this sum to the horseman (as the result of an erroneous court ruling).[44]

As noted at the beginning of this chapter, souls may transmigrate not only into other humans, but also into the animal, vegetable, or inanimate realms. Once R. Zusya and his attendant were travelling along when they found birds pecking at a tree: R. Zusya realized that a soul had transmigrated into the tree, and he effected a *tikun* for it.[45]

The first *gilgul* story to appear in print in the hasidic literature is that of reincarnation as a frog, included in *Shivḥei habesht* in two versions. According to the first, the Ba'al Shem Tov encountered the frog when the tsadik returned from his unsuccessful attempt to go to the Land of Israel. The second version (an alternative signalled as such by the phrase 'and some say') reads as follows:

> Once the rabbi entered a deeply contemplative state [of consciousness], and went about in this manner in the wilderness for three days and three nights, knowing nothing of this. After this, he realized that he was in a great wilderness, far from his place. His having wandered to this desert was wondrous in his eyes; it undoubtedly was not a mere empty region. When he asked the frog: 'Who are you?', it replied that it was a Torah scholar who had returned in this frog. (And then the Ba'al Shem Tov declared: 'You are a Torah scholar', thereby greatly elevating his soul.) He [the frog] also told him that he had been in this animal for five hundred years; although R. Isaac Luria had effected *tikun* for all souls, due to the severity of his transgressions, he had been banished, to wander in an uninhabited region, so that his soul would find no *tikun*. When [the Ba'al Shem Tov] asked him, what was his sin, the latter replied that one time he had made light of the commandment of washing

[43] Bodek, *Pe'er mikedoshim*, §1. For a monetary payment as compensation for troubles caused by two people (in a previous life) to a third individual, see J. Sofer, *Sipurei ya'akov*, ii, §55.

[44] Shenkel, *Ma'asiyot mitsadikim yesodei olam*, §5. *Sefer hakavanot uma'asei nisim*, fo. *6b*, tells of a transmigration for the purpose of putting financial affairs in order. See Nigal, 'Transmigration of Souls' (Heb.).

[45] Reznik, *Mora'im gedolim*, §4, p. 8. See also Brandwein, *Degel maḥaneh yehudah*, §89; A. Stern, *Ḥutim hameshulashim*, 22–3. Cf. the Baghdad tale of transmigration into a pomegranate: Ftayya, *Ruḥot mesaperot*, 9. Elijah ben Solomon Abraham Hakohen (Ha'itamari), *Midrash talpiyot*, letter *gimel*, *gilgul*, fo. 92*c*, writes: 'The harshest transmigration is as an inanimate, dry stone, from which no benefit can issue.'

the hands, and had not fulfilled this obligation properly. Satan had accused him [before the heavenly court], but [the court] responded that this scholar could not be found guilty for a single transgression; rather, one transgression leads to another, and if [Satan] could cause him to commit another sin, then this, too, would be accounted against him.

This scholar went on to misbehave further until he had committed almost every transgression possible. His punishment, therefore, was to be rejected by heaven, with no possibility of repentance. Since he had sinned concerning the washing of the hands, and as a result of his many iniquities had become a drunkard, he was sentenced to be reincarnated as a frog,

that is always in the water, and to be in a place where there are no human beings. For when a Jew were to pass by, or recite some blessing, this would be regarded as a good thought, such that could bring forth what is noble from the worthless. The Ba'al Shem Tov effected a *tikun* for his soul and raised it up, leaving the frog dead.[46]

According to both versions, the Ba'al Shem Tov travelled to a desolate region in order to provide a *tikun* for this soul and enable it to ascend. The story is intended to demonstrate the greatness of the Ba'al Shem Tov, who is capable of effecting *tikunim* even for souls who had not been saved by R. Isaac Luria, the greatest of the repairers of souls. On the other hand, it is plainly derisive of Torah scholars who commit everyday transgressions despite their erudition. The story also displays the motif of *midah keneged midah* (the punishment fitting the crime): one who sins through liquid (in this case, alcohol as well as well as water) is punished through liquid.

Another story has the Ba'al Shem Tov effecting a *tikun* for the soul of a debtor who returned as a horse. It was decreed that he should faithfully serve the creditor to whom he owed money when he died. The Ba'al Shem Tov's request that he be given the horse as a gift was emphatically rejected. However, when the tsadik asked for the late debtor's promissory note, the creditor was happy to agree, since he attributed no worth to a note signed by someone who had already passed away. The Ba'al Shem Tov ripped up the note, and the creditor fully forgave the dead debtor. When they went to the stable, they found the horse dead, for the soul that had entered it had now found its *tikun*.[47]

Souls that have transmigrated into kosher plants and animals find their *tikun* through being consumed at a *se'udat mitsvah* (a meal held in association with the fulfilment of a religious obligation), after the recitation of the blessing over this food, and similar blessings.

[46] *Shivḥei habesht*, ed. Rubinstein, 48. The Yiddish version of *Shivḥei habesht* provides only the version 'Some say'. Cf. [Isaac Dov Baer ben Tsevi Hirsch], *Kahal ḥasidim heḥadash*, §28; Palache, *Torah veḥayim*, fos 10*b*–11*a*. The story from *Shivḥei habesht* was also copied in Vital, *Sha'ar hagilgulim*, ed. Rabinowitz, fos 13*d*–14*a*). *Continued in Appendix.*

[47] See *Shivḥei habesht*, 151; Yehiel Moses of Yadimov, *Likutim ḥadashim*, fo. 19*a*; and, in an abbreviated version, Shenkel, *Sipurei anshei shem*, §12.

R. Ze'ev of Zhitomir, a disciple of the Maggid of Mezirech, had previously been a land tenant in a village. Once, when a Jewish wagon-driver entering the village wished to drink some liquor without first reciting the proper blessing, R. Ze'ev explained to the driver that many people toil exceedingly hard to produce intoxicating drink, and also that myriads of souls transmigrate into the inanimate world. 'You should know', the tsadik told the driver, 'that your father's soul is to be found in this strong drink, and awaits his *tikun* by your recitation of the blessing.' The wagon driver recited the *Shehakol* blessing proper for such drink and the tsadik loudly responded 'Amen'.[48]

It was widely accepted, under the influence of Lurianic kabbalah, that 'most of the righteous transmigrate into fish'.[49] R. Isaac Eisik Safrin wrote that the messiah son of Joseph underwent exile 'for the tsadikim who transmigrate into fish'.[50] R. Simhah Bunem of Pshischa attested of himself: 'Once I was walking by a river, and a large fish cast itself into my bowl. I took the fish, effected a *tikun* for it by myself, and conducted *Kol nidrei* [the renunciation of vows] for it.'[51] During a shortage of fish, a non-Jew brought a fish to R. Joseph Barukh of Neustadt (the son of R. Kalman Kalonymus Epstein of Krakow), who was known as the *guter yid* [the good Jew]. The rabbi ordered that 'the fish be neither skinned not cut up, but rather be cooked whole . . . for there is a great *gilgul* [in it]!'[52] Ten people who ate at the table of R. Barukh of Medzibezh consumed a fish that had been cooked whole, which contained the soul of someone who had drowned himself so as not to succumb to his evil urges.[53] The *magid* R. Abraham of Trisk once purchased a large fish and personally supervised its preparation and cooking. He then ordered his sons to partake of it, declaring that the person whose soul was in the fish had been erudite in the Babylonian and Jerusalem Talmuds, *Sifra*, *Sifrei*, and the Tosefta.[54] R. Joseph, the father of R. Yudel of Chudnov, appeared to his son in a dream on the sabbath night and revealed to him that

[48] See Zeilingold, *Me'orot hagedolim*, 'His Holiness, R. Ze'ev of Zhitomir', §24, p. 91; Libersohn, *Erets haḥayim*, §167, p. 53. *Continued in Appendix.*

[49] Teitelbaum, *Yismaḥ mosheh*, fo. 39*b*: 'This, undoubtedly, refers to minor righteous ones; the great righteous ones, however, do not require any *tikun*.' Cf. Sperling, *Reasons for the Customs* (Heb.), 144; M. M. Sofer, *Sheloshah edrei tson*, 21; Ehrmann, *Devarim arevim*, 'Corrigenda'; ibid., 'Stories from the Holy Rabbi of Lublin', §6. *Continued in Appendix.*

[50] I. Safrin, *Megilat setarim*, 27. A soul that transmigrates into a non-kosher animal is likely to receive its *tikun* if a proper Jew (i.e. one who observes the commandments) makes a garment out of its hide. See Abraham of Slonim, *Beit avraham*, 134.

[51] Samuel of Shinova, *Ramatayim tsofim*, 154 (§43).

[52] Rakats, *Siaḥ sarfei kodesh*, v. 101.

[53] Reznik, *Mora'im gedolim*, §5, pp. 10–11. Cf. [Lemberger], *Magdil yeshuot malko*, 7–8.

[54] Chikernik, *Sipurim uma'amarim yekarim*, 32. Cf. Vital, *Sefer haḥezyonot*, fo. 6*a*. For a haughty scholar who was reincarnated in a fish, for whom the tsadik of Kalev saw that 'there was no possibility of effecting a *tikun*', see Brandwein, *Degel maḥaneh yehudah*, §34. The Holy Jew asked his hasidim to eat a small piece of a rotten (*saruaḥ*) fish, which contained the soul of a Torah scholar who had gone astray (*saraḥ*). See Yehiel Moses of Yadimov, *Likutim ḥadashim*, fo. 19*a*.

he had been reincarnated as a large fish, which the householder whose guest R. Yudel was had purchased for the sabbath. This punishment was inflicted on the father for his having persecuted an informer during his former life. R. Yudel effected a *tikun* for his father's soul by weeping over the drowning of a dog (the reincarnation of the informer), and apparently also by eating the fish.[55]

Other stories recount reincarnation as a goose,[56] or as a rooster;[57] these souls found rest when the animals were eaten. Mention was made earlier of the young man who choked while eating chicken during his wedding feast, thereby effecting a *tikun* for the soul embodied in the chicken, and concluding his own purpose in the world.[58]

One sabbath eve, the wife of the Seer of Lublin had a question regarding whether a chicken was kosher. The Seer was in the ritual bath at the time, and only one of his pupils was in the vicinity. This disciple, whose teachings were approved by the Seer, did not wish to issue a ruling, but when the Seer's wife implored him, he responded that he could not declare the chicken to be fit. Instead of accepting his decision, the wife preferred to await her husband's return, when the Seer permitted the chicken to pass as kosher, on the halakhic grounds that disqualifying it would entail 'considerable loss'. The Seer amazed his disciple when he explained that 'the unfortunate soul that was reincarnated in the chicken has already been waiting for several years, and it begs and pleads that we eat the chicken on the holy sabbath, and thereby effect its *tikun*'.[59]

Cattle also serve as hosts for these wandering souls. The soul of a Jew who sold non-kosher meat as kosher was punished by being reincarnated into non-kosher beasts for four years, again according to the principle of the punishment fitting the crime.[60] R. Yehiel Mikhel of Zlotchev once sent one of his

[55] *Shivḥei habesht*, 177.

[56] I. Safrin, *Megilat setarim*, 39. Cf. Hazan, *Sipurim nifla'im*, 25; Rosenstein, *Pe'er layesharim*, fo. 17*b*. For reincarnation as a small bird, see Lieberson, *Tseror haḥayim*, ch. 1, §14; §70; Libersohn, *Erets haḥayim*, §48, p. 27.

[57] J. Sofer, *Sipurei ya'akov*, ii, §37. See also Reznik, *Mora'im gedolim*, §2. A cat that began to nibble at a chicken that contained a *gilgul* caused R. Nahum of Chernobyl to eat the chicken, together with its bones (Rosenthal, *Hitgalut hatsadikim*, 54). Cf. the Baghdad story of reincarnation in a rooster: Ftayya, *Ruḥot mesaperot*, 12.

[58] Bodek, *Ma'aseh tsadikim*, §2, p. 6. See Tsevi Hirsch of Koidanov, *Kav hayashar*, ch. 2: 'If a person looks at women, his soul will transmigrate in a chicken.'

[59] Ehrmann, *Pe'er vekhavod*, fos 28*b*–29*a*. *Continued in Appendix.*

[60] [Isaac Dov Baer ben Tsevi Hirsch], *Kahal ḥasidim heḥadash*, §203. Cf. Tsevi Hirsch of Koidanov, *Kav hayashar*, ch. 76: 'Whoever commits the sin of unwittingly [drinking] non-kosher wine will later be reincarnated in an ass [*ḥamor*] . . . for the translation of wine is *ḥemer*.' For the three cardinal transgressions for which a person is reincarnated in a non-kosher animal, see Elijah ben Solomon Abraham Hakohen (Ha'itamari), *Midrash talpiyot*, 3: 3, 89*c*. See also Bromberg, *Toledot haniflaot*, 22, for the statement by R. Hayim Meir Yehiel of Mogielnica that several of the city's worthies 'prior to their [latest] birth, had been reincarnated in pigs'.

disciples on a journey, in the course of which he met a small, fine-looking dog, in which his father's soul had been reincarnated;[61] in another instance, a dog that contained a transmigrated soul awaiting its *tikun* lay under the table of R. Akiva Joseph Schlesinger's father-in-law.[62] Reincarnation in a dog is a common punishment for informers. One informer found his *tikun* when the dog in which he had been reincarnated drowned while rescuing R. Yudel of Chudnov.[63] A mitnaged could expect a similar fate, especially if he spoke ill of tsadikim, found fault with them, or mocked them: the author of *Heikhal berakhah*, Isaac Eisik Safrin, cites the observation by R. Naphtali of Ropshits that the soul of anyone who speaks against tsadikim will return as a dog.[64]

A story that reflects this belief describes how a group of hasidim travelling together to the rabbi of Ropshits were barked at and chased by a large dog. They thought that the dog must be the reincarnation of a mitnaged, which barked at them because they were travelling to a tsadik. A carriage that happened to pass by ran over the dog and killed it. When the hasidim arrived at the tsadik's court, he told them: 'You should know, young men, that what the world says about a mitnaged returning as a dog is true.'[65]

Any grave sinner could also expect to be reincarnated in a dog. It is related that R. Isaac Luria was once late for a circumcision ceremony, and gave the following explanation for his tardiness. As he was walking, he was confronted by a dog that came towards him, barking. R. Luria asked the dog who it was, and the animal replied that it was the reincarnation of Gehazi (the servant of the prophet Elisha), who had been punished for his lack of faith and his failure to carry out Elisha's orders: when the prophet commanded him to revive the son of the Shunammite woman with his staff (see 2 Kgs. 4: 29), he doubted that such a miracle could be achieved. On his way,

61 *Shivḥei habesht*, 91–2. *Continued in Appendix.*

62 See A. J. Schwartz, *Derekh hanesher*, 26, citing Schlesinger, *Shimru mishpat*, ii, fo. 72 (I could not find it there); also cited in Klapholz, *Lamed-vav tsadikim nistarim*, ii. 64–6 and Moskowitz, *Otsar hasipurim*, viii, §3. *Continued in Appendix.*

63 *Shivḥei habesht*, 176–7. See Berger, *Eser atarot*, 'R. Meir of Premishlan', §16: the soul of an informer who vexed R. Meir of Premishlan transmigrated into a dog following the death of the tsadik, and collected bones under the table of the latter's son-in-law. For an informer who returned in a mouse, see *Ḥemdat hayamim*, iv, fo. 56*a*.

64 I. Safrin, *Heikhal haberakhah*, 'Nitzavim'. See A. Michelson, *Ohel naftali*, §155; see also Judah Yehiel of Rozdol, *Lev same'aḥ heḥadash*, 36n., which quotes R. Naphtali of Ropshits (following *Heikhal haberakhah*). Vital, *Sefer haḥezyonot*, fo. 13*a*: 'And that person changed into the form of a dog.' See *Sefer hakavanot uma'asei nisim*, fo. 11*a*. Cf. Benayahu, *Sefer toledot ha'ari*, 237–8: the tale of R. Abraham ibn Puah's neighbour, who committed adultery with R. Abraham's wife, and returned as 'a very ugly black dog'. Tsevi Hirsch of Koidanov, who cites the account in *Kav hayashar*, ch. 34, concludes: 'The impudent are punished by *gilgul* in a dog, such as [those who commit] the iniquity of [sexual relations with] a married woman.' The story also appears in *Ḥemdat hayamim*, iv, ch. 4, fo. 56*a*; *Sefer hama'asiyot* (Baghdad), §95, pp. 118–19. Cf. Judah Yehiel of Rozdol, *Lev same'aḥ haḥadash*, 36.

65 Berger, *Eser tsaḥtsaḥot*, 'R. Naphtali of Ropshits', §35; A. Michelson, *Ohel naftali*, §33.

he saw a dead dog and tested the prophet's staff on the animal. The dog did in fact return to life, but the staff was no longer effective on the body of the youth. Gehazi's punishment was reincarnation in a dog.[66]

A special form of transmigration is that of the dybbuk, which is a soul that enters the body of a living person who already possesses a soul of his own.[67] Such an unfortunate person is usually thought to be mad, for at times he utters words that are not his own. On the other hand, it is assumed that this extra soul is receptive to what ordinary mortals do not hear, so that the dybbuk knows things that are hidden from human comprehension, and is capable of transmitting this information to humans. In any event, the tsadik is credited with the power of persuading the dybbuk to leave the body of the living person; at times the dybbuk receives compensation in the form of prayer, a blessing, or study on its behalf (the *tikun* for its soul). During the period before the Ba'al Shem Tov was revealed as a tsadik, his brother-in-law R. Gershon sought to rebuke him. To this end he brought to the tsadik an insane woman who was known for her ability to tell a person his 'abominations [i.e. sins] and good deeds.' The dybbuk insolently told the Ba'al Shem Tov that he did not fear him, since because he had not yet reached the age of 36 (the age at which heaven decreed that he would reveal himself) he was constrained from acting to exorcise the dybbuk. The Ba'al Shem Tov rebuked the dybbuk and threatened the spirit that if he did not willingly go forth, he would convene a heavenly court that would authorize him to act, even if this was still premature. On the positive side, the Ba'al Shem Tov assured the dybbuk that those present would study on his behalf, thereby effecting the necessary *tikun* for the soul. The dybbuk did indeed depart from the woman, without causing her any harm.[68]

A dybbuk that entered the body of the youngest son of a follower of the rabbi of Ruzhin similarly bragged that he feared neither R. Shalom of Belz nor the tsadik of Premishlan, but admitted to being afraid of the tsadik R. Israel of Ruzhin. When the tsadik heard this from the boy's father, he stated confidently that he could exorcise the dybbuk, and moreover that he

[66] See Rakats, *Siaḥ sarfei kodesh*, ii, §475, p. 124. The wandering soul received its *tikun* when the dog jumped into a boiling dish that was poisoned, thus saving the lives of many Jews. See BT *San.* 107*b*; Ben-Yehezkel, *Sefer hama'asiyot*, vi. 288–90.

[67] Tsevi Hirsch of Koidanov, *Kav hayashar*, ch. 40, informs us: 'Know that the matter of transmigration of the soul is divided into two modes. In the first mode, the person does not necessarily die, with his soul transmigrating into another person to effect a *tikun* for the wandering soul; rather, during his lifetime another soul will enter his own body, even though the body already contained one soul, and both souls shall be together, that is, the new soul and his own, joined together, like the foetus within a pregnant [*me'uberet*] woman. Such a *gilgul* within one's lifetime is therefore called the *ibur*. . . . until the blemish is corrected, when the new soul goes to its proper dwelling place; this is the *gilgul* that is not severe.'

[68] See *Shivḥei habesht*, 53. Cf. the statement by the Ba'al Shem Tov in Margolioth, *Kevutsat ya'akov*, fo. 53*b*: 'I cure the mad only with wisdom!' *Continued in Appendix.*

could do so immediately, unlike the tsadik of Belz, who required a number of weeks to accomplish such a task. R. Israel taught the letters of the Hebrew alphabet to the youth, who had been struck dumb since the dybbuk had entered him, and by means of these letters, which were the letters of the Torah, he succeeded in exorcising the dybbuk.[69]

Once a dybbuk entered the body of a virgin, a poor man's daughter, and spoke 'awesome and wondrous' things. Three people, including R. Feibush of Prague, attempted to exorcise the spirit. As they approached, the dybbuk greeted them, and they demanded, with various threats, that the spirit tell them why he had transmigrated. The dybbuk then related that he had fathered many children with non-Jewish women.[70]

Some stories describe in detail the damage inflicted by the dybbuk on the person whose body he enters. One dybbuk would throw a young woman to the ground, cause her neck to elongate, and pull her tongue out of her mouth.[71] In some instances, the dybbuk is depicted not as a transmigrated soul but as a *ba'al davar*, that is, an agent of Satan. One such is the account in which R. Elimelekh intervenes posthumously to rescue a woman from the clutches of Satan.[72] This dybbuk would not allow the woman to engage in any religious activity, and when she visited the synagogue he would lead her to engage in frivolous behaviour, and speak from within her in a non-Jewish tongue. The dead R. Elimelekh saved the woman, who had previously gained only temporary limited relief from a charm she had been given. Scoffing words and profanities were also uttered by another dybbuk that had entered the body of a non-Jewish woman.

I heard from the Ridbaz [R. Raphael Isaac David ben Ze'ev Willowski], may the memory of the righteous be for a blessing, that during his term as rabbi in the city of Slutsk, there was a certain person there by the name of Tanhum. This person, who was frivolous and a scoffer, would trade with the non-Jewish women in eggs and poultry, and was presumed to be a sinner, heaven forfend. Some weeks after his death, a certain non-Jewish woman went mad, and the voice of Tanhum spoke

[69] J. Sofer, *Sipurei ya'akov*, ii, §52. For the case of a fabricated dybbuk inhabitation, in which a maiden, about 20 years old, 'would walk in the streets of the city, barking like a dog, continually throwing herself to the ground, and speaking from her throat', see Zeilingold, *Me'orot hagedolim*, 'His Holiness, the Holy Rabbi, R. Levi Isaac', 15.

[70] Shenkel, *Sipurei anshei shem*, §21. For a dybbuk during the time of R. Isaac Luria who committed adultery and fathered *mamzerim* (illegitimate children), see *Sefer hakavanot uma'asei nisim*, fos 8*b*–10*a*. Breitstein, *Siḥot ḥayim*, 55, tells of a dybbuk that had entered a woman who was then brought before the rabbi of Mogielnica. The dybbuk was punished for having mocked the tsadik; the woman suffered such a fate because she had not taken care to separate *ḥalah* while baking. Cf. ibid. 55–6, 60–1 for the tale of a dybbuk who was punished for having persecuted R. Levi Isaac of Berdichev.

[71] See Breitstein, *Siḥot ḥayim*, §34, pp. 23–4.

[72] See the (forged) letter by R. Elazar of Lizhensk to R. Menahem Mendel of Rymanow, published at the end of N. T. Horowitz, *Imrei shefer*; also cited in Berger, *Eser tsaḥtsaḥot*, 'R. Elimelekh', fo. 20*a*–*b*.

from her mouth, in Yiddish, all the foolishness and profanity that he had been accustomed to speak in his lifetime. Anyone who did not see this non-Jewish woman, but only heard her voice, would think that this was really Tanhum. People came from all around to see this wonder, the dybbuk. Even the maskilim (of little faith) Mordecai ben Hillel Hacohen and Michael Pines (who later went to the Land of Israel, may it be rebuilt and re-established) came from their city to see this. Some weeks later, the non-Jewish woman fell and was killed, and the voice of Tanhum was stilled.[73]

To close this chapter I will present a detailed story of a dybbuk and its exorcism that was told a number of times by R. Moses of Savran.

It happened that a woman who had been possessed by the spirit of a wicked person was brought to the rabbi of Yaryshev for exorcism. The rabbi, of blessed memory, said: 'This is not within my realm, go to the tsadikim of the generation, such as was the rabbi, R. Barukh of Medzibezh, of blessed memory, and the like.' The dybbuk responded from within the woman: 'Rabbi, I am in no need of anyone greater than you; you, too, are capable of effecting a *tikun* for me. If a *minyan* of people among you will recite psalms for ten days, then I will go on my way.' The rabbi said to him: 'If that is so, then I want you to tell me all that has happened to you, from beginning to end.' The dybbuk told the rabbi, of blessed memory: 'I was a Torah scholar. One time, the evil urge entered, me, to make light of the [ritual] washing of the hands. Of what concern is it to me whether or not I wash my hands? After that, I did not wash my hands at all, and one transgression led to another, until I eventually denied the existence of God. Some time later, I took a foreign [i.e. non-Jewish] woman as my wife, and I fathered children. And then, after much time had passed, I thought to myself: What will be my end? What good can be expected by someone who has denied the Lord, the God of Israel? I resolved to return to the Lord and Judaism, but I feared lest I be handed over to the authorities [after having previously converted], and so I sought a place to dwell until the hair of my head and beard grew, and then I would decide what I should do. I came to the house of a certain Jew and asked him to "conceal me in his pavilion" until the hair of my head and beard had grown. He answered me: "What you have said you will do is good. Stay with me in a hidden place." As [we were talking], I heard a voice emerge from another room, and I asked the householder: "Who is the person whose voice I hear?" He answered, "That is my son-in-law, who is a Torah scholar and one who engages in good deeds." Then I heard him recite from chapter 89 of Psalms: "As the moon, established forever, an enduring witness in the sky. *Selah*" [v. 38]. His father-in-law read this incorrectly, and I laughed at him, saying: "Shall such a one be called 'a Torah scholar', who is incapable of reading the words with their proper vocalization?" The young man was embarrassed by what I said, and the householder (who was his father-in-law) was greatly angered with me, and he ordered me: "Leave me, lest I myself deliver you to those who would arise against you. You have been displeasing to the Lord, and you are so now, as well, and you

[73] Mehudar, *Zekhuta de'avraham*, 'Kunteres devarim nifla'im', 130. This dybbuk was exorcised by a mitnagdic rabbi in a mitnagdic environment. *Continued in Appendix.*

shall remain displeasing to the Lord; leave my house." I left his house, and I went to a field in the valley under a great mountain. The houses of non-Jews were there for me to take refuge; I did not want this, but there were no Jewish houses there. I resolved: Whatever the Lord shall find pleasing to do with me, he shall do. I did not desire to enter a non-Jewish house. I saw an outcrop of rock emerging from the mountain close to the earth, and I entered under it lest I be smitten by the pouring rain. And then, suddenly, a torrent of water came from the mountain, I could not get out from under the outcrop of rock, and I drowned in the stormy waters. My soul ascended to heaven, and the heavenly court considered my case. It could find no sin that I had committed in matters between me and the omnipresent [i.e. ritual matters]. Since I could have hidden myself in the house of non-Jews but did not wish to do so, I was considered to have died repentant, and my death atoned for all. But in this I was found guilty, in that I had publicly shamed that young man. The ruling was issued that I would be transmigrated into a chicken. And so it was: I was reincarnated in a chicken of non-Jews, and the head of the chicken was cut off. Then I thought, what shall I do now? If I were to remain in the flesh of the chicken, then the non-Jews would eat me, and it would be extremely difficult for me to ascend to my former place; if I were to enter among the entrails that would be thrown out, even if they might be eaten by a dog or a pig, it would still be easier for me to ascend from them than if I were in the body of a non-Jew. And that is what I did. I entered the entrails, which were discarded outside. In the meantime, the woman passed by, and I entered into her. Accordingly, I am certain that if a quorum of people were to recite psalms for ten days, then I would return to my place.' The rabbi of Yaryshev acted thus, by gathering ten men to recite psalms. Before the conclusion of the ten days, the dybbuk told the rabbi: 'Here, I do not worry for myself, but I am concerned for the woman. Since this horrifying occurrence has become known among the people of the city, and it will be the talk of all, from old to young, the spirits that rove about through the air will hear that I have emerged from the woman after ten days. After my departure, another spirit could enter her: since one has been in her, another could easily enter her afterwards.' The rabbi asked him: 'What do you say will remedy this?' The spirit responded: 'The remedy for this is the following: since there is a corpse here that is to be buried, and when the bier is carried, all the destructive agents and spirits fly about in the air—let your beadle proclaim before all those in the funeral procession, saying: "Know that the spirit that has entered the woman so-and-so is a liar, for having said that he will depart after ten days, in the end, he does not desire to leave!" All the spirits will hear this, and their attention will be diverted from this woman.' And so it was: upon the conclusion of the ten days, the spirit returned to his original place, and the woman remained hale and hearty.[74]

[74] Reznik, *Mora'im gedolim*, §2, pp. 5–7. *Continued in Appendix.*

TEN

THE POWERS OF EVIL AND THE WAR AGAINST THEM

THE SITRA AHRA and the powers of impurity feature in early folk tales, as well as in stories of kabbalists.[1] It is therefore only to be expected that they would be present in hasidic stories, which drew upon these sources. The usual habitat of these evil powers, which are termed *letsim* (literally, 'mockers'), *ḥitsonim* ('external ones'), or *kelipot* (from kabbalistic terminology), was far from any settled human domain: the wilderness, the forest, abandoned buildings, and the like. They could, however, make their presence felt anywhere, and confront a person at any time. If a person follows the paths of Judaism and fears the Lord, he is assured that the powers of holiness will aid him; he will prevail over the dark forces, which will be sent away to their natural abode. For example, the Ba'al Shem Tov drove out demons who sought to attack the shopkeeper's carriage in which he was travelling with a merchant through the forest, and by doing so intensified the shopkeeper's belief in him.[2]

Letsim or *ḥitsonim*, collectively known also as *mezikin* (agents of destruction), were liable to be generated by sins or bad thoughts: we learn, for example, that two *letsim*, a male and a female, were created from the sinful thoughts of an assistant cantor ('a poet [i.e. singer] who was called a bass') and from the women who were in the synagogue.[3] The *mezikin* manifested

[1] For this subject in rabbinic dicta, see Gross, *Otsar ha'agadah*, s.vv. *kishuf* (sorcery), *mezikin* (destructive agents), *sama'el*, *shed* (demon). Demons are active in the night-time: 'A person should not go out alone at night' (BT *Pes.* 112*b*); 'A person may not greet his fellow at night, lest the latter be a demon' (BT *Meg.* 3*a*). Cf. Samuel Hehasid et al., *Sefer ḥasidim*, §939, p. 231. See Basilea, *Emunat ḥakhamim*, fo. 22*a*–*b*: 'One of our people, one of the leading philosophers . . . totally denied the existence of demons. He was shown a certain house in Venice where spirits, who made noises, were heard at night, especially at one window that was open to the air of a narrow alley. The demon would knock upon it at night, but when it was opened, no one was to be found there.' For the forces of impurity in Jewish thought and in the kabbalistic literature, see Tishby, *Wisdom of the Zohar*, ii. 447–546; id., *Doctrine of Evil*.

[2] See *Shivḥei habesht*, 141, where the *letsim* are called *poḥazim* (reckless, wanton ones).

[3] Ibid., 118. A villager came to R. Nehemiah Yehiel (the son of the 'Holy Jew') with his daughter, 'who had been seized by the *ḥitsonim*, heaven forfend, who subjected her to harsh tortures, as is their way'. The tsadik went forth from his home and shouted at the *ḥitsonim*, who

themselves in the women's section of the synagogue; the women feared to pray in their presence, and were compelled to leave.

In other instances, these entities arise as the result of sorcery. For example, R. Moses of Kosov's daughter-in-law, experiencing a difficult childbirth, turned for relief to sorcery. This resulted in a *lets* coming to R. Moses' home, forcing him to leave the house. The *mokhiaḥ* of Polonnoye, Aryeh Leib Geliner, attempted to live there afterwards, but he too was compelled to abandon it by the *lets*, who threw wooden beams from the upper storey,[4] and poured dirt on the books of the *mokhiaḥ*'s companions when they fell asleep while studying.[5] After the *mokhiaḥ*'s departure the house fell into disuse, and various people attempted to remove wooden beams and benches from the deserted ruin; but the *lets* knocked on their windows at night and demanded that they return what they had stolen. Eventually the Ba'al Shem Tov succeeded in quieting the spirit, and thereafter it no longer banged on the walls of people's homes.[6]

A town close to Kotsk was inhabited by a *lets*, who at times would sit on roofs and drum on them, and at others even entered the study hall, all without being seen. At night, when the day's studies were concluded, he would pour water on one of the scholars, and throw straw, dirt, and even stones at another. When the rabbi of Kotsk came to the town he was told of this spirit's mischief, and after the tsadik's visit the townspeople were no longer troubled by the *lets*.[7]

Clearly, then, *letsim* harassed and intimidated people, especially at night. A tax-collector complained to the Ba'al Shem Tov that only half of whatever he had in his house at nightfall, whether money or goods, would still be

departed (Rabinovitz, *Ma'aseh neḥemiyah*, 34). Cf. BT *Eruv.* 18*b*: Adam fathered 'spirits [*ruḥin*], male demons [*shedin*], and she-demons [*lilin*]'. For the connection between a nocturnal emission and demons and spirits, see *Ma'aseh yerushalmi*, ed. Zlotnik, 102–3.

4 Cf. Tsevi Hirsch of Koidanov, *Kav hayashar*, ch. 69: 'They [the *ḥitsonim*] would throw the vessels and the lamps to the ground, but they would not harm any person, they would only confuse the people who dwell there.' See also *Hashaḥar*, 5 (Vienna, 1874), 243; Rodkinsohn, *Toledot ba'alei shem tov*, i, introd., 411. It is noteworthy that Ben-Yehezkel, *Sefer hama'asiyot*, v, does not cite a single hasidic tale in his chapter on 'Demons and Spirits' (pp. 265–89).

5 Cf. Tsevi Hirsch of Koidanov, *Kav hayashar*, ch. 69. The '*ḥitsonim*' would pour 'dirt and dust' into the food in the pots.

6 See *Shivḥei habesht*, 84. The Ba'al Shem Tov ordered his followers to tell the *lets*: 'Israel son of Eliezer [i.e. the Ba'al Shem Tov] is here!'—a proclamation that put an end to the harassment. This also resulted in the *mokhiyaḥ* of Polonnoye becoming a follower of the Ba'al Shem Tov, for he said: 'Since the name Israel son of Eliezer is a [holy] name, we deduce from this that he is a tsadik!' See J. Sofer, *Sipurei ya'akov*, ii, §35; Scholem, 'Historical Image' (Heb.), 341. *Continued in Appendix.*

7 See Rakats, *Siaḥ sarfei kodesh*, i, §286. Cf. *Avot derabi natan*, ch. 37 (*The Fathers According to Rabbi Nathan*, trans. J. Goldin, 153): 'They change their appearance to any likeness they please; and they see, but they themselves are not seen.'

there by the morning. The Ba'al Shem Tov ordered his scribe to write *shemirot* (literally, 'guardings': i.e. amulets),[8] and the members of the household saw that these charms caused the spirit to become agitated; eventually it left the building, going instead to the home of the mill owner, where in its anger it killed two children.[9]

The *ḥitsonim* came to a prison where Jews were being held, and ate, drank, and made merry, 'with drums and dancing', throughout the night; when dawn came, they left without a trace. These *ḥitsonim* greatly feared the Maggid of Koznitz.[10] One householder was driven to his wits' end by a *ḥitsoni* that lived within his house. When R. Solomon of Karlin passed through the area, the householder asked him to visit his home, and gave him a *kvitl* and a *pidyon* against the spirits that infested his house 'and come every night and celebrate and dance there until the light of day'. He also told the tsadik that in the past he had brought a Torah scroll into the house to combat the *ḥitsonim*, but to no avail. R. Solomon gave his staff to his attendant and ordered him to place it next to the window. That night the *ḥitsonim* could not enter through the window, and even 'their "king"', who sought to break through this barrier, was forced to withdraw. In the morning R. Solomon informed the householder that he need no longer fear the *ḥitsonim*, and so it proved.[11]

In the episode referred to above in which destructive agents were brought into existence by sinful thoughts and appeared in the women's section of the synagogue, the preacher of the city sought to drive them out by means of Torah study in the synagogue; not only was the attempt unsuccessful, but the *letsim* attacked and harmed his two children, thereby compelling the preacher to ask for the Ba'al Shem Tov's aid. The destructive agents initially scoffed at the Ba'al Shem Tov, but he succeeded both in rescuing the children and in confining the *letsim* to a place near a certain well, where people never went.[12]

[8] Cf. Tsevi Hirsch of Koidanov, *Kav hayashar*, ch. 69: R. Joel Ba'al Shem Tov also adjured the *ḥitsonim* with holy names. For charms and amulets given by *ba'alei shem* against demons that are liable to harm the inhabitants of a new house, see *Sefer mifalot elohim*, fo. 15; Zechariah of Plungian, *Sefer zekhariyah me'inyanei segulot*, fo. 34; J. Y. Rosenberg, *Rafa'el hamalakh*, 16–17. *Shivḥei habesht*, 52, relates that R. Alexander, the Ba'al Shem Tov's scribe, was alarmed at night by a spirit when he was sent to exorcise the dybbuk tormenting a madman. In his mind he copied divine names 'on a picture of his hand, on each finger'. The Yiddish version of *Shivḥei habesht* (ch. 16) states explicitly that the scribe's function was to write amulets. For the view of R. Isaac Luria, see Vital, *Sha'ar ruaḥ hakodesh*: 'Know that all the names and amulets that are presently written in books are erroneous, and even the names and amulets that were tried and examined by an expert contain many errors, and therefore they may not be used.' See also Ch. 2 above.

[9] *Shivḥei habesht*, 118.

[10] See Gemen, *Sifran shel tsadikim*, ch. 36, §11.

[11] Ibid., §15. For the expulsion of demons from a hotel by R. Tsevi Hirsch of Rymanow, see Kamelhar, *Mevaser tov*, 14.

[12] *Shivḥei habesht*, 118–19. *Continued in Appendix.*

If *letsim* take control of a house or apartment, people are afraid to live there, no one wants to buy it, and its value naturally depreciates. The Ba'al Shem Tov's journey to visit wealthy leaseholders in Slutsk, Lithuania—a vast distance from Ukraine, where he lived—was apparently made in connection with the expulsion of *letsim* and other destructive spirits. These leaseholders had 'built a house surrounded by a wall, but feared to live in it'. Upon the Ba'al Shem Tov's arrival, the wife of one of the leaseholders and her servants led the tsadik to all the buildings, 'and in several places he made movements as if he saw something'.[13] It seems that he was able to discern the destructive spirits and cleanse the premises.

A man in Satanov bought a home which was rumoured to be inhabited by evil spirits. His wife was pregnant at the time, having lost all her previous children, and was afraid to live in the new house; so her husband urged her to travel to the tsadik of Chortkov and request his blessing. Not only did the rabbi bless them, promising that they would live untroubled in their new home; he also informed them that they would have a daughter, and even told them the name they should give the child, one that, the tsadik had written in his books, was effective against an evil spirit.[14] R. Dov Baer of Mezirech advised one of his followers, a wealthy man who had come down in the world, to rent a tavern, but did not reveal its location to him. Taking to the road, the hasid found a group of wagon-drivers standing next to an abandoned tavern. In response to his question, they said that the building stood empty and that no one was willing to rent it, because it was inhabited by demons, who had already harmed many tenants. The hasid rented the building cheaply from its owner, who was pleased to find a tenant, and, thanks to the tsadik's blessing, prospered in his new occupation.[15]

A tax-collector who hired the Ba'al Shem Tov as a teacher for his children told him that the only accommodation he could offer him was 'a single house that is presumed to be impure [i.e. inhabited by evil spirits]'. The Ba'al Shem Tov replied that this would not deter him from living there. He 'designated the upper floor for the *ḥitsonim*, heaven forfend, and when they were cavorting, he rebuked them and they fell silent.'[16] Once a leaseholder who was also an innkeeper came to the tsadik R. Israel of Ruzhin, weeping that *letsim* and destructive spirits had taken up residence in his inn and were causing him trouble, extinguishing the lights every night and putting the benches on the

[13] *Shivḥei habesht*, 133. In accordance with the will of R. David of Makov, the Ba'al Shem Tov slaughtered a calf on the threshold of the house (Wilensky, *Hasidim and Mitnagedim* (Heb.), ii. 242). For the Ba'al Shem Tov's visits to the large land-tenants, see Halpern, 'The Wozczylo Revolt' (Heb.).

[14] Sobelman, *Sipurei tsadikim heḥadash*, §67.

[15] Ibid., §71.

[16] *Shivḥei habesht*, 53. For the purification of the new houses of the 'large land-tenants' in Slutsk, see ibid. 268.

tables. The tsadik blessed the leaseholder, saying that the *letsim* would leave the building and 'would flee to a desert oasis, their place of habitation'.[17] Unfortunately, the tsadik's blessing was not effective, and the leaseholder found relief only when the tsadik himself happened to be in the village on one occasion and spent the night in his house. That night, the *letsim* disturbed R. Israel's rest by playing the flute and making terrifying sounds. The tsadik ordered his attendant to place his pipe and his handkerchief on the window-ledge. This had some effect, but only for a short time, after which they heard the voice of the chief of the *letsim* ordering his minions to continue their harassment of the household. In the morning, the tsadik summoned the leaseholder and gave him amulets to hang on the doors and windows of the inn. This measure did at last put an end to the *letsim*'s malicious activity.[18]

The implication that the tsadik has no fear of demons recurs in the following short story, which also includes a barb directed against the mitnagedim, who are thereby presented as a worse threat than evil spirits. R. Simhah of Lublin bought a ruined building and thought of giving it as a present to R. Jacob Isaac, the Seer of Lublin. It was said that there were demons there, and that the house had been rebuilt several times, but that 'no one could live in it. He [the Seer] said that he feared demons not at all, and he would expel them with a single evening prayer, but he was in trepidation of the mitnagedim.'[19]

In many cases these demons are known by their actions: by the actual damage they cause to people's health or belongings (for example, in the tale cited above in which money and goods would disappear from the tax-collector's house every night); or by their taking control of a person's body, or his thoughts, desires, and deeds. The following tales of sorcery and charms are based on the assumption that evil spirits cause illness, are injurious to human livelihood and possessions, and bear responsibility for natural disasters as well. Physical domination appears in the following two stories. In the first, a person could not leave the forest 'because the *ḥitsonim* prevent

[17] The realm of demons is beyond that of human habitations. Cf. Tsevi Hirsch of Koidanov, *Kav hayashar*, ch. 69, in which the *ḥitsonim* were driven away 'to a place of forests and deserts [i.e. uninhabited places]'. The story is cited (without attribution) in Shenkel, *Ma'asiyot mitsadikim yesodei olam*, §12. *Continued in Appendix.*

[18] Shenkel, *Yeshuot yisra'el*, ii, §19. Judah Yehiel of Rozdol, *Lev same'aḥ heḥadash*, 108: the *ḥitsonim* settled in the inn of a Jew. The innkeeper heard that R. Hanokh Henikh of Alesk (Alik) was travelling to Zlotchev, and he asked R. Hanokh's attendants if the tsadik would spend a night with him. R. Hanokh immediately sensed the presence of these spirits; his anger was aroused for having been brought to 'a place of danger' (see BT *Kid.* 29*b*) and he continued on his way. From that day on, however, the innkeeper knew no evil in his inn.

[19] Rakats, *Siaḥ sarfei kodesh*, v. 103. For an apostate deserting husband who feared demons and spirits when he passed by a ruin every day, see Kaidaner, *Sipurim nora'im*, §59, pp. 74–5.

me', and was rescued only by a *tsetl*, a note written by the tsadik.[20] In the second, a merchant who was about to purchase wine was confused by the demon and found himself standing in a lake, his money having been stolen by the evil spirit;[21] R. Mordecai of Nezkizh forced the demons to return the money.

In many stories, errant behaviour is the result of domination by evil spirits of human thoughts, desires, and actions, and the expulsion of demons saves a Jew from apostasy, adultery, or other serious misconduct.

Often, the evil spirits use enticement to take control of a person's thoughts; the same technique is used by Satan (also known as Samael), who frequently attempts to lead a tsadik into sin. When the Ba'al Shem Tov stayed in Istanbul, on his well-known journey to the Land of Israel, he performed wonders that reached the ears of the royal court, as a result of which he was forced to flee. The Ba'al Shem Tov was ordered by heaven to retrace his steps, and when he refused, he was stripped of 'all the [spiritual] levels', to the extent that he no longer understood the meaning of the letters of the Hebrew alphabet. He accepted all this with love, until his ship sank and 'Samael came to him and said what he said'. Then the Ba'al Shem Tov recited *Shema yisra'el* and began to return, as he had been commanded.[22] In another instance Satan feared the Ba'al Shem Tov, but sought to interfere with the tsadik's disciples by heaping sand and gravel in their way.[23]

The tsadik R. David of Chortkov related in the name of R. Itzikl of Radvil that Satan once argued in heaven that it was difficult for him to succeed because there were tsadikim in the world who increased fear of God and faith, so that few would heed him and sin. When he was asked what he wanted, he replied that he, too, wanted tsadikim of his own, and this was granted him.[24]

One of the hasidim who spent the sabbath with R. Barukh of Medzibezh was present when R. Barukh spoke deprecatingly of R. Levi Isaac of Berdichev's manner of prayer, which entailed much bowing and genuflection. When this hasid took his leave of the tsadik, he reproached R. Barukh for having made fun of the rabbi of Berdichev. R. Barukh responded: 'For

[20] I. Landau, *Zikhron tov*, §3, p. 29. For *ḥitsonim* who torture humans with mud and clay, see the end of the story by R. Nahman of Bratslav, 'The Clever Man and the Simple Man' (included in all collections of R. Nahman's stories; see e.g. *Sipurei ma'asiyot mishanim kadmoniyot*).

[21] I. Landau, *Zikhron tov*, 'The Deeds of the Tsadikim', §30.

[22] I. Safrin, 'Netiv mitsvoteikha', 'Shevil emunah', fo. 4*a*; [Isaac Dov Baer ben Tsevi Hirsch], *Kahal ḥasidim heḥadash*, §23. Jacob Joseph of Polonnoye, *Toledot ya'akov yosef*, makes no mention of Satan; in his version, Ahijah the Shilonite (the Ba'al Shem Tov's mystical teacher) guides the Ba'al Shem Tov back to Istanbul and prompts him to recite *Shema yisra'el*.

[23] Sobelman, *Sipurei tsadikim heḥadash*, §10. Cf. ibid., §32: the Sitra Ahra opens his mouth before R. Menahem Mendel of Vitebsk's ritual slaughterer (to swallow him).

[24] Rapoport, *Divrei david*, fo. 28*b*.

several years Satan has been inciting [meaning: causing commotion on high], claiming that there is no need for the coming of the messiah and the rebuilding of the Temple, since R. Levi Isaac employs all the *kavanot* of the high priest in the Temple. My mockery [of R. Isaac's manner of prayer] was intended to counter this incitement and [thereby] hasten the Redemption.'[25]

Satan seeks to take possession of holy souls, and the fierce war for liberation from his dominion is reflected in a story connected with R. Joel (Halperin) Ba'al Shem of Zamosc. A certain rabbi and his wife, who were childless, set out for the Land of Israel, in the hope that they would be blessed with offspring there. Their ship dropped anchor for a while at an island, but then set out to sea again while the rabbi was still ashore. The rabbi cried out bitterly, but in vain. Then someone came along who claimed that he could put the rabbi back on board the ship, but on one condition: he would have to make a written commitment to give over to this individual the child who would be born to him and his wife in the Land of Israel, when the child reached the age of 13. The rabbi agreed, signed the pledge, and found himself back on the ship again. He kept the agreement a secret, not disclosing it even to his wife. A son was born to them, and as he grew his great intelligence and wisdom became evident. His father, however, could not be happy, because of the promise he had made. The youth, sensing his father's sadness, persistently questioned him about the reason, until eventually he was compelled to divulge the secret. The youth asked his father for travelling expenses and left his parents to study Torah far away, in the hope that the merit of his studies would save him from the man to whom he had been signed over.

The youth arrived in Poland and studied under R. Joel Ba'al Shem. After hearing the youth's history, the tsadik gave him his own staff and ordered him to go to a certain place and there make three circles on the ground. He was then to stand within the third circle and concentrate with intent on the holy names that he gave him. R. Joel also told the youth that wild animals would try to approach him, and 'a boar from the forest' would even enter the first circle, but would not approach the third. After this, bands of demons would come, 'with angels at their head'. The father's signed note was returned to the youth, and when he returned to the *ba'al shem* the latter put *tefilin* on him, even before he had reached the age of 13, thereby delivering the boy from the forces of the Sitra Ahra.[26]

[25] Rapoport, *Divrei david*, fos 8*b*–9*a*.

[26] See Reznik, *Mora'im gedolim*, §13, pp. 27–32. This story was published, with minor changes, in Ehrmann, *Pe'er vekhavod*, fos 19*b*–20*a*. For the circle as a holy realm, in which the powers of evil have no dominion, see Rodkinsohn, *Adat tsadikim*, §4: the Ba'al Shem Tov drew a circle within a circle, and stood within the inner ring, into which the wild animals that had been sent by the sorcerer could not enter. In Bodek(?), *Sipurei kedoshim*, §5, the yeshiva students stand in a circle in the ritual bath, in order to overcome the sorcerer. In another phase of

According to another story, Satan sought to entice a repentant Jew, but was unsuccessful.[27] He similarly attempted (in the guise of a beautiful woman) to seduce R. Jacob Isaac, the Seer of Lublin, while the tsadik was on his way to Lizhensk, again to no avail.[28]

Satan tries to lead the masses astray by presenting them with a so-called 'wonder-worker' who in fact uses the powers of impurity. Once he gave a young man a chest that he claimed was filled with charms containing holy names. The young man was ordered not to open the chest, but, when people came to him with requests, to draw near to the box and pray to the Lord, upon which their requests would be answered. The ruse worked, and people began to stream to the 'wonder-worker', until R. Elimelekh and R. Zusya discovered the deception. They 'made for him a circle with holy adjurations . . . They opened the chest, and it contained serpents and idols. They then neutralized [the power of] the serpents and idols.'[29]

Some tsadikim regarded veneration by their hasidim, or an over-abundance of followers, as a danger put in place by Samael. R. Tsevi Hirsch of Zhidachov proclaimed: 'This world [i.e. the 400–500 people in his entourage] may have been sent to me by Samael, may his name be effaced, to lead me away from you [God]!'[30]

This view is also reflected in a story that is told of R. Shalom of Belz.

Once he told his wife that he did not know what to do, for 'today, the eve of the holy sabbath, towards evening, a renowned rabbi will come to me, dressed in white garments, and he will come to me with his followers. But he, heaven forfend, is from the Sitra Ahra, and many *kelipot* will come with him. And how can I even greet him?' [His wife] said to the holy rabbi: 'But you cannot shame him! After greeting him, go a second time to the ritual bath to immerse.' He replied: 'Very well! But how will I be able to sit with him at the same table?' She answered: 'Perhaps you will be able to subdue him, and show him the error of his ways?' He rejoined: 'That is impossible.' She insisted: 'Nevertheless, you cannot shame him. You can sit together with him, but without drawing near to him at all.' And so he did. He sat together with him the entire holy sabbath, but without looking his guest in the face. Afterwards he told his wife that the Lord had saved him from the forces of impurity, and he had not drawn close to them.[31]

the story, King David encircles Solomon Ephraim, in order to protect the latter from the Sitra Ahra. Cf. the circle made by R. Naphtali Cohen of Frankfurt (the author of *Semikhat ḥakhamim*) around a bridegroom, to protect him from the forces of evil (Weberman, *Ma'aseh nisim*, 67).

[27] J. Sofer, *Sipurei ya'akov*, ii, §38.

[28] See I. Landau, *Zikhron tov*, 'The Deeds of the Tsadikim', §20. Cf. Kleinmann, *Or yesharim*, 7. See also the non-hasidic work Na'im, *Malkhei rabanan*, fo. 35*a*, for a *kelipah* in the form of a black woman who appeared to R. Hayim Abenatar at the Western Wall and pursued him; R. Hayim died that same year.

[29] Ehrmann, *Devarim arevim*, 'Stories of the Holy Brothers R. Elimelekh and R. Zusya', §27.

[30] I. Safrin, *Zohar ḥai*, end of 'Bereshit', cited in Teomim, *Ateret tiferet*, 'His Holiness, the Holy Rabbi, R. Tsevi Hirsch of Zhidachov', §10.

[31] Ehrmann, *Pe'er vekhavod*, 26.

The converse of the idea expressed in the story quoted above about R. Barukh appears in a story that was told by R. Israel of Ruzhin:

Once the Maggid of Mezirech prayed very intensely for the Redemption. From heaven it was asked: 'Who is this who presses matters so strongly? Is there no one greater than him [to do this]?' The Maggid replied that since he was the outstanding tsadik of the generation, it was incumbent upon him to take special pains regarding the Redemption. He was asked: 'How do you know that you are the outstanding tsadik of the generation?' He responded: 'My holy disciples will come and testify.' The Maggid went to his disciples and asked them once, twice, and a third time: 'Who is the tsadik of the generation?' but they remained speechless. The tsadik of Ruzhin remarked: 'They all knew that he was the tsadik of the generation, and if they were silent, this is a sign that the *ba'al davar* [Satan or his agent] was active here.'[32]

Sometimes a person encounters the forces of impurity in the form of beasts. According to *Shivḥei habesht* the Ba'al Shem Tov first confronted the satanic powers before he revealed himself. As a youth, he would bring small children to the teacher's house and to the synagogue for prayers. This work became known in heaven and was a cause of delight there: 'it was a highly propitious hour in heaven'. Satan was immediately aroused, and was apprehensive 'lest the time arrive when he would be swallowed up [i.e. disappear] from the earth'. He sent a sorcerer who turned into a wild animal that set upon the little children when the Ba'al Shem Tov was taking them to prayers. The Ba'al Shem Tov gathered his strength and struck the animal, which fell to the ground lifeless. The following day, the sorcerer was found dead in his home.[33]

An act of religious deception was perpetrated by a demon who held a book in his hands and claimed that it had been written by the Ba'al Shem Tov. It transpired that one of the tsadik's disciples had indeed written teachings that he claimed to have heard from the Ba'al Shem Tov, though in fact he had never spoken such things.[34]

[32] See Rapoport, *Divrei david*, fo. 23*a*. For Satan as impeding repentance and the Redemption, see 'The Spider and the Fly', by R. Nahman of Bratslav (in e.g. *Sipurei ma'asiyot mishanim kadmoniyot*). For Satan's preventing the Ba'al Shem Tov from going to the Land of Israel, see Ch. 17 below.

[33] *Shivḥei habesht*, 41–2. For women as sorcerers, see Samuel Hehasid et al., *Sefer ḥasidim*, §172, p. 70: 'Women were suspected of eating children. . . . Some engage in sorcery, rather, do this [to protect yourselves]: declare that they [all women] are to come to the synagogue, even those who are suspect, and if any child is harmed, then grind their teeth with rocks [i.e. punish the women, for this is proof that they are sorceresses].' See also Tsevi Hirsch of Koidanov, *Kav hayashar*, ch. 29: 'As regards women sorceresses, who are known to harm Israelite children, they should be designated by name, and placed under a strict ban, with a *shofar*, the extinguishing of candles, and the taking out of seven Torah scrolls, and drive them [the sorceresses] out, so that they would have no contact with the sanctity of Israel.'

[34] *Shivḥei habesht*, 144. Cf. Rosenstein, *Pe'er layesharim*, §58, fo. 29*b*: '[R. Pinhas of Korets] related from the Ba'al Shem Tov that there was a person who wrote what he had heard him say,

Sometimes demons appear in human form—as in the story mentioned above of the rabbi separated from his ship. Men fall prey to the lures of female demons; other demons appear in the guise of people familiar to their victims, and thereby succeed in enticing the victim's family and associates. The appearance of male and female demons masquerading as human beings also opens up the possibility of evil spirits marrying humans. It is not surprising that hasidism adopted this notion, which long predated the movement. *Ma'aseh yerushalmi* is the best-known story based on this belief from the medieval period.[35] Many of the hasidic tales containing this motif were undoubtedly influenced by the earlier story of the Jewish goldsmith from Posen during the time that R. Sheftel was the city rabbi. This man engaged in sexual relations with a she-demon, and fathered *letsim* and *ḥitsonim*. These unnatural offspring embittered the lives of all who lived in the goldsmith's house, before they were finally expelled to the wilderness by R. Joel Ba'al Shem of Zamosc and the Posen rabbinical court.[36]

A young man, a follower of the Seer of Lublin, was jealous of another young man who found a beautiful and rich bride. Some time later, he was offered a match that pleased him, since the bride and her parents were of the same sort as his friend's wife and family. The Seer, however, realized that these were not humans, but demons, and he tore up the writ of engagement.[37] The she-demon usually lies on hay, and not in a bed, and by this means can be recognized. Once a *kelipah* in the form of a woman took hold of a man and enticed him. Wishing to save his soul, the man travelled to R. Mordecai of Nezkizh to seek his advice.

He lay down on a haystack to sleep, and this figure came to him, heaven forfend, and invited him: 'Come down to me!' He asked her: 'Why is it that you always come to me, but now you ask me to come to you?' To which she responded: 'Because of [a blade of] grass in the hay on which you are lying, I cannot approach

and when the Ba'al Shem Tov learned of this, he ordered the *mokhiyaḥ* to examine the writings. [The *mokhiaḥ*] asserted that he had written nothing from what the Ba'al Shem Tov had spoken. The Ba'al Shem Tov said that this person had not listened for the sake of heaven, and therefore had been enveloped in a *kelipah*, and he heard other things [that the Ba'al Shem Tov had not spoken].' Scholem cites this in his article 'Historical Image' (Heb.), 14, §42.

[35] See *Ma'aseh yerushalmi*, ed. Zlotnik, chapter entitled 'Marriages between Humans and Demons'; Manasseh ben Israel, *Nishmat ḥayim*, ch. 16, fo. 120*a*; Dan, *Hebrew Story* (Heb.), 95–9, 258, 274. *Continued in Appendix.*

[36] Tsevi Hirsch of Koidanov, *Kav hayashar*, ch. 69; *Sefer hama'asiyot* (Baghdad), §98. *Continued in Appendix.*

[37] See Bodek, *Kahal kedoshim*, §4, fo. 6*b*. Cf. id., *Pe'er mikedoshim*, §5, which mentions Satan (or his surrogate, in the form of a wealthy Jewish merchant who seeks a match with an *ilui* from Prague); *Likutei torah*, MS 789 Mosad Harav Kook, regarding R. Israel of Ruzhin, who saved a Jew who had been compelled to marry a she-demon.

you.' 'Which is it?' he asked her, 'I will cast it aside!' And she told him. Then he took it for himself, and this was a *shemirah* for him.[38]

R. Jacob Kaidaner, author of *Sipurim nora'im*, heard a greatly expanded version of this story from R. David, one of the hasidim of R. Asher of Stolin, who claimed that he 'saw with his own eyes' the man whom the female demon had seduced. After having a sexual relationship with her for some years, the man fell ill, and people advised him to travel to Koznitz to seek the counsel of the tsadik. R. Israel, the Maggid of Koznitz, saw with his mind's eye the man approaching the city in his carriage, and ordered his servant to make it known throughout the city that no one should bring this man into his home. Despite the heavy rain and the bitter cold, and despite the visitor's entreaties, no one disobeyed the tsadik's decree. Since he could not find lodgings in a Jewish home, the man knocked on the door of a non-Jew at the end of the town, seeking a place to spend the night. The non-Jew allowed him to sleep in the barn. The tsadik sent his servant to the visitor with the instruction that he should immediately lie down on the moist hay there, and not move from this spot the entire night. The tsadik told him that the demon would come to him straight away, and that, if she asked him to move from his place, he was not to heed her. When the demon came, seeking to have sexual relations with him, she asked him to move a bit, for where he was, she said, she was not permitted to touch him. The man followed the instructions of the tsadik and did not budge, despite the demon's weeping and wailing that his obstinacy would be the end of her. When she learned that the man was following the commands of R. Israel of Koznitz, a strong wind blew, and the air was filled with a powerful stench. The demon vanished, and in her place the man saw 'a stinking dunghill'. Realizing that the demon was dead, he arose joyfully from the stack of hay, and the next day went to the tsadik, who prescribed a *tikun* for his soul, which had been defiled through his contact with the demon.[39]

[38] Samuel of Shinova, *Ramatayim tsofim*, fo. 42*a*; [Isaac Dov Baer ben Tsevi Hirsch], *Kahal ḥasidim heḥadash*, §88. Cf. I. Landau, *Zikhron tov*, 'The Deeds of the Tsadikim', §31. See also Tsevi Hirsch of Koidanov, *Kav hayashar*, ch. 25, for a woman who married the chief of the demons. Halakhic queries were also raised regarding this topic. See Meir ben Gedaliah, *She'elot uteshuvot maharam milublin*, query 116, fo. 52*a*, regarding 'a woman who engaged in sexual intercourse with a spirit or a demon. . . . He initially had relations with her, [masquerading] as her husband, and the second time as the local *poritz*.'

[39] Kaidaner, *Sipurim nora'im*, §23. R. Nehemiah Yehiel, the son of the 'Holy Jew', spat a number of times at a female demon who approached him when he was lying in the innkeeper's bed while on a journey. After his entreaties and threats, the innkeeper finally admitted that one of the *ḥitsonim* had entered him many years ago, heaven forfend, and every night she came to his bed, and forced him 'to engage in sexual relations with her and do her bidding, heaven forfend' (Rabinovitz, *Ma'aseh neḥemiyah*, 45). [Lemberger], *Niflaot hatsadikim*, 28, presents a non-hasidic account of the marriage of a cat to a female demon. For the sources, see *Sefer hakavanot uma'asei nisim*, fo. 5*a*; Benayahu, *Sefer toledot ha'ari*, 185–7; *Sefer hama'asiyot* (Baghdad), §79. For a person who married a female demon, see I. Levi, 'Un recueil de contes juifs inédits', 51–4.

In some cases a female demon appeared in the guise of a man's wife, and thereby deceived the husband. When Feige Reif immersed herself in the ritual bath after her menstrual period, a demon in her image emerged from the water in her stead, and dwelled in the house of her husband Jacob. This demon, too, was accustomed to sleep on the hay in the upper chamber.[40]

In a similar tale, perhaps influenced by the famous legend of Solomon and Ashmedai (Asmodeus),[41] an evil spirit ruled for an entire year in place of the well-known *poritz* Count Potocki. Neither Potocki's wife nor others close to him realized that this creature was not Potocki, but rather 'a *ḥitsoni* spirit'.[42]

The forces of evil serve sorcerers, and many of the stories attribute dark powers to the enemies of the Jews, including priests. In an encounter between a tsadik and a sorcerer the former is generally victorious, as in the story of the Ba'al Shem Tov taking children to the synagogue. Nevertheless, it seems that not even the Ba'al Shem Tov denied the supernatural powers of sorcerers; in *Shivḥei habesht* the reader encounters sorcerers (of both sexes) and various forms of witchcraft, and feels the tension between those engaging in the black arts and the Ba'al Shem Tov, who represents the forces of holiness.

In response to the request by the townspeople of Medzibezh to act against a priest who had caused a great deal of trouble for the Jews, the Ba'al Shem Tov explains that 'he does not wish to provoke him, for he is a mighty sorcerer'. In the continuation of the tale, the Ba'al Shem Tov seeks to act in moderate fashion, so that the sorcerer will not discover his activity, but to no avail: the priest senses that the Ba'al Shem Tov is seeking to fight him by means of prayer. The second version, which occurs later in the narrative, states explicitly 'that [the priest] employed sorcery against the Ba'al Shem Tov'.[43]

The hasidic story assumes that impure names, like holy ones, have active powers. Every eighty years non-Jews decapitate an *ilui*, a prodigious Talmud scholar, the firstborn of a firstborn, on the day of his bar mitzvah, 'and they place the impure names under his tongue, and he reveals hidden things to them'.[44] In a stratagem that echoes the use of charms containing holy names, sorcerers can also prepare a 'magic paper' that acts upon whoever holds it, or

[40] J. Y. Rosenberg, *Tiferet maharal*, 25 ff.

[41] For Solomon and Ashmodai, see 'A Story of King Solomon, May He Rest in Peace' (Heb.), in Jellinek, *Beit hamidrash*, ii, ch. 2, 86–7.

[42] Bodek, *Pe'er mikedoshim*, §14. For a woman who bore a son to a demon, see Zevin, *Hasidic Tales: Festivals* (Heb.), 534–6.

[43] *Shivḥei habesht*, 137. The identification of priests with sorcerers also is made in a story in Moskowitz, *Otsar hasipurim*, i, §13. According to this tale, a Jew who lived in the time of R. Pinhas of Korets sought to learn the secrets of sorcery from a priest; he subsequently disavowed his actions, and thereby sanctified the Name of God.

[44] Bodek, *Pe'er mikedoshim*, §5, p. 8; Shenkel, *Noraot anshei ma'aseh*, §1.

even touches it. A non-Jewish sorcerer once bribed a tailor to sew such a paper within the garment of a Jewish woman. When she wore the garment, an impure spirit took control of her, and on the night of Yom Kippur, instead of going to the synagogue to hear *Kol nidrei*, she was drawn to the house of the sorcerer. When, however, she removed the item of clothing to which the paper had been attached, the power of the 'magic paper' waned, and she regretted her actions and prayed. A gust of wind arose and bore her back to her home; the act of witchcraft was discovered, and the sorcerer was hanged.[45]

A similar echo of how virtuous powers work is to be found in the story cited above in which a young man, deceived by Satan, was given a chest full of 'serpents and idols'. The supplicants' prayers, directed towards this unclean chest, were effective, thus demonstrating that the powers of impurity are capable of acting in a manner similar to that of the forces of holiness.[46]

A non-Jewish sorcerer who lived near an inn used his powers in such a way that any Jew who rented the inn would die. When R. Shneur Zalman of Lyady recited with great devotion the verse 'there is no augury in Jacob' (Num. 23: 23), the sorcerer and his wife died.[47]

Every year on Purim, R. Pinhas of Korets would tell a story he had heard from the Jewish leaseholder to whom the events described had happened. An antisemitic priest and sorcerer would regularly drink in the Jew's house. Once the Jew asked the priest to teach him the secrets of sorcery. The priest told him to take hold of his belt, and took him into the wilderness (which was regarded as the habitat of the *ḥitsonim*). By the merit of his recitation of the Shema, the demons could not harm him, but it was three years before the Jew succeeded in escaping. Upon his return, he complained to the priest, asking, 'Why did you deceive me?' The priest replied: 'I saw that you were a greater sorcerer than I am, for thousands of *kelipot* fall victim with every *netilat yadayim* [ritual hand-washing] of yours, and every time you wear *tsitsit* [a ritual under-garment].'[48]

The identification of priest with sorcerer also appears in a well-known story, which appears in several versions, related by R. Isaac Judah Yehiel Safrin in the name of his teacher and father-in-law, R. Abraham Mordecai of Pintchov.

In a certain village there was a priest, who was a mighty sorcerer, who employed wizardry to kill Jewish children before their circumcision. One time there was [to

[45] Shenkel, *Ma'asiyot nora'im venifla'im*, §12, pp. 28–9. For the sources of this non-hasidic folktale, see *Ma'asim tovim*, §1; Abraham ben Isaiah Hadayan, *Holekh tamim ufo'el tsedek*. See Ben-Yehezkel, *Sefer hama'asiyot*, iii. 262–4.

[46] See above, n. 29. For an early source, see Jousep (Juspa) Schammes of Worms, *Ma'aseh nisim*, §3.

[47] See Kaidaner, *Sipurim nora'im*, §52.

[48] Milik, *Sipurim nifla'im*, §4, p. 12.

be] a circumcision for [the son of] a certain Jew who lived in that village. Our divine master [the Ba'al Shem Tov] saw that the priest was engaged in preparations to kill the child, and our master travelled there by *kefitsa*[*t haderekh*]. He arrived there with his disciples before nightfall on the day preceding the circumcision, and this Jew greatly honoured him. Our master told the Jew to close the door and any open place, not to leave even a single tiny hole unsealed; he should prepare large, thick staffs, and when he would tell him, 'Strike!' he was to strike with all his might. When night fell, someone knocked at the door to open for him, but the Jew was not willing to do so, as he had been commanded by the man of God. Using black magic, the priest changed his form to that of a cat and non-kosher animals, and he began to dig under the ground of the house. When he poked his head into the house, our master shouted to strike, and the Jew struck him cruel blows, smiting and wounding until his [the priest's] hand and foot were broken. The priest returned to his home, and in the morning there was a great circumcision celebration. When the priest learned that our master was responsible for all that had been done to him, he complained to the authorities, demanding that they should force our master to engage in disputation with him. In the end, the authorities agreed with him and set a date when both would appear. Each would perform a miracle that was to overpower the other, before a large audience. On the appointed day, all the government officials, the priests, and a great crowd assembled. Our master told him: 'You first, do what you can.' The priest brought upon him all manner of spirits, demons, wild beasts, serpents, and scorpions, and all sorts of destructive spirits. Our master quickly took his staff and drew a circle around himself. He stood in the centre, and [the priest] could not cross the circle until he brought a boar from the forest. When our master saw this, he said: 'This [animal] is greatly insolent', and he made haste to draw a ring within the first circle. In its insolence, the boar passed the first circle, but could not pass [the second], retraced its steps, and fled. When the sorcerer saw that all these types of magic were of no use to him [for the purpose of] crossing the circle and harming [the Ba'al Shem Tov], he said to our master: 'You, work [your magic].' He replied: 'I shall do nothing, I shall only call to the children whom you killed, and they will take their revenge of you.' There immediately appeared a very great gathering of little children, who fell upon him, not leaving a single little bone whole.[49]

The following story teaches of the relationship between the Ba'al Shem Tov and the forces of sorcery.

In a time of drought [the Ba'al Shem Tov] prayed for rain. There was a sorceress there with a demon. She cast spells, and no rain fell. The Ba'al Shem Tov upset her sorcery with his prayer, and the demon told her that he had reversed her magic. The sorceress came to his [the Ba'al Shem Tov's] mother, and warned her: 'Tell your son to depart, and leave me alone, for I will work my sorcery against him.' His mother thought that he had quarrelled with her about some business debt

[49] I. Safrin, *Megilat setarim*, 35–6. Cf. Rodkinsohn, *Adat tsadikim*, §4 (copied in A. Walden, *Kahal ḥasidim*); Dan, 'History of the Hebrew *Akdamot* Story' (Heb.), 197 ff. For a black cat, a pig, and a dog as agents of the Sitra Ahra, see J. Y. Rosenberg, *Tiferet maharal*, 8.

concerning strong drink, and she bid him: 'My son, leave this non-Jewess alone, for she is a sorceress.' He replied to his mother: 'I do not fear her.'[50]

Sorcerers and sorceresses were popularly thought to possess superhuman powers, a belief shared here by the Ba'al Shem Tov's mother, who thought that her son was unaware that the woman was a sorceress. The demon carries out the orders of the sorceress, and the contest between the two adversaries ends in victory for the Ba'al Shem Tov. The continuation of this story is instructive: when the sorceress sees the Ba'al Shem Tov pray for rain (a prayer that is apparently answered), she comes to his mother again, and then sends the demon to the Ba'al Shem Tov; but not only is the demon unable to approach the tsadik, he is turned against his mistress: 'The Ba'al Shem Tov said: You dared to come to me, now immediately go and harm the non-Jewess through a little glass window!' The fact that the demon now acts as the agent of the one whom he had initially been ordered to harm attests to the Ba'al Shem Tov's superiority. In the end of the story, the Ba'al Shem Tov incarcerates the demon in a prison in the forest.[51]

The power of the tsadikim, as evident from all the stories quoted here, is expressed in their mastery of the forces of holiness and their triumph over the powers of impurity. However, in certain instances the Ba'al Shem Tov himself used sorcery, although generally he abstained from such activity and rejected its use. 'Once [the Ba'al Shem Tov] raised Samael, for some need of his.' Samael was angry, claiming that he had been raised only three times: when Adam transgressed, at the sin of the Golden Calf, and at the time of the destruction of the Temple. The Ba'al Shem Tov ordered his followers not to cover their faces (the image of God is said to be on a Jew's face), so that Samael would see the image of God on them, and cause them no harm.[52]

As with the patriarch Jacob, angels always went before the Ba'al Shem Tov to his right, and demons to his left. The Ba'al Shem Tov, however, did not wish to make use of these angels, because of their sanctity, nor of the demons, because of their false nature. Once a person wanted to lease some land that until then had been occupied by a widow. The demon that lived in the plot asked the Ba'al Shem Tov to take the lease on this individual's behalf, assuring him that he would cause the man no harm. The evil spirit, however, did not abide by his promise but threw the man off a bridge, and the Ba'al Shem Tov had to save him from drowning.[53]

It is not inconceivable that in time of trouble Jews would turn to the forces of impurity or sorcerers, engage in sorcery themselves, or harness evil

[50] *Shivḥei habesht*, 54–5.

[51] Ibid. According to p. 146 (ibid.), the non-Jewish servant of the Ba'al Shem Tov sought to kill the tsadik. In response to the Ba'al Shem Tov's question, as to how he thought to deceive his master, he replied: 'A demon bit me.'

[52] Shenkel, *Ma'asiyot peliyot*, §11.

[53] See *Shivḥei habesht*, 149.

powers for their needs. R. Jacob Kinder relates that a father once came to R. Shneur Zalman of Lyady with his insane son, having already sought help with no success from several '[Jewish] practitioners of names and [non-Jewish] practitioners of the black arts'.[54] Once the Ba'al Shem Tov was asked to effect a cure for someone who suffered from paralysis. However, when he sensed that 'the members of [the patient's] household had had dealings with non-Jewish sorceresses for his healing', he refused to continue working on behalf of the sick man.[55]

Some tsadikim were themselves suspected by other Jews of engaging in sorcery. A tax-collector who was angry with the Ba'al Shem Tov informed on him to the *poritz*, claiming that he was a sorcerer who could engage in the black arts and might harm him. The *poritz* believed the tax-collector and wrote a letter of complaint to the commissar for permitting the Ba'al Shem Tov to reside in the city. In his reply, the official refuted this accusation.[56] The leading mitnagedic scholars of the city of Brod intended to issue a ban excommunicating the Ba'al Shem Tov from communal life since they suspected that he was not from the Sitra Dekedushah (the side of holiness).[57] An elderly mitnaged wondered whether the Ba'al Shem Tov was a holy person or from the Sitra Ahra.[58]

Even a person's excessive prosperity could render him suspect of sorcery. Thus some butchers wondered whether the business success of a fellow butcher might be a result of the black arts.[59] An adulterous preacher claimed that R. David of Mikoliev was a wizard,[60] and it was said in Lithuania that R. Mordecai of Lachowicze engaged in sorcery.[61]

Amulets occupied a prominent position in the adjuration of evil spirits. An amulet is a piece of parchment or paper containing a secret message with healing properties, or the power to protect against destructive agents. It was usually hung around one's neck, or placed where its help was required.[62] Amulets had been used for a very long time before the emergence of hasidism, being known to the rabbis of the mishnaic and talmudic periods.[63]

[54] Kaidaner, *Sipurim nora'im*, §56. Cf. Sobelman, *Sipurei tsadikim heḥadash*, §25.

[55] *Shivḥei habesht*, 130. Margolioth, *Kevutsat ya'akov*, fo. 54*a–b* (=[Isaac Dov Baer ben Tsevi Hirsch], *Kahal ḥasidim heḥadash*, §15), relates that the Ba'al Shem Tov refused to heal a Jewish land-tenant 'because he was engaged with sorcery and the forces of impurity'.

[56] See *Shivḥei habesht*, 137. Cf. Shenkel, *Ma'asiyot peliyot*, §20, where R. Yehiel of Paris was suspected of engaging in sorcery. The story originated in *Sefer hama'asiyot* (Baghdad), §65, pp. 67–9.

[57] Sobelman, *Sipurei tsadikim heḥadash*, §15.

[58] See ibid., §12.

[59] J. Sofer, *Sipurei ya'akov*, ii, §49.

[60] See Rodkinsohn, *Adat tsadikim*, §9.

[61] Kleinmann, *Or yesharim*, p. 9.

[62] Rodkinsohn, *Adat tsadikim*, §9: an amulet sewn in a skullcap.

[63] See Ben-Yehudah, *Complete Dictionary* (Heb.), xii, s.v. *kemi'a*, *kemi'ah* (amulet). Amulets were used in almost all times and circles. See e.g. the letter by R. Akiva Eger to R. Israel Jonah Landau (I. Landau, *Ein habedolaḥ*, 5; Kamelhar, *Em labinah*, 'Rosh Amana', 18): 'Today the Torah [luminary], our master and teacher Gershon, may his light shine, came to my region

Amulets were used against a diverse range of afflictions and dangers, and to confer blessing in various realms of life. Some charms were intended to ensure a successful conclusion of pregnancy,[64] or of a difficult childbirth;[65] others to bring about the healing or avoidance of illnesses and plagues. R. Elimelekh of Lizhensk would regularly send an emissary to his disciple R. Elimelekh ben Moses of Pshevorsk, with the request that he write an amulet on a piece of a *lulav* (the palm branch used during the Sukkot festival) to cure those suffering from ague.[66] R. David of Talnoye would use amulets to heal the sick and to exorcise dybbuks.[67]

Talismans also have other uses. The Maggid of Koznitz gave a charm to a woman whose problematic menstrual periods prevented her from engaging in sexual relations with her husband,[68] and R. Aaron of Chernobyl wrote an amulet against fear while in the forest.[69] Another charm was used against an infestation of rats, and yet another to protect a person's livelihood. Charms were also used to guarantee the steady flow of water to the ritual bath,[70] to exorcise dybbuks and drive away demons,[71] and as a prophylactic against forbidden actions that might be committed either knowingly or unwittingly.

The amulet given by R. Jonathan Eybeschuetz when he took leave of his son prevented the latter from committing apostasy, and saved him from his inclination to marry a non-Jewish woman.[72] The father of R. Yossele

from the com[munity of] Warsaw, and I heard from him that, with God's help, his wife had been cured by means of an amulet from his exalted Torah excellency. . . . And now there is in the city a certain God-fearing 17-year-old youth, by the name of Samuel, who was born to the woman Hadas, who is enveloped and oppressed by the falling disease [i.e. epilepsy], heaven forfend. . . . May my wish be granted, as my very life, by his excellency: may he do this for me, and send me by the early mail an amulet for him.'

[64] Ehrmann, *Pe'er vekhavod*, fo. *9a*. See *Shivḥei habesht*, 115: R. Shmerl, the father-in-law of R. Falk Hakohen, would take a charm from the Ba'al Shem Tov whenever his wife gave birth. Lieberson, *Tseror haḥayim*, 83: a charm, composed of two letters, for a woman experiencing a difficult childbirth.

[65] Ehrmann, *Pe'er vekhavod*, fo. 13*a*: the tsadik requested that the charm be returned to him after the birth. See Ch. 4 above.

[66] See Rosenthal, *Hitgalut hatsadikim*, 80–1.

[67] See [Isaac Dov Baer ben Tsevi Hirsch], *Kahal ḥasidim heḥadash*, §203. For an amulet that was effaced, and consequently was not effective against an evil spirit, see the (forged?) letter by R. Elazar of Lizhensk at the end of N. T. Horowitz, *Imrei shefer* (also cited in Berger, *Eser tsaḥtsaḥot*, 'R. Elimelekh', fo. 20*a–b*). For the use of charms against a dybbuk, see Graf, *Zera kodesh*, 'An Awesome Act of the Lord', at the end of the book; Donner, *Derekh ha'emunah uma'aseh rav*, 111.

[68] [Isaac Dov Baer ben Tsevi Hirsch], *Kahal ḥasidim heḥadash*, §137.

[69] The wording of this charm is cited in Isaac Dov Baer ben Tsevi Hirsch's *Kahal ḥasidim heḥadash* (§202).

[70] Ehrmann, *Pe'er vekhavod*, fo. 6*b*. Cf. Moskowitz, *Otsar hasipurim*, x, §7.

[71] Rabbinovitch, *Shivḥei rav ye'ivi*, 93–5.

[72] Bodek, *Mifalot hatsadikim*, 12–14. See Pasheles, *Sipurim* (in German), iv: 'Baron Eibenschutz: The Charm', 131.

Hatiner had another son who was about to convert to Christianity; he was given an amulet, and when the son touched it, he wholeheartedly repented.[73]

A Jewish family that lived in the house of the *poritz* was smuggled away when it faced the threat of imprisonment. In all the tumult, the family's baby was forgotten by the smugglers, and it grew up in the home of the *poritz*. Some time later, the boy came to R. Elimelekh and was circumcised. The tsadik gave him an amulet, and ordered him to wear it sewn in his hat, and to open the charm close to his wedding. When the time came, he remembered the tsadik's command and opened the amulet, which read as follows: 'Is it possible that a brother will marry his sister?' Thus an incestuous marriage (for that is what it would have been) was averted.[74]

A charm could also be effective in the next world: the Ba'al Shem Tov promised one of his followers 'a note and a charm' with which he would go unhindered from one gate to the next in the world to come.[75]

The writer of an amulet must be pure and holy, as must the surroundings in which it is written, which must also meet the additional criterion of serenity. On one occasion R. Jacob Joseph showed the Ba'al Shem Tov an amulet that had been written by R. Naphtali, 'and the Ba'al Shem Tov discerned that it had been written while he was in the ritual bath, and while fasting. He said: I shall write such a charm after eating, while sitting on my bed'—that is, without purification, signifying that to him it was a trivial matter.[76] R. Moses Teitelbaum of Ujhely, who frequently gave amulets, also claimed that amulets given by anyone else were ineffective; amulets received their potency from him.[77]

A story about the Ba'al Shem Tov and the giving of an amulet appears in *Megilat setarim* by R. Isaac Eisik Safrin, who heard it from his uncle and teacher, R. Tsevi of Zhidachov.

One time a certain woman came to our master [the Ba'al Shem Tov], [asking him] to give her an amulet to cure her of a certain malady. Our master explained to her

[73] See Abraham of Slonim, *Beit avraham*, 122. Cf. Rapoport, *Divrei david*, fo. 30*b* (see below, n. 78).

[74] See Ehrmann, *Devarim arevim*, 'Stories of the Holy Brothers R. Elimelekh and R. Zusya', §31. See Y.D. of Sudilkov, *Temimei derekh*, 12–17: R. Yehiel Mikhel of Zlotchev wrote for a youth a 'small scroll' that contained the sentence: 'Is it possible that a person shall marry his sister?' Cf. also Kohen, *Shemuot vesipurim*, 212–14: the plot is similar, but the tsadik is the rabbi of Chernobyl. See Kleinmann, *Zikhron larishonim*, 75–81, for an instance during the time of R. Hayim of Sanz. See also 'A Polonnoye Eulogy' (Heb.), in *Otsar hasifrut*, 2 (Krakow, 1888), 124; Ben-Yehezkel, *Sefer hama'asiyot*, ii. 358.

[75] Ehrmann, *Devarim arevim*, 'Stories of the Ba'al Shem Tov', §28.

[76] *Shivḥei habesht*, 148.

[77] Ehrmann, *Pe'er vekhavod*, fo. 5*b*. Cf. Moskowitz, *Otsar hasipurim*, v, §6, for the writing of amulets by R. Moses Teitelbaum, author of *Yismaḥ mosheh*. See also M. M. Sofer, *Sheloshah edrei tson*, 65: the husband of a woman who has lost her mind comes to R. Berish of Oshpetzin to request an amulet. The rabbi, who did not engage in such activity, sends him to R. Teitelbaum, who regularly wrote such charms.

that if she were to give him the sum of fifty zloty, then he would give her the charm. The woman returned home and sold all that she possessed, but she had only thirty zloty. She returned to our master, and told him that she had only thirty zloty, and he did not want to give her a charm.

The tale then relates that the woman turned to the Council of the Four Lands to collect for her the sum she lacked. The members of the Council, however, were angry with the Ba'al Shem Tov, and summoned him to a court of Jewish law. When the Ba'al Shem Tov came before them, he demonstrated for them the outstanding power of the *yiḥudim* in which he was engaged, and they acknowledged his greatness. As a result of her burning desire to give the required sum to the Ba'al Shem Tov, the woman became wealthy. The story ends: 'This, too, was his holy intent.'[78]

The stories give various details of the texts written in amulets. R. Naphtali Katz gave charms in which only his name was written: 'Naphtali Hakohen';[79] R. Abraham of Ulanov gave charms containing acronyms of the names of *tana'im* and *amora'im*;[80] and R. Abraham of Grodizsk used amulets in which he wrote prayers.[81] In a talisman that he gave to a non-Jew for the protection of his livelihood, he wrote: 'and foreigners who come . . .' (Deut. 29: 21).[82] A charm given to a woman experiencing difficulties in childbirth contained the words 'You go forth',[83] and an amulet against mice contained the message, 'I adjure the *sar* [guardian angel] of mice, that they leave this house.'[84]

During a cholera epidemic, R. Menahem Mendel of Kotsk was implored to give a charm. Only after many entreaties did he agree, writing an amulet consisting of a single word of the four Hebrew letters spelling out the word *ḥalera*. These four letters, the Hebrew for 'cholera', are also an acronym for the phrase *ḥatanu lefaneikha raḥem aleinu*: 'We have sinned before You, have mercy on us.'[85]

[78] I. Safrin, *Megilat setarim*, 32–3. Cf. Menahem Nahum of Chernobyl, *Me'or einayim*, 'Naso', fo. 40*d*: 'And the remedies of the Ba'al Shem Tov, may his soul rest in Paradise, were only by means of *yiḥudim*.' See also the letter by R. Gershon of Kutow to his brother-in-law the Ba'al Shem Tov (Hakohen, *Birkat ha'arets*, fo. 63*b*) in which he requested: 'If it were possible to send me a comprehensive amulet, so that there would not be a need for a new one every year, this would be good.'

[79] Berger, *Eser orot*, 'R. David Moses of Chortkov', §16; A. Michelson, *Ohel avraham*, §83. This originates in Rapoport, *Divrei david*, fo. 30*b*, as follows: 'When the Ba'al Shem Tov was in Istanbul, on his way to the Holy Land, he heard people saying that R. Naphtali Hakohen, may his memory be for the life of the world to come, was giving amulets and using holy names. The Ba'al Shem Tov asked someone to bring him an amulet. He opened it up, and he saw that no [divine] name was written there, only his holy name, Naphtali Hakohen.'

[80] Berger, *Eser atarot*, 'R. Abraham of Ulanov', §4.

[81] Shenkel, *Ma'asiyot mitsadikim yesodei olam*, §3. [82] Ehrmann, *Pe'er vekhavod*, fo. 6*b*.

[83] Ibid., fo. 13*a*. Cf. Lieberson, *Tseror haḥayim*, 83: only two letters.

[84] Ehrmann, *Pe'er vekhavod*, fo. 5*b*.

[85] Rakats, *Siaḥ sarfei kodesh*, v. 53; Arten, *Emet ve'emunah*, §682, p. 105. See Rosenstein, *Pe'er layesharim*, fo. 22*b*: R. Pinhas of Korets cured a person of the ague 'without any action, he only

The story quoted above about the Council of Four Lands shows that the giving of charms by the Ba'al Shem Tov was sometimes viewed askance, and this attitude is present in other stories as well. When R. Isaac of Drohobitch was travelling through Medzibezh and heard about the effectiveness of the amulets given by the Ba'al Shem Tov, he thought that the latter was using divine names, and took measures to withdraw the power of these charms, so that they were no longer effective. This situation continued for some ten months. In retaliation, the Ba'al Shem Tov acted to confuse R. Isaac's calendrical calculations, and he erred regarding the days of the week. This confusion led to his being compelled to spend the sabbath in the Ba'al Shem Tov's house. On Saturday night, at the end of the sabbath, the Ba'al Shem Tov asked: 'Why did you take from me the power of the amulets that I give to help people?' R. Isaac replied: 'It is forbidden to use holy names!' The Ba'al Shem Tov then declared: 'No [holy] name or adjuration is written in my amulets; only my own name, Israel ben Sarah Ba'al Shem Tov, is written in them.' R. Isaac did not want to believe the Ba'al Shem Tov, and demanded: 'How is it possible that your name alone effects such very great wondrous actions?' Several amulets were brought before R. Isaac, who opened them and saw that the Ba'al Shem Tov had spoken truthfully. Then R. Isaac said: 'If you will give me a new garment for the holy sabbath, I will restore for you the power of the amulets that they previously possessed.' The Ba'al Shem Tov gave him such a garment, as he had requested, and then R. Isaac opened his mouth and spoke as follows: 'Master of the Universe, when a person enjoys livelihood from his name, of what concern is this to You? Restore to him the active power of the amulets in which his name is written.' And so it was. From that day on, the Ba'al Shem Tov once again effected great and awesome actions with his charms.[86] R. Hirsch of Chortkov also became angry at the Ba'al Shem Tov's writing of charms when he was in Tluste, and the Ba'al Shem Tov showed him that 'Israel ben Sarah' (i.e. his own name) was all that was written in them.[87]

The following story, in contrast, presents different testimony by the Ba'al Shem Tov about his magical activity. This same R. Isaac of Drohobitch asked the Ba'al Shem Tov: 'I heard that his exalted excellency [i.e. the Ba'al Shem

said to one person: "Come and look in my face when I recite *Barekhu*" ['Bless the Lord, the Blessed One', from the morning and evening prayers]—and he was healed'.

[86] Bodek, *Mifalot hatsadikim*, §18; Kleinmann, *Mazkeret shem gedolim*, 'The Light of Isaac', 4–5. Cf. *Shivḥei habesht*, 84.

[87] See J. Sofer, *Sipurei ya'akov*, ii, §35. For a similar approach, see A. Walden, *Shem hagedolim heḥadash*, ch. 1, §16 (R. Abraham Azulai): 'I heard from the rabbi, the holy sage, R. Hayim Abenatar, that he knew the rabbi, of blessed memory, and when a sick person would ask him for a charm, he would take a bit of paper and write on it, in Rashi script: "May it be his will that a complete healing from a certain sickness be sent to so-and-so son of so-and-so. Amen, may it be his will," and no more, without any [divine] name.' See also Ch. 2 n. 86 above.

Tov] writes amulets?', to which the Ba'al Shem Tov replied: 'I give only a blank and [ritually] fit parchment, without any writing in it. If the petitioner merits being answered, then the names of the angels responsible for this matter come by themselves . . . and are to be seen on this blank and fit parchment.'[88]

R. Moses Teitelbaum, author of *Yismaḥ mosheh*, was undecided as to whether or not he should give amulets, since he feared for his soul, lest these charms arouse the *ḥitsonim*. His apprehensions were allayed when he heard a voice telling him: 'Do not fear!', and his charms were subsequently renowned for their efficacy. R. Naphtali of Ropshits was angry with him, because the Seer of Lublin and his circle were not accustomed to write amulets. He wrote a number of letters, but strange things happened to all of them, from which R. Naphtali understood that heaven was impeding him. He therefore sat and wrote a letter to R. Moses in which he encouraged the latter's writing of amulets.[89] Once R. Moses Teitelbaum gave amulets to a woman, but these charms were lost (instead of, as intended, being available for future use). R. Berish of Oshpetzin declared that he used neither '[divine] names nor *yiḥudim*'.[90]

The assumption that a *ba'al mofet* (wonder-worker) uses charms and divine names also lies at the basis of the story cited above about the young man who was deceived by Satan and given a chest full of 'serpents and idols' instead of 'amulets and [divine] names'. Satan warned the young man not to open the chest, reflecting the belief that an amulet loses its mystical power when opened. R. Naphtali Hayim Horowitz gave the parents of an only daughter who had lost her mind an amulet that could be given only once in the recipient's lifetime. He ordered that the girl wear the amulet all her life, without opening it, for its special quality would disappear if opened.[91]

R. Moses Teitelbaum gave an amulet with a blessing for male offspring, cautioning the recipient not to open it. The rabbi in his city, along with the young man who received it, nevertheless opened it, read its contents, and closed it once again. A year passed, but the tsadik's blessing was not fulfilled. The young man travelled to R. Moses, and complained that the charm was not effective. The tsadik demanded: 'Who has dared to open my amulet?'

[88] Ehrmann, *Devarim arevim*, 'Stories of the Ba'al Shem Tov', §29.

[89] [Lemberger], *Magdil yeshuot malko*, 23–4. Moskowitz, *Otsar hasipurim*, ii, §18: the tsadik of Sanz sensed that there was a charm written by R. Moses Teitelbaum, author of *Yismaḥ mosheh*, in the house of a simple village innkeeper. In the past, the innkeeper's wife had had no milk to nurse her infant, and Teitelbaum had given her the charm. The tsadik opened the amulet and read: 'Eldad and Medad', which he regarded to be 'wondrous wisdom'. See Ehrenreich, *Tiyul bapardes*, i. 4: 1; Lischeutz, 'Segulot yisra'el', 8: 25–8. For stories of the charms by R. Teitelbaum, see Moskowitz, *Otsar hasipurim*, iii, §5:2.

[90] Singer, *Seva ratson*, fo. 15*a*. Cf. the statement by the tsadik of Alik: 'I act only by prayer to the Lord, may He be blessed.'

[91] See Moskowitz, *Otsar hasipurim*, xiii. 5.

He gave the charm instead to the young boy Moshele who accompanied the hasid, who benefited from the amulet twenty years later, when it cured him of an illness.[92]

The fundamental dispute concerning the efficacy of amulets was not resolved. The opposing positions in this controversy appear in a story in which R. Tsevi of Zhidachov asks R. Moses Teitelbaum, 'Why should he [i.e. you] give amulets? He could pray . . . and his prayer would undoubtedly be answered', to which the tsadik of Ujhely responded, 'Prayer effects half [see *Lev. Rabbah* 10: 5], and the other half of the request remains!' R. Tsevi then retorted: 'We pray [for] more than what is requested, until all that is requested is granted, and we have no need of any charm!'[93]

[92] Ibid. x, §6.

[93] Teomim, *Ateret tiferet*, 'His Holiness, the Holy Rabbi, R. Tsevi Hirsch of Zhidachov', §18, quoting R. Isaac Safrin in the latter's introduction to *Likutei torah*.

ELEVEN

APOSTASY AND APOSTATES

THE HASIDIC STORYTELLING genre hardly touches upon the subject of non-Jews converting to Judaism, but is replete with tales of apostasy: that is, conversion from Judaism to another religion, usually Christianity. Since apostasy is considered in hasidism (as in Judaism generally) to be the very nadir of moral degeneration, it is frequently portrayed in the broader context of crime: the apostate is variously an adulterer and a murderer, a member of a criminal band, or, at the very least, a deserting husband. One of the stories that will be described in this chapter tells of a ritual slaughterer who, having been dismissed from his position because he murdered a poor man in the city, later became an apostate; another focuses on two adulterers who renounced Judaism for another religion.[1] For women, too, adultery is linked to apostasy: the Ba'al Shem Tov once rescued a young adulteress who was about to convert.[2]

In the hasidic story apostasy is also linked with the Sitra Ahra gaining the upper hand, and the struggle against one is intertwined with the battle against the other. The willing apostate (as opposed to children who were taken captive by non-Jews and did not know of their Jewish origins) is a person who is under Satan's rule, and who is submerged in impurity and crime. The Devil's agents take a particular interest in 'holy souls', such as scholars and tsadikim, who will likely hinder the activity of the Sitra Ahra in this world. One such apostate became a bishop before finally returning to Judaism: 'I was initially a Jew, and then I fell into the depths of the *kelipot*, for I was a great scholar and I possessed a holy soul.'[3] One of the Ba'al Shem Tov's disciples who sinned, and thereby provoked accusations against himself

[1] Zeilingold, *Me'orot hagedolim*, §53, p. 95. The adulterers were a married watchmaker and the wife of a Torah scholar from Karlin. After their apostasy, they lived together for some twenty years, and died destitute.

[2] *Shivḥei habesht*, 163. See Nigal, 'Women in the Book *Shivḥei habesht*' (Heb.), 139. Another instance of apostasy, not connected with adultery, concerned the Seer of Lublin, who saw a cross above the head of his bride, and understood that she would convert. See Sobelman, *Sipurei tsadikim heḥadash*, §28. Cf. A. Michelson, *Shemen hatov*, §25: 'The groom [the Seer] told his fellows that the bride had a face like a non-Jewish woman.' For more concerning a woman's apostasy and death, see Ehrmann, *Devarim arevim*, 'Stories from the Holy Rabbi of Lublin', §12.

[3] Rodkinsohn, *Adat tsadikim*, §8. See Ch. 10 above.

in heaven, was given over to Satan, who sought to entice him to convert. In the end this erring disciple was miraculously saved by the merit of his teacher, the Ba'al Shem Tov. An important role was played in the seduction of Jews away from their religion by the Christian priest, who in these stories embodies Satan and the forces of evil.[4] The efforts of tsadikim (above all, the Ba'al Shem Tov) to return the errant soul to its Jewish source are therefore connected with the struggle to weaken the Sitra Ahra, and their rescue of Jews from apostasy is further expression of the greatness of these hasidic leaders—as it was for the prominent members of the Jewish nation who preceded hasidism. For example, the struggle by the Maharal of Prague and the head of the Pressburg yeshiva to extricate the youthful Solomon Ephraim of Luntshits from the forces of impurity consisted of saving him from apostasy.[5]

The moral decline conducive to apostasy may be that of the individual concerned or that of his family. Stories recounted in Chapter 5 on *agunot* make the point that poor family life is liable to result in the husband's flight from home and desertion of his wife, culminating in apostasy.[6] Thus moral degeneration may begin with trifling matters, continue with serious transgressions and public disgrace, and end with flight from the Jewish nation and faith. Such a decline could begin, for example, with an individual's carelessness concerning the ritual washing of hands, and end in his denying the existence of God and marrying a non-Jewish woman.[7] A disciple of the Ba'al Shem Tov who wished to convert ate and drank in the house of a priest, in contravention of Jewish law.[8] R. Levi Isaac wished to examine the ritual fitness of a knife used by a scholar and slaughterer, but the latter refused, claiming that R. Levi Isaac was unlearned. As time passed, public disquiet arose concerning the slaughterer; people began to gossip about him, and it transpired that there was some reason for the controversy that surrounded him. He was dismissed from his position, after which he went from bad to worse: he murdered a poor Jew in the forest, then moved to London, where he converted to Christianity. Some time later, he came back to R. Levi Isaac, returned to Judaism, and received a *tikun* from the tsadik to effect his repentance.[9] In another instance, a Jew from the city of Shklov was caught

[4] Sobelman, *Sipurei tsadikim heḥadash*, §10, pp. 24 ff. The rescue was performed by the force of the melody *Benei heikhala*, with the words *levatala kol kelipin* (Let all the *kelipot* be nullified). Cf. the story of a rescue by force of the Maggid's exposition at pp. 242–3 below. For more regarding conversion conducted in the priest's residence, see [Lemberger], *Magdil yeshuot malko*, 15.

[5] Bodek(?), *Sipurei kedoshim*, §10, pp. 26–37. Joseph ben R. A., *Mifalot tsadikim heḥadash*, 12–14, tells that the son of R. Jonathan Eybeschuetz was about to marry a non-Jew and convert, but, thanks to a charm that he had been given when he took his leave of his father, he repented and married a Jewish woman.

[6] See e.g. Sobelman, *Sipurei tsadikim heḥadash*, §7.

[7] Zeilingold, *Me'orot hagedolim*, §15, p. 32.

[8] Sobelman, *Sipurei tsadikim heḥadash*, §10.

[9] Bodek(?), *Sipurei kedoshim*, §5, pp. 29 ff.

transgressing with a non-Jewess. He was whipped in public and then placed in the *kine* (stocks) next to the study hall, where every passer-by would spit in his face and curse him. In his shame, he fled to St Petersburg, converted, and became an important government official.[10]

One of the manifestations of moral decline was mocking the tsadik, and this too was likely to end in conversion. It was related that the *ilui* Joseph Tarler, who later (as described below) converted and became a censor, derided R. Tsevi Elimelekh of Dynow. The tsadik observed, 'I am certain that he will convert.' A young Jew, who, so it was related, would later become pope, publicly shamed the rabbi of Vilna while the latter was delivering a sermon, as an indirect result of which the rabbi was forced to divorce his wife and leave the city.

Other factors leading to apostasy included a love affair with a non-Jew. The son of a worthy from Lipovets ran away with the daughter of a non-Jewish neighbour, and all the father's attempts to locate his son were fruitless. When he went to the Maggid of Mezirech, the tsadik advised him to travel to Kiev and search the taverns there, and also gave the father a letter addressed to the son. After searching for weeks, the worthy happened upon a remote tavern where he heard a peasant telling his friend that 'the Jew who lives with the priest will convert some time soon, with his wife'. The worthy bought drinks for the peasant, who finally revealed to him that the couple were living in a monastery. The father managed to get into the building, but when his son saw him, he fled; all the older man could do was leave the letter that he had been given by the Maggid in his son's garments. The son found the letter, in which it was written: 'know the God of your father, and serve him' (1 Chr. 28: 9), and he ran in search of his father. The neighbour's daughter was also rescued from the monastery. The father told his son to divorce his wife and go abroad, and this he did.[11]

Romantic motives for apostasy were often connected with stories of Jews studying at universities,[12] which served as a meeting place for Jewish maskilim and their Christian counterparts.

Sometimes the apostate is a victim of circumstances, such as a Jewish infant who is raised among non-Jews and is unaware of his Jewish origins.

[10] Kaidaner, *Sipurim nora'im*, §56.

[11] Zeilingold, *Me'orot hagedolim*, 36–7. The transmission of a letter is possibly the modern embodiment of the charm. For an amulet that, when touched by an apostate, returned him to Judaism, see Abraham of Slonim, *Beit avraham*, 122.

[12] See Zeilingold, *Me'orot hagedolim*, 'R. Levi Isaac of Berdichev', §1, pp. 11–12. This story contains many modern elements: a Jewish girl is educated among non-Jews; her brother studies at a university; there is soul-searching regarding the act of conversion; a Jewish father wishes to commit suicide if his son converts; the son similarly threatens to do so if he is not allowed to marry the non-Jewish girl. Cf. ibid., §8, pp. 17–19, for a wealthy son who fled with the neighbour's daughter and was about to convert.

Thus, it is related, a Jew who fell into heavy debt to the local *poritz* was forced to give the latter his infant son, who was rescued in a miraculous manner at the age of 13, the time of his bar mitzvah.[13] At times this calamity befell a Jewish baby as the result of a curse placed by a tsadik on the child's father.[14] For example, R. Ezekiel Landau placed a curse on one of the city's worthies, who had not shown him the proper respect, saying that one of his sons would become an apostate. Some time later, this worthy had to go to great lengths to cancel this malediction.[15]

When a Jew converted, the community usually held the convert in contempt; indeed, apostasy was a curse to be hurled at one's enemies. The following tales also reveal the tragic aspect of renouncing one's faith: the sorrow that overwhelms the parents of one who has converted or who plans to do so, and their entreaties to the tsadik to prevent this tragedy, or to return the lost son to the bosom of Judaism. This motif is included in the story about R. Dov Baer of Mezirech, three versions of which are cited below. The tsadik acts after his mother (or, in another version, his father) comes to weep and plead before him. The story portrays the mother's sorrow as well as the difficulties that she overcame in her determination to travel to the tsadik.

The hasidic story also concerns itself with the fate of the apostate. In some instances, he degenerates and lives on the margins of non-Jewish society; in others, he attains prominence in that society, reflecting an unstated assumption that the Jew, even if he abandons his faith, nevertheless possesses outstanding abilities. Mention was made above of the apostate who became a pope, and of Joseph Tarler, who made fun of the tsadik R. Tsevi Elimelekh and became the censor in Lemberg; another case, described in more detail below, is that of a Jewish merchant who converted and married the countess who fell in love with him, and later became a member of the king's court.

The apostate seeks to cut all relations with his family and to deny his origins, and may even become a sworn Jew-hater. In his youth, the censor Tarler had become friends with 'a corrupt person [named] Letteres [Meir Letteres, 1800–71, an author and poet in Galicia], may his name be blotted out, and even before that, heretical books, heaven forfend, had already come out of his pockets'. He prohibited the printing of the books of R. Tsevi Elimelekh, including *Benei yisakhar*, and indeed, the first edition of this work

[13] Bodek, *Mifalot hatsadikim*, §1.

[14] Benjamin Ressler, MS JNUL 5271. See Nigal, 'A Hasidic Manuscript' (Heb.).

[15] Bodek(?), *Sipurei kedoshim*, §15, pp. 59–62. Cf. Drickerman, *Temimei derekh*, 'R. Naphtali', 34–42. Cf. also J. Sofer, *Sipurei ya'akov*, i, §24. For imprisonment in a cellar to prevent the conversion of a youth in the time of R. Judah Hehasid, see *Mayse bukh*, 53–4; 'Beiträge zur jüdischen Sagen- und Spruchkunde im Mittelalter', 28–9.

was printed without the approval of the censor's office.[16] A Jewish tax-collector attested that a Jewish woman who married a wealthy estate owner exhibited even greater hatred of the Jews than that shown by her non-Jewish husband. More common, however is the opposite motif: the apostate who cannot free himself of his Jewishness. It continues secretly to nest within him, and not even an expressed hatred for Jews can shield him from his former religion. His Judaism is awakened within him by particular circumstances such as a meeting with Jews, a sign from heaven, non-Jewish hostility, or persecution of Jews. He is then likely to return to Judaism, and even to die a martyr's death. Chapter 5 included the story of an *agunah* who recognized her husband marching through the streets of Constantinople as the regal figure at the head of a religious procession; the husband eventually returned to Judaism.[17]

The following three stories reflect the influence on the apostate of an encounter with Jews and with Jewish prayer.

In the first, a group of Jewish merchants were compelled to spend the sabbath in the home of a non-Jewish villager. On Friday they saw the villager's aged mother burn two pieces of wood in a strange fashion. They discovered from speaking with her that she had been a Jewess, and had converted when she married a non-Jew. She did not observe the commandments of the Torah, but she never forgot to light sabbath candles, and if she had no candles, she lit splinters of wood. Weeping copiously, the old woman fell to the ground and died. The Jewish merchants took her away, and gave her a Jewish burial.[18]

In the second story,

> [i]t happened that several Jewish artisans travelled deep into Russia, where there were no Jews, and dispersed to seek their livelihood, some in one direction and the rest in another, and they remained there for some time.
>
> When the propitious days [of the month of Elul] approached, and Rosh Hashanah and Yom Kippur were near at hand, they wanted to have a *minyan*, so that they could pray properly. As it transpired, on Yom Kippur eve they were only nine. They rented a house from a certain non-Jew in which to pray, but they were greatly distressed that they could not recite Kaddish or *Barekhu* [prayers requiring a quorum of ten Jews]. When the time for *Kol nidrei* came, a non-Jew who was not

[16] Ehrmann, *Devarim arevim*, §74; A. Michelson, *Ohel naftali*, §274. For Joseph Tarler, see Klausner, *History of Modern Hebrew Literature* (Heb.), ii. 323–4; Bader, *Galician Jewish Celebrities* (Heb.), 105–6. Shenkel, *Ma'asim tovim* (§10) and Chikernik, *Sipurim neḥmadim* (14–15), tell of an apostate who forged a Torah scroll by Ezra the Scribe, writing (Deut. 11: 16) 'ואבדתם [You shall lose]' in place of 'ועבדתם [You shall serve (the Lord)]'.

[17] Kaidaner, *Sipurim nora'im*, §2, pp. 5–7.

[18] Ibid., §56, p. 132. This official later repaid the Jew who had rescued him from the *kine* (cell) in which he had been imprisoned, and helped this Jew to obtain a permit for the printer from Slavuta.

one of the inhabitants of the house appeared, and they were greatly apprehensive. The non-Jew told them: 'Do not be afraid, for I, too, am a Jew! Until now I denied the God of Israel, but now I repent and regret all my actions, and I return with all my heart to the Jewish religion.'[19]

On that frosty day the apostate poured out his heart before his Creator, with the simple words that come from the heart, and then died while praying. After the conclusion of the fast, the artisans smuggled his body away and gave him a Jewish burial.

In the third of these stories (briefly mentioned above), R. Pinhas of Kolomai resolved in his old age to return apostates to the Jewish religion. He learned of a Jewish woman who had married a wealthy estate owner, and he travelled to the place where they lived. A Jewish tax-collector who lived in the vicinity warned him against entertaining any false hopes of returning the woman to Judaism, since her hatred of Jews exceeded even that of her husband and she would not let the tsadik set foot in her house. Nonetheless, R. Pinhas succeeded in making contact with the woman, under the guise of being a grain merchant, and even drew her out of her house into the fields, where he revealed to her that he was not a merchant, but rather a Jew. He asked her to recite the Shema when she arose in the morning and before she went to sleep; in other matters, he permitted her to continue living her life as she had until then. The recitation of the Shema so deeply affected the woman that shortly afterwards she fled from her husband and returned to Judaism.[20]

A sign from heaven was given to a person who, before he had secretly converted, had had the task of blowing the *shofar*. When he tried to blow the ram's horn now, it made no sound. When R. Abraham Hayakhini explained to the man that 'Happy is the people that know the joyful shout [of the *shofar*]' (Ps. 89: 16), he returned to his original faith.[21]

The following story shows how the attitude of non-Jewish society could influence an apostate. A woman came to R. Naphtali Hertzke of Ratzferd and told him that she had been married to a non-Jew for a number of years, 'and they owned property together'. Her husband had recently begun drinking heavily, and he and his brother would brutally beat her. She expressed remorse for her past, and sought the tsadik's advice on how to part from her husband, since he refused to give her her property.[22]

19 Reznik, *Mora'im gedolim*, §11, pp. 24–5. For an apostate who became a local *poritz*, completed a *minyan* on Yom Kippur, and died while praying, see Fishman (Maimon), *Sarei hame'ah*, iii. 143–6.

20 Reznik, *Mora'im gedolim*, §12, pp. 25–7. A young apostate who had married the priest's daughter repented as a result of the tears of an orchard watchman, a Spanish New Christian (Marrano), on Yom Kippur; his non-Jewish wife also decided to convert to Judaism (Kohen, *Shemuot vesipurim*, 5–7).

21 Shenkel, *Ma'asim tovim*, §4.

22 Rotzferd, *Zikhron naftali*, §68, fo. 18*b*.

A blood libel could cause an apostate to repent and motivate him to defend his fellow Jews. R. Isaac of Nezkizh told of a Jewish merchant, who, having fallen in love with a countess, converted and married her. Once, when he was at the royal court, he heard that a blood libel was being concocted. While the other noblemen were confirming in the king's ears that Jews were, indeed, accustomed to slaughter Christians and use their blood for their rituals at Passover, the apostate revolted against this, and told the king that this was a crude libel, without an atom of truth in it. Following this incident, the apostate began to consider repentance, and eventually he returned to Judaism; his wife and children died in a fire.[23]

R. Levi Isaac of Berdichev found in the Vilna communal register an account of an episode that had occurred centuries previously. A wealthy but childless man about 60 years of age became a widower, and married his niece. No children were born from this marriage either, and thus it became known to him, and to everyone in the community, that he was sterile. When his young wife became pregnant, he realized that this was the result of an illicit relationship. The husband shared this information with the rabbi, while outwardly pretending to be overjoyed, and when the woman gave birth he held an ostentatious banquet, as was the practice of those of his social standing. During the circumcision the rabbi, who was performing the ceremony, castrated the infant, and also made a mark in his ear, so that he could be identified in the future. Some time later, the wealthy man passed away. The child excelled in his studies, and was known for both his sharp intellect and his aptness at learning. When he heard other children calling him a *mamzer*, and then the same epithet being voiced in public, he fled from the city and went to a higher yeshiva, where he quickly became one of the most promising students. Some time later, when an extremely distinguished member of the Jewish community of Rome was searching for a husband for his only daughter, this young man was proposed, and the marriage took place.

The rabbi of Vilna happened to be in Rome collecting money to ransom Jewish prisoners. As was customary for important visitors, he delivered a public disquisition on the sabbath, and in the course of this address a young man, the worthy's son-in-law, contradicted the rabbi's teaching and publicly shamed him. Upon the departure of the sabbath, the rabbi spotted the telltale mark on the young man's ear, and he revealed to his father-in-law that his daughter's husband was both a *mamzer* and incapable of fathering children. The young man was forced to divorce his wife, left the city, and converted. He soon began studying to become a priest, once again excelled at his studies, and was eventually elected pope.

[23] I. Landau, *Zikhron tov*, 'On Matters of Faith', §5. Cf. [Isaac Dov Baer ben Tsevi Hirsch], *Kahal ḥasidim heḥadash*, §157.

Some time later, jealous merchants in Rome fabricated a blood libel against an affluent Jewish worthy in the city. The pope heard of the accusation and came to the worthy, in disguise, to raise the latter's spirits, urging him not to abandon hope. The pope asked his slaves to prepare two large bonfires, one at each end of the city. By means of sorcery, he succeeded in reviving the dead child at the centre of the blood libel and refuting the false testimony regarding this worthy. It was then proved that the child's father and a number of his guards were the true murderers. The pope ordered them to be cast into one of the fires, while he himself jumped into the other, having first denounced and reviled Christianity, thus publicly sanctifying the name of God.[24]

R. Uri of Strelisk did not approve of R. Meir of Premishlan, because the latter revealed the esoteric teachings of the Torah. Once, when the two happened to be together, R. Meir spoke of the Inquisition in Spain, and told of a priest who admitted to a Jew who was about to be put to death that he, too, was a clandestine Jew.[25]

Another story involving a pope was told by R. Yerahmiel Moses, a grandson of the Maggid of Koznitz. One of the pupils of R. Joel Sirkes in Krakow converted to Christianity and eventually was elected to the papacy. Being privy to a closely guarded secret (concerning church money that had come to a Jewish widow), he sought to impress the Christians by proving that he knew hidden matters and possessed the spirit of divine inspiration. Obviously, if this secret were to become public knowledge, anti-Jewish riots would result. R. Sirkes caused the apostate to forget all that he knew and lose his mind. He was removed from the papacy and sentenced to be hanged, thus saving the Jews.[26]

A common motif in hasidic stories of conversion is the important force that acts—at times from a great distance—to cause the apostate to repent, or, beforehand, to prevent his conversion: namely, the power of the tsadik. He discerns the forces of the Sitra Ahra that take control of their victim, and he does battle with them, using the various means at his disposal: prayer with the proper *kavanot*; the reciting of chapters from the psalms by himself, by

[24] [Isaac Dov Baer ben Tsevi Hirsch], *Kahal ḥasidim heḥadash*, §105; cf. Shenkel, *Sipurei anshei shem*, §15; Stern, *Ḥutim hameshulashim*, 63. For a Jewish (New Christian) pope who prayed in private with *talit* and *tefilin*, see *Ma'asiyot vesiḥot tsadikim*, 22–3; J. Sofer, *Sipurei ya'akov*, ii, §59. The best-known medieval story of a Jewish pope is that of Elhanan. See *Mayse bukh*, §188, cited in Jellinek, *Bet hamidrash*, v: *Stories*, §12, pp. 148–52. For another version of the story, see ibid., ch. 2, §11, pp. 137–9. For a hostile Christian response to the Jewish story, see A[ppelman], *Das Leben Elchanans*. For traces of a medieval story of a woman who assumed the position of pope, see Slodovnik, *Ma'aseh hagedolim heḥadash*, §37. Cf. Ibn Yahya, *Shalshelet hakabalah*, fo. 90*a*; Rakats, *Siaḥ sarfei kodesh*, ii, §477.

[25] T. H. Rosenberg, *Raza de'uvda*, 'Sha'ar ha'otiyot', 22.

[26] Berger, *Eser atarot*, 'R. Abraham Joshua Heschel', §26, for a person who sought to convert.

his followers, or by the victim and those close to him; close guarding of the victim against evil spirits; and the imposition of obligations connected with repentance. Individuals who lived and were active before hasidism also were gifted with such power. Mention was made above of the Maharal of Prague's efforts on behalf of the young Solomon Ephraim. In another story concerning the Maharal, included in Bodek's *Pe'er mikedoshim*, the son of one of the worthies of Prague was taken on a journey by two other worthies, on the pretext that they were arranging a marriage partner for him. In reality, the youth was brought to a large tower (perhaps a monastery), where he realized that he had been kidnapped by priests. The Maharal proclaimed a fast day, assembled the community in the synagogue, and commanded the people to recite psalms. Finally, he blew a *shofar*, 'and after the conclusion [of the assembly] the youth was brought [by the wind] through a window to the holy *gaon* . . . and he related the episode to the entire congregation'.[27]

A miraculous rescue story is also told of R. Dov Baer of Mezirech, in which he extricated a youth from the clutches of priests. R. Menahem Mendel Bodek refers in *Seder hadorot mitalmidei habesht* to 'a certain booklet' in which

> mention is made . . . of a wondrous episode concerning a woman who had a son who went to convert, heaven forfend. He was already dwelling among the priests in a certain tightly closed house, so that his relatives would not come to entice him to return to the religion of Israel. This youth was truly marvellous in his studies, and his mother wept copiously over him. She went to the holy rabbi, the Maggid, of blessed memory, told him all that had befallen her, and pleaded for her son, that he not sink [into apostasy], heaven forbid. The rabbi ordered her to go home, after which he gathered his pupils who were in attendance, and began to deliver a disquisition on the verse: 'When a person sins' [Lev. 5: 21], and this was a great wonder for them, since this was the eve of the holy sabbath. He assembled them four times that day and expounded on the verse 'When [a person] sins'. At night, as well, the night of the holy sabbath, he delivered three wonderful expositions on the dictum in Scripture, 'When a person sins', and this was a great wonder for the pupils. The seventh time that he delivered a disquisition, a strong wind arose, that splits mountains and shatters rocks. Within this tumult came this young man, and he related all that befallen him that day, for he did not know what had come upon him: suddenly, he had had a change of heart that day, to return to the religion of Israel, but he could not do so, for he had been shut up by the priests. He resolved that early in the morning, when they opened his room, he would flee. During all this, his heart beat strongly, and he found no rest, until he sought to put an end to his life. At one point he became very embittered and wept copiously for what he

[27] Bodek, *Pe'er mikedoshim*, §5, p. 9. Cf. Shenkel, *Noraot anshei ma'aseh*, §1, for the two sons of R. Nethanel who were kidnapped for the purpose of conversion. For a story of Jews in Spain during the time of R. Menahem Mendel of Rymanow, see Ehrmann, *Devarim arevim*, fos 12*a*, 48*b*.

had done, but the door was closed before him, and although he tried with all his strength to smash it, he could not. After this, he resolved to throw himself through the window, and he accepted upon himself self-sacrifice: if he were to fall and die, this would atone for his great sin, for he had sought to be led astray from the living God. And he did so: he threw himself out and fell through the window. By the mercy of God, however, a tempest arose and the wind remained until he stood on his feet, and his life was not dashed out on the ground. The pupils understood the words of their holy master, and his great power to cast light upon those who dwell in darkness and whose path leads through gloom.[28]

Bodek possessed an early written source in which the tale was recounted. A few years after the publication of Bodek's book, a different version of the story appeared in *Sipurim nora'im* by R. Jacob Kaidaner, who attests at the story's conclusion 'that we heard it from the mouth of the holy Old Rebbe'.[29] According to Kaidaner, not only did R. Shneur Zalman of Lyady himself relate the story, he was personally involved, since he lived in the house of the widow whose son converted. The Old Rebbe also helped the unfortunate widow to gain an audience with the Maggid, which was not an easy matter, because the latter's attendant was 'a very difficult person'. When the attendant went to the bathhouse, R. Shneur Zalman opened the door of the Maggid's room and ushered in the widow. In her great excitement, however, the woman was unable to utter a single word, and the Maggid motioned to her to return home. Upon the attendant's return from the bathhouse, while it was still daytime, long before sunset, the Maggid ordered that his disciples be brought in, in order to usher in the sabbath. His disciples found this surprising, since their teacher had never acted in such a manner before. They ate the evening meal 'without leisure', again, contrary to the Maggid's custom, and his great *devekut* also was quite bewildering to the disciples. Following the grace after meals, the Maggid delivered a disquisition, again in an uncharacteristic fashion, with great *devekut* and in a loud voice. (Years later, the Old Rebbe asserted that he himself had not been surprised at all these changes, because he had immediately comprehended that as soon as the widow had left the room, the Maggid began, without delay, to take action for the return of the lost son.) In the middle of his disquisition the Maggid became greatly excited, and a tempest began to rage outdoors. Suddenly, a strong blow was heard against the wall of the house. The Maggid ordered the non-Jewish servant to harness a horse to the carriage,

[28] Bodek, *Seder hadorot mitalmidei habesht*, ch. 2, fo. 11*a*; *Ma'aseh hakedoshim*, §20; Berger, *Eser atarot*, 'R. Baer of Mezirech', §9: 'the awesome matter is known and renowned' (with no reference to the source); Zevin, *Hasidic Tales: On the Torah* (Heb.), 325–6. Cf. Rabbinowich, *Malakhei elyon*, 17: R. Leibele Eiger of Lublin effected the escape from the priests of a female candidate for conversion, by stressing the words *bein yisra'el le'amim* (one [who has distinguished] between Israel and the non-Jewish peoples) during Havdalah.

[29] Kaidaner, *Sipurim nora'im*, §7, 53–7.

and immediately drive to lodgings nearby. The servant found the widow's son there, lying outside, brought him into the lodgings, and heard the entire story from the young man himself. This version by Kaidaner is much more detailed than that of Bodek, but the topic of the Maggid's disquisition is not mentioned.

In a Habad tradition the story appears in a different context.[30] It is reported that during the time of the Old Rebbe a young man by the name of Ze'ev converted, and people came to the tsadik to seek his advice on how to return him to Judaism. R. Shneur Zalman replied that he was unable to be of help himself, but he could tell what had happened during the time of his teacher, the Maggid. The Old Rebbe then related the above episode, which he said had occurred in 1769. His story differs in a number of details from both Bodek's and Kaidaner's versions. According to this version, it is the father of the young man who comes to plead for his son; the Maggid delivers a disquisition on the verse 'When a person sins', and instructs his disciples to recite psalms until the morning. At daybreak, the young man comes to the study hall, but he is asked no questions.

Not only does the tsadik have the power to cause others to repent, even the relating of tales in praise of tsadikim and their actions is likely to advance the process of the apostate's repentance, and attest that his repentance has been accepted in heaven. The following is the complete text of one of the well-known hasidic stories in this vein.

Before his death, the Ba'al Shem Tov, of blessed memory, summoned all his disciples, and commanded them how to conduct themselves, and what would be each one's livelihood; to some he revealed what would happen to them in the future. There was one disciple with him, who was also his attendant, by the name of R. Jacob. The Ba'al Shem Tov called to him, and said: 'You shall travel to all the places where I am known, and you shall tell stories about me to which you were witness, and this shall be your livelihood.' R. Jacob was greatly grieved by this, and he asked, 'What shall be the purpose of being a ceaseless wanderer and a teller of stories?' to which the Ba'al Shem Tov replied: 'Do not worry, for with God's help, you shall become wealthy from this.'

When the holy Ark [i.e. the Ba'al Shem Tov] departed, ascended to heaven, and left us to our lives, his disciples fulfilled all that he had commanded them. R. Joseph travelled everywhere and told stories of the Ba'al Shem Tov, from which he earned a fine livelihood.

Two and a half years after the passing of our master, the Ba'al Shem Tov, of blessed memory, R. Jacob heard that there was a worthy in Italy who would give a gold zloty for every story that he was told about the Ba'al Shem Tov. This R. Jacob resolved to go there and tell him all the stories that he knew of the Ba'al Shem Tov, which would come to a sum of hundreds of zlotys. After this, he would not need to

[30] Glitsenstein, *Rabi duber, harav hamagid mimezirekh*, 107 ff.; id., *Sefer hatoledot rabi menaḥem mendel ba'al hatsemaḥtsedek*, 55–9.

be a constant wanderer for at least a year, or more. He then purchased a horse, along with an attendant, and prepared himself for the journey, for the way was very long. He was delayed on his journey some seven months until he arrived there, for he tarried in every city to gather [money] for his travel expenses.

When he arrived in the city where the worthy resided, he asked the people of the city about the character of the man. They told him that he was exceedingly wealthy, and that his court was like the royal court; he conducted a pious life, and sat and studied the entire day. There were trustees appointed over his business affairs, while he studied and prayed the entire day. At each of the three sabbath meals he requested that he be told stories of the Ba'al Shem Tov, and after the sabbath he would give one gold zloty for each story. R. Jacob enquired regarding the worthy's homeland, whether he had lived here for a long time or not. They replied that he had come there ten years ago and purchased a courtyard from the lord of the city, who was a minister in Rome. [The worthy] settled there and built a synagogue in his courtyard, where the people of the city prayed morning and evening, and on the sabbath most of the people in the city came to his table.

R. Jacob came to him, and asked his officials to inform the worthy that the Ba'al Shem Tov's servant had arrived, and he would tell him many stories of the Ba'al Shem Tov, that his own eyes, and not a stranger, had seen. The official came and told this to the worthy, who responded: 'Let him wait until the sabbath, when he shall tell us [a story].' In the meantime, the worthy ordered that R. Jacob be accommodated, and given a special upper chamber in which he would reside until the sabbath. When the people of the city heard that he was the attendant and disciple of the Ba'al Shem Tov, they all gathered to hear stories from him, since the people of the city had become accustomed, ever since the worthy had taken up residence there, to hear stories of the Ba'al Shem Tov, of blessed memory, every sabbath. When they sat at the sabbath meal, after the *zemirot* [sabbath songs sung at the table], as is customary, the worthy commanded this R. Jacob to tell something of the Ba'al Shem Tov. But R. Jacob completely forgot all the stories, and he could not recall a single episode. He sought to picture in his mind the countenance of the Ba'al Shem Tov, the appearance of the city of Medzibezh, or the appearance of his disciples, so that he would thereby recall some story; he was incapable even of this, for he had completely forgotten everything that had ever happened to him. R. Jacob laboured greatly, attempting to concentrate, but he was completely forgetful of every place where he thought to recall some matter from which a story of the Ba'al Shem Tov could be evoked, as if he had been born that day. His racking his brains to the very end was of no avail, for he could remember nothing at all, and R. Jacob was so confused. All the people of the worthy's household, and all the people of the city, were greatly distressed, for they thought that he had lied about having been with the Ba'al Shem Tov, and that for a certainty he had never seen him. The worthy himself was silent. He told him [R. Jacob], 'Let us wait until tomorrow, perhaps you will be able to recall something.' R. Jacob wept the entire night, and he thought to picture the appearance of the disciples, but to no avail, for he had completely forgotten how to begin telling any story of the Ba'al Shem Tov, as if he had never seen him. During the sabbath morning meal, the worthy asked him once again: 'Perhaps you remember some story?' R. Jacob could say nothing in reply, but he told him: 'It is clear to me that this is not something devoid [of meaning]; nothing like this ever happened to me.' The worthy then said, 'We will wait until the third meal, perhaps you will remember.' But he recalled nothing in the third meal, as well, and he was greatly aggrieved by this. In addition, all of the worthy's entourage wished to show him their contempt, saying: How dare he mock the worthy with his prevarications? All the townspeople were infuriated, and taunted him greatly with their words.

The righteous R. Jacob accepted all this with love, and wondered greatly at this. He laboured to find some reason why this had befallen him, why this was how it was supposed to be, thinking that perhaps the Ba'al Shem Tov had some complaint against him, because he had been unwilling to travel to places where he was known but instead had gone to a foreign land, [whose inhabitants] were not worthy of hearing such stories. He had many similar thoughts, but no reason entered his mind. He wondered greatly at this, and was sorely aggrieved by these events, and he prayed to the Lord the entire sabbath. Upon the departure of the sabbath, the worthy sent a message to him yet again: Perhaps he recalled something that he could tell him. This greatly troubled the righteous [R. Jacob], who was continually asked: 'Have you remembered? Do you know?'

R. Jacob went to his room and wept. He controlled himself and went out, saying: 'Perhaps it is the will of heaven that I not become wealthy, or that stories from the Ba'al Shem Tov will not be told here. All in all, I know that this is not by chance, heaven forfend, and now I shall return home!' The worthy sent him another message, that he should remain until Tuesday, and if he did not then recall anything, he should return to his home. R. Jacob tarried until Tuesday, but recollected nothing. He went to receive the worthy's permission to take his leave, the worthy gave him a respectable present, and he went and sat in the carriage ready for the journey. While he was sitting in the carriage, he remembered an awe-inspiring story of the Ba'al Shem Tov. R. Jacob returned to the worthy's house and sent his attendant to tell [the worthy] that he recalled a precious story. The worthy sent for him, he was brought into his room, and [the worthy] told him: 'Tell it to me, if you please!' R. Jacob related to him, saying:

'Now, one time, before their festival [meaning Easter], the Ba'al Shem Tov was greatly occupied the entire sabbath, and we walked to and fro in his house. Immediately following the third meal, he ordered that the horses be harnessed, and he took three men with him, including myself. We sat in the carriage, and we travelled the entire night. No one knew the purpose of the journey, where it was headed. In the morning light, we came to an exceedingly great city. The horses stopped at a certain large house, whose doors and windows were shuttered. The Ba'al Shem Tov ordered that we knock on the door. An old woman came out, and she cried bitterly: "Why have you come here at this time, for all of you will be led to the slaughter, since on this day the Christians stab every Hebrew who steps outside the threshold of his house, because this is their festival. If they do not find a Hebrew in the streets, then they will cast lots on some Jewish person and will be avenged of their Messiah on him. Woe to the person who will be trapped by their lottery, for they drag him outside from his home, and cruelly torture him, until he falls at their hand, ravaged and beaten. Yesterday they cast lots and the rabbi's son was captured, for Christians know that Hebrews are careful not to walk about in the street on this day. And now, when any of the Christians see you, see that Jews have come here from Poland, why, all of you will be led to the slaughter, even if you have caused no harm. Now, hurry, and flee from the city!" The old woman shouted this as she cried and sighed, while she held her head with her hands. The Ba'al Shem Tov, however, paid no attention to her, and immediately went into the house and ascended to the large upper chamber, where she lived, and ordered that the baggage be brought in. The householders were all in a daze, and lay about, next to the walls of the house. No one spoke a word, out of fear. The old woman entered, wailing and screaming, and she argued with the Ba'al Shem Tov, but he did not answer her. He removed a curtain from one window, where he stood and gazed out. The old woman continued shouting: "Why did you remove the curtain?" He, however, paid her no heed. The Ba'al Shem Tov saw that there was a large platform in the centre of the city, with thirty steps up to it, and a very large crowd had gathered around the platform, where they waited for the bishop. After a little while, the pealing of many bells was heard, announcing the arrival of the bishop.

The Ba'al Shem Tov stood at the window and looked through it. Suddenly, he called to me: "Jacob, go summon the bishop to me, that he come to me quickly." When all those in the house heard what he said, they were so afraid that they were left breathless. They raised their voices against him: "You imbecile, why are you sending a Hebrew man to the slaughter, for all that great crowd will tear him limb from limb." In the bitterness of their souls they continued to curse him, but he paid them no mind, and shouted, "Jacob, go at once! Do not be afraid!" I knew that my master was aware of what he was doing, and I went into the street, without any trepidation. I went to the platform, and no one spoke to me. I told the bishop, in the Hebrew tongue: "The Ba'al Shem Tov is here, he calls upon you to immediately come to him." The bishop replied to me: "I know of his arrival. Tell him that I will come to him presently, after the sermon." I returned, and the people of the house saw from a distance, through holes on the blocked windows, that I was at the platform, and that I spoke with the bishop. They wondered at what they saw, and remained silent, placating the rabbi until my return. He, however, paid no mind, neither to what they had spoken before, nor to their words now. When I delivered the bishop's response, he shouted at me: "Go once again and tell him to come immediately, and do not be a fool!" I returned to the platform, and now he had begun to deliver his sermon. I pulled him by his clothes, and I told him what the Ba'al Shem Tov had said. The bishop told the crowd: "Wait, please. I will shortly return to you." He followed me, and came with me to the Ba'al Shem Tov. The two of them went to a separate room, closed the door, and spoke for some two hours. After this, the Ba'al Shem Tov came out and ordered that the horses be harnessed, and we left straightaway. To this day, I do not know what became of the bishop, nor do I know the name of the city, and the Ba'al Shem Tov did not tell me. Now I remembered what had happened to me then. This episode took place some ten years ago.'

When R. Jacob finished talking, the worthy raised his hands in praise of the Lord. He told R. Jacob: 'I know that your words are true. And as soon as I saw you, I recognized you, but I kept silent. I will tell you the episode. You should know that I was the bishop whom you summoned then, and I had previously been a Jew. After that, I fell into the depths of the *kelipot*, for I was a great sage, and I possessed a holy soul. The Ba'al Shem Tov, in his loving-kindness, extricated me from the depths of the *kelipot*, for I have the merit of my forefathers, since my forefathers were holy. They entreated the Ba'al Shem Tov, and he spoke with me daily, in a dream, that I repent of my ways. That morning, I promised him that I would flee from the city during the morning watch [i.e. the hours preceding the morning], before the masses assembled to hear the sermon. During the sermon I would have spoken so ill of the Lord's people, that the Christians' hearts would become inflamed to kill some Jew. But that morning, when I awakened during the watch, the *kelipah* became very strong. I saw that the Ba'al Shem Tov had already arrived, and I was undecided, until I saw that a very great mass had gathered. As soon as I took a single step from my house, all the bells pealed to proclaim my coming. Then my evil inclination did not allow me to abandon all this honour, and I went to deliver my sermon. When you came and summoned me, I wanted to deliver my sermon first, because I had been overcome by my evil inclination. When, however, you summoned me a second time, I became a totally different person, and I went. The Ba'al Shem Tov gave me a *tikun*, and I completely repented, giving half my riches to the poor, for I was an extremely wealthy person. I also gave one quarter of my money to the king, on condition that he allow me to travel to another land, under some pretext that I told him. The Ba'al Shem Tov commanded me, what I must do to correct my sins every year. He told me: "By this you shall know if your iniquities have been effaced and your sins atoned, if someone shall come and tell you your story." Accordingly, as soon as I saw you, I immediately repented greatly, and when I saw that you had forgotten all the stories, I understood that this was on my account. For I had not yet properly corrected my sin. I did what I did, and my prayer was effective, with the help of God, for you recalled the episode. And now I know that, may the Lord be blessed, my iniquity has been effaced, and I have corrected everything, may the Lord be blessed. As for you, you need not travel around telling stories, for I shall give you many gifts, that will suffice for you your entire life. May it be by the merit of the Ba'al Shem Tov that both of us serve the Creator all the days of our lives, with all our heart and soul, Amen.'[31]

This story has an independent hasidic parallel (version B) that appears in Kaidaner's *Sipurim nora'im*,[32] with a number of striking differences. In version B the attendant, whose name is not mentioned, asks the Ba'al Shem Tov, before the latter's death, what his livelihood shall be. Version A does not

[31] Rodkinsohn, *Adat tsadikim*, §9. Cf. Moskowitz, *Otsar hasipurim*, xvi, §2. R. Jacob, the Ba'al Shem Tov's attendant, is mentioned in *Shivhei habesht*, 144, as the successor of R. Aaron, who left his position as attendant after marrying. R. Jacob told a certain story to R. Gedaliah of Linitz (ibid.). For a tale of the Ba'al Shem Tov marrying off an orphan girl, also related by this R. Jacob, see Fishman (Maimon), *Sarei hame'ah*, iii. 155–8.

[32] Kaidaner, *Sipurim nora'im*, §5, pp. 45–50. *Continued in Appendix.*

specify from whom R. Jacob heard of the wealthy man in Rome, while in version B his informant is a preacher whom the attendant meets in his lodgings. In version A, the attendant recalls this special story only when he is already seated in the carriage that will transport him from the worthy's house, while in version B his memory of this story returns during the third sabbath meal. The two accounts of the story that is told to the wealthy man in Rome differ as follows: according to version B, the Ba'al Shem Tov and those accompanying him travelled by means of *kefitsat haderekh* to a village; version A makes no mention of the miraculous *kefitsat haderekh*, and places their destination in a large city. In version B, the Ba'al Shem Tov and his entourage remain in their lodgings, and their conversation is with the owner of the lodgings and the members of his household; according to version A, they are put up in a large house, where it is an old woman who speaks with the tsadik. Version B speaks of 'a certain priest named Popes', while version A speaks of a bishop. In version A the Ba'al Shem Tov removes the curtain, while in version B he opens the window. Version A has the attendant (R. Jacob) being sent twice to the bishop, to summon him to the Ba'al Shem Tov, while in version B the tsadik gestures to the priest with his finger. An intriguing difference is to be found in the end of the story: in version B the wealthy man secludes himself, counts his money, and gives half to the attendant, none of which is mentioned in version A.

I will end this chapter with a tale about a Jew who did not wish to convert. The Ba'al Shem Tov was informed from heaven that a certain rural Jew ate with greater holy intent than he did. The Ba'al Shem Tov went with his disciples to that village, where they were told by the villager that anyone who could not pay his rent to the *poritz* would be whipped, but if he were willing to convert his debts would be waived. The villager told the Ba'al Shem Tov that he was not willing to convert, and therefore he ate and ate, so that he would be strong enough to withstand the blows that he would receive.[33]

[33] T. H. Rosenberg, *Raza de'uvda*, 'Sha'ar ha'otiyot', 25.

TWELVE

RITUAL SLAUGHTERERS

THE RITUAL SLAUGHTERER (*shoḥet*) is mentioned frequently in hasidic stories, since the provision of kosher meat occupied a prominent place in the thought and practices of the early hasidic leaders.[1] Sometimes hasidim would refuse meat from a ritual slaughterer until they had personally inspected the knife that he used. The importance and sanctity of this position (at times the ritual slaughterer also served as circumciser, or *mohel*) were such that the hasidim considered themselves to be under an especially strict mandate in the realm of *kashrut* and ritual slaughter. Hence their understandable objections to a slaughterer who belonged to the camp of the mitnagedim; R. Aaron of Karlin, for example, opposed the appointment of a mitnaged slaughterer in the community of Horodok, near Pinsk.[2]

The hasidic story reflects a view that many slaughterers do not take proper care regarding the laws governing their work, or are insufficiently God-fearing, and even that some among them are guilty of committing grave sins. The tsadik, who is blessed with the spirit of divine inspiration,[3] is loath to eat meat whose slaughter was flawed, and at times he even succeeds in proving the wickedness of the slaughterer. In such instances the slaughter is relieved of his position, and sometimes also severely punished. In many cases the slaughterer admits to his sin, and the tsadik prescribes a *tikun* for him.

According to the stories of this genre, the sanctity of the position also encouraged the forces of the Sitra Ahra to entrap slaughterers.[4] The dangers that lie in wait for the ritual slaughterer are illustrated by the story of a

[1] See Shmeruk, 'Social Significance of Hasidic *Sheḥitah*' (Heb.); Piekarz, *Beginning of Hasidism* (Heb.), index, s.v. *sheḥitah* (ritual slaughtering), *shoḥatim* (ritual slaughterers).

[2] Zeilingold, *Me'orot hagedolim*, §50, 156–7.

[3] When the tsadik of Gritza was staying with his sister in Warsaw, he sensed, by his spirit of divine inspiration, that the chicken that was served to him was not kosher (Samlung, *Eser zekhuyot*, 'From Our Master of Gritsa', §16). R. Abraham of Stretin would sense by smell if a dish contained some prohibited food; once he smelled that the *shoḥet* had performed ritual slaughter without first immersing himself in the ritual bath (Brandwein, *Degel maḥaneh yehudah*, §82).

[4] Cf. e.g. the story told by the Tsemah Tsedek of Lublin concerning a slaughterer who succeeded in overcoming the *ḥitsonim* by following the counsel of R. Menahem Mendel of Rymanow (Moskowitz, *Otsar hasipurim*, iv, §4, p. 7).

person who asked R. Shmelke to appoint him to this post. The tsadik showed the applicant a person who was standing in the air, between heaven and earth, with a slaughterer's knife in his hand. The tsadik explained to him: 'This person was a slaughterer, and for forty years he has been attempting to correct the flaws that he perpetrated, but he has not yet succeeded.' The applicant immediately withdrew his request for the appointment.[5]

Another version of the story is related by R. Isaac Eisik Safrin, in the name of his father-in-law R. Tsevi of Zhidachov, who in turn heard it from his teacher, R. Yehiel Mikhel of Zlotchev:

Once a person came to our master [the Ba'al Shem Tov] and asked if he would teach him the laws of ritual slaughter, so that he could become a slaughterer. The Ba'al Shem Tov told him: 'My son, come and I will show you something!' He went outside with him, and told him: 'Look at the roof.' This person lifted up his eyes and he saw someone standing by the chimney with a knife in his hand and whetting it. The man was greatly alarmed, and the Ba'al Shem Tov told him: 'My son, this one was a slaughterer several hundred years ago and he unwittingly used a flawed knife, and he still has not received his *tikun*. Afterwards, it was decreed that he was to appear before me and show me a proper knife. For three years he has been standing on the roof, but he cannot show a proper knife. And you want to be a slaughterer?' He replied that he no longer desired this.[6]

In yet a third version the tsadik is R. Menahem Mendel of Rymanow. A person who had learned the work of slaughtering came to the rabbi and requested a *kabalah*, that is, certification as a ritual slaughterer. The tsadik passed his hands over the man's eyes, and asked him to look through the window at the tree that was opposite them. The person looked there, and saw innumerable souls. R. Menahem Mendel told him: 'All those are the souls of slaughterers who came to me to receive a *tikun*!' The person understood the hint, and withdrew his request.[7]

The rabbi of Pshemishel sought to discharge a ritual slaughterer 'because he heard that he was illiterate and that his deeds were not good', although in truth the latter was a hidden tsadik. The continuation of the story teaches that this is merely a variation of the theme of the flawed slaughterer.

5 Ibid. v, §16, p. 32.

6 I. Safrin, *Megilat setarim*, 40.

7 Kamelhar, *Em labinah*, 'Beit menaḥem', 39. On the other hand, some stories feature slaughterers who possessed high spiritual qualities, such as the slaughterer in the vicinity of Shinova who was the author of the book *Raza mehemna*; when R. Moses Teitelbaum, author of *Yismaḥ mosheh*, refused to receive the slaughterer's book, the latter ordered that his books be buried with him. The butchers were angry with him, because he would weep on the necks of the beasts before slaughtering them, and poultry would dance around him, because they wanted to be slaughtered by this tsadik (Ehrmann, *Pe'er vekhavod*, fos 1*b*–2*a*). Cf. what is related about R. Judah Tsevi of Stretin, who had been a ritual slaughterer in his youth: Brandwein, *Degel maḥaneh yehudah*, §18; and ibid., §51, regarding a slaughterer who was a concealed tsadik.

Once a certain young man came to this village [Zuravitch, where the hidden tsadik lived] to ask him to be instructed in the work of ritual slaughtering. He replied that he did not wish to teach him the skill of slaughtering. This young man asked him why he did not wish to teach him to be a ritual slaughterer. Then he led the young man outside, and passed his hand over his face. The young man saw a person standing on the roof, with a knife in his hand, slaughtering himself, with blood pouring from him. After the blood had run out of him, he fell to the ground, and after a few minutes, he [rose] again and stood, again, on the roof and did this same act, and so on, several times. Then he told this young man: 'This one was a slaughterer in his lifetime, and now that he is dead, this is his punishment, for he was not worthy to be such.'[8]

It was only natural that tales concerning sinning slaughterers led the early hasidim to be exacting as regards the preparation of meat, and stories in this vein are told about the Ba'al Shem Tov. When, for example, the Ba'al Shem Tov came to Slutsk, whither he had been invited by wealthy Jewish leaseholders,[9] he asked to examine the slaughterer's knife. This was not an unusual demand for him; but it is not hard to understand the anger aroused by this request, since the local residents regarded the very demand as insulting to the slaughterer and those who had appointed him.[10]

Once, when the Ba'al Shem Tov went to Kostantin with R. David Forkes, the slaughterer arrived while the Ba'al Shem Tov was still praying; since he was pressed for time, he slaughtered the chickens and went on his way. The Ba'al Shem Tov looked at the chickens and said he would eat them, while R. David did not want to. The Ba'al Shem Tov, however, respected R. David's scruples and was not offended by the latter's behaviour.[11]

It was well known among Jews generally that hasidim would ask to examine the slaughterer's knife before eating. Once R. Yudel of Chudnov, a relative of R. Nahman of Kosov, arrived in a mining town and wished to spend the sabbath with a local Jew. The householder suggested that he spend the holy day elsewhere, because he had no fish for the sabbath, 'and he [R. Yudel] would not eat meat, because he had not examined the knife'.[12]

On one occasion the Ba'al Shem Tov stayed with the rabbi of a community for the sabbath. The rabbi's wife was distressed that she had no meat for the sabbath, nor did any of her neighbours. A slaughterer happened to pass by, and, when asked by the rabbi's wife, he answered that only a few hours previously he had slaughtered a tender and good animal.

[8] [Isaac Dov Baer ben Tsevi Hirsch], *Kahal ḥasidim heḥadash*, §58; also cited in Moskowitz, *Otsar hasipurim*, ii, §11, p. 22. See also Piekarz, *Beginning of Hasidism* (Heb.), 70 n. 50.

[9] See Halpern, 'The Wozczylo Revolt' (Heb.), 56–67.

[10] *Shivḥei habesht*, 133.

[11] Ibid. 127. The Ba'al Shem Tov himself engaged in ritual slaughter (ibid. 55).

[12] Ibid. 177.

The Ba'al Shem Tov responded, saying: 'I, too, very greatly love to eat the head, if it would be possible for it to be brought here in its entirety, and have *nikur* [removal of the sciatic nerve] performed here.' The slaughterer concurred: 'This is good!' and he arose and went quickly to bring the head to the rabbi's house. The Ba'al Shem Tov began to speak with the slaughterer: 'The world [i.e. all Jews] says there is a distinctive sign in the teeth. Please count how many teeth it has.' He opened the animal's mouth in order to count its teeth, and it immediately shut its mouth, so that the slaughterer could not extract his hand. The animal pressed on the hand, until the pain became unbearable, and the slaughterer cried out. The Ba'al Shem Tov asked: 'Why are you screaming? There is no life in it!' The Ba'al Shem Tov then shouted at him: 'Wicked one! Make your confession!' And he confessed to his sin, [namely,] that he had never examined the lungs[13]—'as you pleased, you pronounced kosher, and as you pleased, you pronounced [organically] unfit [and therefore non-kosher]'. He [the Ba'al Shem Tov] then prescribed for him a *tikun* for his repentance.[14]

During the time of the Ba'al Shem Tov there was a slaughterer 'who was very frivolous and a drunk'. R. Jacob Joseph of Polonnoye, who took great care not to harm the livelihood of any person, was in no haste to remove him from his position. However, following a hint from the Ba'al Shem Tov a court was convened that heard testimony from the local butcher and decided to dismiss the slaughterer.[15]

Once when the Ba'al Shem Tov was in the vicinity of Kaminka, 'he heard a [heavenly] proclamation' to depose the city's slaughterer, and decided to help the man to find other work. When the Ba'al Shem Tov came, the man had just slaughtered several cattle, and he hung in the corridor one that, in his opinion, was unfit. The Ba'al Shem Tov rejected this opinion and ordered him to prepare a dish from this animal. Since the Ba'al Shem Tov's disciples found it difficult to accept that their master would eat from an animal that the slaughterer had declared unfit, the Ba'al Shem Tov referred the question to R. Samuel, a rabbi in Polonnoye. After the latter also ruled that the animal was fit, he fired the slaughterer, and no longer felt moved to help him find any other means of livelihood.[16]

A certain slaughterer, who had a certificate from the Maggid of Mezirech to engage in this work, once went on a journey, and died on the way. The carriage-driver took the dead man's certificate and knives, and claimed that he was a slaughterer. By force of the certificate from the Maggid, he was appointed slaughterer in a city not far from Ostrog. When the other

[13] The lungs of slaughtered cattle must be examined for lesions.

[14] Ibid. 127–8. The story appears in a modern source: Moskowitz, *Otsar hasipurim*, vi, §3 (in the name of R. Elijah Sternberg); the collector apparently did not remember the primary source. *Continued in Appendix.*

[15] *Shivḥei habesht*, 127. For a reckless and drunkard slaughterer and *kashrut* supervisor, see Rodkinsohn, *Sipurei tsadikim*, §14, pp. 28–9.

[16] *Shivḥei habesht*, 127.

slaughterers saw that he was rendering the animals unfit by his slaughtering, they forced him to come with them to R. Jacob Joseph of Ostrog, who shouted at the impostor, and he latter confessed.[17]

During the time of R. Jacob Joshua Falk (author of *Penei yehoshua*) someone informed the rabbi that the slaughterer was providing the public with unfit animals; the slaughterer was questioned, and he admitted his guilt.[18]

The manner in which slaughterers rendered animals unfit is portrayed in the following two stories. The first relates: 'I heard from the rabbi of our community [R. Gedaliah of Linitz] that the Ba'al Shem Tov had sent [a message] to the rabbi of the holy community of Bichov that his slaughterer belonged to the sect of Shabetai Tsevi, may his name be blotted out, and that he renders animals unfit [by his slaughtering]. [The message continued:] After he showed him his knife, he struck it on a hammer, in order to damage it. The rabbi conducted an inspection afterwards, and so it was.'[19] The second story is also concerned with the damaging of the knife. The Ba'al Shem Tov was invited to a circumcision in Brod, together with R. Hayim Sanzer and R. Moses Ostrer. The slaughterer showed his knife, both to these rabbis and to the Ba'al Shem Tov, and they all agreed that it was fit. During the *se'udat mitsvah*, the Ba'al Shem Tov demurred from partaking of the dishes, claiming that the meat came from an animal that was improperly slaughtered. This declaration aroused great indignation, and the Ba'al Shem Tov was forced to leave the city the following day, and the people of Brod resolved that the name of the Ba'al Shem Tov would never again be mentioned in their city. A disciple of the Ba'al Shem Tov, R. David Forkes, came to the city of Brod, as was his custom, and wished to preach there. The townspeople agreed, on condition that he did not cite any teachings from his master [i.e. the Ba'al Shem Tov]. R. David abided by this condition until his very last sermon in Brod, in which he declared that the Ba'al Shem Tov's teachings were true. The townspeople were infuriated, and a legal ruling was issued, stating that R. David was to apologize to the slaughterer in the presence of ten people. When R. David came to the slaughterer's house on the sabbath, late at night, the slaughterer was found in bed with his daughter-in-law. He was placed under guard, and when he was brought before the rabbinical judges, he stated:

'Know, my masters, that from my arrival here until now I did not improperly slaughter animals. I shall, however, confess to my crime, that for two years I have been sleeping with my daughter-in-law. This is my crime, and this is my sin . . . What the Ba'al Shem Tov said during the circumcision, that this was meat from an improperly slaughtered animal [literally, carrion meat], is the truth. This is what happened: when the beadle came and said that I should prepare an especially good

[17] Rabbinovich, *Shivḥei rav ye'ivi*, 92–3. [18] Kaidaner, *Sipurim nora'im*, §6.
[19] *Shivḥei habesht*, 127.

knife to show to the Ba'al Shem Tov, I greatly feared, thinking perhaps he would know and see my sins. I therefore engaged in mortifications and prepared an especially good knife. When this appeared satisfactory to him, and he neither saw nor knew of my iniquities, then I maliciously made several flaws in the knife, and after this I slaughtered the poultry, so that I could know if he sensed this.' . . . The slaughterer then travelled to the Ba'al Shem Tov, who prescribed a *tikun* to effect repentance for him.[20]

This story's attribution of the additional sin of adultery to the slaughterer who provided the public with improperly slaughtered meat is certainly not coincidental. A slaughterer who refused to show his knife to R. Levi Isaac of Berdichev, claiming that the tsadik was ignorant, was said to engage in similar conduct; in the end, he became an apostate.[21]

R. Meir of Premishlan did not want to eat meat prepared by a certain slaughterer, even though the rabbi of Apta had seen the knife and pronounced it fit. R. Meir related that once, when he was 22 years old, he had gone with R. Moses Leib of Sasov to a circumcision. When they arrived at their lodgings the night before the ceremony, the innkeeper asked R. Moses Leib to remain for the circumcision and receive the honour of acting as *sandak*, but R. Meir discovered (by stirring his cup of tea) that the infant's grandfather had had sexual relations with his daughter-in-law. Here again R. Meir claimed that he was justified in refusing to eat meat prepared by this slaughterer. Indeed, while they were eating the fish during the circumcision banquet, a non-Jewish woman arrived with her child, who she claimed was the son of the slaughterer.[22] Interestingly, R. Meir refused to offer greetings to the slaughterer when the latter showed him his knife, quoting the dictum of the rabbis (BT *Sanhedrin* 81*b*): 'If a person has relations with a heathen woman, he is punished by zealots.' This same law is cited by R. Meir in another story, which depicts how he sought to depose a slaughterer in Atik Hotin who, it was said, had a sexual relationship with a non-Jewish woman. The rabbi of Apta, who happened also to be present, disagreed, and in response to R. Meir's question, explained the rabbinic dictum as follows: '"If a person has relations with a heathen woman, zealots"—that is, the tsadikim

[20] Bodek(?), *Sipurei kedoshim*, §6. Cf. the slightly different version: A. Walden, *Kahal ḥasidim*, fos 25*c*–26*a*. For a slaughterer who provided the public with improperly slaughtered meat and was punished by being reincarnated as a leaf, see Benayahu, *Sefer toledot ha'ari*, 250. For a slaughterer whose penalty for such an offence was to become a dybbuk, see Sharf, *Darkhei yosher*, letter appended to the end of the book.

[21] Zeilingold, *Me'orot hagedolim*, §15, p. 32.

[22] J. Sofer, *Sipurei ya'akov*, ii, §47. A. Michelson, *Ohel avraham*, §12, relates that R. Abraham Abuschel of Frankfurt once participated in a circumcision banquet: 'He was served a portion of chicken, and he said: "This has been improperly slaughtered, by the same knife as the one that is on the table!" An investigation revealed that the maidservant had herself slaughtered [the chicken].'

who are zealous for the Lord—"punish him [*poge'im bo*]", understanding *pegiah* as prayer, as in [Gen. 28: 11]: *vayifga bamakom* [usually translated: 'he came upon a certain place']—the tsadikim must pray for him, to return him as a penitent before the Lord, may he be blessed.'[23]

In his youth, R. Tsevi Elimelekh of Dynow lived in the community of Chotch, in the house of his father-in-law, R. Samuel. He was not pleased by the behaviour of the local slaughterer, and ceased eating meat from animals that the latter had slaughtered. Once R. Tsevi Elimelekh told this to his teacher, the rabbi of Apta. The tsadik expressed his support for his disciple, and told him that a plague was raging at the time in Yaroslav. They went to seek the advice of R. Elimelekh of Lizhensk, who told them: 'I am not a prophet, nor the son of a prophet, but since you have asked, I tell you, from now on closely supervise the ritual slaughterers.' The townspeople accordingly appointed a God-fearing supervisor, who one day, to his surprise, heard the old slaughterer tell a young colleague: 'Now the eyes of the townspeople gaze upon us, therefore, be very precise, and do not act as we have done until now!' The community dismissed the slaughterers, and the plague stopped.[24]

Soon afterwards, a non-Jewish woman filed a lawsuit in the government court, demanding maintenance from the slaughterer of the Chotch community for the son that she had borne him.

[23] Sobelman, *Sipurei tsadikim heḥadash*, §57. Cf. Ze'ev Wolf of Zhitomir, *Or hame'ir*, 22. R. Meir was unwilling to eat meat slaughtered by the butcher in Apta, and claimed that he saw on the knife the *roshem* (remaining impression) of an abomination. A non-Jewish woman arrived and related that she had borne two children by the slaughterer, who had provided for their maintenance but had now abandoned them. This slaughterer, who saw the woman come to complain before the rabbi of Apta, fled and drowned himself in a cistern. Everyone thus saw the wisdom of R. Meir.

[24] Berger, *Eser tsaḥtsaḥot*, 'R. Tsevi Elimelekh', §4; A. Michelson, *Ohel elimelekh*, §169. For R. Solomon Kluger, who hid and saw that the slaughterer was acting improperly, see Schlesinger, *Shimru mishpat*, ii. 16.

THIRTEEN

THE *TAMIM*: THE SIMPLE PERSON

A BELOVED FIGURE in Judaism, who appears in a favourable light in stories from long before the hasidic period, is that of the *tamim*, the simple and innocent person.[1] The hasid is naturally inclined to extol the virtues of the uneducated; one need not be an outstanding scholar, nor a renowned tsadik, for one's prayers to be accepted. The innocent person of pure intent is highly esteemed, even if he does not understand the words of the prayers or does not know how to pray correctly, and even if the manner of his praying violates religious prohibitions.

There was once a drought during the time of the Ba'al Shem Tov, may his memory be for the life of the world to come. He [the Ba'al Shem Tov] saw a common person shouting and praying, reciting this verse, 'He will shut up [*ve'atsar*] the skies so that there will be no rain,'[2] but did not rebuke him, since he saw that his prayer was accepted in heaven.

Afterwards, after rains came, he summoned [this person] and asked him: 'What were you thinking when you recited the verse "He will shut up the skies so that there will be no rain"?' He replied, 'The meaning of *atsar* is to wring out the skies, so that there will be no rain above, for all the rain will fall below; and so, too, the Targum of Onkelos:[3] *va'atsarit*.'[4]

[1] Cf. e.g. Samuel Hehasid et al., *Sefer ḥasidim*, §§5–6, p. 6. Hagiz, *Mishnat haḥakhamim*, §220, includes a story of a New Christian (Marrano) from Portugal who came to Safed and heard a discourse concerning the shewbread that was offered in the Temple every week. The person went and baked *ḥalot*, and on sabbath eve brought them to the synagogue and placed them before the Torah ark. The account also appears in Sperling, *Reasons for the Customs* (Heb.), 528; Shenkel, *Ma'asiyot nora'im venifla'im*, §1; Chikernik, *Sipurim neḥmadim*, 25–8; Moskowitz, *Otsar hasipurim*, ii, §10.

[2] Deut. 11: 17.

[3] See Targum Onkelos on Gen. 40: 11.

[4] Aaron of Apta, *Keter shem tov*, ii, fo. 23*b*; *Erets haḥayim*, §352, p. 102. The story is also cited in Moses Eliakum Briah of Koznitz, *Be'er mosheh*, 'Shemini Atseret', fo. 184*d*; Sperling, *Reasons for the Customs* (Heb.), 528. See also Even-Shemuel, 'From the Thought of R. Israel Ba'al Shem Tov' (Heb.), 84–5, who paraphrases the story, without citing the source; Orian, *The Exalted* (Heb.), 113; Nigal, 'A Primary Source' (Heb.), 139–40. For the literary type, see Ben-Yehezkel, *Kovets lemo'ed sukot*, 37, 'The Prayer of the *Tamim*, a Chapter from One of the Motifs in Jewish Legend'; Scheiber, 'Two Legends' (Heb.), 59–61; Noy, 'Rainmaking Prayer' (Heb.), 34–45; Bar-Yitzhaq, 'The Pattern of Filling Gaps' (Heb.), 62–8. For parallels in non-Jewish folktales, see Heller, '"Gott Wunscht das Herz"', 365–404.

The motif of drought also appears in a hasidic tale of a *tamim* who was a contemporary of R. Isaac Luria. A simple person who lived at that time in the Land of Israel, and whose prayers were 'stuttering and forced', always asked R. Luria how he should act as regards his livelihood. Thanks to the latter's advice, the man became a successful merchant and prospered. Once, during a time of drought, when R. Luria imposed a public fast day, the merchant ate, because he was unaware that a day of fasting had been declared. When R. Luria reproached the *tamim*, the latter apologized to the rabbi, cast his eyes heavenwards, and implored: 'Master of the Universe! Just as I obey you, you, please, obey me, that rain should fall!' The skies immediately grew dark and rain fell.[5]

The following tale accentuates the paramount importance of the intent of the *tamim*, who does not even properly understand a folk saying.

Once the Ba'al Shem Tov spent the sabbath in a certain village with his *minyan*. When the time came for the third sabbath meal, the leaseholder of the village gathered some people [from] the villages, and he sat with them and ate and drank, with sabbath songs and melodies, and praise to the Lord. The Ba'al Shem Tov, may his memory be for the life of the world to come, saw that he was quite pleasing to heaven. After the meal he summoned him, and asked: 'For what reason do you do this, spending so much on the third [sabbath] meal?' The leaseholder responded: 'Why, I heard the world [i.e. people] saying: May my soul go forth among people of Israel [usually meaning: when I die, let there be Jews who will attend to my funeral]. And behold, I heard that on the sabbath every Israelite has an extra soul,[6] and on the departure of the sabbath it leaves him. I, too, said: Let my extra soul go forth among people of Israel. Therefore, I gather people from Israel . . . and I derive great pleasure from this.'[7]

Two more tales show the tsadik's sympathy for the ignorance of the *tamim*. The first concerns the Ba'al Shem Tov's anger with a preacher who defamed the people of Israel, to whom he said, 'You speak ill of the children of Israel? Know that a pure of heart Israelite goes to market on market day, and when it begins to get dark, he is alarmed, and exclaims: Woe is me, that I should allow the time of Minhah [the afternoon prayers] to pass! He enters some house and recites Minhah, without understanding what he says; even the seraphim and *ofanim* [other heavenly creatures] tremble at this!'[8]

The second concerns R. Shalom of Belz:

Once, on the eve of Yom Kippur, the holy rabbi, our master, the rabbi, R. Shalom of Belz, told those close to him: 'Where, then, is the tailor from Brod, for I require

[5] Sobelman, *Sipurei tsadikim heḥadash*, §24. Cf. Ehrmann, *Devarim arevim*, 'Stories of the Ba'al Shem Tov', §30: causing rain to fall, by merit of a drunkard (a hidden tsadik).

[6] See BT *Bets.* 16*a*.

[7] Aaron of Apta, *Keter shem tov*, ii, fo. 23*b*. See also Sperling, *Reasons for the Customs* (Heb.), 181.

[8] *Shivḥei habesht*, 145.

him?' They searched for him among the many people who were there in the synagogue, and they brought him to [the rabbi]. The holy rabbi, may the memory of the righteous be for a blessing, asked him: 'Tell me, what is the meaning of the verse: "Though our iniquities testify against us [*anu banu*]"[9]?' The tailor answered: 'Why does the rabbi not know? Why, the meaning is: "if we possess iniquities", that is, even though we have sinned and transgressed, we nevertheless are your sons [*anu baneinu*].' The tailor was unlettered, and thought that *anu*, [meaning 'testify' and spelled] with the letter *ayin*, is the same as *anu* ['we'], with an *alef*. The holy rabbi, may the memory of the righteous be for a blessing, marvelled at this simple interpretation, and repeated it several times.[10]

The hasidic tale affords a moral and religious dimension to the popular quips and barbs regarding errors made by cantors and worshippers. R. Naphtali Tsevi of Ropshits related that in a certain year unfavourable heavenly decrees were issued against women, and many pregnant women died. 'A certain villager was there, and when he recited the Minhah prayer on the eve of Yom Kippur, in the blessing for a prosperous year, instead of *shanim* [years], he recited *nashim* [women]. He read: "Bless us . . . and bless our women as the good women [instead of: 'and bless our years as the good years']," and his prayer was accepted in heaven.'[11] Not only does a fundamental lack of comprehension of prayer not harm its results, even someone who is totally ignorant of the prayers, but recites the alphabet with full intent, deserves that his prayer be accepted.[12] The most famous story on this theme is that of the youth who contravened the prohibition on playing music on Yom Kippur by playing his flute during the Ne'ilah prayer itself.

A certain villager, who always prayed during the High Holy Days in the study hall of the Ba'al Shem Tov, of blessed memory, had a son who was extremely slow-witted, and could not understand the shapes of the letters, and especially could not recite any holy matter [i.e. he was incapable of reciting the prayers]; nor did his father take him with him to the city on the High Holy Days, for he knew nothing. When he came of bar mitzvah age, he [the father] took him with him for Yom Kippur, so that he would be with him, and he could ensure that he [the son] would not eat on the holy day, due to his lack of knowledge and comprehension. The youth had a flute, which he would always play in the field while herding the sheep

9 Jer. 14: 7.

10 A. Michelson, *Dover shalom*, §94; id., *Ohel elimelekh*, fo. 28*a*; id., *Ohel naftali*, §96.

11 Berger, *Eser tsaḥtsaḥot*, 'R. Naphtali of Ropshits', §56; A. Michelson, *Ohel elimelekh*, fo. 28*a*; id., *Ohel naftali*, §95. Cf. Gemen, *Sifran shel tsadikim*, ch. 9, §8: once R. Elimelekh honoured a villager by asking him to lead the sabbath morning Shaharit service. Instead of reciting 'hala'ag hasha'ananim habuz ligei yonim' ('the scorn of the complacent, the contempt of the haughty'—Ps. 123: 4), the villager read: '. . . ligei yogim', thereby becoming the target of general derision. R. Elimelekh, however, observed that the heavenly entourage 'were pleased by this sweet mistake'.

12 Kleinmann, *Mazkeret shem gedolim*, 201, with omissions, giving as its source: 'ד״ש in an exposition on the Haggadah'. The source being referred to is unclear.

and the lambs. He took the flute in the pocket of his garment, without his father's knowledge. The youth sat during the entire holy day in the study hall, and he was incapable of reciting anything. During the Musaf prayer, he said to his father: 'Father, I have my flute with me, and I greatly desire to play music on my flute.' His father was greatly alarmed and rebuked him, saying: 'Take care, and guard your soul, lest you do this', and he was forced to restrain himself. During the Minhah prayer he asked him, once again, 'Father, let me play music with my flute.' His father soundly cursed him, and warned him severely lest he dare, heaven forfend, to do this. He could not take [the flute] from the youth, because it was *muktseh* [not to be touched on the festival]. After the Minhah prayer, once again he spoke to his father, and requested: 'Whatever, please let me play some tune!' When his father saw how strong was his desire, and his soul greatly longed to play the flute, he asked his son: 'Where do you keep the flute?', and he showed him. His father took the pocket in his hand, and he kept his hand on the pocket and the flute, so that [the son] could not take it out to play. And so he recited the Ne'ilah prayer [concluding service of Yom Kippur], with his hand holding the pocket of the youth's garment that contained the flute. In the middle of the prayer, the youth forcefully pulled out the flute from the pocket and his father's hand, and he played a mighty note on the flute, to the amazement of all who heard. After this note, the Ba'al Shem Tov cut [his prayer] shorter than usual, and declared after his prayer: 'With the music of his flute, this youth has elevated all the prayers, and eased my burden!' He explained the reason for this: 'Since he did not know how to say [i.e. pray] anything, and the entire holy day he saw and heard so much of the prayers of Israel, his holy spark blazed within him like actual fire; the knowledgeable one could engarb the conflagration of holiness and desire within the word of prayer before him, may he be blessed. He [the son], however, knows nothing, and all he could find within himself to slake his thirst was to play his flute before him, may he be blessed, but his father prevented him. The fire of his desire burned within him more strongly each time, until his soul was actually consumed. From the strength of his desire he played the flute from the centre of truth in his heart, with no external reason, but solely for his name, may he be blessed. God desires the heart, and his pure breath was very acceptable to him, may he be blessed, and this thereby elevated all the prayers.'[13]

It transpires, therefore, that what was perceived by the father, and indeed by the entire congregation, as a desecration of Yom Kippur, was not a bad deed, since it was performed innocently and with pure intent. Such acts are holier and purer than the prayers of all the worshippers (including the Ba'al Shem Tov himself); indeed, it was the sound of the flute that paved the way for the prayers of all those in the synagogue, and raised them to the upper spheres.

[13] Margolioth, *Kevutsat ya'akov*, fo. 53*a*; [Isaac Dov Baer ben Tsevi Hirsch], *Kahal ḥasidim heḥadash*, §18. For the influence of the story in the writings of Perets and Berdyczewski, see Unger, *R. Israel Ba'al Shem Tov* (Heb.), 385; for traces of the story in Berdyczewski, see Werses, *Story and Source* (Heb.), 116–17. See also Zevin, *Hasidic Tales: Festivals* (Heb.), 92–3.

A tale with similar themes is told about poor leaseholders who died, leaving a son who was raised by the local *poritz*. The child knew nothing of Judaism, but he was prompted to wonder whether he was Jewish when he saw village Jews coming in their wagons to the town for the High Holy Days. Among his parents' possessions he found the *Korban minḥah* prayer book, from which his mother had been accustomed to pray. The youth's mother and father appeared to him in a dream, night after night, during the Ten Days of Repentance between Rosh Hashanah and Yom Kippur, and emphatically demanded that he return to his religion and his people. When he next saw the Jews arriving in the town, he took the prayer book and fled the *poritz*'s house, arriving at the synagogue at the time of the *Kol nidrei* prayer. 'When he saw all the people were dressed in their white garments, with their holiday prayer books in their hand, praying, confessing, and renouncing [their sins], the child also began to shout bitterly, causing a great uproar in heaven.' The child said: 'Master of the Universe, I do not know what to pray and what to say. Therefore, Master of the Universe, please accept the entire prayer book. As he said this, he opened the prayer book and placed it on the stand, laid his head on it and wept. The Ba'al Shem Tov attested to his disciples that the youth's prayer had a great effect in the heavenly spheres, and his repentance was accepted.[14]

Individuals of the *tamim* type serve as a living example of proper religious and ethical behaviour. The Ba'al Shem Tov took his disciples to Koznitz to meet Reb Shabetai the bookbinder, exhorting them to recognize his sterling qualities and telling them that he was held in high esteem in heaven.[15] In another instance the Ba'al Shem Tov brings his disciples to a *ba'al-bitaḥon* (one who has true faith, an alternative manifestation of the *tamim*), to learn the meaning of genuine trust in the Lord.[16]

R. Levi Isaac of Berdichev once boasted of his Passover Seder, and the mystical intent with which he conducted it.

And word came to him from heaven: 'Why do you aggrandize yourself with your Seder? In this city lives Reb Hayim Trager [i.e. 'the porter'], and he conducts the Seder in a manner finer than yours!' The tsadik sent his disciples to locate the man, and they found him lying drunk in his bed. When he sobered up, the disciples brought him to their master, and they [R. Levi Isaac and the porter] conducted the following conversation: 'Reb Hayim *sertse* [my heart], this sabbath did

[14] Ehrmann, *Devarim arevim*, 'Stories of the Ba'al Shem Tov', §26; Berger, *Eser tsaḥtsaḥot*, 'R. Tsevi Elimelekh of Dynow', §20. *Continued in Appendix.*

[15] See e.g. J. Sofer, *Sipurei ya'akov*, ii, §53: a story about a drawer of water during the time of R. Israel of Ruzhin; ibid. i, §1, about the shaming of a water-carrier by a Torah scholar who wrote a Torah scroll. Cf. Moskowitz, *Otsar hasipurim*, i, §8, pp. 15–18.

[16] Sobelman, *Sipurei tsadikim heḥadash*, §20. See also *Shivḥei habesht*, 117–18.

you recite "We were slaves" [from the Seder; also recited on the sabbath preceding Passover]?' Reb Hayim responded: 'Yes.' 'Did you search for *ḥamets* [leavened food, forbidden on Passover]?' 'Yes.' 'Did you burn the *ḥamets*?' Reb Hayim began to think, and he replied, 'No, because I forgot.' . . . The rabbi asked him: 'Did you conduct the Seder?' He replied: 'Rabbi, I will tell you the truth. I heard that it is forbidden to drink spirits the eight days [of Passover], and this morning I drank enough spirits for all eight days, I became very tired, and I slept. My wife began to awaken me from my sleep, and she asked me: "Why don't you conduct the Seder, like all the Jews?" I said to her: "What do you want from me? I am ignorant, and my father also was ignorant, and I know nothing. I only know this, that the Jews were in exile among the *tsiganers* [= the gypsies], and we have God who brought us forth from there to freedom, and now we, too, are in exile, and, now, too, the Lord will bring us forth from this exile. I saw on the table *matsot*, wine, and eggs. I ate the *matsot* with the eggs, and I drank the wine, and because of my tiredness, I was forced to go back to sleep." '[17]

Another example of the *tamim* is a simple shepherd named Moshe Posterek, who, when his sheep were grazing in the mountains, stood next to a well and said to himself: 'God, how shall I serve you? If you had sheep, I would herd them for free!' Then he jumped over the well, with great enthusiasm, to amuse his creator, as it were, and serve him with his jumping.[18]

I will conclude this chapter with a story that was published only fairly recently. A simple villager wanted to go to the town for Yom Kippur, so that he could pray with a *minyan*. He urged his children to complete their preparations to set out, but when he saw that they were still not ready for the journey, he told them that he was setting out anyway, and asked them to meet him under a certain tree. When he came to the tree, he fell asleep. When the villager awoke, and he realized that he could no longer reach the town before the commencement of the holy day, nor, on the other hand, could he return home without desecrating it, he raised his eyes to heaven and proclaimed: 'Master of the universe! My children have completely forgotten me—I forgive them! In the same way, you, too, forgive your children who have forgotten you!'[19]

As we have seen, the hasidic tale emphasizes the wonderful spiritual instinct of ordinary people, and presents the tsadikim speaking in their praise.[20] In some instances, these simple individuals perform exceptional

[17] *Ma'asiyot vesiḥot tsadikim*, 74; Zevin, *Hasidic Tales: Festivals* (Heb.), 286.

[18] Ehrmann, *Devarim arevim*, 'Stories of the Ba'al Shem Tov', §19.

[19] Kohen, *Shemuot vesipurim*, 70–1. *Continued in Appendix.*

[20] See Rodkinsohn, *Adat tsadikim*, §1, and, in another version, Moskowitz, *Otsar hasipurim*, vi, §5; v, §12: a bookbinder who regarded the paper left over from the production of religious books as holy was rewarded by heaven. See also Rodkinsohn, *Adat tsadikim*, §§5–6; Bodek(?), *Sipurei kedoshim*, §§2–3.

acts, such as the rescue of Jews, that have a profound effect in heaven.[21] The tales of the *tamim* undoubtedly laid the groundwork for the stories of the 'hidden tsadikim' that are the subject of the following chapter.

21 According to a Habad tradition (see *Sefer hasiḥot*, 5 [1943], 168), once the Ba'al Shem Tov stayed in the house of a simple village Jew who was not over-erudite, but, together with his wife, praised the Lord in plain language. The prophet Elijah revealed to the Ba'al Shem Tov that the couple's blessings had a strong effect in heaven, and caused more pleasure 'than the *yiḥudim* of [divine] names recited by the great tsadikim'.

FOURTEEN

HIDDEN TSADIKIM

THE TRADITION of there being thirty-six righteous individuals in the world whose righteousness is hidden is firmly rooted in rabbinic teachings, and stories of people whose deeds and righteousness are wondrous but unknown as such to their contemporaries have been told since early times.[1] However, while the constituent elements of the mythological figure of the hidden righteous individual preceded hasidism, the term *tsadik nistar* or 'hidden righteous/tsadik' (not necessarily referring to a hasidic rabbi), with the emphasis on this person's anonymity, emerged along with the hasidic story. The first group of hasidic tales in Aaron of Apta's *Keter shem tov* speaks of a hasid and a tsadik, one who brings about rainfall by his righteousness, and the other who saves an entire city, with no mention of the adjective 'hidden' or the appellation 'hidden tsadik'.[2] Nor is here any mention of 'hidden' ones in the Hebrew version of *Shivḥei habesht*;[3] however, the Yiddish version of the book relates that the Maggid of Mezirech revealed to R. Yehiel Mikhel of Zlotchev that his carriage-driver was a hidden tsadik, who had already merited a vision of the prophet Elijah.[4]

The majority of hidden tsadik stories are relatively late. The lack of examples from the time of the Ba'al Shem Tov was presumably corrected upon the publication of the Kherson *genizah*.[5] The letters in the *genizah* lead us to conclude that Adam Ba'al Shem Tov of Ropshits believed the Ba'al Shem

[1] For the rabbinic teachings, see BT *Suk.* 45*b*: 'Abaye said, The world never has less than thirty-six righteous ones who are granted a vision of the Divine Presence every day, as it is said [Isa. 30: 18]: "Happy are all who wait for him [*lo*]," and the numerical value of *lo* is thirty-six.' The version in BT *San.* 97*b* reads: 'who are granted a vision of the Divine Presence in every generation'. For thirty righteous ones, see *Gen. Rabbah* 35: 2; JT *AZ* 2: 1; for additional sources, see Schwarzbaum, 'The Thirty-Six Just Hidden Men' (Heb.), 20–8; and for possible sources, see Mach, *Der Zaddik im Talmud und Midrasch*; Scholem, 'Die 36 verborgene Gerechten'; Beer, 'Regarding the Sources' (Heb.), 172–6; Urbach, *The Sages*, 483 ff.; Noy, 'The Hidden Tsadik in Theodicy Legends' (Heb.), 32–40. *Continued in Appendix.*

[2] See Nigal, 'A Primary Source' (Heb.), 138–40.

[3] 1st pub. Korets, 1815.

[4] Korets, 1816, ch. 79.

[5] See Zeitlin, 'New Documents' (Heb.), 9–11, who sees the letters as historical documents, and devotes an extensive discussion to the hidden tsadikim. For a summary of the episode, see Raphael, 'The Kherson *Genizah*' (Heb.).

Tov to be a concealed tsadik, and urged him to reveal himself;[6] according to these letters, the Ba'al Shem Tov was in contact with various hidden tsadikim, and took steps to ensure their livelihood.[7] These imaginary revelations were followed during the succeeding years by a plethora of stories, many of them related by R. Joseph Jacob Schneersohn, the Lubavitch Rebbe.[8] Although no doubt should be cast on the authentic Habad stories that focus on the Ba'al Shem Tov, some of which were related by the Old Rebbe, it would seem that the more fanciful Habad stories about the Ba'al Shem Tov and the hidden tsadikim in his time were based in no small measure on the Kherson *genizah*. The Ba'al Shem Tov is depicted in the Habad stories as being a hidden tsadik, until he revealed himself: he was raised and educated among hidden tsadikim, he performed various missions at the bidding of the leadership of the hidden tsadikim, and, together with other hidden ones, he prepared the groundwork for his later public activity and the dissemination of the teachings of hasidism.

The ideals of these concealed ones included rural settlement by the masses and their occupation in productive labour on the land. According to the Habad world-view, the hidden tsadikim who appeared to be villagers engaging in simple labour were a living example for ordinary people.[9] The character of the hidden tsadik was accepted by the masses because the latter sought an ideal figure with whom they could identify. The Jewish masses were charmed by the concept of a person who appeared coarse, simple, and unlettered, but who in actuality was both righteous in deed and a brilliant scholar. Not only did the figure of the hidden tsadik fire the imagination, it also constituted a response to the accusations of hasidic ignorance and illiteracy advanced by the mitnagedim. If, the hasid said to himself, hidden tsadikim who are familiar with the esoteric teachings are to be found among simple labourers and craftsmen, by what right do the mitnagedim heap abuse upon the simple folk, some of whom are on a higher level than their defamers? Indeed, the world exists by merit of the hidden tsadikim, and not because of those known to be scholars or righteous.

Several stories from the hasidic period about pre-hasidic figures illustrate the superiority of the hidden righteous individual to the revealed ones, that is, the rabbi and the scholar. The story that is told of the friendship between the great halakhic authority R. Moses Isserles and R. Hayim, the brother of

[6] See *Hatamim*, 2 (Warsaw, 1936), letters 7, 11, 13–15, 17, 18, 22, 23, 25, 26. For Adam Ba'al Shem Tov, see Shmeruk, 'Tales about R. Adam Ba'al Shem' (Heb.); id., *Yiddish Literature* (Heb.), 119–46; Koenneker, 'Die Geschichten von Rabbi Adam'.

[7] See e.g. ibid., letters 38, 65.

[8] For the complete Habad story, see Glitsenstein, *Rabi yisra'el ba'al shem tov*, with references to Habad sources. See also Bichovski, *Ginzei nistarot*, 3; Biegeleisen, *Ḥemdah genuzah*, 13; Moskowitz, *Otsar hasipurim*, i, §2.

[9] See e.g. Schneersohn, *Sefer hazikhronot*, 53 ff.

the Maharal of Prague, stresses the difference between the two character types. Elijah studies Torah at night with R. Hayim, who conceals himself from public view in order to study, and who marries the daughter of a simple baker, but is unwilling to study with R. Isserles, since the latter enjoys the trappings of his rabbinical standing.[10] In a similar tale, Elijah refuses to study with the rabbi of Lemberg, claiming that 'he has not yet merited this', while he does study with a simple tailor.[11]

The superiority of the hidden tsadik over his counterpart, the revealed and accepted righteous rabbi, became problematic with the emergence of hasidic tsadikim with their courts and dynasties. The hasidic story has the Ba'al Shem Tov himself raise the question of the standing of the revealed tsadik *vis-à-vis* that of the hidden one: 'Once [the Ba'al Shem Tov] said that, just as there are thirty-six righteous in concealment, there are also thirty-six revealed righteous, and that he was among the revealed thirty-six. He also attested of himself that his concealed aspect is greater than what is known of his revealed self.'[12] The Ba'al Shem Tov therefore assumes that it is possible to be both a hidden and a revealed tsadik simultaneously, a position espoused by R. Mordecai of Lachowicze in response to the question, 'The world says [i.e. it is commonly said] that the thirty-six tsadikim are hidden. If so, then are the tsadikim in our generation not among the thirty-six?' R. Mordecai replied, ironically, 'How fine things would be if we were only what we seem to be!'[13] R. Isaiah Asher Zelig Margolies also heard this distinction between the revealed and hidden tsadik from his teacher, the rabbi of Barniv. The latter related that once when he was in Sanz, R. Hayim passionately exclaimed,

> Do you think that all the thirty-six tsadikim must walk about in torn rags, with sackcloth on their loins? And sit between the oven and the stove, and the like? Some of them have permission to wear fine garments and sit in the upper rows [in the synagogue—a prestigious location], with hundreds of Jews at their table, and to be like any [important] person of their time. They are the ones who shake and agitate all the upper and lower worlds . . . It is they who sacrifice themselves for the sanctification of his name, may he be blessed, and his holy Torah; they flatter no one, but rather rebuke the people of their generation, so that they shall not follow the statutes [i.e. ways] of the non-Jews, and not join together with those who follow their statutes; and they stand in the breach and erect [protective] fences.[14]

[10] Rodkinsohn, *Adat tsadikim*, §22.

[11] Sobelman, *Sipurei tsadikim heḥadash*, §2.

[12] Ehrmann, *Devarim arevim*, 'Stories of the Ba'al Shem Tov', §21. Cf. Kleinmann, *Or yesharim*, 5.

[13] Shalom of Koidanov, *Divrei shalom*, 'Vayikra', fo. 41*a* (trans. from Yiddish). This passage is cited (without mention of the book) in the note by 'Bar-Ami' (B. W. Segel) in *Ost und West* 8 (Berlin, 1908), 165–6. See also Donner, *Derekh ha'emunah uma'aseh rav*, 'Concerning the 36 Tsadikim', 59.

[14] Moskowitz, *Otsar hasipurim*, vii, §36, pp. 23–4.

This view, however, was not characteristic of the hasidim; as we shall see below, the hidden tsadik was usually perceived as coming from the poor masses.

The hasidic story presumes that revealed tsadikim are capable of identifying the hidden ones, and sometimes disclose their identity to their intimate circle. R. Tsevi, the son of the Ba'al Shem Tov, and the *mohel* R. Gedaliah of Zelechow were hidden tsadikim.[15] The Seer of Lublin asserted that R. Reuben Horowitz (author of *Duda'im basadeh*) was the third among the thirty-six tsadikim of his generation.[16] He also stated that R. Alexander Sender of Komarno was one of the thirty-six;[17] the father of the tsadik R. Hirsch Ze'ev of Alik was similarly said to be a hidden tsadik.[18] The rabbi of Kotsk attested that the rabbi of Gostynin, R. Yehiel Meir, was one of the hidden ones,[19] and R. Shalom of Belz discerned that a guest in the synagogue was one of the hidden tsadikim.[20] When the Ketav Sofer (R. Abraham Samuel Benjamin Wolf Sofer) eulogized R. Abraham Shabetai Sheftel Schossberg of Pressburg, he revealed, in the name of his father, the Hatam Sofer, that R. Schossberg was one of the thirty-six hidden tsadikim.[21] During the funeral of a shepherd, a rabbi disclosed that the deceased was one of the hidden tsadikim.[22] Once two hasidim happened to come to the home of R. Isaiah of Kerestir, known as Reb Shaiele, where they spent the night. When they went to bed, they spoke of the hidden tsadikim, and one mentioned that the rabbi of Zhidachov knew these hidden tsadikim, as did the rabbi of Ujhely. At that moment their host, the tsadik, opened the door, and said: 'I, too, know two hidden ones. One: Moshele from Lemberg, and the other: *der riter yankele* [Jacob the Red] in Berlin.'[23]

R. Naphtali Hertzke, the head of the Ratzferd rabbinical court, told a man who complained about moisture in his house to travel to a certain painter in Grosswardein, who would help him. The man did not pay much attention to the tsadik's advice, and when he finally decided to heed him, he was too late: he arrived at Grosswardein to find the painter's funeral in progress, and

[15] [Isaac Dov Baer ben Tsevi Hirsch], *Kahal ḥasidim heḥadash*, §§17, 179, 138; Zevin, *Hasidic Tales: Festivals* (Heb.), 76.

[16] Donner, *Derekh ha'emunah uma'aseh rav*, 60.

[17] A. S. Safrin, *Zikhron devarim*, introd. and note of approbation.

[18] Chikernik, *Sipurim nifla'im uma'amarim kedoshim*, 14.

[19] Kohen, *Shemuot vesipurim*, 43.

[20] Ehrmann, *Pe'er vekhavod*, fos *21b–22a*. See also Weberman, *Derekh tsadikim*, 19–20. Brandwein, *Degel maḥaneh yehudah*, §52, relates, in the name of R. Judah Tsevi of Stratin, that the messiah son of Joseph will be born in Hungary, 'and will be one of the hidden tsadikim'.

[21] Weiss, *Avnei beit hayotser*, ii, §32, p. 66.

[22] Ehrmann, *Devarim arevim*, 'Stories of the Holy Rabbi, the Maggid of Koznitz', §1.

[23] *Mei be'er yeshayahu*, fo. 29*a*, cited in Moskowitz, *Otsar hasipurim*, vii, §44, p. 32. In some instances, a simple person (such as a tailor) has pity on a hidden righteous one and dresses him finely. See Chikernik, *Sipurim neḥmadim*, 15.

learned that shortly beforehand he had been revealed as one of the thirty-six hidden tsadikim.[24]

Since the revealed tsadikim know their hidden counterparts, they care for the latters' physical needs. As noted above, the Ba'al Shem Tov supported them, as did R. Jacob Samson of Shepetovka (who collected money for them),[25] R. Leib Sarahs,[26] and R. Mordecai of Chernobyl.[27] R. Azriel and R. Israel of Polotsk also were seen with R. Mordecai visiting one of the hidden righteous ones.[28] When the hidden tsadikim needed money 'for the commandment of the redemption of captives, for *hakhnasat kalah*, or the like', they would send a note to R. Mordecai with the request that he immediately send them the necessary sum. R. Mordecai consequently needed large amounts of money, which on occasion he would even take by force. Usually he would collect gold and silver items or jewellery for such needs.[29] Tsevi Moskowitz, author of *Otsar hasipurim*, adds that R. Mordecai's sons continued this tradition of providing for hidden tsadikim. R. Abraham of Trisk had a special collection box, known as the *kolelet*, for this purpose.[30] R. Isaac of Skvira said that his father 'knew some of the 36 tsadikim, and supported them.'[31]

The hidden tsadikim were usually poor men, as indicated by their external appearance, occupations, and way of life. They were simple craftsmen and

24 Rotzferd, *Zikhron naftali*, §81.

25 Bodek, *Mifalot hatsadikim*, §21. Cf. Singer, *Seva ratson*, 13. Ehrmann, *Devarim arevim*, 'Stories of the Holy Rabbi, of R. [Joshua] H[eschel] of Apta', §12, relates how R. Samson told the Vilna Gaon that he once asked R. Leib Sarahs to reveal to him where the hidden righteous resided, for he knew that R. Leib provided for their needs. The latter stated that most of them lived in Brod. The wife of one, to whom R. Samson had given money for sabbath expenses, agreed to his request that she and her husband should spend the sabbath with him. Her husband, however, who was therefore compelled to leave his home for the sabbath, took his revenge on the tsadik by appearing in the guise of the *poritz*. For the visit by R. Leib Sarahs to the hidden tsadik R. Itamar Hakohen, see Ze'ev Wolf of Zhitomir, *Or hame'ir*, 14.

26 Rodkinsohn, *Sipurei tsadikim*, §3, p. 7. Cf. Pinhas of Korets, *Beit pinḥas*, §23, p. 38; Rakats, *Siaḥ sarfei kodesh*, iii, §288; Ehrmann, *Devarim arevim*, 'Stories of the Holy Rabbi, of R. [Joshua] H[eschel] of Apta', §1; see also last citation in n. 29 above.

27 Rodkinsohn, *Sipurei tsadikim*, §3; cf. Kleinmann, *Mazkeret shem gedolim*, 159. See also Rakats, *Siaḥ sarfei kodesh*, iii, §288; A. Stern, *Ḥutim hameshulashim*, 58, 80. Ehrmann, *Pe'er vekhavod*, 'Stories of the Martyrs' (in Ehrmann, *Devarim arevim hashalem*, 299), relates that a hasid who was once on his way to R. Mordecai of Chernobyl invited into his carriage a passer-by who was in fact a hidden righteous one. The guest asked the hasid to redeem a promissory note from R. Mordecai that he had in his possession, a request to which the hasid agreed. According to Ehrmann, *Devarim arevim*, 'Stories of the Holy Rabbi, of R. [Joshua] H[eschel] of Apta', §1, a tailor, who was a hidden righteous one, 'ordained' R. Mordecai to be a hasidic tsadik.

28 Rodkinsohn, *Sipurei tsadikim*, §3. See Abraham of Slonim, *Beit avraham*, 198: R. Azriel of Polotsk once heard two hidden tsadikim speaking about R. Zusya's fear of God.

29 Hazan, *Sipurim nifla'im*, §35.

30 Moskowitz, *Otsar hasipurim*, vii. 20.

31 Pinhas of Korets, *Beit pinḥas*, §23, p. 38. In R. Margaliot, *Or hame'ir*, 13, R. Levi Isaac of Berdichev arranges a match for the daughter of the hidden tsadik R. Itamar Hakohen.

labourers, including an ass-drover,[32] a porter and water-bearer,[33] a book-binder,[34] a baker,[35] a tailor,[36] a shoemaker,[37] a distillery worker,[38] a labourer in a flour mill,[39] and a shop assistant.[40] It was related that one hidden tsadik looked 'like a very clumsy field worker'.[41] These hidden ones' clothes were those of the indigent,[42] 'ragged and torn, with sackcloth on their loins',[43] and they generally lived in rented lodgings, or in poor and wretched houses.[44] Their neighbours and workmates usually considered them to be unlettered but honest folk,[45] while in truth they could be great Torah scholars, some of

[32] Chikernik, *Sipurim nifla'im uma'amarim kedoshim*, 14; and, for a cattle herder: R. Margaliot, *Or hame'ir*, 6.

[33] Bodek(?), *Sipurei kedoshim*, §5, p. 35. Cf. Rakats, *Siaḥ sarfei kodesh*, v. 47: when they saw a man carrying water, R. Naphtali of Lizhensk told R. Elimelekh of Rudnik, 'This one, too, is one of the thirty-six righteous.' During the day he drew water for householders, and at night he lay in the study hall 'like an inanimate rock'. He lived in a small, dark apartment at the end of the town, shut in on all sides. The window was blocked, and only through a small peephole could R. Naphtali see that there were lights within the house at night. During the third sabbath meal, he said to himself: 'Fool, leave here, we have already allowed you to look enough, and you are not permitted to see any more', and he went on his way. Ehrmann, *Devarim arevim*, 'Stories of the Holy Rabbi, R. Israel of Ruzhin', §5; id., *Pe'er vekhavod*, 36–7. See also Shimon Rabbi of Tarnow, *Notser te'enah*, §3.

[34] Sobelman, *Sipurei tsadikim heḥadash*, §23.

[35] Rodkinsohn, *Adat tsadikim*, §14. The father-in-law of R. Hayim ben Bezalel was apparently a hidden tsadik. For R. Yekil, the baker in the city of Piltz, see Weinstock, *Peri kodesh hilulim*, 44–6.

[36] See Rodkinsohn, *Sipurei tsadikim*, §3, p. 7; §21, pp. 36–9; Y.D. of Sudilkov, *Temimei derekh*, fo. 26*a–b*. See also Shenkel, *Yeshuot yisra'el*, ii, §18: R. Isaac Luria sent his nephew, who had fallen mute, to a tailor who was a hidden tsadik. See also Pinhas of Korets, *Beit pinḥas*, §24, p. 38. J. Sofer, *Sipurei ya'akov*, ii. 38, tells of a tailor who was a hidden righteous one, and who gave his daughter in marriage to a young thief who had repented of his evil ways; for a hidden one who 'mends garments', see Rakats, *Siaḥ sarfei kodesh*, iii, §288; see also Ehrmann, *Devarim arevim*, 'Stories of the Holy Rabbi, of R. [Joshua] H[eschel] of Apta', §1.

[37] Hazan, *Sipurim nifla'im*, §34; Breitstein, *Siḥot ḥayim*, 40–1.

[38] Bodek, *Mifalot hatsadikim*, §13; cf. Bodek(?), *Sipurei kedoshim*, §17, pp. 64–6. See also *Ma'asiyot mehagedolim vehatsadikim*, 41, for a hidden tsadik whose poverty compelled him to work in a wine distillery.

[39] Bodek[?], *Sipurei kedoshim*, §1.

[40] Shenkel, *Ma'asiyot mitsadikim yesodei olam*, §7: this hidden tsadik brought blessings to his employers. Kamelhar, *Mevaser tov*, 'Va'etḥanan', 38–9; A. Michelson, *Ateret menaḥem*, 70.

[41] Hazan, *Sipurim nifla'im*, §34.

[42] See Gelb, *Beit shelomoh*: 'A shabby *shtreimel* was on his head, and his clothes were simple, like those of the poor'; Moskowitz, *Otsar hasipurim*, vii, §38, p. 25.

[43] Moskowitz, *Otsar hasipurim*, vii. 23–4. Cf. also Chikernik, *Sipurim neḥmadim*, 15.

[44] See Hazan, *Sipurim nifla'im*, §34. Cf. Ehrmann, *Devarim arevim*, 'Stories of the Holy Rabbi, R. Israel of Ruzhin', §5: a wretched house at the end of the city, with its windows blocked on all sides. Cf. Weberman, *Derekh tsadikim*, 35–6.

[45] R. Raphael, who lived in a village near Hamburg, was considered to be unlettered; known to all as 'the *tam*', he in fact studied with his sons in seclusion in the forest. Cf. Bodek(?), *Sipurei kedoshim*, 'The Annals of Ephraim [of Luntshits]', §5; see also Zevin, *Hasidic Tales: On the Torah* (Heb.), 384–6.

whom even merited visions of Elijah.[46] A tailor describes one of the hidden ones, who was a water-drawer, as follows: 'He performs his work honestly. Every day he draws water for the townspeople, and in the evening he returns home like a drunkard, falling asleep and quarrelling with his wife, with the sound of crashing as they fall, fighting, on the floor, and always bickering, weeping, and wailing.'[47] In return for a loan of money to support hidden tsadikim, a young man asked R. Leib Sarahs if he could see one of them. The tsadik instructed him to travel to Berdichev and remain there for the sabbath, and at midnight on Saturday night to enter the only house on a certain street in which a light was still burning; here the young man met a very rough tailor who agreed to mend his torn garment.[48]

Another hidden tsadik, R. Leib Weiner of Brod,[49] 'acted like an animal' in his private life, earning himself the nickname 'Leib, the godly beast'.[50] The hidden tsadik may even not go to the synagogue,[51] getting a reputation as a wicked man. One such man was a wealthy individual who rented a wine distillery: he wore a short coat (like those worn by non-Jews), his *pe'ot* (sidelocks) were short, and he was even suspected of adultery. Despite all these incriminating signs, the Ba'al Shem Tov attested that he was a hidden tsadik.

The uniqueness of the concealed tsadikim lies in their anonymity, which they seek to maintain at any price. One story even declares that 'they are forbidden to reveal themselves all their days'.[52] Their outward appearance and occupation help to keep them in obscurity; if that obscurity is threatened, they go into hiding or move their abode. R. Isaiah Asher Zelig Margolies heard the following account from the rabbi of Barniv, as related by the tsadik of Shinova in Sanz upon his return from the Land of Israel. In the ritual bath of Safed he met a person whom he sensed was one of the thirty-six righteous.

[46] See *Sefer hasiḥot* 5 (1943), 166–7; also nn. 3, 9, 10, and 58 in the current chapter. *Continued in Appendix.*

[47] Ehrmann, *Pe'er vekhavod*, 36–7; id., *Devarim arevim*, 'Stories of the Ba'al Shem Tov', §30 (citing Solomon of Radomsk, *Tiferet shelomoh*, fo. 59).

[48] *Ma'asiyot mehagedolim vehatsadikim*, 41.

[49] See also Ehrmann, *Devarim arevim*, 'Stories of the Holy Rabbi, of R. [Joshua] H[eschel] of Apta', §12, fo. 57*a*: 'I once met our master, the rabbi, R. Leib Sarahs, and I asked him to reveal to me the dwelling place of the thirty-six righteous. He told me that the majority are here in Brod.' Cf. Agnon, *Hakhnasat kalah*, 256.

[50] Joseph ben R. A., *Mifalot tsadikim heḥadash*, 20. Cf. J. H. Lewin, *Aliyot eliyahu*, 62–3 n. 84: 'There was there [in the vicinity of Brod] a certain householder who was perfect in his deeds, and who was truly a Torah scholar, dazzling in his knowledge, who would conduct himself in his affairs as a beast, until he was called "Leib, the godly beast".' His excessive charity led to his own impoverishment, as he was forced to become a worker in a wine distillery, thus his name: 'Leib Weiner'. The Vilna Gaon wanted R. Leib to come with him to the Land of Israel, but R. Leib informed him 'that this was not necessary, for he [the Gaon], too, would return', as indeed he did.

[51] Chikernik, *Ma'asiyot uma'amarim yekarim*, 16–17.

[52] Rodkinsohn, *Sipurei tsadikim*, §3, p. 7.

When he attempted to follow this man, the latter succeeded in evading the tsadik. When the rabbi called to him to stop, the hidden one replied: 'Shinover Rabbi, of what concern is it of yours that I am still alive in the world?' The rabbi of Shinova then attempted to go to the hidden one's apartment, but when he arrived, he learned that the man had left there shortly before the sabbath, and had gone to Ein Zeitim, in the vicinity of Safed. When the tsadik arrived there, he was told that the hidden one had left immediately upon the end of the sabbath.[53] Another story describes how a hidden one, a glazier by trade, sought to escape when he sensed that people were following him. None the less, he revealed to the Jerusalemite who followed him and tried to engage him in conversation that one of the company, that is, one of the thirty-six hidden righteous, prayed in a corner of the study hall in the Hurvat Rabbi Judah Hasid synagogue in Jerusalem.[54]

R. Isaac Meir of Ger told his wife that a hidden one was engaged as a schoolteacher in a certain village. Every night this man would spend hours outside his room, a practice that aroused the curiosity of the landlord. When the householder urged him to say what he was doing, the man replied 'that he was engaged in the conversation of birds', and after much insistent questioning by the householder, he even taught him the language in which the birds spoke. However, once his identity had become known, the hidden one 'was forced to travel somewhere else, to a place where he was not known [to be such a righteous one], for he is a *hidden* tsadik'.[55]

After the wedding of R. Asher, the son of the 'Holy Jew', his father disclosed to him that a shoemaker who was one of the hidden righteous lived in Lemberg, near to the bride's father. The tsadik ordered his son to travel to his father-in-law immediately, in order to meet this shoemaker. R. Asher ordered a pair of shoes from him, and returned to the latter's house every day on various pretexts. On the fifth day the shoemaker was not there, and the householder informed him that he had settled his account for the lodgings and left.[56]

53 Moskowitz, *Otsar hasipurim*, vii, §41, pp. 27–9.

54 Ibid., §42, p. 29. This was R. Isaac Itchele Kolner, who died in 1902; until he passed away, it was not known that he was a concealed tsadik. Nevertheless, though not visible to ordinary people, the hidden tsadikim meet among themselves, e.g. during the seven days of rejoicing following the marriage of a daughter of one of their company, with new concealed ones arriving each day (Y.D. of Sudilkov, *Temimei derekh*, fo. 25*b*).

55 Rakats, *Siaḥ sarfei kodesh*, v. 113. According to the Yiddish version of *Shivḥei habesht* (ch. 79), a hidden tsadik rejected the request by R. Yehiel Mikhel of Zlotchev to study with him, claiming that he must first receive 'approval from heaven'. When R. Yehiel Mikhel came to him once again, the hidden one vanished, together with his wife and children.

56 Breitstein, *Siḥot ḥayim*, 40–1. A. M. Rabinowitz, *Keter hayehudi*, 51, reports an exceptional instance in which the hidden tsadik left his place of residence, not to avoid being revealed, but because he took offence when his employer slapped him on the cheek, thereby publicly shaming him. See also Kamelhar, *Mevaser tov*, 38–9.

The revelation of the hidden righteous one indicates that he has completed his role in this world, and his death is imminent, as we learn from the following story:

Once a terrible case came before R. Solomon Kluger, the Maggid of Brod. Now, a certain woman came before the rabbi to enquire whether a goose that she held in her hand was improperly slaughtered, and the rabbi ruled that it was indeed unfit. The women went home bitter-hearted, because she was poor. As she was walking along, there was a certain porter among those carrying a load, and he called out to the woman: 'Why are you weeping and distressed?' She replied: 'Look, if you will, the rabbi-Maggid declared this goose unfit, and what shall I do?' The porter told her: 'Go back, and tell the rabbi that he should study the *Shulḥan arukh*, and he will see in the place that he marked that the goose is kosher.' The woman went and repeated the porter's words to the rabbi, who read in the *Shulḥan arukh*, and declared that the goose was fit. When the woman came back to the porter, he instructed her: 'Return to the rabbi, and tell him that the goose is unfit, and that he should study such-and-such a section in the *Shulḥan arukh*.' The rabbi perused the *Shulḥan arukh*, and pronounced the goose unfit. The rabbi asked the woman who this man was, but she was unwilling to disclose this, for the porter had adjured her not to reveal his identity. The rabbi commanded her: 'Leave me, and stand with the goose next to the man, and I will see from afar and know that he is the person who sent you to me', and the woman did so. The rabbi summoned the porter to his house, and ordered him to reveal who he was. The porter divulged that he was one of the thirty-six righteous, and the rabbi studied with the porter for a considerable time, until people learned of this. Once this became known, this porter died, and the rabbi-Maggid eulogized him.[57]

Another hidden tsadik, who blessed a childless person with offspring, enjoined him: 'And know, that if this will become known to anyone, then I, you, your wife, and the children that shall be born to you will be in danger, heaven forbid.'[58]

These tales stand in contrast to those of the hidden righteous who were revealed and acted thereafter as manifest tsadikim. As mentioned above, according to the letters of the Kherson *genizah* and certain Habad texts the Ba'al Shem Tov was a hidden tsadik until the age of 36. It is related of R. Moses of Proshovitza: 'This rabbi initially concealed his deeds and manner of worship, and seemed to all the world to be a simple, unlettered

[57] *Ma'asiyot vesiḥot tsadikim*, 90–1. Cf. Ehrmann, *Pe'er vekhavod*, 'Stories of the Martyrs' (in id., *Devarim arevim hashalem*, 300): The rabbi's fierce desire to learn the identity of the hidden tsadik was responsible for the latter's death, after which the rabbi delivered a fitting eulogy.

[58] Ehrmann, *Devarim arevim*, 'Stories of the Holy Rabbi, the Maggid of Koznitz', §1. Cf. ibid., vol. ii, 'Stories of the Holy Rabbi, R. Israel of Ruzhin', §5: a hidden tsadik told R. Elimelekh of Rudnik, who investigated him: 'Enough! You have gazed enough! You are not permitted to look any more!'

person.'[59] Eventually, Elijah informed him that the time had come for him to reveal himself. Similarly, no one knew of R. Shimon Deutsch, who used to hide in the woods and roll about on thorns until his blood flowed. A Jewish scribe who lived in the forest noted his behaviour, 'approached him and said to him: "You cannot conceal yourself from me, when your hidden deeds are known to me. I ask only one thing: what is your name and your place?"'[60] R. Shimon then became a manifest tsadik.

Hidden tsadikim also engage in the esoteric teachings of the Torah. When R. Elimelekh and his brother R. Zusya went into 'exile' (to be together with the Divine Presence that is in exile), their father (who was no longer among the living) appeared to them and told them where each would spend the sabbath. R. Elimelekh was commanded to stay in the rabbi's house, and his brother with a certain shoemaker, who lived at the edge of the city, in a hovel fit only for the poorest. When R. Zusya came and expressed his desire to spend the sabbath with him, the shoemaker's wife said that, as things stood then, they had no food for the sabbath, but she would be happy to accommodate him, provided her husband consented. When the shoemaker, who was a hidden tsadik, returned home, he agreed, on condition that his guest prayed with him in the *minyan* of craftsmen, for they 'pray at dawn, hastily'. R. Zusya was unable to discover the true nature of his host, because the latter prayed 'very quickly, cramming the words together, like one of the simple folk'. During the day R. Zusya looked for the hidden tsadik, but the latter was not in his room. R. Zusya finally found him in the loft, sitting at the table in the company of all the thirty-six hidden righteous (the teller of the story mentions that he had heard that all the thirty-six hidden tsadikim partake of the third sabbath meal together). The hidden ones wondered at the presence of R. Zusya, and asked him not to tell anyone about them. R. Zusya sat with them and heard the most hidden secrets and esoteric teachings. At first, he

[59] Bodek(?), *Sipurei kedoshim*, §17; Bodek, *Mifalot hatsadikim*, §13; Slodovnik, *Ma'aseh hagedolim heḥadash*, §13. Cf. A. Michelson, *Ohel avraham*, §40: R. Abraham Abusch of Frankfurt lived in a village as a hidden tsadik, and Elijah studied with him. Prior to his death, the rabbi of Kariv, who knew the hidden one's true identity, ordered that R. Abraham Abusch be appointed to succeed him. For R. Argeh Leib of Shpola and R. Mordecai of Nezkizh, who were hidden before being known as tsadikim, see A. Stern, *Ḥutim hameshulashim*, 57. For a hidden tsadik who refused a heavenly command to reveal himself, for which he was punished, see Brukman, *Migdal david*, 31.

[60] See [Lemberger], *Niflaot hatsadikim*, 27. When R. Judah Tsevi of Stretin asked to see the knife of a villager who engaged in ritual slaughter, the latter told him: 'Believe me that I have not shown my knife to any rabbi or expert [in the laws of ritual slaughter], except for Elijah, of blessed memory'; it transpired that he was one of the hidden tsadikim (Brandwein, *Degel maḥaneh yehudah*, §51). The knife of a ritual slaughterer who was a hidden tsadik bore the inscription: 'This is the knife [*ma'akhelet*] of the Patriarch Abraham, may the memory of the righteous be for a blessing, by whose merit we eat [*okhlim*]' (Ehrmann, *Devarim arevim*, 'Stories of the Holy Rabbi, R. S[olomon] of Karlin', §6).

honoured his promise, but when R. Elimelekh pressed him, he could not keep his word, and revealed everything to his brother. For this he was sentenced to death by heaven, but the hidden ones took pity on R. Zusya, and were satisfied with an episode that caused him embarrassment, thereby atoning for his misdeed. In this subsequent incident, the shoemaker who was also a hidden tsadik appeared in the guise of a wealthy non-Jew, who accused R. Zusya of stealing his watch. R. Zusya was brought before a non-Jewish judge (who was also in fact a Jew and a concealed tsadik), who finally released him, after explaining to him his sin and its punishment.[61]

Another hidden tsadik taught the secret teachings of the Torah in a ruin far from any town to a disciple of the Maggid of Koznitz, after the latter's death. This hidden one, R. Moses Stashogil, concealed his identity by posing as a worthless individual, the head of a band of robbers. He told his pupil: 'The tsadik of the generation is the one who knows that what I convey to you are my own teachings.'[62]

The hidden tsadik knows concealed matters—even, sometimes, the day on which he himself will die. R. Isaac Eisik, a ritual slaughterer in the village of Zuravitch, was a hidden tsadik; as usual, those around him thought him to be unlettered. Then it became evident to the local rabbi that R. Isaac Eisik knew secret things, for he revealed to the rabbi that the latter had engaged in sexual relations with a woman who was menstrually impure; moreover, towards the end of his life, he knew the date of his own death. This hidden tsadik was the author of several books (*Otiyot derav yitsḥak*, *Raza mehemna*, and *Yesod yitsḥak*) which, because of his modesty, he kept in a chest. R. Aaron of Karlin greatly regretted that he never met R. Isaac Eisik.[63]

A hidden tsadik who lived in a forest and married an orphan who had been raised in the home of the Ba'al Shem Tov knew, when the Ba'al Shem Tov visited him, that the tsadik had treated her poorly. He punished the Ba'al Shem Tov by subjecting him to a terrible sabbath, thereby restoring to him his portion of the world to come.[64]

R. Elijah, the Vilna Gaon, wanted the hidden tsadik R. Leib Weiner of Brod to come with him to the Land of Israel. Weiner refused, and even

[61] Hazan, *Sipurim nifla'im*, §34. See Y.D. of Sudilkov, *Temimei derekh*, fo. 25*b*: a hidden tsadik merited *kefitsat haderekh* on his way to R. Elimelekh of Lizhensk. For the hidden tsadik whom R. Elimelekh and R. Zusya met at a banquet for the poor that a worthy held on his daughter's wedding day, see Mondshein, *Likutei reshimot uma'asiyot*, §207, pp. 37–8.

[62] Bodek, *Mifalot hatsadikim*, §25, fo. 19*a–b*.

[63] [Isaac Dov Baer ben Tsevi Hirsch], *Kahal ḥasidim heḥadash*, §58; this incident is also mentioned in Moskowitz, *Otsar hasipurim*, xx, §11, p. 22 (see also the chapter on ritual slaughterers), and in Agnon, *Sefer sofer vesipur*, 424. Cf. the story that after the Jerusalem shoemaker/hidden tsadik died his chest was found to contain kabbalistic manuscripts: Farhi, *Mora'im gedolim*, 80 (a non-hasidic work).

[64] Bodek, *Mifalot tsadikim*, §26; Zevin, *Hasidic Tales: Festivals* (Heb.), 200–3.

prophesied that the Vilna Gaon would fail in his attempt to go to the Holy Land, a prediction that was realized.[65] Another hidden tsadik, R. Nahum Sofer of Tachov, possessed the spirit of divine inspiration and knew what would happen an entire century after his death. Before his death in 1815 he dictated the text of his tombstone, which ended with the letters תרצ"ה (standing for the year 1915), and it was written in the communal register that 100 years after his death Jews who were in great distress would come to Tachov. One century later, in 1915, during the First World War, Jews came to prostrate themselves at his grave, beginning a practice that continued until the Holocaust.[66]

Like the *tamim* (see Chapter 13), the hidden tsadik protects Jews from oppression, and in many cases saves an entire community. R. Judah of Graydung was once taken to a man who was on his deathbed. Upon his return, he explained to those accompanying him: 'I thought that I was going to visit a sick simple person. I opened the door, and I saw suspended over the head of the sick man a fiery *menorah*, with seven glowing lit branches, that is appropriate for a great tsadik . . . Perhaps he is a hidden one.' Indeed, when speaking with his visitor, the sick man recalled an incident in which he had saved Jewish lives many years previously.[67] R. Hayim, a vineyard watchman, was revealed as one of the hidden righteous when the great kabbalist R. Mordecai Melamed brought Joab ben Zeruiah into this world during a circumcision, but could not then return him to the realm of the dead. R. Hayim entered at that moment and succeeded in saving the city from destruction by returning Joab to his place in the afterworld.[68]

I will conclude this discussion of the hidden righteous with a story, published fairly recently, that was told about the head of the Hayei Olam yeshiva, the late R. Heikel Meletsky, on his son's wedding day. The rabbi, who had difficulty walking,[69] was brought to the wedding ceremony in his bed. The story teaches that his illness resulted from his failure to heed a hidden tsadik. A drunkard, who was known to all as *Itche der shiker* (Itche the

[65] *Ma'asiyot mehagedolim vehatsadikim*, 41. See Moskowitz, *Otsar hasipurim*, i. 13–14; see also above, n. 49. For hidden tsadikim in Lithuania, see Ganuz, 'The Thirty-Six Just Persons' (Heb.), 28–31. For a hidden one in the vicinity of Pinsk who helped *agunot* and performed miracles, see Hampel, 'A Blacksmith' (Heb.), 113–14.

[66] *Melitsei esh* on the months of Av–Elul, §308 (cited in Moskowitz, *Otsar hasipurim*, vii, §31, pp. 20–1).

[67] Sobelman, *Sipurei tsadikim heḥadash*, §21. For light that attests to the presence of the Shekhinah, see Ch. 16 n. 4 below.

[68] Moskowitz, *Otsar hasipurim*, i. §12, p. 22. For Joab, see also Shmeruk, *Yiddish Literature* (Heb.), 143. *Mayse bukh*, §145; *Ma'asiyot mehagedolim vehatsadikim*, 6–10; Jousep (Juspa) Schammes of Worms, *Ma'aseh nisim*, fos 27*b*–29*b*; Nigal, *Magic, Mysticism, and Hasidism*, 9–10.

[69] For testimony regarding the amputation of his leg, see also Lopian, *Lev eliyahu*, i. §2, p. 19.

drunkard), lived in the town of Stutchin. No one knew exactly where he lived, nor did anyone take any particular interest in the man, who spent much of his time in the yeshiva. One day a wagon-driver rushed into the yeshiva to ask the students to help rescue his horse, which was trapped under the overturned wagon and was suffocating. The young men debated whether it was permitted to interrupt Torah study for such a purpose. In the meantime, the driver left the yeshiva to search for help elsewhere. Itche the drunkard, who was sprawled on a bench in the yeshiva, suddenly rose up and commanded the students to help the driver, 'and if you do not go, you will not be able to walk on your legs, heaven forbid'. The wagon-driver, having despaired of finding help elsewhere, returned to the yeshiva, and this time the students decided to assist him.

Some time later, the drunkard asked the teller of the story to come to him at a certain hour and study at his place, telling him that he (Itche) would die this day, at such-and-such an hour. Despite his bewilderment, the storyteller came to Itche's hovel, at the end of the town, and studied there. To his surprise, he found a pair of fine *tefilin* in a chest, having thought until then that Itche had not observed this commandment at all. Itche asked him to convey, after his death, his last request to the rabbi and the burial society: to be interred next to a certain renowned Torah scholar in the old cemetery. Itche also permitted the visitor to show the rabbi his kabbalistic writings, which were in a second chest. Itche died at precisely the time he had specified. The rabbi and the burial society, who had thought the old cemetery was full, were amazed to discover a single burial plot remaining, adjoining that of the Torah scholar next to whom Itche had asked to be interred. The rabbi and a large crowd participated in the funeral, because all understood now that this 'drunkard' was a hidden tsadik.[70]

[70] Kohen, *Shemuot vesipurim*, 205–7. For Elijah the prophet as engaging in the religious duty of burying a hidden tsadik, see Rakats, *Siaḥ sarfei kodesh*, iii, §290; Zevin, *Hasidic Tales: Festivals* (Heb.), 236–7.

FIFTEEN

HOSPITALITY

JEWISH TRADITION puts a high value on hospitality, one of whose attributes is declared by the rabbis to be 'that a person eats [its] fruits in this world, while the principal remains for him in the world to come'.[1] It was only to be expected that it would be similarly praised by leading hasidic figures, such as R. Uri of Strelisk, who ordained that every person should have a guest at his table at every meal, 'and then it will be regarded as if he engaged in all the mystical intents of R. Isaac Luria, of blessed memory'.[2]

Stories on this topic were composed over the ages, and the theme continued into the hasidic genre. R. Abraham Abusch, head of the Frankfurt rabbinical court,[3] is an example of a non-hasidic figure who fulfilled the religious obligation of extending hospitality, even under trying circumstances, such as welcoming a physically repulsive guest.[4]

R. Eliezer, the father of the Ba'al Shem Tov, was put to the test regarding this attribute. It is said that he was 'an extremely hospitable host',[5] and even placed watchmen at the edge of his village to inform him of every visitor's arrival.

Once he was highly praised from heaven above concerning his good attributes, and it was agreed in heaven to put him to the test on some matter. It was asked: 'Who shall go to try him?' And Samael said: 'I will go.' Elijah [the Prophet], of blessed mention [the phrase used is *zakhur latov*, rather than the more usual *zikhrono liverakhah*, so as to suggest the belief that Elijah did not die], said: 'It is not well that you go, I shall go [instead]!' Elijah, of blessed mention, went on a sabbath

1 BT *Shab.* 127*a*, and elsewhere.

2 Uri of Strelisk, *Imrei kodesh*, 21 (pagination added), cited in Agnon, *Elu ve'elu*, 89, 'Vehayah he'akov lemishor'.

3 R. Abraham Abusch was born *c.*1690 in Mezirech, Lithuania, and until 1753 he served as the rabbi in several communities in the Lublin district. From 1759 until his death in 1779 he was the rabbi of Frankfurt am Main. See Piekarz, *Beginning of Hasidism* (Heb.), 35–9.

4 A. Michelsohn, *Birkat avraham* (on *Pesaḥim*), introd.; also cited in id., *Ohel avraham*, §7; Donner, *Derekh ha'emunah uma'aseh rav*, 'Hospitality', §5; Tzitrin, *Shivḥei tsadikim*, ed. Nigal, §30; Shenkel, *Noraot anshei ma'aseh*, §14.

5 Kattina, *Raḥamei ha'av*, §10. See also Slodovnik, *Ma'aseh hagedolim heḥadash*, §18; Shenkel, *Ma'asiyot peliyot*, §15; [Isaac Dov Baer ben Tsevi Hirsch], *Kahal ḥasidim heḥadash*, §25; the story is also related in Agnon, *Elu ve'elu*, 90.

afternoon in the guise of a poor man, with his staff and satchel [thereby violating the sabbath], and came and said: *Shabta taba* [a good sabbath].

R. Eliezer did not reproach the stranger for his violation of the sabbath; on the contrary, he provided him with the third sabbath meal, and after that, the *melaveh malkah*. On the following day, Sunday morning, the tsadik even gave him a handsome present, and again did not reprove him for his desecration of the sabbath. The story ends as follows: 'When Elijah, of blessed mention, saw his good conduct, he revealed himself to him, and said: "Know that I am the prophet Elijah, and I came to put you to the test. As your reward, you will merit having a son who shall illuminate the eyes of Israel."'[6]

R. Yehiel Meir of Gostynin told his followers of his certainty that heaven had tested him regarding his hospitality.[7] The story was as follows. One sabbath night the beadle came to the tsadik and told him that he had seen a guest in the study hall, and he had brought him into the rabbi's house to partake of the sabbath meal. 'And this guest was dressed in garments so disgusting and filthy, and he himself was extremely ugly and coarse, and as dirty as if he had been rolling in the refuse, so that it was impossible to even stand next to him.'[8] The rabbi warmly received the guest, and sat him at his table. The guest did not chant *Shalom aleikhem* to welcome the sabbath angels (as is customary prior to the meal on Friday evening), claiming that he was unable to do so, nor did he recite Kiddush, for the same reason. His inability to perform the sabbath ritual was such that his host was even compelled to recite the *hamotsi* blessing (over bread) with him, word for word, after which 'he ate like a glutton and a beast of the forest, without any human manners'. The guest devoured all the bread, and the tsadik sent someone to ask the neighbours for more, which the guest also consumed at lightning speed. After the meal, the guest claimed that he did not know the Grace after Meals, and lay down in his filthy boots on the sofa.

The host did not question his guest's behaviour, and on the contrary rejoiced at the opportunity to fulfil the commandment of hospitality. He even covered the guest with warm garments, so that he would sleep well. The following morning, when the host came to enquire after his guest, he found that the latter had vanished. Nor had anyone seen him, either before he had come to the rabbi's house or afterwards. 'People said then that this

[6] Tzitrin, *Shivḥei tsadikim*, ed. Nigal, 12. In *Shivḥei habesht*, 39, Elijah speaks in a similar vein to the Ba'al Shem Tov's father, when the latter returned from a foreign land, where he had remained faithful to his people and his religion. In Bodek, *Pe'er mikedoshim* (1991 edn, in: *Sipurim ḥasidi'im*, 162, Elijah comes, in the guise of a pauper, to test a rich man's hospitality, but he is thrown out.

[7] R. Yehiel Meir (d. 1888) was the disciple of R. Mendel of Kotsk, R. Abraham of Chernev, and R. Isaac Meir of Ger, and was known as Ba'al Hatehilim ('master of Psalms', for his recital of psalms the entire day).

[8] Tzitrin, *Shivḥei tsadikim*, ed. Nigal, 91–2.

guest could only have been sent from heaven in such a guise, to put him to the test regarding the commandment of hospitality.'

The Ba'al Shem Tov also put people to the test regarding this commandment. Once he set out, accompanied by his disciples, to examine a hospitable person 'in the land of the West' of whom he had heard great things. They arrived at his house on the Sukkot festival, and their host withstood all the trials to which the Ba'al Shem Tov subjected him.[9] In another instance, the Ba'al Shem Tov heard of a hospitable person in the lands of the East who gave each of his guests 100 roubles.[10] Another story tells of a gracious host during the time of the Ba'al Shem Tov and R. Ze'ev Kiytses.[11]

The subject of hospitality also entered modern Hebrew literature from hasidic thought and the hasidic story. S. Y. Agnon's story 'Vehayah he'akov lemishor' (And the Crooked Shall Be Made Straight) records that Manasseh Hayim, who had lost all his property and was forced to become a wandering beggar, would tell his hosts stories about hospitality.[12] In his retelling of this tale, Agnon copied two paragraphs from the book *Derekh ha'emunah uma'aseh rav*.[13]

An outstanding story on this theme was also used by Agnon,[14] who copied it almost verbatim.

[The tsadik of Nezkizh] related that there was a decent man in Berdichev named R. Lieber, of blessed memory. One winter night, after the fair, a certain person came to his house, seeing that a light was still burning there. R. Lieber received him in a hospitable manner, and he himself made up a bed for him to sleep. The guest asked him: 'Why is his excellency himself troubling himself to prepare it for me?' R. Lieber answered: 'Do you think that I am making it up for you? I am making it up for myself.' He meant by this that he was preparing himself for the world to come.[15]

It would seem reasonable to attribute the large number of stories about hospitality, the emphasis placed upon the importance of this religious obligation, and the tests that the host must sometimes withstand to the fragile socio-economic situation of the majority of east European Jews at the time the stories were composed. I have not cited all the hasidic stories that focus upon the topic of hospitality, but the few mentioned in this chapter constitute a representative sample.

[9] MS JNUL 6289, fo. 55*b*.

[10] *Ma'asiyot mehagedolim vehatsadikim*, 32–3.

[11] Slodovnik, *Ma'aseh hagedolim heḥadash*, §20, p. 44.

[12] Agnon, *Elu ve'elu*, 89.

[13] Donner, *Derekh ha'emunah uma'aseh rav*, 'Hospitality.' See Nigal, *S. Y. Agnon and his Hasidic Sources* (Heb.), 12–13.

[14] Agnon, *Elu ve'elu*, 89.

[15] I. Landau, *Zikhron tov*, 'The Deeds of the Tsadikim', §2, p. 12. Cf. Shenkel, *Sipurei anshei shem*, §22.

SIXTEEN

THE PROPHET ELIJAH

THE HASIDIC STORIES about the prophet Elijah incorporate elements from the Talmud and the Midrash, and from folk tales and kabbalistic literature from the medieval period and later.[1] In all these traditions Elijah appears in various guises and with various purposes: he is the harbinger of good news, frustrates anti-Jewish persecutions, and puts individuals to the test.

The hasidic story is intensely preoccupied with *gilui eliyahu* (the 'vision of Elijah'), which is one of the levels of prophecy. Even in the pre-hasidic tradition this revelation depended on piety, and its level corresponds to that of the individual's devotion. Thus, R. Hayim Vital asserted, regarding 'the conduct of the spirit of divine inspiration at this time', that '[Elijah's] revelations to a person will increase in accordance with his piety'.[2] There are, then, different levels of *gilui eliyahu*, as explained to R. Joseph Karo by the *magid* (his religious and spiritual guide):

> There are three levels here. The first, he saw his [Elijah's] countenance in a dream. The second, he saw while awake, and he greeted him [Elijah], but Elijah did not respond. The third, that he saw Elijah while awake, and Elijah responded. And [when] you shall ascend to the third level, you shall see him while awake, and you shall greet him, but he will come to you only without your being cognizant of this.[3]

Similarly, the well-known *piyut* that is recited on Saturday night at the end of the sabbath, *Eliyahu hanavi* ('The prophet Elijah'), contains the words: 'Happy is the one who sees his countenance in a dream, happy is the one who greets him, and to whom he returns the greeting.'

[1] See Dan, *Hebrew Story* (Heb.), index entry for *Eliyahu*. *Continued in Appendix.*

[2] Vital, *Sha'arei kedushah*, iii, 'Sha'ar' 7, 54–5. For Elijah's appearance in a dream (in the guise of an Ishmaelite) to R. Hayim Vital, see Vital, *Sefer hahezyonot*, §60; see also ibid. pp. 43, 44, 50.

[3] Karo, *Magid meisharim*, 'Bereshit', 13. For Elijah in the life of Karo, see also Werblowsky, *Joseph Caro*, index entry for 'Elijah the Prophet'. Later individuals also merited *gilui eliyahu*: R. Jonathan Eybeschuetz (see I. Safrin, 'Netiv mitsvoteikha', 'Shevil emunah', §11; Shenkel, *Sipurei anshei shem*, §5); the Vilna Gaon (see J. H. Lewin, *Aliyot eliyahu*, introd.); R. Abraham Abusch of Frankfurt (see A. Michelson, *Ohel avraham*, §§40, 44); Elijah Lopian (see Lopian, *Lev eliyahu*, 11–12).

The hasidic story tells us that many hasidic leaders merited *gilui eliyahu*. The prophet appeared to the Ba'al Shem Tov's father upon his return from captivity in a distant land, having withstood many trials, including sexual temptation by the 'daughter of an alien god' (that is, a non-Jewish woman). 'When he was on the way, Elijah, of blessed mention, revealed himself to him, and said to him: "As your reward, you will merit having a son who will illuminate the eyes of Israel, and who will fulfil the verse: 'Israel in whom I glory' [Isa. 49: 3]."'[4]

When the Ba'al Shem Tov was in distress Elijah was revealed to him in a dream, telling him that he would send a non-Jew to help him. The compiler of *Shivḥei habesht* stresses that 'this was the first revelation to him';[5] the hasidim, however, assumed that the Ba'al Shem Tov regularly engaged in conversations with Elijah.[6] According to another story, when the Ba'al Shem Tov was close to death he heard from Ahijah the Shilonite and from Elijah the answer to a question of hasidic theory that had been raised by R. David Forkes.[7] The Maggid, R. Dov Baer of Mezirech, told his disciple R. Solomon of Lutsk that the Ba'al Shem Tov merited *gilui eliyahu* and had related the experience to the Maggid.[8]

The hasidic leaders' claims to have experienced *gilui eliyahu* won them esteem in the hasidic camp, and mockery and derision among the mitnagedim. The rabbis who enjoyed such prestige among the hasidim included R. Elimelekh of Lizhensk, of whom the tsadik R. Shalom of Belz attested: 'Seeing R. Elimelekh in a dream is as if one sees Elijah, of blessed mention.'[9] The following paragraphs describe just a few of the numerous stories about R. Elimelekh.

The rabbi, R. Elimelekh, said that one of the students in his study hall had experienced *gilui eliyahu*. Someone asked him: 'How can this be possible, for the author of

[4] *Shivḥei habesht*, 41. R. Levi Isaac of Berdichev, too, was informed by Elijah of the birth of his son (J. Sofer, *Sipurei ya'akov*, i, §27). *Continued in Appendix.*

[5] *Shivḥei habesht*, 55–6. *Continued in Appendix.*

[6] I. Safrin, *Megilat setarim*, 37. Cf. id., *Notser ḥesed*, fo. 49*c*.

[7] *Shivḥei habesht*, 167. Cf. ibid. 158: the dream by David Forkes in which Elijah came to the Ba'al Shem Tov.

[8] R. Solomon of Lutsk relates, in his introduction to *Magid devarav leya'akov*: 'And I heard from his [the Maggid of Mezirech's] mouth: Why do you wonder that he experienced *gilui eliyahu*, and on the very highest levels, at that. . . . He did not disclose his *gilui eliyahu*, [and did so] possibly only before his death.' R. Hayim Meir Yehiel of Mogielnica, while sitting on Passover eve next to the Maggid of Koznitz, merited seeing the (dead) Maggid of Mezirech when the Maggid of Koznitz was delivering a teaching in the late Maggid's name. R. Hayim, who was about 8 years old at the time, thought that this apparition was Elijah, but his grandfather (the Maggid of Koznitz) told him: 'My son, that was not Elijah, but rather my teacher, R. Baer, of blessed memory, and this is a higher level than *gilui eliyahu*' (Bromberg, *Toledot haniflaot*, 8).

[9] Lieberson, *Tseror haḥayim*, §5; Rabbinovich, *Shivḥei rav ye'ivi*, 91.

the Ibn Ezra [commentary; i.e., R. Abraham Ibn Ezra] does not concede that *gilui eliyahu* exists at the present time, and apparently he himself had not experienced this. In this your excellency [i.e. R. Elimelekh] also will attest, that the author of Ibn Ezra was greater than this person of whom his excellency said that he experienced *gilui eliyahu*?'[10]

R. Elimelekh's response is not relevant to our discussion; at any rate, he insisted that his disciple had merited such a vision of Elijah.[11]

It has already been noted that the mitnagedim responded disdainfully to the hasidim's claims, and various barbed exchanges resulted, such as that between R. Mordecai Ze'ev Ornstein (the head of the Lvov rabbinical court) and R. Elimelekh, described by R. Ornstein's son in the introduction to his book *Yeshuot ya'akov*.[12] R. Elimelekh's response, which contained a subtle taunt at the scholar who addressed the question to him, clearly indicates that the hasidic story ascribed such a revelatory experience to R. Elimelekh himself.

R. Shalom Mordecai, the head of the Berzhan rabbinical court, related:

I heard from an old man that the prophet Elijah and another elder came before the rabbi, R. Elimelekh, on Rosh Hashanah, before the blowing of the shofar, and they informed him of a great [heavenly] accusation [against Israel], and the world was about to be all but destroyed in great upheavals. Two individuals in the generation, however, supported the world, so that it did not fall.[13]

When R. Elimelekh asked who the elder was who accompanied Elijah, the prophet replied that it was Abraham. We learn in the continuation of the tale that the two who saved the world were R. Shmelke of Nikolsburg and R. Elimelekh himself.

The tsadik of Sanz told R. Joseph Schiff:

Since our master, the rabbi, R. Elimelekh, may his merit protect us, was already on a [high spiritual] level when he was a disciple of his holiness, the rabbi, R. Baer, may his merit protect us, Elijah, of blessed mention, would be revealed to him every first night of Rosh Hashanah, and he disclosed to him what was transpiring in heaven. This was so on the night of Rosh Hashanah in [5]533 [= 1772], as well: Elijah was revealed to him, and he informed him that the world is sustained now by three prayers of the greatest of the tsadikim.

10 Meshullam Feivush of Berzhan, *Sefat emet*, 'Matot'. Also cited in Rosenthal, *Tiferet hatsadikim*, 48; Berger, *Eser tsaḥtsaḥot*, 'R. Elimelekh', §31. For a definition of the essential nature of *gilui eliyahu*, see also Israel of Ruzhin, *Irin kadishin*, 'Likutim': 'Elijah in the City'.

11 Mondshein, *Migdal oz*, 245, '*Zikhronot shiloh* by R. Isaiah Halevi Horowitz'. *Continued in Appendix.*

12 Berger, *Eser tsaḥtsaḥot*, 'R. Elimelekh', §22, in the name of R. Aaron Ettinga; cf. the story about Elijah and the tailor (the hidden tsadik) at the end of this chapter.

13 A. Michelson, *Ohel elimelekh*, §9; id., *Shemen hatov*, §10.

R. Elimelekh thought that he was one of these tsadikim and that the second was his brother R. Zusya; R. Joseph Schiff did not recall the name of the third.[14]

Other major hasidic figures are also the subjects of *gilui eliyahu* stories. R. Yehiel Mikhel of Zlotchev came with his son to the Maggid of Mezirech. R. Yehiel Mikhel opened the door and immediately closed it, asking his son: 'Did you not see the prophet Elijah is there with him [the Maggid]?'[15] Several leading tsadikim attested that R. Pinhas, the son of the tsadik R. Jacob Joseph of Ostrog, had experienced *gilui eliyahu* several times;[16] and R. Elimelekh said of R. Naphtali of Ropshits 'that he experiences *gilui eliyahu* whenever he pleases'.[17] R. Shimon Sofer related that his father, the Hatam Sofer (R. Moses Sofer), was once bereaved of a 12-year-old son, and was inconsolable. While R. Shimon was arguing with one of his father's students over who should be the first to enter and offer condolences, a stranger went in and remained with the Hatam Sofer for some considerable time. After he left, R. Moses' mood had considerably improved, and he told R. Shimon and his students that his visitor had been the prophet Elijah. R. Shimon Sofer related this episode to R. Isaac Meir of Ger, and after his departure, the rabbi of Ger told his disciples: 'This was something new for him! I could have showed you Elijah, of blessed mention, every time, provided that I knew that this would be of great benefit to you.'[18]

Once R. Shalom of Belz was acting as host to the rabbi of Podkamen, and he ordered his attendant to bring two additional chairs. In response to the question for whom the second chair was intended, he explained: 'For Elijah!' When his guest expressed his desire to see the prophet, R. Shalom replied: 'The world says that a respectable guest is accompanied by the prophet Elijah, of blessed mention, and whoever is meritorious sees him.'[19]

[14] A. Michelson, *Shemen hatov*, i, §70; Zevin, *Hasidic Tales: Festivals* (Heb.), 23. For a second story of the *gilui eliyahu* of R. Elimelekh, see Meshullam Feivush of Berzhan, *Sefat emet*, 'Matot'; Berger, *Eser tsaḥtsaḥot*, 'R. Elimelekh', §31. See also id., *Eser atarot*, 'R. Solomon Leib of Lantchin', §63.

[15] Shenkel, *Yeshuot yisra'el*, ii, §4; Gemen, *Sifran shel tsadikim*, ch. 4, §3.

[16] A. Michelson, *Shemen hatov*, pt 1, §130.

[17] Ehrmann, *Devarim arevim*, §59; A. Michelson, *Ohel naftali*, §100. Kahana, *Even shetiyah*, 45, asserts that this was said of R. Elimelekh of Rudnik; in *Arba'ah arazim*, 108, it was said of R. Aaron Leib, the son of R. Meir the Great. Ehrmann, *Pe'er vekhavod*, fo. 30*a*, states that R. David Zlatis, one of the disciples of R. Tsevi of Zhidachov and the Seer of Lublin, experienced *gilui eliyahu*. R. Barukh of Medzibezh experienced *gilui eliyahu*, even when angry (Rapoport, *Divrei david*, fo. 35*a*); and it was said of R. Joshua of Dynow that 'Elijah came to him every three days' (Ehrmann, *Devarim arevim*, 'Stories of the Holy Rabbi, Our Master and Teacher, R. Tsevi Elimelekh of Dynow', §16; Berger, *Eser tsaḥtsaḥot*, 'R. Tsevi Elimelekh of Dynow', §1).

[18] Miller, *Beit mordekhai*, i. 61, relates that the Hatam Sofer once acceded to his pupils' request to show them Elijah. A Jew dressed in rags and tatters entered one of his classes; some of the pupils mocked him, others ignored him, and only a third of them greeted him.

[19] A. Michelson, *Dover shalom*, §62.

A person who has not yet attained *gilui eliyahu* eagerly awaits the experience, but even so may not recognize the prophet when it happens. It is related that the Ba'al Shem Tov's disciples asked their rabbi to show them Elijah, and he promised to fulfil their request. One sabbath eve, when the disciples went out into the open fields with their teacher, the Ba'al Shem Tov asked to borrow a pipe for smoking. The disciples met a *poritz*, Pan Shlochtich, and asked him to lend his pipe to their teacher. The *poritz* responded that he knew the rabbi of Medzibezh very well, and would give him the pipe personally. They met and talked of apparently mundane matters, and when the *poritz* left, the Ba'al Shem Tov told his disciples: 'Here, I have kept my word, and shown you Elijah.' The disciples were despondent at not having recognized the *poritz*'s true identity, since they had a fierce desire to study with Elijah. To console them, the Ba'al Shem Tov revealed that his conversation with the *poritz* about grain and the crops was not to be understood literally, but rather concerned *itaruta del-tata* (the 'awakening below', that is, worship) and *itaruta dele'ila* (the heavenly emanation).[20]

Elijah was again revealed as a non-Jew to the Ba'al Shem Tov's disciples in the following story:

> One day, when the disciples had forgotten their request, and the rabbi was riding in a carriage with them, a mounted solder approached them, wearing fine garb. He asked if anyone had a light, so that he could smoke from his pipe. The rabbi told them to oblige him, and they did so. When the disciple gave the light and the soldier gazed into the carriage and saw the Ba'al Shem Tov, he said: 'Oh, master Jew, how are you?', and he fell upon the rabbi's neck and he kissed him, the rabbi also kissed him, and then he went on his way.[21]

Even when Elijah appears in the guise of a Jew, the tsadik's assistance is still required to identify the prophet, for he does not reveal himself to everyone, and even someone whose eyes physically see him may not know who he is. Once the disciples of the Ba'al Shem Tov encountered Elijah at a circumcision (reflecting the belief in Elijah's presence at every circumcision),[22] but he was disguised as a poor person, and they did not recognize him. On the contrary, they suspected him of theft, since he took a Torah scroll out of the study hall, and if the Ba'al Shem Tov had not intervened they would have set about him.[23] So, despite their burning desire to see Elijah, the disciples of the Ba'al Shem Tov never succeeded in identifying him.

[20] Rodkinsohn, *Adat tsadikim*, §11; Zevin, *Hasidic Tales: Festivals* (Heb.), 238–9. Cf. Agnon, *Ha'esh veha'etsim*, 'Fine Stories of R. Israel Ba'al Shem Tov', 97–8. For the appearance of Elijah in the guise of a non-Jew, see BT *Ber. 6b; Midrash rut zuta* 1: 20; *Yalkut rut*, 1, s.v. *hazot naomi*; *Midrash rut zuta* 4: 11; *Yalkut shimoni*, Ruth, 607.

[21] Bodek(?), *Sipurei kedoshim*, §9; Agnon, *Sefer sofer vesipur*, 409. *Continued in Appendix.*

[22] *Pirkei derabi eli'ezer*, ch. 29: *Continued in Appendix.*

[23] J. Sofer, *Sipurei ya'akov*, ii, §50.

Similar episodes are related about others. R. Isaac Eisik Safrin writes in *Megilat setarim* of a time when he was extremely hungry, and his father sent him to their neighbour for some bread.

I was standing there on the threshold, and a non-Jew was sitting there. He asked me: 'My son, do you want bread and strong drink?' and he gave me everything. This was all highly puzzling, but in my great hunger, I was too distracted to understand what all this was. Afterwards, my father told me: 'See, my son, the greatness of your sins, that you merited seeing Elijah only in such a guise.'[24]

R. Solomon Sofer of Dolina related that one of his followers travelled to the Seer of Lublin, to ask the tsadik to show him Elijah.

The rabbi, of blessed memory, directed him: 'Go the ship that is called *pirag* [a ferry], and stand there. Elijah, of blessed mention, will be in the first carriage that travels to the *pirag*.' This hasid went there and waited, and then a certain *poritz* came in a carriage with four horses, driving to the *pirag*. The hasid wondered if this was Elijah, or not. He asked this *poritz* in Polish where he was from. The *poritz* replied: 'One does not speak with a fool', and the hasid went to this rabbi and related this to him. The rabbi explained: 'He spoke well to you, [saying that] you are a fool—why did you speak with him in Polish? You should have greeted him, and asked him to bless you.'[25]

In contrast with the failure of this young man, another succeeded when he asked R. Tsevi of Zhidachov to show him Elijah. The tsadik instructed him:

'On market day, stand next to the house of Abraham Bomel, and when you see a Jew with his loins girded by a rope, go to him and say: "My master, bless me!" And if he tells you: "Leave me, for I shall burn you!", say to him: "The rabbi sent me to you."' The young man went and waited almost the entire day, but no person resembling the description by the tsadik appeared. Close to the afternoon prayers, the young man saw a certain Jew with his loins girded by a rope. He approached the man and said to him: 'My master, bless me!', to which the man responded: 'Leave me, for I shall burn you!' The young man then replied: 'The Grand Rabbi R. Tsevi sent me to you!' Elijah, of blessed mention, then said to him: 'Your Torah shall illuminate the heavens!'[26]

In the next story, told by R. Meir of Premishlan, a failure to identify Elijah leads to thoughts of repentance and reform.

[24] I. Safrin, *Megilat setarim*, 12; Zevin, *Hasidic Tales* (Heb.), 370–1. Elijah also appeared in the guise of a non-Jewish wagon driver when he gave money to the youth Tsevi Elimelekh (the future tsadik of Dynow) (*Ma'asiyot vesiḥot tsadikim*, 25). When the wife of the rabbi of Gostynin was seized by fierce hunger pangs while they were travelling without food, a Jew who sold 'fresh bagels' appeared at the crossroads; her husband was certain that this was Elijah (Rakats, *Siaḥ sarfei kodesh*, i, §192).

[25] *Ma'asiyot vesiḥot tsadikim*, 72. In Rabinovitz, *Ma'aseh neḥemiyah*, 81–2, Elijah appears in the form of a villager who sells a chicken on credit to a village woman; and he appears, in the guise of the Maggid of Stepan, to R. Nehemiah, the son of the 'Holy Jew', when the latter was with the tsadik of Nezkizh (ibid. 92).

[26] Ibid. 73.

When I was a young man, I asked my father, of blessed memory, to show me Elijah, of blessed mention, for I greatly desired to see him. My father, of blessed memory, told me: 'If you study diligently, you will see him.' I sat and studied for a long time, about four weeks, but I did not see him. I complained to my father, of blessed memory: 'Father, did I not request of you, that I desired to see Elijah, of blessed mention?' He responded: 'Go and study.' Once I was sitting in the study hall of my father, of blessed memory, and I thought [i.e. was immersed] in some study, and a ragged pauper came to me, in patchwork, with a strange face, and a large sack over his shoulders. He wanted to set down his bundle in the study hall, but I reproached him, 'My Jewish friend, these are not lodgings for the poor. Go to some teacher, and there you will find lodgings.' The poor man protested, 'But I am very tired, and I want to rest here for a while.' I insisted: 'No! Leave here immediately, lest this anger my father!' As soon as that one had left the study hall, my father, of blessed memory, came there and asked me: 'Did you see Elijah, of blessed mention?' I answered: 'No.' My father, of blessed memory, asked me: 'Was not someone here?' I responded: 'Some indigent was here.' My father, of blessed memory, asked me: 'Did you extend a greeting to him?' I answered: 'No.' My father then told me: 'What have you done, that cannot be amended?' Ever since, I have taken upon myself to greet any poor Jew that I see.[27]

Elijah is depicted in various stories as a deliverer in time of distress, a figure who thwarts anti-Jewish persecutions and protects Jews from danger. The emissary of R. Meir of Premishlan to the tsadik of Butchatch looked around the present company in an attempt to pick out Elijah, but could not identify him. In fact the prophet was there, in the guise of a small person sitting next to the rabbi, and the two annulled an anti-Jewish persecution.[28] The prophet may appear as a non-Jew while fulfilling this function. As noted above, Elijah once dispatched a non-Jew to aid the Ba'al Shem Tov. On another occasion, when the Ba'al Shem Tov and his scribe found themselves on a lonely island and were attacked by brigands, they were rescued by Elijah, who appeared in the guise of the captain of a ship.[29] The Ba'al Shem Tov once sent Elijah, in the guise of a Polish non-Jew, to save R. Gershon of Kutow;[30] at another time, disguised as a German, he rescued two Jews from hanging.[31] Appearing as an Ishmaelite, he delivered R. Gershon when the latter was at sea;[32] and during

[27] *Ma'asiyot vesiḥot tsadikim*, 72.

[28] According to another story, many years ago the rabbi in Jerusalem forgot to give charity for the holiday needs of a poor Torah scholar, and it was decreed in heaven that the city be destroyed, until Elijah mollified the Lord (Shenkel, *Ma'asiyot peliyot*, §14). *Continued in Appendix.*

[29] Rodkinsohn, *Adat tsadikim*, §3. See also Wertheim, *Law and Custom in Hasidism* (Heb.), 176–7.

[30] [Isaac Dov Baer ben Tsevi Hirsch], *Kahal ḥasidim heḥadash*, §33.

[31] *Ma'asiyot vesiḥot tsadikim*, 25. See Brandwein, *Degel maḥaneh yehudah*, §48: Elijah brings a Jew who has no passport across the border.

[32] *Shivḥei habesht*, 70. Cf. Farhi, *Oseh pele*, ii, fo. 72*a*: a youth is stranded on a lonely isle, and Elijah brings him across the ocean.

the time of R. Solomon of Karlin, Elijah acted in the guise of an elderly *poritz* who refused to sign a certain law, thus preventing the enactment of a decree against the Jews.[33]

Elijah is also the harbinger of good tidings, as when he confirmed to a husband who was far from home that his wife had been faithful, and had not succumbed to those who sought to tempt her;[34] and he is the bringer of justice, as when he obtained 20,000 gold roubles from a merchant who had concealed this sum from his partner.[35]

Herzl Bernstein told two people who came to collect money for the redemption of captives how he had become rich. He had once travelled to the fair in Liskovitz with 400 coins in his pocket. When he heard a woman weeping that she had no money to arrange a marriage for her daughter, he gave her all that he had. He then met a dealer in precious stones who gave him copious merchandise on credit, before vanishing without trace the next day. When Bernstein scoured the marketplace in search of this mysterious dealer, people told him not to bother, for it had undoubtedly been Elijah.[36]

When engaged in activities such as these Elijah frequently appears as a pauper (as also in the circumcision story recounted above). Elijah also came to R. Jacob Joseph of Polonnoye in the guise of a simple person,[37] and looked like a mendicant upon leaving the room of R. Israel of Ruzhin.[38] Posing as a beggar, he tried to solicit money from a wealthy man whose son suffered from a mental illness; the son urged the father to support the poor beggar, and the father gave the beggar a handsome donation. Elijah then informed the worried father that at that very moment his son had recovered.[39] Elijah came as a poor person to test a wealthy miser's hospitality, and was thrown out.[40] R. Eliezer, in contrast, withstood a similar trial, and Elijah

[33] Zeilingold, *Me'orot hagedolim*, §11, p. 22. Cf. Moskowitz, *Otsar hasipurim*, v, §11, 27–8. R. Elijah Sternberg told the collector that he had heard from a hasid that R. Solomon ben Yuta (during the time of R. Levi Isaac of Berdichev) was regularly visited by Elijah. Both saw how Elijah, in the guise of an elderly senior government official, sat among the other officials when they discussed an anti-Jewish decree, and stated that he was unwilling to sign the decree; a disagreement erupted, and the edict was rejected.

[34] Sobelman, *Sipurei tsadikim heḥadash*, §4.

[35] Shenkel, *Yeshuot yisra'el*, ii, §18. Two worthies who were waiting before the tsadik's room did not identify Elijah. The tsadik of Ruzhin told them: 'You should regret not having greeted him, and not having gazed on his countenance, for you will not see him again until the advent of the messiah.' Cf. Ze'ev Wolf of Zhitomir, *Or hame'ir*, 9. Elijah revealed himself in the guise of a poor man to R. Aaron Leib the son of R. Meir the Great.

[36] Moskowitz, *Otsar hasipurim*, vol. v. For Elijah in the guise of a householder who gives money to charity, see Kamelhar, *Mevaser tov*, 11.

[37] *Ma'asiyot peliyot nora'im venifla'im*, §10. Cf. Shenkel, *Ma'asiyot peliyot*, 48.

[38] Shenkel, *Niflaot gedolim*, §1. He came as a pauper from the Land of Israel to R. Barukh of Medzibezh (Rapoport, *Divrei david*, fo. 35*a*).

[39] Ehrmann, *Pe'er vekhavod*, fo. 20*b*.

[40] Bodek, *Pe'er mikedoshim*, §8.

promised him a son—the Ba'al Shem Tov; this story was recounted in the previous chapter.[41]

In another story Elijah abrogates a divine decree that had been issued against R. Lieber of Berdichev, a wealthy hasid who was known for his generous hospitality. Once R. Lieber spoke in a sinful manner, and, after the defence put forward on his behalf by Elijah, it was decided in the heavenly court to put him to a test involving the same sin, and enact the decree only if he were to fail this trial. The filthy pauper whom R. Lieber hosted for the sabbath and who gorged himself in a manner not befitting human beings, but without disturbing R. Lieber's equanimity, was none other than Elijah, who had been sent to test him.[42]

In some instances, Elijah comes to teach. Appearing to a cattle merchant as another merchant, he became angry at the latter's not adding the phrase 'God willing' when speaking. Elijah caused the merchant's purse to fall to the ground so that he lost his money and was unable to buy any cattle. After the merchant began to believe in Divine Providence, and no longer ignored heaven when talking, Elijah appeared in the form of a young non-Jew who helped him to drive his cattle through the forest, where the merchant found his lost money.[43]

Elijah plays an important role helping scholars in their studies and delivering halakhic rulings—a motif that was present in earlier rabbinic teachings, and afterwards in the kabbalistic literature. The rabbis portray Elijah's presence in the study hall while the sages are engaged in their learning;[44] he responds to queries that are addressed to him, and at times he himself raises objections.[45] In the stories of the *Mayse bukh*, Elijah teaches Torah to a young man who dwelled in Babylonia,[46] and the kabbalistic literature has him studying with outstanding sages such as R. Shimon bar Yohai and

[41] Kattina, *Raḥamei ha'av*, §3, s.v. *raḥamim* (mercy); [Isaac Dov Baer ben Tsevi Hirsch], *Kahal ḥasidim heḥadash*, §25; Slodovnik, *Ma'aseh hagedolim heḥadash*, §18; Zevin, *Hasidic Tales* (Heb.), 40. Cf. Shenkel, *Ma'asiyot peliyot*, §15; Zeilingold, *Me'orot hagedolim*, §1; and see above, n. 4. *Continued in Appendix.*

[42] Lieberson, *Tseror haḥayim*, §102; Slodovnik, *Ma'aseh hagedolim heḥadash*, §21. *Continued in Appendix.*

[43] Moskowitz, *Otsar hasipurim*, v, §8.

[44] See BT *BM* 85*b*.

[45] See JT *Ber.* 3: 9; *Ruth Rabbah* 4: 1. The rabbis ruled that found articles about which doubt obtains 'shall remain until Elijah comes' (BT *BM* 20*a*, and elsewhere), and the well-known phrase *teko* ('tie', 'draw', in modern Hebrew) that is applied to unresolved halakhic issues is understood as being an acronym for *tishbi yetarets kushiyot uve'ayot* ('the Tishbite [i.e. Elijah] will solve difficulties and problems') (see I. Horowitz, *Shenei luḥot haberit*, 'Oral Law'; Yom Tov Lipmann Heller, *Tosefot yom tov* on Mishnah, *Edu.* 8: 7).

[46] *Mayse bukh* (Amsterdam, 1723), §222; (Nuremburg, 1763), fo. 71*a*. For the student who abandoned his Torah studies because he was not accorded respect, resumed his studies following Elijah's assurance that he would earn wealth and honour, came to realize that these were not true values, and then studied Torah for its own sake, see Shenkel, *Ma'asim tovim*, §8.

R. Isaac Luria.[47] One way in which the hasidic story expresses the greatness of the Ba'al Shem Tov is by showing Elijah learning Torah from him.[48] In the majority of instances the prophet teaches and studies with various individuals. For example, he studied with R. Hayim ben Bezalel (the brother of the Maharal of Prague), when he was in seclusion in a small house in Krakow, but he refused to study with R. Moses Isserles, because the prophet insisted upon studying with the humble, and not with the excessively strict or proud.[49] Elijah taught R. Jacob Joseph of Polonnoye an interpretation of the verse from Psalms (22: 4), 'You are holy, enthroned on the praises of Israel';[50] he studied regularly with R. Joshua of Dynow, the teacher of R. Tsevi Elimelekh of Dynow;[51] and he also studied with the Seer of Lublin.[52] R. Joshua of Belz heard words of Torah from an old man in a dream, before hearing the same teaching from his father, R. Shalom, during a Purim feast. When his father concluded his disquisition, he asked his son: 'Did I state everything as you heard it from the old man [who was none other than the prophet Elijah]?' R. Joshua added that this was one of the many times he sensed the presence of Elijah with his father.[53]

Elijah studied every night with a repentant Jew,[54] and also with R. Moses of Pshevorsk, when the latter was still a concealed tsadik. He told R. Moses when the time had come to reveal himself;[55] he continued to come to

[47] For Shimon bar Yohai, see *Zohar ḥadash*, 'Ki tavo'; also see E. Margaliot, *Elijah the Prophet* (Heb.), 119 ff. *Continued in Appendix.*

[48] R. Jacob Kaidaner writes in his introduction to *Metsaref ha'avodah*, fo. 3*b*, concerning the Ba'al Shem Tov: 'The heavenly angels longed for his teachings, and Elijah, of blessed memory, came to him, to hear Torah from his mouth.'

[49] Rodkinsohn, *Adat tsadikim*, §22; Shenkel, *Niflaot gedolim*, §2. Elijah also revealed himself to R. Jonathan Eybeschuetz; see I. Safrin, 'Netiv mitsvoteikha', 'Shevil emunah', 6, 16*b*; Shenkel, *Sipurei anshei shem*, §5. R. Sender (Alexander) Margoliouth, on the other hand, did not desire 'to interrupt his study and greet him [Elijah]', until his father came to him in a dream and reproached him. See A. Walden, *Shem hagedolim heḥadash*, ch. 60, §3.

[50] Rakats, *Siaḥ sarfei kodesh*, iv, fo. 71*b*; Moskowitz, *Otsar hasipurim*, i. 9–10. When Elijah revealed himself to R. Abraham Zak of Sharigrad and the Ba'al Shem Tov as they studied together, he joined them in their studies. See M. H. Landau, *Ma'amar mordekhai*, introd., 6.

[51] Berger, *Eser tsaḥtsaḥot*, 'R. Tsevi Elimelekh of Dynow', §10. Cf. Ehrmann, *Devarim arevim*, 'Stories of the Holy Rabbi, Our Master and Teacher, R. Tsevi Elimelekh of Dynow', §16. It was said that Elijah revealed himself to R. Aaron Leib, the son of R. Meir the Great, in order to learn with him the esoteric teachings of the Torah, and to open the gates of wisdom, 'but he refused, claiming that he wanted to learn from the mouth of the Holy One, blessed be He, himself' (R. Margaliot, *Or hame'ir*, 9). *Arba'ah arazim*, 108, has a different version: he wanted to study with Ahijah the Shilonite.

[52] See M. M. Walden, *Or haniflaot*, §84.

[53] A. Michelson, *Dover shalom*, §36.

[54] Sobelman, *Sipurei tsadikim heḥadash*, §2.

[55] Bodek(?), *Sipurei kedoshim*, §17; *Mifalot hatsadikim*, §13; Slodovnik, *Ma'aseh hagedolim heḥadash*, §13. Cf. [Isaac Dov Baer ben Tsevi Hirsch], *Kahal ḥasidim heḥadash*, §117. Elijah also studied with R. Abraham Abusch of Frankfurt, when the latter lived as a hidden tsadik in a village near Kariv in the Lublin district (A. Michelson, *Ohel avraham*, §40). Elijah and Elisha came every day to a hidden tsadik who lived during the time of R. Elimelekh of Lizhensk and who was the head of the rabbinical court of a small city (Rakats, *Siaḥ sarfei kodesh*, iv, §48).

R. Moses after the latter had began to act openly, but ceased his visits when R. Moses lost his generosity. Only when he regained this virtue did Elijah return to R. Moses.[56]

When scholars identify a problem and manage to resolve it, they believe that they have been helped by Elijah's presence in the study hall.[57] A young man possessing a sterling character was said to study with Elijah,[58] and the Ba'al Shem Tov declared that a certain preacher learned from the prophet.[59] In other cases, a revelation of Elijah occurs as the result of study: R. Zusya of Hanipoli told R. Nahum of Chernobyl that R. Joseph Karo was revealed to him in a dream, and informed R. Zusya that if he diligently studied the *Beit yosef* (by R. Karo) and completed this commentary within a year, Elijah would be revealed to him. R. Nahum's son R. Moses followed such a regimen of study, and was rewarded with *gilui eliyahu*.[60]

When individuals were compelled by circumstances to cease their Torah study, Elijah would be sent to enable them to continue learning. R. Samuel Shmelke of Nikolsburg once fell asleep while studying at night, and his light was extinguished. When he awoke, he was sorry for having fallen asleep, and searched for someone to rekindle his light. Some time later, it

[56] Rakats, *Siaḥ sarfei kodesh*, iv, §48; Slodovnik, *Ma'aseh hagedolim heḥadash*, §15. For the instance mentioned in the Talmud, in which Elijah stopped coming to a certain pious individual, see BT *BB 7b*. Cf. Berger, *Eser tsaḥtsaḥot*, 'R. Tsevi Elimelekh of Dynow', §10: Elijah would regularly come to study with R. Joshua, the head of the Dynow rabbinical court, but ceased doing so because R. Joshua did not protest against the disparaging comments directed against R. Tsevi Elimelekh.

[57] J. Sofer, *Sipurei ya'akov*, i, §24. By his very sabbath eve Amidah prayer, Elijah offered a hundred resolutions for a difficult question that had troubled R. Menahem Mendel of Kotsk for twenty-two years (Rakats, *Siaḥ sarfei kodesh*, ii, §373). Elijah revealed to R. Zusya the resolution of a difficult Tosafot, so that he would not be shamed by the scholars. When the latter expressed their wonder at R. Zusya's erudition, he disclosed that he had heard the answer from Elijah (*Arba'ah arazim*, 103–4).

[58] J. Sofer, *Sipurei ya'akov*, ii, §59. Cf. *Mayse bukh* (Amsterdam, 1723), §229, for Elijah studying with a certain young man in one of the Babylonian yeshivot.

[59] Shenkel, *Ma'asiyot peliyot*, §7. Cf. Gemen, *Sifran shel tsadikim*, ch. 3, §2: R. Barukh of Medzibezh told of an old man with whom Elijah studied. Cf. also Brawer, *Pe'er yitsḥak*, ch. 9, §3: R. Isaac Eisik of Zhidachov maintained that one was not to expound in public unless 'he had received [these teachings] from Elijah, or, at the least, from a rabbi who had received from him'. He testified of himself that he had received them from a rabbi who had learned Torah from Elijah.

[60] Chikernik, *Ma'asiyot uma'amarim yekarim*, 20; cf. Lieberson, *Tseror haḥayim*, §140. R. Nahum of Chernobyl learned from Elijah how to effect a *tikun* for a 'youthful sin' (i.e. nocturnal pollution) (Weberman, *Derekh tsadikim*, 18, in the name of the end of *Binyan yehoshua*). R. Pinhas of Ginivishov thirsted to study from the book *Tana devei eliyahu*, but he was too poor to purchase it. Elijah manifested himself as a bookseller, who left books with R. Pinhas for him to peruse. When R. Pinhas unsuccessfully searched for the bookseller, the Maggid of Koznitz divulged to him that it was Elijah who had given him his book (Rosenthal, *Hitgalut hatsadikim*, 61).

was revealed to him from heaven that Elijah had been sent to perform this task.[61]

According to another story, Elijah was revealed to R. Samuel Shmelke every night. This was pointed out by the beadle to the important members of the Nikolsburg community, to increase their esteem for the rabbi, whom they sought to expel from the city. In repeating the story, R. Simhah Bunem of Pshischa stressed the humility of the beadle, who saw Elijah every night himself but publicly aggrandized R. Samuel Shmelke on account of the nightly revelations of Elijah that he experienced without mentioning his own nightly revelations.[62]

The traditional belief in Elijah's presence at circumcisions is firmly anchored in classical Jewish sources and features in pre-hasidic tales. According to *Shivḥei ha'ari*, Elijah informed R. Solomon Luria of the birth of his son, the future R. Isaac Luria,[63] but commanded him not to circumcise the infant until he appeared to him.[64] R. Solomon was publicly castigated for delaying the circumcision, but he paid no heed to such protest. Elijah finally appeared to R. Solomon and the latter arranged for the circumcision to take place; Elijah sat on the father's lap before the infant was placed on the latter's knees for the circumcision, and was thus able to hold the infant during the ceremony, but without being seen by any of those in attendance.

The hasidic story accepts Elijah's presence at circumcisions as axiomatic. His encounter with the disciples of the Ba'al Shem Tov at such a ceremony was mentioned earlier in this chapter. R. Gedaliah of Zelechow was about to perform a circumcision and was looking for a man to act as *sandak* and hold the baby during the procedure; he thought that the cobbler facing him was Elijah, the 'angel of circumcision' (because he comes to every such ceremony), when in fact he was the patriarch Abraham.[65] Another tale, which

[61] This story was related by the tsadik's sister Miriam to R. Abraham Joshua Heschel of Apta and R. Ephraim Yehiel Mikhel of the Nimsk community in Moldavia. See T. J. Horowitz, *Semikhut mosheh*, 'introduction by the author's grandson'; Joseph ben R. A., *Mifalot tsadikim heḥadash*, 4–5; Kleinmann, *Mazkeret shem gedolim*, 60–1; Shenkel, *Ma'asim tovim*, fo. 1*a*; Moskowitz, *Otsar hasipurim*, i. 10–11. For the miracle of a candle that burned the entire night for the Maggid of Koznitz, see Bromberg, *Toledot haniflaot*, 34.

[62] Tzitrin, *Shivḥei tsadikim*, §75, fo. 26*a*: 'A Tale of the Holy Rabbi, Rabbi R. Shmelke, of Blessed Memory'.

[63] Solomon of Dreznitz, *Shivḥei ha'ari*, fo. 1*b*. See *Sefer hakavanot uma'asei nisim*, fo. 2*b*; Benayahu, *Sefer toledot ha'ari*, 95–6, 152. Cf. the influence of *Shivḥei ha'ari* on a story in the non-hasidic work *Gedolim ma'asei hashem*, 31. *Continued in Appendix.*

[64] Cf. Shenkel, *Yeshuot yisra'el*, ii, §18: Elijah commands a young man not to wed until his arrival (see below, n. 66).

[65] [Isaac Dov Baer ben Tsevi Hirsch], *Kahal ḥasidim heḥadash*, §138; Moskowitz, *Otsar hasipurim*, i. 5–6. In a pre-hasidic story, Elijah and the fathers of the Israelite people come together to a wedding. See *Mayse bukh* (London, n.d.), §169; for a householder who imagined the tsadik Israel Isaac of Warka, who gave money for the dowry of a villager's daughter, to be Elijah, see Samlung, *Eser zekhuyot*, §21.

was printed in the *Mayse bukh*,[66] exerted great influence upon the hasidic storytelling genre. Once an infant was brought to the synagogue for circumcision, and the entire congregation arose and recited the customary *barukh haba* greeting to the newborn. R. Judah Hehasid, the intended *sandak*, did not, however, rise from his seat. When asked why, he replied that he had not seen Elijah enter with the infant, nor had he seen him sitting on the Chair of Elijah (named in honour of the prophet, where the baby is placed momentarily). According to the explanation given in the tale, when this child would grow up, an evil spirit would come over him, and he would seek to convert.

According to the hasidic variant of this tale, R. Samuel Shmelke of Nikolsburg did not want to accept the role of *sandak* because he did not see Elijah, from which he understood that the newborn was a *mamzer*. The father of the infant, a wealthy and powerful individual, threatened to expel the tsadik from the city if his accusation were not confirmed, and his wife also profusely cursed R. Samuel Shmelke. A dead person, who was summoned to give testimony in the matter, stood behind the partition in the synagogue and declared: 'I did, indeed, do such-and-such, and I committed adultery with her several times. This infant that was born to her is from me.' The dead person requested, and received, a *tikun* for his soul.[67]

Seeing Elijah in a dream (as opposed to seeing him while awake) is a relatively low level of prophecy. Inherent in the story that attests that Elijah came in a dream to the Ba'al Shem Tov is the assumption that this was merely an early phase of the Ba'al Shem Tov's career, after which he met Elijah many times face-to-face. Along with the many who merited seeing Elijah while awake, numerous other individuals had such an experience only while dreaming. Elijah came in a dream to R. Isaac Luria's nephew, commanding him to delay his wedding ceremony until the entry of the prophet.[68] In his dream a repentant tailor saw Elijah, who informed him that his sin had been forgiven.[69] Elijah came in a dream to a synagogue beadle,

[66] *Mayse bukh* (Amsterdam, 1723), §185. Similar stories were later told by R. Abraham Abusch of Frankfurt (a contemporary of the Ba'al Shem Tov). Once he refused to serve as *sandak*, saying: 'If Elijah the prophet is here, I am [willing to be] here [as the *sandak*]; and if Elijah the prophet is not here, the son is undoubtedly flawed [i.e. the issue of a forbidden union].' And it transpired that the latter was the case. See A. Michelson, *Ohel avraham*, §§16, 27, 42: the mother had been raped by a non-Jew; and in §21 the wife of a Frankfurt worthy confessed that her child had been fathered by an army officer.

[67] A. Michelson, *Dover shalom*, 46; Slodovnik, *Ma'aseh hagedolim heḥadash*, §28. Cf. a similar story, without Elijah, in *Shivḥei habesht*, 181.

[68] Shenkel, *Yeshuot yisra'el*, ii, §18. According to another version of the story, the holy forefathers of the Jewish people, including Elijah, taught the revealed and esoteric Torah to R. Isaac Luria's nephew in a forest, and even restored his sight after he went blind. They commanded the youth not to wed until their arrival, and Elijah, in the guise of a shepherd, was the first to arrive on his wedding day. See Bodek(?), *Sipurei kedoshim*, §1.

[69] Sobelman, *Sipurei tsadikim heḥadash*, §2.

whom he requested to open the synagogue doors.[70] R. Isaac Judah Yehiel Safrin attests that he once saw 'a spark of Elijah, of blessed mention, in a dream, and I asked of him: "My lord, greet me!" and he greeted me.'[71]

One exceptionally puzzling tale is told, citing as its source Abraham Mehudar's book *Zekhor le'avraham*. Before his death, the rabbi of Lublin commanded the heads of the community to consult with the first person to die after him regarding his (the rabbi's) successor. The first mortally ill patient to be found after the death of the rabbi was a poor tailor, who claimed that he had no idea what the community's leaders wanted from him. Eventually, he sent them to Ostrog, to take that community's rabbi as their spiritual leader. He instructed then that if the rabbi of Ostrog were to refuse, they were to tell him that the tailor so-and-so of Lublin commanded him to accept the position. When the rabbi of Ostrog learned of the tailor's death, he was very grieved, and accepted the proffered position. To the surprise of the delegation of worthies from Lublin, the rabbi told them how he made the acquaintance of the tailor. Once when he was alone in the study hall, the rabbi saw before him the tailor, who explained that the prophet Elijah had dispatched him to the rabbi, to tell him to lose no time in correcting a certain wrongdoing in the city. The rabbi insisted upon meeting Elijah as a condition for his acting, and despite the tailor's warning that he would be seized by fear and trembling, the rabbi was steadfast in his demand. The tailor passed a handkerchief over the rabbi's face, and when the latter saw Elijah, he became terrified and fell to the ground in a faint.[72]

In addition to the motifs discussed above, this last story also contains the element of Elijah employing agents, in this case, one of the thirty-six hidden righteous. It is not inconceivable that these two motifs, that of Elijah and the hidden righteous, became intertwined in the hasidic story-telling genre, because of their many shared elements: Elijah, like the hidden tsadikim, is not recognized; both Elijah and the hidden tsadikim act on behalf of others.

70 Ibid.

71 I. Safrin, *Megilat setarim*, 23. Cf. Ze'ev Wolf of Zhitomir, *Or hame'ir*, 10–11 (in the name of Kattina, *Raḥamei ha'av*).

72 See *Sipurei tsadikim*, 36–9, which argues that the story was copied from Mehudar, *Zekhor le'avraham*. For an abridged and different version of the tale, see Y.D. of Sudilkov, *Temimei derekh*, fo. 26*a*–*b*.

SEVENTEEN

THE BA'AL SHEM TOV'S UNSUCCESSFUL PILGRIMAGE TO THE LAND OF ISRAEL

A LITTLE-KNOWN and mysterious chapter in the life story of the Ba'al Shem Tov is his unsuccessful pilgrimage to the Land of Israel. Some of the narrative sources tell the tale in detail; others are terse, casting light only on part of the attempted journey and its failure. Scholars have occasionally touched upon the subject,[1] but so far no one has assembled the extant narrative material or compared its parallel formulations and different versions.

The various tales certainly do not add up to a historical documentation of the episode, although the perceptive historian will surely be able to discern the historical facts between the lines of legend. Sometimes, later publications preserve older oral traditions, and hence are more valuable than earlier ones. That the various storytellers, editors, and publishers have added to and deleted from the original content of the tales is quite likely, considering the sensitivity of the subject, namely, the failure of the Ba'al Shem Tov to achieve his intended *aliyah* (literally, 'going up', 'ascent': pilgrimage to the Land of Israel). In this connection we should note Abraham Ya'ari's comment that the 1815 Hebrew version of *Shivḥei habesht* deliberately conceals the failure of the attempt and makes no mention of the journey where some reference to it would have been expected.[2]

Several motifs recur in the hasidic tales in connection with the Ba'al Shem Tov's pilgrimage. Some tales contain just one of them, others combine several. These motifs are:

[1] See A. Ya'ari, 'Three Yiddish Translations' (Heb.); id., 'Two Basic Recensions' (Heb.), 249–72. Ya'ari refers to Drohobitcher's article 'Three Versions' (Heb.), 41–2. In addition to the tales in Rodkinsohn, *Adat tsadikim*, and I. Safrin, 'Netiv mitsvoteikha', discussed in this chapter, Drohobitcher presents version 1, which was told by his family and was based on the various tales presented here. See also Werfel, *Hasidism and the Land of Israel* (Heb.), 11–19. The tales of the Ba'al Shem Tov's *aliyah* have been translated into Yiddish; see Bastomski, *Yiddish Folktales* (Heb.), i. 137–41. Cf. A. Stern, *Ḥutim hameshulashim*, 36–9.

[2] Ya'ari, 'Two Basic Recensions' (Heb.), 261.

(*a*) the motives for the journey;

(*b*) the preparations;

(*c*) the hardships encountered upon the journey and the stay in Istanbul;

(*d*) the spiritual crisis and the physical failures;

(*e*) the overcoming of these failures, the rescue from danger, and the return to spiritual heights;

(*f*) the Ba'al Shem Tov's return home;

(*g*) R. Nahman of Bratslav's pilgrimage.

There is no apparent reason to doubt that the Ba'al Shem Tov did indeed attempt to go to the Holy Land, or that he embarked upon the journey. In respect of his motives, the hasidic tale did not need to spell them out: the yearning for Zion had stirred the hearts of Jews throughout the ages, although few were able to turn the dream into reality. However, according to these tales the Ba'al Shem Tov had an additional particular reason for undertaking his journey: it was explicitly connected with his intention to hasten the redemption and the coming of the messiah. According to hasidic belief, a meeting between the Ba'al Shem Tov and R. Hayim ben Atar, the author of *Or haḥayim* (The Light of Life), who lived in the Land of Israel—a meeting which the Ba'al Shem Tov particularly sought—would have hastened this end. R. Judah Tsevi Hirsch of Stretin relates that the Ba'al Shem Tov wished to obtain the copy of the Book of Psalms in the handwriting of King David which was kept in 'the royal treasury' (apparently the library of the Sultan of Turkey). With this book he intended to go to R. Hayim ben Atar and 'then the messiah, our redeemer, will come'.[3]

R. Hayim ben Atar was greatly admired by the teachers of hasidism. Their frequent quotations from *Or haḥayim* attest to their admiration for the work,[4] an admiration which subsequently grew to the extent that the work was compared to the Zohar. R. David Moses of Chortkov relates (in the name of his father, R. Israel of Ruzhin) that, just as the holy Zohar initially had the power to purify the soul, so the holy *Or haḥayim* had the power to throw light on the Torah and thus purify the soul.[5] He adds that the students

[3] Cf. J. Sofer, *Sipurei ya'akov*, ii, §34, pt 2. Drohobitcher's version (see n. 1) also mentions 'scriptures' which the Ba'al Shem Tov acquired in Istanbul, but was forced to throw into the sea in the tempest.

[4] Cf. e.g. Moses Hayim Ephraim of Sudilkov, *Degel maḥaneh efrayim*, 'Vayetse', 'Vayishlaḥ', 'Devarim', 'Ki tavo'. I have failed to find references that would validate Aron Markus's opinion that the Ba'al Shem Tov declared the *Or haḥayim*, rather than the Zohar, to be the basic statement of hasidic belief.

[5] Cf. Rapoport, *Divrei david*, 22*a*. Markus writes (*Hasidism* (Heb.), 219) that R. Israel of Ruzhin instructed R. Menahem Mendel of Kosov to study *Or haḥayim* instead of the Zohar.

of the tsadik of Ruzhin were required to study a part of *Or haḥayim* every week.

Stories about R. Hayim ben Atar circulated widely among the hasidim. He was said to be the *tsadik hador* (the tsadik of his generation),[6] and it was said that his wife followed the practice (unusual for women) of putting on *tefilin*, as Saul's daughter Michal did.[7] R. Hayim ben Atar was believed to have met the legendary great figures of the lost Ten Tribes,[8] and to have given the Hida (R. Hayim Joseph David Azulai) a letter to place in the cracks of the Western Wall,[9] in order to hasten the redemption of Israel. A letter left in the Western Wall is obviously addressed to the Divine Presence, since that wall is the only place on earth where the Divine Presence constantly resides. However, R. Hayim Joseph forgot to carry out his commission, no doubt because of interference by the Sitra Ahra. A related tale of non-hasidic origin runs as follows: 'When R. Hayim ben Atar in his prayer prostrated himself before the Wall, he saw a woman in black before him. She was an evil spirit (*kelipah*), and she informed him that she had been hunting him for a full year. Within a year R. Hayim died.'[10] He had not been granted permission to see the Shekhinah (the Divine Presence)—which at times takes the form of a woman[11]—at the Wall, nor was any other sign of redemption vouchsafed to him.[12] On the contrary, an evil spirit, representing the power of Satan, showed itself to him, and he, who would have been worthy of bringing an end to the suffering of Israel, passed away.

It is possible that even in their lifetimes the Ba'al Shem Tov and R. Hayim ben Atar (1696–1743) were considered the leading lights of their generation, who would bring redemption to Israel. In a later generation, Michael Levi Rodkinsohn quoted (in the name of his father Alexander Frumkin, who

[6] J. Sofer, *Sipurei ya'akov*, ii, §5. On legends of R. Hayim ben Atar see Tabori, 'Our Master Hayim ben Atar' (Heb.), and Nigal, 'In Praise of R. Hayim ben Atar' (Heb.).

[7] Cf. Shenkel, *Noraot anshei ma'aseh*, §2; Gaon, *Oriental Jews*, 516. Concerning Michal, Saul's daughter, wearing *tefilin*, see *Mekhilta*, 'Bo', 'Masakhta dipasḥa', par. 17; JT *Ber.* 2: 3; BT *Eruv.* 96*a*. [8] J. Sofer, *Sipurei ya'akov*, §6. Cf. Shenkel, *Noraot anshei ma'aseh*, 10–11.

[9] J. Sofer, *Sipurei ya'akov*, §5.

[10] Cf. *Midrash tehilim* 11: 3. R. Abraham Halevi Bruhim saw the Divine Presence in the shape of a woman at the wall. See Assaf, 'Letters from Safed' (Heb.), 123; Benayahu, *Sefer toledot ha'ari*, 49–53.

[11] Cf. Na'im, *Malkhei rabanan*, fo. 35*a*. One of the tales (which originates in Knafo, *Ot berit kodesh*, fo. 10*a*) is about a lion which is about to tear him into pieces in the desert. 'He [R. Hayim] revealed his holy covenant and when the lion saw it he fled from the sight . . . because R. Hayim had never seen *keri* [nocturnal emission].' Cf. Markus, *Hasidism* (Heb.), 317–18.

[12] As opposed to R. Abraham Halevi, a student of R. Isaac Luria (see above, n. 10). Cf. Popirsh, *Or tsadikim*, 'Amud ha'avodah', ch. 17, and Azulai, *Shem hagedolim*, i, §69; I. Safrin, 'Netiv mitsvoteikha', 'Shevil hayiḥud', §4; [Isaac Dov Baer ben Tsevi Hirsch], *Kahal ḥasidim heḥadash*, §106; Shenkel, *Ma'asiyot nora'im venifla'im*, §17: on the eve of Shavuot the Divine Presence, adorned with twenty-four adornments, revealed itself to R. Levi Isaac of Berdichev.

passed them on in the name of his teacher) the Ba'al Shem Tov's words about R. Hayim: 'It is not that he is greater than I am, but he is quicker, because to whatever worlds I ascend, I am told that the author of *Or haḥayim* has just left.'[13] The first to write at length about the connection between the Ba'al Shem Tov and R. Hayim ben Atar was R. Isaac Eizik Safrin of Komarno, who was also the first to ascribe a role in the failure of the planned meeting to the forces of evil. He states that the Sitra Ahra strives to mislead the righteous by setting up all kinds of inimical people against them. In this context R. Isaac Eizik mentions R. Hayim ben Atar, and continues:

Our master the Ba'al Shem Tov said to the holy rabbi [and author of] *Or haḥayim* that his soul was a spark of David's noble spirit, and that every night he was taught Torah from the lips of the Lord, attaining holiness. He was one of the *yoredei merkavah* [mystics; literally, those who have descended from the Heavenly Chariot], able to reveal souls, and was inspired by the Holy Spirit. And our master [the Ba'al Shem Tov], who was of David's noble soul, desired that the soul and spirit should be united and that the higher soul [*neshamah*] should be revealed, thereby bringing the redemption. The Ba'al Shem Tov asked R. Hayim ben Atar through his brother-in-law, the holy R. Gershon of Kutow, whether it was possible for him, the Ba'al Shem Tov, to go to Jerusalem and meet R. Hayim face to face. R. Hayim replied that the Ba'al Shem Tov should let him know whether or not he could see all his limbs and features. The holy teacher answered that he could not see his heels. R. Hayim ben Atar replied that the Ba'al Shem Tov should not trouble himself, because his efforts would be in vain. But the master did not receive this letter, and placing his soul in the hands of the Lord, he set out on the journey. Although he was told by heaven not to go, he decided to imperil himself, and left that winter.[14]

Similarly, Menahem Mendel Bodek writes:

There are different versions concerning the great journey of the Ba'al Shem Tov (blessed be his memory) to the Holy Land to meet with the holy rabbi who wrote the book *Or haḥayim* (blessed be his memory): I was told by a hasid (who had heard it from the holy R. Judah Tsevi Hirsch of Stretin, an outstanding student of the holy and awesome R. Uri of Strelisk, of blessed memory), that the godly Ba'al Shem Tov, blessed be his memory, and the godly [author of] *Or haḥayim*, blessed be his memory, one of whom had the soul of David and the spirit of Solomon, and

[13] Rodkinsohn, *Toledot ba'alei shem tov*, 70 n. 24; Beckmeister, *Sipurei niflaot migedolei yisra'el*, §2. Cf. also Israel ben Sason, *Likutei ma'asiyot*, fos *2a*, *4a–9a*, presents a tale which shows the impact of §12 in Bodek(?), *Sipurei kedoshim*.

[14] I. Safrin, 'Netiv mitsvoteikha', 'Shevil emunah', §1, fo. *4a*. The story is copied in Sperling, *Reasons for the Customs* (Heb.), 292, and in [Isaac Dov Baer ben Tsevi Hirsch], *Kahal ḥasidim heḥadash*, §23. For tales about R. Gershon's meeting with R. Hayim ben Atar, see ibid., §§25–9; I. Landau, *Zikhron tov*, 'Me'avodat hatsadikim', §8; Shenkel, *Noraot anshei ma'aseh*, 12–13. It is, however, doubtful whether R. Gershon of Kutow and R. Hayim ben Atar ever met, since at the time of R. Gershon's *aliyah* in 1747 R. Hayim was no longer alive (he died in 1743). See also Barnai, 'Notes on the Immigration of R. Abraham Gershon Kutower' (Heb.).

the other the soul of Solomon and the spirit of David, loved each other greatly. Had the soul approached the spirit—redemption would have come. Therefore the Ba'al Shem Tov was prevented by heaven, and he was not able to meet with the holy author of *Or haḥayim*, blessed be his memory.[15]

These two hasidic tales link the Ba'al Shem Tov's desire to meet R. Hayim ben Atar with messianic motivations; hence it is clear why Satan placed obstacles in his way. However, while R. Isaac Eizik sees the Sitra Ahra as the cause of the difficulties,[16] Menahem Mendel Bodek speaks of his being 'prevented by heaven'.

Proof that plans existed for the journey is found in the historically reliable story about wealthy leaseholders of Slutsk.[17] A passage here describes the precise plans of the Ba'al Shem Tov and his preparations for the journey to the Land of Israel. The Ba'al Shem Tov seems to have accepted an invitation from the wife of one of the aforesaid leaseholders of Slutsk, and to have made the long journey to Lithuania in the hope of interesting these rich men in financing his travels. In *Shivḥei habesht* the narrator tells us that one of the leaseholders, named Samuel, arranged a meal in honour of his guest the Ba'al Shem Tov and that during the meal the following conversation took place:

[The Ba'al Shem Tov] spoke to him about going to the Holy Land and that he preferred to travel by land. And the leaseholder asked the Ba'al Shem Tov: 'How much do you require in expenses for that?' And he answered that he would need a sum of a thousand [zloty] for expenses. And he replied: 'For me, that is a trifle!' And he promised to send him money annually for his support. The Ba'al Shem Tov answered that he was not concerned with maintenance; the essential thing was to be fortunate enough to merit going to the Holy Land.[18]

This story presents two facts that require further investigation: first, the Ba'al Shem Tov's desire to travel by land; and second, his renunciation of continuing financial support, without which it was virtually impossible to live in the Land of Israel in those days. The latter may be explained by the Ba'al Shem Tov's deep faith in divine succour; however, the former does give rise to questions. Did he originally intend to travel from Constantinople to the Land of Israel by land, or did this story arise later, as a reflection on the misfortunes that befell him during his sea voyage? And if he did initially intend to avoid travelling by sea, could the reason have been fear of drowning?

[15] Bodek, *Seder hadorot heḥadash*, 3*b*. Note that even the tale in J. Sofer, *Sipurei ya'akov*, is told by R. Judah Tsevi of Stretin. For a tale with a similar motif, see *Shivḥei habesht*, ed. Horodezky, 82: R. Eliezer of Amsterdam goes on *aliyah* to meet R. Nahman of Horodenka, saying, 'When we will both be in the Holy Land we shall bring the redeemer.'

[16] See I. Safrin, 'Netiv mitsvoteikha', 'Shevil emunah', §1, fo. 4*a*. See Drohobitcher, 'Three Versions' (Heb.): 'And as they were on the ship the Ba'al Shem Tov saw Satan, who said to him: "Wherefore do you pass me by—lest with sword I came out against you!"'

[17] See Halpern, 'The Wozczylo Revolt' (Heb.).

[18] *Shivḥei habesht*, 133.

In a story that describes an occurrence during the Ba'al Shem Tov's seclusion in a mountain retreat, there are clear indications of the great danger he encountered and of how close he came to catastrophe.

Robbers once came to him and said: 'Our master, we know a shorter way for you to get to the Land of Israel, a way through caves and burrows. If you wish, go with us and we shall be your guides to show you the way.' And he agreed to go with them. As they were going they came to a deep ravine, filled with water and mud and mire. In order to cross the ravine they had to walk over a plank, supporting themselves on a pole which they stuck into the water, and when the Ba'al Shem Tov attempted to cross on the plank he beheld a flaming sword which turned every way. He retreated, for he knew that he would have encountered grave danger in crossing that plank.[19]

According to *Shivḥei habesht* the robbers probably wanted to reward the Ba'al Shem Tov, who had served them as arbitrator and judge in a dispute among themselves, by helping him to reach the Land of Israel. Their offer to take him through a short cut over land may be interpreted as an indication of the Ba'al Shem Tov's fear of the ocean, or alternatively it may be a gloss on the story, composed after the failure of his attempt. The crisis of that journey involves the dangers of spiritual descent and physical drowning. The end result is that the Ba'al Shem Tov returns the way he had come. This tale indicates that the departure, as well as the whole attempted pilgrimage, was a transgression against a divine prohibition. The symbolic figure of the flaming sword which turned every way (*lahat haḥerev hamithapekhet*) echoes that which was placed at the entrance to the Garden of Eden,[20] to prevent man's return to the place from which he was exiled.

It could be argued that the story about the robbers is merely a transposition of a similar crisis experienced by the Ba'al Shem Tov later on his sea journey, and that it serves to indicate another, earlier, attempt by him to get to the Land of Israel. Nevertheless, the stories about the attempt and its failure are not a late invention of the hasidim; they were widespread in the Ba'al Shem Tov's own lifetime.

The Ba'al Shem Tov's journey undoubtedly involved many hardships. According to the hasidic stories he did depart, accompanied by his daughter

[19] Ibid. 48. Cf. also the literary use by Agnon, 'Bilevav yamim', in id., *Elu ve'elu*, 539: 'And Hanania said to the *goy*: "Was it not you who wanted to bring me to the Land of Israel through a cave?" He answered: "Yes, that was me."' The above tale in *Shivḥei habesht* has a parallel in I. Safrin, *Megilat setarim*, 34: 'The robbers, who feared the Ba'al Shem Tov, turned to him with a suggestion: "Holy man, if you wish—go with us on a shorter way to the Holy Land."' In this version the Ba'al Shem Tov accepts the offer: 'and he went with them and they came to a narrow and dangerous passage, and he did not want to rely on a miracle, and turned back.'

[20] Cf. Gen. 3: 24. In the kabbalah this sword symbolizes the *sefirah* of Binah. See Zohar, ii. 27*b* (*tosefta*): 'Binah turns from judgement to mercy'; Vital, *Sha'ar hapesukim*, 'Bereshit', 18, on the passage *vayegaresh et-ha'adam*; Vital, *Ets ḥayim*, §43, ch. 1.

Odel and his two scribes, R. Tsevi Sofer and R. Judah Leib Sofer, and most versions record that he reached Constantinople.[21] In most of the tales the Ba'al Shem Tov spends some time in Constantinople, around Passover.[22] In spite of the many discrepancies, the various stories have one thing in common: they all dwell on the hardships encountered by the Ba'al Shem Tov in the city. Even the Hebrew version of *Shivḥei habesht*, which seeks to avoid the subject of the pilgrimage, contains an odd story which takes place in Constantinople and presents the Ba'al Shem Tov in a strange and unpleasant light.[23] It concerns the mother of a blind child who did not believe in the power of the holy names and scorned the Ba'al Shem Tov; the Ba'al Shem Tov temporarily healed the boy but then caused his blindness to return as punishment for the woman's lack of faith.[24]

The tsadik of Komarno describes how the Ba'al Shem Tov was forced to flee for fear of the authorities: 'During the Passover holiday he was in the city of Constantinople and there he performed wonders and miracles, until this became known in the emperor's palace, and steps were taken, so that he had to make his escape on a ship.'[25] Although the narrator offers no explanation, it is reasonable to surmise that he is not referring to acts of healing the sick and the wretched, but rather to punishing the wicked and thereby hastening the end of sin in the world and the coming of the messiah. A different story about how the Ba'al Shem Tov spent his time in Constantinople is given in Jacob Sofer's book *Sipurei ya'akov*: the Ba'al Shem Tov received the Book of Psalms, in King David's own handwriting, from the Sultan ('the King') as a reward for having healed his daughter. This story goes on to say that a decree was issued against the entire Jewish community, but was cancelled on the eve of Passover.[26]

Two of the tales about the Ba'al Shem Tov's stay in Constantinople revolve around his financial difficulties. According to Michael Levi Rodkinsohn, the tsadik R. Israel Dov Wilednik always used to tell one of these tales on the seventh day of Passover. It relates how the Ba'al Shem Tov's distress was relieved by a guest who visited him on the Seder night.

[21] See J. Sofer, *Sipurei ya'akov*, §34. According to Rodkinsohn, *Adat tsadikim*, §3, R. Tsevi Sofer and the daughter Odel travelled with the Ba'al Shem Tov.

[22] According to the Yiddish version of *Shivḥei habesht*, ch. 62, fos 25*b*–26*a*, almost a year: 'The Ba'al Shem Tov spent a long time in Istanbul, nearly a year.'

[23] See Dan, *Hebrew Story* (Heb.), 107.

[24] *Shivḥei habesht*, 111–12. Cf. Rapoport, *Divrei david*, fo. 30*b*: 'While the Ba'al Shem Tov was in the city of Istanbul on his journey to the Land of Israel, he heard of a name which echoed through the world: that of R. Naphtali Hakohen, blessed be his memory, who gives talismans and uses the holy names.' This also appears in Sperling, *Reasons for the Customs* (Heb.), 303. Cf. Markus, *Hasidism* (Heb.), 316. The Ba'al Shem Tov prostrated himself on the grave of R. Naphtali in Constantinople (= Istanbul).

[25] I. Safrin, 'Netiv mitsvoteikha', 'Shevil emunah', §1, fo. 4*a*.

[26] J. Sofer, *Sipurei ya'akov*, §34.

The visitor brought everything required for the Seder and the holiday, and the Ba'al Shem Tov rewarded him with a blessing of progeny.[27]

Menahem Mendel Bodek's tale connects the Ba'al Shem Tov's financial problems with the salvation of the entire Jewish people. The Ba'al Shem Tov's shortage of money compelled him to interest himself in petty matters, and a wealthy man heard Odel lamenting her father's straitened circumstances. This man invited the Ba'al Shem Tov and his companions to his house and, as a result of his lavish hospitality, the Ba'al Shem Tov's elevated spiritual state returned. That same evening, when he fell asleep, he underwent a spiritual elevation (*aliyat neshamah*) and brought about the revocation of a decree that had been issued against the Jews of the city.[28]

The troubles of the Ba'al Shem Tov, then, involved a spiritual crisis in which his special powers deserted him. According to Bodek, the crisis occurred in Constantinople as a result of 'worries and hardships', but passed when the Ba'al Shem Tov drank good wine, which gladdens the heart, at which point his spiritual powers were restored to their former level. This motif of mental or spiritual decline and recovery does not occur in those stories in which the crisis is a manifestation of divine punishment and/or a means of forcing the Ba'al Shem Tov to turn back and abandon his journey.

According to the Yiddish version of *Shivḥei habesht*, the Ba'al Shem Tov's wisdom and knowledge of Torah, and, most importantly, the efficacy of his prayers,[29] were taken away from him. A detailed description of this affliction is also provided by R. Isaac Eizik Safrin:

> And he was informed by heaven (after being forced to escape from Constantinople by ship) that he should return home, but he did not want to. And his elevated spiritual state left him, and so did his knowledge of Torah and of prayers, to the extent that he did not even know how to read *barukh* [blessed] in the prayer book, nor understand the letters. And he said, 'What of it? I shall travel as a simple ignoramus [*am ha'arets*] and come to the tsadik *Or haḥayim* to the Holy Land.' And he accepted every hardship with loving submission, until the ship was wrecked, and he heard his righteous daughter Odel drowning in the sea and crying out to him: 'Merciful father, where are you at the moment of distress?' At this critical moment, when his powers of holiness had deserted him, the Devil (cursed be he) appeared to him and spoke to him. When he saw that his soul was about to expire he said, 'Hear, O Israel, the Lord is our God, the Lord is one, Lord of the Universe, I shall return home!' And at that moment his patron spirit, Ahijah the Shilonite, appeared before him and consoled him, and in

[27] Rodkinsohn, *Adat tsadikim*, §3.

[28] Bodek, *Ma'aseh tsadikim*, §5, pp. 9–10; *Ma'aseh hakedoshim*, §19, 'Le'oseh niflaot gedolot'. Cf. A. Stern, *Ḥutim hameshulashim*, 36–9.

[29] The Yiddish version of *Shivḥei habesht*, ch. 62, fos 25*b*–26*a*: 'He could pray, but only as a simple man, and not as he used to pray with *kavanot* and *yiḥudim*.'

a moment he brought him back to Constantinople, from where he immediately returned home.[30]

This passage contains some elements that appear as early as R. Jacob Joseph's account (to which I shall turn later in this chapter), and some that can be found in other stories. The spiritual crisis is described in full detail: the Ba'al Shem Tov's mystical powers vanish and he forgets all his learning. In this state, he grows even more rebellious and will not listen to heavenly commands. This motif is not common in stories about the Ba'al Shem Tov. Perhaps he considered the divine prohibition on going to the Land of Israel as an attempt to try his determination. The spiritual decline is followed by physical catastrophe: the ship sinks, and the life of his beloved daughter is in danger. The appearance of Satan at this point is peculiar and is perhaps an indication that the failure of the pilgrimage is, after all, the work of the Devil. It is also possible that he appears to tempt the Ba'al Shem Tov with a promise that if he continued to rebel against heaven, Satan would bring him to his yearned-for destination. However—perhaps as a result of Satan's words—the Ba'al Shem Tov reaffirms divine authority and declares that he will renounce his pilgrimage and return home. At that moment Ahijah the Shilonite appears to comfort and rescue him and his daughter. Again Constantinople is mentioned as a stopping point on the way home.

There is without doubt a close link between R. Isaac Eizik's detailed story and the brief passage on the subject at the end of *Toledot ya'akov yosef*. It is possible that R. Jacob Joseph deliberately gave only an abridged account of the story, and even omitted problematic aspects, while the tsadik of Komarno recorded the whole episode just as it had been transmitted orally since the beginning of hasidism. It is also possible, however, that the tsadik had no other source besides R. Jacob Joseph, and creatively expanded that into a full and exciting tale, embellishing it with imaginary details. Today it is hardly possible to ascertain how the story developed. It can, however, be noted that the other tales about the unsuccessful journey display more similarities to the version by the tsadik of Komarno than to that by R. Jacob Joseph.

According to J. Sofer, whose version in *Sipurei ya'akov* differs from that told by R. Isaac Eizik on several points, the Ba'al Shem Tov left Constantinople on board ship, having obtained the desired Book of Psalms.

And when they were all aboard the ship, and had sailed a few miles, there was a great storm and the ship looked likely to break up. Everyone asked what the cause was for this evil coming upon them. The Ba'al Shem Tov himself said: 'Because of me!' Thereupon they wanted to cast him and his companions overboard, including R. Tsevi Sofer and R. Judah Sofer. At that moment the Ba'al Shem Tov forgot all

[30] I. Safrin, 'Netiv mitsvoteikha', 'Shevil emunah', §1, fo. 4*a*.

the secret *kavanot* [inner meanings] of the Torah, and became like a common ignoramus. And he asked R. Tsevi Sofer and his daughter Odel to remind him of the *kavanot*. They began by reminding him of the *alef-beit* and its mystical meaning, which he had taught them. He began to recite the *alef-beit* with great devotion, and the sea subsided. Then he spread his kerchief upon the water. He sat on his kerchief and his companions on theirs. So they sailed back to Constantinople and this occurred before Passover.[31]

The parallels between this account and the story of Jonah, who also boarded a ship to flee the will of the Lord, are clear. (It is worth noting in passing that the motif of the kerchief has been used by S. Y. Agnon.[32]) A similar episode appears in the versions of R. Israel of Ruzhin, who however credits Ahijah the Shilonite rather than the Ba'al Shem Tov's companions with restoring his spiritual faculties:

The Ba'al Shem Tov once embarked on a ship with his only daughter, and there was a great and mighty tempest, which could uproot mountains, and the ship was about to break up, so that the passengers were compelled to cast lots to determine whom they should cast into the sea to lighten the vessel. And the lot fell upon his daughter Odel, and she was about to be thrown into the sea. At that moment the prophet Ahijah the Shilonite, who was his teacher, came to him and said: 'Did I not teach you the holy names so that you would remember them in a moment of distress?' And the Ba'al Shem Tov answered him that heaven had not allowed him to know what sorrow would come upon them.[33]

There is yet another version of this story which does not mention the shipwreck or the danger of drowning, but instead introduces the motif of capture by robbers. In the story by Rodkinsohn mentioned above, the Ba'al Shem Tov and his companions are celebrating the Seder in Constantinople. The narrative continues:

On the intermediate days of Passover the host respectfully allowed his guests to leave, and the Ba'al Shem Tov said to R. Tsevi [Hirsh] Sofer that he wished to

[31] J. Sofer, *Sipurei ya'akov*, §34. In Rodkinsohn, *Adat tsadikim*, §3 (which also appears later in [Isaac Dov Baer ben Tsevi Hirsch], *Kahal ḥasidim heḥadash*), the Ba'al Shem Tov is quoted as having said to R. Tsevi: ' "At this very moment, I wish to go to the Holy Land." So they went down to the harbour, but could find no ship carrying Jewish travellers. The Ba'al Shem Tov said to R. Tsevi, the scribe, "If you wish, I will spread my handkerchief on the water." '

[32] No doubt Agnon collected material for his stories from the tales about the Ba'al Shem Tov's unsuccessful *aliyah*. In the story 'Bilevav yamim', in id., *Elu ve'elu*, 548, he writes: 'It is well known that every tsadik who comes from abroad to the Land of Israel first has to descend from his initial elevated state . . . until he is given a new mind.' Ibid. 524: 'And a handkerchief was floating as a ship in the midst of the sea, and a man was sitting on the kerchief, his face turned eastward.' Ibid. 540: 'It was the Lord who inspired him [Hanania] to spread the kerchief on the water and sit on it. He spread his kerchief on the water and sat upon it . . . until he reached the Land of Israel.' Ibid. 446: 'I spread my kerchief on the sea and sat down on it until I reached the Land of Israel.' *Continued in Appendix.*

[33] Shenkel, *Yeshuot yisra'el*, i, §6, p. 18.

travel to the Holy Land at once. And they went to the seashore together, but could not find a ship with Jewish travellers. Then the Ba'al Shem Tov said to the scribe R. Tsevi: 'If it pleases you, I shall spread my kerchief on the water; be sure, however, to contemplate the holy name which I shall tell you, and do not cease to meditate on it even for a second, because if, heaven forbid, you should stop thinking of it, I shall be lost together with you and my daughter. I desire to travel, at the risk of my life, so keep it in mind, and we shall go immediately.' But the scribe did not want to endanger the life of the Ba'al Shem Tov, blessed be his memory, and did not allow him to do it. And he forced him to hire a boat, embarking on the first intermediate day of Passover. Immediately a great storm arose, and the boat was tossed helplessly about for two days. They were in great danger and prayed to God for help. On the third day the storm subsided, and they landed on one of the islands. Since the ship's captain did not know the island, they went ashore to explore it. The Ba'al Shem Tov went for a walk on the island with R. Tsevi. They ventured too far, and could not find the way back to the ship. While they were walking backwards and forwards, trying to find the way, robbers, speaking an unknown language, attacked them and tied them up, leaving them while they sharpened their knives. Then the robbers felt weak and sat down to eat. R. Tsevi Sofer said to the Ba'al Shem Tov: 'Why are you silent? Is this a time for silence? Do something, the way you always do in times of danger.' And the Ba'al Shem Tov answered him: 'I know nothing, because my spiritual powers have left me. Perhaps you can remind me of the things I taught you?' And R. Tsevi said: 'I do not remember anything either, except the simple *alef-beit*, which I do remember.' Then the Ba'al Shem Tov cried out: 'And why are you silent? Recite the *alef-beit* to me!' And R. Tsevi Hirsh cried aloud: '*Alef*, *beit*, *gimel*, *dalet*', and the Ba'al Shem Tov repeated after him, aloud, with the great enthusiasm he always showed in holy matters. He did this until all of his former power returned. He had almost cut through his ropes when the sound of bells was heard announcing the sudden appearance of an old captain and his brave men, who scared off the robbers. They freed the captives, and without a word he took the Ba'al Shem Tov and R. Tsevi Sofer back to the ship and accompanied them until they arrived in Constantinople on the seventh day of Passover. It then became clear to the Ba'al Shem Tov that heaven did not permit him to go to the Holy Land, and he returned home.[34]

In this tale it is the human factor, not, as in the other versions, the forces of nature, which interrupts the pilgrimage. Here the Ba'al Shem Tov's spiritual decline is the result of weakness and/or fear, and his powers are restored to him thanks to his scribe R. Tsevi. Like Samson, he is about to break the ropes that bind them, but at that moment the old sea-captain appears, saving them from the robbers. Although the tale does not name this captain, it is clearly the prophet Elijah who effects the miraculous rescue.

The figure of the miraculous rescuer, presumably Elijah, appears also in another version, published by A. Wertheim, a descendant of the Ba'al Shem

[34] Rodkinsohn, *Adat tsadikim*, §3. For a shorter version of this tale, see E. Z. Stern, *Siḥot yekarim*, §9, p. 8.

Tov, who testifies that it had been told in his family.[35] This version does not mention Odel travelling with her father, nor does it say that the ship was wrecked. (On this point Wertheim's version agrees with Rodkinsohn's.) The events described take place during Passover. The ship, on its way to the Land of Israel, drops anchor at a small island. The Ba'al Shem Tov and his scribe R. Tsevi, who are discussing very important matters, forget to return to the ship at the appointed time, failing to hear the bell calling the voyagers back on board, and so are left behind on the island. They are seized by robbers and put in chains. The conversation between the Ba'al Shem Tov and his scribe about the mystical meaning of the *alef-beit* appears here as well. Then the sound of a bell is heard, announcing the arrival of another ship, and the robbers run for their lives, leaving the chained captives behind. The sea-captain takes the Ba'al Shem Tov and the scribe on board this new ship, which returns from the Mediterranean to the shores of the Black Sea. On the seventh day of Passover it drops anchor at a port on the Black Sea in order to allow the Ba'al Shem Tov and his companion to disembark and raise money to pay their fares. At first only the scribe leaves the ship, but later the Ba'al Shem Tov is also allowed ashore. Tired and feeble, he chances upon a Jewish house. The inhabitants are in the synagogue at the time, and, being hungry, the Ba'al Shem Tov eats some dumplings which he finds in a bowl. In the meantime, the scribe returns to the shore with a few Jews of the town to redeem his master. However, the captain and the ship have disappeared. The Ba'al Shem Tov is found asleep in the Jew's house where he has eaten.

To commemorate the miracle, the Ba'al Shem Tov orders a meal of dumplings to be eaten after the end of Passover—not on the seventh day, because dumplings cannot be eaten then because of the prohibition on leaven.

And every year, when the Ba'al Shem Tov was sitting at this meal, retelling the story of the journey to an attentive audience, R. Tsevi would nod his head and say: 'Rebbe, rebbe, why do you insist on calling him "the captain"? Why not use his real name? For we all know that he was no captain at all, but the prophet Elijah himself!'[36]

The differences between this version and Rodkinsohn's are not substantial. The additions serve only to explain the custom of eating dumplings after the last day of Passover; in all other respects the two narratives coincide. Wertheim writes that there was a tradition among the hasidim that 'twice the Ba'al Shem Tov attempted to go to the Land of Israel and both times he failed, because heaven prevented him'.[37]

Thus it appears that the different versions of the story of the attempted pilgrimage can be harmonized.

35 Wertheim, *Law and Custom in Hasidism* (Heb.), 176–7. 36 Ibid. 177. 37 Ibid.

R. Jacob Joseph also speaks of two attempts at pilgrimage by the Ba'al Shem Tov. In a relatively obscure place in his first book, *Toledot ya'akov yosef*, he writes:

Furthermore, I heard in the name of my teacher [the Ba'al Shem Tov] that when he went on his well-known journey, his spiritual mentor [Ahijah the Shilonite] showed him a passage in the Torah where his journey was alluded to, found in the account of the Israelites' sojourn in the desert, that is to say, all man's journeys are alluded to in the Torah. Similarly, when his ship was wrecked and he was greatly aggrieved, his heavenly guide [Ahijah] appeared and showed him the spiritual spheres which he had reached . . . and he took courage to mitigate the [divine] sentence.[38]

So ended the Ba'al Shem Tov's unsuccessful attempt to go to the Holy Land, which has stirred and fascinated the imagination of the hasidim. This tale allows us to understand the various allusions to the role of the Sitra Ahra or Satan in the failure of the journey: everything is determined in heaven, but without Satan's intervention the journey might have been completed.

R. Nahman of Bratslav knew these tales about the pilgrimage, at least in part, and was himself determined to travel anonymously to the Land of Israel.

And in Constantinople he made himself out to be of low and inferior demeanour. He wore ragged clothes, went barefoot and hatless; he became the lowest of the low . . . fought in jest with other people, the way young men will joke with each other . . . and he acted in a hundred ways the part of the fool, all of which cannot be told here. [R. Nahman] also said that the Ba'al Shem Tov and R. Naphtali (of Posen), of blessed memory, were not able to reach the Land of Israel because of the many obstacles they met with, and he, blessed be his memory, met with all of the same obstacles and overcame them all, thanks to his taking on an inferior demeanour; without it he would not have been able to get to his destination.[39]

The hasidic tale, then, assumes that the Ba'al Shem Tov's great-grandson knew of the hardships suffered by his forebear and drew his conclusions accordingly. In order not to rouse the Sitra Ahra, R. Nahman concealed his identity and played the fool, lowering himself to an inferior position; thus he

[38] Jacob Joseph of Polonnoye, *Toledot ya'akov yosef*, fo. 201*a*. 'Shemot Ehyeh' and 'Tserufei Ehyeh' are alternative names for the *sefirah* of Binah, which will always temper justice (the forces of punishment) with mercy. According to this tale, the Ba'al Shem Tov did succeed in 'mitigating judgements and in revoking the decree', but it seems to refer to the rescue from drowning and not to the revocation of the decree against going to the Land of Israel. An indirect testimony that the Ba'al Shem Tov actually departed appears in *Shivḥei habesht*, 61, in the words of R. Jacob Joseph, who tells about the way he approached the Ba'al Shem Tov: 'and afterwards the Ba'al Shem Tov went to the Land of Israel, and I remained desolate until he returned'. Markus, *Hasidism* (Heb.), 316, claims that the Ba'al Shem Tov instituted the practice of reciting Psalm 107 in the prayers after he had been saved from drowning at sea.

[39] Nathan of Nemirov, *Ḥayei moharan*, 'His Journey to the Land of Israel', §11.

outwitted Satan and succeeded in arriving safely in the Land of Israel. There he continued to behave as he had done in Constantinople, and left quickly. It is not impossible that R. Nahman had messianic motives for his pilgrimage, but whereas the hasidic tale of the Ba'al Shem Tov explicitly mentions his wish to bring about the redemption of the Jews, the stories of Bratslav make no mention of any such aim, which can only be read between the lines.

Appendix Supplementary Notes

Chapter 1

note 79 Joseph ben R. A., *Mifalot tsadikim heḥadash*, 9–10, contains a story that was recorded in the communal register, regarding a high official who saved a rabbi. A tale appears in the same book (§5, fo. 4*a*) 'from a reputable person who looked in the book *Hakhnasat oreḥim* in the Vienna library'. See also Ben Ze'ev, son of R.A.Y., *Devarim yekarim*, 4: 'An awesome story copied from an ancient manuscript'. [Isaac Dov Baer ben Tsevi Hirsch], *Kahal ḥasidim heḥadash* (Lvov edn), §105, contains a story that R. Levi Isaac saw in 'the communal register of Vilna'. M. H. Landau, *Ma'amar mordekhai* (bound together with Margolioth, *Kevutsat ya'akov*), includes (p. 6) a story about the Ba'al Shem Tov's study with R. Abraham Zak of Sharigod [Shargorod], and their *gilui eliyahu*, from 'the communal register of Sharigrod'.

note 90 See also the introd. to Yellin, *Derekh tsadikim*: 'For, indeed, such matters, many of which come by word of mouth, are not free, at times, from an error in some detail.' For a more strongly worded formulation of this, see ibid. 23: '[The stories] were copied from one person to another innumerable times, and what is corrupt in them exceeds that which stands [i.e. is unaltered], due to the many mistakes and change and exchange that they suffered when copied from one person to another.' Particularly sharp internal criticism is voiced by R. Hayim of Sanz (Zimetbaum, *Darkhei ḥayim*, introd. 4): 'If a hasid says, "I saw with my own eyes"—then he might have heard, and when a hasid says that he heard—then this undoubtedly never happened!' The anonymous compilers of *Ma'asiyot vesiḥot tsadikim* and Joseph ben R.A. (*Mifalot tsadikim heḥadash*) apologize in their introductions for the lack of chronological order in their respective collections of stories.

Chapter 2

note 2 See Bodek, *Mifalot hatstadikim*, §21, fo. 16*b*; Brandwein, *Degel maḥaneh yehudah*, §84. See also A. M. Rabinowitz, *Keter hayehudi*, 54: while smoking his pipe on Saturday nights, after the departure of the sabbath, the tsadik R. Nehemiah of Bychawa would read the thoughts of all those gathered, doing so 'by the spirit of divine inspiration'. Sobelman, *Sipurei tsadikim heḥadash*, §27, tells of R. Jacob Samson of Shepetovka, who said that the husband of an *agunah* would return; when this came to pass the entire city realized that he had spoken 'with the spirit of divine inspiration'; see Ch. 5 below. For the derision by mitnagedim of the power of the tsadik, see p. 313 n. 26 below. The theme of the power of the tsadik in the hasidic story was apparently influenced by the stories about R. Isaac Luria. For example, Solomon of Dreznitz states in *Shivḥei ha'ari*, fo. 19*a* (my pagination): 'He [Luria] would tell a person what he had done during the past twenty years; what he had done in secret, and what he had thought within the confines of his heart'; fo 19*b*: '. . . until he admitted everything to him'. See also *Sefer hakavanot uma'asei nisim*, fo. 3*b*: '[Luria] also had the ability to know [from] a person's face everything that he had experienced from the day of his birth, the transgressions he had committed, and what he had come to this world to correct'; fo. 6*a*: 'he related to him even a simple conversation that he had with his wife'. Luria also read what was 'written' on people's foreheads. See Vital, *Sefer haḥezyonot*, 152, 165, 173, 182. It was related of R. Elimelekh of Lizhensk that 'if he gazed upon a person, he immediately saw in his face all the sins that he had committed from the day of his birth': Ze'ev Wolf of Zhitomir, *Or hame'ir*, 9.

note 3 Even before R. Abraham (his future father-in-law) had come to the Ba'al Shem Tov, 'he [the Ba'al Shem Tov] saw with the spirit of divine inspiration that his [R. Abraham's] daughter would be his mate'. The attribution of the spirit of divine inspiration to the hasidic masters is firmly anchored in the hasidic theoretical literature as well. See e.g. Meshullam Feivush of Zbarazh, *Likutim yekarim*, fo. 23*c*: 'For we knew that they possess the spirit of divine inspiration; some had a vision of Elijah, of blessed mention, like the Ba'al Shem Tov, of blessed memory, our teacher Menahem Mendel [of Przemysl], and his pupil, our teacher, Dov Baer [of Mezirech], may his memory be for the life of the World to Come.' Samuel of Shinova, *Ramatayim tsofim*, fo. 85*a* (p. 169), relates that R. Moses of Przevorsk was known to possess the spirit of divine inspiration; also (ibid., fo. 91*b* [p. 182]) that the Seer of Lublin told R. Simhah Bunim of Pshischa: 'Hold on to me and you will possess the spirit of divine inspiration from the world of *atsilut*, and all the world will run to you.'

note 31 See I. Safrin, *Netiv mitsvoteikha*, 'Shevil emunah', 5, fo. 14*b*, regarding the grasses of the field that told the future to the rabbi of Apta; Shalom of Koidanov, *Divrei shalom*, introd., fo. 6*a*: R. Solomon of Karlin 'understood the language of birds, the language of trees, the language of the ministering angels'; Brandwein, *Degel maḥaneh yehudah*, §69: R. Judah Tsevi of Stretin 'understood the language of birds, the language of trees, the language of devils, and the language of angels'. For a hidden tsadik who 'engaged in the conversations of birds', see Rakats, *Siaḥ sarfei kodesh*, v. 113. For the source and nature of R. Isaac Luria's knowledge of the 'chirping of birds', see Vital, *Sha'ar ruaḥ hakodesh*, 'Derush', 3; cf. also *Sefer hakavanot uma'asei nisim*, fo. 2*b*: 'He was also worthy to know the language of trees, the language of birds and fire, and the language of the ministering angels; and he knew the language [of] beasts and animals, and of the insects and creeping things that were reincarnated in them.' See also Zevin, *Hasidic Tales: Festivals* (Heb.), 123.

note 64 See also [Isaac Dov Baer ben Tsevi Hirsch], *Kahal ḥasidim heḥadash*, §113; Moskowitz, *Otsar hasipurim*, xvi. 11–12 (for males: on the head; for females: above the head). According to Mondshein, *Likutei reshimot uma'asiyot*, §14, p. 4, R. Levi Isaac placed his hand on women's heads when he blessed them, while Bodek, *Pe'er mikedoshim*, §13, attests that virgin brides were the only women whom R. Shalom of Belz would bless. Cf. also Brawer, *Pe'er yitsḥak*, ch. 12, §1: R. Isaac Eisik of Zhidachov would look at the note, place his hand on the person taking his leave, and grant him 'a blessing from heaven'. Some tsadikim would formulate their blessings as curses (to mitigate the divine decree, or as a means of concealment from the Sitra Ahra): among them were the Grandfather of Shpola (see Ehrmann, *Devarim arevim*, 'Stories of the Holy Rabbi, R. S[olomon] of Karlin', §2) and R. Baruch of Medzibezh, who cursed many people, including tsadikim. Before he died, however, R. Baruch stated that he had not cursed anyone since his curses were, in fact, blessings (see Zeilingold, *Me'orot hagedolim*, 'His Holiness, the Holy Rabbi, R. Baruch of Medzibezh', §28, pp. 58–9). R. Nehemiah Judah, the son of the 'Holy Jew', would vex and curse people, thereby releasing them from harsh heavenly sentences and decrees: see Rabinovitz, *Ma'aseh neḥemiyah*, 69. There were also women who received *kvitlakh*, such as the *rabanit* Sheindel, the widow of the 'Holy Jew', who received a *kvitl* after her husband's death and 'promised succour by the power of her husband'.

note 85 See also Shenkel, *Yeshuot yisra'el*, ii. §10, p. 17: 'Once [R. Israel of Ruzhin] said: "Many say of the Ba'al Shem Tov, may the memory of the righteous and the holy be for a blessing, that he was called *ba'al shem* because he used the holy names, but in truth he was not like this."' A. Rubinstein, '*Hitgalut* Stories' (Heb.), discusses the standing of the *ba'alei shem* in *Shivḥei habesht*, and concludes: 'the redactor of the Hebrew edition acted to obscure and diminish the importance of the Ba'al Shem Tov's activity as a *ba'al shem*', which is not the case in the Yiddish edition. If this was the intent of the Hebrew editor, he was not consistent in implementing it. At any rate, it would seem that the hasidic leaders and writers were ambiguous towards the activity of the Ba'al Shem Tov as a wonder-worker. R. Menahem Nahum of Chernobyl wrote that 'the remedies of the Ba'al Shem Tov, whose soul rests in the heavenly garden, were effected only by means of the *yiḥudim* that he performed' (*Me'or enayim*, 'Naso', fo. 40*d*). R. Isaac Safrin of Komarno emphasizes that the Ba'al Shem Tov 'performed several wondrous things . . . all by his *devekut* [devotion] . . . without [the use of] any [divine] name, for he never used any such name his entire life!' (*Notser ḥesed*, fo. 43*a*). R. Isaac nonetheless concedes that the Ba'al Shem Tov had knowledge of the use of the divine names, and that during his youth his teacher, Ahijah the Shilonite, instructed him in 'all the uses' of the holy names. Once the young Ba'al Shem Tov even sought to cross the Dnieper river on a piece of cloth by means of such a name: he succeeded, but regretted it, repenting and fasting, for the rest of his life. When he had to cross this river a second time, with non-Jews in pursuit, he placed his belt on the river and crossed 'without any name, only with great faith in the God of Israel'. Margolioth, *Kevutsat ya'akov*, contains two stories in which the Ba'al Shem Tov himself opposes the use of holy names. In the first (fo. 52*b*), the Ba'al Shem Tov tells his wife that if he wanted he could turn the stove into gold, 'perhaps you would think, by the use of names? Heaven forbid, only by prayer.' In the second (fo. 53*b*), the Ba'al Shem Tov is quoted as saying: 'I heal the mad only by means of wisdom!'

Chapter 4

note 1 According to Ehrmann, *Zokhreinu leḥayim*, 13, the Ba'al Shem Tov sent R. Tsevi of Chortkov to ask R. Hayim of Sanz to give him a blessing so that

R. Tsevi might have offspring. See also Shenkel, *Ma'asiyot peliyot*, §22. According to Kohen, *Shemuot vesipurim*, 96, R. Levi Isaac of Berdichev would release barren women from their condition with the recitation of *Hodu* ('Give thanks'—a passage from 1 Chr. 16: 8–36 that begins the introductory Pesukei Dezimrah section of the morning prayer service). Cf. also the declaration by R. Isaac Safrin that 'This barren woman shall be remembered [for children] this year, while that one shall never have children!' Every year on the Sukkot holiday, he would assert: 'Now I was answered by the patriarch Abraham, may he rest in peace, regarding four barren women who would be remembered [for children] this year, or five, or more or less, and so it would be every year' (I. Safrin, *Zohar ḥai*, introd.). R. Abraham of Stratin once observed: 'There are some people whose *tikun* consists of their having children, while for others, their *tikun* consists of their not having children, for the grief that a person experiences from not having offspring is the *tikun* for his soul!' (Brandwein, *Degel maḥaneh yehudah*, §85.). Women would also ask the tsadik to grant that they should not miscarry, for which R. Tsevi of Rymanow had a special charm; see Breitstein, *Siḥot ḥayim*, §17, p. 12. For charms used during pregnancy, see J. Y. Rosenberg, *Rafa'el hamalakh*, 29–30.

note 7 Cf. Shenkel, *Ma'asiyot peliyot*, §22; [Isaac Dov Baer ben Tsevi Hirsch], *Kahal ḥasidim heḥadash*, §29; Donner and Wodnik, *Sefer ba'al shem tov*, ii. 169 n. 17; Strisower, *Minḥat yehudah*, 13; Modner, *Kitvei kodesh ramam*, 8; Zevin, *Hasidic Tales: Festivals* (Heb.), 262. In Moskowitz, *Otsar hasipurim*, ii. §2, pp. 5–11, the Ba'al Shem Tov promises a son to a wealthy hasid, on condition that he loses all his property. Afterwards, he raises the child and marries him to the daughter of a poor scribe. In order to explain why he chose the daughter of the scribe, of all possible matches, the Ba'al Shem Tov tells a story about a king's son who converts to Judaism and marries a convert (the daughter of a king): now both are in their second *gilgul* (reincarnation) in the world, in order to complete their first lives. This seems to be the combination of two stories (the story was transmitted in writing to Moskowitz by R. Joseph Hartman of Petah Tikvah, in Israel). For another instance of a childless husband who receives the blessing of the tsadik, see Rabinovitz, *Ma'aseh neḥemiyah*, 42–3.

note 9 For coming down in the world as a condition for the birth of a son, see Gemen, *Sifran shel tsadikim*, 'Ma'arekhet' 1, §5; A. Stern, *Ḥutim hameshulashim*, 16. It is related in *Shivḥei habesht*, 115, that a son was born to R. Shmerl as a result of a blessing by the Ba'al Shem Tov. When R. Shmerl came to the Ba'al Shem Tov after the birth in order to receive a charm from the tsadik, the latter told the new father: 'Know that you will have no more money, for you were given the choice—either money or a son. And I chose well for you, that you would have a son.' For more regarding a blessing for children that was conditional on coming down in the world, in the time of the tsadik R. Judah Tsevi of Stretin, see Brandwein, *Degel maḥaneh yehudah*, §§53, 65. In Breitstein, *Siḥot ḥayim*, §44, pp. 35–7, R. Israel of Ruzhin imposed the condition of the parents' poverty for the birth of a son. After the child was born, their property burned down. Since this child was frivolous, the parents took the Holy One, blessed be He, to court—and won! The father was again successful in business and became rich. Cf. Ehrmann, *Devarim arevim*, 'Stories of the Holy Rabbi, R. I[srael] of Ruzhin', §3.

Chapter 5

note 2 See also *Hamevaser* (ed. Kohen-Zedek), 6 (Lemberg, 1866), no. 5, p. 40; no. 27, p. 212, 'Takanat agunah' (announcement of an *agunah*): the deserting husband stole his wife's *shterntikhel*, earrings, and some money, before fleeing; ibid., no. 36, p. 227; no. 9 (1866), p. 44, 'Halikhot olam' (news). For additional examples see *Hamagid*, 15 (1875), no. 6, p. 6, 'Ishah azuvah' (abandoned wife), containing a response to a rabbi from Torun who was seeking in Russia a deserting husband 'short in stature, with a bit of a beard, who was 45 years old when he left'. See also *Hamagid*, 15 (1875), no. 7, p. 64: 'Takanat agunah', in which a deserting husband aged 52 who had abandoned his wife and baby girl four years previously was sought. The announcement was submitted by the rabbi of Teuringen. See also ibid., 'Hosafah' (additional note), 'Takanat agunah', 'To reconcile sons with their fathers' (see Mal. 3: 24): a young man had fled from his wife, the granddaughter of R. Naphtali of Ropshits. See ibid. no. 12, p. 96, 'Et ba'ali ani mevakeshet' (I seek my husband).

note 26 Cf. the story in which a mitnaged asks the Seer of Lublin about his missing son. When the Seer returns from the toilet, before washing his hands, he informs the mitnaged where his son is to be found. The mitnaged wonders: 'Does the rabbi have the spirit of divine inspiration in the toilet, as well?' The tsadik responds: 'And where will I recall you [mitnagedim], if not in the toilet?' ([Lemberger], *Magdil yeshuot malko*, 42–3). A similar story, in which the mocker himself becomes the subject of derision, is told regarding a cloth merchant who held the Ba'al Shem Tov in low esteem. He nevertheless was forced by his wife, who did believe in the tsadik, to ask the Ba'al Shem Tov about the fate of their son, from whom no word had been received since he set out for Breslau. The mitnaged said, derisively: 'My wife said that you know some things, so I have come, for you to tell me where my son is.' The Ba'al Shem Tov replied: 'For things such as this, I look while in the toilet.' He took a pipe and went to the toilet, where he said: 'I see that he is still in Breslau, and that he is walking about in a German hat.'

note 33 When R. Aaron of Stolin passed through her city, an *agunah* asked the tsadik to act on her behalf. He summoned a furniture mover, who admitted that he and his comrades had murdered her husband, and revealed the location of the grave. When his testimony was confirmed, the woman was released from her status as an *agunah* (Gemen, *Sifran shel tsadikim*, 'Ma'arekhet' 34, §9). In 1944–5 Solomon Michael Nekhes published in Los Angeles a story (based on a story that had appeared in the *Haposek* quarterly) entitled *A ma'aseh fun a agunah* (A Story about an *Agunah*). During the time of R. Meir ben Todros Abulafia (1180–1244), an *agunah* received permission from him to remarry, while an elderly *dayan* vigorously opposed this ruling. On the wedding day, after extensive searches, the latter found the deserting husband and lodged him in his house. In the meantime, R. Abulafia ordered the *dayan* to conduct the wedding ceremony for the *agunah*. Upon returning home, the *dayan* found that the deserting husband had died. R. Abulafia revealed to the *dayan* that this man had died some time previously, but had been brought back to life by heaven to prove to the *dayan* the correctness of the permission granted by the rabbi. Cf. a story from Iraq regarding the revival by a hidden tsadik of a deserting husband who had fallen in battle (Baharav, *Sixty Folktales* (Heb.), 58, 234–6).

Chapter 6

note 19 Another story transfers the test to the realm of the imaginary: 'The rabbi of Nezkizh, of blessed memory, told that when the rabbi of Lublin, of blessed memory, went in his youth to the holy rabbi, R. Elimelekh of Lizhensk, of blessed memory, it happened that rain fell and it was extremely cold. He lost his way at night and saw a house in the forest that was lit up, and he entered it. It was warm and comfortable there, and his soul was revived, after having suffered greatly from the rain and the cold. There was a beautiful woman there, and he did not know what to do, because of [the problem of] *yiḥud*. She sought to entice him to commit a transgression, heaven forfend, and said that she was unmarried and [menstrually] clean. He was greatly distressed by her attempt at seduction, and responded: "I have taken upon myself not to do anything that is permitted, save only that which is pleasing and satisfying to my Creator, and what satisfaction will the Creator derive from this?" As soon as he made this reply, he saw that everything was imaginary, in order to tempt him; there was neither a forest, nor a house, nor a woman.' See Bodek, *Mifalot hatsadikim*, 'The Deeds of the Tsadikim', §20; [Isaac Dov Baer ben Tsevi Hirsch], *Kahal ḥasidim heḥadash*, §131. Cf., with minor changes in wording, Meshullam Feivush of Barezin, *Sefat emet*, 'Vayeshev'; also related in Rosenthal, *Tiferet hatsadikim*, 47. Cf. A. Y. Luria, *Likutim yekarim*, 15–16, §78: R. Joel Ba'al Shem came to a forest on the eve of the sabbath. He saw a palace with a beautiful woman who demanded that he engage in sexual relations with her, but he said that he had cast off all material matters. After the *melaveh malkah*, the palace disappeared, but then the woman came to his home, and he took a vow to do as she requested. When she demanded that he fulfil his vow, he requested that a judgment by Torah law be issued, and the rabbi ruled that R. Joel's vow was null and void. For one of the followers of R. Mordecai of Lachowicze whom the *ba'al davar* (a euphemism for Satan), in the image of a young non-Jewish woman, sought to seduce, but who threw the temptress from his carriage, see Kleinmann, *Or yesharim*, 7. Cf. also the story (BT *Kid.* 81*a*) of R. Me'ir and R. Akiva, to whom the devil appeared in the guise of an alluring woman.

note 32 R. Meir Halevi, head of the Stovnitz rabbinical court, tells of a similar happening in his *Or leshamayim*, 73–4. A husband who returned home after a prolonged absence heard gossip that his wife had engaged in illicit sexual conduct and had given birth as a result. When the woman was questioned about this, she said that she had been employed as a maid in an inn that was owned by a Jew. Once, she was included in a card game, together with the owner of the inn, his wife, and a non-Jewish man. The owner and his wife left the room without her being aware, and the non-Jew put out the light and raped her. She conceived but miscarried. M. Landau, *Toledot yosef*, 9: when R. Menahem Mendel of Bar was appointed *magid meisharim* of this city, the Ba'al Shem Tov came to spend the first sabbath with him, on which occasion a wealthy man held a circumcision for his son. During the ceremony R. Menahem Mendel, who was to be the *sandak*, jumped up and claimed that the child was a *mamzer*, thus arousing the anger of the relatives. The Ba'al Shem Tov intervened, and went with two people to the home of the new mother. The latter admitted that 'the servant seduced her, and she conceived from him'. The child was circumcised at the entrance to the synagogue, as is customary for *mamzerim* (according to *Shulḥan arukh*, 'Yoreh de'ah' 265: 4; see also *Turei zahav*; *Siftei kohen* ad loc.).

Chapter 9

note 8 Sperling, *Reasons for the Customs* (Heb.), 555, relates (in the name of *Sefer nezer hashem*, which I have not seen) that R. Samuel Shmelke of Nikolsburg was the reincarnation of the prophet Samuel. According to Ehrmann, *Devarim arevim*, 'Stories of the Holy Rabbi, Our Master and Teacher, R. N[aphtali] of Ropshits', §8, R. Ze'ev of Zbarazh was the reincarnation of the prophet Jeremiah. R. Ze'ev and his wife were complaining about each other, prompting R. Ze'ev's father, Moharam, to rebuke his daughter-in-law, stating that R. Ze'ev was the soul of Jeremiah. The woman did not heed him, but when her own father heard this he commanded her to mend her ways, thus preventing divorce. Cf. the testimony by R. Isaac Luria that R. Abraham Halevi Berukhim was the reincarnation of Jeremiah (Benayahu, *Sefer toledot ha'ari*, 228; Tsevi Hirsch of Koidanov, *Kav hayashar*, ch. 93; S. Assaf, 'Letters from Safed' (Heb.), 223).

The Maggid of Koznitz called his grandson R. Hayim Me'ir Yehiel (the *saraf* or Angel of Mogielnica) by the name Jeremiah, 'for he said that he saw that he was the *gilgul* of Jeremiah' (Bromberg, *Toledot haniflaot*, 6). Another of the Maggid's grandsons, Moses, who died at the age of 7, was called by his brother the 'Angel': *mein bruderil mosheh rabeinu* (my little brother, Moses our teacher): see ibid. 4. The 'Angel' said that his mother had the soul of a tsadik; he knew the identity of the latter, 'and for what [sin] he received the punishment of returning in a *gilgul* as a female' (ibid. 41). It was related of the Maggid's grandson (the child Berele) that he possessed the soul of the Maggid, Dov Baer of Mezirech (ibid. 39–40).

note 11 R. Abraham Joshua Heschel of Apta attested of himself that he had already been in the world ten times, and that he had been among other things a high priest, a *nasi*, and a king (I. Landau, *Zikhron tov*, 'The Deeds of the Tsadikim', §6). Cf. Rakats, *Siaḥ sarfei kodesh*, ii, §287; Ehrmann, *Devarim arevim*, 'Stories of the Holy Rabbi, of R. [Joshua] H[eschel] of Apta', §3. On Yom Kippur he would say: 'So I would say' (instead of 'So he would say': during the Yom Kippur Musaf service that describes the activity of the high priest in the Temple on this day), and tell of himself that when the Temple stood he had been a high priest, and performed service in the Temple, may it speedily be rebuilt. When he was a youth, he was one of the young men of the priesthood, and he remembered all that. The rabbi of Apta claimed that he knew someone who came to him from that person's first incarnation, when he had sinned and not properly repented. Accordingly, his soul was forced to wander and once again come before the rabbi of Apta (when the latter was the high priest). A. Michelsohn, *Ateret menaḥem*, §143: R. Ezekiel Halberstam, the rebbe of Shinova, would recite Tahanun, even on the *yahrzeit* of tsadikim, and would reproach hasidim who omitted this prayer. He always asked: How can [memorial] lights be kindled for the soul of a tsadik, since he may be reincarnated in this world? On the memorial day of R. Menahem Mendel of

Rymanow, however, he ordered that candles be lit; he related that the rabbi of Rymanow had attested of himself 'that he had already been [in this world] a hundred times, and had been a High Priest at the time of the Temple. . . . he would recite in his prayer of the Temple service, "So I would say"'. He also said of himself that this was his last transmigration in this world, and that he would not return to it again. Consequently, on the *yahrzeit* of R. Menahem Mendel, the holy rabbi Samuel of Shinova ordered that candles be lit (also cited in Moskowitz, *Otsar hasipurim*, xx. 27; Sperling, *Reasons for the Customs* (Heb.), 339; Zevin, *Hasidic Tales: Festivals* (Heb.), 89). According to *Ramatayim tsofim*, fo. 58*a* (p. 115), he said 'that he was now in his third *gilgul*; in the first *gilgul* he was a *nasi*, and in the second, the Exilarch'. See also Brawer, *Pe'er yitsḥak*, ch. 9, §1: R. Isaac Eisik of Zhidachov would scold anyone who interrupted his discourses, and threaten: 'If you will not act properly, I will tell you who [you were] and what your actions were in your previous *gilgulim*, as well!'

Moskowitz, *Otsar hasipurim*, xviii, §8 (p. 24): 'Once the holy rabbi, our master, R. Abraham Joshua Heschel, may the memory of the righteous and the holy be for a blessing, the head of the rabbinical court of Medzibezh and Apta, was sitting, deep in thought, and his followers asked him about this. He replied that he was presently in his tenth *gilgul* in this world, and that he had been a high priest and *nasi*, a king and exilarch.' Teomim, *Menorah hatehorah*, §21: 'We heard from those who speak the truth that every time the holy mouth of the rabbi of Apta would utter during the [recitation of the description of the Temple] service, saying: "So I would say", for he still remembers to the present that he served as high priest in the Temple, and this matter is well known.' See, however, A. Michelson, *Ateret menaḥem*, §143: R. Menahem Mendel of Rymanow would attest of himself that he had already been in the world a hundred times, and he had been a high priest at the time of the Temple, and he therefore recited: 'and so I would say'; he also said of himself that this was the last time that his soul would transmigrate in this world, and that he would not return to it again; also cited in *Otsar hasipurim*, xx. 27.

note 18 In some instances, the soul immediately transmigrates upon a person's death into the body of an infant that is about to be born. It was said of R. Solomon of Karlin: 'The holy rabbi saw with his spirit of divine inspiration regarding this worthy who was about to die, that immediately after his passing his soul would enter the foetus of the woman [who was experiencing a difficult childbirth]; as long as the worthy did not expire, the woman could not give birth' (Gemen, *Sifran shel tsadikim*, 'Ma'arekhet' 12, §13). This child (the dead worthy) would later attend the bar mitzvah celebration of the worthy's young son; he was seated at the table of the indigent, but demanded instead to be seated among the distinguished guests, at the head of the table, and insisted upon receiving a large portion (for he was the head of the family). R. Solomon of Karlin, who saw and understood all this by means of his ability to see from one end of the world to the other, requested that the Lord relieve him of this faculty. In a similar situation, in which the woman experiencing a difficult childbirth was the wife of the Hatam Sofer, the latter refused to pray on her behalf, saying: 'I do not desire to shorten the life of another tsadik' (Yellin, *Derekh tsadikim*, 10). Two *kvitlakh* were given to the rabbi of Kotsk, 'one from a dying person, heaven forfend, and the other from a woman having difficulty in giving birth; one was waiting upon the other, and no more need be said'. The tsadik of Strykow advised the rabbi of Kotsk to ask the Lord to give a new soul to the foetus (Rakats, *Siaḥ sarfei kodesh*, ii, §417). For a month-old infant who recited 'Hear, O Israel' while dying, in the presence of R. Judah Aryeh of Modena, see Azulai, *Shem hagedolim*, ii, 'Ma'arekhet' 10, §72. A girl returned as a bride. The mother-in-law, a widow, hated her daughter-in-law, because of the latter's resemblance to her daughter, who had died fifteen years previously. Her late husband appeared to her in a dream and revealed to her that her daughter-in-law was the reincarnation of their daughter, and from that moment the widow loved her daughter-in-law. See al-Hakam, *Nifla'im ma'asekha*, §81, pp. 74–5.

note 26 A story depicting those who shaved their beards (a vision seen in the desert by Jacob Abulafia, a disciple of R. Isaac Luria) appears in Moskowitz, *Otsar hasipurim*, viii, §4. For the source of this story, see *Sefer hakavanot uma'asei nisim*, fos 7*b*–8*a*; Benayahu, *Sefer toledot ha'ari*, 232–4; cf. the story of the wealthy man in Speyer who cut off his beard with scissors (thereby violating the injunction in Lev. 19: 27), in *Mayse bukh* (1602 edn), §164, fos 104*b*–105*b*. Isaac ben Eliezer Roke'ah of Worms, *Sefer hagan*, fos 9*b*–10*a*, presents the story as it appears in a manuscript written by R. Zalman, the son of R. Judah Hehasid. It is related that R. Judah told that rich man: 'Know that your end [will be] bitter, for after your death demons that resemble cows shall trample the edge of your beard. This is the lot of those who destroy [i.e. shave] the edge of their beard. And know that, similarly, *lo takifu pe'at roshkhem velo tashḥit* [Lev. 19: 27, 'you shall not round off the side-growth on your head, or destroy . . .'] is an acronym for *parot* [cows].' After the death of the sinner, R. Judah Hehasid revived him by means of 'a certain [divine] name'; the dead man described everything that had befallen him after his death, and confirmed the rabbi's warning. The Jerusalemite R. Nathan Shapira copied the story from *Sefer hagan* in *Yayin meshumar*, fo. 35*a*, and R. Elijah ben Solomon Abraham Hakohen (Ha'itamari), in turn, copied it from the later book to *Shevet musar*, ch. 18, fo. 40*b*. The story also appears in *Ḥemdat hayamim*, i, ch. 3, fo. 20*a*, with minor linguistic changes—*haḥakham hanizkar* (the above sage) in place of *aba mori* (my father and teacher), and other alterations, and in Shenkel, *Ma'asiyot peliyot*, 19–20. R. Solomon Bekhor Hozin (who notes that he copied it from *Ḥ*[*emdat*] [*ha*] *y*[*amim*]) quotes the story in *Ma'asim tovim*, fos 20*b*–21*a*. See also Zfatman, 'The *Mayse Bukh*' (Heb.), 144–5.

note 30 Interestingly, most of the transmigrated souls and dybbuks populating the stories in Ftayya, *Ruḥot mesaperot*, committed sins in the realm of sexual misconduct, including incest. Cf. Azikri, *Sefer ḥaredim*, fo. 41*b*. The (anonymous) author of *Ḥemdat hayamim*, iv, fo. 55*d*, writes: 'The kabbalists also stated that there is a sign, by which a person can know for which sin he transmigrated. He examines his actions, [to determine] which sin attracts him more than all the sexual transgressions and [other] sins, and then it is known that he previously . . . had committed that sin.' In Vital, *Sefer haḥezyonot*, 191, the soul of the author of *Magid mishneh* transmigrated because he inadvertently sinned regarding *nidah*; the souls of R. Saul Trishti and R. Joshua Soriano suffered a similar fate, the former for the sin of murder, and the latter for the wilful eating of *ḥelev*.

note 46 Vital, *Sha'ar ruaḥ hakodesh*, 'Derush' 3, 'Hagahah', p. 83: 'Samuel [Vital] said: I recall one Rosh Hodesh, when my master, my father and master [R. Hayim Vital] was delivering a discourse on the water on the day of Tashlikh. We saw a frog coming into the river opposite him, and we began to throw stones at it. . . . My father and master, may the memory of the righteous be for a blessing, had his eyes closed and was discoursing on the Torah, as was his custom. At the sound of the frog croaking, he opened his eyes and rebuked us. He told us that a certain soul had come to hear his discourse, and it came in the garb of a frog. In its honour, he began to deliver a discourse concerning the frog, as to why it is called *tsefarde'a*, meaning *tsefar de'ah* [seeing knowledge].' See the slightly different version in Shenkel, *Sipurei anshei shem*, §8, who copied from Farhi, *Oseh pele*, 196–8. See also Solomon of Radomsk, *Tiferet shelomoh*, for the sabbath of Hanukah, s.v. *le'oseh*. For a father whose soul transmigrated after the death of his son, see Elijah ben Solomon Abraham Hakohen (Ha'itamari), *Midrash talpiyot*, letter *gimel*, *gilgul*, fo. 91*c* (in the name of R. Isaac Luria). For a father who is reincarnated in a patient whom his physician son heals, see Strisower, *Minḥat yehudah*, fo. 19*b*. R. Abraham Jagel writes in *Gei ḥizayon* (§92, fo. 41*a*) of a donkey that says to its master: 'Know that I am not [an ordinary donkey], but I am the soul of your father, your creator.' See also Bergman, *Kotsker Tales* (Yiddish), 77–80, concerning a reincarnated soul of a man who had sinned with a non-Jewish woman during his lifetime, and had eventually become an apostate. The soul transmigrated into a frog, and the Holy Jew and R. Menahem Mendel of Kotsk studied on his behalf and effected his *tikun*. A mitnagedic response to the belief in transmigration and the hasidic stories on this topic appears in the satiric *Gilgul nefesh* by Isaac Erter, in which a soul transmigrates seventeen times (including into a frog and into a dog).

note 48 See Tsevi Hirsch of Koidanov, *Kav hayashar*, ch. 6: 'There are souls that are not accepted [into Paradise] and transmigrate, into grasses, vegetables, and fruits. When a person recites a blessing over a fruit, or engages in words of Torah, then by means of his good speaking, these souls take on the garb of these [words], and are released from the prison of *gilgul* by means of the words of Torah.' Cf. ibid., ch. 88: 'When herbs and grasses begin to sprout from the earth, then the souls of the wicked enter into the plants, so that animals will eat them; and afterwards, when a person consumes the meat, or the plants, and if it [the food] is fit, he thereby effects a *tikun* for the spirit that is reincarnated in the vegetation, or in the meat, and the soul is drawn to holiness by [the recitation of] a blessing.' Bacharach, *Emek hamelekh*, 'The *Tikunim* of Repentance', ch. 5, fo. 17*c*: At the time of the blessing, one must have the intent of 'elevating sparks of purity . . . for this intent regarding the blessing may be the conclusion of its *tikun*, to elevate it by its [the blessing's] merit, to its [the soul's] [proper] place [i.e. in Paradise]. If, however, a person ate it without a blessing, he has broken faith with that soul. . . . Possibly these were the sparks of his father or his brother for whom he had the opportunity to effect a *tikun*, but he caused ruin, and did not know that he does evil to himself.'

note 49 For transmigrations in water, see Vital, *Sha'ar hagilgulim*, introd. 22; id., *Sefer hagilgulim*, 134–6. Bacharach, *Emek hamelekh*, 'The *Tikunim* of Repentance', ch. 4, fo. 17*c*: the fate of 'the righteous Torah scholars . . . is [to be reincarnated] in fish. . . . It therefore is a choice method of observance to eat fish on the sabbath, and especially in the third sabbath meal.' Cf. Vital, *Sefer haḥezyonot*, fo. 6*a*: 'And [the spirit] said to them: I am not like the other spirits, for I am wise and righteous, and I transmigrated only because of a minor sin that remained for me to correct. . . . I entered into a certain fish . . . the daughter ate me, and I entered her, but I caused her no harm.' See also *Sefer hakavanot uma'asei nisim*, fos 11*b*–12*a*; Benayahu, *Sefer toledot ha'ari*, 250; *Sefer hama'asiyot* (Baghdad), paras. 87, 107–10. It is a great merit to transmigrate into a fish, 'which is always kosher' (i.e. does not require ritual slaughter). See Abraham of Slonim, *Beit avraham*, 134. Surprisingly, R. Jacob Nacht devotes an extensive discussion to the eating of fish on the sabbath, but mentions only a single story (credited to Buber) that relates to *gilgulim*; see Nacht, 'Fish' (Heb.), and id., 'The Eating of Fish on the Sabbath' (Heb.).

note 59 Sperling explains (*Reasons for the Customs* (Heb.), 533): 'The reason why ritual slaughter must be conducted with a knife that has been examined and is free of flaws is that the souls of the righteous are reincarnated in cattle or in chicken.' If the chicken becomes unfit as a result of improper slaughtering, this indicates that the heavenly court has found the soul culpable (Rosenthal, *Hitgalut hatsadikim*, 23). An ox (containing a *gilgul*) that was slaughtered was declared non-kosher by the local rabbi, but was pronounced fit for consumption by Rabbi Ye'ivi: see Rabbinovich, *Shivḥei rav ye'ivi*, 28–9. A reincarnation in a duck, which had been declared non-kosher by R. Jacob Joseph of Polonnoye, interfered with his prayers for two weeks (Rosenstein, *Pe'er layesharim*, fo. 17*b*). Cf. a dream concerning reincarnation in a calf and the eating of the calf (Vital, *Sefer haḥezyonot*, fo. 19*a*); cf. also *Ḥemdat hayamim*, iv, ch. 4, fo. 67*b*, for some-one who was reincarnated in an ox in Castile, and who asked his son to redeem the ox, ritually slaughter it, and give the meat to penurious Torah scholars, thus enabling his soul to transmigrate into humans. This story also appears in Elijah ben Solomon Abraham Hakohen (Ha'itamari), *Midrash talpiyot*, letter *gimel*, *gilgul*, fo. 89*c*, citing Azikri, *Sefer ḥaredim* (fo. 41*a*). Elijah ben Solomon Abraham Hakohen also cites it in *Shevet musar*, ch. 18; and in Mehudar, *Zekhor le'avraham*, fo. 74*b* (following *Shevet musar*).

note 61 In this story, the soul transmigrates from the dog to a fish. The fish is eaten by the son of the reincarnated soul, and enters him, to do good for the soul (*mitaber*). By the force of this beneficial entry (*ibur*), the sabbath prayers of the son are 'like [those] of a great and holy man', and he even speaks 'secrets and hidden things of the Torah'. The transmigrated soul 'ascended to its proper place' only after the Saturday night prayer that concludes the sabbath. Cf. Zohar, *Tikunei zohar*, Tikun 70 (fo. 133*a*): 'there is a soul that enters into a dog'; Vital, *Sha'ar ruaḥ hakodesh*, Tikun 20: 'To the one who engages in sexual relations with a non-Jewish woman, know that the rabbis, of blessed memory, said [BT *AZ* 5*a*], concerning one who engages in such relations, "it [the trans-gression] attaches itself to him like a dog". The intent of the rabbis was that the one who engages in relations with a woman who is not Jewish would, after his death, be reincarnated in a dog.' This teaching also appears in Ftayya, *Ruḥot mesaperot*, 18, 39–40, which presents Baghdad stories of reincarnations in dogs. See also *Sefer hakavanot uma'asei nisim*, fo. 6*a*; Elijah ben Solomon Abraham

Hakohen (Ha'itamari), *Shevet musar*, ch. 36. s.v. *vegam nishmato titgalgel bekelev* (His soul, too, shall transmigrate in a dog). R. Abraham Jagel saw in his vision the transmigration of a woman's soul in a wild dog: see Jagel, *Gei ḥizayon*, §89, fos 37*b*–38*b*; Scholem, *Elements of the Kabbalah* (Heb.), 336. Kurzweil wrote, concerning dogs in Agnon's writings: 'Dogs symbolize transgression, desire' (*Essays on the Stories of S. Y. Agnon* (Heb.), 107). This thesis should be examined on the basis of the material presented in the current chapter.

note 62 Cf. R. Margaliot, *Marganita derabi me'ir*, §13: a black dog that was lying under the table of R. Avramchi of Mikulov was a *moser* (pejorative term for informer) who had turned into a dog after being cursed by R. Meir of Peremyshlyany. The same story appears in Ze'ev Wolf of Zhitomir, *Or hame'ir*, 21: R. Me'ir said of an informer in Peremyshlyany, 'I hope that he will collect bones under my son's table', and indeed, a black dog that collected bones came to the third sabbath meal of his son-in-law, R. Abraham Hayim of Mikulov. The hasidim wanted to drive out the dog, but the tsadik prevented them from doing so, and called the dog by the name of the informer: 'Shakhna Drei'. In contrast, the disrespect shown by R. Aryeh Leib (the *mokhiaḥ* of Polonnoye) to the corpse of an informer saved the latter from returning as a dog: *Shivḥei habesht*, 88–9; Zevin, *Hasidic Tales: Festivals* (Heb.), 147.

note 68 J. Sofer, *Sipurei ya'akov*, ii, §36, tells of a dybbuk that revealed the sins of the people of Brod to them. Shenkel, *Noraot anshei ma'aseh*, §6, portrays the soul of the son of R. Nathanel Hasid, who was kidnapped and forced to convert, died in a war, and then entered the body of a simple person and began to reveal hidden things. The soul returned to its repose only after the townspeople conducted a *tikun nefesh* for him. Cf. Vital, *Sefer haḥezyonot*, fo. 6*b*: '[The spirit told] each of the members of the household some of their sins'; Benayahu, *Sefer toledot ha'ari*, 192: 'And tells each one his bad deeds, with signs and wonders.' See also Ftayya, *Ruḥot mesaperot*, 12, for a dybbuk who threatens to reveal the iniquities of those present. Tsevi Hirsch of Koidanov, *Kav hayashar*, ch. 77, presents a story of a woman, in the time of R. Isaac Luria, who falls ill, and it is not known 'if there is within her a spirit or a demon'. Luria determined, after taking her pulse, that her body contained a spirit, and ordered R. Hayim Vital to exorcise it. The spirit revealed to those in attendance that R. Hayim would arrive shortly, but that it did not fear the rabbi. R. Hayim Vital made use of holy names, and the spirit sought to leave through the woman's throat, intending to harm her thereby. Vital, however, forced it to exit from 'the little toe of the left foot'. To those present at the exorcism, the spirit looked 'like a fiery thread'. He had been 'a well-known informer', who had been responsible for the loss of money by Jews to non-Jews. His soul had entered the woman's body because she had been guilty of the sin of profanity, and so was punished with the dybbuk's presence for three years. For the sources of this story, see *Sefer hakavanot uma'asei nisim*, fos 10*a*–*b*; Benayahu, *Sefer toledot ha'ari*, 191–6; Tamar, *Studies* (Heb.), 190. For the concern that no harm should be caused to a person when the spirit exits his body, see *Sefer hakavanot uma'asei nisim*, fo. 10*a*; Benayahu, *Sefer toledot ha'ari*, 196: 'The reason is that the body part through which it exits is completely nullified [i.e. dies]'; ibid., p. 304: 'And from where shall I depart? [the spirit asks], and you shall answer it: depart only from the little toe of the left foot!' Cf. the Baghdad tale in Ftayya, *Ruḥot mesaperot*, 10. These views are reflected in the hasidic story. R. David of Talnoye, who healed the sick and exorcised dybbuks by means of charms, would take pains to ensure that the spirit would leave through 'the little toe', and not harm the person. See Rabbinovich, *Shivḥei rav ye'ivi*, 93–5; [Isaac Dov Baer ben Tsevi Hirsch], *Kahal ḥasidim heḥadash*, §203. *Shivḥei habesht*, 168, in contrast, tells of the spirit of a dead person for whom the Ba'al Shem Tov refused to effect a *tikun*, and who harmed a maiden, the daughter of the beadle. For unsuccessful attempts to exorcise dybbuks, see Bek, *Kunteres dover shalom*, 10–12. For the exorcism of a dybbuk and its departure through the host's little finger and a hole in a window pane, see Lopian, *Lev eliyahu*, 24.

note 73 For additional stories from areas in which mitnagedim were prevalent, see Nigal, *'Dybbuk' Tales in Jewish Literature* (Heb.), which contains more than fifty stories and reports on the subject. Cf. Wildmann, *Magen vetsinah*, ch. 13, fo. 35*a*. For a dybbuk (an apostate, the mistress of a priest) who entered a young non-Jew, was exorcised with the aid of R. Shalom of Belz, and then entered the priest, see A. Michelson, *Dover shalom*, §72. Regarding reactions by maskilim concerning dybbuks, we read in the introduction to Alexander, *Niflaot hasaba kadisha*, ii, that the maskilim derisively ask: 'Why are [dybbuks] not seen at the present, as well?' The author seemingly alludes to S. An-Ski when he answers that they were seen 'until a certain heretic (it's not worthwhile to mention his long name) stood up and made fun of this in theatres and circuses, in order to engage in frivolity'. Alexander then cites proofs for the existence of evil spirits and dybbuks from Manasseh ben Israel, *Nishmat ḥayim* (an incident involving R. Solomon Alkabez), and from Hurwitz, *Sefer haberit.*

note 74 Bromberg, *Toledot haniflaot*, 22–3, observes that, on numerous occasions, R. Hayim Meir Yehiel of Mogielnica exorcised evil spirits, and they feared him. Once he slapped the cheek of a young man who had been possessed by an evil spirit, and the spirit immediately departed. When he was asked by the tsadik of Radoshitz what *kavanot* he used for the exorcism of spirits, he replied: 'Believe me, my master, I do not employ any *kavanot*; rather, these foolish [spirits] fear me, and therefore flee!' For a cantor who enticed youths to engage in homosexual acts and whose soul transmigrated as a dybbuk, see ibid. 26–7. See also ibid. 53–4, for a repentant Jew who became a rabbi and sought to exorcise a dybbuk. The spirit challenged him: 'Are you the one who will tell me to leave this person?' The power of repentance, however, is great, and the dybbuk was eventually compelled to depart. In Shenkel, *Ma'asiyot mitsadikim yesodei olam*, §3, R. Elijah Gutmacher declares that those who think that he is expert in the practical kabbalah are in error. Although he sometimes exorcised a dybbuk, he did so aided by the sanctity of a Torah scroll, and not by other means.

Chapter 10

note 6 According to the Yiddish version of *Shivḥei habesht* (ch. 16), the Ba'al Shem Tov employed the scribe to write an amulet, a fact that was obscured in the Hebrew text (p. 53). In *Hatamim*, 2 (Warsaw, 1936), letter 88, the Ba'al Shem Tov asks R. Tsevi Sofer to write an amulet for a woman who had given birth to stillborn boys. When the Ba' al Shem Tov was in Istanbul, he heard the wife of a worthy (whose only son had lost his sight) speaking disparagingly of 'holy names', and he was infuriated at her not believing in the effectiveness of the names (cf. Rapoport, *Divrei david*, fo. 30*b*); the woman was punished for her disbelief (*Shivḥei habesht*, 111–12). The Ba'al Shem Tov sought to extricate esoteric knowledge from the Sitra Ahra by means of holy names: Bodek, *Mifalot hatsadikim*, §17, fo. 14*b*. He once cautioned his scribe R. Tsevi that, if a demon were to come, he should 'use this holy name that I reveal to you' (Rodkinsohn, *Adat tsadikim*, §3). The responsa literature also writes of the power of the holy names. See e.g. M. Sofer, *Ḥatam sofer*, 'Oraḥ ḥayim', §197.

note 12 Cf. Neubauer, 'Collections from *Divrei Yosef* by R. Joseph ben Isaac Sambari', in id., *Medieval Jewish Chronicles*, 159, regarding R. Samuel ibn Sid (the author of *Kelalei shemuel*), who rid a synagogue in Seville of destructive agents. At first, no one could enter the building, and many died because of these presences. R. Samuel spent the night in the synagogue, and when a demon came to him, with his unsheathed sword in his hand, the rabbi showed him a wooden staff on which the Tetragrammaton was inscribed. Cf. *Lev. Rabbah* 25: 'This may be compared to the king who told his son: "Go forth and engage in business." He replied, "Father, I am afraid of robbers on the road, and pirates at sea." What did his father do? He took a staff, hollowed it out, placed a charm within it, and gave it to his son. He said to him: "Let this staff be in your hand, and you need not fear anyone."' This demon was compelled to convene the other demons, and R. Samuel cast them into a great pit, and decreed that they would not ascend, nor harm anyone. The difficulties entailed in the war against the destructive agents are depicted in Brandwein, *Degel maḥaneh yehudah*, §67: R. Judah Tsevi of Stretin was not informed that the house in which he was spending the night was inhabited by a dangerous *mezik*. During the night the tsadik went to the toilet, remaining there for a long time. Afterwards, he was angry at the inhabitants of the house for not having told him about this destructive agent, 'for the *kelipah* of this *mezik* had three heads', and in the toilet R. Judah Tsevi had succeeded in cutting off only two of them, and it was solely by means of a miracle that he succeeded in getting out of the chamber. When the tsadik left the house, he gave its owner a *shemirah* (literally, 'guarding'; another name for an amulet), and the *mezik* caused no further havoc. *Shivḥei habesht*, 119, attests that the tsadik has the ability to see the destructive agent. The Ba'al Shem Tov saw such a *mezik* that was facing the wall, 'and its appearance was as that of an utterly black cloud', but it was not visible to the *mokhiaḥ* of Polonnoye. Despite the householder's entreaties, the Ba'al Shem Tov was unwilling to drive out the *mezik*.

note 17 Brandwein, *Degel maḥaneh yehudah*, §113, tells of a hasid who had to build a house for himself in the forest. The destructive agents who resided there appeared in his courtyard, and caused him harm. A gigantic demon, holding an unsheathed sword in his hand, could not inflict any injury upon the hasid when the latter was sitting in his hut, but he threatened him and demanded that he leave the forest. The demon vanished upon the cock's crowing, and the *shemirah* that the hasid received from the tsadik put an end to this harassment. For the inhabiting of the forest by humans and its cleansing from demons, cf. *Sefer* *ḥasidim*, ed. Wistinetzki and Freimann, §371, p. 113. Cf. ibid., §1871, p. 453, which tells of Jews in Hungary who were compelled by the threats of a demon to leave the place where they had settled.

note 35 *Sefer hakavanot uma'asei nisim*, fo. 3*b*: 'Also, one day when they were studying, the rabbi [R. Isaac Luria] told the students: I see two adorned she-demons entering a certain room, where there are two young men, to defile them, and I am capable of saving them. Since they brought this upon themselves, for they are engaged in sorcery, I will not save them.' Breitstein, *Siḥot ḥayim*, 24–6, relates a story that had been heard from the rabbi of Mogielnica regarding a hidden tsadik named Shimon Plas who lived during the time of R. Isaac Luria. This concealed tsadik reproached a person who came with a request for a son, for having in his youth placed a ring 'on a [seeming] branch of a tree [that was actually the finger of the she-demon], and said, "Behold, you are betrothed."' He thereby betrothed the evil spirit, and the latter killed his little children. The concealed tsadik gave the man a writ of divorce, and commanded him to place it next to the tree. The rabbi of Mogielnica told the person who had asked him for children that he, too, was punished for having betrothed himself to a maiden who was an evil spirit. The rabbi gave him an amulet, which was his deliverance. See also Ben-Yehezkel, *Sefer hama'asiyot*, ii. 41–4, and sources for the story, ibid. 353–4.

note 36 Cf. Emden, *Birat migdal oz*, 'Aliyat hateva', 244: 'Known and renowned throughout the world is the bad occurrence that happened in the house of our master, may he rest in peace, [R.] Tsoref, in the holy community of Posen, during the time of the father of my father-in-law, the *gaon*, our teacher, the rabbi, R. Naphtali Katz, may the memory of the righteous be for a blessing, and . . . the rabbi, may the memory of the righteous be for a blessing, was an eyewitness. He spoke to me of the strange things done by the *ḥitsonim* in that house, before they were driven away from there.' See also Ben-Yehezkel, *Sefer hama'asiyot*, v. 434–5. Mention should be made here of the contents of 'A Wondrous Story', published in Yiddish in Reischer, *Sha'ar efrayim* in the Altona edn of 1736, but missing from the 1st edn (Fuerth, 1728), which is completely different from the Altona edn: Lilith entered a youth and tortured him for a number of years. R. Ephraim cured him, but said that the first woman that he married would die, since Lilith had dominion over him. And so it was. (My thanks to R. Gershon Kohen of Jerusalem for referring me to this source.)

Chapter 11

note 32 The hasidic story about the attendant of the Ba'al Shem Tov was included in Ehrman (Judaeus), *Der Ba'al Schem von Michelstadt*. It is implied by one of the notes in this composition that the author derived his information about the hero's life from the work by the rabbi's son: Wormser, *Das Leben und Wirken des in Michelstadt verstorbenen Rabbinen Seckel Loeb Wormser*. I examined the one remaining copy of this work in the British Museum, and discovered that it does not mention, or even allude to, the tale of the storytelling attendant. It transpires that on one occasion R. Ehrman met the (unspecified) *admor* of Habad, who had come to Germany for health reasons, and who invited Ehrman to visit Lubavitch. Ehrman travelled to the city and published his impressions from the visit in a newspaper article that was also issued as a separate pamphlet: *Eine Pflanzstaette der Tora, Seperat Abdruck des Aufsatzes 'Bei den Chassidi' von Judaeus, aus dem 'Israelit'*. It may be assumed that he was exposed to the account of the storytelling attendant during his stay in eastern Europe, either orally or through a written text (it should be recalled that both Rodkinsohn and Kaidaner were Habad hasidim), and transferred the story to the *ba'al shem* of Michelstadt. (Incidentally, Ehrman's book *Der Raw*, on the founder of Habad, was undoubtedly influenced by the stories of Habad, and especially by Rodkinsohn's *Shivḥei harav*.) The story appeared in a slightly adapted Yiddish version under the name 'Dem ba'al-shem tovs talmid un der bishaf', in Weitz, *Ba'al-Shem-Tov Motiven*. In striking contrast to this Yiddish adaptation is that by Tiger, *Der tsadik un der ba'al teshuvah*. The most noticeable of the changes introduced in the hasidic story by Tiger is that the storyteller, instead of being R. Jacob, the Ba'al Shem Tov's attendant, is now none other than R. Jacob Joseph of Polonnoye, the Ba'al Shem Tov's disciple.

Chapter 12

note 14 A similar story, disseminated by the pupils of R. Jonathan Eybeschuetz, is cited in Emden, *Beit yehonatan hasofer*, fo. *9a–b*: 'A certain butcher brought meat to sell. Eybeschuetz saw, and called to him, "What is this meat?" He replied, "It is kosher meat, that may be sold to Jews." He told him, "I order you to immediately bring the head of this animal to me." He went and brought it. He told him: "Stick your hand into the mouth of the beast," and he did so. The head closed its mouth and held the butcher's hand with its teeth, and did not want to release it. The butcher sought to free his hand by force, but was unable to do so. He cried bitterly that it was improperly slaughtered . . . Then Eybeschuetz commanded, the beast opened its mouth, and gave the butcher his hand back.' For the slaughterer who rendered animals unfit because of his hatred of butchers, see Gemen, *Sifran shel tsadikim*, 'Ma'arekhet' 36, §11. For the motif of the slaughtered head closing its mouth and trapping the hand of the wicked slaughterer, forcing him to admit that he has slaughtered animals improperly, see also Emden, *Edut beya'akov*, fo. *44a*; *Hashaḥar*, 5 (1874), 248.

Chapter 13

note 14 In Hazan, *Sipurim nifla'im*, §37, pp. 56–7, the rabbi of Lubavitch spoke, in the name of the Ba'al Shem Tov, of the great worth of prayer by simple folk. See E. Z. Stern, *Siḥot yekarim*, §54, pp. 44–5: a shepherd who served the Lord by blowing the *shofar* and in song, tossed up to heaven a coin that he had received as a gift from the local *poritz*, in order to please the Holy One, blessed be He. 'And the Ba'al Shem Tov said that he saw a hand from heaven that received the coin.' See also ibid., §82, pp. 60–1: a simple person, from the area of Koznitz, ate a great deal on the eve of Yom Kippur (in accordance with the commandment), and fell asleep. When he awoke, it was too late to go to Koznitz, and he was greatly distressed because his wife had ridden to the city with the holiday prayer books (assuming that her husband would come on foot), and he was left with nothing from which to pray. He said: 'Master of the Universe, arrange from the *alef-beit* all the prayers in the prayer book and the holiday prayer book', and he recited the letters of the alphabet in order. When the villager came to Koznitz upon the conclusion of the holy day, the Maggid remarked that 'by the recital of the *alef-beit*, all the firmaments were split and the gates of prayer were opened, for "God desires the heart" [BT *San.* 106*b*]!' Cf. Zevin, *Hasidic Tales: Festivals* (Heb.), 22–3: a *tamim*, during the time of R. Isaac Luria, asked the Lord to arrange words and verses from his letters. See Scheiber, 'Two Legends' (Heb.), 59–65.

note 19 Cf. the story appearing in Ehrmann, *Devarim arevim*, 'Stories of the Holy Rabbi, of R. Ts[evi] H[irsch] of Zhidachov', §3: a woman villager was accustomed to come to Berdichev for the Yom Kippur prayers. Once she was late, and R. Levi Isaac delayed the prayers, awaiting her arrival. When she came, the woman was happy that *Kol nidrei* had not yet begun, and she said, emotionally: Holy One, blessed be He! You have acted well with me, and I wish that you will have pleasure from your children! See also Hazan, *Sipurim nifla'im*, §37, pp. 56–7: the tsadik of Lubavitch tells, in the name of the Ba'al Shem Tov, of the virtues of the prayer of the simple and innocent; Beckmeister, *Sipurei niflaot migedolei yisra'el*, §7: a simple person tells the Lord on the eve of Yom Kippur: 'I forgive you for all your sins against me, and you forgive men for all [my] sins!' Moskowitz, *Otsar hasipurim*, xx. 12–13: on his way to the Ba'al Shem Tov on the eve of Yom Kippur, one of his followers sleeps in a forest, and is forced to remain in the forest on Yom Kippur. When, after Yom Kippur is over, he arrives, the Ba'al Shem Tov consoles him, saying that his stay in the forest was decreed (by heaven).

Chapter 14

note 1 I have not found any work examining the question of a connecting link between the rabbinic stories and the hasidic ones that speak of thirty-six hidden righteous ones. Many stories were collected by Klapholz, *The Thirty-Six Hidden Saints*, who, as is usual, is not precise in the citations of his sources. See also the stories by S. Y. Agnon, 'The Hidden Tsadik' (Heb.), in id., *Ir umelo'ah*, 220–7; id., 'What Caused the Ba'al Shem Tov to Become Known in the World' (Heb.), in id., *Ha'esh veha'etsim*, 91–3.

Benjamin Wolf Segel, using the pen-name 'Bar-Ami', wrote a story in German that appeared in *Ost and West* (published by Leo Winz) on the 'Thirty-Six Tsadikim' that was a version of R. Nahman's 'The Rabbi's Son', and claimed that R. Nahman had merely reworked the story of the thirty-six righteous. Segel argued (in a footnote) that the thirty-six 'competed' with the hasidic tsadikim, thus leading to the view that identifies the hidden righteous ones with the hasidic tsadikim. Many early stories of the thirty-six were 'adapted' in the spirit of hasidism, with the hasid replacing the 'hidden [tsadik]' (such as the tsadik assuming the functions of the prophet Elijah). See Bar-Ami, 'Aus der juedischen Sagen- und Maerchenwelt', 769–70, for the story of a hidden tsadik, a miller, who saved the mill owner and lost his standing as tsadik because he had taken advantage of what was told to him from heaven. He went into exile, and repented; he was forgiven, and was permitted to be a renowned *ba'al shem*; thus he was once again a tsadik, but no longer concealed. In a conversation with me, the late Professor D. Sadan told me that Segel was credible, and had received stories orally.

note 46 The hidden tsadik R. Moses Paschishek, a cattle-herder, was considered by the Ba'al Shem Tov to be one of the great ones of the generation. See R. Margaliot, *Or hame'ir*, 6. When the Ba'al Shem Tov came to cleanse the world of Frankists, he went to R. Shabetai of Rashkov, and they agreed that the consent of the two leading tsadikim of the generation must be obtained: namely, R. Hirsch Potoker (the brother of R. Me'ir of Peremyshlyany) and this hidden tsadik. A priest–sorcerer kindled a fire; the cattle-herder feared for his herd, and left the place. Thus the intent of the great ones of the generation to wipe out the Frankists came to naught. It is related (ibid. 13) that R. Uri of Strelisk 'said of the hidden one, R. Itamar Hakohen: "If the Temple were to be rebuilt today, R. Itamar could officiate as the high priest."' It was also said that he gave his daughter in marriage to R. Aaron Leib (the father of R. Me'ir of Peremyshlyany). R. Itamar's daughter married R. Isaac of Kalisz (the brother of R. Me'ir of Peremyshlyany).

Chapter 16

note 1 E. Margaliot collected diverse and important material on this subject in his *Elijah the Prophet* (Heb.), 128–34 ('Elijah and Hasidism'). He did not cite many hasidic stories, probably because of his unfamiliarity with this genre; nor did he use primary sources, relying instead on the studies by Horodezky, Bromberg, and others. A small selection, also taken only in part from primary sources, appears in the chapter on Elijah in hasidism in Menes, *Elijah the Prophet*, 226–45. In contrast, a wealth of material is related in Klapholz, *Stories of Elijah the Prophet*. Unfortunately, the collector of these stories, a Belz hasid, did not include all the hasidic stories about Elijah, and he makes no mention of books such as Bodek's, *Pe'er mikedoshim*, *Mifalot hatsadikim*, or *Ma'aseh tsadikim*, among others. Another book that provides rabbinic teachings and material from kabbalistic sources concerning Elijah is J. Y. Rosenberg, *Eliyahu hanavi*. See also *Yeda-am*, 7 (1962), which is devoted in its entirety to Elijah in Jewish tradition.

note 4 The story of the tidings of the Ba'al Shem Tov's birth may reasonably be assumed to have been influenced by the story of the birth of R. Isaac Luria. See Solomon of Dreznitz, *Shivḥei ha'ari*, fo. 1*a*; cf. fo. 2*a*: 'He said to him: take the child and hold him, for a great light shall come forth from him to the world. Afterwards, his father died, when he was a small child.' See also *Sefer hakavanot uma'asei nisim*, fo. 2*a*; Benayahu, *Sefer toledot ha'ari*, §151: 'And a son was born, and the house was filled with light.' Light at the time of birth, or following it, as was related of Moses (Exod. 34: 33–5; BT *Sot.* 12*a*), attests to the Shekhinah and the greatness of the newborn. When the future author of *Avnei nezer* was born, 'The entire house was filled with light, as is told of Moses' (Rakats, *Siaḥ sarfei kodesh*, v. 101). When R. Judah Tsevi of Stretin came into the world, the house was filled with light (Brandwein, *Degel maḥaneh yehudah*, §14); there was light in the pit in which R. Solomon Ephraim of Luntshits was born (after his parents had been thrown there, because of their debt to the local *poritz*: Bodek(?), *Sipurei kedoshim*, §5). At times light blazes over the head of the tsadik, thus revealing his true identity. See BT *Sot.* 12*b*; *Yalkut shimoni*, 167. There appears to be some influence here from the motif of the radiance of

Moses' face (see Exod. 34: 29–35). *Exodus Rabbah*, 47 (also cited in *Yalkut shimoni*, Exod., 407) asks: 'Whence did Moses take the horns of glory? . . . When he wrote with the quill, some remained, which he passed over his head, from which came forth the horns of glory.' Cf. *Sefer ḥasidim*, ed. Wistinetzky and Freimann, §1059, p. 269. It is related that when R. Gershon of Kutow brought his brother-in-law the Ba'al Shem Tov before the rabbi, so that the latter could reproach the Ba'al Shem Tov (this was before the latter revealed himself), 'When they entered the rabbi's house, the Ba'al Shem Tov removed his veil, the rabbi saw a great light and he rose before him' (*Shivḥei habesht*, 50). Another story of the Ba'al Shem Tov's revealing himself is also connected with the viewing of light and fire. On sabbath eve R. David of Kolomai, who was a guest in the house of the Ba'al Shem Tov (before he revealed himself), saw 'a great light under the oven'. He initially thought that a fire had started, but when he drew near 'he saw that the Ba'al Shem Tov was sitting, with light shining on him . . . The light was over him, like a rainbow' (ibid. 54). Cf. J. Y. Rosenberg, *Tiferet maharal*, 6. See also the following: a lamp burning over the head of R. Abraham Abusch of Frankfurt (A. Michelson, *Ohel avraham*, §5); 'a fiery bow' over the head of the Maggid of Mezirech when he was praying (Kleinmann, *Mazkeret shem gedolim*, 144); the face of R. Tsevi of Zhidachov, which glowed 'as the light of the noonday sun, and extinguished [i.e. overshadowed] the sun' (I. Safrin, *Netiv mitsvoteikha*, 'Shevil emunah', §1); light over the head of R. Nahum of Chernobyl (Kohen, *Shemuot vesipurim*, 233); the blazing light of the Shekhinah seen in the vicinity of the Ba'al Shem Tov's disciples as they danced (*Shivḥei habesht*, 98); fire glowing around those dancing at the wedding of a pair of orphans (A. Michelson, *Ohel elimelekh*, §153); the rabbi of Apta seeing a light over one of the grandchildren of R. Elimelekh (§145). This motif also appears in non-hasidic stories. See e.g. *Sefer hama'asiyot* (Baghdad), §108: a great light over a person's head is a sign that he merits the world to come. For light in non-Jewish literature, see Mach, *Der Zaddik im Talmud und Midrasch*, 66–7.

note 5 According to the Habad tradition (*Sefer hasiḥot* 5 (1943), 166–7), the Ba'al Shem Tov met Elijah during his youth, when he was together with other hidden tsadikim, but he saw the prophet by himself only on his sixteenth birthday, when he was alone in the fields. As he related: 'I was engaged in the *yiḥudim* of the holy names . . . Suddenly, I saw Elijah the prophet standing before me and smiling. I was greatly moved that I had merited *gilui eliyahu* when I was by myself' (from the source in Yiddish). In Letter 34, *Hatamim*, 2 (Warsaw, 1936), Adam Ba'al Shem Tov of Ropshits wrote to the Ba'al Shem Tov in 1735: 'The sign [i.e. proof, of the veracity of what I tell you] is that you have not yet had *gilui eliyahu*, and this year he shall be revealed to you!' For Elijah's coming to the Ba'al Shem Tov on Saturday night, after the departure of the sabbath, in order to deliver a blessing for a good week, see Gemen, *Sifran shel tsadikim*, 'Ma'arekhet' 1, §9. The stories of the visions of Elijah experienced by the Ba'al Shem Tov were probably influenced by similar stories concerning R. Isaac Luria; see e.g. *Sefer hakavanot uma'asei nisim*, fo. 2*b*.

note 11 'I heard from the pupils of R. Johanan Joseph Green, of blessed memory, that the Ba'al Shem Tov, may his merit protect us, was once in Lvov. He was speaking with the rabbi, the *gaon*, R. H[ayim] Kohen Rapoport, may the memory of the righteous be for a blessing, and he said to him: "I heard this from Elijah, of blessed mention." R. H[ayim] asked him: "Why does Elijah not come to me?" The Ba'al Shem Tov replied: "Because his honoured Torah [authority] is too strict, and Elijah does not come to one who is too strict." He replied, "Please tell him that I take it upon myself to abandon excessive strictness, if only Elijah would please come to me." The Ba'al Shem Tov assured him of this, and departed from him. R. H[ayim] had his daily regime, that each day he would sleep [only] a little, for so many hours. Just as soon as he lay down and went to sleep, a villager came to his house, and awakened him with his loud and strange voice. R. H[ayim] seized his pipe and struck him repeatedly with the stem. The following day, when he saw the Ba'al Shem Tov and asked him why Elijah did not come to him, the Ba'al Shem Tov replied that, immediately after his acceptance [of this condition], he had beaten Elijah!'

note 21 In the guise of a non-Jew, Elijah brought an *etrog* and the rest of the Four Species to the Ba'al Shem Tov (J. Sofer, *Sipurei ya'akov*, i, §13). For Elijah as a non-Jewish merchant, see Ehrmann, *Devarim arevim*, 'Stories of the Holy Rabbi, Our Master and Teacher, R. Me'ir of Peremyshlyany', §12. Elijah in the guise of a Polish-speaking non-Jew awarded the 'Holy Jew' his appellation (ibid., 'Luaḥ hatikun' [Corrigenda]). See the derisive maskilic response in *Hashaḥar*, 6 (Vienna, 1875), 3. Cf. BT *Ber.* 6*b*: 'in the guise of an Arab'; BT *Shab.* 109*b*: 'in the guise of a horseman'. The hasidic story does not discriminate against righteous women, several of whom merited *gilui eliyahu*. R. Joseph of Yampol (the son of R. Yehiel Michel of Zloczew) related that his mother had merited such a vision (Sobelman, *Sipurei tsadikim heḥadash*, §50), as did the wife of R. Hirsch of Chortkov and her maidservant (A. Michelson, *Shemen hatov*, 'Stories', §112), and the wife of R. Naphtali of Ropshits (Kamelhar, *Mevaser tov*, 11). Cf. Vital, *Sefer haḥezyonot*, fo. 10*a*, where Elijah appears to the daughter of R. Raphael. A fascinating story of a maidservant who merited seeing Elijah appears in M. H. Landau, *Ma'amar mordekhai*, introd., 6: the communal register of Sharigrad states that the Ba'al Shem Tov studied together with the grandfather of the narrator, R. Abraham Zak of Sharigrad, 'and they experienced *gilui eliyahu*'. Once the maidservant brought them three cups of coffee. When the rabbi asked why she had brought three cups of coffee, since they were only two, the maidservant replied that she saw three rabbis in the room. The Ba'al Shem Tov turned to R. Abraham (who had recently been widowed) and exclaimed: 'I tell you, because she merits seeing Elijah, therefore take her as a wife.' The Ba'al Shem Tov also promised the rabbi that he would have a son who would be both righteous and an outstanding Torah scholar. In response to the townspeople's derision at their rabbi's having married a servant girl, the Ba'al Shem Tov ordered that it be proclaimed: 'Whoever wishes to see Elijah at a circumcision, let him come to the great synagogue, where there is a circumcision, where he shall see Elijah the prophet on the Chair of Elijah.' Cf. what is told about the maidservant in the home of R. Samuel Shmelke of Nikolsburg, who served two glasses (one for Elijah): A. Michelson, *Shemen hatov*, 112). The maidservant of the Hida (R. Hayim Joseph David Azulai) peeped through a crack, and when she saw three guests (one of whom was Elijah), brought four cups of coffee.

'And it was said that apparently because of his [Azulai's] actions, Elijah came to him' (Farhi, *Oseh pele*, 1959 edn, fo. 68*a*). See also a similar story that was told about R. Shalom Sharabi: Weberman, *Ma'aseh nisim*, 42.

note 22 'And so Israel was accustomed to perform circumcision, until they were divided into two kingdoms. The kingdom of Ephraim prevented them from circumcising, and Elijah, of blessed mention, was greatly zealous . . . The Holy One, blessed be He, said to him: You are always zealous [on my behalf]. You were zealous at Shittim for the licentious behaviour there, as it is said: "Phinehas, son of Eleazar [son of Aaron the priest], has turned back my wrath from the Israelites by displaying among them his zealousness for me" [Num. 25: 11; the exposition is based on the identification of Phinehas with Elijah], and here [after the division of the Israelite kingdom] you are zealous. Your life [i.e. I swear], that Israel shall not perform any circumcision until you see with your own eyes [i.e. are present]. This is the source for the rabbinic regulation that a seat of honour is to be prepared for the angel of circumcision, as it is said: "As for the angel of the covenant that you desire, he is already coming" [Mal. 3: 1; this angel is identical with the Elijah who is mentioned at the end of Mal. 3: 'Lo, I will send the prophet Elijah to you'].' Cf. Zohar 1: 93*a*: 'He said to him: I swear to you that every place where my sons will make the holy mark in their flesh, you shall be there, and the mouth that attested that Israel abandoned [the commandment of circumcision] shall attest that Israel observes this.' *Shulḥan arukh*, 'Yoreh de'ah', 265: 'It is customary to prepare at the time of the circumcision a chair for Elijah, who is called the angel of circumcision . . . and when the infant is set down, they recite: "This is the chair of Elijah."'

note 28 Elijah gives a poor woman money to buy what she lacks for Passover (Ehrmann, *Devarim arevim*, 'Stories of the Holy Rabbi, of R. [Joshua] H[eschel] of Apta', §8). In the popular consciousness, Elijah lives as the harbinger of the messiah. The words of the prophet: 'Lo, I will send the prophet Elijah to you' (Mal. 3: 23) were interpreted as referring to the future, to the messianic era, leading to the understanding that Elijah would reveal himself one day before the advent of the messiah (BT *Eruv.* 43*b*, and Tosafot ad loc.; Maimonides, *Mishneh torah*, 'Laws of Kings', 12: 2; JT *Shab.* 1: 3; *Sifrei*, 'Berakhah' 1). Cf. the blessing recited after the *haftarah*: 'Gladden us, O Lord, our God, with Elijah the prophet, your servant, and with the kingdom of the House of David, your anointed.' Most of the stories depict Elijah as advocate and as the harbinger of 'good tidings, salvations, and consolations' (from Grace after Meals).

note 41 Ehrmann, *Devarim arevim*, 'Stories of the Holy Rabbi, of R. Ts[evi] H[irsch] of Zhidachov', §1, relates that Elijah was sent to put one of R. Tsevi Hirsch's hasidim to the test, as regards hospitality, and the hasid successfully withstood the trial. The same paragraph contains a story about *ba'al davar* (Satan) testing the hospitality of a worthy. Cf. Weberman, *Derekh tsadikim*, 'Kunteres menaḥem tsiyon', 42–3. Cf. Ehrmann, *Devarim arevim*, 'Stories of the Holy Rabbi, Our Master and Teacher, R. Me'ir of Peremyshlyany', §15, for a person who did not withstand the test in this realm to which he was subjected by Elijah. For a son born in the father's old age as a reward for his father's hospitality, see Farhi, *Oseh pele*, ii, 1879 edn, fo. 72*a*.

note 42 For another story about a gluttonous guest who was not of this world and who came to test his host, R. Abraham Abusch of Frankfurt, see Shenkel, *Ma'asiyot mitsadikim yesodei olam*, §14; A. Michelson, *Ohel avraham*, §7. The Ba'al Shem Tov said of R. Lieber: 'Even when Elijah the prophet, of blessed mention, wishes to speak with him, the rabbi must greatly trouble himself to find time for this, since he does not always have free time' (Liberson, *Tseror haḥayim*, §99); for another story concerning R. Lieber, see I. Landau, *Zikhron tov*, 'The Deeds of the Tsadikim', §2; Shenkel, *Sipurei anshei shem*, §22; Moskowitz, *Otsar hasipurim*, xvi, §4; Donner, *Derekh ha'emunah uma'aseh rav*, 'Hospitality', §5. Walden, *Shem hagedolim heḥadash*, 'Ma'arekhet: The Great Ones', *lamed*, §93, maintains that he was a disciple of the Maggid of Mezirech. See also Sadan, *Hebrew Literature* (Heb.), 108. For Elijah coming as a guest to the rabbi of Gostynin, who bemoaned his not having a guest in his *sukkah*, see Rakats, *Siaḥ sarfei kodesh*, i, §193.

note 47 For Elijah and R. Isaac Luria, see Bacharach, *Emek hamelekh*, third introd., ch. 1 (fo. 11*a*): 'until Elijah, of blessed mention, came and constantly revealed himself to him, and studied with him'. The writer emphasizes that *gilui eliyahu* is a level immeasurably higher that the appearance of a *magid*, since Elijah 'reveals himself with the Shekhinah, and the two are inseparable'. Cf. Solomon of Dreznitz, *Shivḥei ha'ari*, fos 2*a*–3*b* (pagination added): 'Elijah the prophet, of blessed mention, would at times reveal himself to [R. Isaac Luria], and teach him the esoteric knowledge of the Torah. . . . After two years of the utmost abstinence that he maintained in Egypt, Elijah, of blessed mention, revealed himself to him, and said: "The time of your death has drawn near."' 'Elijah, of blessed mention, was always revealed to him. . . . Elijah the prophet revealed himself to him, and he told him to seclude himself in a place of no speech, where he would have no affairs with any man . . . and there he would merit the spirit of divine inspiration and Elijah, of blessed mention, who would be revealed to him at every and all time, and he revealed the secrets of the Torah to him' (fo. 5*b*). Cf. *Sefer hakavanot uma'asei nisim*, fo. 2*b*: 'Elijah the prophet was revealed to him, and he said: Be strong and resolute in the commandments and the Torah, for if you shall do so, you shall merit the spirit of divine inspiration.'

note 63 Elijah reveals himself to a youth in the guise of a passer-by, accompanies him, and ensures that he will engage in Torah study, in order to annul a heavenly decree that he is to be hanged at the age of 13. Elijah tells him: 'I will reveal to you that I was with you on the way, in human guise, but I am Elijah, of blessed mention. I inform you that, for the second time, your wife shall conceive and give birth to a son; let my recompense for this from you be that you shall not circumcise him until I come and appear to you.' On the day of the circumcision, the father of the newborn asks those present to wait until the arrival of an important guest, 'until Elijah, of blessed mention, manifested himself, but no one other than [the father] saw him. Elijah sat on the chair, and the child's father sat [on Elijah's lap], [while only the father was] in full view of all.'

Chapter 17

note 32 In another well-known story the Ba'al Shem Tov crosses the River Dniester on a belt 'without any *shem*' (mystical holy name). Cf. Moses Hayim Ephraim of

Sudilkov, *Degel maḥaneh efrayim*, 'Vayishlaḥ'; I. Safrin, *Notser ḥesed*, fo. 43*a*; id., *Megilat setarim*, 34; Duner, *Sha'ar ha'emunah*, 1, 14, 63; Liberson, *Erets haḥayim*, §218, p. 72. As Safrin explains in *Notser ḥesed*, the Ba'al Shem Tov crossed the Dniester twice: the first time using one of the holy names, and the second time without using any name, relying solely upon the strength of his belief in God. The message of the passage, cited further on, is clear: it is definitely prohibited to employ holy names and whoever does so commits a sin. After relating some of the wonders worked by the Ba'al Shem Tov, the tsadik of Komarno adds: 'Yet all this is like a drop in a vast ocean, and represents merely a fraction of the great deeds our holy teacher performed among the Jews without the aid of the holy names. For in fact he never used that device. The Ba'al Shem Tov himself related that while he was still very young his great master, the prophet Ahijah the Shilonite, had taught him all the uses of the holy names, which he quickly learned. Since he was still so young, he was curious to know whether he had the spiritual power required to work a wonder. He therefore spread a garment on the face of the Dniester and crossed over, employing one of the names. The Ba'al Shem Tov repented of this act all the days of his life, and never ceased imposing fast-days on himself to expiate this transgression. The penance was finally completed in the following manner: on one occasion he was forced to cross the Dniester to escape from the non-Jews (the sons of Ishmael), who would surely have killed him. He spread a belt on the water of the river, and crossed without employing any holy name, relying entirely upon his great belief in the God of Israel.' Cf. Shalom of Koidanov, *Divrei shalom*, fo. 46*b*, col. *c*. On this subject see Sadan, 'The Story of the Handkerchief' (Heb.); Werses, *Story and Source* (Heb.), 204; Baharav, *Sixty Folktales* (Heb.), 266. Cf. also Farhi, *Mora'im gedolim*, 18 ff.: 'And the old man [Elijah] removed his coat, and spread it upon the face of the water. He said to the boy, "Rise up, and let us go together" . . . and in an instant they found themselves in Salonika.'

Glossary

admor (pl. ***admorim***) 'our master, teacher, and rabbi'; an honorific for a hasidic rabbi

agunah (pl. ***agunot***) a married woman whose husband is absent and who cannot remarry

alef-beit the Hebrew alphabet

aliyah immigration to the Land of Israel

aliyot neshamah out-of-body experiences of the soul leaving the body at night and ascending to the upper spheres

alma dekeshut the 'world of truth', i.e. the world to come

amora'im rabbis of the talmudic period

Ari the pre-eminent kabbalist R. Isaac Luria

asiyat tovah literally, 'performing a boon'; advocacy before the heavenly court by the tsadik on behalf of a dead person

atsilut in kabbalistic thought, the world of emanation

ba'al-bitaḥon a person with perfect trust in the Lord; an alternative manifestation of the *tamim*

ba'al davar agent of Satan

ba'al mofet wonder-worker

ba'al(ei) shem wonder-worker(s)

ba'al ta'avah someone who sins because he cannot control his passions

bedikat ḥamets the final search for *ḥamets* (leavened matter) on the evening preceding Passover

Council of Four Lands the central institution of Jewish self-government in Poland and Lithuania from the sixteenth to the eighteenth centuries

dayan (pl. ***dayanim***) rabbinical court judge(s)

devekut devotion to God

dinim evil decrees or punishing powers

dybbuk a soul that enters the body of a living person who possesses a soul of his or her own

emunat ḥakhamim originally, the traditional belief that the rabbis transmit the Oral Law from one generation to the next; in hasidic thought, this became the faith in the powers of the tsadikim

etrog citron, one of the Four Species taken on the festival of Sukkot

gadlut lit. greatness; mystical–religious level

galaḥ a derogatory term for a priest (literally, someone with a shaven head)

gaon (pl. ***geonim***) genius; as Gaon, honorific applied to Torah scholars

genizah repository of worn-out (or otherwise defective) sacred books

gilgul neshamot transmigration of souls

gilui eliyahu a revelation of the prophet Elijah

haftarah additional scriptural synagogue reading, from the Prophets

hakhnasat kalah the collecting of a bridal fund

ḥalah a portion of dough that is separated each time bread is baked, thus fulfilling a biblical commandment to give part of each batch of dough to the *kohanim*; alternatively, the special sabbath loaf of bread

halakhah the body of Jewish law and ritual

ḥaluka derabanan the spiritual 'cloak' that a person weaves for himself with his good deeds

ḥamets leavened matter, which must be sought out and burned (or otherwise destroyed) before Passover

Haskalah the Jewish Enlightenment

heikhal (pl. ***heikhalot***) the heavenly hall(s) or chamber-palace(s)

ḥelev forbidden animal fat

hilula banquet/celebration held to mark days of festivity

ḥitsonim 'external ones'; evil powers or spirits

ḥol hamo'ed the intermediary days of the festivals of Passover and Sukkot

ḥumash Pentateuch

ilui outstanding student

kashrut laws governing the permitted types and correct preparation of food

kavanah (pl. ***kavanot***) mystical intent

kefitsat haderekh (also ***kefitsat ha'arets***) the miraculous shortening of the way

kelipah (pl. ***kelipot***) literally, 'shell'; a kabbalistic term for the forces of evil and the non-holy

keruz*, *keruzin/m heavenly pronouncement(s)

ketubah wedding contract

kloyz synagogue study hall (literally, 'small room')

kohen a person of the priestly class

kvitl (pl. ***kvitlakh***) written account of one's woes, request for help; esp. a note delivered to the tsadik containing such a request

lamed-vavnik hidden tsadik

letsim 'mockers'; evil powers or spirits

ma'aseh merkavah visions of the divine chariot-throne; mystical contemplation of the divine

magid meisharim preacher

malakhei haḥabalah the destructive angels who seek to kidnap a dead person

mamzer the child of a forbidden union (not to be confused with the 'illegitimate' child in Western culture)

mashgiaḥ spiritual 'supervisor' in a yeshiva

maskil (pl. **maskilim**) adherent of the Haskalah

meḥutan the parent of the person to whom one's child is married

melamed teacher of young children (a profession not held in high regard)

melaveh malkah the festive Saturday night meal that 'accompanies' the departure of the sabbath 'queen'

mezikin agents of destruction; evil spirits

mezonot living expenses

midah keneged midah the punishment fitting the crime

mikveh ritual bath

Minhah the afternoon prayer

minyan quorum of ten adult males required for public prayers; more generally, a congregation

mitnaged (pl. **mitnagedim**) opponent of hasidism

mitsvah commandment; often, good deed

mohel (pl. ***mohalim***) circumciser

mokhiaḥ (pl. ***mokhiḥim***) preacher

musar ethical teachings

nasi literally, 'patriarch'; a title applied to various forms of Jewish leadership positions

netilat yadayim the ritual washing of the hands, upon awakening and before eating

nidah a state of ritual uncleanliness

nikur the removal of various fats, the sciatic nerve, etc., before meat may be consumed

nusaḥ sefarad Sephardi version of the prayers (preferred by hasidim, among others)

parnas synagogue warden

pidyon (pl. ***pidyonot***) literally, 'redemption'; a supplicatory donation

pidyon haben redemption of the firstborn; ceremony following the birth of a firstborn male child

pidyon nefesh monetary contribution accompanying a *kvitl*

piyut liturgical poem

poritz local Polish nobleman for whom the Jews used to collected taxes

posek (pl. ***posekim***) decisor of Jewish law

rabanit rabbi's wife

rebbe hasidic rabbi

Rosh Hodesh the new moon, i.e. the beginning of the Jewish lunar month

rosh yeshivah (pl. ***rashei yeshivot***) head of a yeshiva

sandak the person who holds the infant on his knees during the circumcision

sefirot manifested attributes of the deity

se'udah shelishit third of the three sabbath meals

se'udat mitsvah a meal connected with a religious event

shaliaḥ tsibur lay prayer leader

Shalom aleikhem the traditional greeting between two Jews (literally, 'Peace be unto you')

Shekhinah the Divine Presence

Shema yisra'el the fundamental declaration of faith in the unity of God ('Hear, O Israel')

shemirah (pl. ***shemirot***) 'guarding', i.e. amulet

shevaḥim hagiography

shofar ram's horn

shoḥet ritual slaughterer

shterntikhel ornate head-covering

shtreimel fur hat

siḥah batelah idle talk

siḥot ḥulin mundane talk

Sitra Ahra the 'other side', i.e. evil in all its various manifestations

Sitra Dekedushah the side of holiness

sotah the ritual prescribed for a woman suspected of adultery

talit prayer shawl

tamim simple, innocent person

tana (pl. ***tana'im***) rabbi of the mishnaic period

tena'im marriage conditions; the document specifying these terms

tikun metaphysical 'remedy' for the soul

tikun ḥatsot the prayer recited in the middle of the night for the destroyed Temple. The two variants of this prayer are Tikkun Leah and Tikkun Rahel

tikun nefesh repair of the soul

Tosafot major talmudic commentary

tsadik nistar 'hidden tsadik' (righteous person)

tsetl note

tsitsit ritual fringes

tsiyun headstone

ushpizin the seven 'guests' who visit the sukkah: Abraham, Isaac, Jacob, Joseph, Moses, Aaron, and David

vidui confession recited before death

wachtnacht The night before a circumcision, when people watch over the baby to make sure no harm befalls him

yahrzeit anniversary of a death

yarmulke skullcap

yeshiva talmudic academy

yiḥud the prohibition on a man being alone with a woman to whom he is not married or related

yiḥudim the effecting of a mystical 'union' of the *sefirot* in the upper spheres

zemirot melodies; especially, for the sabbath table

zloty gold coin of high value

Gazetteer of Place Names in Central and Eastern Europe

Bel. = Belarus; Cro.= Croatia; Cz. = Czech Republic; Ger. = Germany; Hung. = Hungary; Lat. = Latvia; Lith. = Lithuania; Mold. = Moldova; Pol. = Poland; Rom.= Romania; Rus. Fed. = Russian Federation; Slov. = Slovakia; Ukr. = Ukraine

Adamow Pol.; 62 km NNW of Lublin
Aleksandrow *see* Aleksandrow Lodzki
Aleksandrow Lodzki Pol.; 13 km WNW of Lodz
Alik *see* Aleksandriya Ukr.; 133 km NW of Rovno
Alikendorf Ger.; 107 km WNW of Leipzig
Altona Ger.; 69 km ENE of Munich
Annopol Ukr.; 50 km ESE of Rovno
Apta *see* Opatow
Atik Hotin possibly Ataki, Mold.; 176 km NW of Kishinev
Azipolia *see* Zhovten

Bar Ukr.; 62 km SW of Vinnitsa
Baranow Sandomierski Pol.; 114 km SSW of Lublin
Barezin *see* Berezhany
Barniv *see* Baranow Sandomierski
Belaya Tserkov Ukr.; 75 km S of Kiev
Belz Ukr.; 62 km N of Lvov
Ber *see* Bar
Berdichev Ukr.; 82 km N of Vinnitsa
Berezhany Ukr.; 82 km ESE of Lvov
Berzhan *see* Berezhany
Bilgoraj Pol.; 82 km S of Lublin
Bilgoray *see* Bilgoraj
Bodrogkeresztur Hung.; 45 km ENE of Miskolc
Bolshevetz *see* Bolshovtsy
Bolshovtsy Ukr.; 94 km SE of Lvov
Bratislava Slov.; 120 km SSE of Brno
Bratslav Ukr.; 56 km SE of Vinnitsa
Breslau *see* Wroclaw
Brno Cz.; 120 km NNW of Bratislava
Brod *see* Brody
Brody Ukr.; 88 km NE of Lvov
Bruen *see* Brno
Brull possibly Bruel, Germ.; 50 km SSW of Rostock, or Bruhl, Germ.; 19 km S. of Koln
Buchach Ukr.; 94 km NW of Chernovtsy
Bucovina A region now in north-eastern Romania and south-western Ukraine; part of the Austro-Hungarian Empire prior to the end of the First World War and then part of Romania until the end of the Second World War.
Bukovina *see* Bucovina
Butchatch *see* Buchach
Bychawa Pol.; 32 km S of Lublin
Bychow possibly Bykhov or perhaps Byckov (Bychawa)
Bykhov Bel.; 133 km NW of Gomel

Cherkassy Ukr.; 157 km ESE of Kiev
Chernev Ukr.; 69 km SE of Lvov
Chernobyl Ukr.; 101 km NNW of Kiev
Chernovtsy Ukr.; 214 km SW of Vinnitsa
Cherny Ostrov Ukr.; 126 km SSE of Rovno
Chervonoarmeisk Ukr.; 88 km SW of Rovno
Chisinau *see* Kishinev
Chmelnik *see* Khmelnic
Chocz Pol.; 82 km ESE of Poznan

Chortkov Ukr.; 82 km N of Chernovtsy
Chotch *see* Chocz
Chrzanow Pol.; 38 km W of Krakow
Chudnov Ukr.; 94 km NNW of Vinnitsa

Danzig *see* Gdansk
Daugavpils Lat.; 189 km ESE of Riga
Debrecen Hung.; 88 km ESE of Miskolc
Dinovitz *see* Dunayevtsy
Dobromil Ukr.; 94 km SW of Lvov
Dolina Ukr.; 107 km S of Lvov
Dorohoi Rom.; 126 km WNW of Iasi
Dreznitz *see* Partizanska Dreznica
Drogichin Bel.; 69 km W of Pinsk
Drogobych Ukr.; 69 km SSW of Lvov
Drohichin *see* Drogichin
Drohobitch *see* Drogobych
Dubno Ukr.; 38 km SW of Rovno
Dubrovno Bel.; 75 km SE of Vitebsk
Dukla Pol.; 82 km SW of Przemysl
Dunaberg *see* Daugavpils
Dunayevtsy Ukr.; 94 km NE of Chernovtsy
Dynow Pol.; 38 km W of Przemysl
Dzerzhinsk Bel.; 38 km SW of Minsk

Friedberg Ger.; 38 km N of Frankfurt am Main

Galicia A region that since the Second World War has been part of southern Poland and Ukraine. Prior to 1772, it constituted the southern part of the Kingdom of Poland, then became part of the Austro-Hungarian empire until the end of the First World War. It was then returned to Poland until the end of the Second World War
Gdansk Pol.; 240 km NNE of Poznan
Ger *see* Gora Kalwaria
Ginivishov *see* Gniewoszow
Gniewoszow Pol.; 62 km WNW of Lublin
Gora Kalwaria Pol.; 38 km SE of Warsaw
Gorodenka Ukr.; 50 km NW of Chernovtsy
Gorodok Bel.; 38 km NW of Vitebsk
Gostynin Pol.; 82 km N of Lodz
Graydung *see* Gorodok
Gritza *see* Grojec
Grodzisk Pol.; 13 km NNE of Warsaw
Grojec Pol.; 50 km S of Warsaw
Grosswardein *see* Oradea
Gusyatin Ukr.; 88 km N of Chernovtsy

Hanipoli *see* Annopol
Horodenka *see* Gorodenka
Horodok *see* Gorodok
Husyatin *see* Gusyatin

Iasi Rom.; 302 km ENE of Cluj
Ilintsy Ukr.; 56 km E of Vinnitsa
Ivano Frankovsk Ukr.; 114 km WNW of Chernovtsy
Izbica Pol.; 56 km ESE of Lublin
Izyaslav Ukr.; 69 km SE of Rovno

Jaroslaw Pol.; 32 km NNW of Przemysl
Jaslo Pol., 94 km WSW of Przemysl
Jassy *see* Iasi

Kaliningrad Rus. Fed.; 586 km SW of Pskov
Kalisz Pol.; 94 km WSW of Lodz
Kalev *see* Nagykallo
Kalyus Ukr.; 107 km NE of Chernovtsy
Kamenets-Podolski *see* Kamenets-Podolskiy
Kamenets-Podolskiy Ukr.; 62 km NE of Chernovtsy
Kamenka Bugskaya Ukr.; 38 km NNE of Lvov
Kaminka *see* Kamenka Bugskaya
Kapust *see* Kopys
Kariv *see* Kurow
Karlin Bel.; 6 km E of Pinsk
Kaunas Lith.; 94 km W of Vilnius
Kazimierz Dolny Pol.; 45 km W of Lublin
Kazmir *see* Kazimierz Dolny
Kerestir *see* Bodrogkeresztur
Kherson Ukr.; 146 km ENE of Odessa
Khmelnic Ukr.; 56 km WNW of Vinnitsa

Kishinev Mold.
Kisvarda Hung.; 94 km ENE of Miskolc
Kleinwardein *see* Kisvarda
Klimentov *see* Klimontow
Klimontow Pol.; 101 km SW of Lublin
Kobrin Bel.; 120 km W of Pinsk
Kock Pol.; 50 km NNW of Lublin
Koidanov *see* Dzerzhinsk
Kolbiel Pol.; 45 km ESE of Warsaw
Kolomai *see* Kolomyya
Kolomyya Ukr.; 69 km WNW of Chernovtsy
Komarno Ukr.; 38 km SW of Lvov
Konigsberg *see* Kaliningrad
Konstantynow Pol.; 107 km S of Bialystok
Koprzywnica Pol.; 101 km SSW of Lublin
Kopys Bel.; 101 km S of Vitebsk
Korets Ukr.; 62 km E of Rovno
Korostyshev Ukr.; 107 km WSW of Kiev
Kosov Ukr.; 62 km W of Chernovtsy
Kostantin *see* Konstantynow
Kotsk *see* Kock
Kovel Ukr.; 126 km WNW of Rovno
Kovla *see* Kovel
Kovno *see* Kaunas
Kozienice Pol.; 82 km WNW of Lublin
Koznitz *see* Koznienice
Krakow Pol.; 94 km SE of Czestochowa
Krivichi Bel.; 101 km NNW of Minsk
Krivitch *see* Krivichi
Krostchov *see* Korostyshev
Kshanev *see* Chrzanow
Kurow Pol.; 32 km WNW of Lublin
Kutow *see* Kuty
Kuty Ukr.; 56 km WSW of Chernovtsy

Lachowicze *see* Lyakhovichi
Lanchin Ukr.; 88 km WNW of Chernovtsy
Lantchin *see* Lanchin
Leczna Pol.; 26 km ENE of Lublin
Leczyca Pol.; 38 km NW of Lodz
Leiden possibly Leidenhofen, Ger.; 75 km N of Frankfurt am Main
Leipzig Ger.; 150 km SSW of Berlin
Lelov *see* Lelow
Lelow Pol.; 38 km ESE of Czestochowa
Lemberg *see* Lvov
Lentchna *see* Leczna
Lesko Pol.; 50 km SSW of Przemysl
Leszno Pol.; 69 km SSW of Poznan
Lezajsk Pol.; 56 km NW of Przemysl
Linitz *see* Ilintsy
Lipovets Ukr.; 38 km E of Vinnitsa
Liskovitz *see* Lyskowice
Lissa *see* Leszno
Litin Ukr.; 32 km WNW of Vinnitsa
Liubar *see* Lyubar
Lizhensk *see* Lezajsk
Lodz Pol.; 114 km N of Czestochowa
Lowicz Pol.; 50 km NNE of Lodz
Lubavichi Rus. Fed.; 75 km S of Smolensk
Lubavitch *see* Lubavichi
Lublin Pol.; 157 km ESE of Warsaw
Luntshits *see* Leczyca
Lutsk Ukr.; 62 km W of Rovno
Lvov Ukr.; 182 km SW of Rovno
Lyady Bel.; 38 km ESE of Minsk
Lyakhovichi Bel.; 107 km N of Pinsk
Lyskowice Pol.; 38 km NE of Lodz
Lyubar Ukr.; 94 km NW of Vinnitsa

Mako Hung.; 26 km E of Szeged
Makov *see* Makow Mazowiecki
Makow Mazowiecki Pol.; 69 km N of Warsaw
Maramaros *see* Sighet
Medzhibozh Ukr.; 82 km W of Vinnitsa
Medzibezh *see* Medzhibozh
Mezhirichi Ukr.; 45 km ENE of Rovno
Mezirech *see* Mezhirichi
Miechov *see* Miechow
Miechow Pol.; 38 km N of Krakow
Mikoliev *see* Nikolayev
Mikulov Cz.; 50 km S of Brno
Mogielnica Pol.; 69 km S of Warsaw
Mukachevo Ukr.; 182 km SSW of Lvov
Munkacs *see* Mukachevo

Nagykallo Hung.; 82 km ESE of Miskolc
Nashelsk *see* Nasielsk

Nasielsk Pol.; 45 km NNW of Warsaw
Nemirov Ukr.; 50 km WNW of Lvov
Nesterov Ukr.; 32 km N of Lvov
Nesukhoyezhe Ukr.; 139 km WNW of Rovno
Nezkizh see Nesukhoyezhe
Nikolayev Ukr.; 144 km NE of Odessa
Nikolsburg *see* Mikulov
Nimigea de Jos Rom.; 75 km NNE of Cluj
Nimsk possibly Nimizshe; *see* Nimigea de Jos
Novyye Veledniki Ukr.; 170 km WNW of Kiev
Nowy Sacz Pol.; 75 km ESE of Krakow
Noyve Strelishcha Ukr.; 50 km SE of Lvov

Opatow Pol.; 94 km SW of Lublin
Oradea Rom.; 133 km W of Cluj
Orsova Rom.; 246 km S of Cluj
Oshpetzin *see* Oswiecim
Ostila *see* Ustilug
Ostraha *see* Ostrog
Ostrog Ukr.; 38 km SE of Rovno
Ostropol Ukr.; 88 km WNW of Vinnitsa
Ostrovy *see* Ostrow Lubelski
Ostrow Lubelski Pol.; 32 km NNE of Lublin
Oswiecim Pol.; 50 km WSW of Krakow

Parczew Pol.; 50 km NNE of Lublin
Partizanska Dreznica Cro.; 101 km SSW of Zagreb
Pavoloch Ukr.; 101 km SW of Kiev
Peremyshlyany Ukr.; 45 km ESE of Lvov
Pilica Pol.; 50 km ESE of Czestochowa
Pilov *see* Pulawy
Piltz *see* Pilica
Pinczow Pol.; 69 km NNE of Krakow
Pinsk Bel.; 221 km SSW of Minsk
Pintchov *see* Pinczow
Piotrkow *see* Piotrkow Trybunalski
Piotrkow Trybunalski Pol.; 45 km SSE of Lodz
Pistin *see* Pistyn
Pistyn Ukr.; 69 km W of Chernovtsy
Plock Pol.; 94 km N of Lodz
Plonsk Pol.; 56 km WNW of Warsaw
Plotsk *see* Plock
Plunge Lith.; 88 km WSW of Siauliai
Plungian *see* Plunge
Podgaytsy Ukr.; 101 km ESE of Lvov
Podgorze Pol.; 13 km SE of Krakow
Podhaitza *see* Podgaytsy
Podkamen Ukr.; 94 km ENE of Lvov
Podolia A region in south-western Ukraine
Pogrebishche Ukr.; 62 km NE of Vinnitsa
Pokshivnitza *see* Koprzywnica
Polonnoye Ukr.; 107 km ESE of Rovno
Polotsk Bel.; 94 km WNW of Vitebsk
Posen *see* Poznan
Poznan Pol.; 157 km N of Wroclaw
Prainsk possibly in Volhynia, NW Ukr.
Premishlan *see* Peremyshlyany
Pressburg *see* Bratislava
Prinsk *see* Prainsk
Probisht *see* Pogrebishche
Proshovitza *see* Proszowice
Proszowice Pol.; 32 km NE of Krakow
Pruzhany Bel.; 120 km WNW of Pinsk
Przemysl Pol.; 163 km S of Lublin
Przeworsk Pol.; 38 km NW of Przemysl
Przysucha Pol.; 94 km ESE of Lodz
Pshemishel *see* Przemysl
Pshevorsk *see* Przeworsk
Pshischa *see* Przysucha
Pulawy Pol.; 45 km WNW of Lublin

Radom Pol.; 101 km W of Lublin
Radomsk *see* Radomsko
Radomsko Pol.; 38 km NNE of Czestochowa
Radoshitz *see* Radoszyce
Radoszyce Pol.; 82 km NE of Czestochowa
Radvil *see* Chervonoarmeisk
Rashkov Mold.; 114 km N of Chisinau
Ratzferd *see* Ujfeherto
Rava Ruska *see* Rava Russkaya
Rava Russkaya Ukr.; 50 km NW of Lvov

Reisha *see* Rzeszow
Riki *see* Ryki
Ropczyce Pol.; 88 km WNW of Przemysl
Ropshits *see* Ropczyce
Rozdol Ukr.; 50 km S of Lvov
Rudnik Pol.; 82 km NW of Przemysl
Ruzhin Ukr.; 75 km NE of Vinnitsa
Ryki Pol.; 62 km WNW of Lublin
Rymanow Pol.; 69 km SW of Przemysl
Rzeszow Pol.; 62 km WNW of Przemysl

Sadgura Ukr.; 6 km N of Chernovtsy
Sadigora *see* Sadgura
Sambor Ukr.; 69 km SW of Lvov
Sanz *see* Nowy Sacz
Sasov Ukr.; 69 km ENE of Lvov
Satanov Ukr.; 107 km N of Chernovtsy
Satmar *see* Satu Mare
Satoraljaujhely Hung.; 75 km NE of Miskolc
Satu Mare Rom.; 126 km NW of Cluj
Savran Ukr.; 75 km S of Uman
Sedeh Lavan *see* Belaya Tserkov
Shargorod Ukr.; 56 km SSW of Vinnitsa
Sharigrad *see* Shargorod
Shchuchin Bel.; 189 km WSW of Minsk
Shedlitz *see* Siedlce
Shepetovka Ukr.; 75 km ESE of Rovno
Sherensk *see* Szrensk
Shevershin *see* Szczebrzeszyn
Shinova *see* Sieniawa
Shklov Bel.; 114 km S of Vitebsk
Shpola Ukr.; 94 km NE of Uman
Siedlce Pol.; 88 km E of Warsaw
Sieniawa Pol.; 50 km NNW of Przemysl
Sighet Rom.; 133 km N of Cluj
Simleu Silvaniei Rom.; 75 km WNW of Cluj
Skalat Ukr.; 133 km N of Chernovtsy
Skarishov *see* Skaryszew
Skaryszew Pol.; 88 km W of Lublin
Skvira Ukr.; 94 km SSW of Kiev
Slavuta Ukr.; 56 km ESE of Rovno
Slonim Bel.; 126 km NW of Pinsk
Slutsk Bel.; 101 km S of Minsk
Sniatin *see* Snyatyn
Snyatyn Ukr.; 32 km WNW of Chernovtsy
Sochaczew Pol.; 56 km WSW of Warsaw
Sochatchev *see* Sochaczew
Stanislav *see* Ivano Frankovsk
Staroselye Ukr.; 101 km WSW of Odessa
Stepan Ukr.; 62 km N of Rovno
Stolin Bel.; 56 km ESE of Pinsk
Stopnica Pol.; 82 km NE of Krakow
Stovnitz *see* Stopnica
Strelisk *see* Noyve Strelishcha
Stretin Ukr.; 69 km ESE of Lvov
Stry *see* Stryy
Strykow Pol.; 26 km NNE of Lodz
Stry Ukr.; 75 km S of Lvov
Stutchin *see* Shchuchin
Sudilkov Ukr.; 82 km ESE of Rovno
Szczebrzeszyn Pol.; 62 km SE of Lublin
Szilagysomlyo *see* Simleu Silvaniei
Szrensk Pol.; 101 km NW of Warsaw

Tachov Cz.; 133 km WSW of Praha
Talnoye Ukr.; 38 km NE of Uman
Tarnopol *see* Ternopol
Tarnow Pol.; 75 km E of Krakow
Ternopol Ukr.; 120 km E of Lvov
Tetiyev Ukr.; 82 km NW of Uman
Ticheniz *see* Tikhinichi
Tikhinichi Bel.; 114 km WNW of Gomel
Tiktin *see* Tykocin
Tishvitz *see* Tyszowce
Tluste *see* Tolstoye
Tolstoye Ukr.; 62 km NNW of Chernovtsy
Tomashevka Bel.; 182 km SW of Pinsk
Tomashov *see* Tomashevka
Torun Pol.; 126 km NE of Poznan
Trisk *see* Turiysk
Tsirin Bel.; 107 km SW of Minsk
Tuchov *see* Tuchow
Tuchow Pol.; 88 km E of Krakow
Turbin *see* Turobin
Turiysk Ukr.; 133 km WNW of Rovno
Turobin Pol.; 50 km SSE of Lublin

Tykocin Pol.; 26 km W of Bialystok
Tyszowce Pol.; 107 km ESE of Lublin

Ujfeherto Hung.; 75 km ESE of Miskolc
Ujhely *see* Satoraljaujhely
Ukmerge Lith.; 69 km NE of Kaunas
Ulanov Ukr.; 56 km NW of Vinnitsa
Ustilug Ukr.; 120 km N of Lvov

Vilkomir *see* Ukmerge
Vilkovisk *see* Volkovysk
Vishnevets Ukr.; 88 km SSW of Rovno
Vishniets *see* Vishnevets
Vitebsk Bel.; 221 km NE of Minsk
Vladnik *see* Novyye Veledniki
Volkovysk Bel.; 163 km WNW of Pinsk
Volozhin Bel.; 75 km W of Minsk

Warka Pol.; 56 km SSE of Warsaw
Wolodni possibly Volodeni, Mold.; 182 km NW of Kishinev
Wroclaw Pol.; 150 km W of Czestochowa

Yampol Ukr.; 114 km S of Vinnitsa
Yarishev *see* Yaryshev
Yaroslav *see* Jaroslaw
Yaryshev Ukr.; 101 km SSW of Vinnitsa
Yadimov *see* Adamow

Zablutov *see* Zabolotov
Zabolotov Ukr.; 50 km WNW of Chernovtsy
Zaleshchiki Ukr.; 45 km NNW of Chernovtsy
Zamosc Pol.; 75 km SE of Lublin
Zaslov *see* Izyaslav
Zbarazh Ukr.; 107 km S of Rovno
Zelechow Pol.; 82 km NW of Lublin
Zhidachov Ukr.; 56 km SSE of Lvov
Zhitomir Ukr.; 120 km N of Vinnitsa
Zholkva *see* Nesterov
Zhovten Ukr.; 107 km SE of Lvov
Zhuravichi Bel.; 94 km NNW of Gomel
Zinkovtsy (Zinkowitz) Ukr.; 69 km NE of Chernovtsy
Zinkowitz *see* Zinkovtsy
Zloczew Pol.; 69 km SW of Lodz
Zlotchev *see* Zolochev
Zolishtchik *see* Zaleshchiki
Zolkiew Pol.; 45 km SE of Lublin
Zolochev Ukr.; 62 km E of Lvov
Zuravitch *see* Zhuravichi

Compiled by Yehudit Malkiel from Gary Mokotoff and Sallyann Amdur Sack, *Where Once We Walked: A Guide to the Jewish Communities Destroyed in the Holocaust* (Teaneck, NJ, 1991).

Bibliography

AARON OF APTA, *Keter shem tov* (Zholkva, 1794/5).

AARON OF ZHITOMIR, *Toledot aharon* (Jerusalem, 1966 [Berditchev, 1817]).

ABRAHAM BEN ISAIAH HADAYAN, *Holekh tamim ufo'el tsedek* (Livorno, 1850).

ABRAHAM OF SLONIM, *Beit avraham* (Jerusalem, 1973).

AGNON, S. Y., *Elu ve'elu* (Jerusalem, 1964).

—— *Ha'esh veha'etsim* (Jerusalem and Tel Aviv, 1966).

—— *Hakhnasat kalah* (Jerusalem, 1959); pub. in English as *The Bridal Canopy*, trans. I. M. Lask (New York, 1967).

—— *Ir umelo'ah* (Jerusalem and Tel Aviv, 1973).

—— *Sefer sofer vesipur* (Jerusalem, 1978).

ALEXANDER, REUBEN HAYIM, *Niflaot hasaba kadisha* (Piotrkow, 1929–37).

AL-HAKAM, JOSEPH HAYIM BEN ELIJAH, *Nifla'im ma'asekha* (Jerusalem, 1912).

AN-SKI, S., *Collected Writings* (Yiddish), vol. xv (Vilna, 1925).

A[PPELMAN], J[OHANN] C[HRISTIAN], *Das Leben Elchanans* (Frankfurt am Main, 1753).

Arba'ah arazim (Benei Berak, n.d.).

ARTEN, ISRAEL JACOB, *Emet ve'emunah* (Jerusalem, 1940).

ASSAF, D., *The Regal Way: The Life and Times of R. Israel of Ruzhin* (Jerusalem, 1997).

ASSAF, SIMHAH, 'Letters from Safed' (Heb.), *Kovets al yad*, 13 (1939), 115–42.

Avot derabi natan, trans. J. Goldin as *The Fathers According to Rabbi Nathan* (New Haven, 1955).

AZIKRI, ELEAZAR, *Sefer ḥaredim* (Venice, 1601; repr. Lublin 1897).

AZULAI, HAYIM JOSEPH DAVID (HIDA), *Shem hagedolim* (Vilna, 1853).

BACHARACH, NAPHTALI, *Emek hamelekh* (Amsterdam, 1648).

BADER, G., *Galician Jewish Celebrities* [Medinah veḥokhmeiha] (New York, 1934).

BAHARAV, Z., *Sixty Folktales Collected from Narrators in Ashkelon* [Shishim sipurei am] (Haifa, 1962).

BANET, MORDECAI, *She'elot uteshuvot parashat mordekhai* (Sighet, 1889).

BAR-AMI [BENJAMIN WOLF SEGEL], 'Aus der juedischen Sagen- und Maerchenwelt', *Ost und West*, 11 (1911), cols 769–70.

BAR-YITZHAQ, H., 'The Pattern of Filling Gaps in Rainmaking Folktales' (Heb.), *Yeda-am*, 19 (1979), 62–8.

Barnai, Y., 'Notes on the Immigration of R. Abraham Gershon Kutower to Eretz-Israel' (Heb.), *Zion*, 42 (1976–7), 111–19.

Basilea, Aviad, *Emunat ḥakhamim* (Mantua, 1730).

Bastomski, S., *Yiddish Folktales and Legends* [Yidishe folksmayses un legenden], 3 vols (Vilna, 1925–7).

Beckmeister, Y., *Sipurei niflaot migedolei yisra'el* (Jerusalem, n.d.).

Beer, M., 'Regarding the Sources of the Number of the 36 *Tsadikim*' (Heb.), *Bar-Ilan, Annual of Bar-Ilan University: Studies in Judaica and the Humanities*, 1 (Ramat Gan, 1963), 172–6.

'Beiträge zur jüdischen Sagen- und Spruchkunde im Mittelalter', *Jahrbücher für Judische Geschichte und Litteratur*, 9 (Frankfurt am Main, 1889), 1–71.

Bek, Shalom Issachar, *Kunteres dover shalom* (New York, n.d.).

Ben Ze'ev, son of R.A.Y., *Devarim yekarim* (Piotrkow, 1905).

Benayahu, M., *Sefer toledot ha'ari* [*Toledot ha'ari* and Luria's *Hanhagot*] (Jerusalem, 1967).

Ben-Yehezkel, M., *Kovets lemo'ed sukot* [anthology on Sukkot] (Jerusalem, 1946).

—— *Sefer hama'asiyot* (Tel Aviv, 1957–9).

Ben-Yehudah, E., *Complete Dictionary of Ancient and Modern Hebrew* [Milon halashon ha'ivrit], xii (Jerusalem and Berlin, 1908).

Berger, Israel, *Eser atarot* [tales of tsadikim] (Piotrkow, 1910).

—— *Eser kedushot* [tales of tsadikim] (Piotrkow, 1906).

—— *Eser orot* [tales of tsadikim] (Piotrkow, 1907).

—— *Eser tsaḥtsaḥot* [tales of tsadikim] (Piotrkow, 1910).

—— *Zekhut yisra'el*: comprises *Eser atarot*, *Eser kedushot*, *Eser orot*, and *Eser tsaḥtsaḥot*.

Berger, Moses, *Divrei elimelekh*, in id., *Ahavat shalom tanina* (Sighet, 1907).

Bergman, Eleazar, *Kotsker Tales* (Yiddish) (Warsaw, 1924).

Bichovski, H. E., *Ginzei nistarot* (Jerusalem, 1924).

Biegeleisen, Joseph Hayim, *Ḥemdah genuzah: A Collection of Letters by the Ba'al Shem Tov and his Holy Company* (Heb.) (Brooklyn, NY, 1944 [*c*.1920]).

Bodek, Menahem Mendel, *Einot mayim* (Lemberg, 1856).

—— *Kahal kedoshim* (Lemberg, 1865).

—— *Ma'aseh tsadikim im divrei tsadikim* (Lemberg, 1864).

—— *Mifalot hatsadikim im divrei meisharim* (Lemberg, 1866?).

—— *Pe'er mikedoshim* (Lemberg, 1865; new edn 1991, ed. G. Nigal).

—— *Seder hadorot heḥadash* (Lemberg, 1865).

—— *Seder hadorot mitalmidei habesht* [The Chronology of the Disciples of the Ba'al Shem Tov] (Lemberg, 1880?).

[——?] *Sipurei kedoshim* (Leipzig?, 1866); ed. G. Nigal (Jerusalem, 1977).

—— *Zikhron menaḥem* [commentary on 'Tikunei hazohar'] (Lemberg, 1875).

Brandwein, Eliezer, *Degel maḥaneh yehudah* (Lemberg, 1912).

Brawer, Michael, *Pe'er yitsḥak* (Lvov, 1928).

Breitstein, Solomon Zalman, *Siḥot ḥayim* (Piotrkow, 1914).

Bromberg, Israel Moses, *Toledot haniflaot* (Warsaw, 1899).

Brukman, Mordecai, *Migdal david* [tales of R. David of Lvov] (Piotrkow, 1930).

Chervinski, Joshua, *Teshuot ḥen*, 2 vols (Jerusalem, 1921).

Chikernik, Isaiah Wolf, *Ma'asiyot uma'amarim yekarim* [hasidic tales] (Zhitomir, 1902).

—— *Ma'asiyot vesipurim yekarim*, in *Sipurei ḥasidut tchernobil* [hasidic tales], ed. G. Nigal (Jerusalem, 1994), 44–5.

—— *Sipurim neḥmadim* [hasidic tales] (Zhitomir, 1903).

—— *Sipurim nifla'im uma'amarim kedoshim* [hasidic tales] (Lemberg, 1908).

—— *Sipurim uma'amarim yekarim* [hasidic tales] (Warsaw, 1903).

Dan, J., *The Hasidic Novella* [Hanovelah haḥasidit] (Jerusalem, 1966).

—— *The Hasidic Story: Its History and Development* [Hasipur haḥasidi] (Jerusalem, 1975).

—— *The Hebrew Story in the Middle Ages* [Hasipur ha'ivri biyemei habeinayim] (Jerusalem, 1974).

—— 'The History of the Hebrew *Akdamot* Story' (Heb.), *Bikoret ufarshanut*, 9–10 (1976), 197–213.

Deinard, Ephraim, *Mashgei ivrim* [Those Who Mislead the Blind] (St. Louis, 1919).

Drickerman, Jacob, *Temimei derekh* (Jerusalem, 1994).

Drohobitcher, Baruch, 'Three Versions of my Ancestor the Ba'al Shem Tov's Journey to the Land of Israel' (Heb.), *Yeda-am*, 6 (1959–60), 41–4.

Dubnow, S., *The History of Hasidism* [Toledot haḥasidut] (Tel Aviv, 1960).

Duner, Jacob Shalom Hakohen, *Derekh ha'emunah uma'aseh rav* [hasidic anthology] (Warsaw, 1899).

Duner, Nathan Neta, *Butsina kadisha* (Piotrkow, 1912).

—— *Derekh ha'emunah uma'aseh rav* (Warsaw, 1899).

—— *Menorat zahav* (Warsaw, 1902).

—— *Rishpei esh hashalem* (Piotrkow, 1904).

—— *Sha'ar ha'emunah* (Warsaw, 1903).

—— and Menahem Mendel Wodnik, *Sefer ba'al shem tov* (Lodz, 1938).

EHRENREICH, SOLOMON ZALMAN, *Tiyul bapardes*, 2 vols (Szilagysomlyon, 1939–40; repr. New York, 1963).

—— *Eine Pflanzstätte der Tora, Seperat Abdruck des Aufsatzes 'Bei den Chassidim' von Judaeus, aus dem 'Israelit'* (Frankfurt am Main, 1920?).

—— *Der Raw* (Frankfurt am Main, 1914).

EHRMANN, DOV BAER, *Devarim arevim* [hasidic tales] (Munkacs, 1903–5).

—— *Devarim arevim hashalem* (Israel, 1973).

—— *Pe'er vekhavod* [hasidic tales] (Munkacs, 1911).

—— *Zokhreinu leḥayim* [hasidic tales] (Munkacs, 1938).

EHRMANN (JUDAEUS), HERZ, *Der Ba'al Schem von Michelstadt* (Frankfurt am Main, 1907).

EISENSTADT, BENZION, *Dor rabanav vesoferav*, 6 vols (Vilna, 1861).

ELEAZAR BEN JUDAH OF WORMS, *Sefer haroke'aḥ* (Jerusalem, 1960).

ELIJAH BEN SOLOMON ABRAHAM HAKOHEN (Ha'itamari), *Midrash talpiyot* (Smyrna, 1736).

—— *Shevet musar* (Constantinople, 1712; Amsterdam, 1732; Jerusalem, 1993).

ELIMELEKH OF LYZHANSK, *No'am elimelekh* (Lemberg, 1788).

EMDEN, JACOB (YAVETS), *Beit yehonatan hasofer* (Altona, 1763?).

—— *Birat migdal oz* (Berdichev, 1831).

—— *Edut beya'akov* (Altona, 1756).

—— *Megilat sefer* (Warsaw, 1896).

Encyclopaedia Judaica, 16 vols, ed. Cecil Roth (Jerusalem, 1971–2).

EPHRATI, DAVID TEVELE, *Toledot anshei shem* (Warsaw, 1875).

EPSTEIN, KALMAN KALONYMUS, *Ma'or vashamesh* [hasidic commentary on the Torah and *megilot*] (Breslau, 1842).

ERTER, ISAAC, *Gilgul nefesh*, in *Hatsofeh leveit yisra'el* (Vienna, 1864).

EVEN-SHEMUEL, J., 'From the Thought of R. Israel Ba'al Shem Tov' (Heb.), in J. L. Maimon (Fishman) (ed.), *Sefer habesht* (Jerusalem, 1960), 84–90.

FARHI, SHABETAI, *Mora'im gedolim* (Warsaw, 1909).

—— *Oseh pele* (Livorno, 1879; Jerusalem, 1959).

FISHMAN (MAIMON), JUDAH LEIB, *Sarei hame'ah*, 6 vols (Tel Aviv, 1978).

FRANKEL, JOAB, and ISAAC FRANKEL, *Ḥen tov zevaḥ tov* (Zolkiew, 1806).

FTAYYA, JUDAH MOSES JESHUA, *Ruḥot mesaperot* (Baghdad, 1933).

GANS, DAVID, *Tsemaḥ david*, ed. M. Breuer (Jerusalem, 1983).

GANUZ, I., 'The Thirty-Six Just Persons in the Jewish Folklore of Lithuania and Beyelo-Russia' (Heb.), *Yeda-am*, 43–4 (1977), 28–31.

GAON, M. D., *Oriental Jews in Palestine* (Jerusalem, 1937).

Gedolim ma'asei hashem (Warsaw, 1909).

GELB, SOLOMON, *Beit shelomoh* (Orsova, 1928).

GELERNTER, ISRAEL DOV BAER, *Revid hazahav* (Przemysl, 1876).

GEMEN, ELIEZER DOV, *Sifran shel tsadikim* [tales of tsadikim] (Warsaw, 1914).

GLITSENSTEIN, A. H., *Rabi duber, harav hamagid mimezirekh* (Brooklyn and Kefar Habad, 1975).

—— *Rabi yisra'el ba'al shem tov* (Kefar Habad, 1975).

—— *Sefer hatoledot rabi menaḥem mendel ba'al hatsemaḥ tsedek* (Brooklyn and Kefar Habad, 1976).

GOLDBERG, R., 'The Hasidic Story as Told by the Tsadik: Literary Form and Idea . . . the Stories of Rabbi Israel of Ruzhin' (Heb.), Ph.D. diss., Hebrew University of Jerusalem, 1997.

GOLDBERGER, ZE'EV WOLF, *Darkhei hatov vehayashar* (Munkacs, 1910).

GOLDSTEIN, MOSES, *Masaot yerushalayim* (Munkacs, 1931).

GOTTLIEB, PESAH, *Ḥidushei maharaf* [talmudic commentary] (Ashdod, 1998).

GRAF, MOSES BEN MENAHEM (PRAEGER), *Zera kodesh* (Fuerth, 1696).

GROSS, M. D., *Otsar ha'agadah*, iii (Jerusalem, 1961).

GUEDEMANN, M., *Hatorah vehaḥayim . . .* (*Geschichte des Erziehungswesens und der Cultur der abendlandischen Juden wahrend des Mittelalters*), i (Warsaw, 1897; photocopied edn Jerusalem, 1972).

HABERMANN, A. M., 'The Gates of Habad' (Heb.), in *Alei Ayin: The Salman Schocken Jubilee Volume* (Jerusalem, 1948–52), 293–370.

Ha'entsiklopediyah ha'ivrit, 37 vols (Jerusalem and Tel Aviv, 1949–95).

HAGER, JACOB, and ISRAEL BERGER, *Ateret ya'akov veyisra'el* (Lvov, 1881).

HAGIZ, MOSES, *Mishnat haḥakhamim* (Chernovtsy, 1864).

HAKOHEN, BARUCH DAVID, *Birkat ha'arets* (Jerusalem, 1904).

HALEVI, ME'IR, *Or leshamayim* (Lvov, 1850).

HALPERIN, JACOB SOLOMON, *Yefeh anaf* (Jerusalem, 1959).

HALPERN, I., 'The Wozczylo Revolt' (Heb.), *Zion*, 22 (1957), 56–67.

HAMPEL, Z., 'A Blacksmith from the Thirty-Six Hidden Saints' (Heb.), *Yeda-am*, 15 (1971), 113–14.

HAZAN, ABRAHAM, *Kokhvei or* (Jerusalem, 1961).

—— *Sipurim nifla'im* (Jerusalem, 1934).

HEILPERIN, MENAHEM MANISH, *Menaḥem meshiv nefesh* (Lemberg, 1900–7).

HELLER, B., ' "Gott Wünscht das Herz". Legenden über Einfältige Andacht und über den Gefährten im Paradies', *Hebrew Union College Annual*, 4 (1927), 365–404.

Ḥemdat hayamim (Venice?, 1793).

HOLTZ, A., *The Tale of Reb Yudel Hasid: From a Yiddish Narrative in 'Nisim veniflaot' to S. Y. Agnon's 'Hakhnasat kalah'* [Ma'aseh r. yudel ḥasid: mereshito be*Nisim veniflaot* ad *Hakhnasat kalah* me'et shai agnon] (New York, 1986).

HORODEZKY, S. A., *Hasidism and Hasidim* [ḥasidut vehaḥasidim], 4 vols (Tel Aviv, 1951).

HOROWITZ, ISAIAH, *Shenei luḥot haberit* (Amsterdam, 1649).

HOROWITZ, NAPHTALI TSEVI, *Imrei shefer* (Lvov, 1884).

HOROWITZ, TSEVI JOSHUA, *Semikhut mosheh* (Przemysl, 1887).

HOROWITZ, Z., *The Horowitz Family: The Great Downfall* [Mishpaḥat horovits: hanefilah hagedolah] (Kiryat Tivon, 1973).

HOZIN, SOLOMON BEKHOR, *Ma'asim tovim* (Baghdad, 1890).

HURWITZ, PHINEHAS ELIJAH, *Sefer haberit* (Bruen, 1797).

IBN YAHYA, GEDALIAH, *Shalshelet hakabalah* (Zolkiew, 1804; repr. Jerusalem 1962).

ISAAC BEN ELIEZER ROKE'AH OF WORMS, *Sefer hagan* (Venice, 1606).

[ISAAC DOV BAER BEN TSEVI HIRSCH], *Kahal ḥasidim heḥadash* [*Emunat tsadikim*] [hasidic tales] (Warsaw, 1900; Lvov, 1902).

ISAAC JUDAH YEHIEL SAFRIN, *Megilat setarim*, 1st edn, from a manuscript (Jerusalem, 1944).

ISRAEL, MAGID OF SLUTSK, *Sefer havikuaḥ* (Warsaw, 1798).

ISRAEL BEN SASON, *Likutei ma'asiyot* (Jerusalem, 1909).

ISRAEL OF RUZHIN, *Irin kadishin* (Warsaw, 1885).

JACOB BEN EZEKIEL HALEVI OF ZLOTOWA, *Shem ya'akov* (Frankfurt, 1716).

JACOB ISAAC (THE SEER OF LUBLIN), *Divrei emet* (Munkacs, 1942).

JACOB JOSEPH OF POLONNOYE, *Ben porat yosef* (Korets, 1781).

—— *Toledot ya'akov yosef* (Korets, 1780).

—— *Tsafenat pane'aḥ* (Korets, 1782), ed. G. Nigal in Jacob Kaidaner, *Sipurim nora'im* (Jerusalem, 1992).

JAGEL, ABRAHAM, *Gei ḥizayon* (Alexandria, 1880).

JELLINEK, A., *Beit hamidrash*, 6 vols (Jerusalem, 1938).

JOSEPH BEN JUDAH YUDEL OF DUBNO, *Yesod yosef* (Shklov, 1785).

JOSEPH BEN R. A., *Mifalot tsadikim heḥadash* (Piotrkow, 1901).

JOUSEP (JUSPA) SCHAMMES OF WORMS, *Ma'aseh nisim* (Amsterdam, 1695).

JUDAH YEHIEL OF ROZDOL, *Lev same'aḥ heḥadash* (Jerusalem, 1963).

KAHANA, HAYIM, *Even shetiyah* (Munkacs, 1930).

KAHANA, Y. Z., *Sefer ha'agunot* (Jerusalem, 1954).

KAIDANER, JACOB, *Metsaref ha'avodah* (Koenigsberg, 1918).

—— *Sipurim nora'im* [hasidic tales] (Lemberg, 1875); ed. G. Nigal (Jerusalem, 1992).

KAMELHAR, YEKUTIEL ARYEH, *Em labinah* (Lemberg, 1909).

—— *Mevaser tov* (Podgorze, 1900).

KARO, JOSEPH, *Magid meisharim* (Jerusalem, 1960).

—— *Shulḥan arukh*, standard edns.

KATTINA, JACOB, *Raḥamei ha'av* (Chernovtsy, 1865).

KAYARA, SHIMON, *Halakhot gedolot* [eighth-century halakhic work] (Berlin, 1890–2).

KLAPHOLZ, I. J., *Lamed-vav tsadikim nistarim*, 2 vols (Tel Aviv, 1968), pub. in part in English as *The Thirty-Six Hidden Saints*, 2 vols, trans. S. Weinbach (Benei Berak, 1981).

—— *Stories of Elijah the Prophet*, trans. A. Nadav, 3 vols (Benei Berak, 1973–9).

KLAUSNER, J., *A History of Modern Hebrew Literature* [Historiyah shel hasifrut ha'ivrit heḥadashah], 6 vols (Jerusalem, 1952).

KLEINMANN, MOSES HAYIM, *Layesharim tehilah* (Piotrkow, 1910).

—— *Mazkeret shem gedolim* [tales of tsadikim] (Piotrkow, 1908).

—— *Or yesharim arba'ah metivei lekhet* [tales of tsadikim] (Warsaw, 1924).

—— *Zikhron larishonim arba'ah metivei lekhet* [tales of tsadikim] (Piotrkow, 1912).

KNAFO, JOSEPH, *Ot berit kodesh* (Livorno, 1884–5).

KOENNEKER, B., 'Die Geschichten von Rabbi Adam und der Fauststoff', *Frankfurter Judaistische Beiträge*, 6 (1978), 91–106.

KOHEN, RAPHAEL NAHMAN, *Shemuot vesipurim* (Kefar Habad, 1972).

KOHEN-TSEDEK, JOSEPH, *Mikha'el hanehefakh lesama'el* ([The Angel] Michael Who Changed into Samael [= the Devil]) (London, 1879).

KURZWEIL, BARUCH, *Essays on the Stories of S. Y. Agnon* [Masot shel shai agnon] (Jerusalem, 1970).

LANDAU, ISAAC, *Zikhron tov* (Piotrkow, 1912).

LANDAU, ISRAEL JONAH, *Ein habedolaḥ* (Piotrkow, 1901).

LANDAU, MATITYAHU, *Toledot yosef* (Berdichev, 1908).

LANDAU, MORDECAI HALEVI, *Ma'amar mordekhai* (Tel Aviv, 1960?).

[LEMBERGER, YEKUTIEL ZALMAN], *Magdil yeshuot malko* [hasidic tales and teachings] (Jerusalem, 1955).

—— *Niflaot hatsadikim* [tales of tsadikim] (Piotrkow, 1911; Warsaw, 1913).

LEVI, G., 'Teshuvat hamishkal', *Yeda-am*, 8 (1963), 63–4.

LEVI, I., 'Un recueil de contes juifs inédits', *Revue des études juives*, 33 (1896), 47–63.

LEWIN, B. M., *Otsar hagaonim* [anthology of geonic material], 13 vols (Jerusalem, 1928–43).

LEWIN, JOSHUA HESHEL, *Aliyot eliyahu* (Vilna, 1874).

LEWINSKI, Y. T., 'Precious Stones and Jewels Stanching Blood (From a Miscellany of Folk Remedies for Stanching Blood)' (Heb.), *Yeda-am*, 2/2–3 (1954), 93–101.

—— 'Water instead of Blood' (Heb.), *Yeda-am*, 9–10 [= vol. 1] (Feb. 1952), 68–70.

LIEBERSON, HAYIM, *Erets haḥayim* (Przemysl, 1927).

—— *Tseror haḥayim* (Bilgoray, 1925).

LIPPE, CH. D., *Bibliographisches Lexikon* (Vienna, 1881).

LISCHEUTZ, SHABETAI, 'Segulot yisra'el', in anon., *Tiyul bapardes* (Simleul-Silvaniei, 1940).

LOPIAN, E., *Lev eliyahu* (Jerusalem, 1972).

LURIA, A. Y., *Likutim yekarim* (printed with Moses Modiner, *Kitvei kodesh ramam*) (Jerusalem, 1966).

Ma'amar kedishin (Munkacs, 1890).

Ma'aseh hakedoshim [hasidic tales] (Lemberg, 1894).

Ma'aseh nora (Warsaw, 1908; Vilna, 1910).

Ma'asim tovim (Baghdad, n.d.).

Ma'asiyot mehagedolim vehatsadikim (Warsaw, 1909).

Ma'asiyot noraot (Munkacs, 1920?).

Ma'asiyot peliyot nora'im venifla'im (Lemberg, 1883; Lublin, 1904).

Ma'asiyot vesiḥot tsadikim [Tales and Discourses of Tsadikim] (Lemberg, 1894).

MACH, R., *Der Zaddik im Talmud und Midrasch* (Leiden, 1957).

MANASSEH BEN ISRAEL, *Nishmat ḥayim* (Amsterdam, 1652).

MARGALIOT, ELAZAR, *Ma'aseh r. zalmene* (Czernowitz, 1863 [1864]).

MARGALIOT, ELIEZER, *Elijah the Prophet in the Literature, Faith, and Spiritual Life of Israel* (Heb.) (Jerusalem, 1960).

MARGALIOT, REUBEN, *Marganita derabi me'ir* (Lemberg, 1927).

—— *Or hame'ir* (Lemberg, 1926).

—— *Tiferet adam* (Lvov, 1933).

MARGOLIES, ELEAZAR, OF SKALAT, *Ma'aseh* (Chernovtsy, 1863; repr. 1864).

MARGOLIOTH, JACOB, *Gedolim ma'asei tsadikim*, ed. G. Nigal (Jerusalem, 1992).

—— *Kevutsat ya'akov* [hasidic tales] (Przemysl, 1896).

MARKUS, ARON, *Hasidism* [Haḥasidut] (Tel Aviv, 1954).

Mayse bukh (Basle, 1602; Amsterdam, 1723; Nuremberg, 1763; Brull, 1889; London, ed. Gaster, n.d.).

MEHUDAR, ABRAHAM, *Zekhor le'avraham* (Lemberg, 1860; repr. Tel Aviv, 1954).
—— *Zekhuta de'avraham* (Tel Aviv, 1958?).
ME'IR BEN GEDALIAH, *She'elot uteshuvot maharam milublin* (Metz, 1769).
MELLER, D., *Besorot tovot* [hasidic tales and discourses] (Bilgoray, 1927).
MENAHEM NAHUM OF CHERNOBYL, *Me'or einayim* (Slavuta, 1798).
MENES, ABRAHAM, *Elijah the Prophet* (Yiddish) (New York, 1955).
MESHULLAM FEIVUSH OF BAREZIN, *Sefat emet* (Lemberg, 1879).
MESHULLAM FEIVUSH OF ZBARAZH, *Likutim yekarim* (Lemberg, 1792).
MICHELSOHN, ABRAHAM HAYIM SIMHAH BUNEM, *Ateret menaḥem* (Bilgoray, 1910).
—— *Birkat avraham* (Warsaw, 1881).
—— *Dover shalom* (Przemysl, 1910).
—— *Mekor ḥayim* (Bilgoray, 1912).
—— *Ohel avraham* (Piotrkow, 1911).
—— *Ohel elimelekh* (Przemysl, 1910).
—— *Ohel naftali* (Lemberg, 1911).
—— *Ohel yehoshua* (Przemysl, 1910).
—— *Shemen hatov* [hasidic commentary and tales] (Piotrkow, 1905; repr. Jerusalem, 1999, ed. G. Nigal).
—— *Tsapaḥat hashemen* [hasidic commentary and tales], booklet appended to *Shemen hatov*.
MICHELSOHN, TSEVI EZEKIEL, *Toledot ya'akov* (Warsaw, 1913).
Midrash tanḥuma, ed. Buber (Vilna, 1885).
MILIK, HAYIM ISAAC, *Sipurim nifla'im* (Satu-Mare, 1940).
MILLER, MORDECAI, *Beit mordekhai*, 2 vols (Jerusalem, 1966).
MONDSHEIN, JOSHUA, *Likutei reshimot uma'asiyot* (Kefar Habad, 1969).
—— *Migdal oz* (Kefar Habad, 1980).
MORIYA, M., *Beit eked sefarim*, 2 vols (Kiryat Shemonah, 1974–6).
MOSES ELIAKUM BRIAH OF KOZNITZ, *Be'er mosheh* (Lvov, 1848).
MOSES HAYIM EPHRAIM OF SUDYLKOW, *Degel maḥaneh efrayim* (Korets, 1810).
MOSES OF KOBRIN, *Amarot tehorot* (Warsaw, 1910).
MOSES MODNER, *Kitvei kodesh r. m[osheh] m[e'odner]* (Jerusalem, n.d.).
MOSKOWITZ, TSEVI, *Otsar hasipurim*, 20 vols (Jerusalem, 1951–9).
NACHT, JACOB, 'The Eating of Fish on the Sabbath' (Heb.), *Sinai*, 11 (1952–3), 139–55.
—— 'Fish' (Heb.), *Sinai*, 8 (1951), 326–33.

NA'IM, JOSEPH BEN ISAAC, *Malkhei rabanan* (Jerusalem, 1931).

NATHAN OF NEMIROV, *Ḥayei moharan* (Lemberg, 1874).

—— *Shivḥei haran* (Ostraha, 1816; repr. Jerusalem, 1961).

—— *Siḥot haran* (Lvov, 1864).

NEKHES, SOLOMON MICHAEL, *A ma'aseh fun a agunah* [A Story about an *Agunah*] (Los Angeles, 1944–5).

NEUBAUER, A., *Medieval Jewish Chronicles* [Seder haḥakhamim vekorot hayamim] (Oxford, 1888).

Niflaot anshei ma'aseh (Podgorze, 1900).

Niflaot hamagid (Yiddish) (Piotrkow, 1911).

NIGAL, GEDALYAH, 'A Chapter in the History of the Hasidic Tale' (Heb.), in Menahem Mendel Bodek, *Sipurei kedoshim*, ed. G. Nigal (Jerusalem, 1977), 87–119.

—— *The Collectors of the Hasidic Story* [Melaktei hasipur haḥasidi] (Jerusalem, 1996).

—— 'The Dybbuk in Jewish Mysticism' (Heb.), *Da'at*, 4 (1980), 75–101.

—— *'Dybbuk' Tales in Jewish Literature* [Sipurei dibuk besifrut yisra'el], 2nd edn (Jerusalem, 1994).

—— *The Hasidic Book and the Jewish Holidays* [Hasipur haḥasidi veheḥagim] (Jerusalem, 2002).

—— 'Hasidic Elements in a Work by Agnon' (Heb.), *Ḥadashot bar-ilan*, 30 (1979), 14–17; repr. in id., *Studies in Hasidism*, ii. 335–46.

—— 'A Hasidic Manuscript from the Early Twentieth Century' (Heb.), *Kiryat sefer*, 52 (1977), 834–42.

—— 'In Praise of R. Hayim ben Atar' (Heb.), in M. Amar (ed.), *Kav lekav* (Jerusalem, 1982), 73–93.

—— *Leader and Congregation* [Manhig ve'edah] (Jerusalem, 1962).

—— *Magic, Mysticism, and Hasidism: The Supernatural in Jewish Thought*, trans. E. Levin (Northvale, NJ, 1994).

—— 'The Master and Teacher of the Ba'al Shem Tov' (Heb.), *Sinai*, 76 (1976), 150–9; repr. in id., *Studies in Hasidism*, i. 80–91.

—— 'New Light on the Hasidic Tale' (Heb.), *Sinai*, 104 (1989), 154–62.

—— 'Nonuniform Moral Standards in Hasidism?' (Heb.), *Shanah beshanah* (2000), 308–13.

—— 'A Primary Source of the Hasidic Story Literature: On the Book *Keter shem tov* and its Sources' (Heb.), *Sinai*, 79 (1976), 132–46.

—— 'On Proverbs and Aphorisms in Nascent Hasidism' (Heb.), in id., *West and East Studies*, 175–82.

—— 'On R. Aaron Samuel Hakohen, One of the Disciples of the Magid of Mezirech' (Heb.), *Sinai*, 78 (1977), 255–62.

—— '*Sefer divrei no'am*: An Apologetic Hasidic Tale' (Heb.), *Sinai*, 63 (2000), 136–9.

—— *Studies in Hasidism* [Meḥkarim baḥasidut], 2 vols (Jerusalem, 1999).

—— *S. Y. Agnon and his Hasidic Sources* [Shai agnon umekorotav haḥasidiyim] (Ramat Gan, 1983).

—— 'Transmigration of Souls to Correct Financial Injustice' (Heb.), *Sinai*, 110 (1990), 63–71; repr. in id., *West and East Studies*, 133–44.

—— *West and East Studies* [Meḥkarei ma'arav umizraḥ] (Jerusalem, 2001).

—— 'Women in the Book *Shivḥei habesht*' (Heb.), *Molad*, 31 (1974), 38–48; repr. in id., *Studies in Hasidism*, ii. 365–78.

Noy, D., 'The Hidden Tsadik in Theodicy Legends' (Heb.), *Yeda-am*, 18 (1977), 32–40.

—— 'The Rainmaking Prayer of the *Tamim*' (Heb.), *Maḥanayim*, 51 (1960), 34–45.

Orian, M., *The Exalted: The Inner World of Hasidism* [Madregot be'olamah shel ḥasidut] (Ramat Gan, 1975).

Palache, Hayim, *Torah veḥayim* (Salonika, 1846).

Pasheles, Wolf, *Sipurim* (German), iv (Prague, n.d.).

Peretz, Isaac Leib, 'Perhaps Even Higher', in *As Once We Were: Selections from the Works of I. L. Peretz*, trans. E. Margolis (Los Angeles, 1951), iv. 98–102.

Pinhas of Dinovitz, *Siftei tsadikim* (Lvov, 1863).

Pinhas of Korets, *Beit pinḥas* (Bilgoray, 1926).

Piekarz, M., *The Beginning of Hasidism* [Biyemei tsemiḥat haḥasidut] (Jerusalem, 1978).

—— *Bratslav Hasidism* (Heb.) (Jerusalem, 1976; 2nd edn Jerusalem, 1996).

Pinkas ostraha (Tel Aviv, 1960).

Pirkei derabi eli'ezer (Constantinople, 1514).

Popirsh, Meir, *Or tsadikim* (Warsaw, 1889).

Potchowsky, Moses Nethanel, *Gan hadasim* (Berdichev, 1910).

Rabbinovich, Eliakim Getzel, *Shivḥei rav ye'ivi* [Jerusalem, 1966].

Rabbinowich, Abraham Isaac, *Malakhei elyon* (Jerusalem, 1966).

Rabinovitz, Menahem Mendel, *Ma'aseh neḥemiyah* (Jerusalem, 1956).

Rabinowitz, Aryeh Mordecai, *Keter hayehudi* (Jerusalem, 1929).

Rabinowitz, Hayim Abraham, *Shemuot tovot razin de'oraita* (Chernovtsy, 1874).

Rakats, Yo'ets Kim Kadish, *Siaḥ sarfei kodesh*, 5 vols in 1 (Lodz, 1927).

—— *Tiferet hayehudi* (Warsaw, 1910).

RAPHAEL, Y., 'The Kherson *Genizah*' (Heb.), *Sinai*, 81 (1977), 129–50.

—— '*Shivḥei habesht*' (Heb.), *Areshet*, 2 (1960), 358–77.

RAPOPORT, ISRAEL, *Divrei david* [hasidic tales and teachings] (Husyatin, 1904).

RECHTMAN, A., *Jewish Ethnography and Folklore* [Yidishe etnografie un folklor] (Buenos Aires, 1958).

REISCHER, EPHRAIM BA'AL SHEM, *Sha'ar efrayim* (Fuerth, 1728; Altona, 1736).

REZNIK, N. Y., *Mora'im gedolim* [hasidic tales] (Przemysl, 1876).

RODKINSOHN, MICHAEL LEVI, *Adat tsadikim* [hasidic tales] (Lemberg, 1864).

—— *Shivḥei harav* [hagiographical tales of R. Shneur Zalman of Lyady] (Lemberg, 1864).

—— *Siftei kedoshim* (Lemberg, 1875).

—— *Sipurei tsadikim mehaḥut hameshulash* [hasidic tales] (Lemberg, 1864).

—— *Toledot ba'alei shem tov*, i: *Or yisra'el* (Königsberg, 1876).

—— *Toledot ba'alei shem tov*, iv: *Toledot amudei haḥabad* (Königsberg, 1876).

ROSENBERG, JUDAH YUDEL, *Divrei hayamim* [tales of King Solomon] (Piotrkow, 1914).

—— *Eliyahu hanavi* [tales of Elijah] (Piotrkow, 1911).

—— *Niflaot hamaharal* [tales of the Maharal of Prague] (Piotrkow, 1909).

—— *Rafa'el hamalakh* [remedies and charms] (Piotrkow, 1911).

—— *Tiferet maharal* [tales of the 'Grandfather of Shpola'] (Lodz, 1912).

ROSENBERG, TSEVI HIRSCH, *Raza de'uvda* (Jerusalem, 1971).

ROSENSTEIN, ISAAC DAVID, *Pe'er layesharim* (Jerusalem, 1921).

ROSENTHAL, SOLOMON GABRIEL, *Hitgalut hatsadikim* [hasidic tales and teachings] (Warsaw, 1901).

—— *Tiferet hatsadikim* [hasidic tales] (Warsaw, 1908).

ROTH, AARON, *Shomer emunim*, 2 vols (Jerusalem, 1961).

ROTZFERD, NAPHTALI HERZKO, *Zikhron naftali* (Kleinwardein [= Kisvarda], 1938).

RUBINSTEIN, A., '*Hitgalut* Stories in the Book *Shivḥei habesht*' (Heb.), *Alei sefer*, 6–7 (1979), 157–86.

—— 'A Possible New Fragment of *Shivḥei habesht*' (Heb.), *Tarbiz*, 35 (1966), 174–91.

RUBINSTEIN, Y., 'Notes on the Book *Shem hagedolim heḥadash*' (Heb.), *Hama'ayan*, 8 (1968), 1–107.

SADAN, D., *Hebrew Literature Borrows and Absorbs* [Bein she'elah ulekinyan] (Tel Aviv, 1968).

—— 'The Story of the Handkerchief' (Heb.), in *Al shai agnon masot uma'amarim* (Tel Aviv, 1979), 79–87.

—— 'The Tailor and his Skullcap' (Yiddish), *Folk un tsiyon*, 29 (1979), 22–3.

SAFRIN, ALEXANDER SENDER OF KOMARNO, *Zikhron devarim* (Lemberg, 1871).

SAFRIN, ISAAC JUDAH YEHIEL (ISAAC EIZIK) OF KOMARNO, *Heikhal haberakhah* (Lemberg, 1869).

—— *Megilat setarim* [personal diary] (1st edn, from a manuscript, Jerusalem, 1944).

—— 'Netiv mitsvoteikha' [introd. to *Otsar haḥayim*] (Lemberg, 1858).

—— *Notser ḥesed* (Lvov, 1856).

—— *Otsar haḥayim* (Przemysl, 1884).

—— *Zohar ḥai* [commentary on the Zohar], 4 vols (Przemysl and Lemberg, 1875–81).

SAMLUNG, AZRIEL HAYIM, *Eser zekhuyot* (Piotrkow, 1931).

SAMUEL HEHASID, JUDAH HEHASID and ELEAZAR OF WORMS, *Sefer ḥasidim* (*Das Buch der Frommen*), ed. J. Wistinetzki and J. Freimann (Frankfurt am Main, 1924).

SAMUEL OF SHINOVA, *Ramatayim tsofim* [commentary on *Tana devei eliyahu*] (Warsaw, 1881).

SCHEIBER, A., 'Two Legends with the Motif: God Wants the Heart' (Heb.), *Yeda-am*, 4 (1957), 59–61.

SCHLESINGER, AKIVA JOSEPH, *Shimru mishpat* (Jerusalem, 1910?).

SCHNEERSOHN, JOSEPH ISAAC, *Sefer hazikhronot* (Memoirs) (Brooklyn, 1955).

SCHOLEM, GERSHOM, 'Die 36 verborgene Gerechten in der Juedischen Tradition', *Judaica*, 1 (Frankfurt am Main, 1963), 216–25.

—— *Elements of the Kabbalah and its Symbolism* [Pirkei yesod behavanat hakabalah usemaleiha] (Jerusalem, 1976).

—— 'The Historical Image of R. Israel Ba'al Shem Tov' (Heb.), *Molad*, 18/144–5 (1960), 335–56.

—— *Major Trends in Jewish Mysticism* (New York, 1961).

—— 'The Neutralisation of the Messianic Element in Early Hasidism', *Journal of Jewish Studies*, 20 (1969–70), 25–55.

SCHWARTZ, ABRAHAM JUDAH, *Derekh hanesher* (Satu-Mare, 1928).

SCHWARTZ, JOSEPH HAKOHEN, *Mo'ed lekhol ḥai* (Grosswardein, 1925).

SCHWARZBAUM, H., 'The Thirty-Six Just Hidden Men in Jewish Folk-Narratives and Folklore' (Heb.), *Yeda-am*, 18 (1977), 20–8.

Sefer hakavanot uma'asei nisim (Constantinople, 1720).

Sefer hama'asiyot (Baghdad, 1866)

Sefer mifalot elohim [Actions by Means of the Holy Names . . . from the Writings of the Kabbalists . . . Our Master and Teacher, R. Joel Ba'al Shem . . . Our Master and Teacher, R. Naphtali Katz] (n.p., 1810).

Sha'ar hapesukim (Jerusalem, 1962–3).

SHALOM OF KOIDANOV, *Divrei shalom* (Vilna, 1882).

SHAPIRA, NATHAN, *Yayin meshumar* (Venice, 1660).

SHARF, MOSES JACOB, *Darkhei yosher* (Brooklyn, 1950).

SHENKEL, ELIEZER, *Ma'asim tovim* [Good Deeds; hasidic tales] (Podgorze, 1900).

—— *Ma'asiyot mitsadikim yesodei olam* [hasidic tales] (Podgorze, 1903).

—— *Ma'asiyot nora'im venifla'im* [hasidic tales] (Krakow, 1896).

—— *Ma'asiyot peliyot* [hasidic tales] (Krakow, 1896).

—— *Niflaot gedolim* [Great Wonders; hasidic tales] (Podgorze, 1900).

—— *Noraot anshei ma'aseh* [The Awesome Acts of Men of Good Deeds; hasidic tales] (Podgorze, 1900).

—— *Sipurei anshei shem* [hasidic tales] (Podgorze, 1903).

—— *Yeshuot yisra'el* [hasidic tales], 2 vols in 1 (Podgorze, 1904).

Shivḥei habesht [In Praise of the Ba'al Shem Tov], ed. S. A. Horodezky (Tel Aviv, 1957); ed. A. Rubinstein (Jerusalem, 1991); first pub. in Heb.: Kapust, 1815; first pub. in Yiddish: Korets, 1816.

SHMERUK, CHONE, 'The Social Significance of Hasidic *Sheḥitah*' (Heb.), *Zion*, 20 (1955), 47–72.

—— 'Tales about R. Adam Ba'al Shem in the Versions of *Shivḥei habesht*' (Heb.), *Zion*, 28 (1963), 86–105.

—— *Yiddish Literature in Poland: Historical Studies and Perspectives* [Sifrut yidish bepolin] (Tel Aviv, 1978).

SIMEON OF DOBROMIL, *Naḥalat shimon* (Laszczow?, 1815).

S[IMEON] R[ABBI] OF TARNOW, *Notser te'enah* [hasidic tales] (Krakow, 1899).

SINGER, ISAAC, *Pe'ulat hatsadikim* [The Activity of the Tsadikim] (Podgorze, 1900).

—— *Seva ratson* [hasidic tales] (Podgorze, 1900).

Sipurei ma'asiyot mishanim kadmoniyot (n.p., 1815)

Sipurei niflaot mehagaon hatsadik hashelaḥ hakadosh (Yiddish) (Warsaw, 1889).

Sipurim ḥadashim ve'amitiyim (Munkacs, 1909).

SLODOVNIK, MATITYAHU TSEVI, *Ma'aseh hagedolim heḥadash* [hasidic tales] (Piotrkow, 1925).

SOBELMAN, ABRAHAM ISAAC, *Sipurei tsadikim heḥadash* [tales of tsadikim] (Yiddish) (Piotrkow, 1909–10).

SOFER, JACOB, *Sipurei ya'akov* [hasidic tales] (vol. i: Husyatin, 1904; vol. ii: Lvov, 1912).

SOFER, MENAHEM MENELI, *Sheloshah edrei tson* [hasidic tales] (Przemysl, 1874).

Sofer, Moses, *Ḥatam sofer* [responsa] (Munkacz, 1912).

Solomon of Dreznitz, 'Writs of Praise and Esteem of the Greatness of R. Isaac Luria, of Blessed Memory', in Joseph Solomon Delmedigo (Yashar) of Candia, *Ta'alumot ḥokhmah* (Basle/Hanau, 1629); also published as *Shivḥei ha'ari* (Ostraha, 1794).

Solomon of Lutsk, *Dibrat shelomoh* (Zholkva, 1849).

—— *Magid devarav leya'akov* (Korets, 1781).

Solomon of Radomsk, *Tiferet shelomoh*, 3 vols (Warsaw, 1867–9).

Sperling, Abraham Isaac, *The Reasons for the Customs and the Sources of the Laws* [Ta'amei haminhagim umekorei hadinim] (Jerusalem, 1961).

Stern, Abraham, *Ḥutim hameshulashim* (Yiddish) (Montreal, 1953).

Stern, Elimelekh Ze'ev, *Siḥot yekarim* (Satu-Mare, 1930).

Strisower, Judah, *Minḥat yehudah* (Jerusalem, 1927).

Tabori, Z., 'Our Master Hayim ben Atar: A Look at his Life and Teachings' (Heb.), *Hado'ar*, 48/11 (New York, 1969), 168–9.

Tamar, T., *Studies in the History of the Jewish People in the Land of Israel and in Italy* [Meḥkarim betoledot hayehudim be'erets yisra'el uve'italiyah] (Jerusalem, 1970).

Teitelbaum, Moses, *Yismaḥ mosheh* (Lemberg, 1849).

Teomim, Judah Aryeh Fraenkel, *Ateret tiferet* (Warsaw, 1910).

—— *Menorah hatehorah* (Przemysl, 1911).

Tiger, Y., *Der tsadik un der ba'al teshuvah (oder 'der schvartzer Bishof')* (London, 1960).

Tishby, Isaiah, *The Doctrine of Evil and the Kelipah in Lurianic Kabbalism* [Torat hara vehakelipah bakabalat ha'ari] (Jerusalem, 1963).

—— *The Wisdom of the Zohar*, trans. David Goldstein, 3 vols (Oxford, 1989).

Tsevi Elimelekh of Dynow, *Igra dekalah* (Lemberg, 1868).

—— *Ma'ayan ganim* (Lemberg, 1863).

Tsevi Hirsch of Koidanov, *Kav hayashar* (Frankfurt am Main, 1705–6).

Tzitrin, Mendel, *Shivḥei tsadikim* [hasidic tales] (Warsaw, 1884), ed. G. Nigal (Jerusalem, 1996).

Unger, Menasheh, *R. Israel Ba'al Shem Tov* (Heb.) (New York, 1963).

Urbach, E. E., *The Sages*, trans. I. Abrahams (Jerusalem, 1975).

Uri of Strelisk, *Imrei kodesh* (Lemberg, 1870).

Vital, Hayim, *Ets ḥayim*.

—— *Sefer hagilgulim* (Przemysl, 1875).

—— *Sefer haḥezyonot, hamekhuneh shivḥei r. ḥayim vital*, ed. A. Z. Aescoly (Jerusalem, 1954).

VITAL, HAYIM, *Sha'ar hagilgulim* (Jerusalem, 1863); ed. Tsevi Me'ir [ben Solomon of Radomsk] Rabinowitz (Przemysl, 1875).

—— *Sha'ar hapesukim* (Jerusalem, 1962–3).

—— *Sha'ar ruaḥ hakodesh* (Jerusalem, 1963).

—— *Sha'arei kedushah* (Piotrkow, 1912).

WALDEN, AARON, *Kahal ḥasidim* [hasidic tales] (n.p., 1860?).

—— *Shem hagedolim heḥadash* (Warsaw, 1864).

WALDEN, MOSES MENAHEM, *Ohel yitsḥak* (Piotrkow, 1914).

—— *Or haniflaot* (Jerusalem, 1954).

WEBERMAN, PINHAS DAVID, *Derekh tsadikim* (Jerusalem, 1967).

—— *Ma'aseh nisim* (Frampol, 1913; repr. Jerusalem, 1966).

WEINER, SAMSON (= SAMSON WERTHEIMER), *Tosafot ḥadashim* (Worms, 1658; Vienna, 1724).

WEINSTOCK, MOSES YAIR, *Peri kodesh hilulim* (Jerusalem, 1961).

WEISS, ISAAC, *Avnei beit hayotser* (Paks, 1900).

WEITZ, ABRAHAM, *Ba'al-Shem-Tov Motiven un andere Dertzeitlungen* (Paris, 1977).

WERBLOWSKY, R. J. Z., *Joseph Caro: Lawyer and Mystic* (Oxford, 1962).

WERFEL, YITSHAK, *Hasidism and the Land of Israel* [Haḥasidut ve'erets yisra'el] (Jerusalem, 1949–50).

WERSES, S., *Story and Source: Studies in the Development of Hebrew Prose* [Sipur veshorasho] (Ramat Gan, 1971).

WERTHEIM, A., *Law and Custom in Hasidism* [Halakhot vehalikhot baḥasidut] (Jerusalem, 1960).

WILDMANN, ISAAC EISIK (HAVER), *Magen vetsinah* (Amsterdam, n.d.).

WILENSKY, M., *Hasidim and Mitnagedim* (Heb.), 2 vols (Jerusalem, 1990).

WORMSER, MICHAEL, *Das Leben und Wirken des in Michelstadt verstorbenen Rabbinen Seckel Loeb Wormser* (Offenbach am Main, 1853).

Writings of the Early Hasidim [Kitvei ḥasidim rishonim] (Jerusalem, 1979).

Y.D. OF SUDILKOV, *Temimei derekh* [Those of Pure Way; hasidic tales] (1866).

YA'ARI, A., 'From Popular Story to Literary Story' (Heb.), *Davar* (26 Aug. 1938), 3–4.

—— 'Miscellaneous Bibliographical Notes' (Heb.), *Kiryat sefer*, 11 (1934–5), 129–31.

—— 'Three Yiddish Translations of *Shivḥei habesht*' (Heb.), *Kiryat sefer*, 12/1 (1935–6), 129–31.

—— 'Two Basic Recensions of *Shivḥei habesht*' (Heb.), *Kiryat sefer*, 39 (1963–4), 249–72, 394–407, 552–62.

Yalkut shimoni (Saloniki/Soncino, 1527).

YASHAR, BARUCH (SCHLICHTER), *Beit komarno* (Jerusalem, 1965).

YEHIEL MOSES OF YADIMOV, *Likutim ḥadashim* (Warsaw, 1899).

YELLIN, ABRAHAM, *Derekh tsadikim* (Piotrkow, 1913).

ZAK, REUBEN, *Beit yisra'el* (Piotrkow, 1912).

—— *Keneset yisra'el* (Warsaw, 1905).

ZECHARIAH OF PLUNGIAN, *Sefer zekhariyah me'inyanei segulot* (Hamburg, 1709).

ZE'EV WOLF OF ZHITOMIR, *Or hame'ir* (Korets, 1787).

ZEILINGOLD, AARON, *Me'orot hagedolim* (Bilgoray, 1911; repr. Jerusalem, 1997).

ZEITLIN, H., 'The New Documents for the History of Hasidism' (Heb.), *Hatur*, 1/26 (Jerusalem, 1921), 9–11.

ZELIGMAN, ELIEZER TSEVI, *Beit tsadik* (Piotrkow, 1910).

ZEVIN, SOLOMON JOSEPH, *Hasidic Tales: Festivals* [Sipurei ḥasidim: mo'adim] (Tel Aviv, 1959).

—— *Hasidic Tales: On the Torah* [Sipurei ḥasidim: parashah] (Tel Aviv, 1964).

ZFATMAN, S., 'The *Mayse Bukh*: An Old Yiddish Literary Genre' (Heb.), *Hasifrut*, 8/2 (1979), 126–52.

ZIMETBAUM, RAPHAEL HALEVI SEGEL, *Darkhei ḥayim* [on R. Hayim Halberstam of Sanz] (Krakow, 1923).

ZLOTNIK, Y. L. (ed.), *Ma'aseh yerushalmi* (Jerusalem, 1947).

Index

C